lonely pl

D0546523

EUROPE'S
BEST TRIPS
40 AMAZING ROAD TRIPS

This edition written and researched by

Belinda Dixon, Isabel Albiston, Oliver Berry,
Stuart Butler, Kerry Christiani, Fionn Davenport,
Marc Di Duca, Peter Dragicevich, Duncan Garwood,
Anthony Ham, Paula Hardy, Catherine Le Nevez,
Sally O'Brien, Josephine Quintero, Daniel Robinson,
Brendan Sainsbury, Andy Symington,
Ryan Ver Berkmoes, Nicola Williams, Neil Wilson

SYMBOLS IN THIS BOOK

✓ Top Tips

📖 History & Culture

📷 Essential Photo

🄢 Link Your Trips

👪 Family

🏃 Walking Tour

🔘 Tips from Locals

🍷 Food & Drink

✖ Eating

↰ Trip Detour

🌳 Outdoors

🛏 Sleeping

📳 Telephone Number

@ Internet Access

🏊 Swimming Pool

🕒 Opening Hours

📶 Wi-Fi Access

👪 Family-Friendly

P Parking

🍃 Vegetarian Selection

❄ Air-Conditioning

MAP LEGEND

Routes
- Trip Route
- Trip Detour
- Linked Trip
- Walk Route
- Tollway
- Freeway
- Primary
- Secondary
- Tertiary
- Lane
- Unsealed Road
- Plaza/Mall
- Steps
-)= = Tunnel
- Pedestrian Overpass
- Walk Track/Path

Boundaries
- ─ ─ ─ International
- ─··─··─ State/Province
- Cliff

Hydrography
- River/Creek
- Intermittent River
- Swamp/Mangrove
- Canal
- Water
- Dry/Salt/ Intermittent Lake
- Glacier

Highway Markers
- ① Highway Marker

Trips
- 1️⃣ Trip Numbers
- 9️⃣ Trip Stop
- 🔗 Walking tour
- ↰ Trip Detour

Population
- ✪ Capital (National)
- ◉ Capital (State/Province)
- ● City/Large Town
- ● Town/Village

Areas
- Beach
- Cemetery (Christian)
- Cemetery (Other)
- Park
- Forest
- Reservation
- Urban Area
- Sportsground

Transport
- ✈ Airport
- Cable Car/ Funicular
- P Parking
- Train/Railway
- Tram

Note: Not all symbols displayed above appear on the maps in this book

CONTENTS

Contents cont.

Italy Duomo, Florence

WELCOME TO
EUROPE

Europe has an embarrassment of riches. To incomparable art and architecture, add a vivid past. To spectacular scenery and vibrant cities, add the finest food and wine. It's a place that helps you do and be what you've always wanted. Hike mountain passes. Savour wine beside sun-ripened vines. Tour *palazzi* and *pueblos*. Linger over lunch-time people watching. Feel you belong.

These riches are best by far discovered by car. And the countless stops we've crafted into 40 road trips are your key to unlocking those experiences. Grip the wheel in white-knuckle mountain routes. Cruise along coast roads. Drive historical timelines. Trace gourmet and vineyard trails.

Trips packed with culture, cities, history, mountains, food, beaches, wine and art – they're all waiting to be discovered and our routes will guide you every stop of the way.

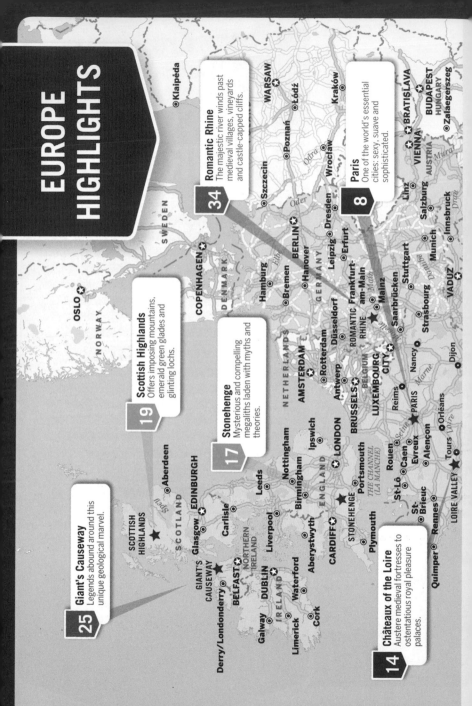

EUROPE HIGHLIGHTS

34 Romantic Rhine
The majestic river winds past medieval villages, vineyards and castle-capped cliffs.

8 Paris
One of the world's essential cities: sexy, suave and sophisticated.

19 Scottish Highlands
Offers imposing mountains, emerald green glades and glinting lochs.

17 Stonehenge
Mysterious and compelling megaliths laden with myths and theories.

25 Giant's Causeway
Legends abound around this unique geological marvel.

14 Châteaux of the Loire
Austere medieval fortresses to ostentatious royal pleasure palaces.

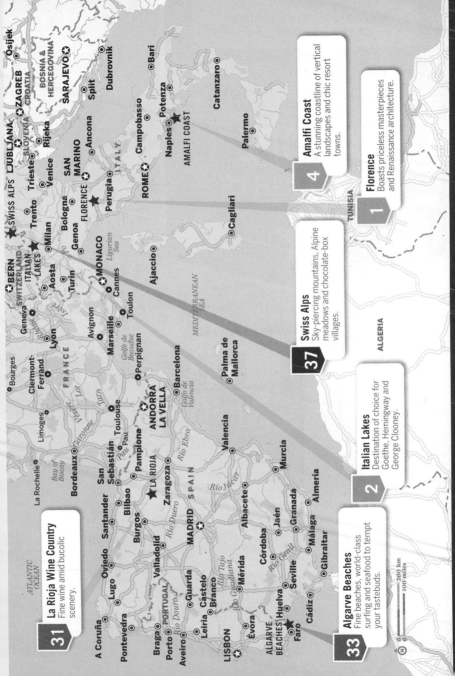

1 Florence
Boasts priceless masterpieces and Renaissance architecture.

4 Amalfi Coast
A stunning coastline of vertical landscapes and chic resort towns.

37 Swiss Alps
Sky-piercing mountains, Alpine meadows and chocolate-box villages.

2 Italian Lakes
Destination of choice for Goethe, Hemingway and George Clooney.

31 La Rioja Wine Country
Fine wine amid bucolic scenery.

33 Algarve Beaches
Fine beaches, world-class surfing and seafood to tempt your tastebuds.

Europe's best sights and experiences, and the road trips that will take you there.

EUROPE
HIGHLIGHTS

★

Italian Lakes

Italy's northern lakes are simply sublime. The most picturesque and least visited is Lago di Como (Lake Como); a highlight of **Trip 2: The Graceful Italian Lakes**, a scenic jaunt around Lakes Maggiore, Orta and Como. Set in the shadow of the Rhaetian Alps, Lago di Como's banks are speckled with Liberty-style villas and fabulous landscaped gardens that burst into blushing colour in April and May.

Trip 2

Italian Lakes Varenna, Lago di Como

Scottish Highlands Urquhart Castle

Scottish Highlands

Scotland's wild places abound in breathtaking vistas: imposing mountains, emerald green glades, glinting lochs – the scenery here is truly awe-inspiring. Drive right into the views on **Trip 19: Royal Highlands & Cairngorms**, which delivers castles, peaks and wildlife galore – and the chance to explore the Royal family's summer holiday haunts.

Trip 19

Paris

What is there to say about the City of Light that hasn't been said a thousand times before? Quite simply, this is one of the world's essential cities: sexy, suave and sophisticated. There's a lifetime of experiences here, from the treasures of the Louvre to the cafes of Montmartre – encounter them on **Trip 8: Essential France**, which steers you all the way from the chic capital to the glistening Med.

Trip 8

The Amalfi Coast

The Amalfi Coast is Italy's most dazzling seafront stretch. Its coastal road – detailed in **Trip 4: The Amalfi Coast** – curves sinuously, linking steeply stacked towns and rocky inlets. All around, cliffs sheer down into sparkling blue waters, lemons grow on hillside terraces, and towering *fichi d'India* (prickly pears) guard silent mountain paths.

Trip 4

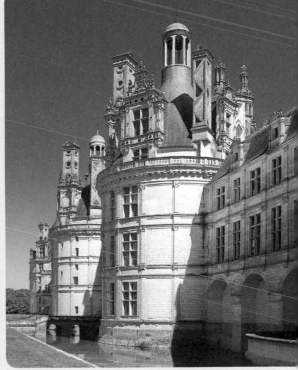

Châteaux of the Loire Château de Chambord

BEST ROADS FOR DRIVING

SS163 The 'Nastro Azzurro' weaves along the precipitous Amalfi Coast. **Trip** 4

Col d'Aubisque A route through the craggy Pyrenees; more like flying than driving. **Trip** 11

A939 Scottish Highlands Motor beside ski slopes at rollercoaster Lecht Pass. **Trip** 19

The São Vicente Coast Road Cliff tops en route to Europe's southwestern-most tip. **Trip** 33

Silvretta High Alpine Road Brave 34 white-knuckle switchbacks 2500m high in the Austrian Alps. **Trip** 39

Châteaux of the Loire

For sky's-the-limit extravagance, don't miss **Trip 14: Châteaux of the Loire**. Constructed by France's aristocratic elite between the 15th and 17th centuries, these lavish mansions were designed to show off their owners' wealth – something they manage to achieve in spectacular fashion. Chambord is the jewel in the crown, but on this trip you'll see plenty of sparkling gems.

Trip 14

13

Stonehenge

Stonehenge

Mysterious and compelling, Stonehenge is Great Britain's most iconic ancient site. People have been drawn to this myth-laden ring of bluestones for the last 5000 years, and we still don't know quite why it was built. Come up with your own theories while gazing at massive megaliths on **Trip 17: The Historic South**, a voyage which crosses the country via a centuries-long timeline through a captivating past.

Trips

BEST SIPS

Castello di Verrazzano Sample Chianti Classico and olive oil at this ancient Italian castle. **Trip** 3

Épernay Explore bottle-packed cellars in the French town dubbed the *capitale du champagne*. **Trip** 13

Rioja Trek Tour a vineyard; sup in a bodega; make your own wine. **Trip** 31

Quinta do Crasto Spectacular, terraced vineyards on a ridge above the Río Douro. **Trip** 32

Engelszell Visit a 13th-century abbey to taste monk-made cheese and beer. **Trip** 40

Swiss Alps View of the Matterhorn from Zermatt

La Rioja Hotel Marqués de Riscal

Swiss Alps

You'd think after motoring through 537km of mind-blowing Alpine scenery on **Trip 37: The Swiss Alps** that you had seen it all. Wrong. After a succession of dramatic green peaks, Alpine lakes, glacial ravines and other hallucinatory natural landscapes, you pull into your final destination: Zermatt, a highly desirable Alpine resort built around the incomperable Matterhorn.

Trip 37

Florence

From Brunelleschi's red-capped Duomo to Michelangelo's *David* and Botticelli's *The Birth of Venus*, Florence boasts priceless masterpieces and a historic centre that looks much as it did in Renaissance times. Art aside, the city is perfect for al fresco dining and wine drinking. And it's only part of **Trip 5: World Heritage Wonders** – an epic exploration of Italy's finest historic cities: Venice, Siena, Pisa and Rome.

Trip 1 3 5

La Rioja Wine Country

La Rioja is the sort of place where you could spend weeks searching out the finest drops. Bodegas offering wine tastings and villages that shelter wine museums are the mainstays. Aside from scenery and fine quaffs, you'll find plenty of surprises (such as a Frank Gehry–designed masterpiece in a tiny village) on **Trip 31: Roving La Rioja Wine Region**.

Trip 31

17

Algarve Beaches

Beach-lovers have much to celebrate on a drive along Portugal's southern coast. Sandy islands, cliffs and shore set the stage for memorable backroad explorations on **Trip 33: Alentejo & Algarve Beaches**. After a day spent surfing or frolicking in the sea, you can roll up to a beautifully sited restaurant for a seafood feast overlooking the crashing waves.

Trip

The Giant's Causeway

The grand geological flourish of the Giant's Causeway is Northern Ireland's most popular attraction and one of the world's most startling natural wonders. Here, you can clamber over some of the 40,000 unique hexagonal basalt columns that trail off into the sea. Discover the rich legends that surround them on **Trip 23: The Long Way Round**; as you circumnavigate enchanting Ireland's entire shore.

Trips

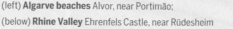

(left) **Algarve beaches** Alvor, near Portimão;
(below) **Rhine Valley** Ehrenfels Castle, near Rüdesheim

DMITRY EAGLE ORLOV/SHUTTERSTOCK ©

STEFVAL/SHUTTERSTOCK ©

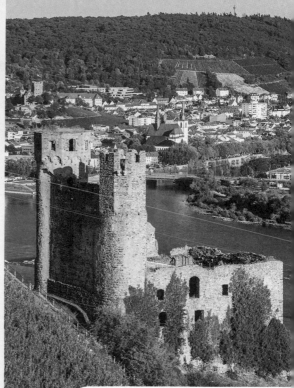

Romantic Rhine

The Rhine has long mesmerised artists, as is illustrated by the 19th-century paintings in Koblenz on **Trip 34: Romantic Rhine**. From Düsseldorf and Cologne, the majestic river snakes through churning whirlpools, medieval villages, vineyards and castle-capped cliffs. Your trail mirrors it, leading to forests and fortresses, and to evenings sipping rieslings under chestnut trees.

Trip

BEST CITIES

- -
London Theatre, history, art, food: Britain's capital has them all. **Trips** `15` `17`
- -
Rome Unique, exquisite, romantic; the one-time capital of the world remains unmissable. **Trips** `1` `5`
- -
Dublin Georgian charm in a vibrant, contemporary city. Plus 1000-plus pubs. **Trips** `22` `23`
- -
Barcelona Playful, historic and flush with unique art. The Spanish city of your dreams. **Trip** `27`

19

IF YOU LIKE

Wine tasting Douro Valley

AGNIESZKA SKALSKA/SHUTTERSTOCK ©

Architecture

Boasting an unparalleled architectural legacy, Europe is home to some of the world's most celebrated masterpieces in building design. Romanesque cathedrals, baroque palaces, Georgian cities, half-timbered cottages, ancient monuments, cutting-edge creations – the wealth of buildings arrayed here will be a memorable part of your trip.

14 Châteaux of the Loire Resplendent châteaux line the banks of the Loire, each one more extravagant than the last.

17 The Historic South Three of England's most spectacular cathedrals, plus London, and Bath's Georgian city-scape.

29 Northern Spain Pilgrimage Showcasing a string of ancient chapels medieval villages and some stunning cathedrals.

Great Views

Awe-inspiring mountains, sun-kissed shores, majestic river valleys, vine-etched hills – Europe can claim superb landscapes linked by ribboning roads. These are truly unforgettable drives.

4 Amalfi Coast Italy's most celebrated shore is a classic Mediterranean pin-up – simply sublime views.

19 Royal Highlands & Cairngorms A sweep of majestic mountains and pine forests encircles the Queen's Scottish summer home.

24 Ring of Kerry Virtually every corner on this iconic Irish drive reveals a vista worthy of a postcard.

37 The Swiss Alps All the big names are here: Matterhorn, Eiger, Jungfrau, Schilthorn, Titlis and Mönch.

Art

Renaissance glories, Impressionist masterpieces, modernist marvels, landmark museums – Europe's astonishing artistic legacy is guaranteed to linger long in the memory after you get home. From Michelangelo to Picasso, Europe is a sheer indulgence for art-lovers and a feast for the eyes.

1 Grand Tour Take in Leonardo's *The Last Supper*, Botticelli's *The Birth of Venus*, Michelangelo's *David* and so much more.

27 Mediterranean Meander See artwork by Spanish greats, from Picasso in Malaga to Catalan giants in Barcelona.

38 Geneva to Zürich Rich and diverse art collections dot this mountanous route – encompassing everything from the Renaissance to Cubism.

Outdoor activities Alpine mountains along the Grossglockner Road

Outdoor Activities

Europe is an adventure playground extraordinaire with landscapes that make pretty much any activity possible. Hike mountain trails, surf gorgeous beaches, go summer-time skiing, windsurfing and white-water rafting – our adrenaline-laced trips enable it all.

16 Britain's Wild Side
A fresh-air fuelled tour of Britain's best wilderness spots, including eight gloriously diverse National Parks.

33 Alentejo & Algarve Beaches Portugal's south-coast stunner, offering cliff-backed shores, seaside villages and great surf.

39 Grossglockner Road
A feat of 1930s Austrian engineering, this road swings giddily around 36 switchbacks – opening up mountain activities galore.

History

In Europe the past is ever present. Everywhere lies evidence of an enthralling heritage stretching back thousands of years – from stone circles and Greek temples to battlefields, chateaux, cathedrals and castles. This history is a seam stitched through the entire continent and our trips unravel the stories for you.

5 World Heritage Wonders Rome's Colosseum and Verona's Arena; a classic cross-country drive.

9 D-Day's Beaches
The events of D-Day still resonate along Normandy's shores; the museums and memorials explain why.

17 The Historic South
Britain's Stonehenge, UNESCO-city Bath, sublime cathedrals and Napoleonic-era ships combine for a truly historic drive.

Food & Wine

With its superb produce and culinary traditions, Europe is a food- and wine-lover's dream destination. Here you can dine al fresco in a medieval piazza, feast on seafood in a historic port, or nibble on cured meats in a Spanish bodega.

3 Tuscan Wine Tour
Savour fine dining in Chianti's picturesque vineyards.

13 Champagne Taster
Chefs cook up a storm while cellars echo to the sound of popping corks.

31 Roving La Rioja Wine Region Bodegas, quality eateries and vineyards to the horizon.

32 Douro Valley Vineyard Trails Northern Portugal's culinary corner boasts sublime views and red wines.

EUROPE
BY REGION

These nine glorious countries have dramatically different characters – each as irresistible and as exciting as the next. What to do and where do go? Here's your guide to getting the very best experiences from each country and its road trips.

Ireland

The emerald isle delivers picture-postcard views that are brooding, dramatic and delightful in turn. It's a place to revel in scenery, history, music-filled pubs and the stillness of village life.

Portugal

Portugal's mix of the medieval and the maritime makes touring a real treat. The legacy of a sometimes turbulent past includes medieval castles, vine-lined terraces and captivating cities. Meanwhile, the pounding Atlantic has sculpted a coast of glorious sandy bays.

Spain

Passionate, sophisticated and devoted to living the good life, Spain showcases sun-baked plains and glittering shores, it also enables leisurely discoveries of heritage, food, wine and art.

Great Britain

From cliff-backed shores and quaint villages, to historic monuments and wild, wild moors., Britain boasts everything from Georgian architecture to 21st-century art.

France

France seduces with a somehow familiar culture woven around cafe terraces, village-square markets and lace-curtained bistros where the *plat du jour* is chalked up outside. Here too find world-class art, architecture and delightfully scenic drives.

Germany

Here the majestic Rhine snakes through churning whirlpools, vast vineyards and medieval villages. And all around storybook castles crown jagged cliffs.

Switzerland

Switzerland is simply spectacular, with dazzling scenery at every turn: pristine lakes, lush meadows, snow-dusted Alps. Add cosmopolitan cities and you have a country making it easy to drive deep into its heart.

Austria

White-knuckle Alpine passes usher in a wealth of adrenaline sports, from year-round skiing to windsurfing and white-water rafting, while pretty castles and dense forests frame the majestic, mighty Danube.

Italy

Epicentre of the Roman Empire and birthplace of the Renaissance, this sun-kissed virtuoso serves up sublime music, food and wine.

Italy

FEW COUNTRIES CAN RIVAL ITALY'S WEALTH OF RICHES. Its historic cities boast iconic monuments and masterpieces at every turn, its food is imitated the world over and its landscape is a majestic patchwork of snow-capped peaks, plunging coastlines, lakes and remote valleys. And with many thrilling roads to explore, it offers plenty of epic driving.

The trips outlined in this section run the length of the country, leading from Alpine summits to southern volcanoes, and from hilltop towns in Tuscany to fishing villages on the Amalfi Coast. They take in heavyweight cities and little-known gems, and cover a wide range of experiences. So whether you want to tour gourmet towns, historic vineyards or idyllic coastlines, we have a route for you.

Italy

GERMANY

AUSTRIA

Innsbruck

SWITZERLAND

Monte Bianco (4810m)

Locarno
Verbania
Lago di Como
Como

Bolzano
Ortles (3905m)
Marmolada (3343m)
Trento

Tarvisio

SLOVENIA

LJUBLJANA

Aosta

Bergamo

Brescia
Verona
Padua

Lago di Garda

2

Milan

1

Piacenza

Venice

5

Trieste

Rijeka

Kvarner Gulf

Turin
Asti
Alessandria

Monte Viso (3841m)

Modena

Monte Croce (1314m)

Valle di Comacchio

FRANCE
Ventimiglia

Genoa

7

MONACO
MONACO

Bologna

Florence

3

Pisa

SAN MARINO

Ancona

CROATIA

Adriatic Sea

Montepulciano
Monte Amiata (1736m)

Lago di Bolsena

Lago Trasimeno

5

Perugia

Ascoli Piceno

Corno Grande (2912m)

Viterbo

L'Aquila

Monte Amaro (2795m)

Vieste

FRANCE

Santa Teresa di Gallura

Olbia

ROME

Monte Cavo (949m)

Frosinone

1

Foggia

Bari

Sassari

Nuoro

Mt Vesuvius (1281m)

Naples
Ischia
Capri
Vico Equense

Salerno

Taranto

Lecce

Oristano

Iglesias

Punta La Marmora (1834m)

Cagliari

Tyrrhenian Sea

Golfo di Salerno

4

Potenza

Monte Pollino (2248m)

Gallipoli

Cosenza

Crotone

Vibo Valentia

Messina

Trapani

Marsala

Palermo

Pizzo Carbonara (1979m)

6

Mt Etna (3340m)

Taormina

Ionian Sea

Catania

Agrigento

Ragusa

Syracuse

MEDITERRANEAN SEA

0   300 km
0   150 miles

Sicily Noto Cathedral

 DON'T MISS

Scrovegni Chapel
See the Renaissance blossoming through the tears in Giotto's moving frescoes for the Scrovegni Chapel on Trip 1

Montalcino
Crowned by a 14th-century fort, this hilltop town produces one of Italy's top red wines. Indulge yourself on Trip 3

Vietri sul Mare
Bring back a piece of the Amalfi Coast from this seaside centre, renowned for its bright-hued ceramics, on Trip 4

Noto
Stroll one of Italy's most beautiful town centres, admiring golden baroque buildings in the southern Sicilian sun on Trip 6

1 **Grand Tour 12–14 Days**
The classic cultural tour – part pilgrimage, part rite of passage. (p29)

2 **The Graceful Italian Lakes 5–7 Days**
The destination of choice for Goethe, Hemingway and George Clooney. (p43)

3 **Tuscan Wine Tour 4 Days**
Red wine fuels this jaunt around historic Chianti vineyards and Tuscan cellars. (p55)

4 **Amalfi Coast 7 Days**
A stunning coastline of vertical landscapes and chic resort towns. (p65)

5 **World Heritage Wonders 14 Days**
Discover the Unesco-listed treasures of Italy's art cities. (p75)

6 **Wonders of Ancient Sicily 12–14 Days**
Unearth Sicily's ancient Greek temples, Byzantine treasures and bewitching baroque towns. (p89)

7 **Italian Riviera 4 Days**
Seaside bastions, palm-fringed promenades, belle époque villas. (p101)

Grand Tour

1

The gap-year journey of its day, the Grand Tour is a search for art and enlightenment, adventure and debauchery.

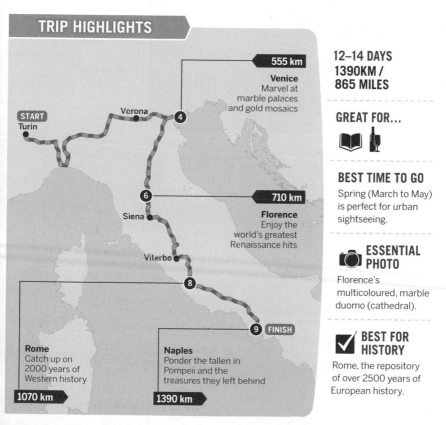

TRIP HIGHLIGHTS

555 km

Venice
Marvel at marble palaces and gold mosaics

Verona

4

START
Turin

710 km

6

Siena

Florence
Enjoy the world's greatest Renaissance hits

Vilerbo

8

9 **FINISH**

Rome
Catch up on 2000 years of Western history

1070 km

Naples
Ponder the fallen in Pompeii and the treasures they left behind

1390 km

**12–14 DAYS
1390KM /
865 MILES**

GREAT FOR...

BEST TIME TO GO
Spring (March to May) is perfect for urban sightseeing.

ESSENTIAL PHOTO
Florence's multicoloured, marble duomo (cathedral).

BEST FOR HISTORY
Rome, the repository of over 2500 years of European history.

Rome Interior of St Peter's Basilica

1 Grand Tour

From the Savoy palaces of Turin and Leonardo's *Last Supper* to the dubious drinking dens of Genoa and the pleasure palaces of Rome, the Grand Tour is part scholar's pilgrimage and part rite of passage. Offering a chance to view some of the world's greatest masterpieces and hear Vivaldi played on 18th-century cellos, it is a rollicking trip filled with the sights, sounds and tastes that have shaped European society for centuries.

❶ Turin

In his travel guide, *Voyage through Italy* (1670), travel writer and tutor Richard Lassels advocated a grand cultural tour of Europe, and in particular Italy, for young English aristocrats, during which the study of classical antiquity and the High Renaissance would ready them for future influential roles shaping the political, economic and social realities of the day.

First they travelled through France before crossing the Alps at Mt Cenis and heading to Turin (Torino), where letters of introduction admitted them to the city's agreeable Parisian-style social whirl. Turin's tree-lined boulevards still retain their elegant, French feel and many turn-of-the century cafes, such as **Caffè San Carlo** (Piazza San Carlo 156, ⊗8am-midnight Tue-Fri, to 1am Sat, to 9pm Mon), still serve Torinese hot chocolate beneath their gilded chandeliers.

Like the Medicis in Florence (Firenze) and the Borghese in Rome (Roma), Turin's Savoy princes had a penchant for extravagant architecture and interior decor. You suspect they also pined for their hunting lodges in Chambéry, France, from where they originated, as they

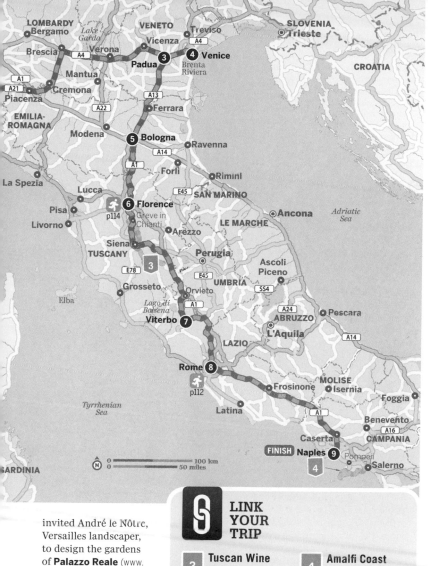

invited André le Nôtre,
Versailles landscaper,
to design the gardens
of **Palazzo Reale** (www.
ilpalazzorealeditorino.it;
Piazza Castello; adult/reduced
€12/6, 1st Sun of month free;
☺8.30am-7.30pm Tue-Sun)
in 1697.

✕ p40

🔗 LINK YOUR TRIP

3 Tuscan Wine Tour

Linger in the bucolic
hills around Florence
and enjoy fine gourmet
dining and world-
renowned wine-tasting.

4 Amalfi Coast

Play truant from
high-minded museums
and head south from
Naples for the Blue
Ribbon drive on the
Amalfi Coast.

The Drive » The two-hour (170km) drive to Genoa is all on autostrada, the final stretch twisting through the mountains. Leave Turin following signs for the A55 (towards Alessandria), which quickly merges with the A21 passing through the pretty Piedmontese countryside. Just before Alessandria turn south onto the A26 for Genoa/Livorno.

---

❷ Genoa

Some travellers, shy of crossing the Alps, might arrive by boat in Genoa (Genova). Despite its superb location, mild microclimate and lush flora, the city had a dubious reputation. Its historic centre was a warren of dark, insalubrious *caruggi* (alleys), stalked by prostitutes and beggars, while the excessive shrewdness of the Genovese banking families earned them a reputation, according to author Thomas Nugent, as 'a treacherous and over-reaching set of people'.

And yet with tourists and businessmen arriving from around the world, Genoa was, and still is, a cosmopolitan place. The **Rolli Palaces**, a collection of grand mansions originally meant to host visiting popes, dignitaries and royalty, made Via Balbi and Strada Nuova (now Via Giuseppe Garibaldi) two of the most famous streets in Europe. Visit the finest of them, the **Palazzo Spinola** (www. palazzospinola.beniculturali. it; Piazza Superiore di Pellicceria 1; adult/reduced €4/2; ⏱8.30am-7.30pm Tue-Sat, from 1.30pm Sun) and the **Palazzo Reale** (www. palazzorealegenova.benicul turali.it; Via Balbi 10; adult/ reduced €4/2; ⏱9am-7pm Tue-Sat, 1.30-7pm Sun). After stop for sweets at **Pietro Romanengo fu Stefano** (www.romanengo.com; Via Soziglia 74r; ⏱3.30-7.30pm Mon, 9am-1pm & 3.15-7.15pm Tue-Sat).

🍴 p40, p107

The Drive » This 365km drive takes most of the day, so stop for lunch in Cremona (p40). Although the drive is on autostrada, endless fields of corn line the route. Take the A7 north out of Genoa and at Tortona exit onto the A21 around industrial Piacenza to Brescia. At Brescia, change again onto the A4 direct to Padua.

---

❸ Padua

Bound for Venice (Venezia), Grand Tourists could hardly avoid visiting Padua (Padova), although by the 18th century international students no longer flocked to **Palazzo del Bò** (☎049 827 30 47; www.unipd. it/en/guidedtours; Via VIII Febbraio, adult/reduced €7/2; ⏱see website for tour times), the Venetian Republic's radical university where Copernicus and Galileo taught classes.

↻ DETOUR: MILAN

Start: ❶ **Turin (p30)**

No Grand Tour would be complete without a detour up the A4 to Milan (Milano) to eyeball Leonardo da Vinci's iconic mural **The Last Supper** (Il Cenacolo; ☎02 9280 0360; www.cenacolovinciano.net; Piazza Santa Maria delle Grazie 2; adult/reduced €6.50/3.25; ⏱8.15am-7pm Tue-Sun; Ⓜ Cadorna). Advance booking is essential (booking fee €1.50).

From his *Portrait of a Young Man* (c 1486) to portraits of Duke Ludovico Sforza's beautiful mistresses, *The Lady with the Ermine* (c 1489) and *La Belle Ferronière* (c 1490), Leonardo transformed the rigid conventions of portraiture to depict highly individual images imbued with naturalism. Then he evolved concepts of idealised proportions and the depiction of internal emotional states through physical dynamism *(St Jerome),* all of which cohere in the masterly *Il Cenacolo.*.

You can visit the university's claustrophobic, wooden **anatomy theatre** (the first in the world), although it's no longer de rigueur to witness dissections on the average tourist itinerary. Afterwards don't forget to pay your respects to the skulls of noble professors who donated themselves for dissection because of the difficulty involved in acquiring fresh corpses. Their skulls are lined up in the graduation hall.

Beyond the university the melancholy air of the city did little to detain foreign visitors. Even Giotto's spectacular frescoes in the **Cappella degli Scrovegni** (Scrovegni Chapel; ☑049 201 00 20; www.cappelladegliscrovegni. it; Piazza Eremitani 8; adult/ reduced €13/6; night ticket €8/6; ⊕9am-7pm), where advance reservations are essential, were of limited interest given medieval art was out of fashion, and only devout Catholics ventured to revere the strange relics of Saint Anthony in the **Basilica di Sant'Antonio** (Il Santo; ☑049 822 56 52; www.ba-silicadelsanto.org; Piazza del Santo; ⊕6.20am-7.45pm Apr-Oct, to 6.45pm Nov-Mar).

The Drive » Barely 40km from Venice, the drive from Padua is through featureless areas of light industry along the A4 and then the A57.

TRIP HIGHLIGHT

➍ Venice

Top of the itinerary, Venice at last! Then, as now, La Serenissima's watery landscape captured the imagination of travellers. At **Carnivale** (www.carni-vale.venezia.it) in February numbers swelled to 30,000; now they number in the hundreds of thousands. You cannot take your car onto the lagoon islands so leave it in a secure garage in Mestre, such as **Garage Europa Mestre** (☑041 95 92 02; www.garageeuro-pamestre.com; Corso del Popolo 55, Mestre; per day €15; ⊕8am-10pm), and hop on the train to Venice Santa Lucia where water taxis connect to all the islands.

Aside from the mind-improving art in the **Gallerie dell'Accademia** (☑041 520 03 45; www. gallerieaccademia.org; Campo della Carità 1050; adult/ reduced €10/8 plus supplement during special exhibitions, first Sun of the month free; ⊕8.15am-2pm Mon, to 7.15pm Tue-Sun; ⓢAccademia) and extraordinary architectural masterpieces such as the **Palazzo Ducale**, the **Campanile**, Longhena's **Chiesa di Santa Maria della Salute** and the glittering domes of the **Basilica di San Marco** (St Mark's Basilica; ☑041 270 83 11; www.basilicasan marco.it; Piazza San Marco; ⊕9.45am-5pm Mon-Sat, 2-5pm Sun summer, to 4pm Sun winter; ⓢSan Marco), Venice was considered an exciting den of debauchery. Venetian wives were notorious for keeping handsome escorts *(cicisbeo)*, courtesans held powerful positions at court and much time was devoted to frequenting casinos and coffeehouses. **Caffè Florian** (☑041 520 56 41; www.caffeflorian.com; Piazza San Marco 56/59; drinks €10-25; ⊕9am-midnight; ⓢSan Marco) still adheres to rules established in the 1700s.

So do as the Venetians would do: glide down the **Grand Canal** on the **No 1 Vaporetto** (ticket €7.50) for an architectural tour of 50 *palazzi* (mansions), gossip in the balconies of the **Teatro La Fenice** (☑041 78 66 72, tours 041 78 66 75; www.teatrolafenice. it; Campo San Fantin 1965; theatre visits adult/reduced €10/7, concert/opera tickets from €15/45; ⓢSanta Maria dei Giglio), or listen for summer thunderstorms in Vivaldi's *Four Seasons,* played by **Interpreti Veneziani** (☑041 27 / 05 61; www.interpretivenezianï. com; Chiesa San Vidal, Campo di San Vidal 2862; adult/reduced €28/23; ⊕doors open 8.30pm; ⓢAccademia).

For more earthly pleasures take a tour of Venice's centuries-old markets with a gourmet food walk.

✕ ⌷ p40, p87

The Drive » Retrace your steps to Padua on the A57 and

WHY THIS IS A GREAT TRIP
PAULA HARDY, WRITER

There's almost no need to explain why the Grand Tour is a classic trip. It is the template for all modern travel itineraries, where for the first time people travelled for curiosity, pleasure and learning. Covering Italy's show-stopping cities, it offers travellers a view of the country's very best art, architecture and antiquities, while transporting them from alpine peaks to sun-struck southern shores.

Top: Anatomy theatre, University of Padua
Left: Hall of Mirrors, Palazzo Reale, Genoa
Right: Teatro La Fenice, Venice

JUSTIN FOULKES/LONELY PLANET ©

A4 and navigate around the ring road in the direction of Bologna to pick up the A13 southwest for this short two-hour drive. After Padua the dual carriageway dashes through wide-open farmland and crosses the Po river, which forms the southern border of the Veneto.

- - - - - - - - - - -

❺ Bologna

Home to Europe's oldest university (established in 1088) and once the stomping ground of Dante, Boccaccio and Petrarch, Bologna had an enviable reputation for courtesy and culture. Its historic centre, complete with 20 soaring towers, is one of the best-preserved medieval cities in the world. In the **Basilica di San Petronio** (www.basilicadisanpetronio.it; Piazza Maggiore; ⊘7.45am-2pm & 3-6pm), originally intended to dwarf St Peter's in Rome, Giovanni Cassini's sundial (1655) proved the problems with the Julian calendar giving us the leap year, while Bolognesi students advanced human knowledge in obstetrics, natural science, zoology and anthropology. You can peer at their strange model waxworks and studiously labelled collections in the **Palazzo Poggi** (www.museopalazzopoggi.unibo.it; Via Zamboni 33; adult/reduced €5/3; ⊘10am-1pm Tue-Sun mid-Jun–mid-Sep, 10am-4pm Tue-Fri, 10.30am-5.30pm Sat & Sun mid-Sep–mid-Jun).

In art as in science, the School of Bologna gave birth to the Carracci cousins Ludovico, Agostino and Annibale, who were among the founding fathers of Italian baroque and were deeply influenced by the Counter-Reformation. See their emotionally charged blockbusters in the **Pinacoteca Nazionale** (www.pinacotecabologna. beniculturali.it; Via delle Belle Arti 56; adult/reduced €4/2; ⏰9am-1.30pm Tue & Wed, 2-7pm Thu-Sun).

✕ ⛺ p41

The Drive » Bologna sits at the intersection of the A1, A13 and A14. Navigate west out of the city, across the river Reno, onto the A1. From here it's a straight shot into Florence for 100km, leaving the Po plains behind you and entering the low hills of Emilia-Romagna and the forested valleys of Tuscany.

TRIP HIGHLIGHT

❻ Florence

From Brunelleschi's red-tiled dome atop Florence's **Duomo** (Cattedrale di Santa Maria del Fiore; www.oper-aduomo.firenze.it; Piazza del Duomo; ⏰10am-5pm Mon-Wed & Fri, to 4pm Thu, to 4.45pm Sat, 1.30-4.45pm Sun) to Michelangelo's and Botticelli's greatest hits, *David* and *The Birth of Venus,* in the **Galleria dell'Accademia** (📞055 29 48 83; www. firenzemusei.it; Via Ricasoli 60; adult/reduced €8/4, incl temporary exhibition €12.50/6.25; ⏰8.15am-6.50pm Tue-Sun) and the **Galleria degli Uffizi** (Uffizi Gallery; www. uffizi.beniculturali.it; Piazzale degli Uffizi 6; adult/reduced €8/4, incl temporary exhibition €12.50/6.25; ⏰8.15am-6.50pm Tue-Sun), Florence, according to Unesco, contains the highest number of artistic masterpieces in the world.

Whereas Rome and Milan have torn themselves down and been rebuilt many times, incorporating a multitude of architectural whims, central Florence looks much as it did in 1550, with stone towers and cypress-lined gardens.

✕ ⛺ p41, p63, p86

TOP TIP: JUMP THE QUEUE IN FLORENCE

In July, August and other busy periods such as Easter, long queues are a fact of life at Florence's key museums. For a fee of €4 each, tickets to the Uffizi and Galleria dell'Accademia (where *David* lives) can be booked in advance. To organise your ticket, go to www.firenzemusei.it or call **Firenze Musei** (📞055 29 48 83; www.firenzemusei.it).

The Drive » The next 210km, continuing south along the A1, travels through some of Italy's most lovely scenery. Just southwest of Florence the vineyards of Greve in Chianti harbour some great farmstays, while Arezzo is to the east. At Orvieto exit onto the SS71 and skirt Lago di Bolsena for the final 45km into Viterbo.

❼ Viterbo

From Florence the road to Rome crossed the dreaded and pestilential campagna (countryside), a swampy, mosquito-infested low-lying area. Unlike now, inns en route were uncomfortable and hazardous, so travellers hurried through Siena, stocking up on wine for the rough road ahead. They also stopped briefly in medieval Viterbo for a quick douse in the thermal springs at the **Terme dei Papi** (📞0761 35 03 90; www.termedeipapi.it; Strada Bagni 12; pool adult/child €12/8, Sun €18/8; ⏰9am-7pm Wed-Mon, plus 9pm-1am Sat), and a tour of the High Renaissance spectacle that is the **Villa Lante** (📞0761 28 80 08; Via Jacopo Barozzi 71; adult/reduced €5/2.50; ⏰8.30am-1hr before sunset Tue-Sun).

The Drive » Rejoin the A1 after a 28km drive along the rural SS675. For the next 40km the A1 descends slowly into Lazio, criss-crossing the river Tevere and keeping the ridge of the Apennines to the left as it darts through tunnels. At Fiano

Romano exit for Roma Nord onto the A1dir for the final 20km descent into the capital.

TRIP HIGHLIGHT

⑧ Rome

In the 18th century Rome, even in ruins, was still thought of as the august capital of the world. Here more than anywhere the Grand Tourist was awakened to an interest in art and architecture, although the **Colosseum** (Colosseo; ☏06 3996 7700; www.coopculture.it; Piazza del Colosseo; adult/reduced incl Roman Forum & Palatino €12/7.50; ☺8.30am-1hr before sunset; Ⓜ Colosseo) was still filled with debris and the Palatine Hill was covered in gardens, its excavated treasures slowly accumulating in the world's oldest national museum, the **Capitoline Museums** (Musei Capitolini; ☏06 06 08; www.museicapitolini.org; Piazza del Campidoglio 1; adult/reduced €12/10; ☺9.30am-7.30pm, last admission 6.30pm; Ⓠ Piazza Venezia).

Arriving through the Porta del Popolo, visitors first spied the dome of St **Peter's** (Basilica di San Pietro; www.vatican.va; St Peter's Sq; ☺7am-7pm summer, to 6.30pm winter; Ⓜ Ottaviano-San Pietro) before clattering along the *corso* to the customs house. Once done, they headed to **Piazza di Spagna**, the city's principal meeting place where Keats penned

his love poems and died of consumption.

Although the **Pantheon** (www.pantheonroma.com; Piazza della Rotonda; ☺8.30am-7.30pm Mon-Sat, 9am-6pm Sun; Ⓠ Largo di Torre Argentina) and **Vatican Museums** (Musei Vaticani; ☏06 6988 4676; http://mv.vatican.va; Viale Vaticano; adult/reduced €16/8, last Sun of month free; ☺9am-4pm Mon-Sat, 9am-12.30pm last Sun of month; Ⓜ Ottaviano-San Pietro) were a must, most travellers preferred to socialise in the grounds of the **Borghese Palace** (☏06 3 28 10; www.galleriaborghese. it; Piazzale del Museo Borghese 5; adult/reduced €11/6.50; ☺8.30am-7.30pm Tue-Sun; Ⓠ Via Pinciana).

Follow their example and mix the choicest sights with more venal pleasures such as fine dining at **Open Colonna** (☏06 4782 2641; www. antonellocolonna.it; Via Milano 9a; meals €20-80; ☺12.30-3.30pm Tue-Sun, 7-11.30pm Tue-Sat; ✱; Ⓠ Via Nazionale) and souvenir shopping

at antique perfumery **Officina Profumo Farmaceutica di Santa Maria Novella** (www.smnovella. it; Corso del Rinascimento 47; ☺10am-7.30pm Mon-Sat; Ⓠ Corso del Rinascimento).

✕ ⑆ p41, p86

The Drive » Past Rome the landscape is hotter and drier, trees give way to Mediterranean shrubbery and the grass starts to yellow. Beyond the vineyards of Frascati, just 20km south of Rome, the A1 heads straight to Naples (Napoli) for 225km, a two-hour drive that often takes much longer due to heavy traffic.

TRIP HIGHLIGHT

⑨ Naples

Only the more adventurous Grand Tourists continued south to the salacious city of Naples. At the time Mt Vesuvius glowed menacingly, erupting six times during the 18th century and eight times in the 19th century. But Naples was the home of opera and *commedia dell'arte* (improvised comedic satire), and

ITALY 1 GRAND TOUR

singing lessons and seats at **Teatro San Carlo** (☎081 797 23 31; www.teatrosancarlo. it; Via San Carlo 98; ☺box office 10am-5.30pm Mon-Sat, to 2pm Sun; ☐R2 to Via San Carlo) were obligatory.

Then there were the myths of Virgil and Dante to explore at Lago d'Averno and **Campi Flegrei** (the Phlegrean Fields). After the discovery of **Pompeii** (☎081 857 53 47; www.pompeiisites.org; entrances at Porta Marina, Piazza Esedra & Piazza Anfiteatro; adult/reduced €13/7.50, incl Herculaneum €22/12; ☺9am-7.30pm summer, to 5pm winter) in 1748, the unfolding drama of a Roman town in its death throes drew throngs of visitors. Then, as now, it was the most popular tourist sight in Italy and its priceless mosaics, frescoes and colossal sculptures filled the **Museo Archeologico Nazionale** (☎081 442 21 49; http://cir.campania.beniculturali. it/museoarcheologiconazionale; Piazza Museo Nazionale 19; adult/reduced €8/4; ☺9am-7.30pm Wed-Mon; Ⓜ Museo, Piazza Cavour).

🛏 p41

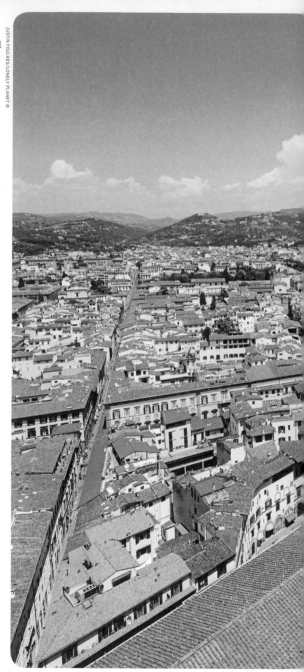

Florence View of the red-tiled dome of the Duomo

Eating & Sleeping

Turin ❶

🍷 Fiorio
Cafe

(Via Po 8; ⊘8.30am-1am Tue-Sun) Garner literary inspiration in Mark Twain's old window seat as you contemplate the gilded interior of a cafe where 19th-century students once plotted revolutions and the Count of Cavour deftly played whist. The bittersweet hot chocolate remains inspirational.

Genoa ❷

✗ Trattoria della Raibetta
Trattoria $$

(📞010 246 88 77; www.trattoriadellaraibetta. it; Vico Caprettari 10-12; meals €35; ⊘noon-2.30pm & 7.30-11pm Tue-Sun) Totally typica Genoese food can be found in the family-run joints hidden in the warren of streets near the cathedral. This, a snug trattoria with a low brick-vaulted ceiling, serves regional classics such as trofiette al pesto or octopus salad alongside excellent fresh fish.

Cremona ❷

✗ La Sosta
Osteria $$

(📞0372 45 66 56; www.osterialasosta.it; Via Sicardo 9; meals €35-40; ⊘12.15-2pm Tue-Sun, 7.15-10pm Tue-Sat) La Sosta is surrounded by violin-makers' workshops and is a suitably harmonious place to feast on regional delicacies such as tortelli di zucca (pumpkin pasta parcels) and baked snails. The entrance is plastered with so many approving restaurant-guide stickers that you can't see through the glass.

Venice ❹

✗ Dalla Marisa
Venetian $$

(📞041 72 02 11; Fondamenta di San Giobbe 652b, Cannaregio; set menu lunch/dinner €15/35; ⊘noon-3pm daily, 7-11pm Thu-Sat; 🚊Crea) At this Cannaregio institution, you'll be seated where there's room and get no menu – you'll have whatever Marisa's cooking. And you'll like it. Lunches are a bargain at €15 for a first, main, side, wine, water and coffee – pace yourself through prawn risotto to finish with steak and grilled zucchini, or Marisa will jokingly scold you over coffee.

✗ Ristoteca Oniga
Venetian $$

(📞041 522 44 10; www.oniga.it; Campo San Barnaba 2852; meals €19-35; ⊘noon-2.30pm & 7-10.30pm Wed-Mon; 🛜; 🚊Ca' Rezzonico) Its menu peppered with organic ingredients, Oniga serves exemplary sarde in saor (sardines in tangy onion marinade), seasonal pastas and the odd Hungarian classic like goulash (a nod to former chef Annika Major). Oenophiles will appreciate the selection of 100-plus wines, handy for toasting to the €19 set lunch menu. Grab a sunny spot in the campo, or get cosy in a wood-panelled corner.

🛏 Ca' Angeli
Boutique Hotel $$

(📞041 523 24 80; www.caangeli.it; Calle del Traghetto de la Madoneta 1434, San Polo; d €95-225, ste from €200; ❄🛜; 🚊San Silvestro) Murano glass chandeliers, a Louis XIV love-seat and namesake 16th-century angels set a refined tone at this restored, canalside palazzo. Guest rooms are a picture with beamed ceilings, antique carpets and big bathrooms, while the dining room looks out onto the Grand Canal. Breakfast includes organic products where possible.

Bologna ⑤

✕ All'Osteria Bottega
Osteria $$

(📞051 58 51 11; Via Santa Caterina 51; meals €35-40; ⏱12.30-2.30pm & 8-10.30pm Tue-Sat) At this *osteria* truly worthy of the name, owners Daniele and Valeria lavish attention on every table between trips to the kitchen for plates of *culatello di Zibello* ham, tortellini in capon broth, pork shank in red wine reduction and other Slow Food delights. Desserts are homemade by Valeria, from the *ciambella* (Romagnola ring-shaped cake) to fresh fruit sorbets.

🛏 Bologna nel Cuore
B&B $$

(📞051 26 94 42; www.bolognanelcuore.it; Via Cesare Battisti 29; s €80-100, d €100-140, apt €125-130; P ❄ 🤶) This centrally located, immaculate and well-loved B&B features a pair of bright, high-ceilinged rooms with pretty tiled bathrooms and endless mod cons, plus two comfortable, spacious apartments with kitchen and laundry facilities. Owner and art historian Maria generously shares her knowledge of Bologna and serves breakfasts featuring jams made with fruit picked near her childhood home in the Dolomites.

Florence ⑥

✕ I Due Fratellini
Sandwiches $

(📞055 239 60 96; www.iduefratellini.com; Via dei Cimatori 38r; panini €3; ⏱10am-7pm) This hole-in-the-wall has been in business since 1875. Wash *panini* down with a beaker of wine and leave the empties on the wooden shelf outside.

🛏 Palazzo Guadagni Hotel
Hotel $$

(📞055 265 83 76; www.palazzoguadagni.com; Piazza Santo Spirito 9; d €130-230; ❄ 🤶) This romantic hotel overlooking Florence's liveliest summertime square is legendary – Zeffirelli shot scenes from *Tea with Mussolini* here. Housed in an artfully revamped Renaissance palace, it has 15 spacious if old-fashioned rooms and an impossibly romantic loggia terrace with wicker chairs and predictably dreamy views.

Rome ⑧

✕ Necci
Cafe $$

(📞06 9760 1552; www.necci1924.com; Via Fanfulla da Lodi 68; dinner around €45, lunch mains around €8; ⏱8am-2am; 🤶; 🚃Via Prenestina) Iconic Necci opened as a gelateria in 1924 and later became a favourite of director Pier Paolo Pasolini. Good for a drink or a meal, it serves up sophisticated Italian cooking to an eclectic crowd of all ages, with a lovely, leafy garden terrace (ideal for families).

✕ Enoteca Regionale Palatium
Ristorante $$$

(📞06 6920 2132; Via Frattina 94; meals €55; ⏱11am-11pm Mon-Sat, closed Aug; 🚃Via del Corso) A rich showcase of regional bounty, run by the Lazio Regional Food Authority, this sleek wine bar serves excellent local specialities, such as *porchetta* (pork roasted with herbs) or *gnocchi alla Romana con crema da zucca* (potato dumplings Roman-style with cream of pumpkin), as well as an impressive array of Lazio wines (try lesser-known drops such as Aleatico).

🛏 Hotel Scalinata di Spagna
Hotel $$

(📞06 6994 0896; www.hotelscalinata.com; Piazza della Trinità dei Monti 17; d €130-260; ❄ @ 🤶; M Spagna) Given its location – perched alongside the Spanish Steps – the Scalinata is surprisingly modestly priced. An informal and friendly place, it's something of a warren, with a great roof terrace and low corridors leading off to smallish, old-fashioned yet romantic rooms. Book early for a room with a view.

Naples ⑨

🛏 Grand Hotel Vesuvio
Hotel $$$

(📞081 764 00 44; www.vesuvio.it; Via Partenope 45; s/d €280/310; ❄ @ 🤶; 🚃128 to Via Santa Lucia) Known for hosting legends – past guests include Rita Hayworth and Humphrey Bogart – this five-star heavyweight is a decadent melange of dripping chandeliers, period antiques and opulent rooms. Count your lucky stars while drinking a martini at the rooftop restaurant.

The Graceful Italian Lakes

2

Writers from Goethe to Hemingway have lavished praise on the Italian lakes, dramatically ringed by snow-powdered mountains and garlanded by grand villas and exotic, tropical flora.

TRIP HIGHLIGHTS

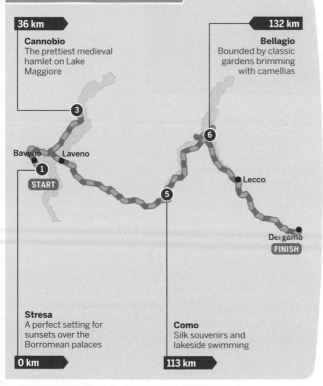

36 km

Cannobio
The prettiest medieval hamlet on Lake Maggiore

132 km

Bellagio
Bounded by classic gardens brimming with camellias

Baveno Laveno
START

Lecco

Dergamo
FINISH

Stresa
A perfect setting for sunsets over the Borromean palaces

0 km

Como
Silk souvenirs and lakeside swimming

113 km

5–7 DAYS
213KM / 132 MILES

GREAT FOR...

BEST TIME TO GO
April to June, when the camellias are in full bloom.

ESSENTIAL PHOTO
The cascading gardens of Palazzo Borromeo.

BEST FOR GLAMOUR
Touring Bellagio's headland in a mahogany cigarette boat.

Bellagio The gardens of Villa Melzi d'Eril on the banks of Lago di Como

43

2 The Graceful Italian Lakes

Formed at the end of the last ice age, and a popular holiday spot since Roman times, the Italian lakes have an enduring natural beauty. At Lago Maggiore (Lake Maggiore) the palaces of the Borromean Islands lie like a fleet of fine vessels in the gulf, their grand ballrooms and shell-encrusted grottoes once host to Napoleon and Princess Diana, while the siren call of Lago di Como (Lake Como) draws Arabian sheikhs and Hollywood movie stars to its discreet forested slopes.

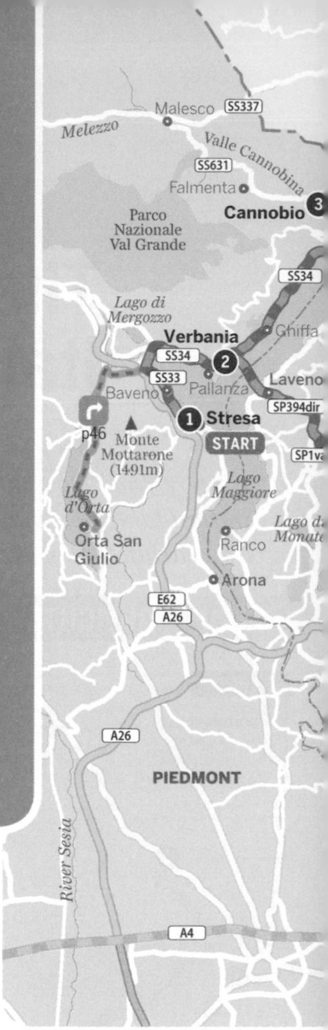

Malesco SS337
Melezzo
Valle Cannobina
SS631
Falmenta
Parco **Cannobio** 3
Nazionale
Val Grande
SS34
Lago di
Mergozzo
Verbania Ghiffa
SS34 2
SS33 Pallanza **Laveno**
Baveno SP394dir
p46 Monte 1 **Stresa**
Mottarone **START**
(1491m) SP1va
Lago Lago
d'Orta Maggiore
Orta San Lago di
Giulio Ranco Monate
Arona
E62
A26

A26

PIEDMONT

River Sesia

A4

TRIP HIGHLIGHT

1 Stresa

More than Como and Garda, Lago Maggiore has retained the belle époque air of its early tourist heyday. Attracted by the mild climate and the easy access the new 1855 railway provided, the European *haute bourgeoisie* flocked to buy and build grand lakeside villas.

The star attractions are the Borromean Islands (Isole Borromee) and their palaces. **Isola Bella** took the name of Carlo III's wife, the *bella* Isabella, in the 17th century, when its centrepiece, **Palazzo Borromeo** (☎0323 3 05 56; www.isoleborromee.it; Isola Bella; adult/child €15/8.50, incl Palazzo Madre adult/child €20.50/10; ☺9am-5.30pm mid-Mar–mid-Oct) was built. Construction of the villa and gardens was thought out in such a way that the island would have the appearance of a vessel, with the villa at the prow and the gardens dripping down 10 tiered terraces at the rear. Inside the palace, the **Galleria dei Quadri** (Picture Gallery) is hung with Old Masters, including Rubens, Titian, Veronese and José Ribera (Spagnoletto).

By contrast, **Isola Madre** eschews ostentation for a more romantic, familial atmosphere. The 16th- to 18th-century **Palazzo Madre**

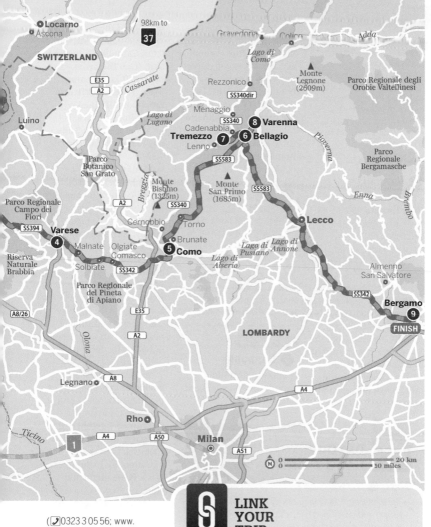

SWITZERLAND

Locarno
Ascona

98km to
37

Gravedona
Colico
Adda

Luino

Lago di Lugano

Cassarate

E35
A2

Lago di Como

Rezzonico

Monte Legnone (2609m)

Parco Regionale degli Orobie Valtellinesi

Menaggio

SS340dir

Piovorna

Cadenabbia

SS340

8 **Varenna**

Tremezzo **7** **6** **Bellagio**

Lenno

Parco Botanico San Grato

SS583

Parco Regionale Bergamasche

Parco Regionale Campo dei Fiori

Breggia

A2

Monte Bisbino (1325m)

SS340

Monte San Primo (1685m)

SS583

Enna

Brembo

SS394

Varese **4**

Cernobbio

Torno

Lago di Pusiano *Lago di Annone*

Lecco

Malnate   Olgiate Comasco

Brunate

5 **Como**

Lago di Alserio

Riserva Naturale Brabbia

Solbiate

SS342

Parco Regionale del Pineta di Apiano

E35

A8/26

Olona

A2

LOMBARDY

Almenno San Salvatore

SS342

Bergamo **9**

FINISH

Legnano

A8

A4

Ticino

1

A4

A50

Rho

Milan (Milano)

A51

N 0 _____ 20 km
   0 _____ 10 miles

(☎0323 3 05 56; www. isoleborromee it adult/child €12/6.50, incl Palazzo Borromeo €20.50/10; ⊙9am-5.30pm mid-Mar–mid-Oct) includes a 'horror' theatre with a cast of devilish marionettes, while Chinese pheasants stalk the English gardens.

✗ p53

LINK YOUR TRIP

1 **Grand Tour**
From Stresa take the A8 to Milan (Milano) from where you can commence your own Grand Tour of Italy.

37 **The Swiss Alps**
From Verbania head north-east for the greatest of the great outdoors: perfect peaks, gorgeous glaciers, verdant valleys.

45

The Drive » Leave Stresa westwards on the Via Sempione (SS33) skirting the edge of the lake for this short, 14km drive. Pass through Baveno and round the western edge of the gulf through the greenery of the Fondo Toce natural reserve. When you reach the junction with the SS34, turn right for Verbania.

❷ Verbania

The late-19th-century **Villa Taranto** (📞0323 55 66 67; www.villataranto.it; Via Vittorio Veneto 111, Verbania Pallanza; adult/reduced €10/5.50; ⏰8.30am-6.30pm mid-Mar–Sep, 9am-4pm Oct; 🅿) sits just outside Verbania. In 1931, royal archer and Scottish captain Neil McEacharn bought the villa from the Savoy family and started to plant some 20,000 species. With its rolling hillsides of purple rhodo-dendrons and camellias, acres of tulip flowers and hothouses full of equatorial lilies it is considered one of Europe's finest botanical gardens. During the last week in April, **Settimana del Tulipano** takes place, when tens of thousands of tulips erupt in magnificent multi-coloured bloom.

🍴 p53

The Drive » Pick up the SS34 again, continuing in a northeasterly direction out of Verbania, through the suburbs of Intra and Pallanza. Once you've cleared the town the 20km to Cannobio are the prettiest on the tour, shadowing the lake shore the entire way with views across the water.

TRIP HIGHLIGHT

❸ Cannobio

Sheltered by a high mountain and sitting at the foot of the Cannobino valley, the medieval hamlet of Cannobio is located 5km from the Swiss border. It is a dreamy place. **Piazza di Vittorio Emanuele III**, lined with pastel-hued houses, is the location of a huge **Sunday market** that attracts visitors from Switzerland. Right in the heart of the historic centre, in a 15th-century monastery that later became the home of the Pironi family, is the atmospheric **Hotel Pironi** (📞0323 7 06 24; www.pironihotel. it; Via Marconi 35; s €120, d €150-195, tr €185-230; 🅿🛜). Behind its thickset walls are rooms with frescoed vaults, exposed timber beams and an assortment of tastefully decorated bedrooms.

You can hire small **sailing boats** (€35/55 per one/two hours) and make an excursion to the ruined **Castelli della Malpaga**, located on two rocky islets to the south of Cannobio. In summer it is a favourite picnic spot.

Alternatively, explore the wild beauty of the Valle Cannobina up the SS631, following the surging Torrente Cannobino stream into the heavily wooded hillsides to Malesco. Just 2.5km along the valley, in Sant'Anna, the torrent forces its way powerfully through a narrow gorge

---

DETOUR: LAGO D'ORTA

Start: ❶ Stresa (p44)

Separated from Lake Maggiore by Monte Mottarone (1492m) and enveloped by thick, dark-green woodlands, Lago d'Orta would make a perfect elopers' getaway. At 13.4km long by 2.5km wide you can drive around the lake in a day. The focal point is the captivating medieval village of **Orta San Giulio**, which sits across from Isola San Giulio, where you'll spy the frescoed, 12th-century **Basilica di San Giulio** (⏰9.30am-6pm Tue-Sun, 2-5pm Mon Apr-Sep, 9.30am-noon & 2-5pm Tue Sun, 2-5pm Mon Oct-Mar). Come during the week and you'll have the place largely to yourself.

known as the **Orrido di Sant'Anna**, crossed at its narrowest part by a Romanesque bridge.

The Drive ≫ The next part of the journey involves retracing the previous 22km drive to Verbania-Intra to board the cross-lake ferry to Laveno. Ferries run every 20 minutes (one-way tickets cost €8 to €13 for car and driver). Once in Laveno pick up the SP394dir and then the SP1var and SS394 for the 23km drive to Varese.

---

❹ Varese

Spread out to the south of the Campo dei Fiori hills, Varese is a prosperous provincial capital. From the 17th century onwards, Milanese nobles began to build second residences here, the most sumptuous being the **Palazzo Estense**, completed in 1771 for Francesco III d'Este, the governor of the Duchy of Milan. Although you cannot visit the palace you are free to wander the vast Italianate **gardens** (open 8am to dusk).

To the north of the city sits another great villa, **Villa Panza** (📞0332 28 39 60; www.fondoambiente. It, Piazza Litta 1; adult/reduced €10/5; ⊗10am-6pm Tue-Sun), donated to the state in 1996. Part of the donation were 150 contemporary canvases collected by Giuseppe Panza di Biumo, mostly by post-WWII American artists. One of the finest

LAGO MAGGIORE EXPRESS

The **Lago Maggiore Express** (📞091 756 04 00; www.lagomaggioreexpress.com; adult/child 1-day tour €34/17, 2-day tour €44/22) is a picturesque day trip you can do without the car. It includes train travel from Arona or Stresa to Domodossola, from where you get the charming *Centovalli* train, crossing 100 valleys, to Locarno in Switzerland and a ferry back to Stresa. The two-day version is perhaps better value if you have the time.

rooms is the 1830 **Salone Impero** (Empire Hall), with heavy chandeliers and four canvases by David Simpson (born in 1928).

The Drive ≫ The 28km drive from Varese to Como isn't terribly scenic, passing through a string of small towns and suburbs nestled in the wooded hills. The single-lane SS342 passes through Malnate, Solbiate and Olgiate Comasco before reaching Como.

TRIP HIGHLIGHT

❺ Como

Built on the wealth of its silk industry, Como is an elegant town and remains Europe's most important producer of silk products. The **Museo della Seta** (Silk Museum; 📞031 30 31 80; www.musoosetacomo.com; Via Castelnuovo 9; adult/reduced €10/7; ⊗10am-6pm Tue-Fri, to 1pm Sat) unravels the town's industrial history, with early dyeing and printing equipment on display. At **A Picci** (📞031 26 13 69; Via Vittorio Emanuele

II 54; ⊗3-7.30pm Mon, 9am-12.30pm & 3-7.30pm Tue-Sat) you can buy top-quality scarves, ties and fabrics for a fraction of the cost you'd pay elsewhere.

After wandering the medieval alleys of the historic centre take a stroll along **Passeggiata Lino Gelpi**, where you pass a series of waterfront mansions, finally arriving at **Villa Olmo** (📞031 25 23 52; Via Cantoni 1; gardens free, villa entry varies by exhibition; ⊗villa during exhibitions 9am-12.30pm & 2-5pm Mon-Sat, gardens 7.30am-11pm summer, to 7pm winter). Set grandly facing the lake, this Como landmark was built in 1728 by the Odescalchi family, related to Pope Innocent XI, and now hosts blockbuster art shows. During the summer the **Lido di Villa Olmo** (📞031 57 08 71; www.lidovillaolmo.it; Via Cernobbio 2; adult/reduced €8/4; ⊗9am-7pm mid-May–Sep), an open-air swimming pool and lakeside bar, is open to the public.

WHY THIS IS A GREAT TRIP
PAULA HARDY, WRITER

Despite centuries of fame as a tourist destination, there's a timeless glamour to the Italian lakes, especially Lago di Como with its mountainous amphitheatre of snow-capped Alps. One of the best ways to see it is to walk the old mule tracks. There are some easy walks with fabulous views around Brunate. Pick up a map showing the trails from the Como tourist office.

Top: Villa Serbelloni, Bellagio, Lago di Como
Left: Market stalls in Cannobio, Lago Maggiore
Right: The gardens of Villa Monastero, Varenna, Lago di Como

On the other side of Como's marina, the **Fu nicolare Como-Brunate** (☎031 30 36 08; www. funicolarecomo.it; Piazza de Gasperi 4; adult one way/return €3/5.50, reduced €2/3.20; ⊙half-hourly departures 6am-midnight summer, to 10.30pm winter) whisks you uphill to the quiet village of **Brunate** for splendid views across the lake.

✗ ⊨ p53

The Drive » The 32km drive from Como to Bellagio along the SS583 is spectacular. The narrow road swoops and twists around the lake shore the entire way and rises up out of Como giving panoramic views over the lake. There are plenty of spots en route where you can pull over for photographs.

- - - - - - - - - - - -

TRIP HIGHLIGHT

⑥ Bellagio

It's impossible not to be charmed by Bellagio's waterfront of bobbing boats, its maze of stone staircases, cypress groves and showy gardens.

Villa Serbelloni (☎031 95 15 55; Piazza della Chiesa 14; adult/child €9/5; ⊙tours 11.30am & 2.30pm Tue-Sun mid-Mar–Oct) **covers much of the promontory on which Bellagio sits.** Although owned by the Rockefeller Foundation, you can still tour the gardens on a guided tour. Otherwise stroll the grounds of neoclassical **Villa Melzi d'Eril** (☎339 4573838; www. giardinidivillamelzi.it; Lungo Lario Manzoni; adult/reduced

€6.50/4; ☺9.30am-6.30pm Apr-Oct), **which run right down to the lake and are adorned with classical statues couched in blushing azaleas.**

Barindelli's (☎338 2110337; www.barindellitaxi boats.it; Piazza Mazzini; tours per hour €140) **operates slick, mahogany cigarette boats in which you can tool around the headland in for a sunset tour (boats seat 10 people).**

🛏 p53

The Drive » The best way to reach Tremezzo, without driving all the way around the bottom of the lake, is to take the ferry from Piazza Mazzini. One-way fares cost €4.60, but for sightseeing you may want to consider the one-day central lake ticket, covering Bellagio, Varenna, Tremezzo and Cadenabbia, for €15.

---

❼ Tremezzo

Tremezzo is high on everyone's list for a visit to the 17th-century **Villa Carlotta** (☎034 44 04 05; www.villacarlotta.it; Via Regina 2; adult/reduced €9/7; ☺9am-7.30pm Apr–mid-Oct), whose botanic gardens are filled with orange trees knitted into pergolas and some of Europe's finest rhododendrons, azaleas and camellias. The villa, which is strung with paintings and fine alabaster-white sculptures (especially lovely are those by Antonio Canova), takes its name from the Prussian princess who was given

Tremezzo Villa Carlotta on the shore of Lago di Como

SEAPLANES ON THE LAKE

For a touch of Hollywood glamour, check out **Aero Club Como** (📞031 57 44 95; www.aeroclubcomo.com; Viale Masia 44; 30min flight from €140), which has been sending seaplanes out over the lakes since 1930. The 30-minute flight to Bellagio from Como costs €140 for two people. Longer excursions over Lake Maggiore are also possible. In summer you need to reserve at least three days in advance.

the palace in 1847 as a wedding present from her mother.

The Drive » As with the trip to Tremezzo, the best way to travel to Varenna is by passenger ferry either from Tremezzo or Bellagio.

---

❽ Varenna

Wander the flower-laden pathway from Piazzale Martiri della Libertà to the gardens of **Villa Cipressi** (📞0341 83 01 13; www.hotelvillacipressi.it; Via IV Novembre 22; adult/child €4/2; ⊙10am-6pm Mar-Oct), now a luxury hotel (singles €140 to €160, doubles €170 to €230), and, 100m further south, **Villa Monastero** (📞0341 29 54 50; www.villamonastero. eu; Via IV Novembre; villa & gardens adult/reduced €8/4, gardens only €5/2; ⊙ gardens 9.30am-7pm year-round, villa 10am-6pm Fri-Sun Mar-May & Oct, 2-6pm Wed, 9.30am-7pm Thu-Sun Jun, Jul & Sep, 9.30am-7pm Aug, 11am-5pm Nov), a former convent turned into a vast residence by the Mornico

family in the 17th century. In both cases, you can stroll through the verdant gardens admiring magnolias, camellias and exotic yuccas.

The Drive » Departing Bellagio, pick up the SS583, but this time head southeast towards Lecco down the other 'leg' of Lago di Como. As with the stretch from Como to Bellagio, the road hugs the lake, offering spectacular views the whole 20km to Lecco. Once you reach Lecco head south out of town down Via Industriale and pick up the SS342 for the final 40km to Bergamo.

---

❾ Bergamo

Although Milan's sky-scrapers are visible on a clear day, historically Bergamo was more close-ly associated with Venice (Venezia). Hence the elegant Venetian-style architecture of **Piazza Vecchia**, appreciated by Le Corbusier for its beautiful and harmonious arrangement.

Behind this secular core sits the **Piazza del Duomo** with its modest baroque cathedral. A great deal more interesting is the **Basilica di Santa Maria Maggiore** (Piazza Duomo; ⊙9am-12.30pm & 2.30-6pm Apr-Oct, shorter hours Nov-Mar) next door. To its whirl of fres-coed, Romanesque apses, begun in 1137, Gothic touches were added as was the Renaissance **Cappella Colleoni** (Piazza Duomo; ⊙9am-12.30pm & 2-6.30pm Mar-Oct, 9am-12.30pm & 2-4.30pm Tue-Sun Nov-Feb), the mausoleum-cum-chapel of the famous mercenary commander, Bartolomeo Colleoni (1696–1770). Demolish-ing an entire apse of the basilica, he commis-sioned Giovanni Antonio Amadeo to create a tomb that is now considered a masterpiece of Lombard art with its exuberant rococo frescoes by Giam-battista Tiepolo.

Also like Venice, Bergamo has a grand art academy. Recently reopened after a seven year renovation, the **Accademia Carrara** (📞035 23 43 96; www. lacarrara.it; Piazza Carrara 82; adult/reduced €10/8; ⊙10am-7pm) is both school and museum, its stunning collection of 1800 Renais-sance paintings amassed by local scholar Count Giacomo Carrara.

🍴 🛏️ p53

Eating & Sleeping

Stresa ❶

✖ Ristorante Il Vicoletto   Ristorante €€

(☎0323 93 21 02; www.ristorantevicoletto.com; Vicolo del Pocivo 3; meals €30-45; ⊗noon-2pm & 6.30-10pm Fri-Wed) Located a short, uphill walk from the centre of Stresa, Il Vicoletto has a commendable regional menu including lake trout, wild asparagus, and traditional risotto with radicchio and Taleggio cheese. The dining room is modestly elegant with bottle-lined dressers and linen-covered tables, while the local clientele speaks volumes in this tourist town.

Verbania ❷

✖ Ristorante Milano   Modern Italian €€€

(☎0323 55 68 16; www.ristorantemilano lagomaggiore.it; Corso Zanitello 2, Verbania Pallanza; meals €50-70; ⊗noon-2pm & 7-9pm Wed-Sun, noon-2pm Mon; ✴) The setting really is hard to beat: Milano directly overlooks Pallanza's minuscule horseshoe-shaped harbour (200m south of the ferry jetty); a scattering of tables sits on lakeside lawns amid the trees. It's an idyllic spot to enjoy lake fish, local lamb and innovative Italian cuisine, such as *risotto ai petali di rosa* (risotto with rose petals).

Como ❺

✖ Osteria del Gallo   Italian €€

(☎031 27 25 91; www.osteriadelgallo-como.it; Via Vitani 16; meals €25-30; ⊗12.30-3pm Mon, to 10pm Tue-Sat) An ageless *osteria* that looks exactly the part. In the wood-lined dining room, wine bottles and other goodies fill the shelves, and diners tuck into traditional local food. The menu is chalked up daily and might include a first course of *zuppa di ceci* (chickpea soup), followed by lightly fried lake fish.

✖ Ristorante Sociale   Italian €€

(☎031 26 40 42; www.ristorantesociale.it; Via Rodari 6; meals €20-30; ⊗noon-2pm & 7-10.30pm Wed-Mon) A workaday street round the back of the *duomo* is an unlikely spot for such a bewitching restaurant. The menu is packed with local meat and lake produce, and might

feature perch and porcini mushrooms. Tuck in under the red-brick barrel ceiling, or in the charming courtyard.

⊨ Avenue Hotel   Boutique Hotel €€

(☎031 27 21 86; www.avenuehotel.it; Piazzolo Terragni 6; d €170-240, ste from €340; P ✴ 🕏) An assured sense of style at this delightful hotel sees ultramodern rooms team crisp white walls with shots of purple or fuchsia-pink. Breakfast is served in a chic courtyard, service is warm but discreet, and you can borrow a bike for free.

Bellagio ❻

⊨ Hotel Silvio   Hotel €€

(☎031 95 03 22; www.bellagiosilvio.com; Via Carcano 10; d from €115-185, meals €30-40; P ✴ 🕏 🞬) Located above the fishing hamlet of Loppia a short walk from the village, this family-run hotel is one of Bellagio's best. Here you can wake up in a contemporary Zen-like room and gaze over the gardens of some of Lago di Como's most prestigious villas. Then spend the morning at Bellagio's *lido;* it's free for hotel guests.

Bergamo ❾

✖ Colleoni & Dell'Angelo   Italian €€€

(☎035 23 25 96; www.colleonidellangelo.com; Piazza Vecchia 7; meals €50-60; ⊗noon-2.30pm & 7-10.30pm Tue-Sun) Grand Piazza Vecchia provides the ideal backdrop to savour truly top-class creative cuisine. Sit at an outside table in summer or opt for the noble 15th-century interior; either way expect to encounter dishes such as black risotto with ricotta and grilled cuttlefish, or venison medallions with chestnut purée and redcurrant jam.

⊨ Hotel Piazza Vecchia   Hotel €€

(☎035 25 31 79; www.hotelpiazzavecchia.it; Via Colleoni 3; d €130-300; ✴ @ 🕏) The perfect Città Alta bolt-hole, this 13th-century townhouse oozes atmosphere, from the honey-coloured beams and exposed stone to the tasteful art on the walls. Rooms have parquet floors and bathrooms that gleam with chrome; the deluxe rooms have a lounge and a balcony with mountain views.

Tuscan Wine Tour 3

Tuscany has its fair share of highlights, but few can match the indulgence of a drive through its wine country – an intoxicating blend of scenery, acclaimed restaurants and ruby-red wine.

TRIP HIGHLIGHTS

START
Florence

34 km

Greve in Chianti
Taste Tuscany's best at Greve's vast cellar

4 — 3 — Panzano in Chianti

Radda in Chianti

Badia a Passignano
Idyllically located wine estate and top restaurant

6 **67 km**

Castello di Ama
Marvel at modern art and Chianti Classico

41 km

Siena

138 km

Montalcino
A fortified hilltown, home of Brunello di Montalcino

7

FINISH
Montepulciano

4 DAYS
185KM / 115 MILES

GREAT FOR...

BEST TIME TO GO
Autumn for earthy hues and the grape harvest.

ESSENTIAL PHOTO
Panoramas from Montalcino's Fortezza.

BEST FOR GOURMETS
Tuscan *bistecca* (steak) in Panzano in Chianti.

Chianti region Vineyards and olive trees

3 Tuscan Wine Tour

Meandering through Tuscany's bucolic wine districts, this classic Chianti tour offers a taste of life in the slow lane. Once out of Florence (Firenze), you'll find yourself on quiet back roads driving through wooded hills and immaculate vineyards, stopping off at wine estates and hilltop towns to sample the local vintages. En route, you'll enjoy soul-stirring scenery, farmhouse food and some captivating Renaissance towns.

❶ Florence

Whet your appetite for the road ahead with a one-day cooking course at the **Food & Wine Academy** (☎055 28 11 03; www.florencecookingclasses. com; Via de' Lamberti 1; 1-day class with market visit & lunch €89), one of Florence's many cookery schools. Once you're done at the stove, sneak out to visit the **Chiesa e Museo di Orsanmichele** (Via dell'Arte della Lana; ☺church 10am-5pm, museum 10am-5pm Mon), an inspirational 14th-century church and one of Florence's lesser-known gems. Over the river, you can stock up on Tuscan wines and gourmet foods at **Obsequium** (☎055 21 68 49; www.obsequium. it; Borgo San Jacopo 17-39; ☺11am-9pm Mon-Sat), a well-stocked wine shop on the ground floor of a medieval tower. Or, explore the old town on foot (p114) before you hit the road.

🍴 🛏 p41, p63, p86

The Drive » From Florence it's about an hour to Verrazzano. Head south along the scenic SR222 (Via Chiantigiana) towards Greve. When you get to Greti, you'll see a shop selling wine from the Castello di Verrazzano and, just before it, a right turn up to the castle.

---

❷ Castello di Verrazzano

Some 26km south of Florence, the **Castello di Verrazzano** (📞055 85 42 43; www.verrazzano.com; Via Citille, Greti; tours €16-115) lords it over a 230-hectare estate where Chianti Classico, Vin Santo, grappa, honey, olive oil and balsamic vinegar are produced. In a previous life, the castle was home to Giovanni di Verrazzano (1485–1528), an adventurer who explored the North American coast and is commemorated in New York by

LINK YOUR TRIP

1 Grand Tour

From Florence head either north or south for to to embark upon your own Grand Tour of Italy.

5 World Heritage Wonders

From Florence pick up the A1 to Siena and towards to Rome, for Unesco-listed beauties.

the Verrazano-Narrows bridge linking Staten Island to Brooklyn.

At the Castello, you can choose from a range of guided tours, including a Classic Wine Tour (1½ hours; adult €18; 10am to 3pm Monday to Friday) and Wine & Food Experience (three hours, adult €58; noon Monday to Friday), which includes a tasting and lunch with the estate wines. Book ahead.

The Drive » From the Castello it's a simple 10-minute drive to Greve in Chianti. Double back to the SR222 in Greti, turn right and follow for about 3km.

❸ Greve in Chianti

The main town in the Chianti Fiorentino, the northernmost of the two Chianti districts, Greve in Chianti has been an important wine centre for centuries. It has an amiable market-town air, and several eater-ies and *enoteche* (wine bars) that showcase the best Chianti food and drink. To stock up on picnic-perfect cured meats, the **Antica Macellerìa Falorni** (www. falorni.it; Piazza Matteotti 71; ⊗9.30am-1pm & 3.30-7.30pm Mon-Sat, from 10am Sun), is an atmospheric butcher's shop-cum-bistro that the Bencistà Falorni family have been running since the early 19th century and which specialises in delicious *finocchiona briciolona* (pork salami made with fennel seeds and Chianti wine). The family also run the Enoteca Falorni (p62), the town's top cellar, where you can sample all sorts of local wine.

The Drive » From Greve turn off the main through road, Viale Giovanni di Verrazzano, near the Esso petrol station, and head up towards Montefioralle. Continue on as the road climbs past olive groves and through woods to Badia a Passignano, about 15 minutes away.

❹ Badia a Passignano

Encircled by cypress trees and surrounded by swaths of olive groves and vineyards, the 11th-century **Badia a Passignano** (📞055 807 12 78; www.osteriadipassignano. com; Badia a Passignano) sits at the heart of a historic wine estate. It's run by the Antinoris, one of Tuscany's oldest and most prestigious winemaking families, and offers a range of guided tours, tastings and cookery courses. Most require a minimum of four people and prior booking, but you can just turn up at the estate's wine shop, **La Bottega** (www.osteria dipassignano.com; Badia di Passignano; ⊗10am-7.30pm Mon-Sat), to taste and buy Antinori wines and olive oil.

✕ 🛏 p63

The Drive » From Badia a Passignano, double back towards Greve and pick up the signposted SP118 for a pleasant 15-minute drive along the narrow tree-shaded road to Panzano.

❺ Panzano in Chianti

The quiet medieval town of Panzano is an essential stop on any

---

✓ **TOP TIP:**
DRIVING IN CHIANTI

To cut down on driving stress, purchase a copy of *Le strade del Gallo Nero* (€2.50), a useful map that shows major and secondary roads and has a comprehensive list of wine estates. It's available at newsstands across the region.

TUSCAN REDS

Something of a viticultural powerhouse, Tuscany excites wine buffs with its myriad of full-bodied, highly respected reds. Like all Italian wines, these are classified according to strict guidelines, with the best denominated *Denominazione di Origine Controllata e Garantita* (DOCG), followed by *Denominazione di Origine Controllata* (DOC) and *Indicazione di Geografica Tipica* (IGT).

Chianti

Cheery, full and dry, contemporary Chianti gets the thumbs up from wine critics. Produced in eight subzones from Sangiovese and a mix of other grape varieties, Chianti Classico is the best known, with its Gallo Nero (Black Cockerel) emblem that once symbolised the medieval Chianti League. Young, fun Chianti Colli Senesi from the Siena hills is the largest subzone; Chianti delle Colline Pisane is light and soft in style; and Chianti Rùfina comes from the hills east of Florence.

Brunello di Montalcino

Brunello is up there at the top with Italy's most prized wines. The product of Sangiovese grapes, it must spend at least two years ageing in oak. It is intense and complex with an ethereal fragrance, and is best paired with game, wild boar and roasts. Brunello grape rejects go into Rosso di Montalcino, Brunello's substantially cheaper but wholly drinkable kid sister.

Vino Nobile di Montepulciano

Prugnolo Gentile grapes (a clone of Sangiovese) form the backbone of the distinguished Vino Nobile di Montepulciano. Its intense but delicate nose and dry, vaguely tannic taste make it the perfect companion to red meat and mature cheese.

Super Tuscans

Developed in the 1970s, the Super Tuscans are wines that fall outside the traditional classification categories. As a result they are often made with a combination of local and imported grape varieties, such as Merlot and Cabernet. Sassacaia, Solaia, Bolgheri, Tignanello and Luce are all super-hot Super Tuscans.

gourmet's tour of Tuscany. Here you can stock up on meaty picnic fare at **L'Antica Macelleria Cecchini** (www.dariocecchini.com; Via XX Luglio 11; ⊗9am-4pm), a celebrated butcher's shop run by the poetry-spouting guru of Tuscan meat, Dario Cecchini. Alternatively, you can eat at one of his three eateries: the **Officina della Bistecca** (☑055 85 21 76; www.dariocecchini.com; Via XX Luglio 11; set menu €50; ⊗sittings at 1pm & 8pm), which serves a simple set menu based on *bistecca;* **Solociccia** (☑055 85 27 27; www.dariocecchini.com; Via Chiantigiana 5; set menus €30 & €50; ⊗sittings at 1pm, 7pm & 9pm), where guests share a communal table to sample meat dishes other than *bistecca;* and **Dario DOC** (www.dariocecchini.com; Via XX Luglio 11; menus €10-20; ⊗noon-3pm Mon-Sat), a casual daytime eatery. Book ahead for the Officina and Solociccia.

The Drive » From Panzano, it's about 20 kilometres to the Castello di Ama. Strike south on the SR222 towards Radda in Chianti, enjoying views off to the right as you wend your way through the green countryside. At Croce, just beyond Radda, turn left and head towards Lecchi and San Sano. The Castello di Ama is signposted after a further 7km.

WHY THIS IS A GREAT TRIP
DUNCAN GARWOOD, WRITER

The best Italian wine I've ever tasted was a Brunello di Montalcino. I bought it directly from a producer after a tasting in the Val d'Orcia and it was a revelation. It was just so thrilling to be drinking wine in the place it had been made. And it's this, combined with the inspiring scenery and magnificent food, that makes this tour of Tuscan wineries so uplifting.

Top: Wine cellar, Castello di Ama
Left: Wine shop, Montalcino
Right: Badia a Passignano

TRIP HIGHLIGHT

❻ Castello di Ama

To indulge in some
contemporary-art
appreciation between
wine tastings, make
for the **Castello di Ama**
(☎0577 74 60 69; www.
castellodiama.com; Località
Ama: guided tours €15, with
wine & oil tasting €35-110;
⊗by appointment) near
Lecchi. The highly
regarded Castello di
Ama estate produces a
fine Chianti Classico and
has an original sculpture
park showcasing 14
site-specific works by
artists including Louise
Bourgeois, Chen Zhen,
Anish Kapoor, Kendell
Geers and Daniel Buren.
Book ahead.

The Drive ›› Reckon on about
1½ hours to Montalcino from
the Castello. Double back to
the SP408 and head south to
Lecchi and then on towards
Siena. Skirt around the east of
Siena and pick up the SR2 (Via
Cassia) to Buonconvento and
hilltop Montalcino, off to the
right of the main road.

TRIP HIGHLIGHT

❼ Montalcino

Montalcino, a pretty
medieval town perched
above the Val d'Orcia,
is home to one of Italy's
great wines, Brunello
di Montalcino (and the
more modest, but still
very palatable, Rosso di
Montalcino). There are
plenty of *enoteche* where

61

you can taste and buy, including one in the **Fortezza** (Piazzale Fortezza; courtyard free, ramparts adult/reduced €4/2; ☺9am-8pm Apr-Oct, 10am-6pm Nov-Mar), the 14th-century fortress that dominates the town's skyline.

For a historical insight into the town's winemaking past, head to the **Museo della Comunità di Montalcino e del Brunello** (☎0577 84 60 21; www.museodelbrunello.it; c/o Fattoria dei Barbi, Località Podernovi 170; €5, with wine tasting €8-10; ☺3.30-7pm Tue-Fri, 11am-1pm & 3.30-7pm Sat & Sun), a small museum off the road to the Abbazia di Sant'Antimo.

✗ ⫟ p63

The Drive » From Montalcino, head downhill and then, after

about 8km, turn onto the SR2. At San Quirico d'Orcia pick up the SP146, a fabulously scenic road that weaves along the Val d'Orcia through rolling green hills, past the pretty town of Pienza, to Montepulciano. Allow about an hour.

WINE TASTING GOES HIGH TECH

One of Tuscany's biggest cellars, the **Enoteca Falorni** (☎055 854 64 04; www.enotecafalorni.it; Piazza delle Cantine 6; ☺10.30am-7.30pm) in Greve in Chianti stocks more than 1000 labels, of which around 100 are available for tasting. It's a lovely, brick-arched place, but wine tasting here is a very modern experience, thanks to a sophisticated wine-dispensing system that preserves wine in an open bottle for up to three weeks and allows tasters to serve themselves by the glass. The way it works is that you buy a prepaid wine card costing from €10 and then use it at the various 'tasting islands' dotted around the cellar. Any unused credit is then refunded when you return the card.

↪ DETOUR: ABBAZIA DI SANT'ANTIMO

Start: ❼ Montalcino (p61)

The striking Romanesque **Abbazia di Sant'Antimo** (www.antimo.it; Castelnuovo dell'Abate; ☺10am-1pm & 3-6pm) lies in an isolated valley just below the village of Castelnuovo dell'Abate, 10.5km from Montalcino. According to tradition, Charlemagne founded the original monastery in 781. The exterior, built in pale travertine stone, is simple but for the stone carvings, which include various fantastical animals. Inside, study the capitals of the columns lining the nave, especially the one representing Daniel in the lions' den.

Music lovers should plan their visit to coincide with the daily services, which include Gregorian chants. Check the website for times.

❽ Montepulciano

Set atop a narrow ridge of volcanic rock, the Renaissance centre of Montepulciano produces the celebrated red wine Vino Nobile. For a drop, head up the main street, called in stages Via di Gracciano nel Corso, Via di Voltaia del Corso and Via dell'Opio nel Corso, to the **Cantine Contucci** (www.contucci.it; Via del Teatro 1; ☺8.30am-12.30pm & 2.30-6.30pm), housed underneath the *palazzo* (mansion) of the same name. A second cellar, the **Cantina de' Ricci** (☎0578 75 71 66; www.dericci.it; Via Collazzi 7; wine tasting plus food €15; ☺9.30am-6pm), occupies a grotto-like space underneath **Palazzo Ricci** near **Piazza Grande**, the town's highest point.

✗ ⫟ p63

Eating & Sleeping

Florence ❶

✕ Il Santo Bevitore   Tuscan €€

(📞055 21 12 64; www.ilsantobevitore.com; Via di Santo Spirito 64-66r; meals €40; ⏱12.30-2.30pm & 7.30-11.30pm, closed Sun lunch & Aug) Reserve or arrive dot on 7.30pm to snag the last table at this ever-popular address, an ode to stylish dining where gastronomes eat by candlelight in a vaulted, whitewashed, bottle-lined interior. The menu is a creative reinvention of seasonal classics: purple cabbage soup with mozzarella cream and anchovy syrup, acacia honey *bavarese* (firm, creamy mousse) with Vin Santo–marinated dried fruits.

Badia a Passignano ❹

✕ Osteria di Passignano   Tuscan €€€

(📞055 807 12 78; www.osteriadipassignano. com; Via di Passignano 33, Badia a Passignano; meals €85, tasting menu €80, with wine €130; ⏱12.15-2.15pm & 7.30-10pm Mon-Sat) Badia a Passignano sits amid a landscape scored by row upon row of vines, and the elegant Michelin-starred eatery in the centre of the village has long been one of Tuscany's most glamorous dining destinations. Intricate, Tuscan-inspired dishes fly the local-produce flag and the wine list is mightily impressive, with Antinori offerings aplenty (by the glass €7 to €35).

🛏 Fattoria di Rignana   Agriturismo €€

(📞0558 5 20 65; www.rignana.it; Via di Rignana 15, Rignana; d fattoria €110-120, without bathroom €95, d villa €140; [P][@][🔊][🏊]) A chic, historic farmhouse with its very own bell tower rewards you for the drive up the long, rutted road. You'll also find glorious views, a large swimming pool and a very decent eatery. Choose between elegant rooms in the 17th-century villa and rustic ones in the *fattoria* (farmhouse). It's 4km from Badia a Passignano and 10km west of Greve.

Montalcino ❼

✕ Ristorante di Poggio Antico   Modern Italian €€€

(📞0577 84 92 00; www.poggioantico.com; Loc Poggio Antico, Montalcino; meals from €50; ⏱noon-2.30pm & 7-9.30pm, closed Mon summer, closed Sun dinner & Mon winter) Located 4.5km outside town on the road to Grosseto, the Poggio Antico vineyard makes award-winning wines, conducts tastings and offers guided tours. Its fine-dining restaurant is one of the best in the area, serving a menu of creative, contemporary Italian cuisine.

🛏 Hotel Vecchia Oliviera   Hotel €€

(📞0577 84 60 28; www.vecchiaoliviera.com; Via Landi 1; s €70-85, d €120-190; [P][✳][🔊][🏊]) Chandeliers, elegant armchairs, polished wooden floors and rich rugs lend this converted oil mill a refined air. The pick of the 11 rooms comes with hill views and a jacuzzi, the pool is in an attractive garden setting, and the terrace has wraparound views.

Montepulciano ❽

✕ Osteria Acquacheta   Tuscan €€

(📞0578 71 70 86; www.acquacheta.eu; Via del Teatro 2; meals €25-30; ⏱12.30-3pm & 7.30-10.30pm Wed-Mon) Hugely popular with locals and tourists alike, this bustling *osteria* specialises in *bistecca alla fiorentina* (chargrilled T-bone steak), which comes to the table in huge, lightly seared and exceptionally flavoursome slabs (don't even *think* of asking for it to be served otherwise). Book ahead.

🛏 Locanda San Francesco   B&B €€

(📞0578 75 87 25; www.locandasanfrancesco. it; Piazza San Francesco 3; d €180-250; [P][✳][@][🔊]) There's only one downside to this B&B: once you check into the supremely welcoming, 14th-century *palazzo*, you might never want to leave. The feel is elegant but also homely: refined furnishings meet well-stocked bookshelves; restrained fabrics are teamed with fluffy bathrobes. The best room has superb views over Val d'Orcia on one side and Val di Chiana on the other.

Amalfi Coast

4

Not for the fainthearted, this trip along the Amalfi Coast tests your driving skill on a 100km stretch, featuring dizzying hairpin turns and pastel-coloured towns draped over sea-cliff scenery.

TRIP HIGHLIGHTS

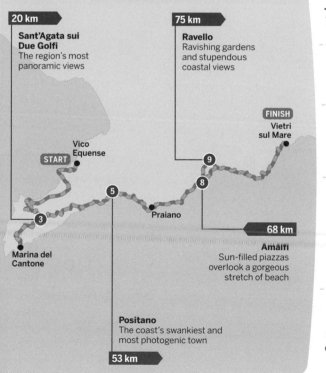

20 km

Sant'Agata sui Due Golfi
The region's most panoramic views

75 km

Ravello
Ravishing gardens and stupendous coastal views

FINISH
Vietri sul Mare

Vico Equense

START

9

8

5

Praiano

3

68 km

Amalfi
Sun-filled piazzas overlook a gorgeous stretch of beach

Marina del Cantone

Positano
The coast's swankiest and most photogenic town

53 km

---

7 DAYS
100KM / 62 MILES

GREAT FOR...

BEST TIME TO GO
Summer for best beach weather, but also peak crowds.

 ESSENTIAL PHOTO
Positano's vertiginous stack of pastel-coloured houses cascading down to the sea.

 BEST FOR OUTDOORS
Hiking Ravello and its environs.

---

4 Amalfi Coast

The Amalfi Coast is about drama, and this trip takes you where mountains plunge seaward in a stunning vertical landscape of precipitous crags, forests and resort towns. Positano and Amalfi are fabulously picturesque and colourful, while mountain-top Ravello is a serenely tranquil place with a tangible sense of history. Cars are useful for inland exploration, as are your own two legs. Walking trails provide a wonderful escape from the coastal clamour.

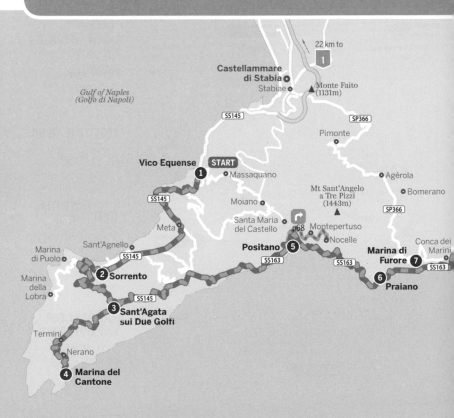

① Vico Equense

The Bay of Naples is justifiably famous for its pizza, which was invented here as a savoury way to highlight two local specialties: mozzarella and sun-kissed tomatoes. Besides its pretty little *centro storico* (historic centre), this little clifftop town overlooking the Bay of Naples boasts some of the region's best pizza, including a by-the-metre version at **Ristorante & Pizzeria da Gigino** (☎081 879 83 09; www.pizzametro. it; Via Nicotera 15; pizza per

metre from €30, meals €15-20; ☺ noon-1.30am, 🅿).

The Drive » From Vico Equense to Sorrento, your main route will be the SS145 roadway for 12km. Expect to hug the sparkling coastline after Marina di Equa before venturing inland around Meta.

TRIP HIGHLIGHT

② Sorrento

On paper, cliff-straddling Sorrento is a place to avoid – a package-holiday centre with few sights, no beach to speak of and a glut of brassy English-style pubs. In reality, it's strangely appealing, its laid-back southern Italian charm resisting all attempts to swamp it in souvenir tat and graceless development.

According to Greek legend, it was in Sorrento's waters that the mythical sirens once lived. Sailors of antiquity were powerless to resist the beautiful song of these charming maidens-cum-monsters, who would lure them to their doom.

✗ 🍴 p73

The Drive » Take the SS145 for 8km to Sant'Agata sui Due Golfi. Sun-dappled village streets give way to forest as you head further inland.

TRIP HIGHLIGHT

③ Sant'Agata sui Due Golfi

Perched high in the hills above Sorrento, sleepy Sant'Agata sui Due Golfi

Cava
Mt Finestra (1145m)
A3
Mt dell'Avvocata (1014m)
Raito
⑪ Vietri sul Mare
SS163 **FINISH**
Ravello ⑨
Scala
Minori
Maiori
⑩ Cetara
p72
SR373
Erchie
SS163
⑧ Atrani
Amalfi
Golfo di Salerno

ⓝ 0 —— 5 km
0 —— 2.5 miles

LINK YOUR TRIP

1 **Grand Tour**
It's a short hop north to Naples, from where you can start your search for enlightenment and adventure.

6 **Wonders of Ancient Sicily**
While you're in the south why not head to Sicily for Arab treasures and Greek splendours .

commands spectacular views of the Bay of Naples on one side and the Bay of Salerno on the other (hence its name, Saint Agatha on the Two Gulfs). The best viewpoint is the **Convento del Deserto** (☎081 878 01 99; Via Deserto; ☺gardens 8am-7pm, lookout 10am-noon & 5-7pm summer, 10am-noon & 3-5pm winter), a Carmelite convent 1.5km uphill from the village centre. It's a knee-wearing hike, but make it to the top and you're rewarded with fabulous 360-degree vistas.

The Drive >> From Sant'Agata sui Due Golfi to Marina del Cantone it's a 9km drive, the last part involving some serious hairpin turns. Don't let the gorgeous sea views distract you.

❹ Marina del Cantone

From **Nerano**, where you'll park, a beautiful hiking trail leads down to the stunning Bay of Ieranto and one of the coast's top swimming spots, Marina del Cantone. This unassuming village with its small pebble beach is a lovely, tranquil place to stay as well as a popular diving destination. The village also has a reputation as a gastronomic hotspot and VIPs regularly catch a boat over from Capri to dine here.

✕ p73

The Drive >> First, head back up that switchback to Sant'Agata sui Due Golfi. Catch the SS145 and then the SS163 as they weave their way

along bluffs and cliff sides to Positano. Most of the 24km involve stunning sea views.

TRIP HIGHLIGHT

❺ Positano

The pearl in the pack, Positano is the coast's most photogenic and expensive town. Its steeply stacked houses are a medley of peaches, pinks and terracottas, and its near-vertical streets (many of which are, in fact, staircases) are lined with voguish shop displays, elegant hotels and smart restaurants. Look closely, though, and you'll find reassuring signs of everyday reality – crumbling stucco, streaked paintwork and occasionally a faint whiff of problematic drainage.

John Steinbeck visited in 1953 and was so bowled over that he wrote of its dream-like qualities in an article for *Harper's Bazaar*.

🛏 p73

The Drive >> From Positano to Praiano it's a quick 6km spin on the SS163, passing Il San Pietro di Positano at the halfway point, then heading southeast along the peninsula's edge.

↱ DETOUR: NOCELLE

Start: ❺ Positano

A tiny, still relatively isolated mountain village above Positano, Nocelle (450m) commands some of the most spectacular views on the entire coast. A world apart from touristy Positano, it's a sleepy, silent place where not much ever happens, nor would its few residents ever want it to. If you want to stay, consider delightful **Villa della Quercia** (☎089 812 34 97; www.villadellaquercia.com; Via Nocelle 5; r €70-80; ☺Apr-Oct; 🛜), a former monastery with spectacular views. Nocelle lies eight very windy kilometres northeast of Positano.

❻ Praiano

An ancient fishing village, a low-key summer resort and, increasingly, a popular centre for the arts, Praiano is a delight. With no centre as such, its whitewashed houses pepper the verdant ridge of Monte Sant'Angelo as it slopes towards Capo Sottile. Exploring involves lots of steps and there are several trails that start from town, including the legendary **Sentiero degli Dei**.

For those willing to take the plunge, the **Centro Sub Costiera Amalfitana** (☎089 81 21 48; www.centrosub.it; Via Marina di Praia; dives from €80; 🚣) runs beginner to expert dives exploring the area's coral, marine life and grottoes.

The Drive ≫ From Praiano, Marina di Furore is just 3km further on, past beautiful coves that cut into the shoreline.

❼ Marina di Furore

A few kilometres further on, Marina di Furore sits at the bottom of what's known as the fjord of Furore, a giant cleft that cuts through the Lattari mountains. The main village, however, stands 300m above, in the upper Vallone del Furore. A one-horse place that sees few tourists, it breathes a distinctly rural air despite the presence of colourful murals and un-likely modern sculpture.

The Drive ≫ From Marina di Furore to Amalfi, the sparkling Mediterranean Sea will be your escort as you drive westward along the SS163 coastal road

WALK OF THE GODS

Probably the best-known walk on the Amalfi Coast is the three-hour, 12km **Sentiero degli Dei**, which follows the high ridge linking Praiano to Positano. The walk commences in the heart of **Praiano**, where a thigh-challenging 1000-step start takes you up to the path itself. The route proper is not advised for vertigo sufferers: it's a spectacular, meandering trail along the top of the mountains, with caves and terraces set dramatically in the cliffs and deep valleys framed by the brilliant blue of the sea. You'll eventually emerge at Nocelle, from where a series of steps will take you through the olive groves and deposit you on the road just east of **Positano**.

for 6km. Look for Vettica Minore and Conca dei Marini along the way, along with fluffy bunches of fragrant cypress trees.

TRIP HIGHLIGHT

❽ Amalfi

It is hard to grasp that pretty little Amalfi, with its sun-filled piazzas and small beach, was once a maritime superpower with a population of more than 70,000. For one thing, it's not a big place – you can easily walk from one end to the other in about 20 min-utes. For another, there are very few historical buildings of note. The explanation is chilling – most of the old city, along with its populace, simply slid into the sea during an earthquake in 1343.

One happy exception is the striking **Cattedrale di Sant'Andrea** (☎089 87 10 59; Piazza del Duomo; ◷7.30am-7pm), parts of which date from the early

THE BLUE RIBBON DRIVE

Stretching from Vietri sul Mare to Sant'Agata sui Due Golfi near Sorrento, the SS163 nicknamed the Nastro Azzurro (Blue Ribbon) remains one of Italy's most stunning roadways. Commissioned by Bourbon king Ferdinand II and completed in 1853, it wends its way along the Amalfi Coast's entire length, snaking round impossibly tight curves, over deep ravines and through tunnels gouged out of sheer rock. It's a magnificent feat of civil engineering – although it can be challenging to drive – and in certain places it's not wide enough for two cars to pass, a fact John Steinbeck alluded to in a 1953 essay.

WHY THIS IS A GREAT TRIP
DUNCAN GARWOOD, WRITER

With its plunging cliffs, shimmering azure waters and picture-book villages, Italy's most celebrated coastline lives up to expectations in spectacular style. The scenery is amazing and its vivid colours are brilliant in the sharp Mediterranean sunlight. Most attention is focussed on the seafront hotspots, but you can always escape the clamour by heading into the hills to take on some of Italy's most jaw-dropping hikes.

Top: Traditional ceramics, Vietri sul Mare
Left: Villa Rufolo, Ravello
Right: Interior of Cattedrale di Sant'Andrea, Amalfi

10th century. Between 10am and 5pm entrance to the cathedral is through the adjacent **Chiostro del Paradiso** (☎089 87 13 24; Piazza del Duomo; adult/reduced €3/1; ☺9am-6pm), a 13th-century Moorish-style cloister.

Be sure to take the short walk around the headland to neighbouring **Atrani**, a picturesque tangle of whitewashed alleys and arches centred on a lively, lived-in piazza and popular beach.

 p73

The Drive » Start the 7km trip to Ravello by heading along the coast to Atrani. Here turn inland and follow the SR 373 as it climbs the steep hillside in a series of second-gear hairpin turns up to Ravello.

- - - - - - - - - - - - - - -

TRIP HIGHLIGHT

❾ Ravello

Sitting high in the hills above Amalfi, refined Ravello is a polished town almost entirely dedicated to tourism. Boasting impeccable artistic credentials – Richard Wagner, DH Lawrence and Virginia Woolf all lounged here – it's known today for its ravishing gardens and stupendous views, the best in the world according to former resident Gore Vidal.

To enjoy these views, head south of Ravello's cathedral to the 14th-century tower that marks the entrance to

Villa Rufolo (☎089 85 76 21; www.villarufolo.it; Piazza Duomo; adult/reduced €5/3; ☺9am-8pm summer, to 4pm winter). Created by Scotsman Scott Neville Reid in 1853, these gardens combine celestial panoramic views, exotic colours, artistically crumbling towers and luxurious blooms.

Also worth seeking out is the wonderful **Camo** (☎089 85 74 61; Piazza Duomo 9, Ravello; ☺10am-noon & 3-5pm Mon-Sat). Squeezed between tourist-driven shops, this very special place is, on the face of it, a cameo shop. And exquisite they are too, crafted primarily out of coral and shell. But don't stop here; ask to see the treasure trove of a museum beyond the showroom.

✕ ⊨ p73

The Drive 》 Head back down to the SS163 for a 19km journey that twists and turns challengingly along the coast to Cetara. Pine trees and a variety of flowering shrubs line the way.

- - - - - - - - - - -

❿ Cetara

Cetara is a picturesque, tumbledown fishing village with a reputation as a gastronomic delight. Since medieval times it has been an important fishing centre, and today its deep-sea tuna fleet is considered one of the Mediterranean's most important. At night, fishermen set out in small boats armed with powerful lamps to fish for anchovies. No surprise then that tuna and anchovies dominate local menus, especially

at **Al Convento** (☎089 26 10 39; www.alconvento. net; Piazza San Francesco 16; meals €30; ☺12.30-3pm & 7-11pm summer, closed Wed winter), a sterling seafood restaurant near the small harbour.

The Drive 》 From Cetara to Vietri sul Mare, head northeast for 6km on the SS163 for more twisting, turning and stupendous views across the Golfo di Salerno.

- - - - - - - - - - -

⓫ Vietri sul Mare

Marking the end of the coastal road, Vietri sul Mare is the ceramics capital of Campania. Although production dates back to Roman times, it didn't take off as an industry until the 16th and 17th centuries. Today, ceramics shopaholics find their paradise at the **Ceramica Artistica Solimene** (☎089 21 02 43; www.ceramicasolimene. it; Via Madonna degli Angeli 7; ☺9am-8pm Mon-Fri, 9am-1.30pm & 4-8pm Sat), a vast factory outlet with an extraordinary glass and ceramic facade.

For a primer on the area's ceramics past, devotees should seek out the **Museo della Ceramica** (☎089 21 18 35; Villa Guerriglia, Via Nuova Raito; ☺9am-3pm Tue-Sat, 9.30am-1pm Sun) in the nearby village of Raito.

↱ DETOUR: RAVELLO WALKS

Start: ❾ Ravello (p71)

Ravello is the starting point for numerous walks that follow ancient paths through the surrounding Lattari mountains. If you've got the legs for it, you can walk down to **Minori** via an attractive route of steps, hidden alleys and olive groves, passing the picturesque hamlet of **Torello** en route. Alternatively, you can head the other way, to Amalfi, via the ancient village of **Scala**. Once a flourishing religious centre with more than a hundred churches and the oldest settlement on the Amalfi Coast, Scala is now a pocket-sized sleepy place where the wind whistles through empty streets, and gnarled locals go patiently about their daily chores.

Eating & Sleeping

Sorrento ②

✗ L'Antica Trattoria   Italian €€

(📞081 807 10 82; www.lanticatrattoria.com; Via
Padre Reginaldo Giuliani 33; lunch menu €19.50,
fixed-price menus €45-80; ⊙noon-11pm) **Head
to the upstairs terrace with its traditional tiles
and trailing grape vines and you seem miles away
from the alleyways outside. With a deserved
reputation as the finest restaurant in town, it has
a mainly traditional menu, with homemade pasta,
a daily fish special and vegetarian options.

🛏 Hotel Cristina   Hotel €€

(📞081 878 35 62; www.hotelcristinasorrento.
it; Via Privata Rubinacci 6, Sant'Agnello; s €130,
d €150-200, tr €220, q €240; ⊙Mar-Oct;
P ✱ 🛜 ⛱) Located high above Sant'Agnello,
this hotel has superb views, particularly from
the swimming pool. The spacious rooms have
sea-view balconies and combine inlaid wooden
furniture with contemporary flourishes like
Philippe Starck chairs. There's an in-house
restaurant and a free shuttle bus to/from
Sorrento's Circumvesuviana train station.

Marina del Cantone ④

✗ Lo Scoglio   Seafood €€€

(📞081 808 10 26; www.hotelloscoglio.com;
Piazza delle Sirene 15, Massa Lubrense; meals
€60; ⊙12.30-5pm & 7.30-11pm) Lo Scoglio is a
favourite of visiting celebs and the food is top
notch (and priced accordingly). Although you can
eat *fettucine al bolognese* and steak here, you'd
be sorry to miss the superb seafood. Options
include a €30 antipasto of raw seafood and
spaghetti al riccio (spaghetti with sea urchins).

Positano ⑤

🛏 Pensione Maria Luisa   Pension €

(📞089 87 50 23; www.pensionemarialuisa.com;
Via Fornillo 42; r €55-120; ⊙Mar-Oct; @ 🛜) The
Maria Luisa is a friendly old-school *pensione*.
Rooms feature shiny blue tiles and simple, no-
frills decor; those with private balconies are well
worth the extra €15 for the bay views. If you can't
bag a room with a view, there's a small communal
terrace offering the same sensational vistas.

Amalfi ⑧

✗ Marina Grande   Seafood €€€

(📞089 87 11 29; www.ristorantemarinagrande.
com; Viale Delle Regioni 4; tasting menu lunch/
dinner €28/60, meals €50; ⊙noon-3pm &
6.30-11pm Wed-Mon Mar-Oct) Run by the third
generation of the same family, this beachfront
restaurant prides itself on its use of locally
sourced organic produce, which, in Amalfi,
means high-quality seafood.

🛏 Hotel Luna Convento   Hotel €€€

(📞089 87 10 02; www.lunahotel.it; Via Pantaleone
Comite 33; s €270-370, d €290-390, ste €490-
590; ⊙Easter-Oct; P ✱ @ 🛜 ⛱) This former
convent was founded by St Francis in 1222 and
has been a hotel for some 170 years. Rooms in
the original building are in the former monks'
cells, but there's nothing poky about the bright
tiles and seamless sea views. The newer wing is
equally beguiling, with religious frescoes. The
cloistered courtyard is magnificent.

Ravello ⑨

✗ Ristorante Pizzeria Vittoria   Pizza €€

(📞089 85 79 47; www.ristorantepizzeriavittoria.
it; Via dei Rufolo 3; meals €30, pizza from €5;
⊙12.15-3pm & 7.15-11pm) Come here for
exceptional pizza, including the Ravellese,
with cherry tomatoes, mozzarella, basil and
courgettes. Other dishes include lasagne with
red pumpkin, smoked mozzarella and porcini
mushrooms, and an innovative chickpea-and-cod
antipasto. The atmosphere is one of subdued
elegance, with a small outside terrace and grainy
historical pics of Ravello on the walls.

🛏 Agriturismo Monte Brusara   Agriturismo €

(📞089 85 74 67; www.montebrusara.com; Via
Monte Brusara 32; s/d €45/90; ⊙year-round)
A working farm, this mountainside *agriturismo*
is located a tough half-hour walk of about 1.5km
from Ravello's centre (call ahead to arrange to
be picked up). It is especially suited to families –
children can feed the pony while you sit back and
admire the views – or to those who simply want
to escape the crowds.

World Heritage Wonders

5

From Rome to Venice, this tour of Unesco World Heritage Sites takes in some of Italy's greatest hits, including the Colosseum and the Leaning Tower of Pisa, and some lesser-known treasures.

TRIP HIGHLIGHTS

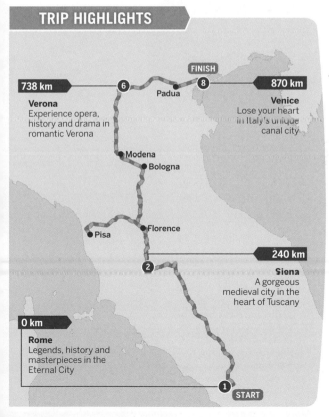

FINISH

738 km ⑥

Padua ⑧

870 km

Verona
Experience opera, history and drama in romantic Verona

Venice
Lose your heart in Italy's unique canal city

● Modena
● Bologna

● Pisa   ● Florence

240 km

②

Siena
A gorgeous medieval city in the heart of Tuscany

0 km

Rome
Legends, history and masterpieces in the Eternal City

① **START**

**14 DAYS
870KM / 540 MILES**

GREAT FOR...

BEST TIME TO GO
April, May and September for ideal sightseeing weather and local produce.

ESSENTIAL PHOTO
Roman Forum from the Palatino.

BEST FOR ART
Florence's Galleria degli Uffizi.

5 World Heritage Wonders

Topping the Unesco charts with 51 World Heritage Sites, Italy offers the full gamut, ranging from historic city centres and man-made masterpieces to snow-capped mountains and areas of outstanding natural beauty. This trip through central and northern Italy touches on the country's unparalleled artistic and architectural legacy, taking in ancient Roman ruins, priceless Renaissance paintings, great cathedrals and, to cap it all off, Venice's unique canal-scape.

TRIP HIGHLIGHT

1 Rome

An epic, monumental metropolis, Italy's capital is a city of thrilling beauty and high drama. According to Unesco, its historic centre boasts some of aniquity's most important monuments and is well worth a stroll. Rome has been a World Heritage Site since 1980, and the **Vatican**, technically a separate state but in reality located within Rome's city limits, has been on the Unesco list since 1984.

Of Rome's many ancient monuments, the most iconic is the **Colosseum** (Colosseo; ☎06 3996 7700; www.coopculture.it; Piazza del Colosseo; adult/reduced incl Roman Forum & Palatino €12/7.50; ☉8.30am-1hr before sunset; Ⓜ Colosseo), the towering 1st-century-AD amphitheatre where gladiators met in mortal combat and condemned criminals fought off wild beasts. Nearby, the **Palatino** (Palatine Hill; ☎06 3996 7700; www.coopculture. it; Via di San Gregorio 30 &

Via Sacra; adult/reduced incl Colosseum & Roman Forum €12/7.50; ⊙8.30am-1hr before sunset; MColosseo) was the ancient city's most exclusive neighbourhood, as well as its oldest – Romulus and Remus supposedly founded the city there in 753 BC. From the Palatino, you can descend to the skeletal ruins of the **Roman Forum** (Foro Romano; ☏06 3996 7700; www.coopculture.it; Largo della Salara Vecchia & Via Sacra; adult/reduced incl Colosseum & Palatino €12/7.50; ⊙8.30am-1hr before sunset; 🚌Via dei Fori Imperiali), the once-beating heart of the ancient city. All three sights are covered by a single ticket.

To complete your tour of classical wonders search out the **Pantheon** (www.pantheonroma. com; Piazza della Rotonda; ⊙8.30am-7.30pm Mon-Sat, 9am-6pm Sun; 🚌Largo di

LINK YOUR TRIP

2 **The Graceful Italian Lakes**

Branch off at Verona and take the A4 for some refined elegance and mountain scenery.

3 **Tuscan Wine Tour**

From Florence head south to Tuscany's Chianti wine country to indulge in some wine tasting at the area's historic vineyards.

Torre Argentina), the best preserved of Rome's ancient monuments. One of the most influential buildings in the world, this domed temple, now a church, is an extraordinary sight with its martial portico and soaring interior.

 p41, p86

The Drive » The easiest route to Siena, about three hours away, is via the A1 autostrada. Join this from the Rome ring road, the GRA (Grande Raccordo Anulare), and head north, past Orvieto's dramatic cliff-top cathedral, to the Valdichiana exit. Take this and follow signs for Siena.

DETOUR: SAN GIMIGNANO

Start: ❷ Siena

Dubbed the medieval Manhattan thanks to its 15 11th-century towers, San Gimignano is a classic hilltop town and an easy detour from Siena. From the car park next to Porta San Giovanni, it's a short walk up to **Palazzo Comunale** (🖉0577 28 63 00; Piazza del Duomo 2; adult/reduced €6/5; ⏰9.30am-7pm summer, 11am-5.30pm winter), which houses the town's art gallery, the **Pinacoteca**, and tallest tower, the **Torre Grossa**. Nearby, the Romanesque basilica, known as the **Collegiata** (Duomo or Basilica di Santa Maria Assunta; Piazza del Duomo; adult/reduced €4/2; ⏰10am-7pm Mon-Fri, to 5pm Sat, 12.30-7pm Sun summer, 10am-4.30pm Mon-Sat ,12.30-4.30pm Sun winter), boasts some remarkable Ghirlandaio frescoes.

Before leaving town, be sure to sample the local Vernaccia wine at the **Museo del Vino** (www. sangimignanomuseovernaccia.com; Via di Fugnano 19; ⏰11.30am-6.30pm Apr-Oct) next to the Rocca (fortress). San Gimignano is about 40km northwest of Siena. Head for Florence on the RA3 until Poggibonsi and then pick up the SS429.

TRIP HIGHLIGHT

❷ Siena

Siena is one of Italy's most enchanting medieval towns. Its walled centre, a beautifully preserved warren of dark lanes, Gothic *palazzi* (mansions) and pretty piazzas, is centred on **Piazza del Campo** (known as Il Campo), the sloping shell-shaped square that stages the city's annual horse race, Il Palio, on 2 July and 16 August.

On the piazza, the 102m-high **Torre del Mangia** (🖉0577 29 26 15; Palazzo Comunale, Piazza del Campo 1; €10; ⏰10am-7pm summer, to 4pm winter) soars above the Gothic **Palazzo Pubblico** (Palazzo Comunale), home to the city's finest art museum, the **Museo Civico** (🖉0577 29 26 15; Palazzo Comunale, Piazza del Campo 1; adult/reduced €9/8; ⏰10am-7pm summer, to 6pm winter). Of Siena's churches, the one to see is the 13th-century **Duomo** (www.operaduomo. siena.it; Piazza del Duomo; summer/winter €4/free, when floor displayed €7; ⏰10.30am-7pm Mon-Sat, 1.30-6pm Sun summer, 10.30am-5.30pm Mon-Sat, 1.30-5.30pm Sun winter), one of Italy's greatest Gothic churches. Highlights include the remarkable white, green and red facade, and, inside, the magnificent inlaid marble floor that illustrates historical and biblical stories.

🍴 🛏 p86

The Drive » There are two alternatives to get to Florence. The quickest, which is via the fast RA3 Siena–Firenze Raccordo, takes about 1½ hours. But if you have the time, we recommend the scenic SR222, which snakes through the Chianti wine country, passing through quintessential hilltop towns and vine-laden slopes. Reckon on at least 2½ hours for this route.

---

❸ Florence

Cradle of the Renaissance and home of

Michelangelo, Machiavelli and the Medici, Florence (Firenze) is magnetic, romantic, unique and busy. A couple of days is not long here but it's enough for a breathless introduction to the city's top sights, many of which can be enjoyed on foot (p114).

Towering above the medieval skyline, the **Duomo** (Cattedrale di Santa Maria del Fiore; www.operaduomo.firenze.it; Piazza del Duomo; ◷10am-5pm Mon-Wed & Fri, to 4pm Thu, to 4.45pm Sat, 1.30-4.45pm Sun) dominates the city centre with its famous red-tiled dome and striking façade. A short hop away, **Piazza della Signoria** opens onto the sculpture-filled **Loggia dei Lanzi** and the **Torre d'Arnolfo** above **Palazzo Vecchio** (☑055 276 82 24; www.musefirenze.it; Piazza della Signoria; museum adult/reduced €10/8, tower €10/8, museum & tower €14/12, guided tour €4; ◷museum 9am-11pm Fri-Wed, to 2pm Thu summer, 9am-7pm Fri-Wed, to 2pm Thu winter), Florence's lavish City Hall.

Next to the *palazzo*, the **Galleria degli Uffizi** (Uffizi Gallery; www.uffizi.beniculturali.it; Piazzale degli Uffizi 6; adult/reduced €8/4, incl temporary exhibition €12.50/6.25; ◷8.15am-6.50pm Tue-Sun) houses one of the world's great art collections, including works by Botticelli,

WORLD HERITAGE SITES

With 51 World Heritage Sites, Italy has more than any other country. But what exactly is a World Heritage Site? Basically it's anywhere that Unesco's World Heritage Committee decides is of 'outstanding universal value' and inscribes on the World Heritage List. It could be a natural wonder such as the Great Barrier Reef in Australia or a man-made icon such as New York's Statue of Liberty, a historic city centre or a great work of art or architecture.

The list was set up in 1972 and has since grown to include 1031 sites from 163 countries. Italy first got in on the act in 1979 when it successfully nominated its first entry – the prehistoric rock drawings of the Valcamonica valley in northeastern Lombardy. The inscription process requires sites to be nominated by a country and then independently evaluated. If they pass scrutiny and meet at least one of 10 selection criteria, they get the green light at the World Heritage Committee's annual meeting. Once on the list, sites qualify for management support and access to the World Heritage Fund.

Italian nominations have generally fared well and since Rome's historic centre and the Chiesa di Santa Maria delle Grazie in Milan were inscribed in 1980, many of the nation's greatest attractions have made it onto the list – the historic centres of Florence, Naples, Siena and San Gimignano; the cities of Venice, Verona and Ferrara; the archaeological sites of Pompeii, Paestum and Agrigento; as well as natural beauties such as the Amalfi Coast, Aeolian Islands, Dolomites and Tuscany's Val d'Orcia.

Leonardo da Vinci, Michelangelo, Raphael and many other Renaissance maestros.

✕ ☵ p41, p63, p86

The Drive ≫ From Florence it's about 1½ hours to Pisa along the A11 autostrada. At the end of the motorway, after the toll booth, head left onto Via Aurelia (SS1) and follow signs to Pisa *centro*.

❹ Pisa

Once a maritime republic to rival Genoa and Venice, Pisa now owes its fame to an architectural project gone horribly wrong. The **Leaning Tower** (Torre Pendente; www.opapisa.it; Piazza dei Miracoli; €18; ◷9am-8pm summer, 10am-5pm winter) is an extraordinary sight and one of Italy's

WHY THIS IS A GREAT TRIP
DUNCAN GARWOOD, WRITER

Every one of the towns and cities on this drive is special. The great treasures of Rome, Florence and Venice are amazing but, for me, it's the lesser-known highlights that make this such an incredible trip – Modena's stunning Romanesque cathedral, the Cappella degli Scrovegni in Padua, and Verona's gorgeous medieval centre.

Top: Replica of Michelangelo's *David*, Piazza della Signoria, Florence
Left: The Duomo and the Leaning Tower, Pisa
Right: Looking towards Torre Ghirlandina, Modena

most photographed monuments. The tower, originally erected as a *campanile* (bell tower) from the late 12th century, is one of three Romanesque buildings on the immaculate lawns of **Piazza dei Miracoli** (also known as Campo dei Miracoli or Piazza del Duomo).

The candy-striped **Duomo** (www.opapisa.it; Piazza dei Miracoli; ⏲10am-8pm summer, to 5pm winter), begun in 1063, has a graceful tiered facade and cavernous interior, while to its west, the cupcake-like **Battistero** (Baptistry; www.opapisa.it; Piazza dei Miracoli, €5, with Camposanto & Museo delle Sinópie 2/3 sights €7/8; ⏲8am-8pm summer, 10am-5pm winter) is something of an architectural hybrid, with a Pisan-Romanesque lower section and a Gothic upper level and dome.

✕ p87

The Drive » It's a 2½-hour drive up to Modena from Pisa. Head back towards Florence on the A11 and then pick up the A1 to Bologna. Continue as the road twists and falls through the wooded Apennines before flattening out near Bologna. Exit at Modena Sud (Modena South) and follow for the *centro*.

- - - - - - - - - - - - -

5 **Modena**

One of Italy's top foodie towns, Modena boasts a stunning medieval centre and a trio of Unesco-listed sights. First up is the gorgeous **Duomo** (www.duomodimodena.it; Corso Duomo; ☺7am-7pm Tue-Sun, 7am-12.30pm & 3.30-7pm Mon), which is widely considered to be Italy's finest Romanesque church. Features to look out for include the Gothic rose window and a series of bas-reliefs depicting scenes from Genesis.

Nearby, the 13th-century **Torre Ghirlandina** (Corso Duomo; €3; ☺9.30am-1pm & 3-7pm Tue-Fri, 9.30am-7pm Sat & Sun summer, 9.30am-1pm & 2.30-5.30pm Tue-Fri, 9.30am-5.30pm Sat & Sun winter), an 87m-high tower topped by a Gothic spire, was named after Seville's Giralda bell tower by exiled Spanish Jews in the early 16th century. The last of the Unesco threesome is **Piazza Grande**, just south of the cathedral. The city's focal square, this is flanked by the porticoed **Palazzo Comunale**, Modena's elegant town hall.

✗ 🛏 p87

The Drive ≫ From Modena reckon on about 1¼ hours to Verona, via the A1 and A22 autostradas. Follow the A22 as it traverses the flat Po valley plain, passing the medieval town of Mantua (Mantova; worth a quick break) before connecting with the A4. Turn off at Verona Sud and follow signs for the town centre.

- - - - - - - - - - - - -

TRIP HIGHLIGHT

❻ Verona

A World Heritage Site since 2000, Verona's historic centre is a beautiful compilation of architectural styles and inspiring buildings. Chief among these is its stunning Roman amphitheatre, the **Arena** (☎045 800 32 04; www.arena.it; Piazza Brà; adult/reduced €10/7.50; ☺8.30am-7.30pm Tue-Sun, from 1.30pm Mon). Dating from the 1st century AD, this is Italy's third-largest amphitheatre after the Colosseum and Capua amphitheatre, and although it can no longer seat 30,000, it still draws sizeable crowds to its opera and concerts.

From the Arena, it's an easy walk to the river Adige and **Castelvecchio** (☎045 806 26 11; https://museodicastelvecchio. comune.verona.it; Corso Castelvecchio 2; adult/reduced €6/4.50; ☺1.30-7.30pm Mon, 8.30am-7.30pm Tue-Sun; 🚻), a picturesque castle housing one of the city's top art museums. Like many of the city's outstanding monuments, this was built during the 14th-century reign of the tyrannical della Scala (Scaligeri) family, whose eye-catching Gothic tombs, the **Arche Scaligere** (Via Arche Scaligere), stand near elegant Piazza dei Signori.

The Drive ≫ To Padua it's about an hour from Verona on the A4 Venice autostrada. Exit at Padova Ovest (Padua West) and join the SP47 after the toll booth. Follow this until you see,

after a road bridge, a turn-off signposted to the *centro*.

- - - - - - - - - - - - -

❼ Padua

Travellers to Padua (Padova) usually make a beeline for the city's main attraction, the **Cappella degli Scrovegni** (Scrovegni Chapel; ☎049 201 00 20; www.cappelladegli scrovegni.it; Piazza Eremitani 8; adult/reduced €13/6, night ticket €8/6; ☺9am-7pm), but there's more to Padua than Giotto frescoes and it's actually the **Orto Botanico** (☎049 827 39 39; www.ortobotanicopd.it; Via dell'Orto Botanico 15; adult/reduced €10/8; ☺9am-7pm daily Apr & May, 9am-7pm Tue-Sun Jun-Sep, to 6pm Tue-Sun Oct, to 5pm Tue-Sun Nov-Mar; 🚻) that represents Padua on Unesco's list of World Heritage Sites. The oldest botanical garden in the world, this dates to 1545 when a group of medical students planted some rare plants in order to study their medicinal properties. A short walk from the garden, Padua's vast **Basilica di Sant'Antonio** (Il Santo; ☎049 822 56 52; www. basilicadelsanto.org; Piazza del Santo; ☺6.20am-7.45pm Apr-Oct, to 6.45pm Nov-Mar) is a major pilgrimage destination, attracting thousands of visitors a year paying homage to St Anthony, the city's patron saint, who is buried here.

ITALIAN ART & ARCHITECTURE

The Ancients
In pre-Roman times, the Greeks built theatres and proportionally perfect temples in their southern colonies at Agrigento, Syracuse and Paestum, whilst the Etruscans concentrated on funerary art, creating elaborate tombs at Tarquinia and Cerveteri. Coming in their wake, the Romans specialised in roads, aqueducts and monumental amphitheatres such as the Colosseum and Verona's Arena.

Romanesque
With the advent of Christianity in the 4th century, basilicas began to spring up, many with glittering Byzantine-style mosaics. The Romanesque period (c 1050–1200) saw the construction of fortified monasteries and robust, bulky churches such as Bari's Basilica di San Nicola and Modena's cathedral. Pisa's striking *duomo* (cathedral) displays a characteristic Tuscan variation on the style.

Gothic
Gothic architecture, epic in scale and typically embellished by gargoyles, pinnacles and statues, took on a more classical form in Italy. Assisi's Basilica di San Francesco is an outstanding early example, but for the full-blown Italian Gothic style check out the cathedrals in Florence, Venice, Siena and Orvieto.

Renaissance
From quiet beginnings in 14th-century Florence, the Renaissance erupted across Italy before spreading across Europe. In Italy, painters such as Giotto, Botticelli, Leonardo da Vinci and Raphael led the way, while architects Brunelleschi and Bramante rewrote the rule books with their beautifully proportioned basilicas. All-rounder Michelangelo worked his way into immortality, producing masterpieces such as *David* and the Sistine Chapel frescoes.

Baroque
Dominating the 17th century, the extravagant baroque style found fertile soil in Italy. Witness the Roman works of Gian Lorenzo Bernini and Francesco Borromini, Lecce's flamboyant *centro storico* (historic centre) and the magical baroque towns of southeastern Sicily.

Neoclassicism
Signalling a return to sober classical lines, neoclassicism majored in the late-18th and early-19th centuries. Signature works include Caserta's Palazzo Reale and La Scala opera house in Milan. In artistic terms, the most famous Italian exponent was Antonio Canova.

The Drive » Traffic permitting, it's about 45 minutes from Padua to Venice, along the A4. Pass through industrial Mestre and over the Ponte della Libertà lagoon bridge to the car park on Piazzale Roma.

TRIP HIGHLIGHT

❽ Venice

The end of the road, quite literally, is Venice (Venezia). Of the city's many must-sees the most famous are on Piazza San Marco, including the **Basilica di San Marco** (St Mark's Basilica; ☏04127083 11; www.basilicasanmarco.it; Piazza San Marco; ⏰9.45am-5pm Mon-Sat, 2-5pm Sun summer, to 4pm Sun winter; 🚤San Marco), **Venice's** great showpiece church. Built originally to house the bones of St Mark, it's a truly awe-inspiring vision with its spangled spires, Byzantine domes, luminous mosaics and lavish marble work. For a bird's-eye view, head to the nearby **campanile** (Bell Tower; www.basilicasanmarco.it; Piazza San Marco; €8; ⊗9am-9pm summer, to 7pm spring & autumn, 9.30am-3.45pm winter; San Marco).

Adjacent to the basilica, the **Palazzo Ducale** (Ducal Palace; 041 271 59 11; www.palazzoducale.visitmuve.it; Piazzetta San Marco 52; adult/reduced incl Museo Correr €19/12; ⊗8.30am-7pm summer, to 5.30pm winter; San Zaccaria) was the official residence of Venice's doges (ruling dukes) from the 9th century. Inside, its lavishly decorated chambers harbour some seriously heavyweight art, including Tintoretto's gigantic *Paradiso* (Paradise) in the Sala del Maggiore Consiglio. Joining the palace to the city dungeons, the **Ponte dei Sospiri** (Bridge of Sighs) was named after the sighs that prisoners – including Casanova – emitted en route from court to cell. If you're hungry, hit the streets on foot for a real taste of the city.

✕ ⌗ p40, p87

VENTDUSUD/GETTY IMAGES ©

Venice Ponte dei Sospiri (Bridge of Sighs)

Eating & Sleeping

Rome ❶

✖ Trattoria Monti — Ristorante $$

(☎06 446 65 73; Via di San Vito 13a; meals €40-45; ⊗1-3pm Tue-Sun, 8-11pm Tue-Sat, closed Aug; Ⓜ Vittorio Emanuele) The Camerucci family runs this elegant brick-arched place, proffering top-notch traditional cooking from Le Marche region. There are wonderful *fritti* (fried things), delicate pastas and ingredients such as *pecorino di fossa* (sheep's cheese aged in caves), goose, swordfish and truffles. Try the egg-yolk *tortelli* pasta. Desserts are delectable, including apple pie with *zabaglione*. Word has spread, so book ahead.

✖ Casa Coppelle — Ristorante $$

(☎06 6889 1707; www.casacoppelle.it; Piazza delle Coppelle 49; meals €45; ⊗noon-3.30pm & 6.30-11.30pm; 🚃Corso del Rinascimento) Exposed brick walls, flowers and subdued lighting set the stage for creative Italian- and French-inspired food at this intimate, romantic restaurant. There's a full range of starters and pastas, but the real tour de force are the rich, decadent meat dishes. Service is attentive and the setting, on a small piazza near the Pantheon, memorable. Book ahead.

🛏 La Piccola Maison — B&B $$

(☎06 4201 6331; www.lapiccolamaison.com; Via dei Cappuccini 30; s €50-180, d €70-200, tr €110-270; ❈ 🛜; Ⓜ Barberini) The excellent Piccola Maison is housed in a 19th-century building in a great location close to Piazza Barberini, and has pleasingly plain, neutrally decorated rooms and thoughtful staff. It's a great deal.

Siena ❷

✖ Enoteca I Terzi — Tuscan $$

(☎0577 4 43 29; www.enotecaiterzi.it; Via dei Termini 7; meals €35-40; ⊗11am-1am summer, 11am-4pm & 6.30pm-midnight winter, closed Sun) A favourite for many locals who head to this historic *enoteca* to linger over lunches, *aperitivi* and casual dinners featuring top-notch Tuscan *salumi* (cured meats), delicate handmade pasta and wonderful wines.

Florence ❸

✖ Trattoria Cibrèo — Tuscan $$

(www.edizioniteatrodelsalecibreofirenze.it; Via dei Macci 122r; meals €30; ⊗12.50-2.30pm & 6.50-11pm Tue-Sat, closed Aug) Dine here and you'll instantly understand why a queue gathers outside before it opens. Once inside, revel in top-notch Tuscan cuisine: perhaps *pappa al pomodoro* (a thick soupy mash of tomato, bread and basil) followed by *polpettine di pollo e ricotta* (chicken and ricotta meatballs). No reservations, no credit cards, no coffee, no pasta and arrive early to snag a table.

✖ L'Osteria di Giovanni — Tuscan $$$

(☎055 28 48 97; www.osteriadigiovanni.it; Via del Moro 22; meals €50; ⊗7-10pm Mon-Fri, 12.30-3pm & 7-10pm Sat & Sun) Cuisine at this smart neighbourhood eatery is sumptuously Tuscan. Imagine truffles, tender steaks and pastas such as *pici al sugo di salsiccia e cavolo nero* (thick spaghetti with a sauce of sausage and black cabbage). Throw in a complimentary glass of *prosecco* and you'll want to return time and again.

🛏 Hotel L'O   Design Hotel €€€

(📞055 27 73 80; www.hotelorologioflorence.
com; Piazza di Santa Maria Novella 24; d from
€150; P ❄ @ 🛜) The type of seductive
address James Bond would feel right at home
in, this super-stylish hotel oozes panache.
Designed as a showcase for the (very wealthy)
owner's (exceedingly expensive) luxury
wristwatch collection, L'O (the hip take on its full
name, Hotel L'Orologio) has four stars, rooms
named after watches and clocks pretty much
everywhere. Don't be late...

Pisa ④

✘ Sottobosco   Cafe $

(www.sottoboscocafe.it; Piazza San Paolo
all'Orto; lunches €15; 🕒3pm-midnight Tue-Fri,
6pm-1am Sat, 6pm-midnight Sun winter, noon-
3pm & 6pm-midnight Tue-Fri, 6pm-1am Sat, 6pm-
midnight Sun summer, closed Jul & Aug) What
a tourist-free breath of fresh air this creative
cafe is! Tuck into a sugary ring doughnut and
cappuccino at a glass-topped table filled with
artists' crayons perhaps, or a collection of
buttons. Lunch dishes (salads, pies and pasta)
are simple and homemade, and come dusk, jazz
bands play or DJs spin tunes.

Modena ⑤

✘ Hosteria Giusti   Gastronomy $$$

(📞059 22 25 33; www.hosteriagiusti.it; Vicolo
Squallore 46; meals €50, with half portions €35;
🕒12.30-2pm Tue-Sat) With only four tables,
a narrow back-alley location, no real signage
and a 90-minute daily opening window, this
perplexingly unassuming osteria isn't really
setting itself up for legendary status. But
tentative whispers turn to exuberant shouts
when regional specialities like cotechino fritto
con zabaglione al lambrusco (fried Modena
sausage with wine-flavoured egg custard) arrive
at your table. Booking essential.

🛏 Hotel Cervetta 5   Hotel $$

(📞059 23 84 47; www.hotelcervetta5.com;
Via Cervetta 5; s €90-115, d €128-215; ❄ 🛜)
Cervetta is about as posh as Modena gets
without pampering to the convention crowd.
A location adjacent to intimate Piazza Grande
is complemented by quasi-boutique facilities,
clean, modern bathrooms and the latest in
TV technology. Fruity breakfasts and wi-fi are
included; garage parking (€15) isn't.

Venice ⑧

✘ All'Arco   Venetian $

(📞041 520 56 66; Calle dell'Ochialer 436, San
Polo; cicheti from €1.50; 🕒8am-8pm Wed-Fri, to
3pm Mon, Tue & Sat; 🚤Rialto-Mercato) Search
out this authentic neighbourhood osteria
(casual tavern) for some of the best cicheti
(bar snacks) in town. Armed with ingredients
from the nearby Rialto market, father-son
team Francesco and Matteo serve miniature
masterpieces such as cannocchia (mantis
shrimp) with pumpkin and roe, and otrega
crudo (raw butterfish) with mint-and-olive-oil
marinade.

✘ Anice Stellato   Venetian $$$

(📞041 72 07 44; www.osterianicestellato.
com; Fondamenta de la Sensa 3272; bar snacks
€13.50, meals €45-50; 🕒10.30am-3.30pm
& 6.30pm-midnight Wed-Sun; 🚤Madonna
dell'Orto) Tin lamps, unadorned rustic tables
and a small wooden bar set the scene for quality
seafood at this excellent canal-side bacaro
(bar). You can munch on bar-side cicheti or go
for the full à la carte menu and swoon over juicy
scampi in saor (vinegar marinade) and grilled
tuna. Reservations recommended.

🛏 Novecento   Boutique Hotel $$$

(📞041 241 37 65; www.novecento.biz; Calle del
Dose 2683/84; d €140-350; ❄ 🛜; 🚤Santa
Maria del Giglio) Sporting a boho-chic look, the
Novecento is a real charmer. Its nine individually
designed rooms ooze style with Turkish kilim
pillows, Fortuny draperies and 19th-century
carved bedsteads. Outside, its garden is a lovely
spot to linger over breakfast.

Wonders of Ancient Sicily

6

More than a trip around la bella Sicilia, this is also a journey through time, from spare Greek temples to Norman churches decked out with Arab and Byzantine finery.

TRIP HIGHLIGHTS

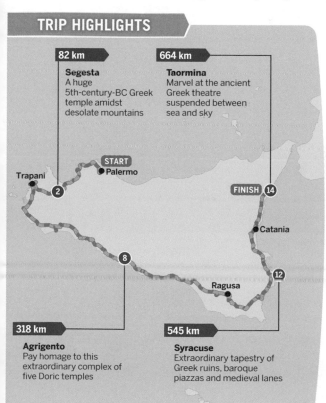

82 km

Segesta
A huge 5th-century-BC Greek temple amidst desolate mountains

664 km

Taormina
Marvel at the ancient Greek theatre suspended between sea and sky

318 km

Agrigento
Pay homage to this extraordinary complex of five Doric temples

545 km

Syracuse
Extraordinary tapestry of Greek ruins, baroque piazzas and medieval lanes

12–14 DAYS
664KM / 412 MILES

GREAT FOR...

BEST TIME TO GO
Spring and autumn are best. Avoid the heat and crowds of high summer.

ESSENTIAL PHOTO
Mt Etna from Taormina's Greek theatre.

BEST FOR HISTORY
Explore layer upon layer of Sicily's past in glorious Syracuse.

Segesta Ruins of the Doric temple

6

Wonders of Ancient Sicily

A Mediterranean crossroads for 25 centuries, Sicily is heir to an unparalleled cultural legacy, from the temples of Magna Graecia to Norman churches made kaleidoscopic by Byzantine and Arab craftsmen. This trip takes you from exotic, palm-fanned Palermo to the baroque splendours of Syracuse and Catania. On the way, you'll also experience Sicily's startlingly diverse landscape, including bucolic farmland, smouldering volcanoes and long stretches of aquamarine coastline.

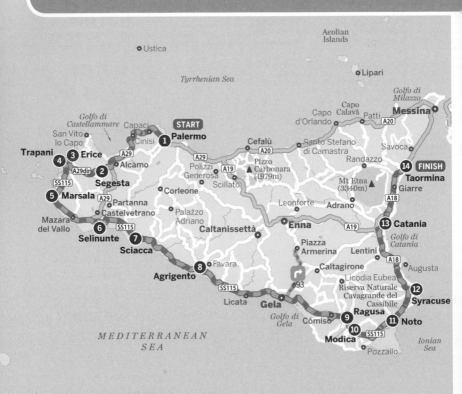

① Palermo

Palermo is a fascinating conglomeration of splendour and decay. Unlike Florence or Rome, many of its treasures are hidden rather than scrubbed up for endless streams of tourists. The evocative history of the city infuses its daily life, lending its dusty backstreet markets a distinct Middle Eastern feel and its architecture a unique East-meets-West look.

A trading port since Phoenician times, the city, which is best explored on foot, first came to prominence as capital of Arab Sicily in the 9th century AD. When the Normans rode into town in the 11th century, they used Arab know-how to turn it into Christendom's richest and most sophisticated city. The **Cappella Palatina** (Palatine Chapel; www.federicosecondo. org; Piazza Indipendenza; adult/reduced Fri-Mon €8.50/6.50, Tue-Thu €7/5; ☺9am-5pm Mon-Sat, 8.30-9.40am & 11.15am-1pm Sun) is the perfect expression of this marriage, with its gold-inflected Byzantine mosaics crowned by a honeycomb *muqarnas* ceiling – a masterpiece of Arab craftsmanship.

For an insight into Sicily's long and turbulent past, the **Museo Archeologico Regionale** (☎091 611 68 07; www. regione.sicilia.it/beniculturali/ salinas; Piazza Olivella 24; ☺9.30am-6.30pm Tue-Fri, to 1pm Sat & Sun) houses some of the island's most valuable Greek and Roman artefacts.

✕ 🛏 p98

The Drive » From Palermo the 82km trip to Segesta starts along the fast-moving A29 as it skirts the mountains west of Palermo, then runs along agricultural plains until you reach the hills of Segesta. The Greek ruins lie just off the A29dir.

TRIP HIGHLIGHT

② Segesta

Set on the edge of a deep canyon in the midst of desolate mountains, the 5th-century-BC ruins of **Segesta** (☎0924 95 23 56; adult/reduced €6/3; ☺9am-7.30pm Apr-Sep, 9am-1hr before sunset Oct-Mar) are a magical site. The city, founded by the ancient Elymians, was in constant conflict with Selinunte, whose destruction it sought with dogged determination and singular success. Time, however, has done to Segesta what violence inflicted on Selinunte; little remains now, save the theatre and the never-completed Doric temple. The latter dates from around 430 BC and is remarkably well preserved. On windy days its 36 giant columns are said to act like an organ, producing mysterious notes.

The Drive » Keep heading along A29dir through a patchwork of green and ochre fields and follow signs for the 40km to Trapani. As you reach its outskirts, you'll head up the very windy SP3 to Erice, with great views of countryside and sea.

---

③ Erice

A spectacular hill town, Erice combines medieval charm with astounding 360-degree views from atop the legendary **Mt Eryx** (750m) – on a clear day, you can see as far as Cape Bon in Tunisia. Wander the medieval streets interspersed with churches, forts and tiny cobbled piazzas. Little remains from its ancient past, though as a centre for the cult of Venus, it has a seductive history.

The best views can be had from the **Giardino del Balio**, which

LINK YOUR TRIP

1 Grand Tour
Head north to Naples where you can start your search for enlightenment and adventure.

4 Amalfi Coast
Don't miss this week-long adventure of hairpin turns and vertical landscapes amid the world's most glamorous stretch of coastline.

overlooks the rugged turrets and wooded hillsides down to the saltpans of Trapani and the sea. Adjacent to the gardens is the Norman **Castello di Venere** (☎366 6712832; www.fondazioneericearte. org/castellodivenere.php; Via Castello di Venere; adult/reduced €4/2; ☺10am-1hr before sunset daily Apr-Oct, 10am-4pm Sat, Sun & holidays Nov-Mar), built in the 12th and 13th centuries over the ancient Temple of Venus.

🏷p98

The Drive ≫ For the 12km to Trapani, it's back down the switchbacks of the SP3.

4 Trapani

Once a key link in a powerful trading network that stretched from Carthage to Venice, Trapani occupies a sickle-shaped spit of land that hugs its ancient harbour. Although Trapani's industrial outskirts are rather bleak, its historic centre is filled with atmospheric pedestrian streets and some lovely churches and baroque buildings. The narrow network of streets remains a Moorish labyrinth, although it takes much of its character from the fabulous 18th-century baroque of the Spanish period.

✖ p98

The Drive ≫ For the 33km trip from Trapani to Marsala, head south on the SS115. Small towns alternate with farmland until

you reach Marsala on Sicily's west coast.

5 Marsala

Best known for its eponymous sweet dessert wines, Marsala is an elegant town of stately baroque buildings within a perfect square of city walls. Founded by Phoenicians escaping Roman attacks, the city still has remnants of the 7m-thick ramparts they built, ensuring that it was the last Punic settlement to fall to the Romans.

Marsala's finest treasure is the partially reconstructed remains of a Carthaginian *liburna* (warship) – the only remaining physical evidence of the Phoenicians' seafaring superiority in the 3rd century BC. You can visit it at the **Museo Archeologico Baglio Anselmi** (☎0923 95 25 35; Lungomare Boeo 30; adult/reduced €4/2; ☺9am-7.30pm Tue-Sat, to 1.30pm Sun & Mon).

✖ p98

The Drive ≫ For this 52km leg, once again head down the SS115, passing through farmland and scattered towns until you reach the A29. Continue on the autostrada to Castelvetrano, then follow the SS115 and SS115dir for the last leg through orchards and fields to seaside Selinunte.

6 Selinunte

Built on a promontory overlooking the sea, the

Greek **ruins of Selinunte** (☎0924 4 62 77; adult/reduced €6/3; ☺9am-6pm Apr-Oct, to 5pm Nov-Mar) are among the most impressive in Sicily, dating to around the 7th century BC. There are few historical records of the city, which was once one of the world's most powerful, and even the names of the various temples have been forgotten and are now identified by letters. The most impressive, **Temple E**, has been partially rebuilt, its columns pieced together from their fragments with part of its tympanum. Many of the carvings, which are on a par with the Parthenon marbles, particularly those from **Temple C**, are now in Palermo's archaeological museum.

The Drive ≫ Head back up to the SS115 and past a series of hills and plains for the 37km trip to Sciacca.

7 Sciacca

Seaside Sciacca was founded in the 5th century BC as a thermal resort for nearby Selinunte. Its healing waters still attract visitors, who come to wallow in the sulphurous vapours and mineral-rich mud. Spas and thermal cures apart, it's a laid-back town with an attractive medieval core and some excellent seafood restaurants.

The Drive ≫ Continue eastwards on the SS115 as it

follows the southern coast onto Porto Empedocle and then 10km inland, Agrigento's hilltop centre. In all, it's about 62km.

TRIP HIGHLIGHT

8 Agrigento

Seen from a distance, Agrigento's unsightly apartment blocks loom incongruously on the hillside, distracting attention from the splendid Valley of Temples below. In the Valley, the mesmerising **ruins** (Valle dei Templi; www.parcovalledeitempli.it; adult/reduced €10/5, incl Museo Archeologico €13.50/7; ⊙8.30am-7pm year-round, plus 7.30-9.30pm Mon-Fri, 7.30-11.30pm Sat & Sun Jul–early Sep) of ancient Akragras boast the best-preserved Doric temples outside of Greece.

The ruins are spread over a 1300-hectare site which is divided into eastern and western halves. Head first to the eastern zone, where you'll find the three best temples: the **Tempio di Hera** (aka the Tempio di Giunone), **Tempio di Ercole** and, most spectacularly, the **Tempio della Concordia** (Temple of Concord). This, the only temple to survive relatively intact, was built around 440 BC and was converted into a Christian church in the 6th century.

Uphill from the ruins, Agrigento's **medieval centre** also has its charms, with a 14th-century cathedral and a number of medieval and baroque buildings.

✗ 🛏 p98

The Drive >> For this 133km leg head back to the SS115, which veers from inland farmland to brief encounters with the sea. Past the town of Gela, you will head into more hilly country, including a steep climb past Comiso, followed by a straight shot along the SP52 to Ragusa.

9 Ragusa

Set amid the rocky peaks northwest of Modica, Ragusa has two faces. Atop the hill sits **Ragusa Superiore**, a busy town with all the trappings of a modern provincial capital, while etched into the hillside is **Ragusa Ibla**. This sloping area of tangled alleyways, grey stone houses and baroque *palazzi* (mansions) is Ragusa's magnificent historic centre.

Like other towns in the region, Ragusa Ibla collapsed after the 1693 earthquake. But the aristocracy, ever impractical, rebuilt their homes on exactly the same spot. Grand baroque churches and *palazzi* line the twisting, narrow lanes, which then open suddenly onto sun-drenched piazzas. Palm-planted Piazza del Duomo, the centre of town, is dominated by the 18th-century baroque **Cattedrale di San Giorgio** (Piazza Duomo; ⊙10am-12.30pm & 4-7pm Jun-Sep, reduced hours rest of year), with its magnificent neoclassical dome and stained-glass windows.

The Drive >> Follow the SS115 for this winding, up-and-down 15km drive through rock-littered hilltops to Modica.

ITALY 6 WONDERS OF ANCIENT SICILY

DETOUR: VILLA ROMANA DEL CASALE

Start: 8 Agrigento

Near the town of Piazza Armerina in central Sicily, the stunning 3rd-century Roman **Villa Romana del Casale** (☎0935 68 00 36; www.villaromanadelcasale. it; adult/reduced €10/5; ⊙9am-6pm Apr-Oct, to 4pm Nov-Mar) is thought to have been the country retreat of Diocletian's co-emperor Marcus Aurelius Maximianus. Buried under mud in a 12th-century flood, the villa remained hidden for 700 years before its floor mosaics – considered some of the finest in existence – were discovered in the 1950s. They cover almost the entire villa floor and are considered unique for their natural, narrative style.

WHY THIS IS A GREAT TRIP
DUNCAN GARWOOD, WRITER

Sicily boasts some of the most spectacular artistic and archaeological treasures you've never heard of. The great Greek ruins of Agrigento and Syracuse might be on many travellers' radars but what about Palermo's Cappella Palatina or Noto's flamboyant baroque streets? These masterpieces are all the more rewarding for being so unexpected, and go to make this round-island trip an amazing and unforgettable experience.

Top: Looking from Trapani across the Tyrrhenian Sea to Mt Eryx and the hilltop town of Erice
Left: Porta Reale, Corso Vittorio Emanuele, Noto
Right: Chiesa di San Giorgio, Modica

IMAGESEF/SHUTTERSTOCK ©

⑩ Modica

Modica is a wonderfully atmospheric town with medieval buildings climbing steeply up either side of a deep gorge. But unlike some of the other Unesco-listed cities in the area, it doesn't package its treasures into a single easy-to-see street or central piazza: rather, they are spread around the town and take some discovering. The highlight has to be the baroque **Chiesa di San Giorgio** (Corso San Giorgio, Modica Alta; ⊘8am-12.30pm & 3.30-6.30pm), which stands in isolated splendour atop a majestic 250-step staircase.

Corso Umberto I is the place to lap up the lively local atmosphere. A wide avenue flanked by graceful palaces, churches, restaurants, bars and boutiques, it is where the locals come to parade during the *passeggiata* (evening stroll). Originally a raging river flowed through town, but after major flood damage in 1902 it was dammed and Corso Umberto was built over it.

🛏 p99

The Drive » Head back onto the SS115, which becomes quite twisty as you close in on Noto, 40km away.

⑪ Noto

Flattened in 1693 by an earthquake, Noto was rebuilt quickly and grandly, and its golden-hued sandstone buildings make it the finest baroque town in Sicily, especially impressive at night when illuminations accentuate its intricately carved facades. The *pièce de résistance* is **Corso Vittorio Emanuele**, an elegantly manicured walkway flanked by thrilling baroque *palazzi* and churches.

Just off Corso Vittorio Emanuele, **Palazzo Nicolaci di Villadorata** (☑338 7427022; www.comune.noto. sr.it/palazzo-nicolaci; Via Corrado Nicolaci; €4; ◷10am-1.30pm & 2.30-7pm) reveals the luxury to which the local nobility were accustomed. The decor is as opulent as the facade, with heavy glass chandeliers, frescoed ceilings and crafty wall paintings designed to look like brocaded wallpaper.

✖ p99

**The Drive ›› ** The 39km drive to Syracuse from Noto takes you down the SP59 and then northeast on the A18, past the majestic Riserva Naturale Cavagrande del Cassibile as you parallel Sicily's eastern coast.

TRIP HIGHLIGHT

⑫ Syracuse

Encapsulating Sicily's timeless beauty, Syracuse is a dense tapestry of overlapping cultures and civilisations. Ancient Greek ruins rise out of lush citrus orchards, cafe tables spill out onto baroque piazzas, and medieval lanes meander to the sea. Your visit, like the city itself, can be split into two easy parts: one dedicated to the archaeological site, the other to Ortygia, the ancient island neighbourhood connected to the modern town by bridge.

It's difficult to imagine now but in its heyday Syracuse was the largest city in the ancient world, bigger even than Athens and Corinth. The **Parco Archeologico della Neapolis** (☑0931 6 62 06; Viale Paradiso 14; adult/reduced €10/5, incl Museo Archeologico €13.50/7; ◷8.30am-1.45pm Mon, last entry 12.45pm, 8.30am-7.30pm Tue-Sun, last entry 6pm) is home to a staggering number of well-preserved Greek (and Roman) remains, with the remarkably intact 5th-century-BC **Teatro Greco** as the main attraction. In the grounds of Villa Landolina, about 500m east of the archaeological park, is the **Museo Archeologico Paolo Orsi** (☑0931 48 95 11; www. regione.sicilia.it/beniculturali/ museopaoloorsi; Viale Teocrito 66; adult/reduced €8/4, incl Parco Archeologico €13.50/7; ◷9am-6pm Tue-Sat, to 1pm Sun).

Despite the labyrinthine streets, it is hard to get lost on **Ortygia**, since it measures less than 1 sq km. And yet it also manages to encompass 25 centuries of history. At its heart, the city's 7th-century **Duomo** (Piazza del Duomo; adult/reduced €2/1; ◷9am-6.30pm Mon-Sat Apr-Oct, to 5.30pm Nov-Mar) lords it over Piazza del

---

THE 1693 EARTHQUAKE

On 11 January 1693, a devastating, 7.4-magnitude earthquake hit southeastern Sicily, destroying buildings from Catania to Ragusa. The destruction was terrible, but it also created a blank palette for architects to rebuild the region's cities and towns out of whole cloth, in the latest style and according to rational urban planning – a phenomenon practically unheard of since ancient times. In fact, the earthquake ushered in an entirely new architectural style known as Sicilian baroque, defined by its seductive curves and elaborate detail, which you can see on display in Ragusa, Modica, Catania and many other cities in the region.

Duomo, one of Sicily's loveliest public spaces. The cathedral was built over a pre-existing 5th-century-BC Greek temple, incorporating most of the original Doric columns in its three-aisled structure. The sumptuous baroque facade was added in the 18th century.

✘ ⌁ p99

The Drive » From Syracuse to Catania, it is a 66km drive north along the A18. This is orange-growing country and you will see many orchards, which can be gorgeously fragrant when in bloom.

- - - - - - - - - - - - -

⓭ Catania

Catania is a true city of the volcano, much of it constructed from the lava that poured down on it during a 1669 eruption. The baroque centre is lava-black in colour, as if a fine dusting of soot permanently covers its elegant buildings, most of which are the work of Giovanni Vaccarini. The

18th-century architect almost single-handedly rebuilt the civic centre into an elegant, modern city of spacious boulevards and set-piece piazzas.

Long buried under lava, the **Graeco-Roman Theatre & Odeon** (☎095 715 05 08; Via Vittorio Emanuele II 262; adult/reduced incl Casa Liberti €6/3; ⊙9am-7pm Mon-Sat, to 1.30pm Sun) remind you that the city's history goes back much further. Picturesquely sited in a crumbling residential area, the ruins are occasionally brightened by laundry flapping on the rooftops of vine-covered buildings that appear to have sprouted organically from the half-submerged stage.

✘ p99

The Drive » The 53km drive to Taormina along the A18 is a coast-hugging northern run, taking in more orange groves as well as glimpses of the sparkling Ionian Sea.

- - - - - - - - - - - - -
TRIP HIGHLIGHT

⓮ Taormina

Over the centuries, Taormina has seduced an exhaustive line of writers and artists, from Goethe to DH Lawrence. The main reason for their swooning? The perfect horseshoe-shaped **Teatro Greco** (☎0942 2 32 20; Via Teatro Greco; adult/reduced €10/5; ⊙9am-1hr before sunset), suspended between sea and sky, with glorious views to brooding Mt Etna through the broken columns. Built in the 3rd century BC, the *teatro* is the most dramatically situated Greek theatre in the world and the second largest in Sicily (after Syracuse).

The 9th-century capital of Byzantine Sicily, Taormina also boasts a well-preserved, if touristy, medieval town – and gorgeous views up and down the Strait of Messina.

Eating & Sleeping

Palermo ①

✖ Trattoria Ai Cascinari
Sicilian €

(☎091 651 98 04; Via d'Ossuna 43/45; meals
€20-25; ☺12.30-2.30pm Tue-Sun, plus
8-10.30pm Wed-Sat) Yes, it's a bit out of the
way, but Ai Cascinari, 1km north of the Cappella
Palatina, is a long-standing Palermitan favourite,
and deservedly so. It's especially enjoyable
on Sunday afternoons, when locals pack the
labyrinth of back rooms and waiters perambulate
non-stop with plates of scrumptious seasonal
antipasti, fresh seafood and desserts from
Palermo's beloved Cappello and Scimone
pasticcerie (pastry shops).

▐ Butera 28
Apartment €€

(☎333 3165432; www.butera28.it; Via Butera
28; apt per day €60-200, per week €400-1320;
❈ 🛜) Delightful multilingual owner Nicoletta
rents 11 comfortable apartments in the 18th-
century Palazzo Lanzi Tomasi, the last home of
Giuseppe Tomasi di Lampedusa, author of The
Leopard. Units range from 30 to 180 sq metres,
most sleeping a family of four or more. Four
apartments face the sea, most have laundry
facilities and all have well-equipped kitchens.

Erice ③

▐ Hotel Elimo
Hotel €€

(☎0923 86 93 77; www.hotelelimo.it; Via Vittorio
Emanuele 75; s €80-110, d €90-130, ste €150-170;
❈ 🛜) Communal spaces at this atmospheric
historic house are filled with tiled beams, marble
fireplaces, intriguing art, knick-knacks and
antiques. The bedrooms are more mainstream,
although many (along with the hotel terrace and
restaurant) have breathtaking vistas south and
west towards the Saline di Trapani, the Egadi
Islands and the shimmering sea.

Trapani ④

✖ Osteria La Bettolaccia
Sicilian €€

(☎0923 2 16 95; www.labettolaccia.it; Via Enrico
Fardella 25; meals €35-45; ☺12.45-3pm Mon-Fri,
plus 7.45-11pm Mon-Sat) Unwaveringly authentic,
this Slow Food favourite just two blocks from
the ferry terminal is the perfect place to try cous
cous con zuppa di mare (couscous with mixed
seafood in a spicy fish sauce, with tomatoes,
garlic and parsley). Even with its newly expanded
dining room, it can still fill up, so book ahead.

Marsala ⑤

✖ Il Gallo e l'Innamorata
Sicilian €€

(☎0923 195 44 46; www.
osteriailgalloelinnamorata.com; Via Bilardello 18;
meals €25-35; ☺12.30-2.30pm & 7.30-10.30pm
Tue-Sun) Warm-orange walls and arched stone
doorways lend an artsy, convivial atmosphere to
this Slow Food–acclaimed eatery. The à la carte
menu features a few well-chosen dishes each
day, including the classic scaloppine al Marsala
(veal cooked with Marsala wine and lemon).

Agrigento ⑧

✖ Kalòs
Modern Sicilian €€

(☎0922 2 63 89; www.facebook.com/ristorante.
kalos; Piazzetta San Calogero; meals €30-45;
☺12.30-3pm & 7-11pm Tue-Sun) For fine dining,
head to this 'smart' restaurant just outside the
historic centre. Five cute tables on little balconies
offer a delightful setting to enjoy homemade
pasta all'agrigentina (with fresh tomatoes, basil
and almonds), citrus shrimp or spada gratinata
(baked swordfish covered in breadcrumbs).
Superb desserts, including homemade cannoli
(pastry shells with a sweet filling) and almond
semifreddi, round out the menu.

▐ PortAtenea
B&B €

(☎349 0937492; www.portatenea.com; Via
Atenea, cnr Via C Battisti; s €35-50, d €50-75, tr

€70-95; ✷ 🛜) This five-room B&B wins plaudits for its panoramic roof terrace overlooking the Valley of the Temples, and its convenient location at the entrance to the old town, five minutes' walk from the train and bus stations. Best of all is the generous advice about Agrigento offered by hosts Sandra and Filippo (witness Filippo's amazing Google Earth tour of nearby beaches!).

Modica ⑩

🛏 Villa Quartarella   Agriturismo €

(📞360 654829; www.quartarella.com; Contrada Quartarella Passo Cane 1; s €40, d €75-80, tr €85-100, q €90-120; P ✷ 🛜 🐾) Spacious rooms, welcoming hosts and ample breakfasts make this converted villa in the countryside south of Modica an appealing choice for anyone travelling by car. Owners Francesco and Francesca are generous in sharing their love and encyclopedic knowledge of local history, flora and fauna and can suggest a multitude of driving itineraries.

Noto ⑪

✗ Ristorante Il Cantuccio   Modern Sicilian €€

(📞0931 83 74 64; www.ristoranteilcantuccio. it; Via Cavour 12; meals €32-36; ⏱12.30-2pm & 7.45-10.30pm Tue-Sun) Tucked into the courtyard of a former noble's palace, this inviting restaurant combines familiar Sicilian ingredients in inspired ways. Perennial favourites such as the exquisite gnocchi al pesto del Cantuccio (ricotta-potato dumplings with basil, parsley, mint, capers, toasted almonds and cherry tomatoes) are complemented by seasonally changing specials such as lemon-stuffed bass with orange-fennel salad or white-wine-stewed rabbit with caponata.

Syracuse ⑫

✗ Bistrot Bella Vita   Italian €€

(📞0931 46 49 38; Via Gargallo 60; sweets €1.50, meals €25; ⏱cafe 7.30am-midnight, restaurant noon-2.30pm & 7-10.45pm Tue-Sun) This casually elegant cafe-restaurant is one of Ortygia's rising stars. Stop by for good coffee (soy milk available) and made-from-scratch cornetti, biscotti and pastries (try the sour orange-and-almond tart). Or book a table in the intimate back dining room, where local, organic produce drives beautifully textured, technically impressive dishes.

🛏 Villa dei Papiri   Agriturismo €

(📞0931 72 13 21; www.villadeipapiri.it; Traversa Cozzo Pantano Testa Pisima 2/c; d €48-108, 2-person ste €68-128, 4-person ste €98-158; P ✷ 🛜) Immersed in an Eden of orange groves and papyrus reeds 8km outside Syracuse, this lovely agriturismo sits next to the Fonte Ciana spring immortalised in Ovid's Metamorphosis. Eight suites are housed in a beautifully converted 19th-century farmhouse, with 16 double rooms dotted around the lush grounds. Breakfast is an extra €7.50 and served in a baronial stone-walled hall.

Catania ⑬

✗ Trattoria di De Fiore   Trattoria €

(📞095 31 62 83; Via Coppola 24/26; meals €15-25; ⏱7pm-12.30am Mon, 1pm-12.30am Tue-Sun) For over 50 years, septuagenarian chef Rosanna has been recreating her great-grandmother's recipes, including the best pasta alla Norma you'll taste anywhere in Sicily. Service can be excruciatingly slow, but for patient souls this is a rare chance to experience classic Catanian cooking from a bygone era. Don't miss Rosanna's trademark zeppoline (sugar-sprinkled ricotta-lemon fritters) at dessert time.

Taormina ⑭

✗ Osteria Nero D'Avola   Sicilian €€

(📞0942 62 88 74; www.osterianerodavola. it; Piazza San Domenico 2b; meals €32-47; ⏱12.30-3pm & 7-11pm Tue-Sun Sep-Jun, 7pm-midnight Jul & Aug) Not only does affable owner Turi Siligato fish, hunt and forage for his smart osteria, he'll probably share anecdotes about the day's bounty and play a few tunes on the piano. Here, seasonality, local producers and passion underscore dishes like the signature cannolo di limone Interdonato (thinly sliced Interdonato lemon with roe, tuna, tomato and chives).

🛏 Hotel Villa Belvedere   Hotel €€€

(📞0942 2 37 91; www.villabelvedere.it; Via Bagnoli Croce 79; s €70-280, d €80-380, ste €120-450; ⏱Mar-late-Nov; ✷ @ 🛜 🐾) Built in 1902, Villa Belvedere was one of Taormina's original grand hotels. Well-positioned with fabulous views and luxuriant gardens, its highlights include a swimming pool complete with century-old palm. Rooms offer neutral hues and understated style. Parking is an extra €16 per day.

Italian Riviera

7

Curving west in a broad arc, backed by the Maritime Alps, the Italian Riviera sweeps down from Genoa through ancient hamlets and terraced olive groves to the French border at Ventimiglia.

TRIP HIGHLIGHTS

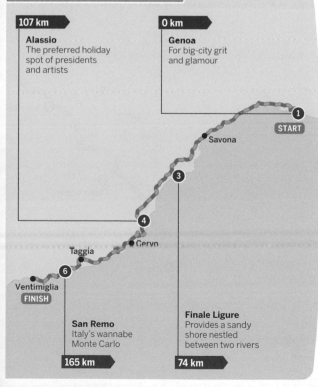

107 km

Alassio
The preferred holiday spot of presidents and artists

0 km

Genoa
For big-city grit and glamour

Savona

START

Taggia

Cervo

Ventimiglia
FINISH

San Remo
Italy's wannabe Monte Carlo

165 km

Finale Ligure
Provides a sandy shore nestled between two rivers

74 km

4 DAYS
214KM / 133 MILES

GREAT FOR...

BEST TIME TO GO
April, May and June for flowers and hiking; October for harvest.

ESSENTIAL PHOTO
Cascading terraces of exotic flowers at Giardini Botanici Hanbury.

BEST FINE DINING
Purple San Remo prawns on the terrace of San Giorgio.

San Remo View over the town

7 Italian Riviera

The contrast between sun-washed, sophisticated coastal towns and a deeply rural, mountainous hinterland, full of heritage farms, olive oil producers and wineries, gave rise to the Riviera's 19th-century fame, when European expatriates outnumbered locals. They amused themselves in lavish botanical gardens, gambled in the casino of San Remo and dined in style in fine art-nouveau villas, much as you will on this tour.

TRIP HIGHLIGHT

❶ Genoa

Like Dr Jekyll and Mr Hyde, Genoa (Genova) is a city with a split personality. At its centre, medieval *caruggi* (alleyways) untangle outwards to the **Porto Antico** and teem with hawkers, merchants and office workers. Along Via Garibaldi and Via XXV Aprile is another Genoa, one of Unesco-sponsored palaces, smart shops and grand architectural gestures like **Piazza de Ferrari** with its

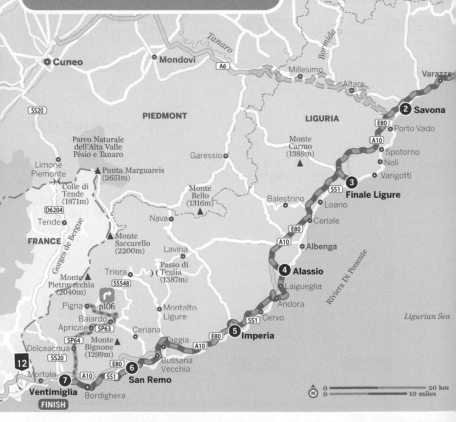

monumental fountain, art nouveau **Palazzo Borsa** (once the city's stock exchange) and the neoclassical **Teatro Carlo Felice** (☏010 538 12 24; www.carlofelice.it; Passo Eugenio Montale 4).

Join the well-dressed *haute bourgeoisie* enjoying high-profile art exhibits in the grand Mannerist halls of the **Palazzo Ducale** (www.palazzoducale.genova.it; Piazza Giacomo Matteotti 9; price varies by exhibition; ☺hours vary), then retire to sip *spritz* amid Bernardo Strozzi's 17th-

century frescoes at **Cambi Cafe** (www.cambi cafe.com; Via Falamonica 9; ☺10am-11pm).

✗ p40, p107

The Drive » Exit Genoa westward, through a tangle of flyovers and tunnels to access the A10 for the first 56km drive to Savona. Once out of the suburbs the forested slopes of the Maritime Alps rise to your right and sea views peep out from the left as you duck through tunnels.

----

❷ Savona

Don't be put off by Savona's horrifying industrial sprawl; the Savonesi were a powerful maritime people and the town centre is unexpectedly graceful. Standing near the port are three of the many medieval towers that once studded the cityscape. As Genoa's greatest rival the town was savagely sacked in 1528, the castle dismantled and most of the population slaughtered, but somehow the **Fortezza del Priamàr** (Piazza Priamar) and the

Cattedrale di Nostra Signora Assunta (Piazza Cattedrale; ☺7.30am-7.30pm) survived.

But you're not here for the architecture – you're here for the food. The covered **market** (Via Pietro Giuria; ☺7am-1.30pm Mon-Sat) is crammed with fruit-and-veg stalls and fish stands stacked with salt cod. **Grigiomar** (Via Pietro Giuria 42r; ☺9am-6pm Mon-Fri, 9am-1pm Sat) salts its own local anchovies. Then there are the local *amaretti* biscuits, made with bitter and sweet almonds, available at **Pasticceria Besio** (www.amarettibesio.com; Via Sormano 16r; ☺2.30-7pm Mon, 9am-7pm Tue-Sat), and the *farinata di grano* (wheat-flour pancakes) at **Vino e Farinata** (Via Pia 15; meals €20; ☺11am-10pm Tue-Sat).

The Drive » Rejoin the A10 and leave the industrial chimneys of Savona behind you. For the first 13km the A10 continues with views of the sea, then at Spotorno it ducks inland for the final 15km to the Finale Ligure exit. Descend steeply for 3km to the Finale hamlets on the coast.

58km to A26
Voltri
A10
Pegli SS1
Arenzano
Genoa
START

Golfo di Genova

❷

LINK YOUR TRIP

2 **The Graceful Italian Lakes**
Heading north from Genoa you're soon in the land of refreshing lakes and mountains.

12 **Riviera Crossing**
Roll right on into France for more beaches, glam cities and glitering seascapes

TRIP HIGHLIGHT

❸ Finale Ligure

Finale Ligure comprises several seaside districts. The marina is narrow and charming, spreading along the sandy shore between two small rivers, the Porra and the Sciusa. East of the Sciusa is Finale Ligure Pia, where you'll find **Alimentari Magnone** (Via Moletti 17), which stocks excellent extra virgin olive oils from local growers. Nearby the Benedictine abbey houses the **Azienda Agricola Apiario Benedettino** (Via Santuario 59; ⊙9am-12.30pm Mon-Sat), where you can buy honey, grappa and organic beauty products.

At the other end of town, **Finalborgo** is the old medieval centre. Each year in March, Finalborgo's cloisters are home to the **Salone dell'Agroalimentare Ligure**, where local farmers hawk seasonal delicacies and vintages.

On Thursday it's worth driving 9km up the coast to picturesque **Noli** for the weekly outdoor market on Corso d'Italia.

✕ 🛏 p107

The Drive » Once again take the high road away from the coast and follow the A10 for a further 35km to Alassio. Near Albenga you'll cross the river Centa and the broad valley where dozens of hothouses dot the landscape.

TRIP HIGHLIGHT

❹ Alassio

Less than 100km from the French border, Alassio's popularity among the 18th- and 19th-century jet set has left it with an elegant colonial character. Its pastel-hued villas range around a broad, sandy beach, which stretches all the way to **Laigueglia** (4km to the south). American president Thomas Jefferson holidayed here in 1787 and Edward Elgar composed *In the South* inspired by his stay in 1904. **Il Muretto**, a ceramic-covered wall, records the names of 550 celebrities who've passed through.

Follow the local lead and promenade along Via XX Settembre or the unspoilt waterfront. Take coffee at **Antico Caffè Pasticceria Balzola** (www.balzola1902.com; Piazza Matteotti 26; ⊙9am-midnight Tue-Sun) and enjoy gelato on the beach beneath a stripy umbrella.

🛏 p107

SAN GIORGIO

Cult restaurant **San Giorgio** (📞0183 40 01 75; www.ristorantesangiorgio.net; Via A Volta 19, Cervo; meals €40-60; ⊙12.30-2pm & 7.30-10pm Wed-Mon, closed Jan) has been quietly wowing gourmets with its authentic Ligurian cooking since the 1950s when mother-and-son team Caterina and Alessandro opened the doors of their home in the *borgo* (medieval town) of **Cervo Alta**. Dine out on the bougainvillea-draped terrace in summer, or in intimate dining rooms cluttered with family silverware and antiques in winter. Below the restaurant, in an old oil mill, is the less formal wine bar and deli **San Giorgino**.

Genoa Fountain in the Piazza de Ferrari

The Drive » If you have
time take the scenic coast
road, SS1 (Via Roma), from
Alassio through Laigueglia and
Marina di Andora to Imperia.
It is a shorter and more scenic
jaunt when traffic is light. The
alternative, when traffic is heavy,
is to head back to the A10.

❺ Imperia

Imperia consists of two
small seaside towns,
Oneglia and Porto Maur-
izio, on either side of the
Impero river.

Oneglia, birthplace
of Admiral Doria, the
Genoese Republic's
greatest naval hero, is
the less attractive of the
two, although **Piazza**

Dante, with its arcaded
walkways, is a pleasant
place to grab a coffee.
This is also where the
great olive-oil dynasties
made their name. Visit
the **Museo dell'Olio** (www.
museodellolivo.com; Via
Garessio 13; adult/reduced
€5/2.50; ☺9am-12.30pm &
3-6.30pm Mon-Sat), housed
in a lovely art-nouveau
mansion belonging to
the heritage Fratelli Carli
factory. The museum is
surprisingly extensive
and details the history
of the Ligurian industry
from the 2nd century BC.
Buy quality oil here or
anywhere in town.

West of Oneglia is
pirate haven **Porto Mau-
rizio**, perched on a rocky
spur that overlooks a
yacht-filled harbour.

The Drive » Rejoining the A10
at Imperia, the landscape begins
to change. The olive terraces
are dense, spear-like cypresses
and umbrella pines shade
the hillsides, and the fragrant
maquis (Mediterranean scrub)
is prolific. Loop inland around
Taggia and then descend slowly
into San Remo.

TRIP HIGHLIGHT

❻ San Remo

San Remo, Italy's wan-
nabe Monte Carlo, is a
sun-dappled Mediterra-
nean resort with a grand

DETOUR: L'ENTROTERRA

Start: ➐ Ventimiglia

The designation 'Riviera' omits the pleated, mountainous interior – *l'entroterra* – that makes up nine-tenths of Liguria. Harried by invasions, coast-dwellers took to these vertical landscapes over a thousand years ago, hewing their perched villages from the rock face of the Maritime Alps. You'll want to set aside two extra days to drive the coiling roads that rise up from Ventimiglia to **Dolceacqua**, **Apricale** and **Pigna**. If you do make the effort, book into gorgeous boutique hotel **Apricus Locanda** (☑339 6008622; www.apricuslocanda.com; Via IV Novembre 5, Apricale; s/d €95/105; P🐾); it's worth it for the breakfast and see-forever panoramas.

belle-époque **casino** (www.casinosanremo.it; Corso degli Inglesi) and lashings of Riviera-style grandeur.

During the mid-19th century the city became a magnet for European exiles such as Czar Nicolas of Russia, who favoured the town's balmy winters. They built an onion-domed **Russian Orthodox church** (Via Nuvoloni 2; €1; ☺9.30am-noon & 3-6pm) reminiscent of Moscow's St Basil's Cathedral, which still turns heads down by the seafront. Swedish inventor Alfred Nobel also maintained a villa here, the **Villa Nobel** (Corso Felice Cavallotti 112; adult/reduced €5.50/4; ☺10am-12.30pm Tue-Thu, 10am-12.30pm & 5-8pm Fri-Sun Jun-Sep), which now houses a museum dedicated to him.

Beyond the waterfront, San Remo hides a little-visited old town, a labyrinth of twisting lanes that cascade down the Ligurian hillside. Curling around the base is the **Italian Cycling Riviera**, a path that tracks the coast as far as Imperia. For bike hire, enquire at the **tourist office** (www.visit rivieradeifiori.it; Largo Nuvoloni 1; ☺9am-7pm Mon-Sat, 9am-1pm Sun; 👣).

✖ 🛏 p107

The Drive » For the final 17km stretch to Ventimiglia take the SS1 coastal road, which hugs the base of the mountains and offers uninterrupted sea views. In summer and at Easter, however, when traffic is heavy, your best bet is the A10.

➐ Ventimiglia

Despite its enviable position between the glitter of San Remo and the Côte d'Azur, Ventimiglia is a soulful but disorderly border town, its Roman past still evident in its bridges, amphitheatre and ruined baths. Now it's the huge **Friday market** (☺8am-3pm Fri) that draws the crowds.

If you can't find a souvenir here then consider one of the prized artisanal honeys produced by **Marco Ballestra** (☑0184 35 16 72; www.ilmieledel brichetto.it; Via Girolamo Rossi 5), which has hives in the hills above the Valle Roya. There are over a dozen different types.

To end the tour head over to the pretty western suburb of Ponte San Ludovico to the **Giardini Botanici Hanbury** (www.giardinihanbury.com; Corso Montecarlo 43; adult/reduced €9/7.50; ☺9.30am-6pm), the 18-hectare estate of English businessman Sir Thomas Hanbury; he planted it with an extravagant 5800 botanical species from five continents.

✖ p107

Eating & Sleeping

Genoa ❶

✗ Il Marin — Seafood €€€

(Eataly Genova; ☎010 869 87 22; www.eataly.
net; Porto Antico; meals €50; ☺noon-3pm &
7-10.30pm) Eating by the water often means a
compromise in quality, but Eataly's 3rd-floor
fine-dining space delivers both panoramic port
views and Genoa's most innovative seafood
menu. Rustic wooden tables, Renzo Piano–
blessed furniture and an open kitchen make
for an easy, relaxed glamour, while dishes use
unusual Mediterranean-sourced produce and
look gorgeous on the plate.

Finale Ligure ❸

✗ Osteria ai Cuattru Canti — Osteria €

(Via Torcelli 22; set menus €20; ☺noon-2pm
& 8-10pm Tue-Sun) Simple and good Ligurian
specialities are cooked up at this rustic place in
Finalborgo's historic centre.

⌂ Val Ponce — Agriturismo €

(☎329 3154169; www.valleponci.it; Val Ponci
22, Localita Verzi; d/apt €85/165) Only 4km
from the beach, Val Ponce feels deliciously wild,
tucked away in a rugged Ligurian valley. Horses
graze, grapevines bud and the restaurant turns
out fresh Ligurian dishes, with vegetables
and herbs from a kitchen garden. On weekend
evenings and Sunday lunch, there's live music
or classic vinyl. Rooms are simple but show the
keen eye of the Milanese escapee owners.

⌂ Hotel Florenz — Hotel €€

(☎019 69 56 67; www.hotelflorenz.it; Via Celesia
1; s/d €86/132; ☺closed Nov & Feb; P @ 🌊)
This rambling 18th-century former convent just
outside Finalborgo's village walls (800m from
the sea) is simple and homey but one of the
area's most atmospheric spots to sleep.

Alassio ❹

⌂ Villa della Pergola — Boutique Hotel €€€

(☎0182 64 61 30; www.villadellapergola.com;
Via Privata Montagu 9/1; d from €315; P 🌊)
Sitting in a tropical garden that rivals the
famous Villa Hanbury, Villa della Pergola was the
home of eminent Victorian, General McMurdo.
He bought the plot in 1875 and designed the
villa in Anglo-Indian style with large airy rooms,
broad verandahs and cascading terraces with
peerless sea views.

San Remo ❻

✗ Ristorante Urbicia Vivas — Ligurian €€

(☎0184 57 55 66; Piazza Dolori 5; meals €30;
☺10.30am-midnight) Basking in a quiet
medieval square in San Remo's remarkable old
town, Urbicia is slavishly faithful to old Ligurian
recipes with a strong bias towards seafood.
There's a €12 lunch deal and Friday night is
risotto night.

⌂ Hotel Liberty — Hotel €

(☎0184 50 99 52; www.hotellibertysanremo.
com; Rondò Garibaldi 2; s €55, d €85-100;
P 🌊) A 10-room hotel is set in a Liberty-style
villa off a small traffic circle about 100m from
the train station. It's quiet, clean and run by
helpful young owners.

Ventimiglia ❼

✗ Pasta & Basta — Ligurian €

(☎0184 23 08 78; www.pastaebastaventimiglia.
com; Via Marconi 20; meals €20; ☺noon-3pm
& 7-10pm Tue-Sun, lunch only Mon) Duck into
the underpass near the seafront on the border
side of town to the perpetually redeveloping
port area. Various house-made fresh pasta can
be mixed and matched with a large menu of
sauces, including a good pesto or salsa di noci
(walnut purée), and washed down with a carafe
of pale and refreshing Pigato, a local white.

NEED ^{TO} KNOW

CURRENCY
Euro (€)

LANGUAGE
Italian

VISAS
Generally not required for stays of up to 90 days (or at all for EU nationals); some nationalities need a Schengen visa.

FUEL
You'll find filling stations on autostradas and major roads. Reckon on €1.49 for a litre of unleaded petrol and €1.33 for diesel.

HIRE CARS
Avis (www.avis.com)
Europcar (www.europcar.com)
Hertz (www.hertz.it)
Maggiore (www.maggiore.it)

IMPORTANT NUMBERS
Ambulance (☎118)
Emergency (☎112)
Police (☎113)
Roadside Assistance (☎803 116; ☎800 116 800 from a foreign mobile phone)

Climate

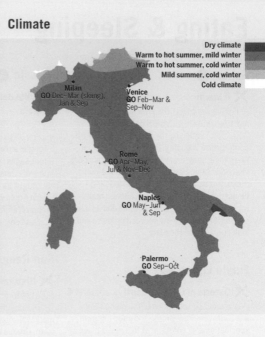

Dry climate
Warm to hot summer, mild winter
Warm to hot summer, cold winter
Mild summer, cold winter
Cold climate

Milan
GO Dec–Mar (skiing), Jan & Sep

Venice
GO Feb–Mar & Sep–Nov

Rome
GO Apr–May, Jul & Nov–Dec

Naples
GO May–Jun & Sep

Palermo
GO Sep–Oct

When to Go

High Season (Jul–Aug)
» Queues at big sights and on the road, especially in August.
» Prices also rocket for Christmas, New Year and Easter.
» Late December to March is high season in the Alps and Dolomites.

Shoulder (Apr–Jun & Sep–Oct)
» Good deals on accommodation, especially in the south.
» Spring is best for festivals, flowers and local produce.
» Autumn provides warm weather and the grape harvest.

Low Season (Nov–Mar)
» Prices up to 30% less than in high season.
» Many sights and hotels closed in coastal areas.
» A good period for cultural events in large cities.

Daily Costs

Budget: Less than €100

» Dorm bed: €15–30

» Double room in a budget hotel: €50–110

» Pizza or pasta: €6–12

Midrange: €100–250

» Double room in a hotel: €110–200

» Local restaurant dinner: €25–50

» Admission to museum: €4–15

Top End: More than €250

» Double room in a four- or five-star hotel: €200–450

» Top restaurant dinner: €50–150

» Opera ticket: €40–200

Eating

Restaurants (Ristoranti) Formal service and refined dishes, with prices to match.

Trattorias Informal, often family-run, places with classic regional cooking.

Vegetarians Most places offer good vegetable starters and side dishes.

Price indicators for a two-course meal with a glass of house wine and *coperto* (cover charge).

€	less than €25
€€	€25–45
€€€	more than €45

Sleeping

Hotels From luxury boutique palaces to modest family-run *pensioni* (small hotels).

B&Bs Rooms in restored farmhouses, city townhouses or seaside bungalows.

Agriturismi Farmstays range from working farms to luxury rural retreats.

Room Tax A nightly occupancy tax is charged on top of room rates.

Price indicators for a double room with private bathroom (breakfast included) in high season:

€	less than €110
€€	€110–200
€€€	more than €200

Arriving in Italy

Leonardo da Vinci (Fiumicino) Airport (Rome)

Rental cars Agencies are located near the multilevel car park.

Trains & buses Run every 30 minutes from 6.23am to 11.23pm.

Night buses Departures at 1.15am, 2.15am, 3.30am and 5am.

Taxis Set fare to centre €48; 45 minutes.

Malpensa Airport (Milan)

Rental cars Agencies in the Arrivals sections of Terminals 1 and 2.

Trains & buses Run every 30 minutes from 5.45am to 11.30pm.

Night buses Limited services from 12.15am to 5am.

Taxis Set fare €90; 50 minutes.

Capodichino Airport (Naples)

Rental cars Contact agencies via an intercom in the Arrivals hall.

Buses Run every 20 minutes from 6am to 11.40pm.

Taxis Set fare €16 to €23; 30 minutes.

Mobile Phones (Cell Phones)

Local SIM cards can be used in European, Australian and some unlocked US phones. Other phones must be set to roaming.

Internet Access

Free wi-fi is available in most hotels, B&Bs, *pensioni* etc and in many bars and cafes.

Money

ATMs at every airport, most train stations and widely available in towns and cities. Credit cards accepted in most hotels and restaurants.

Tipping

Not obligatory but round up the bill in pizzerias and trattorias; 10% is normal in upmarket restaurants.

Useful Websites

Italia (www.italia.it) Comprehensive tourism site.

Michelin (www.viamichelin.it) A useful route planner.

Agriturismi (www.agriturismi. it) Guide to farmstays.

Lonely Planet (www. lonelyplanet.com/italy) Destination lowdown.

Language

Italian sounds can all be found in English. If you read our coloured pronunciation guides as if they were English, you'll be understood. Note that ai is pronounced as in 'aisle', ay as in 'say', ow as in 'how', dz as the 'ds' in 'lids', and that r is strong and rolled. If the consonant is written as a double letter, it's pronounced a little stronger, eg *sonno* *son·no* (sleep) versus *sono* *so·no* (I am). The stressed syllables are indicated with italics.

BASICS

Hello.	*Buongiorno.*	bwon·*jor*·no
Goodbye.	*Arrivederci.*	a·ree·ve·*der*·chee
Yes./No.	*Sì./No.*	see/no
Excuse me.	*Mi scusi.*	mee *skoo*·zee
Sorry.	*Mi dispiace.*	mee dees·*pya*·che
Please.	*Per favore.*	per fa·*vo*·re
Thank you.	*Grazie.*	*gra*·tsye

You're welcome.
Prego. .... *pre*·go

Do you speak English?
Parli inglese? .... *par*·lee een·*gle*·ze

I don't understand.
Non capisco. .... non ka·*pee*·sko

How much is this?
Quanto costa questo? .... *kwan*·to *kos*·ta *kwe*·sto

ACCOMMODATION

Do you have a room?
Avete una camera? .... a·*ve*·te oo·na *ka*·me·ra

Want More?

For in-depth language information and handy phrases, check out Lonely Planet's *Italian Phrasebook*. You'll find it at **shop.lonelyplanet.com**, or you can buy Lonely Planet's iPhone phrasebooks at the Apple App Store.

How much is it per night/person?
Quanto costa per .... *kwan*·to *kos*·ta per
una notte/persona? .... oo·na no·te/per·*so*·na

DIRECTIONS

Where's ...?
Dov'è ...? .... do·*ve* ...

Can you show me (on the map)?
Può mostrarmi .... pwo mos·*trar*·mee
(sulla pianta)? .... (soo·la *pyan*·ta)

EATING & DRINKING

What would you recommend?
Cosa mi consiglia? .... *ko*·za mee kon·*see*·lya

I'd like ..., please.
Vorrei ..., per favore. .... vo·*ray* ... per fa·*vo*·re

I don't eat (meat).
Non mangio (carne). .... non *man*·jo (*kar*·ne)

Please bring the bill.
Mi porta il conto, ... mee *por*·ta eel *kon*·to
per favore? .... per fa·*vo*·re

EMERGENCIES

Help!
Aiuto! .... a·*yoo*·to

I'm lost.
Mi sono perso/a. (m/f) .... mee so·no per·so/a

I'm ill.
Mi sento male. .... mee *sen*·to *ma*·le

Call the police!
Chiami la polizia! .... *kya*·mee la po·lee·*tsee*·a

Call a doctor!
Chiami un medico! .... *kya*·mee oon *me*·dee·ko

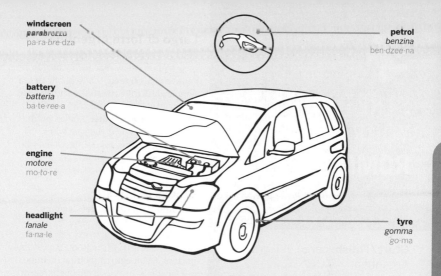

windscreen
parabrezza
pa·ra·bre·dza

petrol
benzina
ben·dzee·na

battery
batteria
ba·te·ree·a

engine
motore
mo·to·re

headlight
fanale
fa·na·le

tyre
gomma
go·ma

ON THE ROAD

I'd like to hire a/an ...	Vorrei noleggiare ...	vo·ray no·le·ja·re ...
4WD	un fuoristrada	oon fwo·ree·stra·da
automatic/ manual	una macchina automatica/ manuale	oo·na *ma* kee·na ow·to·ma·tee·ka/ ma·noo·a·le
motorbike	una moto	oo·na mo·to

How much is it ...?	Quanto costa ...?	kwan·to kos·ta ...
daily	al giorno	al jor·no
weekly	alla settimana	a·la se·tee·ma·na

Does that include insurance?
E' compresa l'assicurazione?
e kom·pre·sa la·see·koo·ra·tsyo·ne

Does that include mileage?
E' compreso il chilometraggio?
e kom·pre·so eel kee·lo·me·tra·jo

What's the city/country speed limit?
Qual'è il limite di velocità in città/campagna?
kwa·le eel lee·mee·te dee ve·lo·chee·ta een chee·ta/kam·pa·nya

Is this the road to (Venice)?
Questa strada porta a (Venezia)?
kwe·sta stra·da por·ta a (ve·ne·tsya)

(How long) Can I park here?
(Per quanto tempo) Posso parcheggiare qui?
(per kwan·to tem·po) po·so par·ke·ja·re kwee

Where's a service station?
Dov'è una stazione di servizio?
do·ve oo·na sta·tsyo·ne dee ser·vee·tsyo

Please fill it up.
Il pieno, per favore.
eel pye·no per fa·vo·re

I'd like (30) litres.
Vorrei (trenta) litri.
vo·ray (tren·ta) lee·tree

Please check the oil/water.
Può controllare l'olio/ l'acqua, per favore?
pwo kon·tro·la·re lo·lyo/ la·kwa per fa·vo·re

I need a mechanic.
Ho bisogno di un meccanico.
o bee·zo·nyo dee oon me·ka·nee·ko

The car/motorbike has broken down.
La macchina/moto si è guastata.
la ma·kee·na/mo·to see e gwas·ta·ta

I had an accident.
Ho avuto un incidente.
o a·voo·to oon een·chee·den·te

111

STRETCH YOUR LEGS
ROME

Start/Finish: Largo di Torre Argentina

Distance: 1.7km

Duration: Three hours

The best way to explore Rome's historic centre, much of which is closed to unauthorised traffic, is on foot. Park near Stazione Termini, then head into the centre by bus. As you walk you'll discover picturesque cobbled lanes, showboating piazzas, basilicas and ancient ruins.

Take this walk on Trips

Largo di Torre Argentina

Start in **Largo di Torre Argentina**, a busy square easily reached by bus. In its sunken central area, the Republican-era templesdate to between the 2nd and 4th centuries BC. On the piazza's western flank, **Teatro Argentina**, Rome's premier theatre, stands near the spot where Julius Caesar was assassinated in 44 BC.

The Walk » From the square, head east along Corso Vittorio Emanuele II to Piazza del Gesù.

Chiesa del Gesù

The landmark **Chiesa del Gesù** (www.chiesadelgesu.org; Piazza del Gesù; ☉7am-12.30pm & 4-7.45pm, St Ignatius rooms 4-6pm Mon-Sat, 10am-noon Sun) is Rome's most important Jesuit church. Behind its imposing facade is an awe-inspiring baroque interior. Headline works include the swirling vault fresco by Il Baciccia and Andrea del Pozzo's opulent tomb for Ignatius Loyola, the Jesuits' founder.

The Walk » Cross Corso Vittorio Emanuele II and follow Via del Gesù north. Then turn left onto Via Santa Caterina da Siena.

Basilica di Santa Maria Sopra Minerva

Trumpeted by Bernini's much-loved **Elefantino** statue, this **basilica** (www.santamariasopraminerva.it; Piazza della Minerva 42; ☉7.30am-7pm Mon-Fri, 7.30am-12.30pm & 3.30-7pm Sat, 8am-12.30pm & 3.30-7pm Sun) is Rome's only Gothic church. However, little remains of the original 13th-century structure and these days the main drawcard is a minor Michelangelo sculpture and its colourful, art-rich interior.

The Walk » From the basilica, it's an easy stroll up Via della Minerva to Piazza della Rotonda.

Pantheon

A remarkable 2000-year-old temple, now church, the **Pantheon** (www.pantheonroma.com; Piazza della Rotonda; ☉8.30am-7.30pm Mon-Sat, 9am-6pm Sun) is the best preserved of Rome's ancient monuments. Built by Hadrian over Marcus Agrippa's earlier 27 BC temple, it has stood since around AD 125. t's an exhilarating

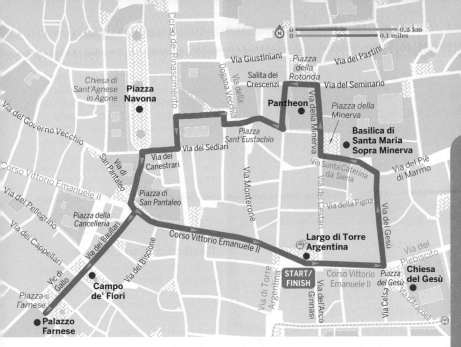

experience to pass through its vast bronze doors and gaze up at the largest unreinforced concrete dome ever built.

The Walk >> Follow the signs to Piazza Navona, stopping en route for a quick coffee at **Caffè Sant'Eustachio** (Piazza Sant'Eustachio 82; ⏱8.30am-1am Sun-Thu, to 1.30am Fri, to 2am Sat).

Piazza Navona

With its ornate fountains, baroque *palazzi* (mansions) and colourful cast of street artists, hawkers and tourists, **Piazza Navona** is central Rome's elegant showpiece square. Its grand centrepiece is Bernini's **Fontana dei Quattro Fiumi**, an ornate, showy fountain featuring personifications of the rivers Nile, Ganges, Danube and Plate.

The Walk >> Exit the piazza to the south, cross Corso Vittorio Emanuele II and continue up Via dei Baullari.

Campo de' Fiori

Noisy, colourful **Campo de' Fiori** is a major focus of Roman life: by day it hosts one of Rome's best-known

markets, while at night it morphs into a raucous open-air pub. Amidst the chaos look out for a sinister statue of a hooded monk. This is the heretic philosopher Giordano Bruno who was burned at the stake here in 1600.

The Walk >> Head up to Piazza Farnese, a matter of metres away.

Palazzo Farnese

The formidable **Palazzo Farnese** (www.inventerrome.com; Piazza Farnese; €9; ⏱guided tours 3pm, 4pm & 5pm Mon, Wed & Fri) is one of Rome's finest Renaissance buildings. Now home to the French Embassy, it can only be visited on a guided tour (for which you need to pre-book; see the website for details), but it's worth it to marvel at a series of frescoes by Annibale Carracci that are said by some to rival Michelangelo's in the Sistine Chapel.

The Walk >> To get back to Largo di Torre Argentina, double back to Corso Vittorio Emanuele II and head right.

STRETCH YOUR LEGS
FLORENCE

Start/Finish: Galleria dell'Accademia

Distance: 2.5km

Duration: One day

To get the best out of Florence (Firenze), park your car at Piazza della Libertà, and head into the city's historic centre on foot. This tour provides a great introduction to the city, passing through its headlining piazzas, basilicas and galleries.

Take this walk on Trips

Galleria dell'Accademia

Before heading into the heart of the historic centre, take time to salute Florence's fabled poster boy. Michelangelo's *David* (1504), arguably the most famous sculpture in the Western world, stands in all his naked glory in the **Galleria dell'Accademia** (www.firenzemusei.it; Via Ricasoli 60; adult/reduced €8/4, incl temporary exhibition €12.50/6.25; ⏱8.15am-6.50pm Tue-Sun). He originally guarded Palazzo Vecchio but was moved here in 1873.

The Walk ⟩⟩ From the gallery, head south along Via Ricasoli, past the Carabé gelateria, down to Via de' Pucci. Turn right, skirting past Palazzo Pucci, as you continue on to Piazza San Lorenzo.

Basilica di San Lorenzo

A fine example of Renaissance architecture, the **Basilica di San Lorenzo** (Piazza San Lorenzo; €5, incl Biblioteca Medicea Laurenziana €7.50; ⏱10am-5.30pm Mon-Sat, plus 1.30-5pm Sun winter) is best known for its **Sagrestia Vecchia** (Old Sacristy). Around the corner, at the rear of the basilica, the **Museo delle Cappelle Medicee** (Medici Chapels; www.firenzemusei. it; Piazza Madonna degli Aldobrandini 6; adult/reduced €6/3; ⏱8.15am-1.50pm, closed 2nd & 4th Sun & 1st, 3rd & 5th Mon of month) has some exquisite Michelangelo sculptures.

The Walk ⟩⟩ From Piazza Madonna degli Aldobrandini, head down Via de' Conti and its continuation Via F Zanetti to Via de' Cerretani. Hang a left and soon you'll see Piazza del Duomo ahead.

Duomo

Florence's 14th-century **Duomo** (www. operaduomo.firenze.it; Piazza del Duomo; ⏱10am-5pm Mon-Wed & Fri, to 4pm Thu, to 4.45pm Sat, 1.30-4.45pm Sun) is the city's most iconic landmark with its pink, white and green marble facade and red-tiled **dome** (adult/reduced incl cupola, baptistry, campanile, crypt & museum €15/3; ⏱8.30am-7pm Mon-Fri, to 5.40pm Sat). Nearby, you can climb the **campanile** (⏱8.30am-7.30pm) and admire the bas-reliefs on the 11th-century **Battistero** (Baptistry; ⏱11.15am-7pm Mon-Sat, 8.30am-2pm Sun & 1st Sat of month).

The Walk >> It's a straightforward 400m or so down Via dei Calzaiuoli to Piazza della Signoria.

Piazza della Signoria

This lovely cafe-lined piazza is overlooked by the **Torre d'Arnolfo**, the high point of **Palazzo Vecchio** (www.musefirenze .it; museum adult/reduced €10/8, tower €10/8, museum & tower €14/12, guided tour €4; ⊙ museum 9am-11pm Fri-Wed, to 2pm Thu, tower 9am-9pm Fri-Wed, to 2pm Thu, shorter hours winter), Florence's medieval City Hall. It still houses the mayor's office but you can visit its lavish apartments.

The Walk >> To get to the Galleria degli Uffizi takes a matter of seconds, although we can't vouch for how long it'll take to get inside. The gallery is just off the piazza's southeastern corner, in a grey porticoed *palazzo* (mansion).

Galleria degli Uffizi

The **Uffizi** (www.uffizi.beniculturali.it; Piazzale degli Uffizi 6; adult/reduced €8/4, incl temporary exhibition €12.50/6.25; ⊙8.15am-6.50pm Tue-Sun) boasts one of Italy's greatest art collections, bequeathed to Florence in 1743 by the Medici family on condition that it never leave the city. The highlight is the stash of Renaissance art, including Botticelli's *La nascita di Venere* (Birth of Venus), Leonardo da Vinci's *Annunciazione* (Annunciation) and Michelangelo's *Tondo doni* (Holy Family).

The Walk >> Pick up Via Lambertesca, over the way from the gallery entrance, and follow it to Via Por Santa Maria. Go left and it's a short hop to the river.

Ponte Vecchio

Florence's celebrated bridge has twinkled with the wares of jewellers since the 16th century when Ferdinando I de' Medici ordered them to replace the the town butchers, who were wont to toss malodorous unwanted leftovers into the river. The bridge as it stands was built in 1345 and was the only one in Florence saved from destruction by the retreating Germans in 1944.

The Walk >> To get back to the Galleria dell'Accademia, pick up bus C1 from Lungarno Generale Diaz and head up to Piazza San Marco.

France

ICONIC MONUMENTS, FABULOUS FOOD, WORLD-CLASS WINES there are so many reasons to plan your very own French voyage.

Whether you're planning on cruising the corniches of the French Riviera, getting lost among the snowcapped mountains or tasting your way around Champagne's hallowed vineyards, this is a nation that's made for road trips and full of unforgettable routes that will plunge you straight into France's heart and soul.

There's a trip for everyone here: family travellers, history buffs, culinary connoisseurs and outdoors adventurers.

Buckle up, and bon voyage – you're in for quite a ride.

Champagne region Phare de Verzenay

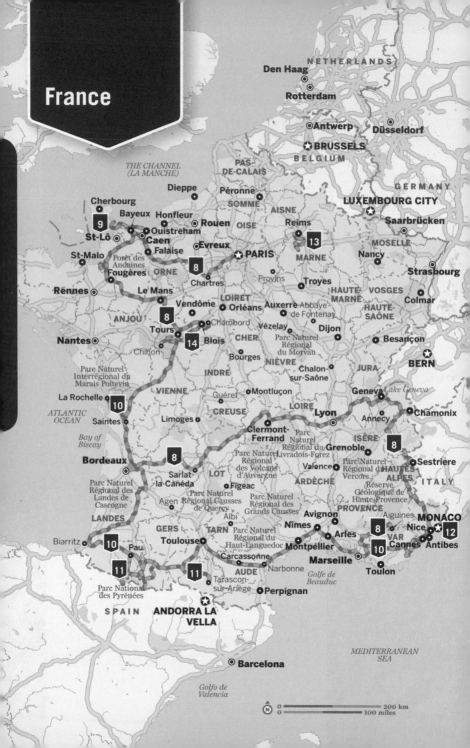

The Pyrenees Lac de Gaube

 DON'T MISS

Longues-sur-Mer

See where parts of the
famous D-Day film, *The
Longest Day* (1962),
was filmed on Trip **9**

Lac de Gaube

One of the Pyrenees'
finest trails leads to the
glittering Lac de Gaube.
Catch the cable car to
the trail on Trip **11**

Fenocchio

Enjoy some original
flavours at this iconic
ice-cream parlour on
Trip **12**

Château de Chambord

The Loire's star
expression of
Renaissance
architecture, capped
by its world-famous
double-helix staircase.
Discover it on Trip **14**

Essential France

8

City to city, coast to coast, this grand tour visits some of France's most unmissable sights. There's some epic driving involved, but this is one trip you won't forget in a hurry.

TRIP HIGHLIGHTS

335 km

Bayeux
Check out the world's longest comic strip

4 Caen

START ✪ PARIS

2100 km

Chamonix
Savour sky-high views of Mont Blanc

Poitiers

10

Clermont-Ferrand

8

FINISH

13

Cannes

1445 km

Sarlat-la-Canéda
Explore the medieval heart of this gorgeous Dordogne town

Gorges du Verdon
Experience France's answer to the Grand Canyon

3060 km

21 DAYS
3060KM /
1902 MILES

GREAT FOR...

BEST TIME TO GO
April to June

ESSENTIAL PHOTO

Overlooking the Parisian panorama from the Basilique du Sacré-Coeur.

BEST FOR FAMILIES

Brave the space-age rides and roller-coaster thrills of Futuroscope.

Gorges du Verdon Ravine through Haute-Provence

121

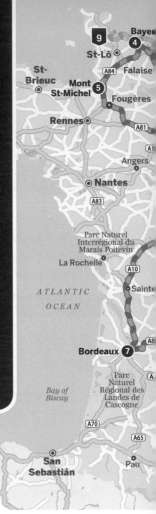

8 | Essential France

This is the big one – an epic trek that travels all the way from the chilly waters of the English Channel to the gleaming blue Mediterranean. Along the way, you'll stop off at some of France's most iconic sights: the château of Versailles, the abbey of Mont St-Michel, the summit of Mont Blanc and the beaches of the French Riviera. *Allez-y!*

❶ Paris

For that essentially Parisian experience, it's hard to beat Montmartre – the neighbourhood of cobbled lanes and cafe-lined squares beloved by writers and painters since the 19th century. This was once a notoriously ramshackle part of Paris, full of bordellos, brothels, dance halls and bars, as well as the city's first can-can clubs. Though its hedonistic heyday has long since passed, Montmartre still retains a villagey charm, despite the throngs of tourists.

The centre of Montmartre is **place du Tertre**, once the village's main square, now packed with buskers and portrait artists. You can get a sense of how the area would once have looked at the **Musée de Montmartre** (☎01 49 25 89 39; www.museede montmartre.fr; 12 rue Cortot, 18e; adult/child €9.50/5.50; ◷10am-6pm; Ⓜ Lamarck-Caulaincourt), which details the area's bohemian past. It's inside Montmartre's oldest building, a 17th-century manor house once occupied by Renoir and Utrillo.

Nearby, Montmartre's finest view unfolds from the dome of the **Basilique du Sacré-Coeur** (☎01 53 41 89 00; www.sacre-coeur-montmartre.com; place du Parvis du Sacré-Cœur; dome adult/child €6/4, cash only; ◷6am-10.30pm, dome 8.30am-8pm May-Sep, to 5pm

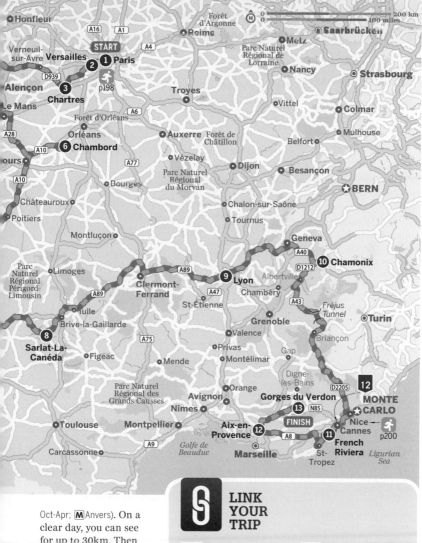

Oct–Apr; Ⓜ Anvers). On a
clear day, you can see
for up to 30km. Then
head to the riverbank for
a stroll through Paris'
history (p198).

✕ 🍽 p130

The Drive » Drive From the
centre of Paris, follow the A13
west from Porte d'Auteuil and
take the exit marked 'Versailles
Château'. Versailles is 28km
southwest of the city.

🔗 LINK YOUR TRIP

9 **D-Day's Beaches**
Take a side trip
from Caen to follow
the course of the WWII
invasion on Normandy's
beaches.

12 **Riviera Crossing**
Combine this
journey with our jaunt
down the French Riviera,
which begins in Cannes.

❷ Versailles

Louis XIV transformed his father's hunting lodge into the **Château de Versailles** (☎01 30 83 78 00; www.chateauversailles. fr; place d'Armes; adult/child passport ticket incl estate-wide access €18/free, with musical events €25/free, palace €15/free; ⏲9am-6.30pm Tue-Sun Apr-Oct, to 5.30pm Tue-Sun Nov-Mar; Ⓜ RER Versailles-Château–Rive Gauche) in the mid-17th century, and it remains France's most majestic palace. The royal court was based here from 1682 until 1789, when revolutionaries massacred the palace guard and dragged Louis XVI and Marie Antoinette back to Paris, where they were ingloriously guillotined.

The architecture is truly eye-popping. Highlights include the **Grands**

Appartements du Roi et de la Reine (State Apartments) and the famous **Galerie des Glaces** (Hall of Mirrors), a 75m-long ballroom filled with chandeliers and floor-to-ceiling mirrors. Outside, the vast park incorporates terraces, flower beds, paths and fountains, as well as the **Grand and Petit Canals**.

Northwest of the main palace is the **Domaine de Marie-Antoinette** (Marie Antoinette's Estate; www. chateauversailles.fr; Château de Versailles; adult/child €10/free, with passport ticket free; ⏲noon-6.30pm Tue-Sun Apr-Oct, to 5.30pm Tue-Sat Nov-Mar), where the royal family would have taken refuge from the intrigue and etiquette of court life.

The Drive » The N10 runs southwest from Versailles through pleasant countryside and forest to Rambouillet. You'll

join the D906 to Chartres. All told, it's a journey of 76km.

❸ Chartres

You'll know you're nearing Chartres long before you reach it thanks to the twin spires of the **Cathédrale Notre Dame** (www.cathedrale-chartres. org; place de la Cathédrale; ⏲8.30am-7.30pm daily year-round, also to 10pm Tue, Fri & Sun Jun-Aug), considered to be one of the most important structures in Christendom.

The present cathedral was built during the late 12th century after the original was destroyed by fire. It's survived wars and revolutions remarkably intact, and the brilliant-blue stained-glass windows have even inspired their own shade of paint (Chartres blue). The cathedral also houses the Sainte Voile (Holy Veil), supposedly worn by the Virgin Mary while giving birth to Jesus.

The best views are from the 112m-high **Clocher Neuf** (New Bell Tower; Cathédrale Notre Dame; adult/child €7.50/free; ⏲9.30am-12.30pm & 2-6pm Mon-Sat, 2-6pm Sun May-Aug, 9.30am-12.30pm & 2-5pm Mon-Sat, 2-5pm Sun Sep-Apr).

✕ ⨮ p130

The Drive » Follow the D939 northwest for 58km to Verneuil-sur-Avre, then take the D926 west for 78km to Argentan –

VISITING VERSAILLES

Versailles is one of the country's most popular destinations, so planning ahead will make your visit more enjoyable. Avoid the busiest days of Tuesday and Sunday, and remember that the château is closed on Monday. Save time by pre-purchasing tickets on the château's website, or arrive early if you're buying at the door – by noon queues spiral out of control.

You can also access off-limits areas (such as the Private Apartments of Louis XV and Louis XVI, the Opera House and the Royal Chapel) by taking a 90-minute **guided tour** (☎01 30 83 77 88; www. chateauversailles.fr; tours €7, plus palace entry; ⏲English-language tours 9.30pm Tue-Sun).

both great roads through typical Norman countryside. Just west of Argentan, the D158/N158 heads north to Caen, then turns northwest on the N13 to Bayeux, 94km further.

TRIP HIGHLIGHT

④ Bayeux

The **Tapisserie de Bayeux** (☏02 31 51 25 50; www.bayeux museum.com; rue de Nesmond; adult/child incl audioguide €9/4; ◷9am-6.30pm Mar-Oct, to 7pm May-Aug, 9.30am-12.30pm & 2-6pm Nov–Feb) is without doubt the world's most celebrated (and ambitious) piece of embroidery. Over 58 panels, the tapestry recounts the invasion of England in 1066 by William I, or William the Conqueror, as he's now known.

Commissioned in 1077 by Bishop Odo of Bayeux, William's half-brother, the tapestry retells the battle in fascinating detail: look for Norman horses getting stuck in the quicksands around Mont St-Michel, and the famous appearance of Halley's Comet in scene 32. The final showdown at the Battle of Hastings is particularly graphic, complete with severed limbs, decapitated heads, and the English King Harold getting an arrow in the eye.

The Drive >> Mont St-Michel is 125km southwest of Bayeux; the fastest route is along the D6 and then the A84 motorway.

⑤ Mont St-Michel

You've already seen it on a million postcards, but nothing prepares you for the real **Mont St-Michel** (☏02 33 89 80 00; www. monuments-nationaux.fr; adult/child incl guided tour €9/ free; ◷9am-7pm, last entry 1hr before closing). It's one of France's architectural marvels, an 11th-century island abbey marooned in the middle of a vast golden bay.

When you arrive, you'll be steered into one of the Mont's huge car parks. You then walk along the causeway (or catch a free shuttle bus) to the island itself. Guided tours are included, or you can explore solo with an audioguide.

The **Église Abbatiale** (Abbey Church) is reached via a steep climb along the **Grande Rue**. Around the church, the cluster of buildings known as **La Merveille** (The Marvel) includes the cloister, refectory, guest hall, ambulatory and various chapels.

For a different perspective, take a guided walk across the sands with **Découverte de la Baie du Mont-Saint-Michel** (☏02 33 70 83 49; www.decou vertebaie.com; 1 rue Montoise, Genêts; adult/child from €8/5) and **Chemins de la Baie** (☏02 33 89 80 88; www. cheminsdelabaie.com; 34 rue de l'Ortillon, Genêts; adult/ child from €7.30/5), both

based in Genêts. Don't be tempted to do it on your own – the bay's tides are notoriously treacherous.

📖 p130

The Drive >> Take the A84, N12 and A81 for 190km to Le Mans and the A28 for 102km to Tours, where you can follow a tour through the Loire Valley if you wish. Chambord is about 75km from Tours via the D952.

⑥ Chambord

If you only have time to visit one château in the Loire, you might as well make it the grandest – and **Chambord** (☏info 02 54 50 40 00; tour & show reservations 02 54 50 50 40; www. chambord.org; adult/child €11/9, parking near/distant €6/4; ◷9am-5pm or 6pm; ⛟) is the most lavish of them all. It's a showpiece of Renaissance architecture, from the double-helix staircase up to the turret-covered rooftop. With over 440 rooms, the sheer scale of the place is mindboggling – and in the Loire, that's really saying something.

The Drive >> It's 425km to Bordeaux via Blois and the A10 motorway. You could consider breaking the journey with stop-offs at Futuroscope and Poitiers, roughly halfway between the two.

⑦ Bordeaux

When Unesco decided to protect Bordeaux's medieval architecture in 2007, it simply listed half the city in one fell swoop.

PETER RICHARDSON / ROBERTHARDING / GETTY IMAGES ©

DOUG PEARSON / GETTY IMAGES ©

CÈPES

WHY THIS IS A GREAT TRIP
OLIVER BERRY, WRITER

It's an epic in every sense: in scale, views, time and geography. This once-in-a-lifetime journey covers France from every possible angle: top to bottom, east to west, city and village, old-fashioned and modern, coast and countryside. It links together many of the country's truly unmissable highlights, and by the end you'll genuinely be able to say you've seen the heart and soul of France.

Top: Produce market, Aix-en-Provence
Left: Sausages for sale, Sarlat-la-Canéda
Right: Cathédrale St-André, Bordeaux

Covering 18 sq km, this is the world's largest urban World Heritage Site, with grand buildings and architectural treasures galore.

Top of the heap is the **Cathédrale St-André**, known for its stone carvings and generously gargoyled belfry, the **Tour Pey-Berland** (place Jean Moulin; adult/child €5.50/ free; ⏰10am-1.15pm & 2-6pm Jun-Sep, 10am-12.30pm & 2-5.30pm Oct-May). But the whole old city rewards wandering, especially around the **Jardin Public** (cours de Verdun), the pretty squares of **esplanade des Quinconces** and **place Gambetta**, and the city's 4km-long **riverfront esplanade**, with its playgrounds, paths and paddling pools.

✕ 🛏 p130

The Drive » Sarlat-la-Canéda is a drive of 194km via the A89 motorway, or you can take a longer but more enjoyable route via the D936.

- - - - - - - - - - -

TRIP HIGHLIGHT

❽ Sarlat-la-Canéda

If you're looking for France's heart and soul, you'll find it among the forests and fields of the Dordogne. It's the stuff of French fantasies: river-bank châteaux, medieval villages, wooden-hulled *gabarres* (flat-bottomed barges) and market stalls groaning with foie gras, truffles, walnuts and wines. The medieval town of Sarlat-la-Canéda makes the perfect base, with a beautiful medieval centre and lots of lively markets.

It's also ideally placed for exploring the Vézère Valley, about 20km to the northwest, home to France's finest cave paintings. Most famous of all are the ones at the **Grotte de Lascaux** (🖉05 53 51 95 03; www.semitour. com; Montignac; adult/child €9.90/6.40, combined ticket with Le Thot €13.50/9.40; ⊙ guided tours 9am-7pm Jul & Aug, 9.30am-6pm Apr-Jun, Sep & Oct, 10am-12.30pm & 2-5pm Nov-Mar, closed Jan), although to prevent damage to the paintings, you now visit a replica of the cave's main sections in a nearby grotto.

The Drive » The drive east to Lyon is a long one, covering well over 400km and travelling across the spine of the Massif Central. A good route is to follow the A89 all the way to exit 6,

then turn off onto the N89/D89 to Lyon. This route should cover between 420km and 430km.

- - - - - - - - - - -

❾ Lyon

Fired up by French food? Then you'll love Lyon, with its *bouchons* (small bistros), bustling markets and fascinating food culture. Start in **Vieux Lyon** and the picturesque quarter of **Presqu'île**, then catch the funicular to the top of **Fourvière** to explore the city's Roman ruins and enjoy cross-town views.

Film buffs will also want to make time for the **Musée Lumière** (🖉04 78 78 18 95; www.institut-lumiere. org; 25 rue du Premier Film, 8e; adult/child €6.50/5.50; ⊙10am-6.30pm Tue-Sun; Ⓜ Monplaisir-Lumière), where the Lumière Brothers (Auguste and Louis) shot the first reels of the world's first motion picture, *La Sortie des*

Usines Lumières, on 19 March 1895.

🍴 🛏 p131

The Drive » Take the A42 towards Lake Geneva, then the A40 towards St-Gervais-les-Bains. The motorway becomes the N205 as it nears Chamonix. It's a drive of at least 225km.

- - - - - - - - - - -

TRIP HIGHLIGHT

❿ Chamonix

Snuggling among snow-clad mountains – including Europe's highest summit, Mont Blanc – adrenaline-fuelled Chamonix is an ideal springboard for the French Alps. In winter, it's a mecca for skiers and snowboarders, and in summer, once the snows thaw, the high-level trails become a trekkers' paradise.

There are two really essential Chamonix experiences. First, catch the dizzying cable car to the top of the **Aiguille du Midi** to snap a shot of Mont Blanc.

Then take the combination mountain train and cable car from the **Gare du Montenvers** (🖉04 50 53 22 75; www. compagniedumontblanc.fr; 35 place de la Mer de Glace; adult/child return €31/26.40; ⊙10am-4.30pm) to the **Mer de Glace** (Sea of Ice), France's largest glacier. Wrap up warmly if you want to visit the glacier's sculptures and ice caves.

The Drive » The drive to the Riviera is full of scenic thrills.

FUTUROSCOPE

Halfway between Chambord and Bordeaux on the A10, 10km north of Poitiers, **Futuroscope** (🖉05 49 49 11 12; www.futuroscope.com; av René Monory, Chasseneuil-du-Poitou; adult/child €43/35; ⊙10am-11.15pm Jul, 9am-11.15pm Aug, shorter hours rest of year, closed Jan–mid-Feb) is one of France's top theme parks. It's a futuristic experience that takes you whizzing through space, diving into the ocean depths, racing around city streets and on a close encounter with creatures of the future. Note that many rides have a minimum height of 120cm.

You'll need at least five hours to check out the major attractions, or two days to see everything. The park is in the suburb of Jaunay-Clan; take exit 28 off the A10.

An attractive route is via the D1212 to Albertville, and then via the A43, which travels over the Italian border and through the Tunnel de Fréjus. From here, the N94 runs through Briançon, and a combination of the A51, N85 and D6085 carries you south to Nice. You'll cover at least 430km.

PETER BARNETT / GETTY IMAGES ©

French Riviera The winding coastline

⑪ French Riviera

If there's one coast road in France you simply have to drive, it's the French Riviera, with its rocky cliffs, maquis-scented air and dazzling Med views. Sun-seekers have been flocking here since the 19th century, and its scenery still never fails to seduce.

Lively **Nice** and cinematic Cannes make natural starts, but for the Riviera's loveliest scenery, you'll want to drive down the gorgeous **Corniche de l'Estérel** to **St-Tropez**, still a watchword for seaside glamour. Summer can be hellish, but come in spring or autumn and you'll have its winding lanes and fragrant hills practically to yourself. For maximum views, stick to the coast roads: the D6098 to Antibes and Cannes, the D559 around the Corniche de l'Estérel, and the D98A to St-Tropez. It's about 120km via this route.

The Drive › From St-Tropez, take the fast A8 for about 230km west to Aix-en-Provence.

⑫ Aix-en-Provence

Sleepy Provence sums up the essence of *la douce vie* (the gentle life). Cloaked in lavender and spotted with hilltop villages, it's a region that sums up everything that's good about France.

Cruising the back roads and browsing the markets are the best ways to get acquainted. **Carpentras** and **Vaison-la-Romaine** are particularly detour-worthy, while artistic **Aix-en-Provence** encapsulates the classic Provençal vibe, with its pastel buildings and Cézanne connections.

✕ ⌷ p131

The Drive › The gorges are 230km northeast of Aix-en-Provence, via the A51 and D952.

TRIP HIGHLIGHT

⑬ Gorges du Verdon

Complete your cross-France adventure with an unforgettable expedition to the **Gorges du Verdon** – sometimes known as the Grand Canyon of Europe. This deep ravine slashes 25km through the plateaus of Haute-Provence; in places, its walls rise to a dizzying 700m, twice the height of the Eiffel Tower (321m).

The two main jumping-off points are the villages of **Moustiers Ste-Marie**, in the west, and **Castellane**, in the east. Drivers and bikers can take in the canyon panorama from two vertigo-inducing cliffside roads, but the base of the gorge is only accessible on foot or by raft.

Eating & Sleeping

Paris ❶

✖ Holybelly International €

(www.holybel.ly; 19 rue Lucien Sampaix, 10e; breakfast €5-11.50, lunch mains €13.50-16.50; ⊙9am-6pm Thu, Fri, Mon, from 10am Sat & Sun; Ⓜ Jacques Bonsergent) This outstanding barista-run coffee shop and kitchen is always rammed with a buoyant crowd, who never tire of Holybelly's exceptional service, Belleville-roasted coffee and cuisine. Sarah's breakfast pancakes served with egg, bacon, homemade bourbon butter and maple syrup are legendary, while her lunch menu features everything from traditional braised veal shank to squid *à la plancha*.

🛏 Hôtel Amour Boutique Hotel €€

(☏01 48 78 31 80; www.hotelamourparis.fr; 8 rue Navarin, 9e; d €170-230; 🛜; ⓂSt-Georges, Pigalle) Craving romance in Paris? The inimitable black-clad Amour ('Love') features original design and nude artwork in each of the rooms, some more explicit than others. The icing on the cake is the hip ground-floor bistro with summer patio garden, a tasty spot for breakfast, lunch or dinner and everything in between. Rooms don't have a TV, but who cares when you're in love?

Chartres ❸

✖ Le Tripot Bistro €€

(☏02 37 36 60 11; www.letripot.wixsite.com/chartres; 11 place Jean Moulin; 2-/3-course lunch menus €15/18, 3-course dinner menus €29.50-45, mains €13.50-22; ⊙noon-1.45pm & 7.30-9.15pm Tue & Thu-Sat, noon-1.45pm Sun) Tucked off the tourist trail and easy to miss, even if you do chance down its narrow street, this atmospheric space with low beamed ceilings is a treat for authentic and adventurous French fare like saddle of rabbit stuffed with snails, and grilled turbot in truffled hollandaise sauce. Locals are onto it, so booking ahead is advised.

🛏 Le Grand Monarque Hotel €€€

(☏02 37 18 15 15; www.bw-grand-monarque. com; 22 place des Épars; d €145-215, f €275; ✴ @ 🛜) With its teal-blue shutters gracing its 1779 façade, lovely stained-glass ceiling, and treasure trove of period furnishings, old B&W photos and knick-knacks, the refurbished Grand Monarque (with air-con in some rooms) is a historical gem and very central. A host of hydrotherapy treatments are available at its spa. Its elegant restaurant, **Georges** (☏02 37 18 15 15; www.bw-grand-monarque.com; 22 place des Épars; 4-course menu from €75, 8-course tasting menu €95, mains €38-41; ⊙noon-2pm & 7.30-10pm Tue-Sat), has a Michelin star. Staff are charming.

Mont St-Michel ❺

🛏 Vent des Grèves B&B €

(☏Estelle 02 33 48 28 89; www.ventdesgreves. com; 7-9 chemin des Dits, Ardevon; s/d/tr/q incl breakfast €42/52/62/72) This friendly, family-run B&B has five modern rooms, furnished simply, with magical views of the Mont. Outstanding value. Situated an easily walkable 1km east of the shuttle stop in La Caserne.

Bordeaux ❼

✖ Le Petit Commerce Seafood €€

(05 56 79 76 58; 22 rue Parlement St-Pierre; 2-course lunch menu €14, mains €15-25; ⊙noon-midnight) This iconic bistro, with dining rooms both sides of a narrow pedestrian street and former Michelin-starred chef Stéphane Carrade in the kitchen, is the star turn of the trendy St-Pierre quarter. It's best known for its excellent seafood menu that embraces everything from Arcachon sole and oysters to eels, lobsters and *chipirons* (baby squid) fresh from St-Jean de Luz.

Mama Shelter
Design Hotel €€

([☎]05 57 30 45 45; www.mamashelter.com/en/bordeaux; 19 rue Poquelin Molière; d/tr from €79/129) With personalised iMacs, video booths and free movies in every room, Mama Shelter leads the way in cutting-edge sleep. Crisp white rooms come in small, medium or large, with family-friendly XL doubles touting a sofa bed. The ground-floor restaurant (mains €13 to €29) sports the same signature rubber rings strung above the bar as other Philippe Starck–designed hotels, and weekends usher concerts, gigs and other cultural happenings onto the small stage.

Lyon ❾

Le Poêlon d'Or
Bouchon €€

([☎]04 78 37 65 60; www.lepoelondor-restaurant.fr; 29 rue des Remparts d'Ainay, 2e; lunch menus €17-20, menus €27-32; ⊙noon-2pm & 7.30-10pm Mon-Fri; [M]Ampère-Victor Hugo) This upmarket *bouchon*, around the corner from the Musée des Tissus, is well known among local foodies who recommend its superb *andouillette* (chitterlings) and pike dumplings. Save room for the delicious chocolate mousse or the vanilla crème brûlée. Yummy. Well worth the detour.

Cour des Loges
Hotel €€€

([☎]04 72 77 44 44; www.courdesloges.com; 2-8 rue du Bœuf, 5e; d €200-350; ste €250-600; [✳][@][🛜][🏊]; [M]Vieux Lyon) Four 14th- to 17th-century houses wrapped around a *traboule* (secret passage) with preserved features such as Italianate loggias make this an exquisite place to stay. Individually decorated rooms woo with designer bathroom fittings and bountiful antiques, while decadent facilities include a spa, a Michelin-starred restaurant (menus €95 to €115), a swish cafe and a cross-vaulted bar.

Aix-en-Provence ⓬

Le Petit Verdot
French €€

([☎]04 42 27 30 12; www.lepetitverdot.fr; 7 rue d'Entrecasteaux; mains €19-25; ⊙7pm-midnight Mon-Sat) Great Provençal food and great Provençal wines – really, what more do you want from a meal in this part of France? It's all about hearty, honest dining here, with table tops made out of old wine crates, and a lively chef-patron who runs the place with huge enthusiasm. Expect slow-braised meats, seasonal veg, sinful desserts and some super wines to go with.

Villa Gallici
Historic Hotel €€€

([☎]04 42 23 29 23; www.villagallici.com; 18 av de la Violette; r from €350; [P][✳][🛜][🏊]) Baroque and beautiful, this fabulous villa was built as a private residence in the 18th century, and it still feels marvellously opulent. Rooms are more like museum pieces, stuffed with gilded mirrors, toile-de-jouy wallpaper and filigreed furniture. There's a lovely lavender-filled garden for breakfast, plus a super pool for lazy evening swims. It even has its own wine cellar.

D-Day's Beaches

9

Explore the events of D-Day, when Allied troops stormed ashore to liberate Europe from Nazi occupation. From war museums to landing beaches, it's a fascinating and sobering experience.

TRIP HIGHLIGHTS

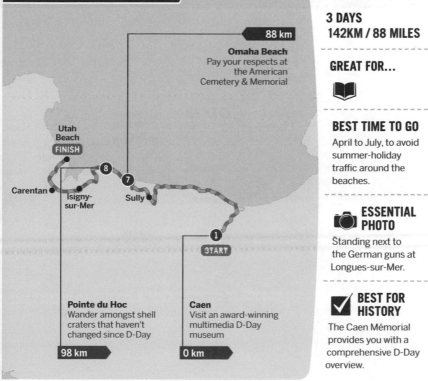

88 km

Omaha Beach
Pay your respects at the American Cemetery & Memorial

Utah Beach
FINISH

Carentan

Isigny-sur-Mer

Sully

8

7

1
START

Pointe du Hoc
Wander amongst shell craters that haven't changed since D-Day

98 km

Caen
Visit an award-winning multimedia D-Day museum

0 km

3 DAYS
142KM / 88 MILES

GREAT FOR...

BEST TIME TO GO
April to July, to avoid summer-holiday traffic around the beaches.

ESSENTIAL PHOTO
Standing next to the German guns at Longues-sur-Mer.

BEST FOR HISTORY
The Caen Mémorial provides you with a comprehensive D-Day overview.

9 D-Day's Beaches

The beaches and bluffs are quiet today, but on 6 June 1944 the Normandy shoreline witnessed the arrival of the largest armada the world has ever seen. This patch of the French coast will forever be synonymous with D-Day (known to the French as Jour-J), and the coastline is strewn with memorials, museums and cemeteries – reminders that though victory was won on the Longest Day, it came at a terrible price.

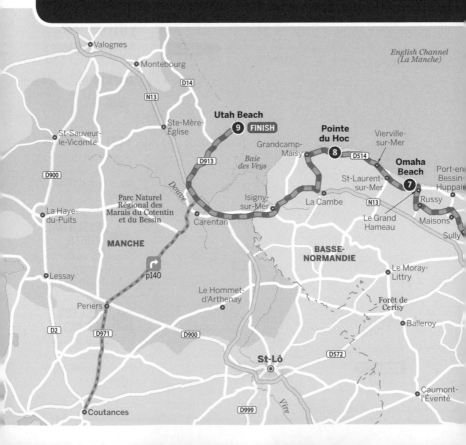

① Caen

Situated 3km northwest of Caen, the award-winning **Mémorial – Un Musée pour la Paix** (Memorial – A Museum for Peace; 02 31 06 06 44; www.memorial-caen.fr; esplanade Général Eisenhower; adult/child €20/17; 9am-7pm daily early Feb-early Nov, 9.30am-6.30pm Tue-Sun early Nov-early Feb, closed 3 weeks in Jan) is a brilliant place to begin with some background on the historic events of D-Day, and the wider context of WWII. Housed in a purpose-designed building covering 14,000 sq metres, the memorial offers an immersive experience, using sound, lighting, film, animation and audio testimony to evoke the grim realities of war, the trials of occupation and the joy of liberation.

The visit begins with a whistle-stop overview of Europe's descent into total war, tracing events from the end of WWI through to the rise of fascism in Europe, the German occupation of France and the Battle of Normandy. A second section focuses on the Cold War. There's also the well-preserved original bunker used by German command in 1944.

On your way around, look for an original Typhoon fighter plane and a full-size Sherman tank.

p141

The Drive » From the museum, head northeast along Esplanade Brillaud de Laujardière, and follow signs to Ouistreham. You'll join the E46 ring road; follow it to exit 3a (Porte d'Angleterre), and merge onto the D515 and D84 to Ouistreham. Park on the seafront on bd Aristide Briand. In all it's a trip of 18km.

② Ouistreham

On D-Day, the sandy seafront around Ouistreham was code named **Sword Beach** and was the focus

LINK YOUR TRIP

8 Essential France

Join this grand tour at the island abbey of Mont St-Michel, about 140km from the Normandy coastline via the A84 motorway.

13 Champagne Taster

For a change in focus head east, about four hours from Caen, to the cellars of Épernay for a fizz-fuelled tour.

of attack for the British 3rd Infantry Division.

There are precious few reminders of the battle today, but on D-Day the scene was very different: most of the surrounding buildings had been levelled by artillery fire, and German bunkers and artillery positions were strung out along the seafront. Sword Beach was the site of some of the most famous images of D-Day – including the infamous ones of British troops landing with bicycles, and bagpiper Bill Millin piping troops ashore while under heavy fire.

The Drive » Follow the seafront west onto rue de Lion,

following signs for 'Overlord – L'Assaut' onto the D514 towards Courseulles-sur-Mer, 18km west. Drive through town onto rue de Ver, and follow signs to 'Centre Juno Beach'.

- - - - - - - - - - - -

③ Juno & Gold Beaches

On D-Day, Courseulles-sur-Mer was known as **Juno Beach**, and was stormed mainly by Canadian troops. It was here that the exiled French General Charles de Gaulle came ashore after the landings – the first 'official' French soldier to set foot in mainland Europe since 1940. He was followed by Winston Churchill on 12 June and

King George VI on 16 June. A Cross of Lorraine marks the historic spot.

The area's only Canadian museum, the **Juno Beach Centre** (☎02 31 37 32 17; www.junobeach. org; voie des Français Libres, Courseulles-sur-Mer; adult/child €7/5.50, incl guided tour of Juno Beach €11/9; ☺9.30am-7pm Apr-Sep, 10am-5pm Oct-Mar, closed Jan) has exhibits on Canada's role in the war effort and the landings, and offers guided tours of Juno Beach (€5.50) from April to October.

A short way west is **Gold Beach**, attacked by the British 50th Infantry on D-Day.

The Drive » Drive west along the D514 for 14km to Arromanches. You'll pass a carpark and viewpoint marked with a statue of the Virgin Mary, which overlooks Port Winston and Gold Beach. Follow the road into town and signs to Musée du Débarquement.

- - - - - - - - - - -

④ Arromanches

This seaside town was the site of one of the great logistical achievements of D-Day. In order to unload the vast quantities of cargo needed by the invasion forces without capturing one of the heavily defended Channel ports, the Allies set up prefabricated marinas off two landing beaches, code named **Mulberry Harbour**. These consisted of 146 massive cement caissons towed

D-DAY IN FIGURES

Code named 'Operation Overlord', the D-Day landings were the largest military operation in history. On the morning of 6 June 1944, swarms of landing craft – part of an armada of more than 6000 ships and 13,000 aeroplanes – hit the northern Normandy beaches, and tens of thousands of soldiers from the USA, the UK, Canada and elsewhere began pouring onto French soil. The initial landing force involved some 45,000 troops; 15 more divisions were to follow once successful beachheads had been established.

The majority of the 135,000 Allied troops stormed ashore along 80km of beaches north of Bayeux that were codenamed (from west to east) Utah, Omaha, Gold, Juno and Sword. The landings were followed by the 76-day Battle of Normandy, during which the Allies suffered 210,000 casualties, including 37,000 troops killed. German casualties are believed to have been around 200,000; another 200,000 German soldiers were taken prisoner. About 14,000 French civilians also died.

For more background and statistics, see www.normandiememoire.com and www.6juin1944.com.

over from England and sunk to form a semi-circular breakwater in which floating bridge spans were moored. In the three months after D-Day, the Mulberries facilitated the unloading of a mind-boggling 2.5 million men, four million tonnes of equipment and 500,000 vehicles.

At low tide, the stanchions of one of these artificial quays, **Port Winston** (named after Winston Churchill), can still be seen on the sands at Arromanches.

Beside the beach, the **Musée du Débarquement** (Landing Museum; 📞02 31 22 34 31; www.musee-arromanches.fr; place du 6 Juin; adult/child €7.90/5.80; ⏱9am-12.30pm & 1.30-6pm Apr-Sep, 10am-12.30pm & 1.30-5pm Oct-Mar, closed Jan) **explains the logistics and importance of Port Winston.**

The Drive » Continue west along the D514 for 6km to the village of Longues-sur-Mer. You'll see the sign for the Batterie de Longues on your right.

- - - - - - - - - - - - -

⑤ Longues-sur-Mer

At Longues-sur-Mer you can get a glimpse of the awesome firepower available to the German defenders in the shape of two 150mm artillery guns, still housed in their concrete casements. On D-Day they were capable of hitting targets more than 20km away – including Gold Beach (to the

east) and Omaha Beach (to the west).

Parts of the classic D-Day film, *The Longest Day* (1962), were filmed here.

The Drive » Backtrack to the crossroads and head straight over onto the D104, signed to Vaux-sur-Aure/Bayeux for 8km. When you reach town, turn right onto the D613, and follow signs to the 'Musée de la Bataille de Normandie'.

- - - - - - - - - - - - -

⑥ Bayeux

Though best known for its medieval tapestry, Bayeux has another claim to fame: it was the first town to be liberated after D-Day (on the morning of 7 June 1944).

It's also home to the largest of Normandy's 18 Commonwealth military cemeteries – the **Bayeux War Cemetery**, situated on bd Fabien Ware. It contains 4848 graves of soldiers from the UK and 10 other countries – including Germany. Across the road is a memorial for 1807 Commonwealth

soldiers whose remains were never found. The Latin inscription reads: 'We, whom William once conquered, have now set free the conqueror's native land'.

Nearby, the **Musée Mémorial de la Bataille de Normandie** (Battle of Normandy Memorial Museum; 📞02 31 51 46 90; www.bayeux museum.com; bd Fabien Ware; adult/child €7/4; ⏱9.30am-6.30pm May-Sep, 10am-12.30pm & 2-6pm Oct-Apr, closed Jan-mid-Feb) **explores the battle through photos, personal accounts, dioramas and film.**

✕ 🏠 p141

The Drive » After overnighting in Bayeux, head northwest of town on the D6 towards Port-en-Bessin-Huppain. You'll reach a Super-U supermarket after about 10km. Go round the roundabout and turn onto the D514 for another 8km. You'll see signs to the 'Cimetière Americain' near the hamlet of Le Bray. Omaha Beach is another 4km further on, near Vierville-sur-Mer.

D-DAY DRIVING ROUTES

There are several signposted driving routes around the main battle sites – look for signs for 'D-Day-Le Choc' in the American sectors and 'Overlord – L'Assaut' in the British and Canadian sectors. A free booklet called *The D-Day Landings and the Battle of Normandy*, available from tourist offices, has details on the eight main routes.

Maps of the D-Day beaches are available at *tabacs* (tobacconists), newsagents and bookshops in Bayeux and elsewhere.

WHY THIS IS A GREAT TRIP
OLIVER BERRY, WRITER

You'll have heard the D-Day story many times before, but there's nothing quite like standing on the beaches where this epic struggle played out. D-Day marked the turning point of WWII and heralded the end for Nazism in Europe. Paying your respects to the soldiers who laid down their lives in the name of freedom is an experience that will stay with you forever.

Top: Arromanches and Gold Beach
Left & Right: Normandy American Cemetery & Memorial

TRIP HIGHLIGHT

❼ Omaha Beach

If anywhere symbolises the courage and sacrifice of D-Day, it's Omaha – still known as 'Bloody Omaha' to US veterans. It was here, on the 7km stretch of coastline between Vierville-sur-Mer, St-Laurent-sur-Mer and Colleville-sur-Mer, that the most brutal fighting on D-Day took place. US troops had to fight their way across the beach towards the heavily defended cliffs, exposed to underwater obstacles, hidden minefields and withering crossfire. The toll was heavy: of the 2500 casualties at Omaha on D-Day, more than 1000 were killed, most within the first hour of the landings.

High on the bluffs above Omaha, the **Normandy American Cemetery & Memorial** (📞02 31 51 62 00; www.abmc. gov; Colleville-sur-Mer; ⊕9am-6pm mid-Apr–mid-Sep, to 5pm mid-Sep–mid-Apr) **provides a sobering reminder of the human cost of the battle. Featured in the opening scenes of *Saving Private Ryan*, this is the largest American cemetery in Europe, containing the graves of 9387 American soldiers, and a memorial to 1557 comrades 'known only unto God'.**

Start off in the very thoughtfully designed visitor centre, which has moving portrayals of some of the soldiers buried here. Afterwards, take in the expanse of white marble crosses and Stars of David that stretch off in seemingly endless rows, surrounded by an immaculately tended expanse of lawn.

The Drive » From the Vierville-sur-Mer seafront, follow the rural D514 through quiet countryside towards Grandcamp-Maisy. After about 10km you'll see signs to 'Pointe du Hoc'.

TRIP HIGHLIGHT

8 Pointe du Hoc

West of Omaha, this craggy promontory was the site of D-Day's most audacious military exploit. At 7.10am, 225 US Army Rangers command-ed by Lt Col James Earl Rudder scaled the sheer 30m cliffs, where the Germans had stationed a battery of artillery guns trained onto the beaches of Utah and Omaha. Un-fortunately, the guns had already been moved in-land, and Rudder and his men spent the next two days repelling counter-attacks. By the time they were finally relieved on 8 June, 81 of the rangers had been killed and 58 more had been wounded.

Today the **site** (☎02 31 51 90 70; www.abmc.gov;

DETOUR: COUTANCES

Start: 9 Utah Beach

The lovely old Norman town of **Coutances** makes a good detour when travelling between the D-Day beaches and Mont St-Michel. At the town's heart is its Gothic **Cathédrale de Coutances** (http://cathedralecoutances.free.fr; parvis Notre-Dame; ⊙8.30am-noon & 2-5.30pm). Interior highlights include several 13th-century windows, a 14th-century fresco of St Michael skewering the dragon, and an organ and high altar from the mid-1700s. You can climb the lantern tower on a tour (adult/child €7/4).

Coutances is about 50km south of Utah Beach by the most direct route.

⊙9am-6pm mid-Apr–mid-Sep, to 5pm rest of year), which France turned over to the US government in 1979, looks much as it did on D-Day, complete with shell craters and crum-bling gun emplacements.

The Drive » Stay on the D514 to Grandcamp-Maisy, then continue south onto the D13 dual carriageway. Keep going till you reach the turn-off for the D913, signed to St-Marie-du-Mont/Utah Beach. It's a 44km drive.

---

9 Utah Beach

The D-Day tour ends at St-Marie-du-Mont, also known as **Utah Beach**, which was assaulted by soldiers of the US 4th and 8th Infantry Divisions. The beach was relatively lightly defended, and by midday the landing force had linked with para-troopers from the 101st Airborne. By nightfall, some 20,000 men and 1700 vehicles had arrived on French soil, and the road to European libera-tion had begun.

Today the Utah Beach site is marked by military memorials and the **Musée du Débarquement** (Utah Beach Landing Museum; ☎02 33 71 53 35; www.utah-beach.com; Ste-Marie du Mont; adult/child €8/4; ⊙9.30am-7pm Jun-Sep, 10am-6pm Oct-May, closed Jan) inside the former German com-mand post.

Eating & Sleeping

Caen ❶

✕ À Contre Sens

Modern French €€

(☏02 31 97 44 48; www.acontresenscaen.fr; 8 rue Croisiers; mains €30-35, menus €25-54; ☺noon-1.15pm Wed-Sat & 7.30-9.15pm Tue-Sat) A Contre Sens's stylish interior and serene atmosphere belie the hotbed of seething creativity happening in the kitchen. Under the helm of chef Anthony Caillot, meals are thoughtfully crafted and superbly presented. Recent selections included pollack cooked in seawater with risotto of oysters, cabbage and coconut, and a juicy thick-cut pork chop with carmelised onions.

✕ Café Mancel

Norman €€

(☏02 31 86 63 64; www.cafemancel.com; Château de Caen; menus €18-36; ☺noon-10pm Tue-Sat, to 2pm Sun) In the same building as the Musée des Beaux-Arts, stylish Café Mancel serves up delicious, traditional French cuisine – everything from pan-fried Norman-style beefsteak to hearty Caen-style tripes. Has a lovely sun terrace, which also makes a fine spot for a drink outside of busy meal times.

⊨ Hôtel des Quatrans

Hotel €€

(☏02 31 86 25 57; www.hotel-des-quatrans.com; 17 rue Gémare; d from €100; ☏) This typically modern hotel has 47 comfy, unfussy rooms in white and chocolate. Promotional deals are often available online.

Bayeux ❻

✕ Alchimie

Modern French €€

(lunch menu €12) On a street lined with restaurants, Alchimie has a simple but elegant design that takes nothing from the beautifully presented dishes. Choose from the day's specials listed on a chalkboard menu, which might include hits like brandade de morue (baked codfish pie). It's a local favourite, so call ahead.

✕ Au Ptit Bistrot

Modern French €€

(☏02 31 92 30 08; 31 rue Larcher; lunch menu €17-20, dinner menu €27-33, mains €16-19; ☺noon-2pm & 7-9pm Tue-Sat) Near the cathedral, this friendly, welcoming eatery whips up creative, beautifully prepared dishes that highlight the Norman bounty without a lick of pretension. Recent hits include chestnut soup, duck breast and bulgur with seasonal fruits and roasted pineapple, and black cod with spinach and spicy guacamole. Reservations are essential.

⊨ Les Logis du Rempart

B&B €

(☏02 31 92 50 40; www.lecornu.fr; 4 rue Bourbesneur; d €60-105, tr €110-130; ☏) The three rooms of this delightful maison de famille ooze old-fashioned cosiness. Our favourite, the Bajocasse, has parquet flooring, a canopy bed and Toile de Jouy wallpaper. The shop downstairs is the perfect place to stock up on top-quality, homemade cider and calvados (apple brandy). Two-night minimum stay.

⊨ Villa Lara

Boutique Hotel €€€

(☏02 31 92 00 55; www.hotel-villalara.com; 6 place de Québec; d €190-360, ste €390-520; P ✳☏) Newly constructed in the past decade, this 28-room hotel, Bayeux's most luxurious, sports minimalist colour schemes, top-quality fabrics and decor that juxtaposes 18th- and 21st-century tastes. Amenities include a bar and a gym. Most rooms have cathedral views.

Atlantic to Med

10

Salty Atlantic ports, pristine mountain vistas, the heady bouquet of fine wine, reminders of Rome and Hollywood glam: this classic sea-to-sea trip takes you through the best of southern France.

TRIP HIGHLIGHTS

0 km

La Rochelle
Made for waterfront mooching, lunching and sunset drinks

1 START

175 km

St-Émilion
Wine tasting and shopping for some of the world's finest drops

2 St-Émilion

FINISH
Nice

Montpellier

6   **8**

Bayonne

Narbonne

Carcassonne
Walk the ramparts of France's most magnificent fortress city

863 km

Marseille
Visit MuCEM, icon of modern Marseille, with stunning views to boot

1158 km

10 DAYS
1498KM /
931 MILES

GREAT FOR...

BEST TIME TO GO

Spring or autumn, for warm weather sans the crowds.

ESSENTIAL PHOTO

Pose like a film star on the steps of Cannes's Palais des Festivals et des Congrès.

BEST FOR FAMILIES

La Rochelle, with its child-friendly attractions and boats.

10 Atlantic to Med

In May the film starlets of the world pour into Cannes to celebrate a year of movie-making. Let them have their moment of glam – by the time you've finished scaling Pyrenean highs, chewing Basque tapas, acting like a medieval knight in a turreted castle and riding to the moon in a spaceship, you too will have the makings of a prize-winning film.

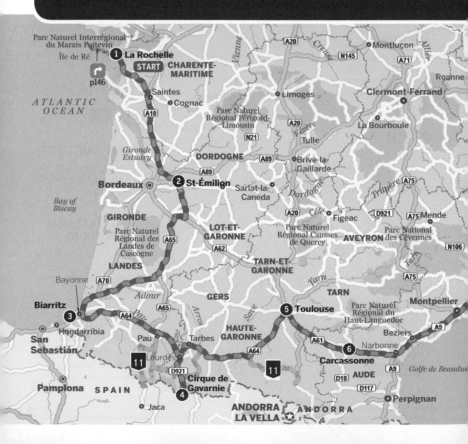

❶ La Rochelle

Known as La Ville Blanche (the White City), La Rochelle is home to luminous limestone facades, arcaded walkways, half-timbered houses and ghoulish gargoyles glowing in the bright coastal sunlight. One of France's foremost seaports from the 14th to the 17th centuries, it remains a great seafaring centre and one of France's most attractive cities.

There are several defensive towers around the **Vieux Port** (Old Port), including the lacy **Tour de la Lanterne** (rue sur les Murs; adult/child €6/free, 3 towers €8.50/free; ⏱10am-1pm & 2.15-6.30pm Apr-Sep, to 5.30pm Oct-Mar), that once served to protect the town at night in times of war. Scale their sturdy stone heights for fabulous city and coastal views.

La Rochelle's number-one tourist attraction is its state-of-the-art **aquarium** (www.aquarium-larochelle.com; quai Louis Prunier; adult/child €16/12; ⏱9am-11pm Jul & Aug, 9am-8pm Apr-Jun & Sep, 10am-8pm Oct-Mar) with UFO-like rays and fearsome sharks, teeth-gnashing piranhas, timid turtles and the bizarre half-newt. Equally fun for families is the **Musée Maritime** (Maritime Museum; ☎05 46 28 03 00; www.museemaritimelarochelle.fr; place Bernard Moitessier; adult/child €8/5; ⏱10am-7pm Jul & Aug, to 6.30pm Apr-Jun & Sep, shorter hours rest of year), with its fleet of boats to explore; and a trip out to sea with **Croisières Inter-Îles** (☎08 25 13 55 00; www.inter-iles.com; cours des Dames) to admire the unusual iceberg of an island fortress, Fort Boyard.

🛏 p151

The Drive » Using the main A10 toll road it's 187km (about 2½ hours) to St-Émilion. Turn off the A10 at exit 39a, signed for Libourne. Skirt this industrial town and follow the D243 into St-Émilion.

LINK YOUR TRIP

11 The Pyrenees

Take a side trip east or west from the A64 to further explore this majestic mountain landscape.

12 Riviera Crossing

Starting from Nice, this drive takes you further along the coast through the glitzy, glam French Riviera.

TRIP HIGHLIGHT

❷ St-Émilion

Built of soft honey-coloured rock, medieval St-Émilion produces some of the world's finest red wines. Visiting this pretty town, and partaking in some of the tours and activities on offer, is the easiest way to get under the (grape) skin of Bordeaux wine production. The **Maison du Vin de St-Émilion** (www. maisonduvinsaintemilion.com; place Pierre Meyrat; ⊘9.30am-12.30pm & 2-6.30pm) runs wine-tasting classes and has a superb exhibition covering wine essentials.

Guided tours of the town (adult/child from €8/free) and surrounding chateaux are run by the **tourist office** (⌨05 57 55 28 28; www.saint-emilion-tourisme. com; place des Créneaux; ⊘9.30am-7.30pm Jul & Aug, shorter hours rest of year); reserve ahead in season. Several tours include tastings and vineyard visits.

✕ ⇧ p151

The Drive » Leave St-Émilion on the D243 to Libourne, cross the town, then pick up the D1089 signposted 'Agen, Bergerac, Bordeaux'. Continue on the N89 towards Bordeaux until you see signs for the A630 toll road – at which point sit back and hit cruise control for the remaining 226km to Biarritz. Count 240km and about 2½ hours in all.

❸ Biarritz

Biarritz is as ritzy as its name suggests. This coastal town boomed as a resort in the mid-19th century, when regularly visited by Napoléon III and his Spanish-born wife, Eugénie. Along its rocky coastline are architectural hallmarks of this golden age, and the belle-époque and art-deco eras that followed.

Biarritz is all about its fashionable beaches, especially the central **Grande Plage** and **Plage Miramar**. In the heat of summer you'll find them packed end to end with sun-loving bathers.

↱ DETOUR: ÎLE DE RÉ

Start: ❶ La Rochelle (p145)

Bathed in the southern sun, drenched in a languid atmosphere and scattered with villages of green-shuttered, whitewashed buildings with red Spanish-tile roofs, Île de Ré is one of the most delightful places on the west coast of France. The island spans just 30km from its most easterly and westerly points, and just 5km at its widest section. But take note: the secret's out and in high season it can be almost impossible to move around and even harder to find a place to stay.

On the northern coast about 12km from the toll bridge that links the island to La Rochelle is the quaint fishing port of **St-Martin-de-Ré**, the island's main town. Surrounded by 17th-century fortifications (you can stroll along most of the ramparts) constructed by Vauban, the port town is a mesh of streets filled with craft shops, art galleries and sea-spray ocean views.

The island's best beaches are along the southern edge – including unofficial naturist beaches at **Rivedoux Plage** and **La Couarde-sur-Mer** – and around the western tip (northeast and southeast of Phare-des-Baleines). Many beaches are bordered by dunes that have been fenced off to protect the vegetation.

From La Rochelle it's 24km and a half-hour drive to St-Martin-de-Ré via the toll bridge, Pont de l'Île de Ré (www.pont-ile-de-re.com; return ticket €16 mid-June to mid-September, €8 rest of the year).

**The Drive ›› ** It's 208km (2¾ hours) to the village of Gavarnie. Take the A63 and A64 toll roads to exit 11, then the D940 to Lourdes (worth a look for its religious Disneyland feel). Continue south along D913 and D921.

❹ Cirque de Gavarnie

The Pyrenees doesn't lack impressive scenery, but your first sight of the Cirque de Gavarnie is guaranteed to raise a gasp. This breathtaking mountain amphitheatre is one of the region's most famous sights, sliced by thunderous waterfalls and ringed by sawtooth peaks, many of which top out at above 3000m.

There are a couple of large car parks in the village of Gavarnie, from where it's a two-hour walk to the amphitheatre. Wear proper shoes, as snow lingers along the trail into early summer. Between Easter and October you can go by horse or donkey (around €25 return).

**The Drive ›› ** Retrace your steps to Lourdes, then take the N21 toward Tarbes and veer onto the A64 to reach Toulouse. It takes nearly three hours to cover the 228km.

❺ Toulouse

Elegantly sited at the confluence of the Canal du Midi and Garonne River, the vibrant southern city of Toulouse is often known as La Ville Rose, a reference to the distinc-tive pink stone used in many of its buildings.

Toulouse's magnificent main square, **place du Capitole**, is the city's literal and metaphorical heart. To its south is the city's **Vieux Quartier** (Old Quarter), a tangle of lanes and leafy squares that beg exploration on foot. Then, of course, there are the soothing twists and turns of the Garonne River and mighty Canal du Midi – laced with footpaths and likewise clearly created with stretching your legs in mind.

The sky's the limit at the fantastic **Cité de l'Espace** (www.cite-espace. com/en; av Jean Gonord; adult €21-25.50, child €15.50-19; ☺10am-7pm daily Jul & Aug, to 5pm or 6pm Sep-Dec & Feb-Jun, closed Mon Feb, Mar & Sep-Dec, closed Jan). Since WWII, Toulouse has been the centre of France's aerospace industry, developing many important aircraft (including Concorde and the Airbus A380) as well as components for many international space programs. The museum brings this interstellar industry vividly to life through hands-on exhibits including a shuttle simulator, a planetarium, a 3D cinema and a simulated observatory.

✕ ⌷ p151

**The Drive ›› ** It's an easy 95km (one hour) down the fast A61 to Carcassonne. Notice how the vegetation becomes suddenly much more Mediterranean about 15 minutes out of Toulouse.

❻ Carcassonne

Perched on a rocky hilltop and bristling with zigzagging battlements, stout walls and spiky turrets, from afar the fortified city of Carcassonne is most people's perfect idea of a medieval castle. Four million tourists a year stream through its city gates to explore **La Cité** (enter via Porte Narbonnaise or Porte d'Aude; ☺24hr), visit **Château Comtal** (place du Château, La Cité; adult/child €8.50/free; ☺10am-6.30pm Apr-Sep, 9.30am-5pm Oct-Mar) and ogle at stunning views along the city's ancient ramparts.

**The Drive ›› ** Continue down the A61 to the Catalan-flavoured town of Narbonne, where you join the A9 (very busy in summer) and head east to Nîmes. From there the A54 will take you into Arles. Allow just over two hours to cover the 223km and expect lots of toll booths.

❼ Arles

Arles' poster boy is the celebrated impressionist painter Vincent van Gogh. If you're familiar with his work, you'll be familiar with Arles: the light, the colours, the landmarks and the atmosphere, all faithfully captured. But long before Van Gogh rendered this grand Rhône River locale on canvas, the Romans valued its worth. Today it's the reminders of Rome that are probably the town's most memorable attractions.

WHY THIS IS A GREAT TRIP
NICOLA WILLIAMS, WRITER

I'm a sucker for the big blue and fine wine, so this seafaring trip is right up my alley. Feasting on fresh oysters on the seashore aside, I strongly advise lingering over lunch at La Terrasse Rouge (p151) near St-Émilion. This spectacular vineyard restaurant was borne out of Jean Nouvel's designer revamp of Château La Dominique's wine cellars: dining on its uber-chic terrace overlooking a field of dark-red glass pebbles is the ultimate French road-trip reward.

Top & Left: St-Emilion
Right: Cathedral & MuCEM, Marseilles

JEAN-PIERRE LESCOURRET ©

At **Les Arènes** (Amphithéâtre; www.arenes-arles.com; Rond-Point des Arènes; adult/child €6/free, incl Théâtre Antique €9/free; ⊙9am-8pm Jul & Aug, to 7pm May-Jun & Sep, shorter hours rest of year) slaves, criminals and wild animals (including giraffes) met their dramatic demise before a jubilant 20,000-strong crowd during Roman gladiatorial displays.

The **Théâtre Antique** (☎04 90 96 93 30; bd des Lices; ⊙9am-7pm May-Sep, shorter hours rest of year), which dates from the 1st century BC, is still regularly used for al fresco concerts and plays.

✕ ⊨ p151

The Drive 》 From Arles take the scenic N568 and A55 route into Marseille. It's 88km (an hour's drive) away.

TRIP HIGHLIGHT

❽ Marseille

With its history, fusion of cultures, *souq*-like markets, millennia-old port and *corniches* (coastal roads) along rocky inlets and sun-baked beaches, Marseille is a captivating and exotic city.

Ships have docked for more than 26 centuries at the city's birthplace, the colourful Vieux Port (Old Port), which remains a thriving harbour to this day. Guarding it are **Bas Fort St-Nicolas** on the south side and, across the water, **Fort St-Jean**, founded in the 13th century by

149

the Knights Hospitaller of St John of Jerusalem. A vertigo-inducing footbridge links the latter with the stunning **Musée des Civilisations de l'Europe et de la Méditerranée,** (MuCEM; www.mucem.org; 7 Promenade Robert Laffont; adult/family/child €9.50/14/ free; ⊙10am-8pm Wed-Mon Jul & Aug, 11am-7pm Wed-Mon Sep, Oct, May & Jun, 11am-6pm Wed-Mon Nov-Apr) the icon of modern Marseille. Its vast anthropological collection is housed in a bold, contemporary building known as J4, designed by Algerian-born, Marseille-educated architect Rudi Ricciotti.

From the Vieux Port, hike up to the fantastic history-woven quarter of **Le Panier**, dubbed Marseille's Montmartre as much for its sloping streets as its artsy ambi-

ence. It's a mishmash of lanes hiding artisan shops, *ateliers* (workshops) and terraced houses strung with drying washing.

The Drive » To get from Marseille to Cannes, take the northbound A52 and join the A8 toll road just east of Aix-en-Provence. It's 181km and takes just under two hours.

---

❾ Cannes

The eponymous film festival only lasts for two weeks in May, but thanks to regular visits from celebrities the buzz and glitz are in Cannes year-round.

The imposing **Palais des Festivals et des Congrès** (1 bd de la Croisette; guided tour adult/child €4/ free) is the centre of the glamour. Climb the red carpet, walk down the auditorium, tread the stage and learn about

cinema's most prestigious event on a 1½-hour guided tour run by the **tourist office** (📞04 91 13 89 00; www.marseille-tourisme.com; 11 La Canebière; ⊙9am-7pm Mon-Sat, 10am-5pm Sun).

🍴 🛏 p172

The Drive » Weave along the D6007 to Nice, taking in cliffs, turquoise waters and the yachties' town of Antibes. It's 31km and, on a good day, takes 45 minutes.

---

❿ Nice

You don't need to be a painter or artist to appreciate the extraordinary light in Nice. Matisse, Chagall et al spent years lapping up the city's startling luminosity and radiance, and for most visitors to Nice, it is this magical light that seduces. The city has a number of world-class sights, but the star attraction is probably the seafront **Promenade des Anglais**. Atmospheric, beautiful and photogenic, it's a wonderful place to stroll (p200) or watch the world go by, so make sure you leave yourself plenty of time to soak it all in.

🍴 🛏 p151, p172

DETOUR: AIX-EN-PROVENCE

Start: ❼ Arles (p147)

Aix-en-Provence is to Provence what the Left Bank is to Paris: an enclave of bourgeois-bohemian chic. Art, culture and architecture abound here. A stroller's paradise, the highlight is the mostly pedestrian old city, **Vieil Aix**. South of cours Mirabeau, **Quartier Mazarin** was laid out in the 17th century, and is home to some of Aix's finest buildings. Central Place des Quatre Dauphins, with its fish-spouting fountain (1667), is particularly enchanting. Further south still is the peaceful **Parc Jourdan**, where locals gather beneath plane trees to play *pétanque*.

From Arles it's a 77km (one-hour) drive down the A54 toll road to Aix-en-Provence. To rejoin the main route take the A51 and A7 for 32km (30 minutes) to Marseille.

Eating & Sleeping

La Rochelle ❶

🛏 Hôtel St-Nicolas   Boutique Hotel €€

(☎05 46 41 71 55; www.hotel-saint-nicolas.com; 13 rue Sardinerie et place de la Solette; d/tr €125/145; 🅿 ❄ 🛜) This stylish hotel, tucked in a peaceful courtyard with delightful summer terrace, has smart comfortable rooms with ultra-modern bathrooms – think giant rain showers, heated towel rails and sweet-smelling welcome products. A handful of rooms are across the courtyard in an equally inviting annexe, and breakfast (€12) is served in an indoor tropical garden. Check its website for excellent-value deals.

St-Émilion ❷

🍴 La Terrasse Rouge   French €€

(☎05 57 24 47 05; www.laterrasserouge.com; 1 Château La Dominique; lunch menu €28; 🕑 noon-2.30pm & 7-11pm Jun-Sep, noon-2.30pm & 7-11pm Fri & Sat, noon-2.30pm Sun-Thu Oct-May) Foodies adore this spectacular vineyard restaurant. Chefs work exclusively with small local producers to source the seasonal veg, fruit and so on used in their creative cuisine. Oysters are fresh from Cap Ferret, caviar comes from Neuvic in the Dordogne and the wine list is, naturally, extraordinary.

Toulouse ❺

🍴 Le Genty Magre   French €€€

(☎05 61 21 38 60; www.legentymagre.com; 3 rue Genty Magre; mains €18-30, menu €38; 🕑12.30-2.30pm & 8-10pm Tue-Sat) Classic French cuisine is the order of the day here, but lauded chef Romain Brard has plenty of modern tricks up his sleeve, too. The dining room feels inviting, with brick walls, burnished wood and sultry lighting. It's arguably the best place in the city to try rich, traditional dishes such as *confit de canard* (duck confit) or *cassoulet* (stew).

🛏 Hôtel Albert 1er   Hotel €€

(☎05 61 21 47 49; www.hotel-albert1.com; 8 rue Rivals; d €65-145; ❄ 🛜) The Albert's central location and eager-to-please staff are a winning

combination. A palette of maroon and cream, with marble flourishes here and there, bestows a regal feel on comfortable rooms. Bathrooms are lavished with ecofriendly products. The breakfast buffet is largely organic. Some recently upgraded rooms have mod cons such as USB ports and coffee makers.

Arles ❼

🛏 Le Cloître   Design Hotel €€

(☎04 88 09 10 00; www.hotel-cloitre.com; 18 rue du Cloître; s €105, d €130-185; @ 🛜) Proving you don't need to spend a fortune for originality and imagination, the 19 rooms at this zingy hotel next to the Cloître Ste-Trophime combine history and modern design to winning effect: bold colours, funky patterns and retro furniture abound, and the rooftop terrace is a stunning sundowner spot. The lavish breakfast spread is (unusually) worth the €14 price tag.

Nice ❿

🍴 Le Bistrot d'Antoine   Modern French €€

(☎04 93 85 29 57; 27 rue de la Préfecture; menus €25-43, mains €15-25; 🕑 noon-2pm & 7-10pm Tue-Sat) A quintessential French bistro, right down to the checked tablecloths, streetside tables and impeccable service – not to mention the handwritten blackboard, loaded with classic dishes like rabbit pâté, pot-cooked pork, blood sausage and duck breast. For classic French food, this is a treat.

🛏 Nice Garden Hôtel   Boutique Hotel €€

(☎04 93 87 35 62; www.nicegardenhotel.com; 11 rue du Congrès; s €75, d €90-123, tr €138; 🕑 reception 8am-9pm; ❄ 🛜) Behind heavy iron gates hides this gem: nine beautifully appointed rooms – the work of the exquisite Marion – are a subtle blend of old and new and overlook a delightful garden with a glorious orange tree. Amazingly, all this charm and peacefulness is just two blocks from the promenade. Breakfast €9.

The Pyrenees

11

Traversing hair-raising roads, sky-top passes and snow-dusted peaks, this trip ventures deep into the unforgettable Pyrenees. Buckle up – you're in for a roller coaster of a drive.

TRIP HIGHLIGHTS

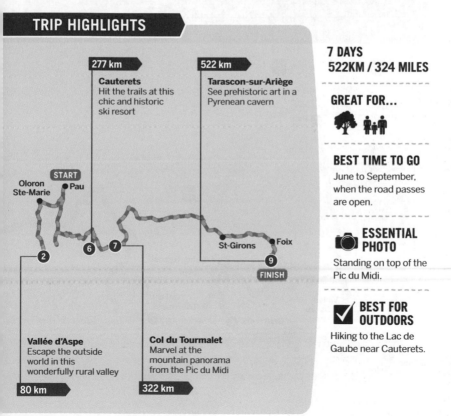

277 km

Cauterets
Hit the trails at this chic and historic ski resort

522 km

Tarascon-sur-Ariège
See prehistoric art in a Pyrenean cavern

Oloron Ste-Marie

START Pau

St-Girons   Foix

FINISH

Vallée d'Aspe
Escape the outside world in this wonderfully rural valley

80 km

Col du Tourmalet
Marvel at the mountain panorama from the Pic du Midi

322 km

7 DAYS
522KM / 324 MILES

GREAT FOR...

BEST TIME TO GO
June to September, when the road passes are open.

ESSENTIAL PHOTO
Standing on top of the Pic du Midi.

BEST FOR OUTDOORS
Hiking to the Lac de Gaube near Cauterets.

11 The Pyrenees

They might not have the altitude of the Alps, but the Pyrenees pack a mighty mountain punch, and if you're an outdoors-lover, you'll be in seventh heaven here. With quiet villages, rustic restaurants, spectacular trails and snowy mountains galore, the Pyrenees are a wild adventure – just remember to break in your hiking boots before you arrive.

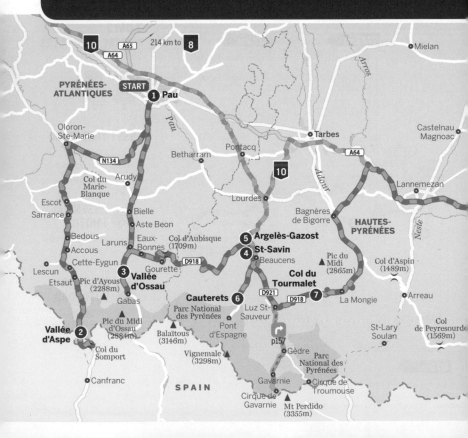

❶ Pau

Palm trees might seem out of place in this mountainous region, but Pau (rhymes with 'so') has long been famed for its mild climate. In the 19th century this elegant town was a favourite wintering spot for wealthy Brits and Americans, who left behind many grand villas and smart promenades.

Its main sight is the **Château de Pau** (☎05 59 82 38 00; www.chateau-pau. fr; 2 rue du Château; adult/child €7/free; ☺9.30am-12.15pm & 1.30-5.45pm, gardens open longer hrs), built by the monarchs of Navarre and transformed into a Renaissance château in the 16th century. It's home to a fine collection of Gobelins tapestries and Sevres porcelain.

Pau's tiny old centre extends for around 500m around the Château de Pau, and boasts many attractive medieval and Renaissance buildings.

LINK YOUR TRIP

10 **Atlantic to Med**
From Foix, head just over an hour northeast to Carcassone and then east for the balmy Med or west for the slower-paced Atlantic coast.

8 **Essential France**
From Foix, it's four hours' drive east to Aix-en-Provence, where you can commence the grand tour of France in reverse.

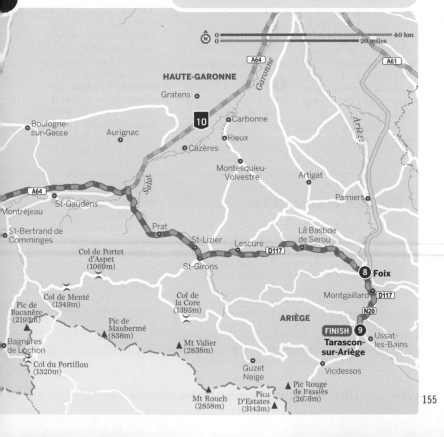

Central street parking is mostly *payant* (chargeable), but there's free parking on place de Verdun and the street leading west of there (av du 18 Régiment d'Infanterie).

✗ ⊨ p161

The Drive 》 To reach the Vallée d'Aspe from Pau, take the N193 to Oloron-Ste-Marie. The first 30km are uneventful, but over the next 40km south of Oloron the mountain scenery unfolds in dramatic fashion, with towering peaks stacking up on either side of the road.

TRIP HIGHLIGHT

❷ Vallée d'Aspe

The westernmost of the Pyrenean valleys makes a great day trip from Pau. Framed by mountains and bisected by the Aspe River, it's awash with classic Pyrenean scenery. The main attraction here is soaking up the scenery. Allow yourself plenty of time for photo stops, especially around pretty

villages such as **Sarrance**, **Borcé** and **Etsaut**.

Near the quiet village of **Bedous**, it's worth detouring up the narrow road to **Lescun**, a tiny hamlet perched 5.5km above the valley, overlooking the peak of **Pic d'Anie** (2504m) and the cluster of mountains known as the **Cirque de Lescun**.

The valley ends 25km further south near the **Col du Somport** (1631m), where a controversial tunnel burrows 8km under the Franco-Spanish border. The return drive to Pau is just over 80km.

The Drive 》 To reach the Vallée d'Ossau from Pau, take the N134 south of town, veering south onto the D934 towards Arudy/Laruns. From Pau to Laruns, it's about 42km.

❸ Vallée d'Ossau

More scenic splendour awaits in the Vallée d'Ossau, which tracks the course of its namesake river for a spectacular

60km. The first part of the valley as far as Laruns is broad, green and pastoral, but as you travel south the mountains really start to pile up, before broadening out again near Gabas.

Halfway between Arudy and Laruns, you can spy on some of the Pyrenees' last griffon vultures at the **Falaise aux Vautours** (Cliff of the Vultures; 📞05 59 82 65 49; www.falaise-aux-vautours.com; adult/child €6/4; ⊙10.30am-12.30pm & 2-6.30pm Jul & Aug, 2-5.30pm Apr-Jun & Sep). Once a common sight, these majestic birds have been decimated by habitat loss and hunting; they're now protected by law. Live CCTV images are beamed from their nests to the visitors centre in Aste-Béon.

The ski resort of **Artouste-Fabrèges**, 6km east of Gabas, is linked by cable car to the **Petit Train d'Artouste** (📞05 59 05 36 99; www.altiservice. com/excursion/train-artouste; adult/child €25/21; ⊙Jun–mid-Sep), a miniature mountain railway built for dam workers in the 1920s. The train is only open between June and September; reserve ahead and allow four hours for a visit.

The Drive 》 The D918 between Laruns and Argelès-Gazost is one of the Pyrenees' most breathtaking roads, switchbacking over the lofty Col d'Aubisque. The road feels exposed, but it's a wonderfully

THE TRANSHUMANCE

If you're travelling through the Pyrenees between late May and early June and find yourself stuck behind a cattle-shaped traffic jam, there's a good chance you may have just got caught up in the Transhumance, in which shepherds move their flocks from their winter pastures up to the high, grassy uplands.

This ancient custom has been a fixture on the Pyrenean calendar for centuries, and several valleys host festivals to mark the occasion. The spectacle is repeated in October, when the flocks are brought back down before the winter snows set in.

scenic drive. You'll cover about 52km, but allow yourself at least 1½ hours. Once you reach Argelès-Gazost, head further south for 4km along the D101 to St-Savin.

---

❹ St-Savin

After the hair-raising drive over the Col d'Aubisque, St-Savin makes a welcome refuge. It's a classic Pyrenean village, with cobbled lanes, quiet cafes and timbered houses set around a fountain-filled main square.

It's also home to one of the Pyrenees' most respected hotel-restaurants, **Le Viscos** (☎05 62 97 02 28; www.hotel-leviscos.com; 1 rue Lamarque, St-Savin; menus €49-75; ⊙12.30-2.30pm Tue-Sun & 7.30-9.30pm daily; 🅿❄🛜), run by celeb chef Jean-Pierre St-Martin, known for his blend of Basque, Breton and Pyrenean flavours (as well as his passion for foie gras). After dinner, retire to one of the cosy country rooms and watch the sun set over the snowy mountains.

🛏 p161

The Drive » From St-Savin, travel back along the D101 to Argelès-Gazost. You'll see signs to the Parc Animalier des Pyrénées as you approach town.

---

❺ Argelès-Gazost

Spotting wildlife isn't always easy in the Pyrenees, but thankfully the **Parc Animalier**

des Pyrénées (☎05 62 97 91 07; www.parc-animalier-pyrenees.com; adult/child €18/13; ⊙9.30am-6pm or 7pm Apr-Oct) does all the hard work for you. It's home to a menagerie of endangered Pyrenean animals including wolves, marmots, lynxes, giant ravens, vultures, racoons, beavers and even a few brown bears (the European cousin of the grizzly bear).

The Drive » Take the D921 south of Argelès-Gazost for 6km to Pierrefitte-Nestalas. Here, the road forks; the southwest branch (the D920) climbs up a lush, forested valley for another 11km to Cauterets.

TRIP HIGHLIGHT

❻ Cauterets

For alpine scenery, the century-old ski resort of Cauterets is perhaps the signature spot in the Pyrenees. Hemmed in by mountains and forests, it

has clung on to much of its *fin-de-siècle* character, with a stately spa and grand 19th-century residences.

To see the scenery at its best, drive through town along the D920 (signed to the 'Pont d'Espagne'). The road is known locally as the **Chemins des Cascades** after the waterfalls that crash down the mountainside; it's 6.5km of nonstop hairpins, so take it steady.

At the top, you'll reach the giant car park at **Pont d'Espagne** (cable cars adult/child €13/10.50). From here, a combination *télécabine* and *télésiege* (adult/child €13/10.50) ratchets up the mountainside allowing access to the area's trails, including the popular hike to the sapphire-tinted **Lac de Gaube**.

🍴🛏 p161

↪ DETOUR: CIRQUE DE GAVARNIE

Start: ❻ Cauterets

For truly mind-blowing mountain scenery, it's well worth taking a side trip to see the Cirque de Gavarnie, a dramatic amphitheatre of mountains 20km south of Luz-St-Saveur. It's a return walk of about two hours from the village, and you'll need to bring sturdy footwear.

There's another spectacular circle of mountains 6.5km to the north, the **Cirque de Troumouse**. It's reached via a hair-raising 8km toll road (€5 per vehicle; open April to October). There are no barriers and the drops are really dizzying, so drive carefully.

PHILIPPE COHAT / GETTY IMAGES ©

ESCUDERO PATRICK / GETTY IMAGES ©

WHY THIS IS A GREAT TRIP
OLIVER BERRY,
WRITER

The craggy peaks of the Pyrenees are home to some of France's rarest wildlife and most unspoilt landscapes, and every twist and turn in the road seems to reveal another knockout view – one of my personal favourites is the amazing road over the Col d'Aubisque, which feels closer to flying than driving. I love the traditional way of life here, too. Visit during the Transhumance to be treated to one of France's great rural spectacles.

Top: Col d'Aubisque
Left: Château de Pau
Right: Cauterets ski resort

The Drive » After staying overnight in Cauterets, backtrack to Pierrefitte-Nestalas, and turn southeast onto the D921 for 12km to Luz-St-Saveur. The next stretch on the D918 is another mountain stunner, climbing up through Barèges to the breathtaking Col du Tourmalet.

- - - - - - - - - - - - - - - -

TRIP HIGHLIGHT

❼ Col du Tourmalet

Even in the pantheon of Pyrenean road passes, the Col du Tourmalet commands special respect. At 2115m, it's the highest road pass in the Pyrenees, and usually only opens between June and October. It's often used as a punishing mountain stage in the Tour de France, and you'll feel uncomfortably akin to a motorised ant as you crawl up towards the pass.

From the ski resort of La Mongie (1800m), a cable car climbs to the top of the soaring **Pic du Mıdı** (www.picdumidi.com; adult/child €36/23; ⊙9am-7pm Jun-Sep, 10am-5.30pm Oct, Dec-Apr). This high-altitude observatory commands otherworldly views – but it's often blanketed in cloud, so make sure you check the forecast before you go.

The Drive » The next stage to Foix is a long one. Follow the D918 and D935 to Bagnères-de-Bigorre, then the D938 and D20 to Tournay, a drive of 40km. Just before Tournay, head west onto the A64 for 82km. Exit onto the D117, signed to St-Girons. It's another 72km to Foix.

ROAD PASSES IN THE PYRENEES

The high passes between the Vallée d'Ossau, the Vallée d'Aspe and the Vallée de Gaves are often closed during winter. Signs are posted along the approach roads indicating whether they're *ouvert* (open) or *fermé* (closed). The dates given below are approximate, and depend on seasonal snowfall.

Col d'Aubisque (1709m, open May-Oct) The D918 links Laruns in the Vallée d'Ossau with Argèles-Gazost in the Vallée de Gaves. An alternative that's open year-round is the D35 between Louvie-Juzon and Nay.

Col de Marie-Blanque (1035m, open most of year) The shortest link between the Aspe and Ossau valleys is the D294, which corkscrews for 21km between Escot and Bielle.

Col du Pourtalet (1795m, open most of year) The main crossing into Spain generally stays open year-round except during exceptional snowfall.

Col du Tourmalet (2115m, open Jun-Oct) Between Barèges and La Mongie, this is the highest road pass in the Pyrenees. If you're travelling east to the Pic du Midi (for example from Cauterets), the only alternative is a long detour north via Lourdes and Bagnères-de-Bigorre.

⑧ Foix

Foix is a quiet mountain town, but it's an excellent base for exploring the eastern Pyrenees. Looming above town is the triple-towered **Château de Foix** (☎05 61 05 10 10; adult/child €5.60/3.80; ⏰10am-6pm summer, shorter hours rest of year), constructed in the 10th century as a stronghold for the counts of Foix. The interior is rather bare, but there's a small museum, and the view from the battlements is glorious. There's usually at least one daily tour in English in summer.

Afterwards, head 4.5km south to **Les Forges de Pyrène** (☎05 34 09 30 60; adult/child €9/6; ⏰10am-6.30pm), a fascinating 'living museum' exploring Ariège folk traditions. Spread over 5 hectares, it illustrates traditional trades such as glass blowing, tanning, thatching and nail making, and even has its own blacksmith, baker and cobbler.

🛏 p161

The Drive » Spend the night in Foix, then head for Tarascon-sur-Ariège, 17km south of Foix on the N20. Look out for brown signs to the Parc de la Préhistoire.

TRIP HIGHLIGHT

⑨ Tarascon-sur-Ariège

Thousands of years ago, the Pyrenees were home to thriving communities of hunter-gatherers, who used the area's caves as shelters and left behind many stunning examples of prehistoric art.

Near Tarascon-sur-Ariège, the **Parc de la Préhistoire** (☎05 61 05 10 10; adult/child €11/8.30; ⏰10am-7pm, closed Nov-Mar) provides a handy primer on the area's ancient past. It's a mix of multimedia exhibits and hands-on outdoor displays, exploring everything from prehistoric carving to the art of animal-skin tents and ancient spear-throwing.

About 6.5km further south, the **Grotte de Niaux** (www.sites-touristiques-ariege. fr; adult/child €12/8) is home to the Pyrenees' most precious cave paintings. The centrepiece is the **Salon Noir**, reached after an 800m walk through the darkness and decorated with bison, horses and ibex. To help preserve the delicate paintings, there's no artificial light inside; you're given a torch as you enter. The cave can only be visited with a guide. From April to September there's usually a daily tour in English at 1.30pm. Bookings advised.

Eating & Sleeping

Pau ❶

✕ Les Papilles Insolites
Bistro €€

(📞05 59 71 43 79; www.lespapillesinsolites.
blogspot.co.uk; 5 rue Alexander Taylor; lunch/
dinner menu €22/45, mains around €23;
🕐12.15-2pm & 8-9.30pm Wed-Sat) Run by a
former Parisian sommelier, this cosy bar-bistro
pitches itself between a bistro and a wine shop.
It serves beautifully prepared, ingredient-rich
dishes like Galician-style octopus with potatoes,
fennel and olive tapenade, or beef with leeks,
tempura and lemongrass-raspberry reduction.
Complete the experience with the owner's
choice of one of the 350-odd wines stacked
around the shop. Gorgeously Gallic.

🛏 Hôtel Bristol
Hotel €€

(📞05 59 27 72 98; www.hotelbristol-pau.
com; 3 rue Gambetta; s €55-100, d €80-110,
f €120-130; P 📶) A classic old French hotel
with surprisingly up-to-date rooms, all wrapped
up in a fine 19th-century building. Each room
is uniquely designed, with stylish decor,
bold artwork and elegant furniture; while big
windows fill the rooms with light. Ask for a
mountain-view room with balcony. Breakfast
costs €12.

St-Savin ❹

🛏 Hôtel des Rochers
Hotel €€

(📞05 62 97 09 52; www.lesrochershotel.com; 1
place du Castillou; d €60-68, tr €95-100; P 📶)
In the idyllic village of St-Savin, 16km south of
Lourdes, this handsomely landscaped hotel
makes a perfect mountain retreat. It's run by an
expat English couple, John and Jane, who have
renovated the rooms in clean, contemporary
fashion – insist on one with a mountain view.
Half-board is available.

Cauterets ❻

✕ La Grande Fache
Traditional French €€

(📞06 08 93 76 30; 5 rue Richelieu; fondue per
person €18-23; 🕐noon-2.30pm & 7-10pm)
You're in the mountains, so really you should be
eating artery-clogging, cheese-heavy dishes
such as *tartiflette* (potatoes, cheese and bacon
baked in a casserole), *raclette* and fondue. This
family-run restaurant crammed with mountain
memorabilia will oblige.

🛏 Hôtel du Lion d'Or
Hotel €€

(📞05 62 92 52 87; www.liondor.eu; 12 rue
Richelieu; s €76-86, d €80-162, with half-board s/d
from €119/144; 📶) This Heidi-esque hotel oozes
mountain character from every nook and cranny.
In business since 1913, it is deliciously eccentric,
with charming old rooms in polkadot pinks, sunny
yellows and duck-egg blues, and mountain-
themed knick-knacks dotted throughout, from
antique sleds to snowshoes. Breakfast includes
homemade honey and jams, and the restaurant
serves hearty Pyrenean cuisine.

Foix ❽

🛏 Hôtel Eychenne
Hotel €€

(📞05 61 65 00 04; www.hotel-eychenne.com;
11 rue Peyrevidal; s/d €50/60; 📶) In a good
location in the centre of Foix, Hôtel Eychenne
has simple, carpeted rooms with wooden
shutters and bathrooms of a vaguely futuristic
(circa 1960s) design, with capsule-like showers.
There's an easygoing bar downstairs.

🛏 Hôtel Restaurant Lons
Hotel €€

(📞05 34 09 28 00; www.hotel-lons-foix.com; 6
place Dutilh; r €79-103) One of the better hotels
in Foix is an old-fashioned affair with rambling
corridors and functional but comfy rooms, some
of which look onto the river, while the others face
Foix's shady streets. The riverside restaurant
offers good-value half-board (*menus* €18 to €36).

Riviera Crossing

12

French road trips just don't get more glamorous than this: cinematic views, searing sunshine, art history aplenty and the Med around every turn.

TRIP HIGHLIGHTS

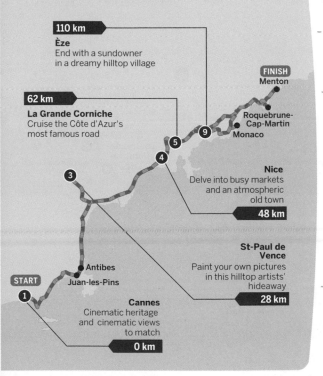

110 km
Èze
End with a sundowner in a dreamy hilltop village

FINISH
Menton

62 km
La Grande Corniche
Cruise the Côte d'Azur's most famous road

Roquebrune-Cap-Martin

Monaco

Nice
Delve into busy markets and an atmospheric old town

48 km

St-Paul de Vence
Paint your own pictures in this hilltop artists' hideaway

28 km

Antibes

START

Juan-les-Pins

Cannes
Cinematic heritage and cinematic views to match

0 km

4 DAYS
110KM / 68 MILES

GREAT FOR...

BEST TIME TO GO
Anytime, but avoid July and August's heavy traffic.

ESSENTIAL PHOTO
Standing beneath Augustus' monumental Trophée des Alpes, with Monaco and the Med far below.

BEST FOR GLAMOUR
Strolling the Croisette in Cannes and fulfilling those film-star fantasies.

Menton Seaside town of peaceful gardens and belle-époque mansions

12 Riviera Crossing

Cruising the Côte d'Azur is the French road trip everyone has to do at least one in their lifetime. From film town Cannes to down-to-earth Nice via the corkscrew turns of the Corniches and into millionaire's Monaco, it's a drive that you'll remember forever (and hopefully not because of the dreadful summer traffic). Filmmakers, writers, celebs and artists have all had their hearts stolen by this glittering stretch of coastline: by the end of this trip, you'll understand why.

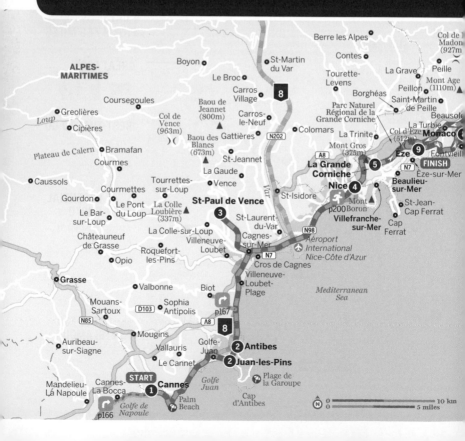

① Cannes

What glitzier opening could there be to this Côte d'Azur cruise than Cannes, which is just as cinematic as its reputation suggests. Come July during the film festival, the world's stars descend on **boulevard de la Croisette** (aka La Croisette) to stroll beneath the palms, plug their latest opus and hobnob with the media and movie moguls. Getting your picture snapped outside the **Palais des Festivals** is

a must-do, as is a night-time stroll along the boulevard, illuminated by coloured lights.

Outside festival time, Cannes still feels irresistibly ritzy. Private beaches and grand hotels line the seafront; further west lies old Cannes. Follow rue St-Antoine and snake your way up **Le Suquet**, Cannes' atmospheric original village. Pick up the region's best produce at **Marché Forville**, a couple of blocks back from the port.

Not seduced? Then head to the **Îles de Lérins**, two islands a 20-minute boat ride away. Tiny and traffic-free, they're perfect for walks or a picnic. Boats for the islands leave from quai des Îles, on the western side of the harbour.

 p172

The Drive » The most scenic route to Antibes is via the coastal D6007. Bear right onto av Frères Roustan before Golfe Juan. With luck and no tailbacks, you should hit Juan-les-Pins in 30 minutes or so.

② Antibes & Juan-les-Pins

A century or so ago, Antibes and Juan-les-Pins were a refuge for artists, writers, aristocrats and hedonistic expats looking to escape the horrors of post-WWI Europe. They came in their droves – F Scott Fitzgerald wrote several books here, and Picasso rented a miniature castle (it's now a museum dedicated to him).

First stop is the beach resort of **Juan-les-Pins**. It's a long way from the fashionable resort of Fitzgerald's day, but the beaches are still good for sun-lounging (even if you do have to pay).

Then it's on around the peninsula of **Cap d'Antibes**, where many of the great and good had their holiday villas: the Hotel Cap du Eden Roc was one of their favourite fashionable haunts. Round the peninsula is pretty **Antibes**, with a harbour full of pleasure boats and an old town ringed by medieval

Castellar LIGURIA Roverino
e-Agnès Ventimiglia
bio Garavan Mortola
uebrune ⑦ **Menton**
Carnolès
⑥ **Roquebrune-**
Cap **Cap-Martin**
Martin
e d'Azur

LINK YOUR TRIP

8 **Essential France**
This trip makes a natural extension of our grand tour of France's unmissable sights.

10 **Atlantic to Med**
Cover the whole south of France by combining these coastal trips which intersect at Cannes and Nice.

ramparts. Aim to arrive before lunchtime, when the atmospheric **Marché Provençal** will still be in full swing, and then browse the nearby **Musée Picasso** (⏱04 92 90 54 20; www.antibes-juanlespins. com/culture/musee-picasso; Château Grimaldi, 4 rue des Cordiers; adult/concession €6/3; ⏰10am-6pm Tue-Sun mid-Jun–mid-Sep, 10am-noon & 2-6pm Tue-Sun mid-Sep–mid-Jun) to see a few of the artist's Antibes-themed works.

✕ 🛏 p172

The Drive ›› Brave the traffic on the D6007 and avoid signs to turn onto the A8 motorway: it's the D2 you want, so follow signs for Villeneuve-Loubet. When you reach the town, cross the river. You'll pass through a tunnel into the outskirts of Cagnes-sur-Mer;

now start following signs to St-Paul.

- - - - - - - - - -

TRIP HIGHLIGHT

❸ St-Paul de Vence

Once upon a time, hilltop St-Paul de Vence was just another village like countless others in Provence. But then the artists moved in: painters such as Marc Chagall and Pablo Picasso sought solitude here, painted the local scenery and traded canvases for room and board (this is how the **Colombe d'Or** (⏱04 93 32 80 02; www.la-colombe-dor .com; place de Gaulle; d €250-430; ⏰restaurant noon-2.30pm & 7.30-10.30pm late Dec-Oct; ❋ 🛜 🛏) hotel came by its stellar art collection).

It's now one of the Riviera's most exclusive locations, a haven for artists, film stars and celebrities, not to mention hordes of sightseers, many of whom are here to marvel at the incredible art collection at the **Fondation Maeght** (⏱04 93 32 81 63; www.fondation-maeght.com; 623 chemin des Gardettes; adult/child €15/10; ⏰10am-7pm Jul-Sep, to 6pm Oct-Jun). Created in 1964 by collectors Aimé and Merguerite Maeght, it boasts works by all the big 20th-century names – Miró sculptures, Chagall mosaics, Braque windows and canvases by Picasso, Matisse and others.

While you're here, it's worth taking a detour northwards to Vence, where the marvellous **Chapelle du Rosaire** (Rosary Chapel; ⏱04 93 58 03 26; 466 av Henri Matisse; adult/child €6/3; ⏰2-5.30pm Mon, Wed & Sat, 10-11.30am & 2-5.30pm Tue & Thu, closed mid-Nov–early Dec) was designed by an ailing Henri Matisse. He had a hand in everything here, from the stained-glass windows to the altar and candlesticks.

The Drive ›› Return the way you came, only this time follow the blue signs onto the A8 motorway to Nice. Take exit 50 for Promenade des Anglais, which will take you all 18km along the Baie des Anges. The views are great, but you'll hit nightmare traffic at rush hour.

DETOUR: CORNICHE DE L'ESTÉREL

Start: ❶ Cannes (p165)

West of Cannes, the winding coast road known as the **Corniche de l'Estérel** (sometimes known as the Corniche d'Or, the Golden Road) is well worth a side trip if you can spare the time. Opened in 1903 by the Touring Club de France, this twisting coast road is as much about driving pleasure as getting from A to B; it runs for 30 unforgettable coastal kilometres all the way to St-Raphael. En route you'll pass seaside villages, secluded coves (sandy, pebbled, nudist, cove-like, you name it) and the rocky red hills of the Massif de l'Estérel, dotted with gnarly oaks, juniper and wild thyme. Wherever you go, the blue Mediterranean shimmers alongside, tempting you to stop for just one more swim. It's too much to resist.

④ Nice

With its mix of real-city grit, old-world opulence and year-round sunshine, Nice is the undisputed capital of the Côte d'Azur. Sure, the traffic's horrendous and the beach is made entirely of pebbles (not a patch of sand in sight!), but that doesn't detract from its charms. It's a great base, with loads of hotels and restaurants, and character in every nook and cranny.

Start with a morning stroll (p200) through the huge food and flower markets on **cours Saleya**, then delve into the winding alleyways of the old town, **Vieux Nice**, with many backstreet restaurants where you can try local specialities such as *pissaladière* (onion tart topped with olives and anchovies) and *socca* (chickpea-flour pancake). Stop for an ice cream at famous Fenocchio (p172) – flavours include tomato, lavender, olive and fig – then spend the afternoon sunbathing on the beaches along the seafront **Promenade des Anglais** before catching an epic sunset.

If you have the time, the city has some great museums too – you'll need at least an afternoon to explore all of the modern masterpieces at the **Musée d'Art Moderne et d'Art Contemporain** (MAMAC;

04 97 13 42 01; www.mamac-nice.org; place Yves Klein; ⏰10am-6pm Tue-Sun).

✕ 🍴 p151, p172

The Drive » Head out of the city through Riquier on the D2564. You don't want the motorway – you want to hit bd Bischoffsheim, which becomes bd de l'Observatoire as it climbs up to the summit of Mont Gros. Take it all in, stop for the pancity views, then get ready to really drive. The next 12km are thrilling, twisting past the Parc Naturel Régional de la Grande Corniche. Pull over and make use of the picnic tables if you wish, or take a break for a hilly hike, then continue to La Turbie.

⑤ La Grande Corniche

Remember that sexy scene from Hitchcock's *To Catch A Thief*, when Grace Kelly and Cary Grant cruised the hills in a convertible, enjoying sparkling banter and searing blue Mediterranean views? Well you're about to tackle the very same drive – so don your shades, roll down the windows and hit the asphalt.

It's a roller coaster of a road, veering through hairpins and switchbacks as it heads into the hills above Nice. There are countless picnic spots and photo opportunities along the way, including the **Col d'Èze**, the road's highest point at 512m. Further on you'll pass the monumental Roman landmark known as the **Trophée des Alpes** (☎04 93 41 20 84; http://la-turbie. monuments-nationaux.fr; 18 av Albert Ier, La Turbie; adult/child

FRANCE **12** RIVIERA CROSSING

↱ ## DETOUR: BIOT

Start: ② Antibes & Juan-les-Pins (p165)

This 15th-century hilltop village was once an important pottery-manufacturing centre. The advent of metal containers brought an end to this, but Biot is still active in handicraft production, especially glassmaking. At the foot of the village, the **Verrerie de Biot** (☎04 93 65 03 00; www.verreriebiot.com; chemin des Combes; museum adult/child €3/1.50; ⏰9.30am-7.30pm Mon-Sat, 10.30am-1pm & 2.30-7.30pm Sun Apr-Sep, to 6pm Oct-Mar) produces bubbled glass by rolling molten glass into baking soda; bubbles from the chemical reaction are then trapped by a second layer of glass. You can watch skilled glass-blowers at work and browse the adjacent art galleries and shop. There are also guided tours (€6), during which you get the chance to try your hand at a spot of glass-blowing – and learn why it's probably best left to the professionals.

WHY THIS IS A GREAT TRIP
OLIVER BERRY, WRITER

If there were a top 10 of French road trips, this would have to figure near the top. It takes in most of the quintessential sights of the Côte d'Azur, from seaside cities to hilltop villages, and tackles the hairpin turns and hair-raising drops of the three clifftop roads known as the Corniches. The views are simply stunning – simply put, it's one of the world's must-do drives.

Top: St-Paul de Vence
Left: Èze
Right: Harbour, Cannes

€5.50/free; 9.30am-1pm & 2.30–6.30pm Tue–Sun mid May–mid-Sep, 10am-1.30pm & 2.30-5pm rest of year), a magnificent triumphal arch built to commemorate Augustus' victory over the last remaining Celtic-Ligurian tribes who had resisted conquest. The views from here are jaw-dropping, stretching all the way to Monaco and Italy beyond.

The Drive » Monte Carlo may sparkle and beckon below, but keep your eyes on the road; the principality will keep for another day. Stay on the D2564 to skirt Monaco for another amazing 10km, then turn right into the D52 to Roquebrune.

- - - - - - - - - -

⑥ Roquebrune-Cap-Martin

This village of two halves feels a world away from the glitz of nearby Monaco: the coastline around **Cap Martin** remains relatively unspoilt, as if Roquebrune had left its clock on medieval time. The historic half of the town, Roquebrune itself, sits 300m high on a pudding-shaped lump. It towers over the Cap, but they are, in fact, linked by innumerable, very steep steps.

The village is delightful, free of tack, and there are sensational views of the coast from the main village square, **place des Deux Frères**. Of all Roquebrune's steep streets, **rue Moncollet** –

with its arcaded passages and stairways carved out of rock – is the most impressive. Scurry upwards to find architect Le Corbusier's grave at the cemetery at the top of the village (in section J, and, yes, he did design his own tombstone).

The Drive » Continue along the D52 towards the coast, following promenade du Cap-Martin all the way along the seafront to Menton. You'll be there in 10 minutes, traffic permitting.

- - - - - - - - - - -

❼ Menton

Last stop on the coast before Italy, the beautiful seaside town of Menton offers a glimpse of what the Riviera once looked like, before the high rises, casinos and property developers moved in. It's ripe for wandering, with peaceful gardens and belle-èpoque mansions galore, as well as an attractive yacht-filled harbour. Meander the historic quarter all the way to the **Cimetière du Vieux Château** (montée du Souvenir; ⊗7am-8pm May-Sep, to 6pm Oct-Apr) for the best views in town.

Menton's miniature microclimate enables exotic plants to flourish here, many of which you can see at the **Jardin Botanique Exotique du Val Rahmeh** (⏾04 93 35 86 72; http://jardinvalrahmeh. free.fr; av St-Jacques; adult/child €6.50/5; ⊗10am-12.30pm & 3.30-6.30pm Wed-Mon May-Aug, 10am-12.30pm & 2-5pm Wed-Mon Sep-Apr), where terraces overflow with fruit trees, and the beautiful, once-abandoned **Jardin de la Serre de la Madone** (⏾04 93 57 73 90; www.serredelamadone. com; 74 rte de Gorbio; adult/child €8/4; ⊗10am-6pm Tue-Sun Apr-Oct, to 5pm Jan-Mar, closed Nov-Dec), overgrown with rare plants. The tourist office's garden website (www.jardins-menton.fr) has a list and opening times.

Spend your second night in town.

✕ 🛏 p173

PERFUME IN GRASSE

Up in the hills to the north of Nice, the town of Grasse has been synonymous with perfumery since the 16th century, and the town is still home to around 30 makers – several of which offer guided tours of their factories, and the chance to hone your olfactory skills.

It can take up to 10 years to train a *perfumier*, but since you probably don't have that much time to spare, you'll have to make do with a crash course. Renowned maker **Molinard** (⏾04 93 36 01 62; www.molinard.com; 60 bd Victor Hugo; 30min/1hr workshops €30/69; ⊗9.30am-6.30pm) runs workshops ranging from 30-minute sessions to two hours, during which you get to create your own custom perfume (sandalwood, vanilla, hyacinth, lily of the valley, civet, hare and rose petals are just a few of the potential notes you could include). At the end of the workshop, you'll receive a bottle of *eau de parfum* to take home. **Galimard** (⏾04 93 09 20 00; www.galimard.com; 73 rte de Cannes; workshops from €49; ⊗9am-12.30pm & 2-6pm) and **Fragonard's Usine Historique** (⏾04 93 36 44 65; www.fragonard.com; 20 bd Fragonard; ⊗9am-7pm Jul & Aug, 9am-12.30pm & 2-6pm Sep-Jun) offer similar workshops.

For background, it's also worth making time to visit the **Musée International de la Parfumerie** (MIP; ⏾04 97 05 58 11; www.museesdegrasse.com; 2 bd du Jeu de Ballon; adult/child €4/free; ⊗10am-7pm May-Sep, 10.30am-5.30pm Oct-Apr; 🚻) and its nearby **gardens** (⏾04 92 98 02 69; www.museesdegrasse.com; 979 chemin des Gourettes, Mouans-Sartoux; adult/child €4/free; ⊗10am-7pm May-Aug, 10am-5.30pm mid-Mar-Apr & Sep-mid-Nov, closed mid-Nov-mid-Mar), where you can see some of the many plants and flowers used in scent-making. Needless to say, the bouquet is overpowering.

The Drive » Leave Menton on the D6007, the Moyenne Corniche, skirting the upper perimeter of Monaco. When you're ready turn off into Monaco, take your pick of the car parks (they all charge the same rate, capped at €20 per day). Good options include the Chemin des Pêcheurs and Stade Louis II for old Monaco, or the huge underground Casino car park by allées des Boulingrins for central Monte Carlo.

- - - - - - - - - - -

⑧ Monaco

This pint-sized principality (covering barely 200 hectares) is ridiculous, absurd, ostentatious and fabulous all at once. A playground of the super-rich, with super-egos to match, it's the epitome of Riviera excess – especially at the famous **Casino de Monte Carlo**, where cards turn, roulette wheels spin and eye-watering sums are won and lost.

For all its glam, Monaco's not all show. Up in the hilltop quarter of **Le Rocher**, shady streets surround the **Grimaldi Palace**, the wedding-cake castle of Monaco's royal family (time your visit for the pomptastic changing of the guard at 11.55am). Nearby is the impressive **Musée Océanographique de Monaco**, stocked with all kinds of deep-sea denizens. It even has a 6m-deep lagoon complete with circling sharks.

Round things off with a stroll around the cliffside **Jardin Exotique** and the obligatory photo of Monaco's harbour, bristling with over-the-top yachts.

The Drive » Pick up where you left off on the Moyenne Corniche (D6007), and follow its circuitous route back up into the hills all the way to Èze.

- - - - - - - - - - -

TRIP HIGHLIGHT

⑨ Èze

This rocky little village perched on an impossible peak is the jewel in the Riviera crown. The main attraction is technically the medieval village, with small higgledy-piggledy stone houses and winding lanes (and, yes, galleries and shops).

It's undoubtedly delightful but it's the everpresent views of the coast that are truly mesmerising. They just get more spectacular from the **Jardin Exotique d'Èze** (☏ 04 93 41 10 30; adult/child €6/2.50; ⏰ 9am-7.30pm Jul-Sep, to 6.30pm Apr-May & Jun, to 5.30pm rest of year), a surreal cactus garden at the top of the village, so steep and rocky it may have been purpose-built for mountain goats. It's also where you'll find the old castle ruins; take time to sit, draw a deep breath and gaze, as few places on earth offer such a panorama.

Èze gets very crowded between 10am and 5pm; if you prefer a quiet wander, plan to be here early in the morning or before dinner. Or even better, treat yourself to a night and a slap-up supper at the swish **Château Eza**, a fitting finish to this most memorable of road trips.

🛏 p173

Eating & Sleeping

Cannes ❶

✖ Bobo Bistro　　　　Mediterranean €

(📞04 93 99 97 33; 21 rue du Commandant André; pizza €12-16, mains €15-20; ⊗ noon-3pm & 7-11pm Mon-Sat, 7-11pm Sun) Predictably, it's a 'bobo' (bourgeois bohemian) crowd that gathers at this achingly cool bistro in Cannes' fashionable Carré d'Or (Golden Sq). Decor is stylishly retro, with attention-grabbing *objets d'art* like a tableau of dozens of spindles of coloured yarn. Cuisine is local, seasonal and invariably organic: artichoke salad, tuna carpaccio with passion fruit, roasted cod with mash *fait masion* (homemade).

🛏 Hôtel Le Mistral　　　　Boutique Hotel €€

(📞04 93 39 91 46; www.mistral-hotel.com; 13 rue des Belges; s €89-109, d €99-129; ❄ 🛜) For super-pricey Cannes, this little 10-roomer is quite amazing value. Rooms are small but decked out in flattering red and plum tones – Privilege rooms have quite a bit more space, plus a fold-out sofa bed. There are sea views from the top floor, and the hotel is just 50m from La Croisette. There's no lift, though.

🛏 Villa Garbo　　　　Boutique Hotel €€€

(📞04 93 46 66 00; www.villagarbo-cannes.com; 62 bd d'Alsace; d from €230; ❄ @ 🛜) For a taste of Cannes' celeb lifestyle, this indulgent stunner is hard to beat. Rooms are more like apartments, offering copious space, plus kitchenettes, king-size beds, sofas and more. The style is designer chic – acid tones of puce, orange and lime contrasted with blacks and greys, supplemented by quirky sculptures and *objets d'art*. Unusually, rates include breakfast.

Antibes ❷

✖ La Badiane　　　　Fusion €

(📞04 93 34 45 41; 3 traverse du 24 Août; lunch menus €17-18.50, mains €13-15; ⊗ lunch Mon-Fri) This little side street behind Antibes' bus station has a clutch of great lunchtime restaurants, including this exotic Moroccan-tinged diner, which serves up yummy treats like chicken tagine, crispy *pastillas* (filled pastries) and spicy quiches. Shame it's only open for lunch on weekdays.

🛏 Hôtel La Jabotte　　　　B&B €€

(📞04 93 61 45 89; www.jabotte.com; 13 av Max Maurey; d from €120; ❄ @ 🛜) A couple of kilometres south of the old town on the coastal bd James Wyllie towards Cap d'Antibes, this pretty little hideaway makes a cosy base. Hot pinks, sunny yellows and soothing mauves dominate the homey, feminine decor, and there's a sweet patio where breakfast is served on sunny days. There's a minimum stay of three nights in summer.

Nice ❹

✖ Fenocchio　　　　Ice Cream €

(📞04 93 80 72 52; www.fenocchio.fr; 2 place Rossetti; 1/2 scoops €2.50/4; ⊗9am-midnight Feb-Oct) There's no shortage of ice-cream sellers in the old town, but this *maître glacier* (master ice-cream maker) has been king of the scoops since 1966. The array of flavours is mind-boggling – olive, tomato, fig, beer, lavender and violet are just a few to try. Dither too long over the 70-plus flavours and you'll never make it to the front of the queue. For a Niçois twist, ask for *tourte de blette* (a sweet chard tart with raisins, pine kernels and parmesan).

✕ Le Bistrot d'Antoine
Modern French €€

(☎04 93 85 29 57; 27 rue de la Prefecture; menus €25-43, mains €15-25; ⊗noon-2pm & 7-10pm Tue-Sat) A quintessential French bistro, right down to the checked tablecloths, streetside tables and impeccable service – not to mention the handwritten blackboard, loaded with classic dishes like rabbit pâté, pot-cooked pork, blood sausage and duck breast. If you've never eaten classic French food, this is definitely the place to start; and if you have, you're in for a treat.

🛏 Hôtel Le Genève
Hotel €€

(☎04 93 56 84 79; www.hotel-le-geneve-nice. com; 1 rue Cassini; r €135-169; ✱ 🛜) Situated just off place Garibaldi, this renovated corner hotel is bang in the middle of Nice's lively Petit Marais *quartier*. Bedrooms look sleek in cool greys, crimsons and charcoals; bathrooms are modern and well-appointed. Breakfast is served in the ground-floor cafe, brimful of vintage bric-a-brac and mismatched furniture. Bars and cafes abound here.

🛏 Hôtel Villa Rivoli
Boutique Hotel €€

(☎04 93 88 80 25; www.villa-rivoli.com; 10 rue de Rivoli; s €96, d €116-178, f €254; ✱ 🛜) This charming but strangely shaped villa dates back to 1890, and it's packed with period detail – gilded mirrors, fireplaces, cast-iron balconies and old-world wallpapers, as well as little conifer trees on the balconies and a sweeping marble staircase. Rooms are on the small side, and some are showing their age. There's a small garden and car park beside the hotel.

Menton ❼

✕ Le Cirke
Seafood €€

(☎04 89 74 20 54; www.restaurantlecirke. com; 1 square Victoria; menus lunch €26 & €29, dinner €30 & €45, mains €18-35; ⊗noon-1.30pm & 7.15-9.30pm Wed-Mon) From paella to bouillabaisse, grilled fish to fried calamari, this smart Italian-run restaurant is the place to turn to for delicious seafood. The wine list is a mix of Italian and French wines, and the service is as sunny as Menton itself.

🛏 Hôtel Napoléon
Boutique Hotel €€

(☎04 93 35 89 50; www.napoleon-menton.com; 29 porte de France; d €95-330; ✱ @ 🛜 ☰) Standing tall on the seafront, the Napoléon is Menton's most stylish sleeping option. Everything from the pool, the restaurant-bar and the back garden (a heaven of freshness in summer) has been beautifully designed. Rooms are decked out in white and blue, with Cocteau drawings on headboards. Sea-facing rooms have balconies but are a little noisier because of the traffic.

Èze ❾

🛏 Château Eza
Luxury Hotel €€€

(☎04 93 41 12 24; www.chateaueza.com; rue de la Pise; d from €360; ✱ 🛜) If you're looking for a place to propose, well, there can be few more memorable settings than this wonderful clifftop hotel, perched dramatically above the glittering blue Mediterranean. There are only 12 rooms, so it feels intimate, but the service is impeccable, and the regal decor (gilded mirrors, sumptuous fabrics, antiques) explains the sky-high price tag.

Champagne Taster

13

From musty cellars to vine-striped hillsides, this Champagne adventure whisks you through the heart of the region to explore the world's favourite celebratory tipple. It's time to quaff!

TRIP HIGHLIGHTS

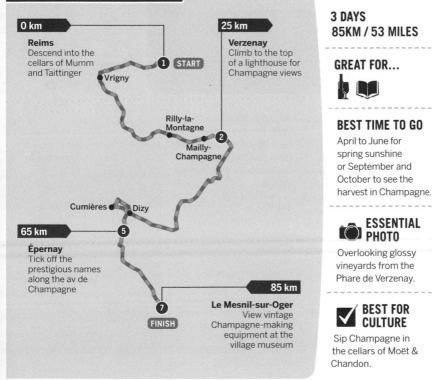

0 km

Reims
Descend into the cellars of Mumm and Taittinger

① START

Vrigny

25 km

Verzenay
Climb to the top of a lighthouse for Champagne views

Rilly-la-Montagne

②

Mailly-Champagne

Cumières ● ● Dizy

65 km

⑤

Épernay
Tick off the prestigious names along the av de Champagne

85 km

⑦

FINISH

Le Mesnil-sur-Oger
View vintage Champagne-making equipment at the village museum

**3 DAYS
85KM / 53 MILES**

GREAT FOR...

BEST TIME TO GO

April to June for spring sunshine or September and October to see the harvest in Champagne.

ESSENTIAL PHOTO

Overlooking glossy vineyards from the Phare de Verzenay.

BEST FOR CULTURE

Sip Champagne in the cellars of Moët & Chandon.

13 Champagne Taster

'My only regret in life is that I didn't drink enough Champagne,' wrote the economist John Maynard Keynes, but by the end of this tour, you'll have drunk enough bubbly to last several lifetimes. Starting and ending at the prestigious Champagne centres of Reims and Épernay, this fizz-fuelled trip includes stops at some of the world's most famous producers – with ample time for tasting en route.

- - - - - - - - - - - - - -

TRIP HIGHLIGHT

❶ Reims

There's nowhere better to start your Champagne tour than the regal city of **Reims**. Several big names have their *caves* (wine cellars) nearby. **Mumm** (☎03 26 49 59 70; www.mumm.com; 34 rue du Champ de Mars; tours incl tasting €20-45; ☺tours 9.30am-1pm & 2-6pm daily, shorter hours & closed Sun Oct-Mar), pronounced 'moom', is the only *maison* in central Reims. Founded in 1827, it's the world's third-largest Champagne producer. One-hour tours explore its enormous cellars, filled with 25 million bottles of bubbly, and include tastings of several vintages.

North of town, **Taittinger** (☎03 26 85 45 35; www.taittinger.com; 9 place St-Niçaise; tours €17-45; ☺9.30am-5.30pm, shorter hours & closed weekends Oct-Mar) provides an informative overview of how Champagne is actually made – you'll leave with a good understanding of the production process, from grape to bottle. Parts of the cellars

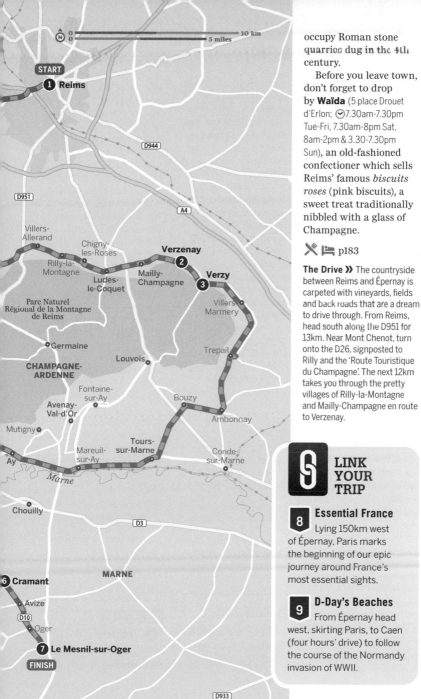

occupy Roman stone quarries dug in the 4th century.

Before you leave town, don't forget to drop by **Waïda** (5 place Drouet d'Erlon; ⏰7.30am-7.30pm Tue-Fri, 7.30am-8pm Sat, 8am-2pm & 3.30-7.30pm Sun), an old-fashioned confectioner which sells Reims' famous *biscuits roses* (pink biscuits), a sweet treat traditionally nibbled with a glass of Champagne.

✕ 🛏 p183

The Drive ≫ The countryside between Reims and Épernay is carpeted with vineyards, fields and back roads that are a dream to drive through. From Reims, head south along the D951 for 13km. Near Mont Chenot, turn onto the D26, signposted to Rilly and the 'Route Touristique du Champagne'. The next 12km takes you through the pretty villages of Rilly-la-Montagne and Mailly-Champagne en route to Verzenay.

LINK YOUR TRIP

8 **Essential France**
Lying 150km west of Épernay, Paris marks the beginning of our epic journey around France's most essential sights.

9 **D-Day's Beaches**
From Épernay head west, skirting Paris, to Caen (four hours' drive) to follow the course of the Normandy invasion of WWII.

TRIP HIGHLIGHT

❷ Verzenay

Reims marks the start of the 70km **Montagne de Reims Champagne Route**, the prettiest (and most prestigious) of the three signposted road routes that wind their way through the Champagne vineyards. Of the 17 *grand cru* villages in Champagne, nine lie on and around the Montagne, a hilly area whose sheltered slopes and chalky soils provide the perfect environment for viticulture (grape growing).

Most of the area's vineyards are devoted to the pinot noir grape. You'll pass plenty of producers offering *dégustation* (tasting) en route. It's up to you how many you choose to visit – but whatever you do, don't miss the panorama of vines seen from the top of the **Phare de Verzenay** (Verzenay Lighthouse; www. lepharedeverzenay.com; D26; lighthouse adult/child €3/2, museum €8/4, combined ticket €9/5; ☺10am-5pm Tue-Fri, to 5.30pm Sat & Sun, closed Jan), a lighthouse constructed as a publicity gimmick in 1909. Nearby, the **Jardin Panoramique** demonstrates the four authorised techniques for tying grapevines to guide wires.

The Drive ⟩⟩ Continue south along the D26 for 3km.

❸ Verzy

This village is home to several small vineyards that provide an interesting contrast to the big producers. **Étienne and Anne-Laure Lefevre** (☎03 26 97 96 99; www.champagne-etienne-lefevre.com; 30 rue de Villers; ☺9-11.30am & 1.30-5.30pm Mon-Sat) run group tours of their family-owned vineyards and cellars – if you're on your own, ring ahead to see if you can join a pre-arranged tour. There are no flashy videos or multimedia shows – the emphasis is firmly on the nitty-gritty of Champagne production.

For a glass of fizz high above the treetops, seek out the sleek **Perching Bar** (www.perchingbar. eu; Forêt de Brise-Charrette; ☺noon-2pm & 4-8pm Wed-Sun mid-Apr–mid-Dec) deep in the forest.

The Drive ⟩⟩ Stay on the D26 south of Verzy, and enjoy wide-open countryside views as you spin south to Ambonnay. Detour west onto the D19, signed to Bouzy, and bear right onto the D1 along the northern bank of the Marne River. When you reach the village of Dizy, follow signs onto the D386 to Hautvillers. It's a total drive of 32km or 45 minutes.

❹ Hautvillers

Next stop is the hilltop village of Hautvillers, a hallowed name among Champagne aficionados:

it's where a Benedictine monk by the name of Dom Pierre Pérignon is popularly believed to have created Champagne in the late 16th century. The great man's tomb lies in front of the altar of the **Église Abbatiale**.

The village itself is well worth a stroll, with a jumble of lanes, timbered houses and stone-walled vineyards. On place de la République, the **tourist office** (☎03 26 57 06 35; www.tourisme-hautvillers. com; place de la République; ☺9.30am-1pm & 1.30-5.30pm Mon-Sat, 10am-4pm Sun, shorter hours winter) hands out free maps detailing local vineyard walks; one-hour guided tours cost €3 (€5 with a tasting).

Steps away is **Au 36** (www.au36.net; 36 rue Dom Pérignon; ☺10.30am-6pm Tue-Sun, closed Christmas-early Mar), a wine boutique with a 'wall' of Champagne quirkily arranged by aroma. There's a tasting room upstairs; a two-/three-glass session costs €12/16.

The Drive ⟩⟩ From the centre of the village, take the rte de Cumières for grand views across the vine-cloaked slopes. Follow the road all the way to the D1, turn left and follow signs to Épernay's *centre-ville*, 6km to the south.

TRIP HIGHLIGHT

❺ Épernay

The prosperous town of **Épernay** is the self-proclaimed *capitale du champagne* and is home to many of the most illustrious Champagne houses. Beneath the streets are an astonishing 110km of subterranean cellars, containing an estimated 200 million bottles of vintage bubbly.

Most of the big names are arranged along the grand av de Champagne. **Moët & Chandon** (☎03 26 51 20 20; www.moet.com; 20 av de Champagne; adult incl 1/2 glasses €23/28, 10-18yr €10; ☺ tours 9.30-11.30am & 2-4.30pm Apr–mid-Nov, 9.30-11.30am & 2-4.30pm Mon-Fri mid-Nov–Mar) **offers**

frequent and fascinating one hour tours of its prestigious cellars, while at nearby **Mercier** (☎03 26 51 22 22; www.champagne mercier.fr; 68-70 av de Champagne; adult incl 1/2/3 glasses €14/19/22 Mon-Fri, €16/21/25 Sat & Sun, 12-17yr €8; ☺ tours 9.30-11.30am & 2-4.30pm, closed mid-Dec–mid-Feb)

CHAMPAGNE KNOW-HOW

Types of Champagne

» **Blanc de Blancs** Champagne made using only chardonnay grapes. Fresh and elegant, with very small bubbles and a bouquet reminiscent of 'yellow fruits' such as pear and plum.

» **Blanc de Noirs** A full-bodied, deep golden Champagne made solely with black grapes (despite the colour). Often rich and refined, with great complexity and a long finish.

» **Rosé** Pink Champagne (mostly served as an aperitif) with a fresh character and summer-fruit flavours. Made by adding a small percentage of red pinot noir to white Champagne.

» **Prestige Cuvée** The crème de la crème of Champagne. Usually made with grapes from Grand Cru vineyards and priced and bottled accordingly.

» **Millésimé Vintage** Champagne produced from a single crop during an exceptional year. Most Champagne is nonvintage.

Sweetness

» **Brut** Dry; most common style; pairs well with food.

» **Extra Sec** Fairly dry but sweeter than Brut; nice as an aperitif.

» **Demi Sec** Medium sweet; goes well with fruit and dessert.

» **Doux** Very sweet; a dessert Champagne.

Serving & Tasting

» **Chilling** Chill Champagne in a bucket of ice for 30 minutes before serving. The ideal serving temperature is 7°C to 9°C.

» **Opening** Grip the bottle securely and tilt it at a 45-degree angle facing away from you. Rotate the bottle slowly to ease out the cork – it should sigh, not pop.

» **Pouring** Hold the flute by the stem at an angle and let the Champagne trickle gently into the glass – less foam, more bubbles.

» **Tasting** Admire the colour and bubbles. Swirl your glass to release the aroma and inhale slowly before tasting the Champagne.

WHY THIS IS A GREAT TRIP
KERRY CHRISTIANI, WRITER

You can sip Champagne anywhere, but a road trip really slips under the skin of these Unesco-listed vineyards. Begin with an eye-opening, palate-awakening tour and tasting at *grande maison* cellars in Épernay and Reims. I love the far-reaching view from Phare de Verzenay and touring the back roads in search of small producers, especially when the aroma of new wine hangs in the air and the vines are golden in autumn.

Top: Fortress, Champagne
Left: Glasses of Champagne
Right: Marne River with Épernay in background

tours take place aboard a laser-guided underground train.

Serious quaffers might prefer the intimate tours at **Champagne Georges Cartier** (☏03 26 32 06 22; www.georgescartier.com; 9 rue Jean Chandon Moët; adult incl 1/2 glasses €12/16, 2-glass Grand Cru €22, 3-glass vintage €35; ☺tours 10.30am, noon, 2.30pm, 4pm Tue-Sun), whose warren of cellars and passageways, hewn out of the chalk in the 18th century, is incredibly atmospheric. Look out for the fascinating WWII graffiti. Tours are followed by a tasting of the *maison*'s Champagnes.

Finish with a climb up the 237-step tower at **De Castellane** (☏03 26 51 19 11; www.castellane.com; 57 rue de Verdun; adult incl 1 glass €14, under 12yr free; ☺tours 10am-11pm & 2-5pm, closed Christmas–mid Mar), which offers knockout views over the town's rooftops and vine-clad hills.

✕ ⮕ p183

The Drive ⟫ Head south of town along av Maréchal Foch or av du 8 Mai 1945, following 'Autres Directions' signs across the roundabouts until you see signs for Cramant. The village is 10km southeast of Épernay via the D10.

- - - - - - - - - -

6 Cramant
You'll find it hard to miss this quaint village, as the northern entrance is heralded

THE SCIENCE OF CHAMPAGNE

Champagne is made from the red pinot noir (38%), the black pinot meunier (35%) or the white chardonnay (27%) grape. Each vine is vigorously pruned and trained to produce a small quantity of high-quality grapes. Indeed, to maintain exclusivity (and price), the designated areas where grapes used for Champagne can be grown and the amount of wine produced each year are limited.

Making Champagne according to the *méthode champenoise* (traditional method) is a complex procedure. There are two fermentation processes, the first in casks and the second after the wine has been bottled and had sugar and yeast added. Bottles are then aged in cellars for two to five years, depending on the *cuvée* (vintage).

For two months in early spring the bottles are aged in cellars kept at 12°C and the wine turns effervescent. The sediment that forms in the bottle is removed by *remuage*, a painstakingly slow process in which each bottle, stored horizontally, is rotated slightly every day for weeks until the sludge works its way to the cork. Next comes *dégorgement:* the neck of the bottle is frozen, creating a blob of solidified Champagne and sediment, which is then removed.

by a two-storey-high Champagne bottle. From the ridge above the village, views stretch out in all directions across the Champagne countryside, taking in a patchwork of fields, farmhouses and rows upon rows of endless vines. Pack a picnic and your own bottle of bubbly for the perfect Champagne country lunch.

The Drive » Continue southeast along the D10 for 7km, and follow signs to Le-Mesnil-sur-Oger.

TRIP HIGHLIGHT

❼ Le Mesnil-sur-Oger

Finish with a visit to the excellent **Musée de la Vigne et du Vin** (🖉03 26 57 50 15; www.champagne-launois.fr; 2 av Eugène Guillaume, cnr D10; adult incl 3 flutes €12; ☺tours 10am Mon-Fri, 10.30am Sat & Sun), where a local wine-growing family has assembled a collection of century-old Champagne-making equipment. Among the highlights is a massive 16-tonne oak-beam grape

press dating to 1630. Reservations can be made by phone or online; ask about the availability of English tours when you book.

Round off your trip with lunch at **La Gare** (🖉03 26 51 59 55; www.lagarelemesnil.com; 3 place de la Gare; menus €18-26; ☺noon-1.30pm Mon-Wed, noon-1.30pm & 7-9pm Thu-Sat; 🖷), which prides itself on serving bistro-style grub prepared with seasonal produce, simple as pork tenderloin with cider and potatoes. There's a €9 menu for *les petits*.

Eating & Sleeping

Reims ❶

✕ Brasserie
Le Boulingrin   Brasserie €€

(☎03 26 40 96 22; www.boulingrin.fr; 29-31 rue de Mars; menus €20-29; ⊙noon-2.30pm & 7-10.30pm Mon-Sat) A genuine, old-time brasserie – the decor and zinc bar date back to 1925 – whose ambience and cuisine make it an enduring favourite. From September to June, the culinary focus is on *fruits de mer* (seafood) such as Breton oysters. There's always a €9.50 lunch special.

✕ l'Assiette
Champenoise   Gastronomy €€€

(☎03 26 84 64 64; www.assiettechampenoise. com; 40 av Paul-Vaillant-Couturier, Tinqueux; menus €95-255; ⊙noon-2pm & 7.30-10pm Thu-Mon, 7.30-10pm Wed) Heralded far and wide as one of Champagne's finest tables and crowned with the holy grail of three Michelin stars, L'Assiette Champenoise is headed up by chef Arnaud Lallemen. Listed by ingredients, his intricate, creative dishes rely on outstanding produce and play up integral flavours – be it Breton lobster, or milk-fed lamb with preserved vegetables. One for special occasions.

⇚ Les Telliers   B&B €€

(☎09 53 79 80 74; http://telliers.fr; 18 rue des Telliers; s €67-84, d €79-120, tr €116-141, q €132-162; [P][🛜]) Enticingly positioned down a quiet alley near the cathedral, this bijou B&B extends one of Reims' warmest *bienvenues*. The high-ceilinged rooms are big on art-deco character, and handsomely decorated with ornamental fireplaces, polished oak floors and the odd antique. Breakfast costs an extra €9 and is a generous spread of pastries, fruit, fresh-pressed juice and coffee.

Épernay ❺

✕ La Cave à
Champagne   Regional Cuisine €€

(☎03 26 55 50 70; www.la-cave-a-champagne. com; 16 rue Gambetta; menus €20-38; ⊙noon-2pm & 7-10pm Thu-Mon; [👪]) 'The Champagne Cellar' is well regarded by locals for its *champenoise* cuisine (snail-and-pig's-trotter casserole, fillet of beef in pinot noir), served in a warm, traditional, bourgeois atmosphere. You can sample four different Champagnes for €28.

✕ La Grillade
Gourmande   French €€

(☎03 26 55 44 22; www.lagrilladegourmande. com; 16 rue de Reims; menus €19-59; ⊙noon-2pm & 7.30-10pm Tue-Sat) This chic, red-walled bistro is an inviting spot to try chargrilled meats and dishes rich in texture and flavour, such as crayfish pan-fried in Champagne and lamb cooked in rosemary and honey until meltingly tender. Diners spill out onto the covered terrace in the warm months.

⇚ La Villa
Eugène   Boutique Hotel €€€

(☎03 26 32 44 76; www.villa-eugene.com; 84 av de Champagne; s €160-177, d €216-343, ste €380-398; [P][❄][🛜][🏊]) Sitting handsomely astride the av de Champagne in its own grounds with an outdoor pool, La Villa Eugène is a class act. It's lodged in a beautiful 19th-century town mansion that once belonged to the Mercier family. The roomy doubles exude understated elegance, with soft, muted hues and the odd antique. Splash out more for a private terrace or four-poster bed.

Châteaux of the Loire

14

For centuries, France's longest river has been a backdrop for royal intrigue and extravagant castles. This trip weaves nine of the Loire Valley's most spectacular and sublimely beautiful châteaux.

TRIP HIGHLIGHTS

189 km

Chambord
France's château superstar, a royal hunting lodge on steroids

120 km

Amboise
Charles VIII's Loire-side birthplace and Da Vinci's last home

Blois — **9** FINISH

6

Villandry — **5**

4

Chinon
START

Azay-le-Rideau
A Renaissance jewel on a lovely island

52 km

Chenonceaux
Wander a fairy-tale landscape of reflected arches and riverside gardens

107 km

5 DAYS
189KM / 118 MILES

GREAT FOR...

BEST TIME TO GO
May and June for good cycling weather; July for gardens and special events.

ESSENTIAL PHOTO
Château de Chenonceau's graceful arches reflected in the Cher River.

BEST TWO DAYS
The stretch between Chenonceau and Chambord takes in the true classics.

Chenonceaux Château de Chenonceau

14 Châteaux of the Loire

From warring medieval warlords to the kings and queens of Renaissance France, a parade of powerful men and women have left their mark on the Loire Valley. The result is France's most magnificent collection of castles. This itinerary visits nine of the Loire's most iconic châteaux, ranging from austere medieval fortresses to ostentatious royal pleasure palaces. Midway through, a side trip leads off the beaten track to four lesser-known châteaux.

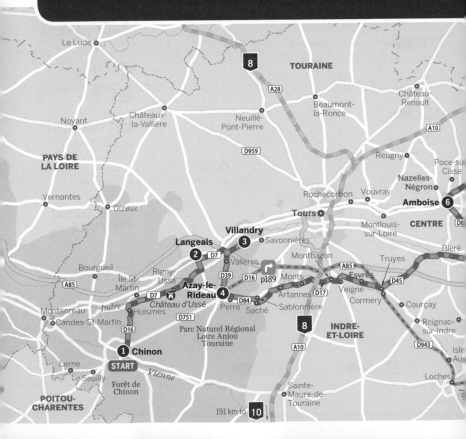

➊ Chinon

Tucked between the medieval **Forteresse Royale de Chinon** (☎02 47 93 13 45; www.forteressechinon. fr; adult/child €8.50/6.50; ⊙9.30am-7pm May-Aug, to 5pm or 6pm Sep-Apr) – a magnificent hilltop castle – and the Vienne River, Chinon is forever etched in France's collective memory as the venue of Joan of Arc's first meeting with Charles VII, future king of France, in 1429. Highlights include superb panoramas from the castle's ramparts and, down in the medieval part of town (along rue Voltaire), several fine buildings dating from the 15th to 17th centuries.

🛏 p193

The Drive » Follow the D16 north of Chinon for 10km, then head 15km east on the D7 past the fairy-tale Château d'Ussé (the inspiration for the fairy tale *Sleeping Beauty*) to Lignières, where you catch the D57 3km north into Langeais.

➋ Langeais

The most medieval of the Loire châteaux, the **Château de Langeais** (☎02 47 96 72 60; www. chateau-de-langeais.com; adult/child €9/5; ⊙9.30am-6.30pm Apr–mid-Nov, 10am-5pm mid-Nov–Mar) – built in the 1460s – is superbly preserved inside and out, looking much as it did at the tail end of the Middle Ages, with crenellated ramparts and massive towers dominating the surrounding village. Original 15th-century furniture and Flemish tapestries fill its flagstoned chambers. In one room, a life-size wax-figure tableau portrays the marriage of Charles VIII and Anne of Brittany, held here on 6 December 1491, which brought about the historic union of France and Brittany.

Langeais presents two faces to the world. From the town you see a fortified castle, nearly windowless, with machicolated

LOIRE ・ FINISH

20 km
10 miles

A10 — Blois ➐ — Huisseau-sur-Cosson — ➒ **Chambord** — D112 Domaine National de Chambord

Forêt de Blois

Forêt de Russy — Bracieux

Onzain — D952 — D765 — D102 Tour-en-Sologne

Cande-sur-Beuvron — ➑ **Cheverny**

D952 — Chaumont-sur-Loire

D952

LOIR-ET-CHER

Pontlevoy — ● Contres

Montrichard

➎ D176 — Monthou-sur-Cher — A85

henonceaux

uzille — *Cher* — St-Aignan — *Sauldre*

Montpoupon — D675

➟ p189

● Montrésor — ● Valençay

Nouans-les-Fontaines

➑ **Essential France**
From Chambord either head north for Versailles and Paris, or south for a longer trip taking in wine, the Alps and the Med.

➓ **Atlantic to Med**
Head south-east to La Rochelle (a little over 200km) to begin a leisurely meander from coast to coast.

LINK YOUR TRIP

FRANCE **14** CHÂTEAUX OF THE LOIRE

walls rising forbiddingly from the drawbridge. But the sections facing the courtyard have large windows, ornate dormers and decorative stonework designed for more refined living.

Behind the château is a ruined stone **keep** constructed in 994 by warlord Foulques Nerra, France's first great château builder. It is the oldest such structure in France.

✂ p193

The Drive » Backtrack south across the Loire River on the D57, then follow the riverbank east 10km on the D16 to Villandry.

➌ Villandry

The six glorious landscaped gardens at the **Château de Villandry** (📞02 47 50 02 09; www. chateauvillandry.com; 3 rue Principale; chateau & gardens adult/child €10.50/6.50, gardens only €6.50/4.50, audio-guides €4; ⏱9am-btwn 5pm & 7pm year-round, château interior closed mid-Nov–mid-Dec & early Jan-early Feb) are among the finest in France, with over 6 hectares of cascading flowers, ornamental vines, manicured lime trees, razor-sharp box hedges and tinkling fountains. Try to visit when the gardens are blooming, between April and October; midsummer is most spectacular.

Wandering the pebbled walkways, you'll see the classical **Jardin d'Eau** (Water Garden), the

Labyrinthe (Maze) and the **Jardin d'Ornement** (Ornamental Garden), which depicts various kinds of love (fickle, passionate, tender and tragic). But the highlight is the 16th-century-style **Jardin des Simples** (Kitchen Garden), where cabbages, leeks and carrots are laid out to create nine geometrical, colour-coordinated squares.

For bird's-eye views across the gardens and the nearby Loire and Cher Rivers, climb to the top of the **donjon** (keep), the only medieval remnant in this otherwise Renaissance-style château.

The Drive » Go southwest 4km on the D7, then turn south 7km on the D39 into Azay-le-Rideau.

TRIP HIGHLIGHT

➍ Azay-le-Rideau

Romantic, moat-ringed **Azay-le-Rideau** (📞02 47 45 42 04; www.azay-le-rideau. fr; adult/child €8.50/free. audioguide €4.50; ⏱9.30am-6pm Apr-Sep, to 7pm Jul & Aug, 10am-5.15pm Oct-Mar) is one of France's absolute gems, wonderfully adorned with elegant turrets, delicate stonework and steep slate roofs, and surrounded by a shady, landscaped park. Built in the 1500s, the château's most famous feature is its Italian-style **loggia staircase** overlooking the central courtyard, decorated with the royal salamanders and ermines of François I and Queen

Claude. The interior decor is mostly 19th century; the **Salon de Biencourt** was given historically coherent furnishings and comprehensively restored in 2016. The lovely English-style gardens were restored and partly replanted in 2015.

The Drive » Follow the D84 east 6km through the tranquil Indre valley, then cross the river south into Saché, home to an attractive château and Balzac museum. From Saché continue 26km east on the D17, 11km northeast on the D45 and 9km east on the D976. Cross north over the Cher River and follow the D40 east 1.5km to Chenonceaux village and the Château de Chenonceau.

TRIP HIGHLIGHT

➎ Chenonceaux

Spanning the languid Cher River atop a supremely graceful arched bridge, the **Château de Chenonceau** (📞02 47 23 90 07; www.chenonceau.com; adult/child €13/10, with audio-guide €17.50/14; ⏱9am-7pm or later Apr-Sep, to 5pm or 6pm Oct-Mar) is one of France's most elegant châteaux. It's hard not to be moved and exhilarated by the glorious setting, the formal gardens, the magic of the architecture and the château's fascinating history. The interior is decorated with rare furnishings and a fabulous art collection.

This extraordinary complex is largely the work of several remarkable women (hence its nickname, Le Château des Dames). The distinctive arches and the eastern formal garden were added by Diane de Poitiers, mistress of King Henri II. Following Henri's death, Catherine de Médicis, the king's scheming widow, forced Diane (her second cousin) to exchange Chenonceau for the rather less grand Château de Chaumont. Catherine completed the château's construction and added the yew-tree maze and the western rose garden. Chenonceau had an 18th-century heyday under the aristocratic Madame Dupin, who made it a centre of fashionable society; guests included Voltaire and Rousseau.

The château's pièce de résistance is the 60m-long, chequerboard-floored **Grande Gallerie** over the Cher. From 1940 to 1942 it served as an escape route for refugees fleeing from German-occupied France (north of the Cher) to the Vichy-controlled south.

The Drive › Follow the D81 north 13km into Amboise; 2km south of town, you'll pass the Mini-Châteaux theme park, whose intricate scale models of 44 Loire Valley châteaux are great fun for kids!

DETOUR: SOUTH OF THE LOIRE RIVER

Start: ❹ Azay-le-Rideau

Escape the crowds by detouring to four less-visited châteaux between Azay-le-Rideau and Chenonceaux.

First stop: **Loches**, where Joan of Arc, fresh from her victory at Orléans in 1429, famously persuaded Charles VII to march to Reims and claim the French crown. The undisputed highlight here is the **Cité Royale** (🖉02 47 59 01 32; www.chateau-loches.fr; ◷24hr), a vast citadel that spans 500 years of French château architecture in a single site, from Foulques Nerra's austere 10th-century **keep** to the Flamboyant Gothic and Renaissance styles of the **Logis Royal**. To get here from Azay-le-Rideau, head 55km east and then southeast along the D751, A85 and D943.

Next comes the quirky **Château de Montrésor** (🖉02 47 92 60 04; www.chateaudemontresor.fr; Montrésor; adult/child €8/4; ◷10am-7pm Apr–mid-Nov, 10am-6pm Sat & Sun mid-Nov–Mar), 19km east of Loches on the D760, still furnished much as it was over a century ago, when it belonged to Polish-born count, financier and railroad magnate Xavier Branicki. The eclectic decor includes a Cuban mahogany spiral staircase, a piano once played by Chopin and a treasury room filled with Turkish hookahs, plus other spoils from the 17th-century Battle of Vienna.

Next, head 20km north on the D10 and D764 to the **Château de Montpoupon** (🖉02 47 94 21 15; www.chateau-loire-montpoupon.com; adult/child €9/5; ◷10am-7pm Apr-Sep, shorter hours winter), idyllically situated in rolling countryside. Opposite the castle, grab lunch at the wonderful **Auberge de Montpoupon** (🖉02 47 59 01 18; www.chateau-loire-montpoupon.com; Céré-la-Ronde; mains €11.50-18.50; ◷lunch Tue-Sun, dinner Tue-Sat Apr-Oct).

Continue 12km north on the D764 to **Château de Montrichard**, another ruined 11th-century fortress constructed by Foulques Nerra. After visiting the château, picnic in the park by the Cher River or taste sparkling wines at **Caves Monmousseau** (🖉02 54 32 35 15; www.monmousseau.com; 71 route de Vierzon, Montrichard; ◷10am-12.30pm & 1.30-6pm Apr-Oct, 10am-noon & 2-5pm Mon-Sat Nov-Mar).

From Montrichard, head 10km west on the D176 and D40 to rejoin the main route at Chenonceaux.

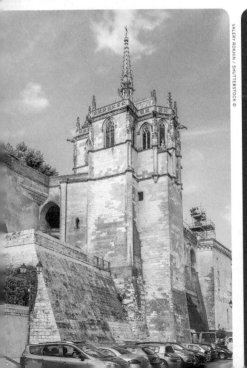

WHY THIS IS A GREAT TRIP
DANIEL ROBINSON, WRITER

Travel doesn't get more quintessentially French – or splendidly pampering – than this tour of the most famous Loire Valley châteaux, which brings together so many of the things I love most about France: supremely refined architecture, richly dramatic history, superb cuisine and delectable wines. My family especially enjoys the forbidding medieval fortresses of Langeais and Loches, which conjure up a long-lost world of knights, counts and court intrigue.

Top: Le Close Lucé
Left: Chapelle St-Hubert
Right: Château Royal d'Amboise

TRIP HIGHLIGHT

6 Amboise

Perched on a rocky escarpment above town, the **Château Royal d'Amboise** (☎02 47 57 00 98; www.chateau-amboise.com; place Michel Debré; adult/child €11.20/7.50, incl audioguide €15.20/10.50; ⏱9am-6pm or 7.30pm Mar–mid-Nov, 9am-12.30pm & 2-5.15pm mid-Nov–Feb) was a favoured retreat for all of France's Valois and Bourbon kings. The ramparts afford thrilling views of the town and river, and you can visit the furnished **Logis** (Lodge) and the Flamboyant Gothic **Chapelle St-Hubert** (1493), where Leonardo da Vinci's presumed remains have been buried since 1863.

Amboise's other main sight is **Le Clos Lucé** (☎02 47 57 00 73; www.vinci-closluce.com; 2 rue du Clos Lucé; adult/child €15/10.50; ⏱9am-7pm or 8pm Feb-Oct, 9am or 10am-5pm or 6pm Nov-Jan; 👶), the grand manor house where Leonardo da Vinci (1452–1519) took up residence in 1516 and spent the final years of his life at the invitation of François I. Already 64 by the time he arrived, Da Vinci spent his time sketching, tinkering and dreaming up ingenious contraptions. Fascinating models of his many inventions are on display inside the home and around its lovely 7-hectare gardens.

✕ 🛏 p193

The Drive » Follow D952 northeast along the Loire's northern bank, enjoying 35km of beautiful river views en route to Blois. The town of Chaumont-sur-Loire makes a pleasant stop for its imposing château and gardens.

- - - - - - - - - - - -

❼ Blois

Seven French kings lived in **Château Royal de Blois** (www.chateaudeblois.fr; place du Château; adult/child €10/5, audioguide €4/3; ☉9am-6pm or 7pm Apr-Oct, 9am-noon & 1.30-5.30pm Nov-Mar), whose four grand wings were built during four distinct periods in French architecture: Gothic (13th century), Flamboyant Gothic (1498–1501), early Renaissance (1515–20) and classical (1630s). You can easily spend half a day immersing yourself in the château's dramatic and bloody history and extraordinary architecture.

In the Renaissance wing, the most remarkable feature is the spiral **loggia staircase**, decorated with fierce salamanders and curly Fs, heraldic symbols of François I. The **King's Bedchamber** was the setting for one of the bloodiest episodes in the château's history. In 1588 Henri III had his arch-rival, Duke Henri I de Guise, murdered by royal bodyguards (the king is said to have hidden behind a tapestry while the deed was done). Dramatic and graphic oil paintings illustrate these events next door in the Council Room.

✖ p193

The Drive » Cross the Loire and head 16km southeast into Cheverny via the D765 and D102.

- - - - - - - - - - - -

❽ Cheverny

Perhaps the Loire's most elegantly proportioned château, **Cheverny** (www. chateau-cheverny.fr; av du Château; château & gardens adult/child €10.50/7.50; ☉9.15am-7pm Apr-Sep, 10am-5.30pm Oct-Mar) represents the zenith of French classical architecture: the perfect blend of symmetry, geometry and aesthetic order. Inside are some of the most sumptuous and elegantly furnished rooms anywhere in the Loire Valley. Highlights include the formal **Dining Room**, with panels depicting the story of Don Quixote; the **King's Bedchamber**, with ceiling murals and tapestries illustrating stories from Greek mythology; and a children's **playroom** complete with toys from the time of Napoléon III.

Cheverny's **kennels** house pedigreed hunting dogs; feeding time, known as **Soupe des Chiens**, takes place most days at 11.30am. Behind the château, the 18th-century **Orangerie**, which sheltered priceless artworks, including the *Mona Lisa*, during WWII, is now a warm-season tearoom.

Tintin fans may recognise the château's façade as the model for Captain Haddock's ancestral home, Marlinspike Hall.

🛏 p193

The Drive » Take the D102 10km northeast into Bracieux, then turn north on the D112 for the final 8km run through forested Domaine National de Chambord, the largest walled park in Europe. Catch your first dramatic glimpse of France's most famous château on the right as you arrive in Chambord.

- - - - - - - - - - - -

TRIP HIGHLIGHT

❾ Chambord

A crowning achievement of French Renaissance architecture, **Château de Chambord** (www.chambord. org; adult/child €11/9, parking €4-6; ☉9am-5pm or 6pm; 🚻) – with 440 rooms, 365 fireplaces and 84 staircases – is by far the largest, grandest and most visited château in the Loire Valley. Begun in 1519 by François I (r 1515–47) as a weekend hunting lodge, it quickly grew into one of the most ambitious and expensive architectural projects ever attempted by a French monarch.

Rising through the centre of the structure, the world-famous **double-helix staircase** – reputedly designed by Leonardo da Vinci – ascends to the great **lantern tower** and rooftop, where you can marvel at a skyline of cupolas, domes, turrets, chimneys and lightning rods and gaze out across the vast grounds.

Eating & Sleeping

Chinon ❶

🛏 Hôtel de France   Hotel €€

(☎02 47 93 33 91; www.bestwestern-hoteldefrance-chinon.com; 47 place du Général de Gaulle, aka place de la Fontaine; d €99-139, apt €175; ❄ 🛜) Run impeccably by the same couple since 1979, this Best Western–affiliated hotel, right in the centre of town, has 30 rooms arrayed around an inner courtyard. Tastefully decorated in a contemporary style, many have views of the château – as does the magnificent, flowery terrace on the roof. Offers enclosed bicycle parking. No lift.

Langeais ❷

✗ Au Coin des Halles   Bistro €€

(☎02 47 96 37 25; www.aucoindeshalles.com; 9 rue Gambetta; lunch menus €16.50, other menus €26-55; ☺12.15-2pm & 7.15-9pm Fri-Tue) Half a block from the entrance to the château, this elegant eatery is *mi-bistrot, mi-gastro* (half-bistro, half-gastronomic restaurant), serving delicious *cuisine du marché* (cuisine based on what's available fresh in the markets) grown and raised by local producers.

Amboise ❻

✗ La Fourchette   French €€

(☎06 11 78 16 98; 9 rue Malebranche; lunch/dinner menus €17/30; ☺noon-1.30pm Tue-Sat, 7-8.30pm Fri & Sat, plus Tue & Wed evenings summer) Hidden away in a back alley off rue Nationale, this is Amboise's favourite address for family-style French cooking – chef Christine will make you feel as though you've been invited to her house for lunch. The menu has just two entrées, two mains and two desserts. It's small, so reserve ahead.

Chinon (cont.)

🛏 Le Vieux Manoir   B&B €€

(☎02 47 30 41 27; www.le-vieux-manoir.com; 13 rue Rabelais; d incl breakfast €150-220, f €330, cottages €260-310; ☺late Mar-1 Nov; 🅿 ❄ 🛜) Set in a lovely walled garden, this restored mansion has oodles of old-time charm. The six rooms and two cottages, decorated with antiques, get lots of natural light, and owners Gloria and Bob (expat Americans who once ran an award-winning Boston B&B) are generous with their knowledge of the area.

Blois ❼

✗ L'Orangerie du Château   Gastronomy €€€

(☎02 54 78 05 36; www.orangerie-du-chateau.fr; 1 av Dr Jean Laigret; menus €38-84; ☺noon-1.45pm & 7-9.15pm Tue-Sat; 🅿) This Michelin-starred restaurant serves *cuisine gastronomique inventive* inspired by both French tradition and culinary ideas from faraway lands. The wine list comes on a tablet computer. For dessert try the speciality, soufflé.

Cheverny ❽

🛏 La Levraudière   B&B €

(☎02 54 79 81 99; www.lalevraudiere.fr; 1 chemin de la Levraudière; d incl breakfast €80, 5-person ste €150; 🛜) In a peaceful farmhouse from 1892, amid 3.5 hectares of grassland, La Levraudière's four rooms are comfortable and homey and come with king-size beds. Sonia Maurice, the friendly owner, speaks English and is happy to supply local cycling maps. Situated 2.5km south of the Château de Cheverny.

NEED ^{TO} KNOW

CURRENCY
Euro (€)

LANGUAGE
French

VISAS
Generally not required for stays of up to 90 days (or at all for EU nationals); some nationalities need a Schengen visa.

FUEL
Petrol stations are common around main towns and larger towns. Unleaded costs around €1.28 per litre; *gazole* (diesel) is usually at least €0.15 cheaper.

RENTAL CARS
ADA (www.ada.fr)

Auto Europe (www.autoeurope.com)

Avis (www.avis.com)

Europcar (www.europcar.com)

Hertz (www.hertz.com)

IMPORTANT NUMBERS
Ambulance (SAMU) ✆15

Police ✆17

Fire ✆18

Europe-wide emergency ✆112

Climate

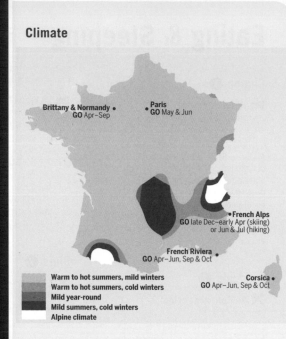

Brittany & Normandy •
GO Apr–Sep

• Paris
GO May & Jun

• French Alps
GO late Dec–early Apr (skiing)
or Jun & Jul (hiking)

French Riviera •
GO Apr–Jun, Sep & Oct

Corsica •
GO Apr–Jun, Sep & Oct

Warm to hot summers, mild winters
Warm to hot summers, cold winters
Mild year-round
Mild summers, cold winters
Alpine climate

When to Go

High Season (Jul & Aug)
» Queues at big sights and on the road, especially August.

» Christmas, New Year and Easter equally busy.

» Late December to March is high season in Alpine ski resorts.

» Book accommodation and tables in the best restaurants well in advance.

Shoulder (Apr–Jun & Sep)
» Accommodation rates drop in southern France and other hot spots.

» Spring brings warm weather, flowers and local produce.

» The *vendange* (grape harvest) is reason to visit in autumn.

Low Season (Oct–Mar)
» Prices up to 50% lower than high season.

» Sights, attractions and restaurants open fewer days and shorter hours.

» Hotels and restaurants in quieter rural regions (such as the Dordogne) are closed.

Your Daily Budget

Budget: less than €130
» Dorm bed: €18–30

» Double room in budget hotel: €90

» Admission to many attractions first Sunday of month: free

» Lunch *menus*: less than €20

Midrange: €130–220
» Double room in a midrange hotel: €90–190

» Lunch *menus* in gourmet restaurants: €20–40

Top end: more than €220
» Double room in a top-end hotel: €190–350

» Top restaurant dinner: *menu* €65, à la carte €100–150

Eating

Restaurants & bistros Range from traditional to contemporary minimalist; urban dining is international, rural dining staunchly French.

Brasseries Open from dawn until late, these casual eateries are great for dining in between standard meal times.

Cafes Ideal for breakfast and light lunch; many morph into bars after dark.

Price ranges refer to the average cost of a two-course meal:

€	less than €20
€€	€20–40
€€€	more than €40

Sleeping

B&Bs Enchanting properties with maximum five rooms.

Hostels New-wave hostels are design-driven, lifestyle spaces with single/double rooms as well as dorms.

Hotels Hotels embrace every budget and taste. Refuges and *gîtes d'étape* (walkers' lodges) for hikers can be found on trails in mountainous areas.

Price ranges refer to a double room in high season, with private bathroom, excluding breakfast:

€	less than €90
€€	€90–190
€€€	more than €190

Arriving in France

Aéroport de Charles de Gaulle (Paris)
Trains, buses and RER suburban trains run to the city centre every 15 to 30 minutes between 5am and 11pm; night buses kick in from 12.30am to 5.30am. Fares are €9.75 by RER, €6 to €17.50 by bus and €8 by night bus. Flat fare of €50/55 for 30-minute taxi journey to right-/left-bank central Paris (15% higher between 5pm and 10am, and Sundays).

Aéroport d'Orly (Paris)
Linked to central Paris by Orlyval rail then RER (€12.05) or bus (€7.50 to €12.50) every 15 minutes between 5am and 11pm. Or T7 tram to Villejuif-Louis Aragon then metro to the centre (€3.60). The 25-minute journey by taxi costs €35/30 to right-/left-bank central Paris (15% more from 5pm to 10am, and Sundays).

Mobile Phones

European and Australian phones work, but only American mobiles (cells) with 900 and 1800 MHz networks are compatible. Use a French SIM card with a French number to make cheaper calls.

Internet Access

Wi-fi is available at major airports, in most hotels, and at many cafes, restaurants, museums and tourist offices.

Money

ATMs at every airport, most train stations and on every second street corner in towns and cities. Visa, MasterCard and Amex widely accepted.

Tipping

By law, restaurant and bar prices are *service compris* (ie include a 15% service charge), so there's no need to leave a *pourboire* (tip).

Useful Websites

French Government Tourist Office (www.france.fr) Sights, activities, transport and special-interest holidays.

Lonely Planet (www. lonelyplanet.com/france) Travel tips, accommodation, forum and more.

Mappy (www.mappy.fr) Mapping and journey planning.

Opening Hours

Banks 9am–noon and 2–5pm Monday to Friday or Tuesday to Saturday

Restaurants noon–2.30pm and 7–11pm six days a week

Cafes 7am–11pm

Bars 7pm–1am

Shops 10am–noon and 2–7pm Monday to Saturday

Language

The sounds used in spoken French can almost all be found in English. There are a couple of exceptions: nasal vowels (represented in our pronunciation guides by o or u followed by an almost inaudible nasal consonant sound m, n or ng), the 'funny' u (ew in our guides) and the deep-in-the-throat r. Bearing these few points in mind and reading our pronunciation guides below as if they were English, you'll be understood just fine.

BASICS

Hello.	*Bonjour.*	bon·zhoor
Goodbye.	*Au revoir.*	o·rer·vwa
Yes./No.	*Oui./Non.*	wee/non
Excuse me.	*Excusez-moi.*	ek·skew·zay·mwa
Sorry.	*Pardon.*	par·don
Please.	*S'il vous plaît.*	seel voo play
Thank you.	*Merci.*	mair·see

You're welcome.
De rien.   der ree·en

Do you speak English?
Parlez-vous anglais?   par·lay·voo ong·glay

I don't understand.
Je ne comprends pas.   zher ner kom·pron pa

How much is this?
C'est combien?   say kom·byun

ACCOMMODATION

Do you have any rooms available?
Est-ce que vous avez   es·ker voo za·vay
des chambres libres?   day shom·brer lee·brer

How much is it per night/person?
Quel est le prix   kel ay ler pree
par nuit/personne?   par nwee/per·son

DIRECTIONS

Can you show me (on the map)?
Pouvez-vous m'indiquer   poo·vay·voo mun·dee·kay
(sur la carte)?   (sewr la kart)

Where's ...?
Où est ...?   oo ay ...

EATING & DRINKING

What would you recommend?
Qu'est-ce que vous   kes·ker voo
conseillez?   kon·say·yay

I'd like ..., please.
Je voudrais ...,   zher voo·dray ...
s'il vous plaît.   seel voo play

I'm a vegetarian.
Je suis végétarien/   zher swee vay·zhay·ta·ryun/
végétarienne. (m/f)   vay·zhay·ta·ryen

Please bring the bill.
Apportez-moi   a·por·tay·mwa
l'addition,   la·dee·syon
s'il vous plaît.   seel voo play

EMERGENCIES

Help!
Au secours!   o skoor

I'm lost.
Je suis   zhe swee·
perdu/perdue. (m/f)   pair·dew

Want More?

For in-depth language information and handy phrases, check out Lonely Planet's *French Phrasebook*. You'll find it at **shop.lonelyplanet.com**, or you can buy Lonely Planet's iPhone phrasebooks at the Apple App Store.

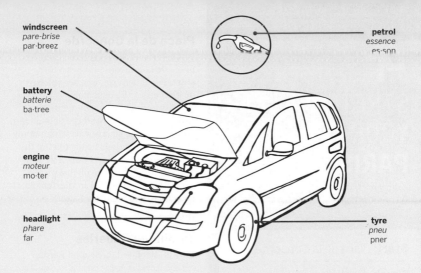

windscreen
pare-brise
par·breez

petrol
essence
es·son

battery
batterie
ba·tree

engine
moteur
mo·ter

headlight
phare
far

tyre
pneu
pner

Signs

Cédez la Priorité	Give Way
Sens Interdit	No Entry
Entrée	Entrance
Péage	Toll
Sens Unique	One Way
Sortie	Exit

I'm ill.
Je suis malade. zher swee ma·lad

Call the police!
Appelez la police! a·play la po·lees

Call a doctor!
Appelez un médecin! a·play un mayd·sun

ON THE ROAD

I'd like to hire a/an ...	*Je voudrais louer ...*	zher voo·dray loo·way ...
4WD	*un quatre-quatre*	un kat·kat
automatic/ manual	*une automatique/ manuel*	ewn o·to·ma·teek/ ma·nwel
motorbike	*une moto*	ewn mo·to

How much is it daily/weekly?
Quel est le tarif par jour/semaine? kel ay ler ta·reef par zhoor/ser·men

Does that include insurance?
Est-ce que l'assurance est comprise? es·ker la·sew·rons ay kom·preez

Does that include mileage?
Est-ce que le kilométrage est compris? es·ker ler kee·lo·may·trazh ay kom·pree

What's the speed limit?
Quelle est la vitesse maximale permise? kel ay la vee·tes mak·see·mal per·meez

Is this the road to ...?
C'est la route pour ...? say la root poor ...

Can I park here?
Est-ce que je peux stationner ici? es·ker zher per sta·syo·nay ee·see

Where's a service station?
Où est-ce qu'il y a une station-service? oo es·keel ya ewn sta·syon·ser·vees

Please fill it up.
Le plein, s'il vous plaît. ler plun seel voo play

I'd like (20) litres.
Je voudrais (vingt) litres. zher voo·dray (vung) lee·trer

Please check the oil/water.
Contrôlez l'huile/l'eau, s'il vous plaît. kon·tro·lay lweel/lo seel voo play

I need a mechanic.
J'ai besoin d'un mécanicien. zhay ber·zwun dun may·ka·nee·syun

The car/motorbike has broken down.
La voiture/moto est tombée en panne. la vwa·tewr/mo·to ay tom·bay on pan

I had an accident.
J'ai eu un accident. zhay ew un ak·see·don

197

STRETCH YOUR LEGS
PARIS

Start: Place de la Concorde

Finish: Panthéon

Distance: 4.5km

Duration: 3 hours

Paris is one of the world's most strollable cities, whether that means window-shopping on the boulevards or getting lost among the lanes of Montmartre. This walk starts by the Seine, crosses to the Île de la Cité and finishes in the Latin Quarter, with monuments and museums aplenty en route.

Take this walk on Trip

8

Place de la Concorde

If it's Parisian vistas you're after, the place de la Concorde makes a fine start. From here you can see the Arc de Triomphe, the Assemblée Nationale (the lower house of parliament), the Jardin des Tuileries and the Seine. Laid out in 1755, the square was where many aristocrats lost their heads during the Revolution, including Louis XVI and Marie Antoinette. The obelisk in the centre originally stood in the Temple of Ramses at Thebes (now Luxor).

The Walk » Walk east through Jardin des Tuileries.

Jardin des Tuileries

This 28-hectare landscaped **garden** (⊙7am-11pm Jun-Aug, shorter hours Sep-May; ⬧; Ⓜ Tuileries, Concorde) was laid out in 1664 by André Le Nôtre, who also created Versailles' gardens. Filled with fountains, ponds and sculptures, the gardens are now part of the Banks of the Seine World Heritage Site, created by Unesco in 1991.

The Walk » Walk across place du Carrousel onto the Cour Napoléon.

Musée du Louvre

Overlooking the Cour Napoléon is the mighty Louvre, with its controversial 21m-high glass **Grande Pyramide**, designed by IM Pei in 1989. Nearby is the **Pyramide Inversée** (Upside-Down Pyramid), which acts as a skylight for the underground Carrousel du Louvre shopping centre.

The Walk » Continue southeast along riverside Quai du Louvre to the Pont Neuf metro station.

Pont Neuf

As you cross the Seine, you'll walk over Paris' oldest bridge – ironically known as the 'New Bridge', or Pont Neuf. Henri IV inaugurated the bridge in 1607 by crossing it on a white stallion.

The Walk » Cross the Pont Neuf onto the Île de la Cité. Walk southeast along Quai des Horloges, and then turn right onto bd du Palais.

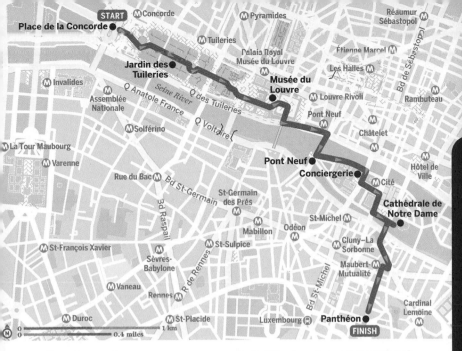

Conciergerie

On bd du Palais, elegant **Conciergerie**
(www.monuments-nationaux.fr; 2 bd du Palais,
1er; adult/child €8.50/free, joint ticket with
Sainte-Chapelle €15; ⏰9.30am-6pm; MCité)
is a royal palace that became a prison
and torture chamber for enemies of
the Revolution. The 14th-century Salle
des Gens d'Armes (Cavalrymen's Hall)
is Europe's largest surviving medieval
hall. The nearby church of **Sainte-
Chapelle** (joint ticket with Conciergerie €15)
has stunning stained glass.

The Walk ≫ Continue east along rue de Lutèce,
then cross place du Parvis Notre Dame and walk
towards the cathedral.

Cathédrale de Notre Dame

At the eastern end of Île de la Cité, show-
stopper **Notre Dame** (www.cathedraledeparis.
com; 6 place du Parvis Notre Dame, 4e; cathedral
free, towers adult/child €8.50/free; ⏰cathedral
8am-6.45pm Mon-Fri, to 7.15pm Sat & Sun; MCité)
is the heart of Paris – it's from here that
all distances in France are measured.

Built in stages between the 11th and
15th centuries, it's on a gargantuan scale;
the interior is 130m long, 48m wide and
35m high. Don't miss the three rose windows, the 7800-pipe organ and a walk up
the gargoyle-covered Gothic towers.

The Walk ≫ Cross the river on Pont au Double
and follow rue Lagrange to bd St-Germain. Then
take rue des Carmes and rue Valette south to the
place du Panthéon.

Panthéon

Once you reach the left bank you're in
the Latin Quarter, the centre of Parisian
higher education since the Middle Ages,
and home to the city's top university, the
Sorbonne. Here you'll find the **Panthéon**
(www.monum.fr; place du Panthéon, 5e; adult/
child €8.50/free; ⏰10am-6.30pm; MMaubert-
Mutualité or RER Luxembourg), the neoclassical mausoleum where some of France's
greatest thinkers are entombed, including Voltaire, Rousseau and Marie Curie.

The Walk ≫ Walk east to place Monge, take line
7 to Palais Royal Musée du Louvre, then line 1 west
to Concorde.

STRETCH YOUR LEGS
NICE

Start Hotel Negresco, Promenade des Anglais

Finish Promenade des Anglais

Distance 5.8km

Duration 2 hours

Get to know Nice's bustling heart with this walk that begins with a seaside stroll, then takes you into the tangled alleys of the old town, and finally up and over the city's soaring headland to the port. Along the way shop, eat and drink with the fun-loving Niçois.

Take this walk on Trips

[10] [12]

Promenade des Anglais

Nice personified, the Prom seductively blends hedonism with history, pumping beach clubs with quiet seaside gazing. English expats paid out-of-work citrus farmers to build the Prom in 1822 – a civic win-win. Don't miss the palatial facades of belle époque **Hôtel Negresco** and art deco **Palais de la Méditerranée**.

The Walk ›› Turn up av de Verdun past palms and posh shops to place Masséna. Take in the elegant Italian architecture, then head down the steps. Take rue de l'Opéra, a quick walk to our next stop.

Rue St-François de Paule

Window-shop, pick up snacks or shop for gifts on this elegant street just back from the seaside. First stop: **Moulin à Huile d'Olive Alziari** (www.alziari.com.fr; 14 rue St-François de Paule; ◷8.30am-12.30pm & 2.15-7pm Mon-Sat) for superb local olive oil, tapenade (olive spread) and olives. Head west to the florid **Opera House**; across the road is **Henri Auer Confiserie** (www.maison-auer.com; 7 rue St-François de Paule; ◷9am-6pm Tue-Sat), a film-set-perfect sweet shop; pick up *amandes enrobé* (cocoa-dredged chocolate-covered almonds).

The Walk ›› Continue on past soap sellers and wine bars and into the open square. This eventually becomes cours Saleya.

Cours Saleya

A top tourist destination that remains Niçois to the core, this bustling market square does different moods according to the hour. Greet the day with espresso and a banter with the produce and flower sellers, lunch with locals or get rowdy after dark with the town's cool kids and students.

The Walk ›› Any of the streets running away from the beach take you to rue de la Préfecture.

Vieux Nice

Soak in the labyrinthine streets of Nice's old town, stumbling upon Baroque gems like **Cathédrale Ste-Réparate** (place Rossetti). Stop to eat – book **Le Bistrot d'Antoine** (☎04 93 85 29 57; 27 rue de la Préfecture; menus €25-43,

mains €15-25; ⊘noon-2pm & 7-10pm Tue-Sat),
or grab an aperitif at **Les Distilleries
Idéales** (www.lesdistilleriesideales.fr; 24 rue
de la Préfecture; ⊘9am-12.30am) and snack
at **Lou Pilha Leva** (☑04 93 13 99 08; 10 rue
du Collet; small plates €3-5; ⊘9am-midnight;
✎). Grab a delicious ice-cream cone at
Fenocchio (www.fenocchio.fr; 2 place Rossetti;
1/2 scoops €2.50/4; ⊘9am-midnight Feb-Oct).

The Walk 》 Take the stairs at rue Rossetti, or
the lift at rue des Ponchettes to avoid the climb.

Colline du Château

On a rocky outcrop towering over Vieux
Nice, the **Parc du Château** (⊘8.30am-
8pm Apr-Sep, to 6pm Oct-Mar) offers a panorama of the whole city – Baie des Anges
on one side, the port on the other. Fabulous for picnics (there's a waterfall) or to
let the kids loose in the playground.

The Walk 》 Follow the path north through the
park towards the cemetery, then follow Allée
Font aux Oiseaux and the Montée du Château
back into the old town. Find your way along the
backstreets to bd Jean Jaurès, and cross the road
into Promenade du Paillon.

Promenade du Paillon

It's hard to imagine that this beautifully
landscaped park was once a bus station
and multi-storey car park. The park
unfolds from the Théâtre National to
place Masséna with a succession of green
spaces, play areas and water features,
and is now a favourite among Niçois for
afternoon or evening strolls. Local kids
love playing in the fountains, too.

The Walk 》 Follow the park as it heads
northeast and exit onto av St-Sébastien.

Musée d'Art Moderne et d'Art Contemporain (MAMAC)

Nice's flagship modern art **museum**
(www.mamac-nice.org; place Yves Klein;
⊘10am-6pm Tue-Sun) focuses is on European and American avant-garde from
the 1950s to the present, with works
by leading artists such as Niki de Saint
Phalle, César, Arman and Yves Klein.
The building's rooftop is also an exhibition space (with knockout panoramas
of the city). Then it's back to the Promenade des Anglais for a post-walk *pastis*.

Great Britain

GREAT BRITAIN OVERFLOWS WITH UNFORGETTABLE EXPERIENCES AND SPECTACULAR SIGHTS. There's the grandeur of Scotland's mountains, England's quaint villages and country lanes, and the haunting beauty of Welsh coast. You'll also find wild northern moors, the exquisite university colleges of Oxford and Cambridge, and a string of vibrant cities boasting everything from Georgian architecture to 21st-century art.

From the world famous to the well hidden, our trips will help you discover all the elements that make Britain truly great. History, cities, food, scenery, the arts – we've unearthed the best experiences and crafted them into superb drives.

Loch Ness Urquhart Castle
HIPPRODUCTIONS/SHUTTERSTOCK ©

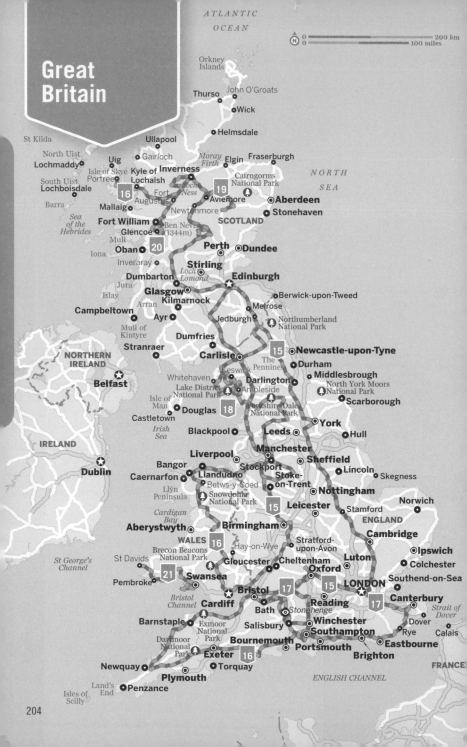

Great Britain

Bath

 DON'T MISS

Hardknott Pass & Wrynose Pass
Drive England's two steepest road routes, where gradients reach 30%, on Trip 18

Cairngorm Sled-Dog Centre
Hanging on for dear life as a team of huskies careers along forest trails (even when there's no snow), on Trip 19

Kinlochleven
Tackling the ladders and bridges of the 500m via ferrata climbing route, which weaves through the crags of Grey Mare's Tail, on Trip 20

Kidwelly Castle
The battlements of lesser-known Kidwelly prove particularly satisfying to clamber around on Trip 21

The Best of Britain

15

Swing through three countries and several millennia of history as you take in a greatest hits parade of Britain's chart-topping sights.

716 miles

Edinburgh
Delve into the tangle of alleyways around the Scottish capital's Royal Mile

0 miles

London
This electrifying metropolis is one of the world's great cities

284 miles

Cardiff
Visit the Welsh capital's castle, museums and sci-fi sights

Carlisle

York

Manchester

Cambridge

Oxford

Bath

Salisbury

Winchester

START/FINISH

21 DAYS
1128 MILES /
1815KM

GREAT FOR...

BEST TIME TO GO
Myriad festivals take place between May and September.

 ESSENTIAL PHOTO
Britain's biggest city spread below the London Eye.

BEST FOR HISTORY
Follow atmospheric footpaths through the world's largest stone circle at Avebury.

Edinburgh View of the city from Calton Hill

207

15 The Best of Britain

London's bright lights and blockbuster attractions bookend this epic expedition around the British mainland. In between, you'll encounter ancient sights, learn about fabled figures from King Arthur to Shakespeare, and visit masterpiece-filled museums and galleries and celebrated football stadiums – interleaved by quaint villages, patchworked farmland and glorious rolling green open countryside, along with the best of British drinking, dining and nightlife.

TRIP HIGHLIGHT

1 London

Gear up for your trip with at least a couple of days in Britain's most exhilarating city. Traversed by the serpentine River Thames, London is awash with instantly recognisable landmarks and open spaces, from **Trafalgar Square** (⊖Charing Cross) to the **London Eye** (☎0871 781 3000; www.londoneye. com; adult/child £21.20/16.10; ⊗10am-8pm, to 9.30pm in summer; ⊖Waterloo). Other unmissable sights incude:

Houses of Parliament (www.parliament.uk; Parliament Sq, SW1; ⊖Westminster), topped by the **Big Ben** clock tower.

Westminster Abbey (☎020-7222 5152; www. westminster-abbey.org; 20 Dean's Yard, SW1; adult/child £20/9, verger tours £5, cloister & gardens free; ⊗9.30am-4.30pm Mon, Tue, Thu & Fri, to 7pm Wed, to 2.30pm Sat; ⊖Westminster)

St James's Park (www. royalparks.org.uk; The Mall, SW1; deckchairs per hr/day £1.50/7; ⊗5am-midnight, deckchairs daylight hours

Mar–Oct; 🚇St James's Park or Green Park) **and Palace** (www.royal.gov.uk; Cleveland Row, SW1; 🚇Green Park)

Buckingham Palace

(📞020-7766 7300; www.royalcollection.org.uk; Buckingham Palace Rd, SW1; adult/child/under-5 £21.50/12.30/free; ⏲9.30am-7.30pm late Jul–Aug, to 6.30pm Sep; 🚇St James's Park, Victoria or Green Park)

Hyde Park (www.royalparks.org.uk/parks/hyde-park; ⏲5am-midnight; 🚇Marble Arch, Hyde Park Corner or Queensway)

Kensington Gardens

(www.royalparks.org.uk/parks/kensington-gardens; ⏲6am-dusk; 🚇Queensway or Lancaster Gate) **and Palace** (www.hrp.org.uk/kensingtonpalace; Kensington Gardens, W8; adult/child

LINK YOUR TRIP

19 Royal Highlands & Cairngorms

Take a detour mid-trip to to explore classic Scottish countryside: from Edinburgh head two hours north through Perthshire to the lovely village of Braemar.

18 Classic Lakes

Break up the long drive between Manchester and Edinburgh by turning west off the M6 onto the A590 to tour the charming Lake District.

£16.30/free; ⏰10am-6pm Mar-Oct, to 5pm Nov-Feb; ⊖High St Kensington)

World-leading, often-free museums and art galleries include the **Tate Modern** (www.tate.org.uk; Queen's Walk, SE1; ⏰10am-6pm Sun-Thu, to 10pm Fri & Sat; ♿; ⊖Blackfriars, Southwark or London Bridge) and the **British Museum** (📞020-7323 8299; www.british museum.org; Great Russell St, WC1; ⏰10am-5.30pm Sat-Thu, to 8.30pm Fri; ⊖Russell Sq or Tottenham Court Rd).

London's drinking, dining and nightlife options are limitless (Soho and Shoreditch make great starting points), as are its entertainment venues, not least grand theatre stages such as **Shakespeare's Globe** (📞020-7401 9919; www.shakespearesglobe. com; 21 New Globe Walk, SE1; seats £10-43, standing £5; ⊖Blackfriars or London Bridge).

🏃 p219

The Drive » Take the M40 northwest through High Wycombe and the Chilterns

AONB (Area of Outstanding Natural Beauty) to Oxford (59 miles in total).

- - - - - - - - - - - -

❷ Oxford

Oxford's elegant honey-toned buildings of the university's colleges, scattered throughout the city, wrap around tranquil courtyards and along narrow cobbled lanes. The oldest colleges date back to the 13th century and little has changed inside since, although there's a busy, lively world beyond the college walls. **Christ Church** (📞01865-276492; www.chch. ox.ac.uk; St Aldate's; adult/child £8/7; ⏰10am-4.15pm Mon-Sat, 2-4.15pm Sun) is the largest of all of Oxford's colleges, with the grandest quad. From the quad, you access 12th-century **Christ Church Cathedral** (📞01865-276150; www.chch. ox.ac.uk/cathedral; St Aldate's; admission free; ⏰10am-4.15pm Mon-Sat, 2-4.15pm Sun), originally the abbey church and then the college chapel, before it was

declared a cathedral by Henry VIII.

Other highlights include Oxford's **Bodleian Library** (📞01865-287400; www.bodleian.ox.ac.uk/bodley; Catte St; tours £6-14; ⏰9am-5pm Mon-Sat, 11am-5pm Sun), one of the oldest public libraries in the world, and Britain's oldest public museum, the 1683-established **Ashmolean Museum** (📞01865-278000; www.ashmolean.org; Beaumont St; ⏰10am-5pm Tue-Sun), second in repute only to London's British Museum.

The Drive » Head southwest on the A420 to Pusey and continue southwest on the B4508. You'll reach the car park for the White Horse 2.3 miles southwest of Uffington off the B4507, a 24-mile journey altogether.

- - - - - - - - - - - -

❸ Uffington White Horse

Just below Oxfordshire's highest point, the highly stylised **Uffington White Horse** (NT; www.national-trust.org.uk; White Horse Hill; ⏰dawn-dusk) image is the oldest chalk figure in Britain, dating from the Bronze Age. It was created around 3000 years ago by cutting trenches out of the hill and filling them with blocks of chalk; local inhabitants have maintained the figure for centuries. Perhaps it was planned for the gods: it's best seen from the air above. It's a half-mile walk east through

fields from the hillside
car park

The Drive » It's a 49-mile
trip to Winchester: return to
the B4507 and drive southeast
to Ashbury and take the
B4000 southeast to join the
southbound A34.

➍ Winchester

Set in a river valley,
this ancient cathedral
city was the capital of
Saxon kings and a power
base of bishops, and
evokes two of England's
mightiest myth-makers:
famous son Alfred the
Great (commemorated
by a **statue**) and King
Arthur (a 700-year-old
copy of the round table
resides in Winchester's
cavernous **Great Hall**
(📞01962-846476; www.
hants.gov.uk/greathall; Castle
Ave; suggested donation £3;
⏰10am-5pm), the only
part of 11th-century Win-
chester Castle that Oliver
Cromwell spared from
destruction).

Winchester's archi-
tecture is exquisite,
from the handsome
Elizabethan and Regency
buildings in the narrow
streets to the wondrous
Winchester Cathedral
(📞01962-857225; www.
winchester-cathedral.org.uk;
The Close; adult/child incl cathedral body & crypt tours £8/
free; ⏰9.30am-5pm Mon-Sat,
12.30-3pm Sun) at its core.
One of southern Eng-
land's most awe-inspiring
buildings, the 11th-
century cathedral has a
fine Gothic facade, one
of the longest medieval

naves in Europe (164m),
and highlights includ-
ing intricately carved
medieval choir stalls,
Jane Austen's grave
(near the entrance, in
the northern aisle) and
one of the UK's finest
illuminated manuscripts,
the dazzling, four-volume
Winchester Bible dating
from the 12th century.
Book ahead for excellent
tours of the ground floor,
crypt and tower.

The Drive » From Winchester,
hop on the B3049 then the A30
for the 26-mile drive west to
Salisbury.

➎ Salisbury

Salisbury has been an
important provincial city
for more than a thousand
years, and its streets form
an architectural timeline
ranging from medieval
walls and half-timbered
Tudor town houses to
Georgian mansions
and Victorian villas. Its
centrepiece is the majestic
13th-century **Salisbury
Cathedral** (📞01722-555120;
www.salisburycathedral.org.
uk; Cathedral Close; requested
donation adult/child £7.50/
none; ⏰9am-5pm Mon-
Sat, noon-4pm Sun). This
early English Gothic–style
structure has an elaborate
exterior decorated with
pointed arches and flying
buttresses, and is topped
by Britain's tallest spire at
123m, which was added
in the mid-14th century.
Beyond the cathedral's
highly decorative West
Front, a small passageway
leads into the 70m-long

nave. In the north aisle
look out for a fascinating
medieval clock dating
from 1386, probably the
oldest working timepiece
in the world. Don't miss
the cathedral's original,
13th-century copy of
the **Magna Carta** (www.
salisburycathedral.org.uk;
Cathedral Close; ⏰9.30am-
4.30pm Mon-Sat, noon-3.45pm
Sun) in the chapter house,
or a 90-minute tower tour
(adult/child £12.50/8; pre-
booking essential), which
sees you climbing 332
vertigo-inducing steps
to the base of the spire
for jaw-dropping views
across the city and the
surrounding countryside.

The Drive » It's just 9.6
miles northwest from Salisbury
via the A360 to otherworldly
Stonehenge.

➏ Stonehenge

Despite countless
theories about this site's
purpose, ranging from
a sacrificial centre to a
celestial timepiece, no
one knows for sure what
drove prehistoric Britons
to expend so much time
and effort constructing
Stonehenge (EH; 📞0370
333 1181; www.english-heritage.
org.uk; adult/child on-the-day
tickets £18/11, advance booking
£15.50/9.30; ⏰9am-8pm
Jun-Aug, 9.30am-7pm Apr, May
& Sep, 9.30am-5pm Oct-Mar;
🅿); it is one of Britain's
great archaeological mys-
teries. The first phase of
building started around
3000 BC, when the outer
circular bank and ditch
were erected. A thousand

WHY THIS IS A GREAT TRIP
CATHERINE LE NEVEZ, WRITER

A trip titled Best of Britain is bound to be a classic, but what seals it for me is its incredible sweep of history. From neolithic-era stone circles to a Bronze Age chalk figure, Roman baths, medieval walls and mighty cathedrals, wonky black-and-white Tudor towns, multilayered cityscapes and futuristic developments, every era of British endeavour is represented along this journey.

Top: Tower Bridge
Left: Stone circle, Avebury
Right: St James's Park, London

MARK THOMAS / GETTY IMAGES ©

years later, an inner circle of granite stones, known as bluestones, was added.

An ultramodern makeover has brought an impressive visitor centre and the closure of an intrusive road (now restored to grassland). The result is a far stronger sense of historical context; dignity and mystery returned to an archaeological gem. A pathway frames the ring of massive stones. Although you can't walk in the circle, unless on a recommended **Stone Circle Access Visit** (📞0370 333 0605; www.english-heritage.org.uk; adult/child £32/19), you can get close-up views. Admission is through timed tickets – secure a place well in advance.

The Drive » Drive east to Durrington and take the A345 north, climbing over the grassy Pewsey Downs National Nature Reserve (home to another chalk figure, the Alton Barnes White Horse, dating from 1812), to reach Avebury (24 miles in total).

- - - - - - - - - - - - -

❼ Avebury

With a diameter of 348m, **Avebury** (NT; 📞01672-539250; www.nationaltrust.org.uk; ⏰24hr; 🅿) is the largest stone circle in the world, and is also one of the oldest, dating from 2500 to 2200 BC. Though it lacks the dramatic trilithons of its sister site Stonehenge, the massive stone circle is at least as rewarding to visit. Today, more than 30 stones are in place (pillars show where missing stones would have been) and a large section of the village is actually inside the stones – footpaths wind around them, allowing you to really soak up the extraordinary atmosphere. National Trust–run guided walks (£3) take place most days.

📖 p219

The Drive ››› It's a 27-mile drive along the A4 past patchwork fields, country pubs and a smattering of villages to the Georgian streetscapes of Bath.

---

⑧ Bath

World Heritage–listed Bath was founded on top of natural hot springs and has been a tourist draw for some 2000 years. Its 18th-century heyday saw the construction of magnificent Georgian architecture from the 18th century. The best way to explore the city's Roman Baths complex and beautiful neoclassical buildings is on foot (p294).

Bath is known to many as a location in Jane Austen's novels, including *Persuasion* and *Northanger Abbey*. Although Austen lived in Bath for only five years, from 1801 to 1806, she remained a regular visitor and a keen student of the city's social scene. At the **Jane Austen Centre** (📞01225-443000; www.janeausten.co.uk; 40

Gay St; adult/child £11/5.50; ⏰9.45am-5.30pm Apr-Oct, 10am-4pm Nov-Mar), guides in Regency costumes regale you with Austen-esque tales as you tour memorabilia relating to the writer's life in Bath.

The Drive ››› It's 56.5 miles from Bath to the Welsh capital. Take the A46 north and join the westbound M4 over the Severn Estuary on the six-lane, cable-stayed Second Severn Crossing bridge (westbound bridge traffic incurs a £6.60 toll, payable by cash, debit card or credit card).

TRIP HIGHLIGHT

⑨ Cardiff

Set between an ancient fort and ultramodern waterfront, Cardiff has been the capital of Wales since only 1955, but has embraced the role with vigour and is now one of Britain's leading urban centres, as you can see on a stroll through its compact streets.

The huge success of the reinvented classic TV series *Doctor Who* has brought Cardiff to the attention of sci-fi fans worldwide. You can find yourself sucked through a crack in time and thrown into the role of the Doctor's companion at the interactive, highly entertaining **Doctor Who Experience** (📞0844 801 2279; www.doctorwhoexperience.com; Porth Teigr; adult/child £15/11; ⏰10am-5pm Jul & Aug, Tue-Sun Mar-Jun, Sep & Oct, Wed-Sun Nov-Feb, last admission 3.30pm daily) exhibition, located next

to the BBC studios where the series is filmed (look for the TARDIS outside).

If you time it right, you can catch a fired-up rugby test at Cardiff's **Principality Stadium** (Millennium Stadium; 📞029-2082 2432; www.principalitystadium.wales; Westgate St; tours adult/child £13/9).

📖 p219

The Drive ››› Take the A48 northeast for 32 miles, bypassing Newport, to riverside Chepstow.

---

⑩ Chepstow

Nestled in an S-bend in the River Wye, Chepstow (Welsh: Cas-gwent) was first developed as a base for the Norman conquest of southeast Wales, later prospering as a port for the timber and wine trades. As river-borne commerce gave way to the railways, Chepstow's importance diminished to reflect its name, which means 'market place' in Old English.

One of Britain's oldest castles, imposing **Chepstow Castle** (Cadw; www.cadw.gov.wales; Bridge St; adult/child £4.50/3.40; ⏰9.30am-5pm Mar-Oct, 10am-4pm Nov-Feb) perches atop a limestone cliff overhanging the river, guarding the main river crossing from England into South Wales. Building commenced in 1067, less than a year after William the Conqueror invaded England, and it was extended over the centuries. Today there are plenty of towers, battlements and wall walks to explore. A cave in the cliff below the castle is one of many places where legend says King Arthur and his knights are napping until the day they're needed to save Britain.

The Drive » Farmland makes up most of this 68-mile drive. Head northeast on the A48 along the River Severn to Gloucester then continue northeast on the A46 to Stratford-upon-Avon.

- - - - - - - - - - -

⓫ Stratford-upon-Avon

Experiences linked to the life of Stratford's fêted son William Shakespeare range from the touristy – medieval re-creations and Bard-themed tearooms – to the humbling, such as Shakespeare's modest grave in **Holy Trinity Church** (☏01789-266316; www.stratford-upon-avon.org; Old Town; Shakespeare's grave adult/child £2/1; ⏰8.30am-6pm Mon-Sat, 12.30-5pm Sun Apr-Sep, shorter hours Oct-Mar). There's also a sublime play by the **Royal Shakespeare Company** (RSC; ☏box office 01789-403493; www.rsc.org.uk; Waterside; tours adult £6.50-8.50, child £3-4.50, tower adult/child £2.50/1.25; ⏰tour times vary, tower 10am-6.15pm Sun-Fri 10am-12.15pm & 2-6.15pm Sat Apr-Sep, 10am-4.30pm Sun-Fri, 10am-12.15pm & 2-4.30pm Sat Oct-Mar).

One of the best ways to get a feel for the area's Tudor streets and willow-lined riverbanks is on foot.

Combination tickets are available for the three houses associated with Shakespeare in town – Shakespeare's Birthplace, Shakespeare's New Place and Hall's Croft. If you also visit the childhood home of Shakespeare's wife, **Anne Hathaway's Cottage** (☏01789-204016; www.shakespeare.org.uk; Cottage Lane, Shottery; adult/child £10.25/6.50; ⏰9am-5pm mid-Mar–Oct, closed Nov–mid-Mar), and his mother's farm, **Mary Arden's Farm** (☏01789-204016; www.shakespeare.org.uk; Station Rd, Wilmcote; adult/child £13.25/8.50; ⏰10am-5pm mid-Mar–Oct, closed Nov–mid-Mar), you can buy a combination ticket covering all five properties.

Don't miss a pint with the locals at Stratford's oldest and most atmospheric pub, the 1470-built **Old Thatch Tavern** (www.oldthatchtavernstratford.co.uk; Greenhill St; ⏰11.30am-11pm Mon-Sat, noon-6pm Sun; ☏).

The Drive » The fastest route from Stratford-upon-Avon to Manchester is to head northwest on Birmingham Rd and pick up the northbound M42, which becomes the M6. You'll see the hilly Peak District National Park to your east. It's a 116-mile journey; this stretch incurs road tolls totalling £3.

- - - - - - - - - - -

⓬ Manchester

A rich blend of history and culture is on show in this Northern Powerhouse's museums, galleries and innovative, multigenre art centres such as **HOME** (☏0161-200 1500;

BRITAIN'S BEST FESTIVALS

In London, see stunning blooms at the Royal Horticultural Society's **Chelsea Flower Show** (www.rhs.org.uk/chelsea; Royal Hospital Chelsea; admission from £23; ⏰May), military bands and bear-skinned grenadiers during the martial pageant **Trooping the Colour** (⏰Jun), or steel drums, dancers and outrageous costumes at the famous multicultural Caribbean-style street festival, **Notting Hill Carnival** (www.thenottinghillcarnival.com; ⏰Aug).

Wales' **National Eisteddfod** (☏08454-090900; www.eisteddfod.cymru; ⏰Aug) is descended from ancient Bardic tournaments. It's conducted in Welsh, but welcomes all entrants and visitors. It moves about each year, attracting some 150,000 visitors.

Edinburgh's most famous happenings are the **International Festival** (☏0131-473 2000; www.eif.co.uk) and **Fringe** (☏0131-226 0026; www.edfringe.com), but August also has an event for anything you care to name – books, art, theatre, music, comedy, marching bands... (www.edinburghfestivals.co.uk).

http://homemcr.org; 2 Tony Wilson Pl, First St; tickets £5-20; ☺ box office noon-8pm; bar 10am-11pm Mon-Thu & Sun, to midnight Fri & Sat).

The **Manchester Art Gallery** (☎0161-235 8888; http://manchesterartgallery. org; Mosley St; tours 20min/ 1hr free/£80; ☺10am-5pm Mon-Wed & Fri-Sun, to 9pm Thu) has a superb collection of British art and a hefty number of European masters. The older wing has an impressive selection that includes 37 Turner watercolours, as well as the country's best assemblage of Pre-Raphaelite art, while the newer gallery is home to 20th-century British art starring Lucien Freud, Francis Bacon, Stanley Spencer, Henry Moore and David Hockney. A wonderful collection of British watercolours are displayed at Manchester's **Whitworth Art Gallery** (☎0161-275 7450; www. whitworth.manchester.ac.uk; Oxford Rd, University of Manchester; ☺10am-5pm, to 9pm Thu; 🖳), which also has an exceptional collection of historic textiles.

Manchester is famed for its rival football teams **Manchester United** (☎0161-868 8000; www. manutd.com; Sir Matt Busby Way; tours adult/child £18/12; ☺ museum 9.30am-5pm, tours every 10min 9.40am-4.30pm except match days) and **Manchester City** (www. mcfc.co.uk; Etihad Campus), and its **National Football Museum** (☎0161-605 8200;

www.nationalfootballmuseum. com; Corporation St, Urbis, Cathedral Gardens; ☺10am-5pm) **FREE** charts British football's evolution.

The city is also world renowned for its live-music scene, with gigs in all genres most nights of the week.

🛏 p219

The Drive » This trip's longest drive, at 216 miles, takes you northwest via the M61 and M6, passing between the Yorkshire Dales National Park to the east and the Lake District National Park to the west. Once you cross into Scotland the road becomes the A74 and climbs into the Southern Uplands, then becomes the A702 as it leads into Edinburgh.

- - - - - - - - - - -

TRIP HIGHLIGHT

⑬ Edinburgh

The Scottish capital is intimately entwined with its landscape, with buildings and monuments perched atop crags and overshadowed by cliffs. From the Old Town's picturesque jumble of medieval tenements piled high along the Royal Mile, its turreted skyline strung between the black, bull-nosed Castle Rock and the russet palisade of Salisbury Crags, to the New Town's neat neoclassical grid, the city offers a constantly changing perspective.

Along with a walk through the Old Town, unmissable experiences here include visiting **Edinburgh Castle** (www.

MAREMAGNUM/GETTY IMAGES ©

edinburghcastle.gov.uk; Castle Esplanade; adult/child £16.50/9.90, audioguide additional £3.50; ☺9.30am-6pm Apr-Sep, to 5pm Oct-Mar, last admission 1hr before closing; 🖳23, 27, 41, 42), which has played a pivotal role in Scottish history, both as a royal residence – King Malcolm Canmore (r 1058–93) and Queen Margaret first made their home here in the

Cardiff Principality Stadium

11th century – and as a military stronghold; and climbing to the hilltop **Arthur's Seat** (Holyrood Park; 🚌6, 35) for city panoramas.

Edinburgh has 700-plus pubs, more per square mile than any other UK city. Sample a dram of Scottish whisky at icons like **Malt Shovel** (📞0131-225 6843; www.taylor-walker.co.uk; 11-15 Cockburn St; 🕐11am-11pm Sun-Thu, to 1am Fri & Sat; 🛜🚻; 🚌36, 41), with over 100 single malts behind the bar.

🛏 p219

The Drive » Drive southeast on the A68, passing through the Scottish Borders, and enter Northumberland National Park at the English border. Join the southbound A1 at Darlington, then take the eastbound A59 to York (191 miles altogether).

⑭ York

A magnificent ring of 13th-century walls encloses York's medieval narrow streets. At its heart lies the immense, awe-inspiring **York Minster** (www.yorkminster.org; Deangate; adult/child £10/free, incl tower £15/5; 🕐9am-5.30pm Mon-Sat, 12.45-5pm Sun, last admission 30min before closing). Built mainly between 1220 and 1480, it encompasses all the major stages of Gothic architectural development. The transepts (1220–55) were built in Early English style; the octagonal chapter house (1260–90) and nave (1291–1340) in the Decorated style; and the west towers, west front and central (or lantern) tower (1470–72) in Perpendicular style.

Don't miss a walk on York's City Walls, which follow the line of the original Roman walls and give a new perspective on the city. Allow 1½ to two hours for the full circuit of 4.5 miles.

York is considered England's most haunted city, from the ghosts of Roman soldiers marching through the **Treasurer's House** (NT; www.nationaltrust.org.uk; Chapter House St; adult/child £8/4; ☺11am-4.30pm Apr-Oct) to manifestations in pubs including the **Old White Swan** (www.nicholsonspubs.co.uk; 80 Goodramgate; ☺10am-midnight Sun-Thu, to 1am Fri & Sat); even shops like the **Antiques Centre** (www.theantiquescentreyork.co.uk; 41 Stonegate; ☺9am-5.30pm Mon-Sat, to 4pm Sun) are said to be haunted.

🛏 p219

The Drive ⟫ From York, it's 156 miles to Cambridge. Take the A64 southwest to join onto the A1 heading southeast.

- - - - - - - - - - - -

⑮ Cambridge

Surrounded by meadows, Cambridge is a university town extraordinaire, with a tightly packed core of ancient colleges and riverside 'Backs' (college gardens), which you can stroll around (p292).

The colossal neoclassical pile containing the **Fitzwilliam Museum** (www.fitzmuseum.cam.ac.uk; Trumpington St; donation requested; ☺10am-5pm Tue-Sat, noon-5pm Sun) was built to house the fabulous treasures that the seventh Viscount Fitzwilliam bequeathed to his old university. Standout exhibits include Roman and Egyptian grave goods, artworks by many of the great masters and some quirkier collections such as banknotes and literary autographs.

For the full Cambridge experience, rent a river boat from operators such as **Scudamore's Punting** (☎01223-359750; www.scudamores.com; Granta Place; chauffeured punt per 45 min per person £16-19, 6-person self-punt per hr £22-28; ☺9am-dusk).

🛏 p219

The Drive ⟫ Hop on the M11 for the 55-mile zip to London.

Eating & Sleeping

London ❶

🛏 Hoxton Hotel   Hotel ££

(☑020-7550 1000; www.hoxtonhotels.com; 81 Great Eastern St, EC2; r from £49; ✳ @ 🛜; ⊖Old St) In the heart of hip Shoreditch, this sleek hotel takes the easyJet approach to selling its rooms – book long enough ahead and you might pay just £49. The 210 renovated rooms are small but stylish, with flatscreen TVs, a desk, fridge with complimentary bottled water and milk, and breakfast (orange juice, granola, yoghurt, banana) in a bag delivered to your door.

Avebury ❼

🛏 Manor Farm   B&B ££

(☑01672-539294; www.manorfarmavebury. com; High St; s £70-80, d £90-100; P 🛜) A rare chance to sleep in style inside a stone circle – this red-brick farmhouse snuggles just inside Avebury henge. The elegant, comfy rooms blend old woods with bright furnishings, while the windows provide spine-tingling views of those 4000-year-old standing stones.

Cardiff ❾

🛏 Lincoln House   Hotel ££

(☑029-2039 5558; www.lincolnhotel.co.uk; 118 Cathedral Rd, Pontcanna; r £90-150; P 🛜) Walking a middle line between a large B&B and a small hotel, Lincoln House is a generously proportioned Victorian property with heraldic emblems in the stained-glass windows of its sitting room, and a separate bar. For added romance, book a four-poster room.

Manchester ❶❷

🛏 King Street Townhouse   Boutique Hotel £££

(☑0161-667 0707; www.eclectichotels. co.uk; 10 Booth St; r from £350, ste from £350; ✳ @ 🛜 ⛶) Arguably the city centre's finest lodgings is in this beautiful 1872 Italian renaissance-style former bank, now an exquisite boutique hotel with 40 bedrooms ranging from snug to suite. Furnishings are the perfect combination of period elegance and contemporary style. On the top floor is a small spa with an infinity pool overlooking the town hall; downstairs is a nice bar and restaurant.

Edinburgh ❶❸

🛏 Southside Guest House   B&B ££

(☑0131-668 4422; www.southsideguesthouse. co.uk; 8 Newington Rd; s/d from £80/105; 🛜; 🚌 all Newington buses) Though set in a typical Victorian terrace, the Southside transcends the traditional guest-house category and feels more like a modern boutique hotel. Its eight stylish rooms ooze interior design, standing out from other Newington B&Bs through the clever use of bold colours and modern furniture. Breakfast is an event, with Bucks fizz (cava mixed with orange juice) on offer to ease the hangover!

York ❶❹

🛏 Hedley House Hotel   Hotel ££

(☑01904-637404; www.hedleyhouse.com; 3 Bootham Tce; d/f from £105/115; P 🛜 ♿) This redbrick terrace-house hotel sports a variety of smartly refurbished, family-friendly accommodation, including rooms that sleep up to five, and some self-catering apartments – plus it has a sauna and spa bath on the outdoor terrace at the back, and is barely five minutes' walk from the city centre through the Museum Gardens.

Cambridge ❶❺

🛏 Worth House   B&B ££

(☑01223-316074; www.worth-house.co.uk; 152 Chesterton Rd; s £75-85, d £95-145; P 🛜) The welcome is wonderfully warm, the great-value rooms utterly delightful. Soft grey and cream meets candy-stripe reds, fancy bathrooms boast claw-foot baths and tea trays are full of treats. There's also a three-person, self-catering apartment (per week £550) two doors down.

Britain's Wild Side

16

Take a drive on the wild side on this tri-country trip through Britain's glorious national parks and protected Areas of Outstanding Natural Beauty.

TRIP HIGHLIGHTS

1290 miles

Cairngorms National Park
Explore Britain's biggest – and loftiest – national park

1007 miles

Kielder Water & Forest Park
Stargaze at state-of-the-art Kielder Observatory

432 miles

Brecon Beacons National Park
Discover the four completely different facets of the Brecon Beacons

21 DAYS
1435 MILES / 2310KM

GREAT FOR...

BEST TIME TO GO
June to September offers the best conditions for outdoor activities.

ESSENTIAL PHOTO
Cornwall's Bedruthan Steps at sunset.

BEST FOR WILDLIFE
Spot wild red deer, especially in autumn, at Exmoor National Park.

Cairngorms National Park River Spey, Aviemore

221

16 Britain's Wild Side

Leave the city lights behind on this adventure into Britain's natural heartland. On this intrepid trip you'll get up close to soaring mountain peaks, desolate moorland, sea-sprayed beaches, scalloped bays, lush hills, green dales, high, barren fells, and glassy lakes, all teeming with wildlife. Along the way, opportunities abound to get out and explore the breathtaking countryside on foot, bicycle, horseback and kayak.

❶ New Forest

With typical, accidental, English irony the New Forest is anything but new – it was first proclaimed a royal hunting preserve in 1079. It's also not much of a forest, being mostly heathland ('forest' is from the Old French for 'hunting ground'). For an overview of New Forest, which was designated a national park in 2005, stop by the **New Forest Museum** (www.newforestcentre.org. uk; main car park, Lyndhurst; ⊙10am-5pm Apr-Oct, to 4pm Nov-Mar). Wild ponies mooch around pretty scrubland, deer flicker in the distance and rare birds flit among the foliage. Genteel villages dot the landscape, connected by a web of walking and cycling trails. **Lyndhurst tourist office** (☏02380-282269; www.thenewforest. co.uk; main car park, Lyndhurst; ⊙10am-5pm Easter-Oct, to 4pm Nov-Easter) stocks maps and guides; they're also available from its website. New Forest is also a popular spot for horse riding; **Burley Villa**

(Western Riding: ☎01425-
610278; www.burleyvilla.
co.uk; near New Milton; per hr
from £35) organises rides
using traditional English
and also Western saddle
styles (per 90 minutes
£48).

🛏 p233

The Drive »» Take the A31
southwest to Weymouth
and Chesil Beach. Follow the
Jurassic Coast northwest along
the B3157 to Lyme Regis (81
miles in total).

----

❷ Lyme Regis

Fossils regularly emerge
from the unstable cliffs
surrounding Lyme Regis,
exposed by the landslides
of a retreating shoreline,
making this a key stop
along the Unesco-listed
Jurassic Coast.

For an overview, **Dino-
saurland** (☎01297-443541;
www.dinosaurland.co.uk;

§ **LINK
YOUR
TRIP**

17 **The Historic South**
Soak up some of
England's rich heritage
before starting your wild
trip – it's an hour and a
half south on the A34 from
Oxford to the New Forest.

20 **Great Glen**
Do this lake-and-
mountain themed ramble
through the Scottish
Highlands in reverse from
Inverness.

Coombe St; adult/child £5/4; ◷10am-5pm mid-Feb–mid-Oct) overflows with fossilised remains; look out for belemnites, a plesiosaurus and an impressive locally found ichthyosaur. Kids love the lifelike dinosaur models, rock-hard tyrannosaur eggs and 73kg dinosaur dung.

Three miles east of Lyme, the **Charmouth Heritage Coast Centre** (☏01297-560772; www.charmouth.org; Lower Sea Lane, Charmouth; ◷10.30am-4.30pm daily Easter-Oct, Thu-Sun Nov-Easter) runs one to seven fossil-hunting trips a week (adult/child £7.50/3). In Lyme itself, **Lyme Regis Museum** (☏01297-443370; www.lymeregismuseum.co.uk; Bridge St; adult/child £4/free; ◷10am-5pm Easter-Oct, 11am-4pm Wed-Sun Nov-Easter) organises three to seven walks a week (adult/child £11/6); local expert **Brandon Lennon** (☏07854 377519; www.lymeregisfossil walks.com; adult/child £8/6; ◷Sat-Mon) also leads expeditions. Book walks in advance.

The Drive » Drive west on the A3052 through the dazzling East Devon AONB (Area of Outstanding Natural Beauty) to Exeter and take the B3212 up into Postbridge, a small village in the middle of Dartmoor National Park (52 miles all up).

❸ Dartmoor National Park

Covering 368 sq miles, this vast **national park** (☏01626-834684; www.visitdartmoor.co.uk) feels like it's tumbled straight out of a Tolkien tome, with its honey-coloured heaths, moss-covered boulders, tinkling streams and eerie granite tors (hills).

On sunny days Dartmoor is idyllic: ponies wander and sheep graze beside the road, as seen in Steven Spielberg's WWI epic *War Horse*. But Dartmoor is also the setting for Sir Arthur Conan Doyle's *The Hound of the Baskervilles*, and in sleeting rain and swirling mists the moor morphs into a bleak wilderness where tales of a phantom hound seem very real. Be aware too that the military uses live ammunition in its training ranges (p225).

Dartmoor is a haven for outdoor activities, including hiking, cycling, riding, climbing and white-water kayaking; the **Dartmoor National Park Authority** (DNPA; www.dartmoor.gov.uk) has detailed information. And there are plenty of rustic pubs to cosy up in when the fog rolls in.

🛏 p233

The Drive » Head west through Tavistock to pass through the Tamar Valley, another AONB, on the A390. At Dobwalls, pick up the A38 and drive west along the forested River Fowey to join the southwest-bound A30. Take the Victoria turn-off and travel northwest past Newquay Cornwall Airport to the Bedruthan Steps (62 miles altogether).

❹ Bedruthan Steps

On Cornwall's surf-pounded coast loom the stately rock stacks of **Bedruthan** (Carnewas; NT; www.nationaltrust.org.uk/car newas-and-bedruthan-steps). These mighty granite pillars have been carved out by thousands of years of wind and waves, and the area is now owned by the National Trust. The beach itself is accessed via a steep staircase and is submerged at high tide. Towards the north end is a rocky shelf known as Diggory's Island, which separates the main beach from another little-known cove.

The Drive » Drive east to join the northeast-bound A39, which runs parallel to the Cornish coast, to the town of Lynmouth in Exmoor National Park (94 miles in total).

❺ Exmoor National Park

In the middle of Exmoor National Park is the higher moor, an empty, expansive, other-worldly landscape of tawny grasses and huge skies.

Exmoor supports one of England's largest wild red deer populations, best experienced in autumn when the annual 'rutting' season sees stags bellowing, charging at each other and clashing horns in an attempt to impress prospective mates. The Exmoor National Park Authority (ENPA; www.exmoor-nationalpark.gov.uk) runs regular wildlife-themed guided walks (free), which include evening deer-spotting hikes. Or head out on an organised jeep safari.

The open moors and a profusion of marked bridleways offer excellent hiking. Cycling is also popular here; **Exmoor Adventures** (☑07976-208279; www.exmoor adventures.co.uk) runs a five-hour mountain-biking skills course (£50) and also hires bikes (per day £25).

The Drive ≫ From Lynmouth to Libanus in the Brecon Beacons National Park it's 143 miles. Take the A39 east along the coast to join the M5 at Bridgwater. Take the Second Severn Crossing bridge (westbound bridge traffic incurs a £6.60 toll, payable by cash, debit card or credit card) and head west towards Cardiff to join the northwest-bound A470.

TRIP HIGHLIGHT

➏ Brecon Beacons National Park

Brecon Beacons National Park (Parc Cenedlaethol Bannau Brycheiniog) ripples for 45 miles from the English border to near Llandeilo in the west. High mountain plateaus of grass and heather, their northern rims scalloped with glacier-scoured hollows, rise above wooded, waterfall-splashed valleys and green, rural landscapes.

Within the park there are four distinct regions: the wild, lonely **Black Mountain** (Mynydd Du) in the west, with its high moors and glacial lakes; **Fforest Fawr** (Great Forest), whose rushing streams and spectacular waterfalls form the headwaters of the Rivers Tawe and Neath; the **Brecon Beacons** (Bannau Brycheiniog) proper, a group of very distinctive, flat-topped hills that includes Pen-y-Fan (886m),

the park's highest peak; and the rolling heath-land ridges of the **Black Mountains** (Y Mynyddoedd Duon) – not to be confused with the Black Mountain (singular) in the west. The park's main **visitor centre** (☑01874-623366; www.breconbeacons.org; Libanus; ⊙9.30am-5pm Easter-Sep) has details of walks, hiking and biking trails, outdoor activities, wildlife and geology (call first to check it's open).

🛏 p233

The Drive ≫ Drive north along the A470 to reach the southern boundary of Snowdonia National Park at Mallwyd (79 miles altogether).

➐ Snowdonia National Park

Wales' best-known and most-visited slice of nature, Snowdonia National Park (Parc Cenedlaethol Eryri) became the country's first national park in 1951. Every year more than 350,000 people walk, climb or

---

✓ **TOP TIP: WARNING: DARTMOOR MILITARY RANGES**

Live ammunition is used on Dartmoor's training ranges. Check locations with the **Firing Information Service** (☑0800 458 4868; www.mod.uk/access) or tourist offices. Red flags fly at the edges of in-use ranges by day; red flares burn at night. Beware unidentified metal objects lying in the grass. Don't touch anything; report finds to the **Commandant** (☑01837-650010).

WHY THIS IS A GREAT TRIP
CATHERINE LE NEVEZ, WRITER

For a relatively small island, Britain's landscapes have an astonishing diversity and this classic trip offers a taste, from wooded forests to windswept moors, and coastal cliffs to tranquil lakes, with opportunities all along the route for more in-depth exploration. Bring rain gear at any time of year as getting out into Britain's great outdoors invariably means encountering classic British weather.

Top: Sea kayaker, Skye
Left: Reindeer, Cairngorms National Park
Right: Isle of Anglesey

take the rack-and-pinion **railway** ([☎]01286 870223; www.snowdonrailway.co.uk; Llanberis; adult/child return diesel £29/20, steam £37/27; [🕑]9am-5pm mid-Mar–Nov) to the 1085m summit of Snowdon. The park's 823 sq miles embrace stunning coastline, forests, valleys, rivers, bird-filled estuaries and Wales' biggest natural lake. The **Snowdonia National Park Information Centre** ([☎]01690-710426; www.eryri-npa.gov.uk; Royal Oak Stables; [🕑]9.30am-5.30pm Easter-Oct, to 4pm rest of year) is an invaluable source of information about walking trails, mountain conditions and more.

The Drive » Continue north on the A470 and take the A5 northwest to Bangor. Cross Robert Stephenson's 1850-built Britannia Bridge over the Menai Strait and take the A545 northwest to Beaumaris (a 72-mile trip).

❽ Isle of Anglesey

The 276-sq-mile Isle of Anglesey (Ynys Môn) offers miles of inspiring coastline, hidden beaches and the country's greatest concentration of ancient sites.

Almost all of the Anglesey coast has been designated as an AONB (Area of Outstanding Natural Beauty). Beyond the handsome Georgian town of Beaumaris (Biwmares), there are hidden gems scattered all over the island. It's very much a living centre of Welsh culture, too, as you can see for yourself at **Oriel Ynys Môn** (📞01248-724444; www.orielynysmon.info; 🕙10.30am-5pm; **P**). A great, introductory day walk from Beaumaris takes in the ancient monastic site of **Penmon Priory** (Cadw; www.cadw.wales.gov.uk; Penmon; parking £2.50; 🕙10am-4pm; **P**), Penmon Point with views across to Puffin Island, and Blue Flag beach Llanddona.

🛏 p233

The Drive ≫ Return to the mainland and take the A55 northeast, crossing the border into England where the road becomes the M56. Continue northeast towards Manchester before turning off on the southeast-bound M6. At Sandbach turn east on the A534 and follow the signs to Leek, then take the A53 northeast before turning east towards Longnor then Bakewell (138 miles all-up).

9 Peak District National Park

Founded in 1951, the Peak District was England's first national park and is Europe's busiest. But even at peak times, there are 555 sq miles of open country-side in which to soak up the scenery. Caving and climbing, cycling and, above all, walking (including numerous short walks) are the most popular activities. The **Peak District National Park Authority** (📞01629-816200; www.peakdistrict.gov.uk; bicycle hire per half-day/day adult £14/17, child £10/12) has reams of information about the park and also operates several cycle-hire centres. The charming town of Bakewell also has a helpful **tourist office** (📞01629-816558; www.visitpeakdistrict.com; Bridge St; 🕙9.30am-5pm Apr-Oct, 10.30am-4.30pm Nov-Mar).

🛏 p233

TOP TIP: WALKING SAFETY TIPS

The British countryside can appear gentle, and often is, but conditions can deteriorate quickly. Year-round on the hills or open moors carry warm waterproof clothing, a map and compass, and high-energy food (eg chocolate) and drinks. If you're really going off the beaten track, leave your route details with someone.

The Drive ≫ From Bakewell take the A623 northwest towards Manchester and pick up the northbound M66, then at Burnley take the northeast-bound M65 to Skipton. Enter the Yorkshire Dales National Park on the B6265 to Grassington and head northwest on the B6160 to Aysgarth. Then take the A684 along the River Ure to Hawes (a total of 118 miles).

10 Yorkshire Dales National Park

Protected as a national park since the 1950s, the glacial valleys of the Yorkshire Dales (named from the old Norse word *dalr*, meaning 'valleys') are characterised by a distinctive landscape of high heather moorland, stepped skylines and flat-topped hills above valleys patchworked with drystone dykes and little barns. Hawes is home to the **Wensley-dale Creamery** (www.wensleydale.co.uk; adult/child £2.50/1.50; 🕙10am-4pm; **P** 🚻), producing famous Wensleydale cheese. In the limestone country of the southern Dales you'll encounter extraordinary examples of karst scenery (created by rainwater dissolving the underlying limestone bedrock).

The Drive ≫ Head southwest on the B6255 to Ingleton. Take the A65 northwest to Sizergh then the A590 southwest to the Lake District's southern reaches at Newby Bridge. Drive north along Lake Windermere before veering northwest to Hawkshead (53 miles all up).

Cornwall Bedruthan Steps

⑪ Lake District National Park

The Lake District (or Lakeland, as it's commonly known round these parts) is by far the UK's most popular national park. Ever since the Romantic poets arrived in the 19th century, its postcard panorama of craggy hilltops, mountain tarns and glittering lakes has stirred visitors' imaginations. It's awash with outdoor opportunities, from lake cruises to mountain walks.

Many people visit for the region's literary connections: among the many writers who found inspiration here are William Wordsworth, Samuel Taylor Coleridge, Arthur Ransome and, of course, Beatrix Potter, a lifelong lover of the Lakes, whose delightful former farmhouse, **Hill Top** (NT; ☎015394-36269; www.nationaltrust.org.uk/ hill-top; adult/child £10/5, admission to garden & shop free; ⊙ house 10am-5.30pm Mon-Thu, 10am-4.30pm Fri-Sun, garden 10am-5.45pm Mon-Thu, 10am-5pm Fri-Sun), inspired many of her tales including *Peter Rabbit*.

🛏 p233, p259

The Drive ≫ Drive northwest on the A591 to join the A595 to Carlisle. Then take the A689 and A69 northeast to Walltown along Hadrian's Wall (72 miles altogether).

⑫ Hadrian's Wall

Hadrian's Wall is one of Britain's most revealing and dramatic Roman ruins, its 2000-year-old procession of abandoned forts, garrisons, towers and milecastles marching across the wild and lonely landscape of northern England. This wall was about defence and control, but this edge-of-empire barrier also symbolised the

229

boundary of civilised order – to the north lay the unruly land of the marauding Celts, while to the south was the Roman world of orderly taxpaying, underfloor heating and bathrooms. There's an excellent visitor centre at **Walltown** (Northumberland National Park Visitor Centre; ☎01697-747151; www.northumberlandnational park.org.uk; Greenhead; ⏱10am-6pm Apr-Sep, to 5pm Oct, 10am-4pm Sat & Sun Nov-Mar). The finest sections of the wall run along the southern edge of remote Northumberland National Park.

The Drive ≫ Follow the B6318 northeast along Hadrian's Wall. Turn north on the B6320 to Bellingham. Continue northwest alongside the North Tyne river and Kielder Water lake to the village of Kielder (a 43-mile journey).

TRIP HIGHLIGHT

⑬ Kielder Water & Forest Park

Adjacent to Northumberland National Park, the Kielder Water & Forest Park is home to the vast artificial lake Kielder Water, holding 200,000 million litres. Surrounding its 27-mile-long shoreline is England's largest plantation forest, with 150 million spruce and pine trees. Kielder Water is a water-sports playground (and midge magnet; bring insect repellent), and also has walking and cycling as well as great birdwatching. Comprehensive information is available at www.visitkielder.com.

The lack of population here helped see the area awarded dark-sky status by the International Dark Skies Association in 2013 (the largest such designation in Europe), with controls to prevent light pollution. For the best views of the Northumberland International Dark Sky Park, attend a stargazing session at state-of-the-art, 2008-built **Kielder Observatory** (☎0191-265 5510; www.kielderobservatory.org; Black Fell, off Shilling Pot; public observing session adult/child £16.50/15; ⏱ by reservation). Book ahead and dress warmly as it's seriously chilly here at night.

The Drive ≫ It's a 139-mile drive from Kielder to Balloch on the southern shore of Loch Lomond. Head north into Scotland and join the A68 towards Edinburgh. Take the M8 to Glasgow and then the A82 northwest to Balloch.

⑭ Loch Lomond

Loch Lomond is mainland Britain's largest lake and, after Loch Ness, the most famous of Scotland's lochs. It's part of the **Loch Lomond & the Trossachs National Park** (www.lochlomond-trossachs.org), which became the heart of Scotland's first national park, created in 2002. The park extends over a huge area, from Balloch north to Tyndrum and Killin, and from Callander west to the forests of Cowal.

From Balloch, **Sweeney's Cruises** (☎01389-752376; www.sweeneyscruiseco.com; Balloch Rd) offers a range of trips including a one-hour return cruise to Inchmurrin (adult/child £10.20/7, five times

Kielder Water & Forest Park Mountain-biking through the forest

daily April to October, twice daily November to March), and a two-hour cruise (£18/10.20 twice daily May to September plus weekends April and October) around the islands. **CanYou Experience** (☎01389-756251; www.canyouexperience.com; Loch Lomond Shores; ☺10am-5.30pm Easter-Oct) also arranges boat trips and water- and land-based activities from various bases around Loch Lomond.

The Drive » Follow the A82 along Loch Lomond's western shoreline and pick up the northeast-bound A85 at Crianlarich. Then take the northwest-bound A9 to Aviemore (a total of 141 miles).

TRIP HIGHLIGHT

⑮ Cairngorms National Park

The vast Cairngorms National Park (www.cairngorms.co.uk) stretches from Aviemore in the north – with a handy **tourist office** (☎01479-810930;

OUTER HEBRIDES

If you're not ready to return to the mainland after visiting the Isle of Skye, consider a trip to the Outer Hebrides (aka the Western Isles; Na h-Eileanan an Iar in Gaelic) – a 130-mile-long string of islands west of Skye. More than a third of Scotland's registered crofts are here, and no less than 60% of the population are Gaelic speakers. With limited time, head straight for the west coast of Lewis with its prehistoric sites, preserved blackhouses, beautiful beaches, and arts and crafts studios – the **Lochmaddy Tourist Office** (☎01867-500321; Pier Rd; ☻10am-5pm Mon-Sat Apr-Oct) can provide a list. Ferries (car £30, driver and passenger £6.10 each) run once or twice daily from Uig on Skye to Lochmaddy (1¾ hours) and Tarbert (1½ hours).

www.visitaviemore.com; The Mall, Grampian Rd; ☻9am-5pm Mon-Sat, 10am-4pm Sun year-round, longer hrs Jul & Aug) – to the Angus Glens in the south, and from Dalwhinnie in the west to Ballater and Royal Deeside in the east.

The park encompasses the highest landmass in Britain – a broad mountain plateau, riven only by the deep valleys of the Lairig Ghru and Loch Avon, with an average altitude of over 1000m and including five of the six highest summits in the UK. This wild mountain landscape of granite and heather has a sub-Arctic climate and supports rare alpine tundra vegetation and high-altitude bird species, such as snow bunting, ptarmigan and dotterel.

Lower down, scenic glens are softened by beautiful open forests of native Scots pine, home to rare animals and birds such as pine martens, wildcats, red squirrels, ospreys, capercaillies and crossbills.

🛏 p233

The Drive » Take the A9 northwest to Inverness, then the southwest-bound A82 along Loch Ness (keeping an eye out for mythical beasts). At Invermoriston join the westbound A887, which becomes the A87, and continue to Kyle of Lochalsh where you'll cross the Skye Bridge to the Isle of Skye. Continue along the A87 to reach Portree (a 145-mile journey all up).

- - - - - - - - - -

⑯ **Isle of Skye**

The Isle of Skye (an t-Eilean Sgiathanach in Gaelic) takes its name from the old Norse *sky-a*, meaning 'cloud island', a Viking reference to the often-mist-enshrouded Cuillin Hills. It's a 50-mile-long patchwork of velvet moors, jagged mountains, sparkling lochs and towering sea cliffs. Lively Portree (Port Righ) has the island's only **tourist office** (☎01478-612992; www.visitscotland.com; Bayfield Rd; ☻9am-6pm Mon-Sat, 10am-4pm Sun Jun-Aug, shorter hours Sep-May; 🛜).

Skye offers some of the finest walking in Scotland, including some short, low-level routes. The sheltered coves and sea lochs around the coast of Skye provide magnificent sea-kayaking opportunities. **Skyak Adventures** (☎01471-820002; www.skyakadventures.com; 29 Lower Breakish, Breakish; 1-day course per person from £100) runs expeditions and courses for both beginners and experienced paddlers to otherwise inaccessible places.

Skye's stunning scenery is the main attraction, but when the mist closes in there are plenty of castles, crofting museums and cosy pubs and restaurants, along with dozens of art galleries and craft studios.

Eating & Sleeping

New Forest ❶

🛏 The Pig   Boutique Hotel £££
(📞0345 225 9494; www.thepighotel.co.uk;
Beaulieu Rd, Brockenhurst; r £175-265; 🅿 🛜)
One of the New Forest's classiest hotels remains
an utter delight: log baskets, croquet mallets and
ranks of guest gumboots give things a country-
house air; espresso machines and minilarders
lend bedrooms a luxury touch. The effortless
elegance makes it feel like you've just dropped by
a friend's (very stylish) rural retreat.

Dartmoor National Park ❸

🛏 Tor Royal Farm   B&B ££
(📞01822-890189; www.torroyal.co.uk; Tor
Royal Lane, near Princetown; s £60, d £80-100;
🅿 🛜) An easygoing, country cottage–styled
farmhouse packed with lived-in charm. The
rooms are rather old-fashioned – cream-and-
white furniture, puffy bedspreads, easy chairs
– but they're cosy, and the sumptuous afternoon
tea (£14) is reason to stay here alone.

Brecon Beacons National Park ❻

🛏 Peterstone Court   Hotel £££
(📞01874-665387; www.peterstone-court.com;
Llanhamlach; r from £150; 🅿 🛜 🏊) At this
elegant Georgian manor house, the rooms are
large and comfortable, and the views across the
valley to the Beacons are superb. The boutique
spa centre is a big drawcard. It also has an
excellent **restaurant** (breakfast £8-14, lunch
£15-17, dinner £14-21; ⏱7.30-9.30am & noon-
9.30pm). Llanhamlach is 3 miles southeast of
Brecon, just off the A40.

Isle of Anglesey ❽

🛏 Ye Olde Bulls Head
Inn & Townhouse   Hotel ££
(📞01248-810329; www.bullsheadinn.co.uk;
Castle St; d inn/townhouse from £90/110; 🛜)
These sister properties, located just across the
road from each other, provide quite a contrast.
Where the Bulls Head accommodation –
occupying the oldest pub in town – is historic
and elegant, the townhouse is contemporary,
high-tech and design driven. Breakfast for both
is served at the old inn.

Peak District National Park ❾

🛏 Melbourne House &
Easthorpe   B&B ££
(📞01629-815357; www.bakewell-
accommodation.co.uk; Buxton Rd; d from £70;
🅿 🛜) Occupying a picturesque, creeper-
covered building (Melbourne House) dating
back more than three centuries and a new annex
(Easthorpe), with uncluttered, neutral-toned
rooms, this inviting B&B is handily situated on
the main road leading to Buxton.

Lake District National Park ⓫

🛏 Summer Hill
Country House   Hotel ££
(📞015394-36180; www.summerhillcountry
house.com; Hawkshead Hill, d £102-122;
🅿 @ 🛜) On Hawkshead Hill, this 1700s house
has a wonderfully out-of-the-way setting, 3
miles from both Coniston and Hawkshead. The
five rooms vary in shape and size, but all feature
posh bath products and net-connected Mac
Minis for getting online or watching DVDs. The
garden boasts sculptures and a summerhouse
that belonged to John Ruskin.

Cairngorms National Park ⓯

🛏 Old Minister's House   B&B £££
(📞01479-812181; www.theoldministershouse.
co.uk; Ski Rd, Inverdruie; s/d £125/140; 🅿 🛜)
This former manse dates from 1906 and has
five rooms with a luxurious, country-house
atmosphere. It's in a lovely setting amid Scots
pines on the banks of the River Druie, southeast
of Aviemore.

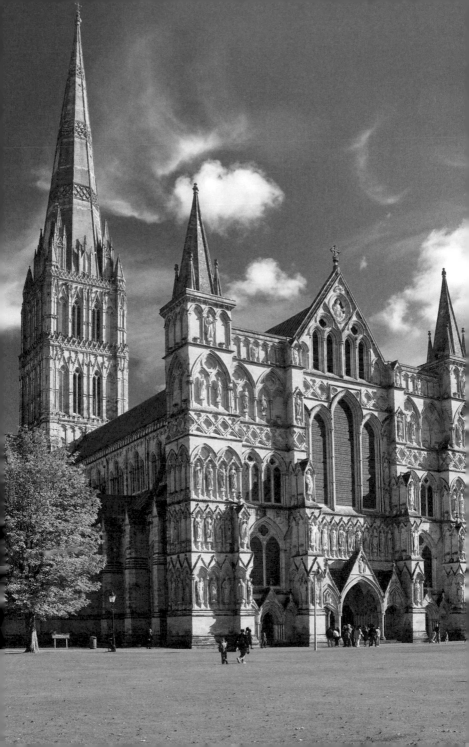

The Historic South

17

England's rich heritage runs like a glittering seam through this remarkable road trip. Discovering sights nautical, archaeological and architectural, you'll travel the ages as you clock up the miles.

TRIP HIGHLIGHTS

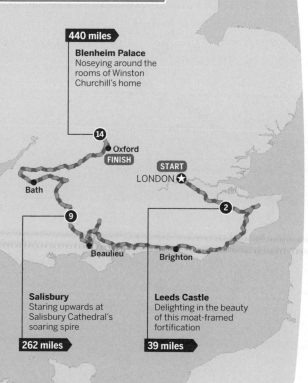

440 miles

Blenheim Palace
Noseying around the rooms of Winston Churchill's home

14

Oxford
FINISH

START
LONDON

Bath

9

2

Beaulieu

Brighton

Salisbury
Staring upwards at Salisbury Cathedral's soaring spire

262 miles

Leeds Castle
Delighting in the beauty of this moat-framed fortification

39 miles

9–11 DAYS
450 MILES / 720KM

GREAT FOR...

BEST TIME TO GO
Spring and autumn. Summer if you don't mind more crowds.

ESSENTIAL PHOTO
Lounging in a punt with a backdrop of Oxford's divine buildings.

BEST FOR SURPRISES
The world's biggest stone circle: Avebury (not Stonehenge).

Salisbury Cathedral A 13th-century building with the tallest spire in England

17 The Historic South

Stand by to tour some of the world's most beautiful castles and most memorable archaeological sites. Take in three of England's most impressive cathedrals, Georgian cityscapes, Churchill's palace and Oxford's spires. Discover guerilla art and this country's fine tradition of seaside kitsch. Motor to a motor museum, explore unspoiled villages and encounter 14th-century fellow travellers' tales. In short, take a road trip through the very best of Britain's past.

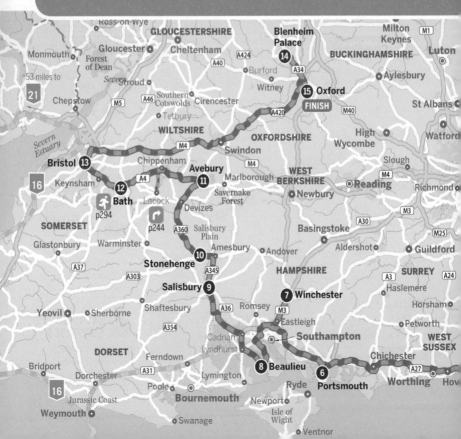

① London

Vibrant London is so packed with historic sights, where's best to start? In the capital's touchstone: **St Paul's** (☎020-7246 8350; www. stpauls.co.uk; St Paul's Churchyard, EC4; adult/child £18/8; ◷8.30am-4.30pm Mon-Sat; ⊖St Paul's). Designed by Sir Christopher Wren in 1675 after the Great Fire, its vast dome is famed for avoiding Luftwaffe raids during the Blitz. Head inside and up 257 steps to the walkway called the Whispering Gallery, then to the Golden Gallery at

the top for unforgettable London views. Next explore the city's rich past at the **Museum of London** (www.museumoflondon. org.uk; 150 London Wall, EC2; ◷10am-6pm; ⊖Barbican). Then head east to elegant Tower Bridge to learn in its **exhibition** (☎020-7403 3761; www.towerbridge.org.uk; Tower Bridge, SE1; adult/child £9/3.90, incl Monument £11/5; ◷10am-6pm Apr-Sep, 9.30am-5.30pm Oct-Mar, last admission 30min before closing; ⊖Tower Hill) just how they raise the arms – and the road – to let ships through.

🔖 p219

The Drive ⟫ London's streets and suburbs meet bursts of the Kent countryside; you're heading for the A20 towards Sidcup, then the M20 towards Dover. Shortly after Maidstone leave the motorway behind, picking up A20 signs for Lenham and then Leeds Castle, some 40 miles from the capital.

TRIP HIGHLIGHT

② Leeds Castle

Immense and moat-ringed, for many **Leeds Castle** (www.leeds-castle. com; adult/child £24.50/16.50; ◷10am-6pm Apr-Sep, to 5pm Oct-Mar) is one of the world's most romantic. The formidable, intricate structure balancing on two islands is known as something of a 'ladies castle'. This stems from the fact that in its more than 1000 years of history, it has been home to a who's who of medieval

LINK YOUR TRIP

21 **West Wales: Swansea to St Davids**

From Oxford, head west on the M4 to Swansea for the sweeping beaches and vast sand dunes of the Welsh coast.

16 **Britain's Wild Side**

It's an hour and a half south from Oxford to the New Forest to pick up this exploration of Britain's glorious national parks.

queens, most famously Henry VIII's first wife, Catherine of Aragon.

The Drive » Next up is a 25-mile cruise, high up over the vast chalk ridge of the North Downs. You're headed northeast, largely along the A252/A28 – the Canterbury Rd which echoes the old pilgrim footpath to the cathedral city.

---

❸ Canterbury

Canterbury tops the charts for English cathedral cities – and no wonder. Here medieval alleyways frame exquisite architecture, with **Canterbury Cathedral** (www.canterbury-cathedral.org; adult/concession £12/10.50, tours £5/4, audioguide £4/3; ⊙9am-5.30pm Mon-Sat, 12.30-2.30pm Sun) the centrepiece. This towering Gothic cathedral features fine stonework, a cavernous crypt and the site of English history's most famous murder: Archbishop Thomas Becket was killed here in 1170 after 'hints' from King Henry II, drawing

thousands of pilgrims for more than 800 years. The **Canterbury Tales** (www.canterburytales.org.uk; St Margaret's St; adult/child £9.75/7.50; ⊙10am-5pm Mar-Oct, to 4.30pm Nov-Feb) exhibition uses animatronics and audio guides to explore Chaucer's stories of these 14th-century travellers. For a taste of even older Canterbury, head to the mosaics of the **Roman Museum** (www.canterburymuseums.co.uk; Butchery Lane; adult/child £8/free; ⊙10am-5pm).

🛏 p245

The Drive » Now for a 35-mile drive. Head back up and over the North Downs on the A28 towards Ashford. Then plunge down to roll, along the A2070, through the verdant valley of the Weald of Kent. Soon you're edging the flat-lands of Romney Marsh and arriving at Rye.

---

❹ Rye

Welcome to one of England's prettiest towns. Here cobbled lanes, wonky Tudor buildings

and tales of smugglers abound. The best place to start stretching your legs is **Mermaid Street**. It bristles with 15th-century timber-framed houses with quirky names such as 'The House with Two Front Doors' and 'The House Opposite'. A short walk away the 13th-century **Ypres Tower** (www.ryemuseum.co.uk; Church Sq; adult/child £4/free; ⊙10.30am-5pm Apr-Oct, to 3.30pm Nov-Mar) affords views of Rye Bay, the marshes and sometimes France. The **Rye Heritage Centre** (☎01797-226696; www.ryeheritage.co.uk; Strand Quay; ⊙10am-5pm Apr-Oct, shorter hours Nov-Mar) offers themed walking tours.

The Drive » The next 50-mile leg sees you taking a string of A roads west. They lead past the woods and farms of the High Weald AONB up to another chalk ridge, this time the amphitheatre of hills that is the South Downs. Eventually, it's time to descend to Brighton on the shore.

---

❺ Brighton

Famously hedonistic, exuberant and home to the UK's biggest gay scene, Brighton rocks. The bright n' breezy seafront boasts the grand, century-old **Brighton Pier** (www.brightonpier.co.uk; Madeira Dr), complete with fairground rides, amusement arcades and candy floss stalls. Stroll inland to the magnificent **Royal Pavilion** (☎03000-290901; http://brightonmuseums.org.uk/royalpavilion; Royal

---

THE CANTERBURY TALES

The Canterbury Tales is the best-known work of English literature's father figure: Geoffrey Chaucer (1342–1400). Chaucer was the first English writer to introduce characters – rather than 'types' – into fiction. They feature strongly in *The Canterbury Tales*, an unfinished series of 24 vivid stories told by a party of pilgrims travelling between London and Canterbury. The text remains one of the pillars of the literary canon. But more than that, it's a collection of rollicking good yarns of adultery, debauchery, crime and edgy romance, and is filled with Chaucer's witty observations about human nature.

Pavilion Gardens; adult/child £12.30/6.90, ⊙9.30am 5.45pm Apr-Sep, 10am-5.15pm Oct-Mar), the glittering palace of Prince George (later King George IV). It's one of the most opulent buildings in England, and Europe's finest example of early-19th-century chinoiserie. Take in the Salvador Dalí sofa modelled on Mae West's lips at the **Brighton Museum & Art Gallery** (www.brighton-hove-museums.org.uk; Royal Pavilion Gardens; adult/child £5.20/3; ⊙10am-5pm Tue-Sun), then gear up for a lively night out by shopping amid the boutiques of the tightly packed **Brighton Lanes**.

🛏 p245

The Drive » Next is a 50-mile blast due west, largely along A roads, to the historic port of Portsmouth. As the 170m-high Spinnaker Tower gets closer on the horizon, pick up signs for the Historic Dockyard Car Park.

❻ Portsmouth

Portsmouth's blockbuster **Historic Dockyard** sees you gazing at the hulk of Henry VIII's flagship, the **Mary Rose** (www.maryrose. org; adult/child £18/13; ⊙10am-5.30pm Apr-Oct, to 5pm Nov-Mar), and jumping aboard **HMS Victory** (www.hms-victory.com; adult/child £18/13; ⊙10am-5.30pm Apr-Oct, to 5pm Nov-Mar) – the warship Nelson captained at the Battle of Trafalgar. Then there's the Victorian

🡒 **DETOUR: BEACHY HEAD**

Start: ❹ Rye

An 8-mile detour off your route leads to a truly remarkable view. Around 25 miles west of Rye, peel off the A27 onto the A22 to Eastbourne. Head to the seafront to take the signed route that climbs to **Beachy Head**. Pick a parking spot and follow the footpaths to the cliffs themselves. These 162m-tall sheer chalk faces are the highest point of cliffs that slice across the rugged coastline at the southern end of the South Downs. Far below sits a squat red-and-white-striped lighthouse. Appealing walks include the 1.5 mile hike west to the beach at Birling Gap.

HMS Warrior (www.hmswarrior.org; adult/child £18/13; ⊙10am 5.30pm Apr Oct, to 5pm Nov-Mar) and a wealth of imaginative, maritime-themed museums, along with waterborne **harbour tours** (☎02392-839766; www.historicdockyard.co.uk; adult/child £7/5; ⊙ hours vary). Round it all off with the WWII-era submarine **HMS Alliance** (www.submarine-museum.co.uk; Haslar Rd, Gosport; adult/child £14/10; ⊙10am-5.30pm Apr-Oct, 10am-4.30pm Wed-Sun Nov-Mar) or by strolling around the defences in the historic **Point district** and by climbing the sail-like **Spinnaker Tower** (☎02392-857520; www.spinnakertower.co.uk; Gunwharf Quays; adult/child £10/8; ⊙10am-6pm) for 23-mile views.

The Drive » Time to head inland; a 30-mile motorway cruise (the M27 then the M3) takes you to Winchester.

❼ Winchester

Calm, collegiate Winchester is a mellow must-see. One of southern England's most awe-inspiring buildings, 11th-century **Winchester Cathedral** (☎01962-857225; www.winchester-cathedral.org. uk; The Close; adult/child incl cathedral body & crypt tours £8/free; ⊙9.30am-5pm Mon-Sat, 12.30-3pm Sun) sits at its core. It boasts a fine Gothic facade, one of the longest medieval naves in Europe (164m) and intricately carved medieval choir stalls, sporting everything from mythical beasts to a mischievous green man. Jane Austen's grave is near the entrance, in the northern aisle. The fantastical crumbling remains of **Wolvesey Castle** (EH; ☎0370-333 1181; www.english-heritage.org. uk; College St; ⊙10am-5pm Apr-Oct) sit nearby, as

WHY THIS IS A GREAT TRIP

BELINDA DIXON, WRITER

For me, great trips need classic sights, and this journey delivers in spades. As well as the big-name attractions, you also get intriguing insights and some surprises: the stone circle preferred by purists; hip, hedonistic Brighton's seaside heritage; and some of this nautical nation's most important ships, the *Mary Rose*, HMS *Victory* and Brunel's pioneering SS *Great Britain*. If only history lessons at school had been this much fun.

Above: Traditional wooden punts, Oxford
Right: Blenheim Palace

does one of England's most prestigious private schools: **Winchester College** (☎01962-621209; www.winchestercollege.org; College St; adult/child £7/free; ⊙tours 10.15am, 11.30am, 2.15pm, 3.30pm Mon, Wed, Fri-Sun), which you can visit on a tour.

🛏 p245

The Drive ≫ Leave Winchester's ancient streets to take the motorways towards

OLGA_ANOURINA / GETTY IMAGES ©

VISITBRITAIN / BRITAIN ON VIEW / GETTY IMAGES ©

Southampton (initially the M3). After 14 miles turn off onto the A35 towards Lyndhurst. From here it's 9-miles to Beaulieu through the New Forest's increasingly wooded roads.

⑧ Beaulieu

The vintage car museum and stately home at **Beaulieu** (☏01590-612345; www.beaulieu.co.uk; adult/child £24/12; ☺10am-6pm Apr-Sep, to 5pm Oct-Mar) is centred on a 13th-century Cistercian monastery that fell to the ancestors of the current proprietors, the Montague family, after Henry VIII's 1536 monastic land-grab. Today its **motor museum** includes F1 cars and jet-powered land-speed record-breakers and wheels driven by James Bond and Mr Bean. The **palace** began life as a 14th-century Gothic abbey gatehouse, and received a 19th-century Scottish makeover in the 1860s.

The Drive ⟫ The SatNav wants to start this 28-mile leg by routing you onto the A326. Resist! Opt for the A and B roads that wind through the villages of Lyndhurst, Cadnam, Brook and North Charford, revealing the New Forest's enchanting blend of woods and open heath. Eventually join the A338 to Salisbury.

most famous stone circle will soon pop into view. The entry to the site is just beyond.

⑨ Salisbury

Salisbury's skyline is dominated by the tallest spire in England, which soars from its central, majestic 13th-century **cathedral** (☎01722-555120; www.salisburycathedral.org.uk; Cathedral Close; requested donation adult/child £7.50/none; ⏰9am-5pm Mon-Sat, noon-4pm Sun). This early English Gothic–style structure's elaborate exterior is decorated with pointed arches and flying buttresses, while its statuary and tombs are outstanding. Don't miss the daily **tower tours** and the cathedral's original, 13th-century copy of the **Magna Carta** (⏰9.30am-4.30pm Mon-Sat, noon-3.45pm Sun). The surrounding **Cathedral Close** has a hushed, other-worldly feel. Nearby, the hugely important finds at **Salisbury Museum** (☎01722-332151; www.salisburymuseum.org.uk; 65 Cathedral Close; adult/child £8/4; ⏰10am-5pm Mon-Sat year-round, plus noon-5pm Sun Jun-Sep) include Iron Age gold coins, a Bronze Age gold necklace and the **Stonehenge Archer**, the bones of a man found in the ditch surrounding the stone circle.

🛏 p73, p151

The Drive » Next: a 10-mile drive taking you back 5000 years. The A345 heads north. Soon after joining the A303, detail a passenger to watch the right windows – the world's

⑩ Stonehenge

Welcome to Britain's most iconic archaeological site: **Stonehenge** (EH; ☎0370 333 1181; www.english-heritage.org.uk; adult/child on-the-day tickets £18/11, advance booking £15.50/9.30; ⏰9am-8pm Jun-Aug, 9.30am-7pm Apr, May & Sep, 9.30am-5pm Oct-Mar; P), a compelling ring of monolithic stones that dates, in parts, back to 3000 BC. Head into the **Visitor Centre** to see 300 finds from the site and experience an impressive 360-degree projection of the stone circle through the ages and seasons. Next hop on a trolley bus (or walk; it's 1.5 miles) to the monument. There, as you stroll around it, play 'spot-the-stone': look out for the **bluestone horseshoe** (an inner semi-circle), the **trilithon horseshoe** (sets of two vertical stones topped by a horizontal one) and the **Slaughter Stone** and **Heel Stone** (set apart, on the northeast side). Then try to work out what on earth it all means. Note that entrance is by timed ticket; secure yours well in advance.

The Drive » Now for a 24-mile, A-road meander through rural England. After dodging through Devizes, it's not long before signs point left to Avebury's main car park.

⑪ Avebury

A two-minute stroll from the car park (£7 per day) leads to a ring of stones that's so big an entire village sits inside. Fringed by a massive bank and ditch and with a diameter of 348m, **Avebury** (NT; ☎01672-539250; www.nationaltrust.org.uk; ⏰24hr; P) is the largest stone circle in the world. Dating from 2500 to 2200 BC, more than 30 stones are still in place and you can wander between them and clusters of other stones at will. On the fringes, 16th-century **Avebury Manor** (NT; ☎01672-539250; www.nationaltrust.org.uk; adult/child £6.75/3.35; ⏰11am-5pm Apr-Oct, to 4pm mid-Feb–Mar, 11am-4pm Thu-Sun Nov & Dec) is home to interiors spanning five periods, ranging from Tudor, through Georgian, to the 1930s.

🛏 p219

The Drive » Next a cruise due west; as the A4 winds for 30 miles past fields and through villages to the city of Bath.

⑫ Bath

Sophisticated, stately and ever-so-slightly snooty, Bath is graced with some of Britain's finest Georgian architecture. Wandering around the streets (p294) is a real joy. For an insight into how the city came to have the shape it does, head to the **Museum of Bath Architecture**

(☎01225-333895; www.
museumofbatharchitecture.org.
uk; The Vineyards, The Paragon;
adult/child £5.50/2.50; ⏱2-
5pm Tue-Fri, 10.30am-5pm Sat &
Sun mid-Feb–Nov). The **Bath
Assembly Rooms** (www.
nationaltrust.org.uk; 19 Bennett
St; ⏱10.30am-5pm Mar-Oct,
to 4pm Nov-Feb), where
socialites once gathered,
gives an insight into the
Georgian world. Discover
the city's culinary heritage
at **Sally Lunn's** (☎01225-
461634; www.sallylunns.co.uk; 4
North Pde Passage; mains £6-17;
⏱10am-9.30pm Sun-Thu, to
10pm Fri & Sat), which bakes
the famous Bath Bun
(a brioche-meets-bread
treat). For a free glass
of the spring water that
made the city rich, stop
by the **Pump Room** (www.
romanbaths.co.uk; Stall St;
⏱10am-5pm). Then perhaps
soak in it: at **Thermae
Bath Spa** (☎01225-331234;
www.thermaebathspa.com;
Hot Bath St; Mon-Fri £34, Sat &
Sun £37; ⏱9am-9.30pm, last
entry 7pm), steam rooms,
waterfall showers and a
choice of swimming pools
(including a gorgeous
rooftop one) will help you
relax.

🛏 p245

The Drive ❯❯ It's a 13-mile blast
from Bath to Bristol along the
A36/A4.

- - - - - - - - - - - - -

⑬ Bristol

In Bristol a fascinating
seafaring heritage meets
an edgy, contemporary
vibe. The mighty **SS
Great Britain** (☎0117-926

0680; www.ssgreatbritain.
org; Great Western Dock, Gas
Ferry Rd; adult/child £14/8;
⏱10am-5.30pm Apr-Oct, to
4.30pm Nov-Mar) sits on
the city's waterfront.
Designed in 1843 by engi-
neering genius Isambard
Kingdom Brunel, its inte-
rior has been impeccably
refurbished, including
the galley, the surgeon's
quarters and a working
model of the original
steam engine. The whole
vessel is contained in
an air-tight dry dock,
dubbed a 'glass sea'. At
the **Bristol Museum & Art
Gallery** (☎0117-922 3571;
www.bristolmuseums.org.uk;
Queen's Rd; ⏱10am-5pm Mon-
Fri, to 6pm Sat & Sun) take
in the *Paint-Pot Angel*
by world-famous street
artist Banksy. In the
suburb of **Clifton** explore
Georgian architecture,
especially in Cornwallis
and Royal York Cres-
cents. The **Clifton Observatory** (☎0117-974 1242;
www.cliftonobservatory.com;
Litfield Rd, Clifton Down; adult/
child £2.50/1.50; ⏱10am-5pm

SITES AROUND STONEHENGE

As you drive the roads around Stonehenge it's worth
registering that the site forms part of a huge complex
of ancient monuments. North of Stonehenge
and running roughly east–west is the **Cursus**,
an elongated embanked oval; the smaller **Lesser
Cursus** is nearby. Two clusters of burial mounds, the
Old Barrow and the **New Kings Barrow**, sit beside
the ceremonial pathway **The Avenue**. This routeway
originally linked the site with the River Avon, 2 miles
away. Theories abound as to what these sites were
used for, ranging from ancient sporting arenas to
processional avenues for the dead.

Feb-Oct, to 4pm Nov-Jan),
meanwhile, features a
rare *camera obscura*
which offers incredible
views of the deep fissure
that is the Avon Gorge.

🍴 p245

The Drive ❯❯ Travelling partly
on motorways and partly on
A-roads, the next 80-mile leg
sees you skirting Oxford (for
now) and arriving at the tree-
lined avenue that leads to one of
Britain's finest stately homes.

- - - - - - - - - - - - -

TRIP HIGHLIGHT

⑭ Blenheim Palace

A monumental baroque
fantasy designed by
Sir John Vanbrugh
and Nicholas Hawks-
moor, **Blenheim Palace**
(☎01993-810530; www.blen
heimpalace.com; Woodstock;
adult/child £24.90/13.90, park
& gardens only £14.90/6.90;
⏱ palace 10.30am-5.30pm,
park & gardens 9am-6pm;
🅿) was built between
1705 and 1722. The house
is stuffed with statues,
tapestries, ostentatious
furniture, priceless china
and giant oil paintings.

DETOUR: LACOCK

Start: ⑪ Avebury (p242)

Around 16 miles into your Avebury-to-Bath cruise, consider a detour south. A drive of just 4 extra miles leads to a real rarity: a medieval village that's been preserved in time. In Lacock, the sweet streets framed by stone cottages, higgledy-piggledy rooftops and mullioned windows are a delight to stroll around. Unsurprisingly, it's a popular movie location – it's popped up in the Harry Potter films, *The Other Boleyn Girl* and a BBC adaptation of *Pride and Prejudice*. The 13th-century former Augustinian nunnery of **Lacock Abbey** (NT; ☎01249-730459; www.nationaltrust. org.uk; Hither Way; adult/child £12/6; ⊙10.30am-5.30pm Mar-Oct, 11am-4pm Nov-Feb) is a must-see: its deeply atmospheric rooms and stunning Gothic entrance hall are lined with bizarre terracotta figures – spot the scapegoat with a lump of sugar on its nose. The **Fox Talbot Museum** (NT; ☎01249-730459; www.nationaltrust. org.uk; Hither Way; adult/child £12/6, includes entry to Lacock Abbey; ⊙10.30am-5.30pm Mar-Oct, 11am-4pm Nov-Feb) features an intriguing display on early photography, while the **George Inn** (www.georgeinnlacock.co.uk; 4 West St; mains £10-16; ⊙food noon-2.30pm & 6-9pm Mon-Sat, 6-8pm Sun) is an atmospheric pub in which to re-fuel.

Highlights include the **Great Hall**, a soaring space topped by a 20m-high ceiling adorned with images of the first duke. Britain's legendary WWII prime minister, Sir Winston Churchill, was born here in 1874 – the **Churchill Exhibition** is dedicated to his life, work, paintings and writings. The house is encircled by vast, lavish **gardens** and **parklands**, parts of which were landscaped by the great Lancelot 'Capability' Brown. A minitrain (50p) whisks you to the **Pleasure Gardens**, which feature a yew **maze**, adventure playground, lavender garden and butterfly house.

The Drive ≫ From Blenheim's grandeur, it's a 10-mile pootle down the A44/A4144 to Oxford's dreaming spires.

----

⑮ Oxford

One of the world's most famous university towns, the centre of Oxford is rich in history and studded with august buildings. The city has 38 colleges – **Christ Church** (☎01865-276492; www.chch. ox.ac.uk; St Aldate's; adult/child £8/7; ⊙10am-4.15pm Mon-Sat, 2-4.15pm Sun) is the largest, with 650 students, and has the grandest quad. Founded in 1524 by Cardinal Thomas Wolsey, alumni include Albert Einstein and 13 British prime ministers. It's also famous for the Harry Potter films. At the **Ashmolean** (☎01865-278000; www.ashmolean.org; Beaumont St; ⊙10am-5pm Tue-Sun), Britain's oldest public museum showcases treasures such as Egyptian mummies, Indian textiles and Islamic art. Beautiful **Magdalen College** (☎01865-276000; www.magd.ox.ac.uk; High St; adult/child £5/4, 45min tours £6; ⊙1-6pm Oct-Jun, noon-7pm Jul-Sep, tours 6pm daily Jul-Sep) is worth a visit for its medieval chapel, 15th-century cloisters and 40-hectare grounds. Nearby, let someone else navigate for a bit: head to **Magdalen Bridge Boathouse** (☎01865-202643; www.oxfordpunting.co.uk; High St; chauffeured 4-person punt per 30min £30, punt rental per hour £24; ⊙9.30am-dusk Feb-Nov) for a ride on a chauffeured punt.

🛏 p245

Eating & Sleeping

Canterbury ❸

🛏 Cathedral Gate Hotel Hotel ££
(📞01227-464381; www.cathgate.co.uk; 36 Burgate; s/d £50/112, without bathroom £50/81.50; 📶) Predating the spectacular cathedral gate it adjoins, this quaint 15th-century hotel is a medieval warren of steep staircases and narrow passageways leading to 27 pleasingly old-fashioned rooms with angled floors, low doors and cockeyed walls. Some have cathedral views, while others overlook pretty Buttermarket. There's no lift.

Brighton ❺

🛏 Artist Residence Boutique Hotel £££
(📞01273-324 302; www.artistresidence brighton.co.uk; 33 Regency Sq; d £129-260; 📶) Eclectic doesn't quite describe the rooms at this wonderful 23-room townhouse hotel, set amid the splendour of Regency Sq. As befits the name, every bedroom is a work of funky art with bold wall murals, bespoke and vintage furniture, rough wood cladding and in-room roll-top baths. The Set Restaurant downstairs has a glowing reputation. Book direct and breakfast is free.

Winchester ❼

🛏 St John's Croft B&B ££
(📞01962-859976; www.st-johns-croft.co.uk; St John's St; s/d/f £55/90/120; 🅿 📶) You may fall in love with this oh-so-casually stylish, rambling Queen Anne townhouse, where rattan carpets are teamed with bulging bookcases, and Indian art with shabby-chic antiques. The rooms are vast, the garden is tranquil and breakfast is served beside the Aga in the country-house kitchen.

Salisbury ❾

🛏 Chapter House Inn ££
(📞01722-412028; www.thechapterhouseuk. com; 9 St Johns St; r £100-140) In this 800-year-old boutique beauty, wood panels and wildly wonky stairs sit beside duck-your-head beams. The cheaper bedrooms are swish but the posher ones are stunning, starring slipper baths and the odd heraldic crest. The pick is room 6, where King Charles is reputed to have stayed.

Bath ⓬

🛏 Queensberry Hotel Hotel £££
(📞01225-447928, www.thequeensberry. co.uk; 4 Russell St; r £125-185, ste £225-275; 📶) Award-winning, quirky Queensberry is Bath's best boutique spoil. Four Georgian town houses have been combined into one seamlessly stylish whole where heritage roots meet snazzy designs; expect everything from gingham checks and country creams to bright upholstery, original fireplaces and free-standing tubs. Rates exclude breakfast; parking is £7.

Bristol ⓭

✗ Riverstation British ££
(📞0117-914 4434; www.riverstation.co.uk; The Grove; lunch 2/3 courses £14/17, dinner mains £15-18; ⏱ noon-2.30pm & 6-10.30pm) Riverstation is one of Bristol's original dining-out destinations, and still leads the pack. The waterside location is hard to beat, with a view over the Floating Harbour, but it's the food that keeps the punters coming back: classic in style with a strong European flavour, from French fish soup to steak à la béarnaise.

Oxford ⓯

🛏 Burlington House B&B ££
(📞01865-513513; www.burlington-hotel-oxford co.uk; 374 Banbury Rd, Summertown; s/d from £70/96; 🅿 📶) Twelve elegantly contemporary rooms with patterned wallpaper, immaculate bathrooms and luxury touches are available at this beautifully refreshed Victorian merchant's house. Personal service is as sensational as the delicious breakfast, complete with organic eggs and homemade bread. It's 2 miles north of central Oxford, with good public transport links.

Classic Lakes

18

Beloved of poets and painters, this road trip takes in the scenic wonders of the UK's largest and loveliest national park.

TRIP HIGHLIGHTS

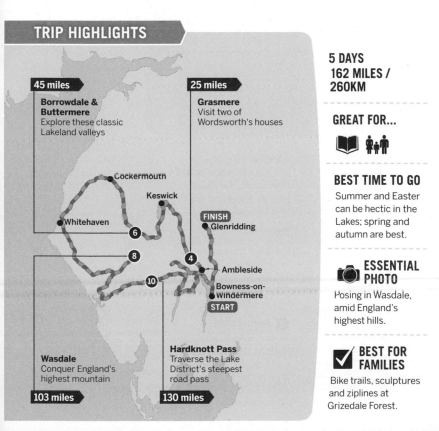

45 miles

Borrowdale & Buttermere
Explore these classic Lakeland valleys

25 miles

Grasmere
Visit two of Wordsworth's houses

Cockermouth

Keswick

FINISH
Glenridding

Whitehaven

6

8

4

10

Ambleside

Bowness-on-Windermere

START

Wasdale
Conquer England's highest mountain

103 miles

Hardknott Pass
Traverse the Lake District's steepest road pass

130 miles

**5 DAYS
162 MILES /
260KM**

GREAT FOR...

BEST TIME TO GO
Summer and Easter can be hectic in the Lakes; spring and autumn are best.

ESSENTIAL PHOTO
Posing in Wasdale, amid England's highest hills.

BEST FOR FAMILIES
Bike trails, sculptures and ziplines at Grizedale Forest.

Lake District Blea Tarn, near Wrynose Pass

18 Classic Lakes

William Wordsworth, Samuel Taylor Coleridge and Beatrix Potter are just a few of the literary luminaries who have fallen in love with the Lake District. It's been a national park since 1951, and is studded by England's highest hills (fells), including the highest of all, Scafell Pike (978m). This drive takes in lakes, forest, hills and valleys, with country houses, hill walks and cosy pubs thrown in for good measure.

❶ Bowness-on-Windermere

England's largest lake, at nearly 9 miles long, Windermere makes an obvious starting point for a Lakeland road trip. The town is actually split into two: Windermere, a mile or so uphill from the lake, and waterfront Bowness-on-Windermere. Cruising the lake is the classic pastime here: **Windermere Lake Cruises** (☎015394-43360; www.windermere-lakecruises.co.uk; tickets from £2.70) offers regular trips, or you can hire your own rowing boat beside the jetty and travel at your own leisurely pace.

🛏 p259

The Drive » From Bowness, follow Rayrigg Rd north until it joins the A591 which rolls all the way to Ambleside, 6 miles north.

❷ Ambleside

Around Windermere's upper end lies the old mill town of Ambleside. It's a pretty place, well stocked with outdoors shops and some excellent restaurants: don't miss a meal at the Lake Road Kitchen (p259), run by an imaginative chef who trained at the legendary Noma in Copenhagen. Afterwards, work off some calories with a walk up to the waterfall of **Stock Ghyll Force**.

🍴 p259

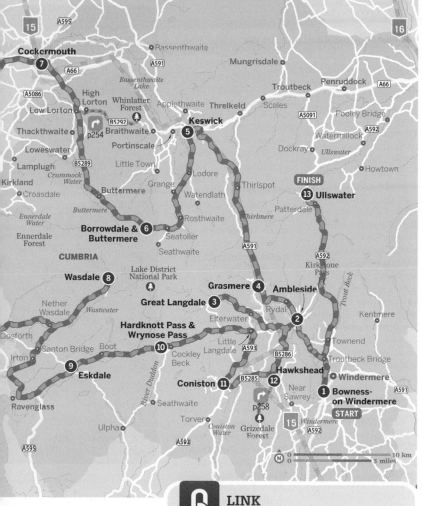

The Drive » Take the A593 west towards Skelwith Bridge, and follow signs to Elterwater and Great Langdale. It's a wonderful 8-mile drive that gets wilder and wilder the deeper you head into the valley. There's a large car park beside the Old Dungeon Ghyll Hotel, but it gets busy in summer; there's usually overflow parking available in a nearby field.

LINK YOUR TRIP

15 The Best of Britain

Start this circuit of Britain's greatest hits by picking up the M6 at Penrith between Manchester and Edinburgh.

16 Britain's Wild Side

Head north or south along the A591 to visit more of the Britain's glorious natural beauty spots.

❸ Great Langdale

The Lake District has some truly stunning valleys, but Great Langdale definitely ranks near the top. As you pass through the pretty village of **Elterwater** and its village green, the scenery gets really wild and empty. Fells stack up like dominoes along the horizon, looming over a patchwork of barns and fields. If you're up for a hike, then tackle the multi-peak circuit around the **Langdale Pikes**. Alternatively, the more sedentary option is to just admire the view over a pint of ale from the cosy bar of the **Old Dungeon Ghyll** (☎015394-37272; www.odg.co.uk; Great Langdale; s £58, d £116-132; 🅿🛜♿), a classic hikers' haunt.

The Drive » Retrace the road to Ambleside and head north to Grasmere on the A591 for 5 miles.

TRIP HIGHLIGHT

❹ Grasmere

The lovely little village of Grasmere is inextricably linked with the poet William Wordsworth, who made it his home in the late 18th century and never left unless he really had to. Two of his houses are now open to the public. The most famous is **Dove Cottage** (☎015394-35544; www.wordsworth.org.uk; adult/child £7.50/4.50; ⏱9.30am-5.30pm), a tiny house where he lived with his sister Dorothy, wife Mary and three children between 1798 and 1807. Guided tours explore the house, and next door the Wordsworth Museum has lots of memorabilia relating to the Romantic poets (including haunting life masks of John Keats and Wordsworth).

A little way south of Grasmere is the house where Wordsworth spent most of his adult life, **Rydal Mount** (☎015394-33002; www.rydalmount.co.uk; adult/child £7.50/3.50, grounds only £4.50; ⏱9.30am-5pm Mar-Oct, 11am-4pm Wed-Mon Nov, Dec & Feb). It's still owned by the poet's descendants, and is a much grander affair than Dove Cottage: you can have a look around the library, visit the poet's attic study and wander around the gardens he designed. Below the house, **Dora's Field** is filled with daffodils in springtime; it was planted in memory of Wordsworth's daughter, who died of tuberculosis.

If you have a sweet tooth, you'll also want to pick up a souvenir at **Sarah Nelson's Gingerbread Shop** (☎015394-35428; www.grasmeregingerbread.co.uk; Church Cottage; ⏱9.15am-5.30pm Mon-Sat, 12.30-5pm Sun), which still makes its gingerbread

to a recipe formulated in 1854.

🛏 p259

The Drive » From Grasmere, continue north on the A591. You'll pass through the dramatic pass known as Dunmail Raise, where a great battle is said to have taken place between the Saxons and the Celtic king Dunmail, who was slain near the pass. Stay on the road past the

Grizedale Forest Woodland stream

lake of Thirlmere all the way to Keswick (13 miles).

- - - - - - - - - - -

❺ Keswick

Another of the Lake District's classic market towns, Keswick is a place that revolves around the great outdoors. Several big fells lie on its doorstep, including the imposing lump of **Skid-daw** and the dramatic

TOP TIP: NATIONAL TRUST MEMBERSHIP

Being a National Trust (www.nationaltrust.org.uk) member comes in very handy in the Lake District. The Trust owns several key attractions, including Hill Top and the Beatrix Potter Gallery near Hawkshead, Wordsworth House in Cockermouth and Fell Foot and Wray Castle near Windermere. Best of all, you get to park for free at all the NT's car parks – handy in celebrated beauty spots like Buttermere, Borrowdale, Wasdale, Gowbarrow Park and Tarn Hows.

WHY THIS IS A GREAT TRIP
OLIVER BERRY, WRITER

For classic English scenery, nowhere quite compares to the Lake District. With its fells and waterfalls, valleys and villages, lakes and meadows, it's like a postcard that's come to life. It's visited by some 13 million people every year, but it's still easy to find peace and serenity – whether it's rowing across a lake, cycling through the countryside or standing atop a fell. Pack spare memory cards – you'll need them.

Left: A classic ploughman's lunch
Above: Grasmere, home to poet William Wordsworth
Right: Hiking around Tarn Hows

ridge of **Blencathra**, but it's the lake of **Derwentwater** that really draws the eye: it was said to be Beatrix Potter's favourite, and she supposedly got the idea for Squirrel Nutkin while watching red squirrels frolicking on its shores. The **Keswick Launch** (☏017687-72263; www.keswick-launch.co.uk; round-the-lake adult/child/family £10.25/5.15/24) travels out around the lake year-round.

Back in town, don't miss a visit to **George Fisher** (☏017687-72178; www.georgefisher.co.uk; 2 Borrowdale Rd; ⊙9am-5.30pm Mon-Sat, 10am-4pm Sun), the most famous outdoors shop in the Lake District: if you need a new pair of hiking boots, this is definitely the place to come.

🏠 p259

The Drive » The drive into Borrowdale on the B5289 is a beauty, passing several pretty villages as it travels through the valley. You can't get lost en route to Honister Pass (10 miles from Keswick) – there's only one road to take; Buttermere lies on the other side of the pass. You'll want to stop for numerous photos on the way.

- - - - - - - - - - - - - - -

TRIP HIGHLIGHT

⑥ Borrowdale & Buttermere

South of Keswick, the B5289 tracks along the eastern side of Derwentwater and enters the bucolic valley of Borrowdale, a classic Lakeland canvas of fields, fells, streams and endless drystone walls. It's worth stopping off to see the geological oddity of the **Bowder Stone**, a huge boulder deposited by a glacier, and for a quick hike up to the top of **Castle Crag**, which has the best views of the valley.

Then it's up and over the perilously steep **Honister Pass**, where the Lake District's last working **slate mine** (☎017687-77230; www.honister-slate-mine.co.uk; mine tour adult/child £12.50/7.50; ☺tours 10.30am, 12.30pm & 3.30pm Mar-Oct) is still doing a thriving trade. You can take a guided tour down into the mine or brave the heights along the stomach-upsetting Via Ferrata, and pick up slate souvenirs in the shop.

Nearby Buttermere has a sparkling twinset of lakes, **Buttermere** and **Crummock Water**,

and is backed by a string of impressive fells. The summit of **Haystacks** is a popular route: it was the favourite fell of Alfred Wainwright, who penned the definitive seven-volume set of guidebooks of the Lake District's fells between the 1950s and '70s. It's a two- to three-hour return walk from Buttermere.

The Drive ≫ From Buttermere village, bear left on the B5289 signed towards Loweswater and Crummock Water, which continues into the Lorton Valley. At Low Lorton, stay on the B5289, which continues 4 miles to Cockermouth. Total distance: 11 miles.

- - - - - - - - - - - - - -

❼ Cockermouth

Grasmere might be Wordsworth central, but completists will want to visit the poet's **childhood home** (NT; ☎01900-824805; Main St; adult/child

£7.20/3.60; ☺11am-5pm Sat-Thu Mar-Oct) in Cockermouth. Now owned by the National Trust, it's been redecorated in period style according to details published in Wordsworth's own father's accounts: you can wander round the drawing room, kitchen, pantry and garden, and see the rooms where little Willie and his brother John slept.

Cockermouth is also the home of local beer-maker **Jennings Brewery** (☎01900-821011; www.jenningsbrewery.co.uk; adult/child £9/4.50; ☺guided tours 1.30pm Wed-Sat), where you can take a guided tour and learn about the brewing process, then sample a couple of ales such as Cocker Hoop and the excellently named Sneck Lifter. Just a snifter, mind – you're driving, after all.

The Drive ≫ Head west on the A66 and detour onto the A595, which tracks the coast all the way to Whitehaven. To reach Wasdale (35 miles all up), turn off at Gosforth, and then follow signs to Nether Wasdale and Wasdale Head. It's quite easy to miss the turning, so keep your eyes peeled; sat-navs can be very unreliable here.

- - - - - - - - - - - - - -

TRIP HIGHLIGHT

❽ Wasdale

Wild Wasdale is arguably the most dramatic valley in the national park. Carving its way for 5 miles from the coast,

---

DETOUR: WHINLATTER FOREST PARK

Start: ❻ Buttermere (p253)

Encompassing 1200 hectares of pine, larch and spruce, **Whinlatter** (www.forestry.gov.uk/whinlatter) is England's only true mountain forest, rising sharply to 790m about 5 miles from Keswick. The forest is a designated red squirrel reserve; you can check out live video feeds from squirrel cams at the visitor centre. It's also home to two exciting mountain-bike trails and a tree-top assault course. You can hire bikes next to the visitor centre.

To get to Whinlatter Forest Park from Buttermere, look out for the right turn onto the B5292 at Low Lorton, which climbs up to Whinlatter Pass.

It was gouged out by a long-extinct glacier during the last Ice Age, if you look closely, you can still see glacial marks on the scree-strewn slopes above Wastwater. Most people come for the chance to reach the summit of **Scafell Pike**, England's highest point; it's a tough six- to seven-hour slog, but the views from the top are quite literally as good as they get (assuming the weather plays ball, of course).

Afterwards, reward yourself with a meal at the **Wasdale Head Inn** (☎019467-26229; www. wasdale.com, s £59, d £118-130, tr £177; P 🤶), a gloriously olde-worlde hostelry with lashings of mountain heritage: it was here that the sport of rock climbing was pioneered in the mid-19th century.

The Drive ❯❯ Retrace your route to Gosforth, and take the coast road (A595) south to Ravenglass and follow signs to Eskdale (22 miles). Alternatively, there's a shortcut into Eskdale via Nether Wasdale and Santon Bridge, but it's easy to get lost, especially if you're relying on sat-nav; a good road map is really handy here.

- - - - - - - - - - -

⑨ Eskdale

The valley of Eskdale was once a centre for mineral-mining, and a miniature steam train was built to carry ore down from the hillsides to the

DETOUR: ST BEES HEAD

Start: ❼ Cockermouth

Cumbria's coastline might not have the white sandy beaches of Wales or the epic grandeur of the Scottish coast, but it has a bleak beauty all of its own – not to mention a renowned seabird reserve at **St Bees Head** (RSPB; stbees.head@rspb.org.uk), where you can spot species including fulmars, herring gulls, kittiwakes and razorbills. You can also look for England's only nesting black guillemots at nearby Fleswick Bay. Just try and forget the fact that one of the UK's largest nuclear reactors, Sellafield, is round the corner.

The village of St Bees is 5 miles south of White-haven, and the headland is signposted from there.

coast. Now known as the **Ravenglass & Eskdale Railway** (☎01229-717171; www.ravenglass-railway.co.uk; adult/child/family return £13.50/6.75/38; 🚂), its miniature choo-choos are a beloved Lakeland attraction. They chuff for 7 miles along the valley from the station at Ravenglass to the final terminus at Dalegarth. Nearby, the **Boot Inn** (☎019467-23224; www. thebooteskdale.co.uk; Boot; mains £10-18; P) makes a pleasant stop for lunch.

The Drive ❯❯ Since you're driving, the most sensible idea is to park near Dalegarth Station, ride the train to Ravenglass and back, and then set off for Hardknott Pass. There's only one road east. Take it and get ready for a hair-raising, white-knuckle drive. It's 6 (very steep!) miles from Eskdale to Hardknott Pass.

TRIP HIGHLIGHT

❿ Hardknott Pass & Wrynose Pass

At the eastern end of Eskdale lie England's two steepest road passes, Hardknott and Wrynose. Reaching 30% gradient in some places, and with precious few passing places on the narrow, single-file road, they're absolutely not for the faint-hearted or for nervous drivers – but the views are amazing, and they're doable if you take things slow (although it's probably best to leave the caravan or motor home in the garage). Make sure your car has plenty of oil and water, as you'll do much of the road in 1st gear, and the strain on the engine can be taxing. Take it slow, and take breaks – you need to keep your focus on the road ahead.

From Eskdale, the road ascends via a series of very sharp, steep switchbacks to the remains of **Hardknott Fort**, a Roman outpost where you can still see the remains of some of the walls. Soon after you reach **Hardknott Pass** at 393m (1289ft). The vistas here are magnificent: you'll be able to see all the way to the coast on a clear day. Next you'll drop down into Cockley Beck before continuing the climb up to **Wrynose Pass** (393m/1289ft). Near the summit is a small car park containing the **Three Shire Stone**, where the counties of Cumberland, Westmorland and Lancashire historically met. Then it's a slow descent down through hairpins and corners to the packhorse Slaters Bridge and on into the valley of **Little Langdale**. Phew! You made it.

The Drive » Once you reach Little Langdale, follow the road east until you reach the A593, the main road between Skelwith Bridge and Coniston. Turn right and follow it for 5 miles.

- - - - - - - - - - - - - -

⓫ Coniston

South of Ambleside, the old mining village of Coniston is dominated by its hulking fell, the **Old Man of Coniston**, an ever-popular objective for hikers, but it's perhaps best known for the world speed record attempts made here by father and son Malcolm and Donald Campbell between the 1930s and 1960s. Though they jointly broke many records, in 1967 Donald was tragically killed during an attempt in his jet-boat *Bluebird*; the little **Ruskin Museum** (www.ruskinmuseum.com; adult/child £6/3; ☺10am-5.30pm Easter–mid-Nov, 10.30am-3.30pm Wed-Sun mid-Nov–Easter) has the full story.

Coniston Water is also said to have been the inspiration for Arthur Ransome's classic children's tale, *Swallows and Amazons*. The best way to explore is aboard the **Steam Yacht Gondola** (NT; ☎015394-63850; www.nationaltrust.org.uk/steam-yacht-gondola; Coniston Jetty; half lake adult/child return £11/5.50, full lake adult/child/family £21.50/10/51), a beautifully restored steam yacht built in 1859. It travels over the lake to the stately home of **Brantwood** (☎015394-41396; www.brantwood.org.uk; adult/child £7.50/free, gardens only £4.95/free; ☺10.30am-5pm mid-Mar–mid-Nov, to 4pm Wed-Sun mid-Nov–mid-Mar), owned by the Victorian polymath, critic, painter and inveterate collector John Ruskin. The house is packed with furniture and crafts, and the gardens are glorious.

🛏 p259

HILL TOP

Two miles from Hawkshead in the tiny village of Near Sawrey, the idyllic cottage at **Hill Top** (NT; ☎015394-36269; www.nationaltrust.org.uk/hill-top; adult/child £10/5, admission to garden & shop free; ☺house 10am-5.30pm Mon-Thu, 10am-4.30pm Fri-Sun, garden 10am-5.45pm Mon-Thu, 10am-5pm Fri-Sun) is the most famous house in the whole of the Lake District. It belonged to Beatrix Potter, and was used as inspiration for many of her tales: the house features directly in *Samuel Whiskers, Tom Kitten, Pigling Bland* and *Jemima Puddleduck*, and you will doubtless recognise the kitchen garden from *Peter Rabbit*.

Following her death in 1943, Beatrix bequeathed Hill Top (along with more than 4000 acres of land) to the National Trust, with the proviso that the house be left with her belongings and decor untouched. The house formed the centrepiece for celebrations to mark the author's 150th birthday in 2016.

Entry is by timed ticket; it's very, very popular, so try visiting in late afternoon or on weekdays to avoid the worst crowds.

Ambleside Bar at the historic Drunken Duck pub

The Drive » Heading north from Coniston, turn right onto the B5285 up Hawkshead Hill. You'll pass Tarn Hows and the Drunken Duck en route to Hawkshead, about 4 miles east.

---

⑫ Hawkshead

If you're searching for the perfect chocolate-box lakeland village, look no further – you've found it in Hawkshead, an improb-ably pretty confection of whitewashed cottages, winding lanes and slate roofs. It's car-free, so you can wander at will: don't miss the **Beatrix Potter Gallery** (NT; www.national-trust.org.uk/beatrix-potter-gal-lery; Red Lion Sq; adult/child £6/3; ⊙10.30am-5pm Sat-Thu mid-Mar–Oct), which has a collection of the artist's original watercolours and botanical paintings (she had a particular fascination with fungi).

Nearby, make a detour via the manmade lake of **Tarn Hows** before stopping for lunch at the Lake District's finest dining pub, the wonder-fully named Drunken Duck.

✗ p259

The Drive » Head back to Ambleside and then follow the A591 back towards Windermere. Just before you reach it, take the turn-off onto the A592 to Troutbeck Bridge, which climbs up to the lofty Kirkstone Pass – at 454m this is the highest mountain pass in Cumbria that's open to road traffic. It's steep, but it's a main A-road so it's well maintained.

⓭ Ullswater

From the windlashed heights of Kirkstone Pass, the A592 loops down towards the last stop on this jaunt around the Lake District: stately Ullswater, the national park's second-largest lake (after Windermere). It's an impressive sight, its silvery surface framed by jagged fells and plied by the puttering **Ullswater 'Steamers'** (☏017684-82229; www.ullswater-steamers.co.uk; round-the-lake adult/child £13.90/6.95); you can also hire your own vessels from the Glenridding Sailing Centre.

DETOUR: GRIZEDALE FOREST

Start: ⓬ Hawkshead (p257)

Stretching for 6000 acres across the hilltops between Coniston Water and Esthwaite Water, **Grizedale Forest** (www.forestry.gov.uk/grizedale) is a wonderful place for a wander. It's criss-crossed by cycling trails, and is also home to more than 40 outdoor sculptures created by artists over the last 30 years, including a xylophone and a man of the forest. There's an online guide at www.grizedalesculpture.org.

As you leave the Hawkshead car park, you'll immediately see a brown sign for Grizedale, heading right onto North Lonsdale Rd. Just follow the brown signs from here – it's 3 miles' drive from the village.

As you skirt up the lake's western edge, it's worth stopping for a walk around **Gowbarrow Park**, where there's a clattering waterfall to admire called **Aira Force**, and impressive displays of daffodils in springtime (Wordsworth dreamt up his most famous poem while walking nearby, the one which starts 'I wandered lonely as a cloud...').

For an epic end to the trip, strap on your hiking boots and tackle the famous ridge climb via Striding Edge to the summit of **Helvellyn**, the Lake District's third-highest mountain at 950m. You'll need a head for heights, but you'll feel a real sense of achievement: you've just conquered perhaps the finest hill walk in all of England.

Eating & Sleeping

Bowness-on-Windermere ❶

🛏 Cranleigh   Hotel £££

(☎015394-43293; www.thecranleigh.com; Kendal Rd, Bowness-on-Windermere; d £119-189, ste £305-515; P 🛜) This guesthouse has gone all out on the decor, but strip away the snazziness and it's still just a B&B. It's worth bumping up to the superior for the spacious bathrooms or maybe blowing the budget on one of the two over-the-top suites (check out the Sanctuary, complete with Bose stereo, glass bath and picture-fireplace).

Ambleside ❷

🍴 Lake Road Kitchen   Bistro £££

(☎015394-22012; www.lakeroadkitchen.co.uk; Lake Rd; 5-/8-course tasting menu £50/80; ⏰6-9.30pm Wed-Sun) This much-lauded new bistro has brought some dazzle to Ambleside's dining scene. Its Noma-trained head chef James Cross explores the 'food of the north', and his multicourse tasting menus are chock full of locally sourced, seasonal and foraged ingredients, from shore-sourced seaweed to forest-picked mushrooms. Presentation is impeccable, flavours are experimental, and the Scandi-inspired decor is just so. A meal not to miss.

Grasmere ❹

🛏 How Foot Lodge   B&B ££

(☎015394-35366; www.howfootlodge.co.uk; Town End; d £76-85; P) Just a stroll from Dove Cottage, this stone house has six rooms finished in fawns and beiges; the nicest are the deluxe doubles, one with a sun terrace and the other with a private sitting room. Rates are an absolute bargain considering the location.

Keswick ❺

🛏 Howe Keld   B&B ££

(☎017687-72417; www.howekeld.co.uk; 5-7 The Heads; s £60-85, d £112-130; P 🛜) This gold-standard B&B pulls out all the stops: goose-down duvets, slate-floored bathrooms, chic colours and locally made furniture. The best rooms have views across Crow Park and the golf course, and the breakfast is a pick-and-mix delight. Free parking is available on The Heads if there's space.

Coniston ⓫

🛏 Bank Ground Farm   B&B ££

(☎015394-41264; www.bankground.com; East of the Lake; d from £90; P) This lakeside farmhouse has literary cachet: Arthur Ransome used it as the model for Holly Howe Farm in *Swallows and Amazons*. Parts of the house date back to the 15th century, so the rooms are snug. Some have sleigh beds, others exposed beams. The tearoom is a beauty too, and there are cottages for longer stays. Two-night minimum.

Hawkshead ⓬

🍴 Drunken Duck   Pub Food £££

(☎015394-36347; www.drunkenduckinn.co.uk; Barngates; lunch mains £7-12, dinner mains £22; ⏰noon-2pm & 6-10pm; P 🛜) Long one of the Lakes' premier dining destinations, the Drunken Duck blends historic pub and fine-dining restaurant. On a wooded crossroads on the top of Hawkshead Hill, it's renowned for its luxurious food and home-brewed ales, and the flagstones and sporting prints conjure a convincing country atmosphere. Book well ahead for dinner or take your chances at lunchtime.

If you fancy staying, you'll find the rooms (£105 to £325) are just as fancy as the food. The pub's tricky to find: drive along the B5286 from Hawkshead towards Ambleside and look out for the brown signs.

Royal Highlands & Cairngorms

19

The heart of the Scottish Highlands features a feast of castles and mountains, wild rollercoaster roads, ancient Caledonian pine forest, and the chance to see Highland wildlife up close and personal.

TRIP HIGHLIGHTS

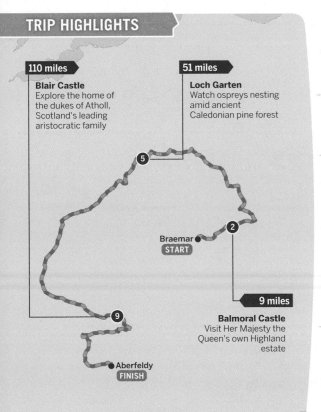

110 miles

Blair Castle
Explore the home of the dukes of Atholl, Scotland's leading aristocratic family

51 miles

Loch Garten
Watch ospreys nesting amid ancient Caledonian pine forest

5

Braemar ●
START

2

9 miles

Balmoral Castle
Visit Her Majesty the Queen's own Highland estate

9

● Aberfeldy
FINISH

4–5 DAYS
149 MILES / 238KM

GREAT FOR...

BEST TIME TO GO

July and August mean good weather and all attractions are open.

ESSENTIAL PHOTO

The gorgeous view of Schiehallion mountain from Queen's View on Loch Tummel.

BEST FOR WILDLIFE

Watching the nesting ospreys at Loch Garten.

Balmoral Castle One of the royal family's residences

261

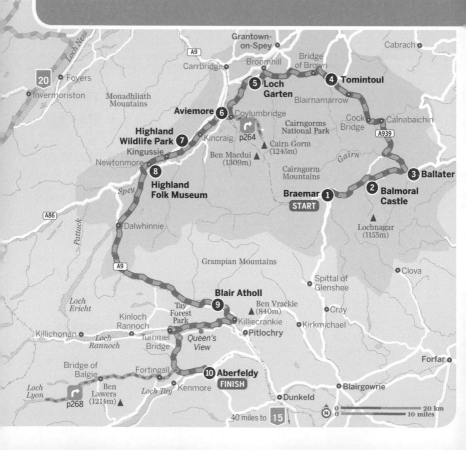

19 Royal Highlands & Cairngorms

You'll tick off the highlights of Royal Deeside and the central Highlands as you make this circuit around Cairngorms National Park. Queen Victoria kickstarted the Scottish tourism industry when she purchased Balmoral Castle in the middle of the 19th century, and her descendants still holiday here. Later, heed the call of the great outdoors with a visit to an osprey nesting site, and a funicular ride to a mountain top.

Loch Ness

20 Foyers
Invermoriston

Monadhliath Mountains

Grantown-on-Spey
Cabrach

A9
Carrbridge
Broomhill
Bridge of Brown

5 Loch Garten
4 Tomintoul

Blairnamarrow

Aviemore 6
Coylumbridge
Cock Bridge
Calnabaichin
A939

Highland Wildlife Park 7
Kincraig
p264
Cairngorms National Park
Cairn Gorm (1245m)

Kingussie
Ben Macdui (1309m)
Gairn

Newtonmore
8
Cairngorm Mountains

Highland Folk Museum
Braemar 1
START
2 Balmoral Castle
3 Ballater

A86
Spey
Pattack
Lochnagar (1155m)

Dalwhinnie

A9
Grampian Mountains

Loch Ericht
Spittal of Glenshee
Clova

Blair Atholl
9
Ben Vrackie (840m)
Cray

Kinloch Rannoch
Tay Forest Park
Killiecrankie
Kirkmichael

Killichonan
Loch Rannoch
Tummel Bridge
Queen's View
Pitlochry

Bridge of Balgie
Fortingall
10 Aberfeldy
FINISH
Forfar

Loch Lyon
p268
Ben Lawers (1214m)
Loch Tay
Kenmore
Blairgowrie

Dunkeld

40 miles to 15
N
0   20 km
0   10 miles

❶ Braemar

Braemar is a pretty little village with a grand location on a broad plain ringed by mountains where the Dee valley and Glen Clunie meet. In winter this is one of the coldest places in the country – temperatures as low as -29°C have been recorded.

Just north of the village, turreted **Braemar Castle** (www.braemarcastle. co.uk; adult/child £8/4; ⏰10am-4pm daily Jul & Aug, Wed-Sun Apr-Jun, Sep & Oct; P) dates from 1628 and served as a government garrison after the 1745 Jacobite rebellion. It was taken over by the local community in 2007, and now offers guided tours of the historic castle apartments.

LINK YOUR TRIP

20 **Great Glen**
The stirring wilderness of the northwest Highlands awaits – it's an hour and three-quarters west to Glen Coe.

15 **The Best of Britain**
Head an hour and a half south to Edinburgh to begin our epic loop of Britain's greatest hits at its midpoint.

There are Highland games in many towns and villages throughout the summer, but the best known is the **Braemar Gathering** (www.brae margathering.org), which takes place on the first Saturday in September.

🍴 🛏 p269

The Drive » The upper valley of the River Dee stretches east from Braemar to Aboyne. Made famous by its long association with the monarchy, the region is often called Royal Deeside. Head east from Braemar on the A93 for 9 miles to the car park at the entrance to Balmoral Castle.

TRIP HIGHLIGHT

❷ Balmoral Castle

Built for Queen Victoria in 1855 as a private residence for the royal family, **Balmoral Castle** (☎01339-742534; www. balmoralcastle.com; Crathie; adult/child £11.50/5; ⏰10am-5pm Apr-Jul, last admission 4.30pm; P) kicked off the revival of the Scottish Baronial style of architecture that characterises so many of Scotland's 19th-century country houses. The admission fee includes an interesting and well-thought-out audioguide, but the tour is very much an outdoor one through garden and grounds.

As for the castle itself, only the ballroom, which displays a collection of Landseer paintings and royal silver, is open to the public. Don't expect to see the Queen's private

quarters! The main attraction is learning about Highland estate management, rather than royal revelations.

You can buy a booklet that details several waymarked walks within Balmoral Estate; the best is the climb to **Prince Albert's Cairn**.

The Drive » Continue east on the A93 for another 8 miles to Ballater.

---

❸ Ballater

The attractive village of Ballater owes its 18th-century origins to the curative waters of nearby Pannanich Springs (now bottled commercially as Deeside Natural Mineral Water), and its prosperity to nearby Balmoral Castle.

The village recently received a double dose of misfortune when the **Old Royal Station** (its main tourist attraction) burned down in May 2015, followed by the worst flooding in living memory in January 2016. Most businesses were open again by summer 2016, but the the station may remain closed until 2018.

There are many pleasant walks in the surrounding area. The steep woodland walk up **Craig-endarroch** (400m) takes just over one hour; ask at the tourist office for more info. If you'd rather cycle, you can hire bikes from **CycleHighlands** (☏01339-755864; www.cyclehighlands.com; The Pavilion, Victoria Rd; bicycle hire per half-day/day £12/18; ⊙9am-6pm) and **Bike Station** (☏01339-754004; www.bikestationballater.co.uk; Station Sq; bicycle hire per 3hr/day £12/18; ⊙9am-6pm), which also offer guided bike rides and advice on local trails.

🛏 p269

The Drive ⟫ The A939 strikes north through the mountains from Ballater to Tomintoul (25 miles). The section beyond Cock Bridge is a magnificent rollercoaster of a road, much loved by motorcyclists, summiting at the Lecht pass

(637m) where there's a small skiing area (it's usually the first road in Scotland to be blocked by snow when winter closes in).

----

❹ **Tomintoul**

Tomintoul (tom-in-towel) is a pretty, stone-built village with a grassy, tree-lined main square. It was built by the Duke of Gordon in 1775 on the old military road that leads over the Lecht pass from Corgarff, a route now followed by the A939. The village's recently refurbished and extended **museum** (☏01807-580285; The Square; ⊙10am-5pm Apr-Oct) celebrates local history, with reconstructions of a crofter's kitchen and a blacksmith's forge.

There's excellent mountain biking at the **BikeGlenlivet** (www.glen-livetest.co.uk; trails free, parking £3) trail centre, 4.5 miles north of Tomintoul, off the B9136 road.

✗ 🛏 p269

The Drive ⟫ Continue northwest from Tomintoul on the A939 for 8.5 miles before turning left on a minor road to the village of Nethy Bridge. In the village, turn left towards Aviemore on the B970 then, after 600m, turn left again on a minor road to Loch Garten (total 17 miles).

DETOUR: CAIRNGORM MOUNTAIN

Start: ❻ Aviemore

Cairngorm Mountain (1245m), 10 miles southeast of Aviemore, is the sixth-highest summit in the UK and home to Scotland's biggest ski area. A funicular railway ferries skiers almost to the top of the mountain, and continues to operate throughout the summer so that visitors can get a taste of the high mountain plateau.

The **Cairngorm Mountain Railway** (☏01479-861261; www.cairngormmountain.org; adult/child return £11.50/7.50; ⊙every 20min 10am-4pm May-Nov, 9am-4.30pm Dec-Apr; P) is the national park's most popular attraction, whisking you to the edge of the Cairngorm plateau (altitude 1085m) in just eight minutes. The bottom station is at the Coire Cas car park at the end of Ski Rd; at the top is an exhibition, a shop (of course) and a restaurant. For environmental and safety reasons, you're not allowed out of the top station in summer unless you book a guided walk or mountain-bike descent; check the website for details.

Six miles east of Aviemore, on the road to Cairngorm Mountain, **Loch Morlich** is surrounded by some 8 sq miles of pine and spruce forest that make up the Glenmore Forest Park. Its attractions include a sandy beach (at the east end) and a watersports centre.

Nearby, the **Cairngorm Reindeer Centre** (www.cairngormreindeer.co.uk; Glenmore; adult/child £14/8; ⊙closed early Jan–mid-Feb; 🚼) runs guided walks to see and feed Britain's only herd of reindeer, who are very tame and will even eat out of your hand. Walks take place at 11am daily (weather-dependent), plus another at 2.30pm from May to September, and a third at 3.30pm Monday to Friday in July and August.

5 Loch Garten

A car park on the shores of Loch Garten, amid beautiful open forest of Scots pine, gives access to the **RSPB Loch Garten Osprey Centre** (☎01479-831694; www.rspb. org.uk/lochgarten; Tulloch; osprey hide adult/child £5/2; ☺ osprey hide 10am-6pm Apr-Aug). Ospreys nest in a tall pine tree on the reserve – you can watch from a hide as the birds feed their young, and see live CCTV feeds from the nest. These rare and beautiful birds – the only bird of prey in the world that eats only fish – migrate here each spring from Africa, arriving in April and leaving in August (check the website to see if they're in residence).

The Drive » The minor road leads back to the B970, where you turn left along the banks of the River Spey to Coylumbridge; turn right here to reach Aviemore (11 miles).

6 Aviemore

The gateway to the Cairngorms, Aviemore may not be the prettiest town in Scotland – the main attractions are in the surrounding area – but when bad weather puts the hills off-limits, Aviemore fills up with hikers, cyclists and climbers (plus skiers and snowboarders in winter) cruising the outdoor-equipment shops or recounting their latest adventures in the cafes and bars.

Strathspey Steam Railway (☎01479-810725; Station Sq; return adult/child £14.25/7.15; **P**) runs steam trains on a section of restored line between Aviemore and Broomhill, 10 miles to the northeast, via Boat of Garten. There are four or five trains daily from June to August, and a more limited service in April, May, September, October and December.

The **Cairngorm Sled-Dog Centre** (☎07767-270526; www.sled-dogs. co.uk; Ski Rd; 🐾) will take you on a 30-minute sled tour of local forest trails in the wake of a team of huskies, or a three-hour sled-dog safari. The sleds have wheels, so snow's not necessary.

🛏 p269

The Drive » From Aviemore drive south on the B99152, which follows the valley of the River Spey; after 8.5 miles, soon after passing through the village of Kincraig, you'll see a sign on the right for the Highland Wildlife Park.

7 Highland Wildlife Park

The **Highland Wildlife Park** (☎01540-651270; www. highlandwildlifepark.org; Kincraig; adult/child £15.40/11.55; ☺10am-6pm Jul & Aug, to 5pm Apr-Jun & Sep-Oct, to 4pm Nov-Mar; **P**) features a drive-through safari park as well as animal enclosures that offer the chance to view rarely seen native wildlife, such as Scottish wildcats, capercaillies, pine martens and red squirrels, as well as species that once roamed the Scottish hills but have long since disappeared, including wolves, lynx, wild boars, beavers and European bison. Last entry is two hours before closing.

The Drive » Continue southwest on the B9152 through Kingussie to the Highland Folk Museum (6.5 miles).

8 Highland Folk Museum

The old Speyside towns of Kingussie (kin-yew-see) and Newtonmore sit at the foot of the great heather-clad humps known as the Monadhliath Mountains. Newtonmore is best known as the home of the excellent **Highland Folk Museum** (☎01540-673551; www.high landfolk.museum; Kingussie Rd, Newtonmore; ☺10.30am-5.30pm Apr-Aug, 11am-4.30pm Sep & Oct; **P**), an open-air collection of historical buildings and artefacts revealing many aspects of Highland culture and lifestyle. Laid out like a farming township, it has a community of traditional thatch-roofed cottages, a sawmill, a schoolhouse, a shepherd's

WHY THIS IS A GREAT TRIP

NEIL WILSON,
WRITER

Pretty much everything about this trip screams classic Scotland – romantic castles set amid forest-fringed hills (including the British royal family's own holiday home); picturesque Highland villages beside salmon-filled rivers; hiking and mountain biking amid wild mountain scenery in the heart of Britain's biggest national park; iconic Scottish wildllife experiences (think ospreys, reindeer, wildcats); there's even a whisky distillery thrown in for good measure!

Top: Wild red deer
Left: A road through Cairngorms National Park
Right: Loch Garten

bothy (hut) and a rural post office.

The Drive » Join the main A9 Inverness to Perth road and follow it south for 35 miles to Blair Atholl, passing through bleak mountain scenery and climbing to a high point of 460m at the Pass of Drumochter

---

TRIP HIGHLIGHT

❾ Blair Atholl

The village of Blair Atholl dates only from the early 19th century, built by the Duke of Atholl, head of the Murray clan, whose seat – magnificent **Blair Castle** (☏01796-481207; www.blair-castle.co.uk; adult/child £10.70/6.40, family £28.90; ⏰9.30am-5.30pm Easter-Oct, 10am-4pm Sat & Sun Nov-Mar; P 🚻) – is one of the most popular tourist attractions in Scotland.

Thirty rooms are open to the public and they present a wonderful picture of upper-class Highland life from the 16th century on. The original tower was built in 1269, but the castle underwent significant remodelling in the 18th and 19th centuries. Highlights include the 2nd-floor **Drawing Room** with its ornate Georgian plasterwork and Zoffany portrait of the 4th duke's family, complete with a pet lemur (yes, you read that correctly) called Tommy; and the **Tapestry Room** draped with

17th-century wall hangings created for Charles I. The **dining room** is sumptuous – check out the 9-pint wine glasses – and the **ballroom** is a vast oak-panelled chamber hung with hundreds of stag antlers.

🛏 p269

The Drive ≫ Follow the B8079 southeast out of Blair Atholl for a few miles, past the historic battle site of Killiecrankie, and turn right on the B8019 Strathtummel road. This gloriously scenic road leads along Loch Tummel (stop for photographs at Queen's View) to Tummel Bridge; turn left here on the B846 over the hills to Aberfeldy (29 miles).

- - - - - - - - - - - - -

⑩ Aberfeldy

Aberfeldy is the gateway to Breadalbane (the historic region surrounding Loch Tay), and a good base: adventure sports, angling, art and castles all feature on the menu here. It's a peaceful, pretty place on the banks of the Tay, but if it's moody lochs and glens that steal your heart, you may want to push further west into **Glen Lyon**.

You arrive in the town by crossing the River Tay via the elegant **Wade's Bridge**, built in 1733 as part of the network of military roads designed to tame the Highlands. At the eastern end

of town is **Aberfeldy Distillery** (www.dewars.com; tour adult/child £9.50/4.50; ☺10am-6pm Mon-Sat, noon-4pm Sun Apr-Oct, 10am-4pm Mon-Sat Nov-Mar; 🅿), home of the famous Dewar's whisky; tours include an entertaining interactive

blending session. More expensive tours allow you to try venerable Aberfeldy single malts and others.

🛏 p269

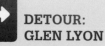

DETOUR: GLEN LYON

Start: ⑩ **Aberfeldy**

The 'longest, loneliest and loveliest glen in Scotland', according to Sir Walter Scott, stretches for 32 unforgettable miles of rickety stone bridges, native woodland and heather-clad hills, becoming wilder and more uninhabited as it snakes its way west. The ancients believed it to be a gateway to Faerieland, and even the most sceptical of visitors will be entranced by the valley's magic.

There are no villages in the glen – the majestic scenery is the main reason to be here – just a cluster of houses at Bridge of Balgie, where the **Bridge of Balgie Tearoom** (📞01887-866221; Bridge of Balgie; snacks £3-5; ☺10am-5pm Apr-Oct; 🅿🛜🐾), with a suntrap of a terrace overlooking the river, serves as a hub for walkers, cyclists and motorists. The owner is a fount of knowledge about the glen, and her pistachio and almond cake is legendary.

There are several waymarked woodland walks beginning from a car park a short distance beyond Bridge of Balgie, and more challenging hill walks into the surrounding mountains (see www.walkhighlands.co.uk/perthshire).

From Abefeldy, the B846 leads to the pretty village Fortingall, famous for its ancient yew tree, where a narrow minor road strikes west up the glen; another steep and spectacular route from Loch Tay crosses the hills to meet it at Bridge of Balgie. The road continues west as far as the dam on Loch Lyon, passing a memorial to Robert Campbell (1808–94), a Canadian explorer and fur trader, who was born in the glen.

Eating & Sleeping

Braemar ❶

🛏 St Margarets   B&B £

(📞01339-741697; soky37@hotmail.com; 13 School Rd; s/tw £34/56; 🛜) Grab this place if you can, but there's only one room: a twin with a serious sunflower theme. The genuine warmth in the welcome is delightful. It's tucked behind the church on the south side of the A93 road.

🛏 Craiglea   B&B ££

(📞01339-741641; www.craigleabraemar.com; Hillside Dr; d/f from £76/105; P🛜) Craiglea is a homely B&B set in a pretty stone cottage with three en suite bedrooms. Vegetarian breakfasts are available and the owners can rent you a bike and give advice on local walks.

Ballater ❸

🛏 Auld Kirk   Hotel ££

(📞01339-755762; www.theauldkirk.com; Braemar Rd; s/d from £80/115; P🛜🐾) Here's something a little out of the ordinary – a seven-bedroom hotel housed in a converted 19th-century church. The interior blends original features with sleek modern decor – the pulpit now serves as the reception desk, while the breakfast room is bathed in light from leaded Gothic windows.

Tomintoul ❹

🛏 Argyle Guest House   B&B ££

(📞01807-580766; www.argyletomintoul.co.uk; 7 Main St; d/f from £65/115; 🛜🐾) Comfortable accommodation for walkers, and the best porridge in the Cairngorms!

🍴 Clockhouse Restaurant   Scottish ££

(The Square; mains £10-14; 🕐 noon-2pm & 6-8pm) Serves light lunches and bistro dinners made with fresh Highland lamb, venison and salmon.

Aviemore ❻

🛏 Cairngorm Hotel   Hotel ££

(📞01479-810233; www.cairngorm.com; Grampian Rd; s/d from £72/104; P🛜) Better known as 'the Cairn', this long-established hotel is set in the fine old granite building with the pointy turret opposite the train station. It's a welcoming place with comfortable rooms and a determinedly Scottish atmosphere, with tartan carpets and stags' antlers. There's live music on weekends, so it can get a bit noisy – not for early-to-bedders.

Blair Atholl ❾

🛏 Atholl Arms Hotel   Hotel ££

(📞01796-481205; www.athollarms.co.uk; r from £90; P🛜🐾) This hotel, near Blair Atholl train station, is convenient for the castle, with rooms of a high standard; book ahead on weekends. The Bothy Bar here is the sibling pub of the Moulin Hotel in Pitlochry, snug with booth seating, an enormous fireplace and bucket-loads of character; there's no better place to be when the rain is lashing down outside.

Aberfeldy ❿

🛏 Tigh'n Eilean Guest House   B&B ££

(📞01887-820109; www.tighneilean.com; Taybridge Dr; s/d from £48/78; P🛜🐾) Everything about this property screams comfort. It's a gorgeous place overlooking the Tay, with individually designed rooms – one has a Jacuzzi, while another is set on its own in a cheery yellow summer house in the garden, giving you a bit of privacy. The garden itself is fabulous, with hammocks for lazing in, and the riverbank setting is delightful.

Great Glen

20

This lake-and-mountain themed trip leads you through some of the Highlands' scenic hotspots, and along the shores of world-famous Loch Ness – here be monsters!

TRIP HIGHLIGHTS

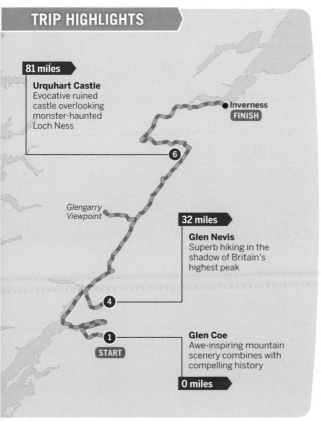

81 miles

Urquhart Castle
Evocative ruined castle overlooking monster-haunted Loch Ness

● **Inverness**
FINISH

6

Glengarry Viewpoint

32 miles

Glen Nevis
Superb hiking in the shadow of Britain's highest peak

4

1
START

Glen Coe
Awe-inspiring mountain scenery combines with compelling history

0 miles

2–3 DAYS
147 MILES/235KM

GREAT FOR...

BEST TIME TO GO
April to see snow on the mountains, October for autumn colours in the forests.

ESSENTIAL PHOTO

Failing a shot of the Loch Ness monster, crossing the wire bridge at Steall Meadows.

BEST FOR FAMILIES

A Nessie-hunting cruise from Fort Augustus.

Glen Nevis Crossing the wire bridge through Nevis Gorge

271

20 Great Glen

The Great Glen is a geological fault running in an arrow-straight line across Scotland, filled by a series of lochs including Loch Ness. This trip follows the A82 road along the glen (completed in 1933 – a date that coincides with the first sightings of the Loch Ness Monster!) and links two areas of outstanding natural beauty – Glen Coe to the south, and Glen Affric to the north.

TRIP HIGHLIGHT

❶ Glen Coe

Scotland's most famous glen is also one of its grandest. The A82 road leads over the **Pass of Glencoe** and into the narrow upper glen. The southern side is dominated by three massive, brooding spurs, known as the **Three Sisters**, while the northern side is enclosed by the continuous steep wall of the knife-edged **Aonach Eagach** ridge, a classic mountaineering challenge.

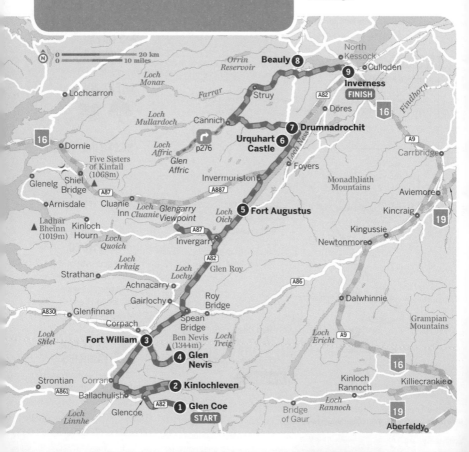

Glencoe Visitor Centre

(NTS; ☎01855-811307; www.glencoe-nts.org.uk; adult/child £6.50/5; ⏰9.30am-5.30pm Easter-Oct, 10am-4pm Thu-Sun Nov-Easter; 🅿) provides comprehensive information on the geological, environmental and cultural history of Glencoe, charts the development of mountaineering in the glen, and tells the story of the Glencoe Massacre in all its gory detail.

🍴 🛏 p277

The Drive » From Glencoe village at the foot of the glen, head east on the B863 for 7 miles along the southern shore of Loch Leven to Kinlochleven.

- - - - - - - - - - - - - -

❷ Kinlochleven

Kinlochleven is hemmed in by high mountains at the head of beautiful Loch Leven, where the West Highland Way

LINK YOUR TRIP

 19 Royal Highlands & Cairngorms

Get your fill of Scottish splendour by beginning with this tour of castles and mountains before heading west to Glen Coe.

 16 Britain's Wild Side

Explore more of Britain's natural beauty spots by taking this trip in reverse from Inverness.

brings a steady stream of hikers through the village. It is also the starting point for walks up the glen of the River Leven, through pleasant woods to the **Grey Mare's Tail** waterfall, and harder mountain hikes into the Mamores.

Scotland's first **Via Ferrata** (☎01855-413200; www.glencoeactivities.com; per person/family £55/170) – a 500m climbing route equipped with steel ladders, cables and bridges – snakes through the crags around the Grey Mare's Tail, allowing non-climbers to experience the thrill of climbing (you'll need a head for heights, though!).

🍴 p277

The Drive » Return west along the north side of Loch Leven, perhaps stopping for lunch at the excellent Lochleven Seafood Cafe, then head north on the A82 to Fort William (22 miles).

- - - - - - - - - - - - - -

❸ Fort William

Basking on the shores of Loch Linnhe amid magnificent mountain scenery, Fort William has one of the most enviable settings in the whole of Scotland. If it wasn't for the busy dual carriageway crammed between the less-than-attractive town centre and the loch, and one of the highest rainfall records in the country, it would be almost idyllic. Even so,

the Fort has carved out a reputation as 'Outdoor Capital of the UK' (www.outdoorcapital.co.uk).

The small but fascinating **West Highland Museum** (☎01397-702169; www.westhighlandmuseum.org.uk; Cameron Sq; ⏰10am-5pm Mon-Sat Apr-Oct, to 4pm Mar & Nov-Dec, closed Jan & Feb) is packed with all manner of Highland memorabilia. Look out for the secret portrait of Bonnie Prince Charlie – after the Jacobite rebellions, all things Highland were banned, including pictures of the exiled leader, and this tiny painting looks like nothing more than a smear of paint until viewed in a cylindrical mirror.

🍴 🛏 p277

The Drive » At the roundabout on the northern edge of Fort William, take the minor road that runs into Glen Nevis; it leads to a car park at the far end of the glen, 6.5 miles away.

- - - - - - - - - - - - - -

TRIP HIGHLIGHT

❹ Glen Nevis

Scenic Glen Nevis – used as a filming location for *Braveheart* and the Harry Potter movies – wraps around the base of Ben Nevis, Britain's highest mountain. The **Glen Nevis Visitor Centre** (☎01397-705922; www.bennevisweather.co.uk; ⏰8.30am-6pm Jul & Aug, 9am-5pm Apr-Jun, Sep & Oct, 9am-3pm Nov-Mar; 🅿) is situated 1.5 miles up the glen, and provides information on hiking, weather forecasts, and specific advice on climbing **Ben Nevis**.

From the car park at the end of the road, there is an excellent 1.5-mile walk through the spectacular Nevis Gorge to **Steall Meadows**, a verdant valley dominated by a 100m-high bridal-veil waterfall. You can reach the foot of the falls by crossing the river on a wobbly, three-cable wire bridge – one cable for your feet and one for each hand – a real test of balance!

The Drive » Return down Glen Nevis and head north on the A82. At Invergarry, turn left onto the A87 which climbs high above Loch Garry; stop at the famous Glengarry Viewpoint (layby on left). By a quirk of perspective, the lochs to the west appear to form the map outline of Scotland. Return to the A87 and continue to Fort Augustus (44 miles).

❺ Fort Augustus

Fort Augustus, at the junction of four old military roads, was originally a government garrison and the headquarters of General George Wade's road-building operations in the early 18th century. Today it's a neat and picturesque little place bisected by the Caledonian Canal.

Boats using the canal are raised and lowered 13m by a 'ladder' of five consecutive locks. It's fun to watch, and the neatly landscaped canal banks are a great place to soak up the sun. The **Caledonian Canal Centre** (☎01320-366493; Ardchattan House, Canalside; ◷10am-4pm), beside the lowest lock, has information on the history of the canal.

Cruise Loch Ness (☎01320-366277; www.cruiselochness.com; adult/child £14/8; ◷hourly 10am-4pm Apr-Oct, 1 & 2pm only Nov-Mar), at the jetty beside the canal bridge, operates one-hour cruises on Loch Ness accompanied by the latest high-tech sonar equipment so you can keep an underwater eye open for the Loch Ness monster.

The Drive » It's a straightforward but scenic 17-mile drive along the shores of Loch Ness to Urquhart Castle.

- - - - - - - - - - - - -

TRIP HIGHLIGHT

❻ Urquhart Castle

Commanding a superb location with outstanding views over Loch Ness, **Urquhart Castle** (HS; ☎01456-450551; adult/child £8.50/5.10; ◷9.30am-6pm Apr-Sep, to 5pm Oct, to 4.30pm Nov-Mar; **P**) is a popular Nessie-hunting hot spot. A huge visitor centre (most of which is beneath ground level) includes a video theatre (with a dramatic 'reveal' of the castle at the end of

the film) and displays of medieval items discovered in the castle. The five-storey tower house at the northern point is the most impressive remaining fragment and offers wonderful views across the water.

The Drive » A short hop of 2 miles leads to Drumnadrochit.

Loch Ness Fort Augustus Abbey

🕖 Drumnadrochit

Deep, dark and narrow, Loch Ness stretches for 23 miles between Inverness and Fort Augustus. Its bitterly cold waters have been extensively explored in search of Nessie, the elusive Loch Ness monster, but most visitors see her only in the form of a cardboard cutout at Drumnadrochit's monster exhibitions.

The **Loch Ness Centre** (📞01456-450573; www.lochness.com; adult/child £7.95/4.95; ⏰9.30am-6pm Jul & Aug, to 5pm Easter-Jun, Sep & Oct, 10am-3.30pm Nov-Easter; 🅿️👶) adopts a scientific approach that allows you to weigh the evidence for yourself. Exhibits include the original equipment – sonar survey vessels, miniature submarines, cameras and sediment coring tools – used in various monster hunts, as well as original photographs and film footage of sightings. You'll find out about hoaxes and optical

DETOUR: GLEN AFFRIC

Start: ❼ Drumnadrochit (p275)

Glen Affric (www.glenaffric.org), one of the most beautiful glens in Scotland, extends deep into the hills beyond Cannich, halfway between Drumnadrochit and Beauly. The upper reaches of the glen, now designated as **Glen Affric Nature Reserve**, is a scenic wonderland of shimmering lochs, rugged mountains and native Scots pine forest, home to pine martens, wildcats, otters, red squirrels and golden eagles.

A narrow, dead-end road leads southwest from Cannich; about 4 miles along is **Dog Falls**, a scenic spot where the River Affric squeezes through a narrow, rocky gorge. A circular walking trail (red waymarks) leads from Dog Falls car park to a footbridge below the falls and back on the far side of the river (2 miles, allow one hour).

The road continues beyond Dog Falls to a parking area and picnic site at the eastern end of **Loch Affric**, where there are several short walks along the river and the loch shore. The circuit of Loch Affric (10 miles, allow five hours walking, two hours by mountain bike) follows good paths right around the loch and takes you deep into the heart of some very wild scenery.

illusions, as well as learning a lot about the ecology of Loch Ness – is there enough food in the loch to support even one 'monster', let alone a breeding population?

The Drive ›› Head west on the A831 which leads to the village of Cannich – jumping-off point for the Glen Affric detour – before turning north along lovely Strathglass to reach Beauly (30 miles).

❽ Beauly

Mary, Queen of Scots is said to have given this village its name in 1564 when she visited, exclaiming in French: 'Quel beau lieu!' (What a beautiful place!). Founded in 1230, the red-sandstone **Beauty Priory** is now an impressive ruin, haunted by the cries of rooks nesting in a magnificent centuries-old sycamore tree.

Corner on the Square (p277) makes a good place to break your journey.

✕ p277

The Drive ›› Drive east on the A862 for 12 miles to Inverness.

❾ Inverness

Inverness has a great location astride the River Ness at the northern end of the Great Glen. In summer it overflows with visitors intent on monster hunting at nearby Loch Ness, but it's worth a visit in its own right for a stroll along the picturesque River Ness, a cruise on Loch Ness, and a meal in one of the city's excellent restaurants.

The main attraction in Inverness is a leisurely stroll along the river to the **Ness Islands**. Planted with mature Scots pine, beech and sycamore, and linked to the river banks and each other by elegant Victorian footbridges, the islands make an appealing spot. They're a 20-minute walk south of the castle – head upstream on either side of the river (the start of the Great Glen Way), and return on the opposite bank.

🛏 p277

Eating & Sleeping

Glen Coe ❶

🛏 Clachaig Inn
Hotel ££

(📞01855-811252; www.clachaig.com; s/d £53/106; P 🛜) The Clachaig, 2 miles east of Glencoe village, has long been a favourite haunt of hill walkers and climbers. As well as comfortable en suite accommodation, there's a smart, modern lounge bar with snug booths and high refectory tables, mountaineering photos and bric-a-brac, and climbing magazines to leaf through.

✖ Glencoe Café
Cafe £

(📞01855-811168; www.glencoecafe.co.uk; Glencoe village; mains £4-8; ⏰10am-4pm daily, to 5pm May-Sep, closed Nov; P 🛜) This friendly cafe is the social hub of Glencoe village, serving breakfast fry-ups till 11.30am (including vegetarian versions), light lunches based around local produce (think Cullen skink, smoked salmon quiche, venison burgers), and the best cappuccino in the glen.

Kinlochleven ❷

✖ Lochleven Seafood Cafe
Seafood ££

(📞01855-821048; www.lochlevenseafoodcafe. co.uk; mains £11-23, whole lobster £40; ⏰meals noon-3pm & 6-9pm, coffee & cake 10am-noon & 3-5pm mid-Mar–Oct; P 👪) This outstanding place serves superb shellfish freshly plucked from live tanks – oysters on the half shell, razor clams, scallops, lobster and crab – plus a daily fish special and some non-seafood dishes. For warm days, there's an outdoor terrace with a view across the loch to the Pap of Glencoe, a distinctive conical mountain.

Fort William ❸

🛏 Grange
B&B £££

(📞01397-705516; www.grangefortwilliam.com; Grange Rd; d £145; P 🛜) An exceptional 19th-century villa set in its own landscaped grounds, the Grange is crammed with antiques and fitted with log fires, chaise lounges and Victorian roll-top baths. The Turret Room, with its window seat in the turret overlooking Loch Linnhe, is our favourite. It's 500m southwest of the town centre. No children.

✖ Lime Tree
Scottish ££

(📞01397-701806; www.limetreefortwilliam. co.uk; Achintore Rd; mains £16-20; ⏰6.30-9.30pm; P 🛜) Fort William is not over-endowed with great places to eat, but the restaurant at this small hotel and art gallery has put the UK's Outdoor Capital on the gastronomic map. The chef turns out delicious dishes built around fresh Scottish produce, ranging from Loch Fyne oysters to Loch Awe trout and Ardnamurchan venison.

Beauly ❽

✖ Corner on the Square
Cafe £

(📞01463-783000; www.corneronthesquare. co.uk; 1 High St; mains £7-13; ⏰8.30am-5.30pm Mon-Fri, 8.30am-5pm Sat, 9.30am-5pm Sun) Beauly's best lunch spot is this superb little delicatessen and cafe that serves breakfast (till 11.30am), daily lunch specials (11.30am to 4.30pm) and excellent coffee.

Inverness ❾

🛏 Heathmount Hotel
Boutique Hotel ££

(📞01463-235877; www.heathmounthotel. com; Kingsmills Rd; s/d from £75/105; P 🛜) Small and friendly, the Heathmount combines a popular local bar and restaurant with eight designer hotel rooms, each one different, ranging from a boldly coloured family room in purple and gold to a slinky black velvet four-poster double. Five minutes' walk east of the city centre.

West Wales: Swansea to St Davids

21

This route links two distinctly Welsh cities – one large and one beyond tiny – by way of Wales' two most famously beautiful stretches of coast.

TRIP HIGHLIGHTS

125 miles

St Davids
Historic micro-city set in an ancient landscape

10
St Davids
FINISH

● Haverfordwest

● Carmarthen

Pembroke ● **7** ● Tenby

Llanelli ●

START
Swansea

Rhossili **4**

86 miles

Tenby
Postcard-perfect beach town with a medieval core

Rhossili
Miles of golden sand backed by steep-sloped downs

20 miles

---

4 DAYS
125 MILES / 201KM

GREAT FOR...

BEST TIME TO GO
June, July and August offer the best beach weather; although there's no assurances of sun.

ESSENTIAL PHOTO
The view of Three Cliffs Bay from Pennard Castle.

BEST FOR FAMILIES
Splashing about on the beach at Tenby.

Pembrokeshire Coast Elegug Stack Rocks

21 | West Wales: Swansea to St Davids

The broad sandy arc of Swansea Bay is only a teaser for what is to come. Once you escape the city sprawl, the wild beauty of the Welsh coast immediately begins to assert itself. Waves crash against sheer cliffs painted from a rapidly changing palate of grey, purple and inky black. In between are some of Britain's very best beaches: glorious sandy stretches and tiny remote coves alike.

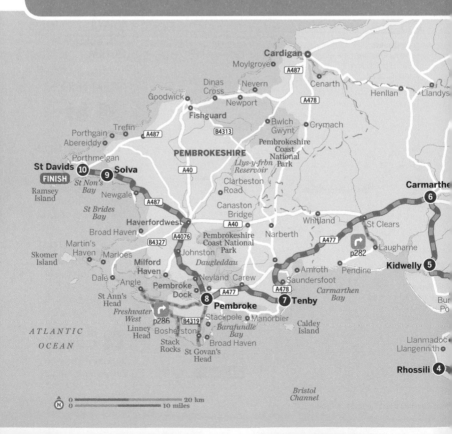

① Swansea

Although it's not the most immediately attractive place, Wales' second biggest city has its own workaday charm and an enviable setting on 5-mile-long, sandy, Swansea Bay. An active bar scene is enthusiastically supported by a large student population, while a new brace of affordable ethnic eateries has improved the city's once drab dining options no end.

Fuel up on Welsh cakes hot off the griddle at **Swansea Market** (www. swanseaindoormarket.co.uk; Oxford St; ⊙8am-5.30pm Mon-Sat), then dive into the whizz-bang **National Waterfront Museum** (☎0300 111 2333; www.museumwales.ac.uk; South Dock Marina, Oystermouth Rd; ⊙10am-5pm) and the charmingly old-fashioned **Swansea Museum** (☎01792-653763; www.swanseamuseum.co.uk; Victoria Rd; ⊙10am-5pm Tue-Sun). Fans of Welsh poet Dylan Thomas can tour his **birthplace** (☎01792-472555; www.dylanthomasbirthplace.com; 5 Cwmdonkin Dr, Uplands; adult/child £8/6; ⊙ tours 11am, 1pm & 3pm), explore his legacy at the **Dylan Thomas Centre** (☎01792-463980; www.dylanthomas.com; Somerset Pl; ⊙10am-4.30pm), catch a show at the **Dylan Thomas Theatre** (☎01792-473238; www.dylanthomastheatre.org.uk; Gloucester Pl), where he once trod the boards, and visit some of the many pubs he famously frequented. If you've got an interest in antiquities, seek out the fascinating **Egypt Centre** (www.egypt.swan.ac.uk; Mumbles Rd, Skotty; ⊙10am-4pm Tue-Sat) at Swansea University.

🛏 p289

The Drive ›› Broad Oystermouth Rd traces the edge of Swansea Bay, changing its name to Mumbles Rd halfway along. It's only 4 miles from central Swansea to the heart of the Mumbles strip.

② The Mumbles

Swansea's swanky seaside suburb sprawls along the western curve of Swansea Bay and terminates in the pair of rounded hills which may have gifted the area its unusual name (from the French *Les Mamelles* – 'the breasts'). **Oystermouth Castle** (☎01792-635478; www.swansea.gov.uk/oystermouthcastle; Castle Ave; adult/child £3/1.50; ⊙11am-5pm Easter-Sep) is well worth a visit – a Norman fortress standing guard over the fashionable Newton Rd bar and shopping strip.

Pick up an ice cream at **Joe's** (☎01792-368212; www.joes-icecream.com; 526

LINK YOUR TRIP

17 **The Historic South**
Sample some heritage and culture before hitting the wild coast: from Oxford, it's two and a half hours west on the M4 to Swansea.

15 **The Best of Britain**
The Welsh coast tour is an obvious side-trip from our grand tour of the best sights of Britain – it's an hour's drive between Swansea and Cardiff.

Lampeter

Llanybydder

Llangadog

Llandeilo

Ammanford

38 miles to 15

Pontarddulais

70 miles to 17

Llanelli

START
Swansea
①

nolston

A4118 ③
Parkmill

② Mumbles

Mumbles Rd; ☺10.30am-5.30pm), a Swansea institution since it was founded by an Italian immigrant in 1922, and take a stroll along the waterside promenade to the Victorian **pier** (☎01792-365225; www.mumbles-pier.co.uk; Mumbles Rd). There's a pretty little sandy beach tucked just beneath it. If you're peckish there are some good cafes and restaurants spread along the waterfront, and plenty of pubs and bars too.

🛏 p289

The Drive » From the Mumbles it's 6 miles to Parkmill on the Gower Peninsula. Head uphill on Newton Rd, following the Gower signs. Eventually the houses give way to fields and,

at the village of Murton, a sharp right-hand turn leads to the B4436 and on to the A4118, the main Gower road.

- - - - - - - - - - - -

❸ Parkmill

The spectacular coastal landscape of the Gower Peninsula was recognised by officialdom when it was declared the UK's first 'Area of Outstanding Natural Beauty' in 1956.

In the village of Parkmill, historic mill buildings have been converted into the **Gower Heritage Centre** (☎01792-371206; www.gowerheritagecentre.co.uk; Parkmill; adult/child £6.80/5.80; ☺10am-5.30pm; 🐾). Despite its worthy-sounding name, it's a great place to take kids, incorporating a petting

zoo and a puppet theatre. Nearby **Parc-le-Breos** (Parkmill) contains the remains of a 5500-year-old burial chamber.

However, the real reason to stop in Parkmill is to take a stroll to **Three Cliffs Bay**. Recognised as one of Britain's most beautiful beaches, Three Cliffs has a memorable setting, with a ruined 13th-century castle above and a triple-pointed rock formation framing a natural arch at its eastern end.

The Drive » From Parkmill, continue west on the A4118, following the signs to Rhossili. Eventually the road turns left towards the village of Scurlage and the Rhossili turn-off. All up it's a distance of 10 miles along good roads, but it's quite likely

---

DETOUR: LAUGHARNE

Start: ❻ Carmarthen (p285)

While shooting down the highway between Carmarthen and Tenby, it's worth considering taking a left at St Clears to visit the small town of Laugharne (pronounced '*larn*') on the Taf estuary. Perched picturesquely above the reed-lined shore, **Laugharne Castle** (Cadw; www.cadw.gov.wales; Wogan St; adult/child £3.80/2.85; ☺10am-5pm Apr-Oct) is a hefty 13th-century fortress which was converted into a mansion in the 16th century.

Swansea may have been Dylan Thomas' birthplace but Laugharne is where he chose to live out his final years, providing the inspiration for his classic play for voices *Under Milk Wood*. Many fans make the pilgrimage here to visit the **boathouse** (☎01994-427420; www.dylanthomasboathouse.com; Dylan's Walk; adult/child £4.20/2; ☺10am-5pm May-Oct, 10.30am-3pm Nov-Apr) where he lived, the shed where he wrote and his final resting place in the graveyard of St Martin's Church. Also worth a look is cosy **Brown's Hotel** (☎01994-427688; www.browns-hotel.co.uk; King St; pizza £8-10; ☺11am-11pm), one of his favourite watering holes.

Laugharne is situated 4 miles off the highway and you're best to allocate at least a couple of hours to explore it properly. Although you can continue southwest from here on narrow roads, you're better off backtracking to the A477 to get to Tenby.

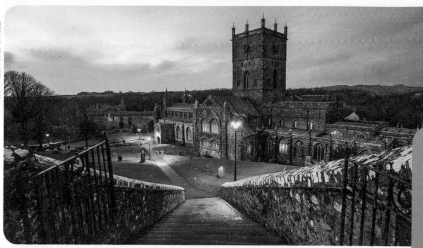

JOE DANIEL PRICE / GETTY IMAGES ©

St Davids St Davids Cathedral

you'll be stuck behind a slow-moving campervan or tractor at some point along the way.

TRIP HIGHLIGHT

❹ Rhossili

It can be dangerous for swimmers but the three miles of surf-battered golden sands of Rhossili Bay make it the Gower Peninsula's most dramatic and spectacular beach. Surfers tend to congregate at the village of Llangennith near the north end of the beach, but Rhossili village to the south makes for a better casual stop. There's a National Trust **visitor centre** (☏01792-390707; www.nationaltrust.org.uk/gower; Coastguard Cottages, Rhossili; ⏱10.30am-4pm) here, and the excellent Bay Bistro & Coffee House (p289), if you're after a meal or a snack.

This end of the beach is abutted by **Worms Head**, a dragon-shaped promontory which turns into an island at high tide and is home to seals and a variety of sea birds. It's safe to explore it on foot for 2½ hours either side of low tide, but keep an eye on the time and mind you don't get cut off by the incoming tide.

✗ p289

The Drive 》 It's only 31 miles from Rhossili to Kidwelly, but allow an hour as the narrow lanes leading out from the Gower Peninsula will slow you down. The first part of the journey zigzags along tiny lanes to the peninsula's northern edge. Before and after motoring through the scraggly outskirts of Llanelli, it's a pleasantly rural drive.

- - - - - - - - - - - - - -

❺ Kidwelly

Castles are a dime a dozen in this part of Wales – a legacy of a time when Norman 'Marcher' lords were given authority and a large degree of autonomy to subjugate the Welsh in the south and along the English border. The cute little Carmarthenshire town of Kidwelly has a particularly well-preserved example.

Originally erected in 1106, only 40 years after the Norman invasion of England, **Kidwelly Castle** (Cadw; www.cadw.gov.wales; Castle Rd, Kidwelly; adult/child £4/3; ⏱9.30am-5pm Mar-Oct, 10am-4pm Nov-Feb) got its current configuration of imposing stone walls in the 13th century. Wander around and explore its remaining towers and battlements, or just stop by to take a photo of the grey walls looming above the peaceful river far below.

The Drive 》 From Kidwelly, take the A484 north for 10 miles through the green fields of Carmarthenshire. Eventually

WHY THIS IS A GREAT TRIP
PETER DRAGICEVICH, WRITER

As well as traversing two of Wales' most acclaimed beauty spots – the Gower Peninsula and the Pembrokeshire Coast – this journey offers the perfect introduction to contemporary Welsh life. You'll get a taste of a large post-industrial city, visit tiny fishing villages, travel through fertile farmland and wash up in St Davids – a place as close to the Welsh soul as any could claim to be.

Top: Rhossili Bay, Gower Peninsula
Left: Colourful buildings in Solva
Right: Picturesque Tenby Harbour

B.LV STO:K, SHUTTERSTOCK ©

you'll see Carmarthen in the distance, straddling a hill above the River Tywi.

- - - - - - - - - - - - -

❻ Carmarthen

Although it has ancient provenance, there's not an awful lot to see in Carmarthenshire's county town. Still, it's worth stopping to stretch your legs with a stroll through its historic centre. Call into **Castle House** (Nott Sq; ⏲9.30am-4.30pm Mon-Sat) to examine the few sections that remain of a once mighty fortress. **Carmarthen Market** (www.carmarthen shiremarkets.co.uk; Market Way; ⏲9.30am-4.30pm Mon-Sat) has existed since Roman times. It's a good place to sample the local specialty, Carmarthen ham – an air-dried meat that's very similar to prosciutto. Carmarthenshire is a largely agricultural county, and the market remains an important hub for local producers.

The Drive » Twenty-six miles of verdant farmland separate Carmarthen from Tenby. Take the A40 to St Clears, where you can either detour to Laugharne or branch off on the A477 and enter Pembrokeshire. Past Kilgetty, turn left onto the A478, which leads directly to Tenby.

- - - - - - - - - - - - -

`TRIP HIGHLIGHT`

❼ Tenby

Sandy, family-friendly beaches spread out in either direction from the pretty pastel-striped resort town occupying the headland. Tenby's historic core is still partly enclosed by Norman walls, although all that's left of its castle is a meagre collection of ruins gazing over the sea.

The beach is the big attraction here, but if the weather's not co-operating, pop into **Tenby Museum & Art Gallery** (☎01834-842809; www.tenbymuseum.org.uk; Castle Hill; adult/child £4.95/free; ◷10am-5pm daily Apr-Dec,

Tue-Sat Jan-Mar) and the National Trust's restored **Tudor Merchant's House** (NT; ☎01834-842279; www.nationaltrust.org.uk; Quay Hill; adult/child £5/2.50; ◷11am-5pm Wed-Mon Easter-Jul, Sep & Oct, daily Aug, Sat & Sun Nov-Easter). If you've got the time, take a boat trip out to **Caldey Island** (☎01834-844453; www.caldey-island.co.uk; adult/child £12/6; ◷Mon-Sat May-Sep, Mon-Thu Apr & Oct), home to seals, seabirds, beaches

and a community of Cistercian monks.

🛏 p289

The Drive » From Tenby it's a short and sweet 10-mile hop to Pembroke. From the town centre, head west on Greenhill Rd, head under the railway bridge and turn right at the roundabout. Follow Hayward Lane (the B4318) through a patchwork of fields until you reach the Sageston roundabout. Turn left onto the A477 and then veer left on the A4075.

DETOUR: WEST OF PEMBROKE

Start: ❽ Pembroke

The remote peninsula that forms the bottom lip of the long, deep-sea harbour of Milford Haven has some of the Pembrokeshire Coast's most dramatic geological features and blissful little beaches. The National Trust–managed **Stackpole Estate** (NT; ☎01646-661359; www.nationaltrust.org.uk; ◷dawn-dusk) covers 8 miles of coastline south and west of Pembroke. It includes the golden sands of **Barafundle Bay** and **Broad Haven South**, and a network of walking tracks around the **Bosherston Lily Ponds**.

Continue past Bosherston to the coast and a short steep path leads to the photogenic shell of **St Govan's Chapel**, wedged into a slot in the cliffs just above the pounding waves. There's a natural rock arch here, one of many along this stretch of coast. Sadly, the coast to the west of here is part of a military firing range. When the red flags are flying there's no public access to some of the Pembrokeshire Coast's most arresting natural sights – the **Elegug Stack Rocks** and the gigantic arch known as the **Green Bridge of Wales**.

After sidestepping the firing range, the road continues on to **Freshwater West** – a moody, wave-battered stretch of coast that has provided a brooding backdrop for movies such as *Harry Potter and the Deathly Hallows* and Ridley Scott's *Robin Hood*. It's widely held to be Wales' best surf beach, but also one of the most dangerous for swimmers.

From Pembroke it's 4 miles to the Stackpole Estate and 8 miles to Freshwater West. If it's beach weather, you could easily make a day of it. Take the B4319 heading south from Pembroke; Stackpole, Bosherston and the Ellegug Stack Rocks are reached from narrow country lanes branching off it. The B4319 continues past Freshwater West and terminates at the B4320, where you can turn right to head back to Pembroke.

Parkmill Pennard Castle

❽ Pembroke

The little town of Pembroke is completely dominated by hulking **Pembroke Castle** (☏01646-684585; www.pembroke-castle.co.uk; Main St; adult/child £6/5; ⏰10am-5pm; 🚼), which looms over the end of its main street. The fortress is best viewed from the Mill Pond, a pretty lake which forms a moat on three sides of the craggy headland from which the castle rises. Pembroke played a leading role in British history as the birthplace of the first Tudor king, Henry VII. Compared to many of its contemporaries, the castle is in extremely good nick, with lots of well-preserved towers, dungeons and wall-walks to explore. Needless to say, kids love it.

A strip of mainly Georgian and Victorian buildings leads down from the castle, including among them some good pubs and the excellent **Food at Williams** (☏01646-689990; www.foodatwilliams.co.uk; 18 Main St; mains £5-8.50; ⏰9am-4.30pm Mon-Sat, 10am-3pm Sun, 🚼) cafe.

🛏 p289

The Drive » The 24-mile journey to Solva heads through the port town of Pembroke Dock, crosses the Daugleddau estuary and then heads up through Pembrokeshire's nondescript county town of Haverfordwest. Exit Haverfordwest on the A487, which traverses farmland before reaching the coast at Newgale, a surf beach backed by a high bank of pebbles. From here the road shadows the coast.

❾ Solva

Clustered around a hook-shaped harbour, Solva is the classic Welsh fishing village straight out of central casting. Pastel-hued cottages line the gurgling stream running through its lower reaches, while Georgian town houses cling to the cliffs above. When the tide's out, the water disappears completely from the harbour, leaving the sailing fleet striking angular poses on the sand.

There's not much to do here except to stroll about perusing the antique shops and galleries, or to settle in somewhere cosy for a meal. Our favourite for the latter is the **Cambrian Inn** (☏01437-721210; www.thecambrianinn.co.uk; 6 Main St; mains £11-21, s/d £70/95; ⏰noon-3pm & 6-9pm; 🚼), an upmarket pub known for its gourmet burgers and meat pies.

If you need to burn off some calories afterwards, a 1-mile walk will take you upstream to the **Solva Woollen Mill** (☎01437-721112; www.solvawoollenmill.co.uk; Middle Mill; ⏰9.30am-5.30pm Mon-Fri Oct-Jun, 9.30am-5.30pm Mon-Sat, 2-5.30pm Sun Jul-Sep), which is the oldest working mill of its kind in Pembrokeshire.

🛏 p289

The Drive » You really can't go wrong on the 3-mile drive to St Davids. Just continue west.

TRIP HIGHLIGHT

⑩ St Davids

A city only by dint of its prestigious cathedral, pretty St Davids feels more like a small town or an oversized village. Yet this little settlement looms large in the Welsh consciousness as the hometown of its patron saint.

Fascinating **St Davids Cathedral** (www.stdavidscathedral.org.uk; suggested donation £3, tours £4; ⏰8.30am-6pm Mon-Sat, 12.45-5.30pm Sun) stands on the site of the saint's own 6th-century religious settlement. Wonderful stone and wooden carvings decorate the interior, and

there's a treasury and historic library hidden within. Right next to the cathedral are the ruins of a spectacular medieval **bishop's palace** (Cadw; www.cadw.gov.wales; adult/child £3.50/2.65; ⏰9.30am-5pm Mar-Oct, 10am-4pm Nov-Feb).

St David was born at **St Non's Bay**, a ruggedly beautiful section of coast with a holy well and a cute little chapel, a short walk from the centre of town. If it's a swim or

surf you're after, head to broad, beautiful **Whitesands Bay** (Porth Mawr).

Also not to be missed is **Oriel y Parc** (Landscape Gallery; ☎01437-720392; www.orielyparc.co.uk; cnr High St & Caerfai Rd; ⏰10am-4pm), an architecturally interesting visitor centre and art gallery showcasing landscape paintings from the collection of the National Museum Wales.

🛏 p289

💬 LOCAL KNOWLEDGE: ST DAVID'S DAY

St David's Day is to the Welsh what St Patrick's Day is to the Irish – a day to celebrate one's essential Welshiness, albeit somewhat more soberly than their Celtic brethren from across the way. If you're in Wales on 1 March, there's no better place to be than the saint's own city, St Davids. All around the cathedral a host of golden daffodils explodes into flower seemingly right on cue; people pin leek, daffodil or red dragon badges to their lapels; the streets are strung with flags bearing the black and gold St David's cross; and *cawl* (a traditional soupy stew) is consumed in industrial qualities. Of course, the focus of more solemn events is the cathedral, where the saint's remains lie in a recently restored shrine, a replica of one which was destroyed during the Reformation.

Eating & Sleeping

Swansea ❶

🛏 Christmas Pie B&B
B&B ££

(📞01792-480266; www.christmaspie.co.uk;
2 Mirador Cres, Uplands; s/d £53/82; P 📶)
The name suggests something warm and
comforting, and this suburban villa does not
disappoint. The three en-suite bedrooms are all
individually decorated. Plus there's fresh fruit
and an out-of-the-ordinary, vegetarian-friendly
breakfast selection.

The Mumbles ❷

🛏 Patricks
with Rooms
Boutique Hotel £££

(📞01792 360199; www.patrickswithrooms.
com; 638 Mumbles Rd; r £120-175; 📶) Patricks
has 16 individually styled bedrooms in bold
contemporary colours, with art on the walls,
fluffy robes and, in some of the rooms, roll-top
baths and sea views. Some are set back in
a separate annexe. Downstairs there's an
upmarket restaurant and bar.

Rhossili ❹

✖ Bay Bistro & Coffee House
Bistro £

(📞01792-390519; www.thebaybistro.co.uk;
mains £6-12; ⏰10am-5.30pm; 🖊) A buzzy
beach cafe with a sunny terrace, good surfy
vibrations and the kind of drop-your-panini
views that would make anything taste good –
although the roster of burgers, sandwiches,
cakes and coffee stands up well regardless. On
summer evenings it opens for alfresco meals.

Tenby ❼

🛏 Southside
Hotel ££

(📞01834-844355; www.southsidetenby.
co.uk; Picton Rd; s/d £45/80; 📶) Rooms are
spacious, comfortable and not at all chintzy
at this friendly little private hotel just outside

the town walls. Three of the four rooms have en
suites, while the other has a private bathroom
accessed from the corridor.

Pembroke ❽

🛏 Woodbine
B&B ££

(📞01646-686338; www.
pembrokebedandbreakfast.co.uk; 84 Main St; s/d
from £50/65; 📶) This well-kept, forest-green
Georgian townhouse presents a smart face to
Pembroke's main drag. The three pretty guest
rooms are tastefully furnished, with original
fireplaces and contemporary wallpaper. Two
have en suites, while the family room has its
bathroom out on the corridor.

Solva ❾

🛏 Haroldston House
B&B ££

(📞01437-721404; www.haroldstonhouse.co.uk;
29 High St; r £80-90; P 📶) Set in a lovely old
Georgian merchant's house, this wonderful
B&B offers chic modern style. The simple but
tastefully decorated rooms feature art by
owner Ian McDonald as well as other Welsh or
Wales-based artists. There's a free electric-car
charging point, discounts for guests arriving by
public transport, and tasty, inventive breakfast
options.

St Davids ❿

🛏 Twr y Felin
Hotel £££

(📞01437-725555; www.twryfelinhotel.com;
Caerfai Rd; r/ste from £160/240) Incorporating
an odd circular tower that was once a windmill,
this chic boutique hotel is St Davids' most
upmarket option. The entire building is lathered
with contemporary art, with dozens of pieces
in the lounge-bar and restaurant alone. The
21 bedrooms are all luxurious, but the most
spectacular is the three-level circular suite in
the tower itself.

NEED <u>TO</u> KNOW

CURRENCY
Pound sterling (£)

LANGUAGE
English; also Scottish Gaelic and Welsh

VISAS
Generally not needed for stays of up to six months. Not a member of the Schengen Zone.

FUEL
Urban petrol (gas) stations are plentiful; service stations are regularly spaced on motorways. Fill up before heading into rural areas, where they're scarcer.

Expect to pay around £1.10 per litre.

RENTAL CARS
Avis www.avis.co.uk
Budget www.budget.co.uk
Europcar www.europcar.co.uk
Thrifty www.thrifty.co.uk

IMPORTANT NUMBERS
Emergency (☏ 112 or ☏ 999) Police, fire, ambulance, mountain rescue, coastguard
AA (☏ 0800 88 77 66) Roadside assistance
RAC (☏ 800 197 7815) Roadside assistance

Climate

Warm to hot summers, mild winters

Fort William
GO May or Sep

Aberdeen
GO May–Sep

Edinburgh
GO Any time

Brecon
GO May–Sep

Norwich
GO May–Sep

London
GO Any time

Exeter
GO Apr–Oct

When to Go

High Season (Jun–Aug)
》 Weather at its best.

》 Accommodation rates peak.

》 Busy roads, especially in seaside areas, national parks and big-draw cities.

Shoulder (Mar–May & Sep–Oct)
》 Crowds reduce.

》 Prices drop.

》 Weather often good.

Low Season (Nov–Feb)
》 Wet and cold.

》 Snow falls in mountain areas.

》 Outside London, opening hours often reduced.

Your Daily Budget

Budget: Less than £55
» Dorm beds: £15–30

» Cheap cafe and pub meals: £7–11

Midrange: £55–120
» Double hotel or B&B room: £65–130 (London £100–200)

» Restaurant main meal: £10–20

Top End: More than £120
» Four-star hotel room: from £130 (London from £200)

» Three-course meal in a good restaurant: around £40

» Car rental per day: from £35

Eating

Restaurants From cheap-and-cheerful to Michelin-starred, covering all cuisines.

Pubs Serve reasonably priced meals, some are top notch.

Cafes Good daytime option for casual breakfasts, lunch or afternoon tea.

Vegetarian Find meat-free restaurants in towns and cities. But rural menus may contain just one 'choice'.

In reviews, the following price ranges refer to a main dish. Prices are slightly higher in London.

£	less than £10
££	£10–£20
£££	more than £20

Sleeping

Hotels From small townhouses to grand mansions; from

budget to corporate offerings to boutique.

B&Bs Range from a room in someone's house (with shared bathroom) to luxury spoils.

Inns Rooms above rural pubs; can be a cosy choice.

Hostels Bare-bones, often dorm-style, accommodation.

Reviews of places to stay use the following price ranges, all based on double room with private bathroom in high season.

	LONDON	OTHER
£	less than £100	less than £65
££	£100–£200	£65–£130
£££	more than £200	more than £130

Arriving in Great Britain

Heathrow airport Trains, London Underground (tube) and buses to central London from 5am to around midnight (night buses run later) are £5.70–21.50. Taxis to central London cost £45 to £85.

Gatwick airport Trains to central London from 4.30am to 1.35am £10–20; 24hr buses (hourly) to central London from £5. Taxis to central London: £100.

Eurostar trains from Paris or Brussels Arrive at London St Pancras International station.

Buses from Europe Arrive at London Victoria Coach Station.

Mobile Phones

The UK uses the GSM 900/1800 network, which covers Europe, Australia and New Zealand, but isn't compatible with the North American GSM 1900, although most modern mobiles can function on both networks.

Internet Access

» 3G and 4G mobile broadband coverage is good in urban centres, but limited in rural areas.

» Many accommodation providers have wi-fi access (free or up to £6 per hour).

» Internet cafes (from £1 per hour) are rare away from tourist spots.

Money

ATMs ('cash machines') are common in cities and towns. Visa and MasterCard are widely accepted, although some B&Bs take cash or cheque only.

Tipping

Restaurants Around 10–15% in eateries with table service.

Pubs & Bars If you order and pay at the bar, tips are not expected. If you order a meal at the table and pay afterwards, then 10% is usual.

Taxis Roughly 10%.

Useful Websites

Lonely Planet (www.lonelyplanet.com/great-britain) Destination information, hotel bookings, traveller forums.

Visit Britain (www.visitbritain.com) Comprehensive tourist info.

STRETCH YOUR LEGS
CAMBRIDGE

Start/Finish: Grand Arcade

Distance: 3 miles

Duration: Three hours

University city Cambridge is a place in which to walk. This tour takes in a prestigious college, magnificent chapels, an ancient library, a cosy teashop and gardens lining a river filled with punts.

Take this walk on Trip

15

Grand Arcade

Browse some of the 60 prestigious shops in Cambridge's glitzy Grand Arcade. It's one of the few places you can park centrally, so it's a good place to start.

The Walk » Head for the Lion Yard entrance; exit onto Petty Cury, crossing the square to emerge onto stately King's Parade. Cut left to King's College Chapel.

King's College Chapel

In a city crammed with showstopping buildings, **King's College Chapel** (☎01223-331212; www.kings.cam.ac.uk/chapel; King's Pde; adult/child £9/6; ⊙9.30am-3.15pm Mon-Sat & 1.15-2.30pm Sun term time, 9.30am-4.30pm daily, to 3.30pm Dec, Jan & university holidays) is the scene-stealer. The grandiose structure is one of England's most extraordinary examples of Gothic architecture. Its intricate 80m-long, fan-vaulted ceiling is the world's largest.

The Walk » Stroll north up King's Parade.

Great St Mary's Church

A major expansion of **Great St Mary's** (www.gsm.cam.ac.uk; Senate House Hill; ⊙10am-4pm Mon-Sat, 1-4pm Sun) between 1478 and 1519 resulted in the late-Gothic Perpendicular style you see today. Striking features include the mid-Victorian stained-glass windows, seating galleries and two organs. Climb the **tower** (adult/child £3.90/2.50) for superb vistas.

The Walk » Dodge bicyclists and touting tour guides to marvel at the ornate gates of Gonville & Caius College. Soon Trinity's elaborate Tudor entrance way towers up on the left.

Trinity College

The largest of Cambridge's colleges, elegant **Trinity College** (www.trin.cam.ac.uk; Trinity St; adult/child £3/1; ⊙10am-4.30pm, closed early Apr–mid-Jun) features a sweeping Great Court: the biggest of its kind in the world. It also boasts the renowned **Wren Library** (⊙noon-2pm Mon-Fri, plus 10.30am-12.30pm Sat term time only), containing 55,000 books dated before 1820. Works include those by Shakespeare and Swift.

And an original *Winnie the Pooh*, written by Trinity graduate AA Milne.

The Walk » Head back through Trinity's entrance and pass the front of gorgeous St John's College.

Round Church

Cambridge's intensely atmospheric **Round Church** (www.christianheritage.org.uk; Bridge St; £2.50; ◷10am-5pm Mon-Fri, 1.30-5pm Sat, 1.30-4pm Sun) is one of only four such structures in England. It was built by the mysterious Knights Templar in 1130.

The Walk » Cut right down sweet, narrow Portugal Pl and onto wide Jesus Green. Pass tennis players to stroll the wooden boardwalk beside the river and ranks of punts. After crossing the bridge by Magdelene College, it's not long before you reach the Backs.

The Backs

From here you'll see the stately sweep of **St John's College** amid the trees; Trinity sits next door. Welcome to 'the Backs', a series of riverside parks behind the colleges' grandiose facades and stately courts – picture-postcard snapshots of graceful bridges and student life.

The Walk » Nip up Garret Hostel Lane for closer college views. Next come the gates of Clare College, then glimpses of the impressive King's College Chapel; the Palladian Fellows' Building is to the right. After curving beside Queens' College, cut left.

Mathematical Bridge

From Silver St's bridge, look left to spy the **Mathematical Bridge**, a flimsy-looking wooden construction built in 1749.

The Walk » Look out for the fleets of about-to-embark punts on the right as you head up Silver St.

Fitzbillies

Cambridge's oldest bakery, **Fitzbillies** (www.fitzbillies.com; 52 Trumpington St; mains £6-12; ◷8am-6pm Mon-Fri, 9am-7pm Sat, 10am-6pm Sun) has a soft spot in the hearts of generations of students, thanks to its ultrasticky Chelsea buns.

The Walk » Stroll up King's Parade, passing now-familiar King's College. Turn right just before Great St Mary's, retracing your steps back to the car.

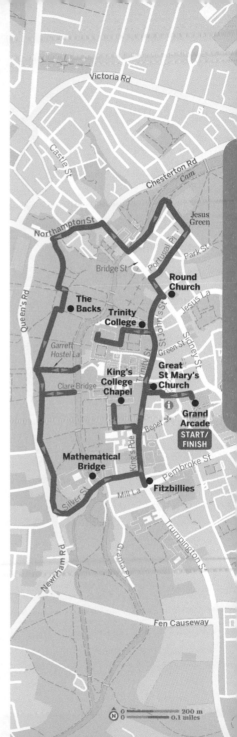

STRETCH YOUR LEGS
BATH

Start/Finish: SouthGate

Distance: 2½ miles

Duration: Three hours

Bath's cityscape is simply sumptuous – so stunning it has World Heritage site status. On this walk you'll encounter architecture ranging from Roman baths via a medieval cathedral to exquisite Georgian designs.

Take this walk on Trips

SouthGate

On cruising into Bath, follow signs to SouthGate car park. It's set beneath a new shopping centre which aims to echo the city's Georgian architecture.

The Walk 》 Exit into St Lawrence St and head north, to join Stall St, before cutting right down Abbeygate St towards the Roman Baths.

Roman Baths

The Romans built a complex of bath-houses (p150) above three natural hot springs, which emerge at a toasty 46°C (115°F). They form one of the best-preserved ancient Roman spas in the world. A tour reveals the **Great Bath** (a lead-lined pool filled with steaming water), bathing pools, changing rooms and excavated sections revealing the hypocaust heating system.

The Walk 》 From Bath's baths it's a few steps east to the city's abbey.

Bath Abbey

Towering **Bath Abbey** (p196) was built between 1499 and 1616, making it the last great medieval church raised in England. On the striking west facade angels climb up and down stone ladders, commemorating a dream of the founder, Bishop Oliver King. You can also take tower tours.

The Walk 》 Cross the square south of Bath Abbey, then wind onto Parade Gardens passing the Empire Hotel (1901) and the rushing weir to Pultney Bridge (1773), a rarity in that it features shops. Then duck up Green St.

Tasting Room

High-class vintages, tapas and piled-high platters of meats and cheese are the modi operandi of the **Tasting Room** (☏01225-483070; www.tastingroom.co.uk; 6 Green St; mains £6-13; ⊗10.30am-11pm Wed-Sat, to 4.30pm Mon & Tue), a slinky cafe-bar set above a wine merchant.

The Walk 》 Turn into elegant Milsom St, browsing its chic shops as you make your way, via George St, into narrow Bartlett St, a trendy enclave.

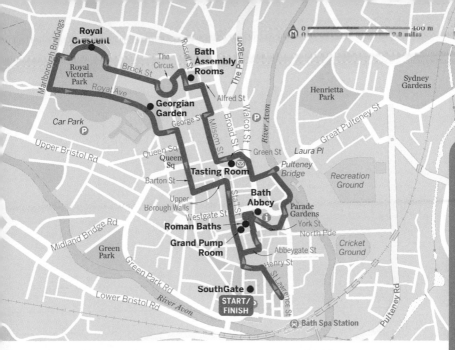

Bath Assembly Rooms

When they opened in 1771, Bath's **Assembly Rooms** (NT; www.nationaltrust.org.uk; 19 Bennett St; ☺10.30am-5pm Mar-Oct, to 4pm Nov-Feb) were where fashionable socialites gathered to waltz, play cards and listen to the latest chamber music. Tour the card room, tearoom and ballroom.

The Walk » Next it's into The Circus (1768), a gorgeous ring of 33 houses divided into semicircular terraces. From there gracious Brock St gradually reveals Bath's exquisite Royal Crescent.

Royal Crescent

The imposing, impeccably grand Royal Crescent (p196) curls around private lawns. Designed by John Wood the Younger (1728–82) and built between 1767 and 1775, the houses appear perfectly symmetrical from the outside, but no two houses are quite the same inside.

The Walk » From the Crescent's far end, stroll back along Royal Ave. Opposite the bowling green pavilion, cut left from the main road, up an easy-to-miss path to hunt out the gate in the wall leading into the Georgian Garden.

Georgian Garden

The tiny, walled **Georgian Garden** (off Royal Ave; ☺9am-5pm) features period plants and gravel walkways. They've been carefully restored, providing an intriguing insight into what would have lain behind the Circus' grand facades.

The Walk » Pass through Queen Sq, the oldest of Bath's Georgian squares to skirt the elaborate Theatre Royal (1805). Upper Borough Walls marks medieval Bath's northern edge; from here it's a short stroll to the Pump Room.

Grand Pump Room

The centre of the grand 19th-century **Pump Room** (www.romanbaths.co.uk; Stall St; ☺10am-5pm) is filled with restaurant tables, but the interior also shelters an ornate spa fountain from which Bath's famous hot springs flow. Ask staff for a (free) glass; it will be startlingly warm – an impressive 38°C (100°F).

The Walk » Cut down Stall St, back into St Lawrence St and back to your car.

Ireland

YOUR MAIN REASON FOR VISITING? TO EXPERIENCE IRELAND OF THE POSTCARD – captivating peninsulas, dramatic wildness and undulating hills. Scenery, history, culture, bustling cosmopolitanism and the stillness of village life – you'll visit blockbuster attractions and replicate famous photo ops. But there are plenty of surprises too – and they're all within easy reach of each other. Whether you want to drive through the wildest terrain or sample great food while hopping between spa treatments, we've got something for you.

Ring of Kerry Ruined cottage on the seashore
REMIZOV/SHUTTERSTOCK ©

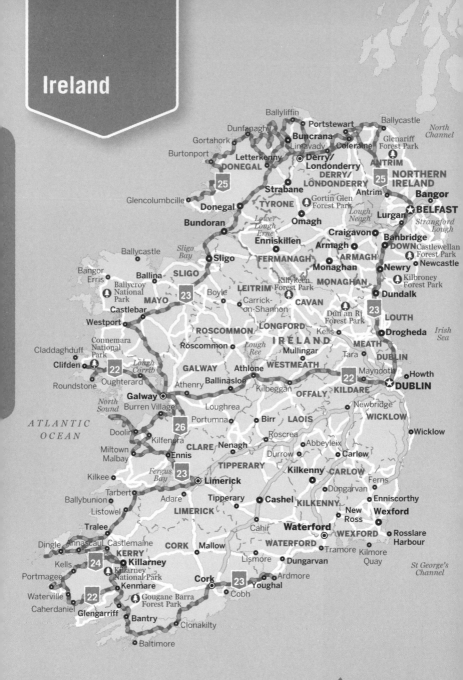

Ireland

Ballyliffin
Portstewart
Ballycastle
North Channel
Dunfanaghy
Buncrana
Glenariff
Forest Park
Gortahork
Limavady
Coleraine
Burtonport
Letterkenny
Derry/
ANTRIM
NORTHERN
25
DONEGAL
Londonderry
25
IRELAND
DERRY/
LONDONDERRY
Antrim
Bangor
Strabane
TYRONE
Lurgan
☆**BELFAST**
Glencolumbcille
Donegal
Gortin Glen
Forest Park
Lough
Neagh
Strangford
Lough
Bundoran
Omagh
Lower
Lough
Erne
Craigavon
Banbridge
DOWN
Castlewellan
Forest Park
Enniskillen
Armagh
DOWN
Newcastle
Sligo Bay
FERMANAGH
ARMAGH
Ballycastle
Sligo
Newry
Kilbroney
Forest Park
Killykeen
Forest Park
Bangor
Erris
Ballina
SLIGO
LEITRIM
MONAGHAN
Monaghan
Dundalk
Ballycroy
National
Park
MAYO
23
Boyle
Carrick-
on-Shannon
CAVAN
Dún an Rí
Forest Park
23
LOUTH
Castlebar
ROSCOMMON
LONGFORD
Kells
Drogheda
Irish
Sea
Westport
Roscommon
Lough
Ree
IRELAND
Connemara
National
Park
22
Lough
Corrib
Mullingar
MEATH
DUBLIN
Claddaghduff
Oughterard
GALWAY
Athlone
WESTMEATH
Tara
22
Maynooth
Howth
Clifden
Ballinasloe
Kilbeggan
☆**DUBLIN**
Roundstone
Athenry
Galway
OFFALY
KILDARE
North
Sound
Burren Village
Loughrea
Newbridge
26
Portumna
Birr
LAOIS
WICKLOW
ATLANTIC
OCEAN
Doolin
Kilfenora
CLARE
Nenagh
Roscrea
Abbeyleix
Carlow
Wicklow
Miltown
Malbay
Ennis
Durrow
CARLOW
Kilkee
TIPPERARY
Kilkenny
Ferns
Fergus Bay
23
◎**Limerick**
KILKENNY
Enniscorthy
Tarbert
Adare
Tipperary
Cashel
New
Ross
Wexford
Ballybunion
Listowel
LIMERICK
Cahir
WEXFORD
Rosslare
Harbour
Tralee
Waterford
Dingle
Annascaul
Castlemaine
CORK
Mallow
WATERFORD
Tramore
Kilmore
Quay
Kells
Killarney
Lismore
Dungarvan
St George's
Channel
24
Killarney
National Park
Cork
23
Ardmore
Portmagee
Kenmare
◎**Cork**
Youghal
Waterville
22
Gougane Barra
Forest Park
Cobh
Caherdaniel
Glengarriff
Bantry
Clonakilty
Baltimore

Ⓝ 0 ⸻ 50 km
0 ⸻ 25 miles

Galway Traditional Irish pub

 Iconic Ireland 7 Days
The best of Ireland's five-star cultural and natural attractions. (p301)

23 **The Long Way Round 14 Days**
Ireland's crenellated coastlines, vibrant port cities and island treasures. (p315)

24 **Ring of Kerry 4 Days**
Weave your way past jaw-dropping scenery as you circumnavigate the Iveragh Peninsula. (p329)

 The North in a Nutshell 10 Days
Big cities, big-name sights, hidden beaches, tiny islands – an epic drive. (p341)

 Musical Landscapes 5 Days
A ride round County Clare's hottest trad-music spots. (p353)

✔ DON'T MISS

Killarney Jaunting Cars
Clip-clop in a traditional horse-drawn jaunting car on Trip **24**

Belfast
When previously warring communities have the courage to strive for peace, it's inspiring. Witness that transformation on Trip **25**

Arranmore Island
Ancient pubs, turf fires and late-night music sessions make overnighting special. Do a Robinson Crusoe on Trip **25**

Ennistymon
This authentic market town in County Clare gives a genuine taste of country living. Savour its fine bars on Trip **26**

Galway
You may find it hard to leave the City of Tribes. Go for its culture, conviviality and craic on Trip **26**

Iconic Ireland

22

This trip gives you a glimpse of the very best Ireland has to offer, including the country's most famous attractions, most spectacular countryside, and most popular towns and villages.

TRIP HIGHLIGHTS

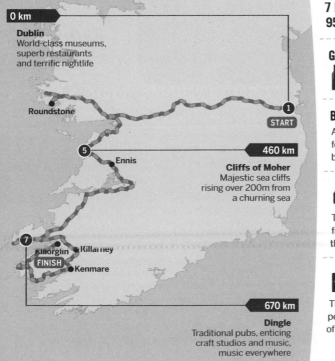

0 km

Dublin
World-class museums, superb restaurants and terrific nightlife

460 km

Cliffs of Moher
Majestic sea cliffs rising over 200m from a churning sea

670 km

Dingle
Traditional pubs, enticing craft studios and music, music everywhere

7 DAYS
959KM / 596 MILES

GREAT FOR...

BEST TIME TO GO
April to September, for the long days and best weather.

ESSENTIAL PHOTO

The Lakes of Killarney from Ladies' View on the Ring of Kerry.

BEST TWO DAYS

The Connemara peninsula and the Ring of Kerry.

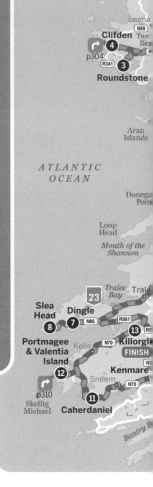

22 | Iconic Ireland

Every time-worn truth about Ireland will be found on this trip: the breathtaking scenery of stone-walled fields and wave-dashed cliffs; the picture-postcard villages and bustling towns; the ancient ruins that have stood since before history was written. The trip begins in Ireland's storied, fascinating capital and transports you to the wild west of Galway and Connemara before taking you south to the even wilder folds of County Kerry.

TRIP HIGHLIGHT

❶ Dublin

World-class museums, superb restaurants and the best collection of entertainment in the country – there are plenty of good reasons why the capital is the ideal place to start your trip. Get some sightseeing in on a walking tour (p366) before 'exploring' at least one of the city's storied – if not historic – pubs.

Your top stop should be the grounds of **Trinity College** (☎01-896 1000;

www.tcd.ie; ⏰ 8am-10pm), home to the gloriously illuminated Book of Kells. It's kept in the Old Library's stunning 65m **Long Room** (www.tcd.ie/visitors/book-of-kells; East Pavilion, Library Colonnades, Trinity College; adult/student/child €10/9/free; ⏰9.30am-5pm Mon-Sat, 9.30am-4.30pm Sun May-Sep, 9.30am-5pm Mon-Sat, noon-4.30pm Sun Oct-Apr; 🚌all city centre).

✕ 🛏 p312, p326

The Drive 》It's a 208km trip to Galway city across the country along the M6 motorway, which has little in terms of visual highlights beyond green fields, which get greener and a little more wild the further west you go. Twenty-four kilometres south of Athlone (about halfway) is a worthwhile detour to Clonmacnoise.

❷ Galway City

The best way to appreciate Galway is to amble – around Eyre Sq and

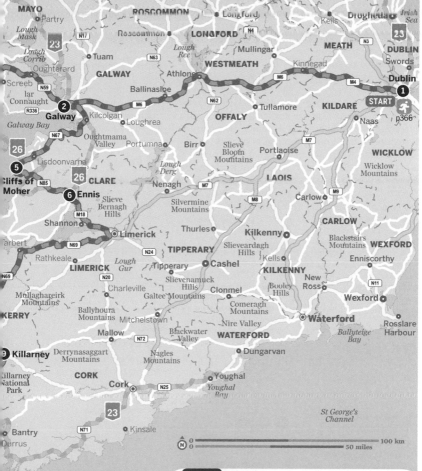

down Shop St towards the Spanish Arch and the River Corrib, stopping off for a little liquid sustenance in one of the city's classic old pubs. Top of our list is **Tig Cóilí** (Mainguard St; ⊘10.30am-midnight Mon-Thu, to 12.30am Fri & Sat, to 11pm Sun), a fire-engine-red pub that draws

LINK YOUR TRIP

23 The Long Way Round

For comprehensive coverage of the best of south and north, combine these two trips making a loop from Galway.

26 Musical Landscapes

Take a detour from Galway through County Clare's hottest trad music spots, picking up the trail again in Lisdoonvarna.

them in with its two live *céilidh* (traditional music and dancing sessions) each day. A close second is the cornflower blue **Tigh Neachtain** (www.tigh neachtain.com; 17 Upper Cross St; ⏰10.30am-11.30pm Mon-Thu & Sun, 10.30am-12.30am Fri & Sat), known simply as Neachtain's (*nock*-tans) or Naughtons – stop and join the locals for a pint.

✕ 🛏 p312

The Drive ≫ The most direct route to Roundstone is to cut through Connemara along the N59, turning left on the Clifden Rd – a total of 76km. Alternatively, the 103km coastal route, via the R336 and R340, winds its way around small bays, coves and lovely seaside hamlets.

- - - - - - - - - -

❸ Roundstone

Huddled on a boat-filled harbour, Roundstone (Cloch na Rón) is one of Connemara's gems. Colourful terrace houses and inviting pubs overlook the dark recess of Bertraghboy Bay, which is home to lobster trawl-

ers and traditional *currachs* with tarred canvas bottoms stretched over wicker frames.

Just south of the village, in the remains of an old Franciscan monastery, is Malachy Kearns'. Kearns is Ireland's only full-time maker of traditional bodhráns (handheld goatskin drums). Watch him work and buy a tin whistle, harp or booklet filled with Irish ballads; there's also a small free folk museum and a cafe.

The Drive ≫ The 22km inland route from Roundstone to Clifden is a little longer, but the road is better (especially the N59) and the brown, barren beauty of Connemara is yours to behold. The 18km coastal route along the R341 brings you through more speckled landscape; to the south you'll have glimpses of the ocean.

- - - - - - - - - -

❹ Clifden

Connemara's 'capital', Clifden (An Clochán) is an appealing Victorian-

era country town with an amoeba-shaped oval of streets offering evocative strolls. It presides over the head of the narrow bay where the River Owenglin tumbles into the sea. The surrounding countryside beckons you to walk through woods and above the shoreline.

✕ 🛏 p312

The Drive ≫ It's 154km to the Cliffs of Moher; you'll have to backtrack through Galway city (take the N59) before turning south along the N67. This will take you through the unique striated landscape of the Burren, a moody, rocky and at times fearsome space accented with ancient burial chambers and medieval ruins.

- - - - - - - - - -

TRIP HIGHLIGHT

❺ Cliffs of Moher

Star of a million tourist brochures, the Cliffs of Moher (Aillte an Mothair, or Ailltreacha Mothair) are one of the most popular sights in Ireland.

The entirely vertical cliffs rise to a height of 203m, their edge falling away abruptly into the constantly churning sea. A series of heads, the dark limestone seems to march in a rigid formation that amazes, no matter how many times you look.

Such appeal comes at a price: crowds. This is check-off tourism big time and bus-loads come and go constantly in summer. A vast **visitor centre** (www.cliffsofmoher.ie;

**DETOUR:
THE SKY ROAD**

Start: ❹ Clifden

If you head directly west from Clifden's Market Sq you'll come onto the Sky Road, a 12km route tracing a spectacular loop out to the township of Kingston and back to Clifden, taking in some rugged, stunningly beautiful coastal scenery en route. It's a cinch to drive, but you can also easily walk or cycle it.

Skellig Michael View to Little Skellig

WHY THIS IS A GREAT TRIP
FIONN DAVENPORT, WRITER

The loop from Dublin west to Galway and then south through Kerry into Cork explores all of Ireland's scenic heavy hitters. It's the kind of trip I'd make if I was introducing visiting friends to the very best Ireland has to offer, the kind of appealing appetiser that should entice them to come back and visit the country in greater depth.

Top: Staigue Fort
Left: Clifden
Right: The road between Kenmare and Killarney

10am 0pm Jul & Aug, to 7.30pm June, to 7pm May & Sep, to 6.30pm Apr, to 6pm Mar & Oct, to 5pm Nov-Feb; admission to site adult/child €6/free) handles the hordes.

Like so many over-popular natural wonders, there's relief and joy if you're willing to walk for 10 minutes. Past the end of the 'Moher Wall' south, there's a trail along the cliffs to Hag's Head – few venture this far.

The Drive » The 39km drive to Ennis goes inland at Lahinch (famous for its world-class golf links); it's then 24km to your destination, through flat south Clare. Dotted with stone walls and fields, it's the classic Irish landscape.

- - - - - - - - - - - - - -

6 Ennis

As the capital of a renowned music county, Ennis (Inis) is filled with pubs featuring trad music. In fact, this is the best reason to stay here. Where's best changes often; stroll the streets pub-hopping to find what's on any given night.

If you want to buy an authentic, well-made Irish instrument, pop into **Custy's Music Shop** (☎065-682 1727; www.custys music.com; Cook's Lane, off O'Connell St; ☺10am-6pm Mon-Sat), which sells fiddles and other musical items as well as giving general info about the local scene.

✕ ⊨ p312, p361

The Drive »It's 186km to Dingle if you go via Limerick city, but only 142km if you go via the N68 to Killimer for the ferry across the Shannon estuary to Tarbert. The views get fabulous when you're beyond Tralee on the N86, especially if you take the 456m Connor Pass, Ireland's highest.

TRIP HIGHLIGHT

❼ Dingle Town

In summer, Dingle's hilly streets can be clogged with visitors, there's just no way around it; in other seasons, its authentic charms are all yours to savour. Many of Dingle's pubs double as shops, so you can enjoy Guinness and a singalong among such items as screws and nails, wellies and horseshoes.

✕ ⊨ p313

The Drive »It's only 17km to Slea Head along the R559. The views – of the mountains to the north and the wild ocean to the south and west – are a big chunk of the reason you came to Ireland in the first place.

LOCAL KNOWLEDGE: ENNIS' BEST TRAD SESSION PUBS

Cíaran's Bar (1 Francis St; ⏱10.30am-11.30pm Mon-Thu, to 12.30am Fri & Sat, 12.30-11pm Sun) Slip into this small place by day and you can be just another geezer pondering a pint. At night there's usually trad music. Bet you wish you had a copy of the Guinness mural out front!

Brogan's (24 O'Connell St; ⏱10.30am-11.30pm Mon-Thu, to 12.30am Fri & Sat, 12.30-11pm Sun) On the corner of Cooke's Lane, Brogan's sees a fine bunch of musicians rattling even the stone floors from about 9pm Monday to Thursday, plus even more nights in summer.

Cruise's Pub (Abbey St; ⏱noon-2am) There are trad music sessions most nights from 9.30pm.

Poet's Corner Bar (Old Ground Hotel, O'Connell St; ⏱11am-11.30pm Mon-Thu, 11-12.30am Fri & Sat, noon-11pm Sun) This old pub often has massive trad sessions on Fridays.

O'Dea's (66 O'Connell St; ⏱10.30am-11.30pm Mon-Thu, to 12.30am Fri & Sat, 12.30-11pm Sun) Unchanged since at least the 1950s, this plain-tile-fronted pub is a hideout for local musicians serious about their trad sessions. Gets some of Clare's best.

❽ Slea Head

Overlooking the mouth of Dingle Bay, Mt Eagle and the Blasket Islands, Slea Head has fine beaches, good walks and superbly preserved structures from Dingle's ancient past, including **beehive huts**, forts, inscribed stones and church sites. Dunmore Head is the westernmost point on the Irish mainland and the site of the wreckage in 1588 of two Spanish Armada ships.

The Iron Age **Dunbeg Fort** is a dramatic example of a promontory fortification, perched atop a sheer sea cliff about 7km southwest of Ventry on the road to Slea Head. The fort has four outer walls of stone. Inside are the remains of a house and a beehive hut, as well as an underground passage.

The Drive »The 88km to Killarney will take you through Annascaul (home to a pub once owned by Antarctic explorer Tom Crean) and Inch (whose beach is seen in *Ryan's Daughter*). At Castlemaine, turn south towards Miltown then take the R563 to Killarney.

❾ Killarney

Beyond its proximity to lakes, waterfalls, woodland and moors dwarfed by 1000m-plus peaks, Killarney has many charms of its own as well as being the gateway to the Ring of Kerry,

Dingle Peninsula Sheep pasture

perhaps *the* outstanding highlight of many a visit to Ireland.

Besides the breathtaking views of the mountains and glacial lakes, highlights of the 10,236-hectare Killarney National Park include Ireland's only wild herd of native red deer, the country's largest area of ancient oak woods and

19th-century Muckross House.

✕ ⌗ p313, p339

It's 27km along the N71 to Konmaro, much of it through Killarney National Park with its magnificent views – especially Ladies' View (at 10km; much loved by Queen Victoria's ladies-in-waiting) and, 5km further on, Moll's Gap, a popular stop for photos and food.

⑩ Kenmare

Picturesque Kenmare carries its romantic reputation more stylishly than does Killarney, and there is an elegance about its handsome central square and attractive buildings. It still gets very busy in summer, all the same. The town stands where the delightfully named Finnihy,

Roughty and Sheen Rivers empty into Kenmare River. Kenmare makes a pleasant alternative to Killarney as a base for visiting the Ring of Kerry and the Beara Peninsula.

 p313, p339

The Drive » The 47km to Caherdaniel along the southern stretch of the Ring of Kerry duck in and out of view of Bantry Bay, with the marvellous Beara Peninsula to the south. Just before you reach Caherdaniel, a

4km detour north takes you to the rarely visited Staigue Fort, which dates from the 3rd or 4th century.

- - - - - - - - - - - -

⓫ Caherdaniel

The big attraction here is **Derrynane National Historic Park** (☑ 066-947 5113; www.heritageireland. ie; ☉10.30am-6pm Apr-Sep, 10am-5pm Wed-Sun mid-Mar–end Mar & Oct, 10am-4pm Sat & Sun Nov; adult/child €4/2), the family home

of Daniel O'Connell, the campaigner for Catholic emancipation. His ancestors bought the house and surrounding parkland, having grown rich on smuggling with France and Spain. It's largely furnished with O'Connell memorabilia, including the restored triumphal chariot in which he lapped Dublin after his release from prison in 1844.

↱ DETOUR: SKELLIG MICHAEL

Start: ⓬ Portmagee & Valentia Island

The jagged, 217m-high rock of **Skellig Michael** (www.heritageireland.ie; ☉mid-May–Sep) (Archangel Michael's Rock; like St Michael's Mount in Cornwall and Mont Saint Michel in Normandy) is the larger of the two Skellig Islands and a Unesco World Heritage Site. It looks like the last place on earth where anyone would try to land – let alone establish a community – yet early Christian monks survived here from the 6th until the 12th or 13th century. Influenced by the Coptic Church (founded by St Anthony in the deserts of Egypt and Libya), their determined quest for ultimate solitude led them to this remote, wind-blown edge of Europe.

In 2015, Skellig Michael featured as Luke Skywalker's secret retreat in *Star Wars: The Force Awakens* (and will feature in subsequent episodes of the third trilogy), attracting a whole new audience to the island's dramatic beauty.

It's a tough place to get to, and requires care to visit, but is worth every effort. You'll need to do your best grizzly sea-dog impression ('Argh!') on the 12km crossing, which can be rough. There are no toilets or shelter, so bring something to eat and drink, and wear stout shoes and weatherproof clothing. Due to the steep (and often slippery) terrain and sudden gusts, it's not suitable for young children or people with limited mobility.

Be aware that the island's fragility requires limits on the number of daily visitors. The 15 boats are licensed to carry no more than 12 passengers each, for a maximum of 180 people at any one time. It's wise to book ahead in July and August, bearing in mind that if the weather's bad the boats may not sail (about two days out of seven). Trips usually run from Easter until September, depending, again, on the weather.

Boats leave Portmagee, Ballinskelligs and Derrynane at around 10am and return at 3pm, and cost about €45 per person. Boat owners generally restrict you to two hours on the island, which is the bare minimum to see the monastery, look at the birds and have a picnic. The crossing takes about 1½ hours from Portmagee, 35 minutes to one hour from Ballinskelligs and 1¾ hours from Derrynane.

The Drive » Follow the N70 for about 18km and then turn left onto the R567, cutting through some of the wildest and most beautiful scenery on the peninsula, with the ragged outline of Skellig Michael never far from view. Turn left onto the R565; the whole drive is 35km long.

⑫ Portmagee & Valentia Island

Portmagee's single street is a rainbow of colourful houses, and is much photographed. On summer mornings, the small pier comes to life with boats embarking on the choppy crossing to the Skellig Islands.

A bridge links Portmagee to 11km-long **Valentia Island** (Oileán Dairbhre), an altogether homier isle than the brooding Skelligs to the southwest. Like the Skellig Ring it leads to, Valentia is an essential, coach-free detour from the Ring of Kerry. Some lonely ruins are worth exploring.

Valentia was chosen as the site for the first transatlantic telegraph cable. When the connection was made in 1858, it put Caherciveen in direct contact with New York. The link worked for 27 days before failing, but went back into action years later.

Derrynane Estuary Horseriding near Caherdaniel

The island makes an ideal driving loop. From April to October, there's a frequent, quick ferry trip at one end, as well as the bridge to Portmagee on the mainland at the other end.

The Drive » On the 55km drive between Portmagee and Killorglin, keep the mountains to your right (south) and the sea – when you're near it – to your left (north). Twenty-four kilometres along is the unusual Glenbeigh Strand, a tendril of sand protruding into Dingle Bay with views of Inch Point and the Dingle Peninsula.

⑬ Killorglin

Killorglin (Cill Orglan) is a quiet enough town, but that all changes in mid-August, when the town erupts in celebration for Puck Fair, Ireland's best-known extant pagan festival.

First recorded in 1603, with hazy origins, this lively (read: boozy) festival is based around the custom of installing a billy goat (a poc, or puck), the symbol of mountainous Kerry, on a pedestal in the town, its horns festooned with ribbons. Other entertainment ranges from a horse fair and bonny baby competition to street theatre, concerts and fireworks; the pubs stay open until 3am.

Author Blake Morrison documents his mother's childhood here in *Things My Mother Never Told Me*.

Eating & Sleeping

Dublin ❶

✖ 101 Talbot — Modern Irish €€

(www.101talbot.ie; 100-102 Talbot St; mains €17-24; ◷noon-3pm & 5-11pm Tue-Sat; 🖳all city centre) This Dublin classic has expertly resisted every trendy wave and has been a stalwart of good Irish cooking since opening more than two decades ago. Its speciality is traditional meat-and-two-veg dinners, but with vague Mediterranean and even Middle Eastern influences: roast Wicklow venison with sweet potato, lentil and bacon cassoulet and a sensational Morcoccan-style lamb tagine. Superb.

⌂ Number 31 — Guesthouse €€€

(☎01-676 5011; www.number31.ie; 31 Leeson Close; s/d incl breakfast €200/240; 🅿🛜; 🖳all city centre) The city's most distinctive property is the former home of modernist architect Sam Stephenson, who successfully fused '60s style with 18th-century grace. Its 21 bedrooms are split between the retro coach house, with its coolly modern rooms, and the more elegant Georgian house, where rooms are individually furnished with tasteful French antiques and big comfortable beds. Gourmet breakfasts with kippers, homemade breads and granola are served in the conservatory.

Galway City ❷

✖ Quays — Irish €€

(Quay St; mains lunch €11-14, dinner €17-22; ◷11am-10pm) This sprawling pub does a roaring business downstairs in its restaurant, which has hearty carvery lunches and more ambitious mains at night. The cold seafood platter stars the bounty from Galway Bay. Students on dates and out celebrating get rowdier as the pints and hours pass.

⌂ House Hotel — Hotel €€€

(☎091-538 900; www.thehousehotel.ie; Spanish Pde; r €140-220; 🅿🛜) There's a hip and cool array of colour in the lobby at this smart and stylish boutique hotel. Public spaces contrast modern art with trad details and bold accents. Cat motifs abound. The 40 rooms are small but plush, with bright colour schemes and quality fabrics. Bathrooms ooze comfort.

Clifden ❹

✖ Mitchell's — Seafood €€

(☎095-21867; www.mitchellsrestaurantclifden.com; Market St; lunch mains €7-15, dinner mains €17-28; ◷noon-10pm Mar-Oct) Seafood takes centre stage at this elegant spot. From a velvety chowder right through a long list of ever-changing and inventive specials, the produce of the surrounding waters is honoured. The wine list does the food justice. Lunch includes sandwiches and casual fare. Book for dinner.

⌂ Dolphin Beach — B&B €€

(☎095-21204; www.dolphinbeachhouse.com; Lower Sky Rd; s from €90, d €130-180, dinner €40; 🅿🛜) This exquisite B&B, set amid some of Connemara's best coastal scenery, does everything right. The emphasis is on style, tranquillity, relaxation and gorgeous views, a formula that can be hard to tear yourself away from. It's 5km west of Clifden, tucked away off the Lower Sky Road.

Ennis ❻

✖ Rowan Tree Cafe Bar — Mediterranean €€

(www.rowantreecafebar.ie; Harmony Row; mains €11-23; ◷10.30am-11pm; 🛜) There's nothing low rent about the excellent Med-accented fare served at this cafe-bar on the ground floor of the namesake hostel. The gorgeous main dining room has high ceilings and a wondrous old wooden floor from the 18th century; tables outside have river views. Ingredients are locally and organically sourced.

🛏 Old Ground Hotel   Hotel €€

(☎065-682 8127; www.flynnhotels.com; O'Connell St; s/d from €120/150; P@🛜) A seasoned, charming and congenial space of polished floorboards, cornice-work, antiques and open fires, the lobby is always a scene: old friends sinking into sofas, deals cut at the tables, and ladies from the neighbouring church's altar society exchanging gossip over tea. Parts of this smart and rambling landmark date back to the 1800s. The 83 rooms vary greatly in size and decor – ask to inspect a few. On balmy days, retire to tables on the lawn.

Dingle ❼

✖ Idás   Irish €€€

(☎066-915 0885; John St; mains €27-31; ⏲5.30-9.30pm Tue-Sun) Chef Kevin Murphy is dedicated to promoting the finest of Irish produce, much of it from Kerry, taking lamb and seafood and foraged herbs from the Dingle peninsula and creating delicately flavoured concoctions such as braised John Dory fillet with fennel dashi cream, pickled cucumber, wild garlic and salad burnet. An early-bird menu offers two/three courses for €24.50/28.50.

✖ Out of the Blue   Seafood €€€

(☎066-915 0811; www.outoftheblue.ie; The Wood; mains lunch €12.50-20, dinner €21-37; ⏲5-9.30pm Mon-Sat, 12.30-3pm & 5-9.30pm Sun) 'No chips', reads the menu of this funky blue-and-yellow, fishing-shack-style restaurant on the waterfront. Despite its rustic surrounds, this is one of Dingle's best restaurants, with an intense devotion to fresh local seafood (and only seafood); if they don't like the catch, they don't open. With seafood this good, who needs chips?

🛏 Pax House   B&B €€

(☎066-915 1518; www.pax-house.com; Upper John St; d from €120; ⏲Mar-Nov; P@🛜) From its highly individual decor (including contemporary paintings) to the outstanding views over the estuary from room balconies and terrace, Pax House is a treat. Choose from less expensive hill-facing accommodation,

rooms that overlook the estuary, and two-room family suites opening onto the terrace. It's 1km southeast of the town centre.

Killarney ❾

✖ Brícín   Irish €€

(www.bricin.com; 26 High St; mains €19-26; ⏲6-9pm Tue-Sat) Decorated with fittings from a convent, an orphanage and a school, this Celtic deco restaurant doubles as the town museum, with Jonathan Fisher's 18th-century views of the national park taking pride of place. Try the house speciality, boxty (traditional potato pancake). Two-/three-course dinner for €22/25 before 6.45pm.

🛏 Crystal Springs   B&B €€

(☎064-663 3272; www.crystalspringsbb.com; Ballycasheen Cross, Woodlawn Rd; s/d €70/95; P🛜) The timber deck of this wonderfully relaxing B&B overhangs the River Flesk, where trout anglers can fish for free. Rooms are richly furnished with patterned wallpapers and walnut timber; private bathrooms (most with spa baths) are huge. The glass-enclosed breakfast room also overlooks the rushing river. It's about a 15-minute stroll into town.

Kenmare ❿

✖ Horseshoe   Pub Food €€

(☎064-664 1553; www.thehorseshoekenmare. com; 3 Main St; mains €14-26; ⏲kitchen 5-10pm Thu-Mon) Flower baskets brighten the entrance to this popular gastropub, which has a short but excellent menu that runs from Kenmare Bay mussels in creamy apple cider sauce to braised Kerry lamb on mustard mash.

🛏 Parknasilla Resort & Spa   Hotel €€€

(☎064-667 5600; www.parknasillaresort. com; Parknasilla; d/f/ste from €139/179/229; P@🛜🏊) This hotel has been wowing guests (including George Bernard Shaw) since 1895 with its pristine resort on the tree-fringed shores of the Kenmare River with views to the Beara Peninsula. From the modern, luxuriously appointed bedrooms to the top-grade spa, private 12-hole golf course and elegant restaurant, everything here is done just right. It's 3km southeast of Sneem.

The Long Way Round

23

Why go in a straight line when you can perambulate at leisure? This trip explores Ireland's jagged, scenic and spectacular edges; a captivating loop that takes in the whole island.

TRIP HIGHLIGHTS

244 km

Giant's Causeway
One of the natural wonders of the world

③

Belfast

600 km

Westport
Photogenic Georgian town with a musical reputation

⑥

Dublin
START

⑨ **The Burren**
Doolin

Ring of Kerry

Inishmór
Wind-lashed, cliff-protected World Heritage island

740 km

⑭ FINISH

1300 km

Ardmore
Secluded seaside village with ancient Christian ruins

---

14 DAYS
1300KM /
807 MILES

GREAT FOR...

BEST TIME TO GO
You'll have the best weather (and crowds) in June and August, but September is ideal.

ESSENTIAL PHOTO
Killahoey Beach from the top of Horn Head.

BEST TWO DAYS
Stops 7 to 9 allow you to experience the very best of the wild west, including a day trip to the Aran Islands.

23 The Long Way Round

There's a strong case to be made that the very best Ireland has to offer is closest to its jagged, dramatic coastlines: the splendid scenery, the best mountain ranges (geographically, Ireland is akin to a bowl, with raised edges) and most of its major towns and cities – Dublin, Belfast, Galway, Sligo and Cork. The western edge – between Donegal and Cork – corresponds to the Wild Atlantic Way driving route.

- - - - - - - -

① Dublin

From its music, art and literature to the legendary nightlife that has inspired those same musicians, artists and writers, Dublin has always known how to have fun and does it with deadly seriousness. Start your sightseeing with a walk (p366).

Should you tire of the city's more highbrow offerings, the **Guinness Storehouse** (www.guinness storehouse.com; St James's Gate, South Market St; adult/ student/child €18/16/6.50, connoisseur experience €48;

⊙9.30am-5pm Sep-Jun, to 7pm Jul & Aug; 🚌21A, 51B, 78, 78A, 123 from Fleet St, 🚉James's) is the most popular place to visit in town; a beer-lover's Disneyland and multi-media bells-and-whistles homage to the country's most famous export and the city's most enduring symbol. The old grain storehouse is a suitable cathedral in which to worship the black gold; shaped like a giant pint of Guinness, it rises seven impressive storeys around a stunning central atrium.

Campbeltown

Giant's
Causeway
Ballycastle
Dunfanaghy
Buncrana
Coleraine
North
Channel
Rosses Bay
Letterkenny
Derry
Larne
Strabane
Ballymena
Antrim
Belfast
Lisburn
Donegal
Omagh
Dromore
Donegal Bay
Bundoran
Armagh
Banbridge
Sligo
Enniskillen
Monaghan
Newry
Ballysadare
Dundalk
Dundalk Bay
Charlestown
Longford
Irish Sea
Drogheda
Roscommon
Mullingar
Tuam
Swords
Ballinasloe
Athlone
Dublin START
Tullamore
Naas
Bray
Birr
Greystones
Portlaoise
Wicklow
Nenagh
Carlow
Arklow
Thurles
Kilkenny
Limerick
Cashel
Enniscorthy
Tipperary
Clonmel
New Ross
Wexford
Waterford
Rosslare Harbour
Mallow
Dungarvan
St George's Channel
Youghal
Ardmore
Cork
FINISH
Cobh

ATLANTIC OCEAN

0   80 km
0   50 miles

p312, p326

The Drive » It's 165km of motorway to Belfast – M1 in the Republic, A1 in Northern Ireland – but remember that the speed limit changes from kilometres to miles as you cross into the North.

------

② Belfast

Belfast is in many ways a brand-new city. Once lumped with Beirut, Baghdad and Bosnia as one of the four 'Bs' for travellers to avoid, in recent years it has pulled off a remarkable transformation from bombs-and-bullets pariah to a hip-hotels-and-hedonism party town.

The old shipyards on the Lagan continue to give way to the luxury apartments of the Titanic Quarter, whose centrepiece, the stunning, star-shaped edifice housing

IRELAND **23** THE LONG WAY ROUND

LINK YOUR TRIP

22 Iconic Ireland
For comprehensive coverage of the best of north and south, combine these two trips making a loop from Galway.

26 Musical Landscapes
Take a detour from Galway through County Clare's hottest trad music spots, picking up the trail again in Ennis.

the **Titanic Belfast** (www.
titanicbelfast.com; Queen's
Rd; adult/child £17.50/7.25;
🕙9am-7pm Jun-Aug, to 6pm
Apr, May & Sep, 10am-5pm Oct-
Mar) centre, covering the
ill-fated liner's construction here, has become the
city's number-one tourist
draw.

New venues keep pop-
ping up – already this
decade historic **Crumlin
Road Gaol** (🕿028-9074
1501; www.crumlinroadgaol.
com; 53-55 Crumlin Rd; day
tour adult/child £8.50/6.50,
evening tour £7.50/5.50;
🕙10am-5.30pm, last tour
4.30pm, evening tour 6pm)
and **SS Nomadic** opened
to the public, and WWI
warship **HMS Caroline**
became a floating muse-

um in 2016. They all add
to a list of attractions
that includes beauti-
fully restored Victorian
architecture, a glittering
waterfront lined with
modern art, a fantastic
foodie scene and music-
filled pubs.

If you're keen on learn-
ing more about the city's
troubled history, take
a walking tour of West
Belfast.

🍴 🛏 p326

The Drive » The *fastest* way to
the causeway is to take the A26
north, through Ballymena, before
turning off at Ballymoney – a
total of 100km – but the longer
(by 16km), more scenic route is
to take the A8 to Larne and follow
the coast through handsome

Cushendall and popular
Ballycastle.

- - - - - - - - - -

TRIP HIGHLIGHT

❸ Giant's Causeway

When you first see it
you'll understand why
the ancients believed the
causeway was not a natu-
ral feature. The vast ex-
panse of regular, closely
packed, hexagonal stone
columns dipping gently
beneath the waves looks
for all the world like the
handiwork of giants.

This spectacular rock
formation – a national
nature reserve and
Northern Ireland's only
Unesco World Heritage
Site – is one of Ireland's
most impressive and

DETOUR:
GIANT'S CAUSEWAY TO BALLYCASTLE

Start: ❸ Giant's Causeway

Between the Giant's Causeway and Ballycastle lies the most scenic stretch of the
Causeway Coast, with sea cliffs of contrasting black basalt and white chalk, rocky
islands, picturesque little harbours and broad sweeps of sandy beach. It's best
enjoyed on foot, following the 16.5km of waymarked **Causeway Coast Way** (www.
walkni.com) between the Carrick-a-Rede car park and the Giant's Causeway, although
the main attractions can also be reached by car or bus.

About 8km east of the Giant's Causeway is the meagre ruin of 16th-century
Dunseverick Castle, spectacularly sited on a grassy bluff. Another 1.5km on is the
tiny seaside hamlet of **Portbradden**, with half a dozen harbourside houses and the
tiny, blue-and-white **St Gobban's Church**, said to be the smallest in Ireland. Visible
from Portbradden and accessible via the next junction off the A2 is the spectacular
White Park Bay, with its wide, sweeping sandy beach.

The main attraction on this stretch of coast is the famous (or notorious,
depending on your head for heights) **Carrick-a-Rede Rope Bridge** (www.nationaltrust.
org.uk; Ballintoy; adult/child £5.90/3; 🕙9.30am-7pm Apr-Aug, to 6pm Mar, Sep & Oct, to 3.30pm
Nov-Feb). The 20m-long, 1m-wide bridge of wire rope spans the chasm between the
sea cliffs and the little island of Carrick-a-Rede, swaying gently 30m above the rock-
strewn water.

DETOUR: HORN HEAD

Start: ❹ Dunfanaghy

Horn Head has some of Donegal's most spectacular coastal scenery and plenty of birdlife. Its dramatic quartzite cliffs, covered with bog and heather, rear over 180m high, and the view from their tops is heart-pounding.

The road circles the headland; the best approach by car is in a clockwise direction from the Falcarragh end of Dunfanaghy. On a fine day, you'll encounter tremendous views of Tory, Inishbofin, Inishdooey and tiny Inishbeg islands to the west; Sheep Haven Bay and the Rosguill Peninsula to the east; Malin Head to the northeast; and the coast of Scotland beyond. Take care in bad weather as the route can be perilous.

atmospheric landscape features, but it can get very crowded. If you can, try to visit midweek or out of season to experience it at its most evocative. Sunset in spring and autumn is the best time for photographs.

Visiting the Giant's Causeway itself is free of charge but you pay to use the car park on a combined ticket with the **Giant's Causeway Visitor Experience** (☎028-2073 1855; www.nationaltrust.org. uk; adult/child with parking £9/4.50, without parking £7/3.25; ☺9am-7pm Apr-Sep, to 6pm Feb, Mar & Oct, to 5pm Nov-Jan); parking-only tickets aren't available.

✖ p326

The Drive » Follow the A29 and A37 as far as Derry/ Londonderry, then cross the invisible border into the Republic and take the N13 to Letterkenny before turning northwest along the N56 to Dunfanaghy. It's a total of 136km.

❹ Dunfanaghy

Huddled around the waterfront beneath the headland of Horn Head, Dunfanaghy's small, attractive town centre has a surprisingly wide range of accommodation and some of the finest dining options in the county's northwest. Glistening beaches, dramatic coastal cliffs, mountain trails and forests are all within a few kilometres.

✖ p326

The Drive » The 145km south to Sligo town will take you back through Letterkenny (this stretch is the most scenic), after which you'll follow the N13 as far as Ballyshannon and then, as you cross into County Sligo, the N13 to Sligo town.

❺ Sligo Town

It's 100km to Westport, across the western edge of County Clare – as you follow the N17 (and the N5 once you pass Charlestown), the landscape is flat, the road flanked by fields, hedge rows and clusters of farmhouses. Castlebar, 15km before Westport, is a busy county town.

✖ ⊨ p326

The Drive » It's 100km to Westport, across the western edge of County Clare – as you follow the N17 (and the N5 once you pass Charlestown), the landscape is flat, the road flanked by fields, hedge rows and clusters of farmhouses. Castlebar, 15km before Westport, is a busy county town.

TRIP HIGHLIGHT

❻ Westport

There's a lot to be said for town planning, especially if 18th-century architect James Wyatt was the brains behind the job. Westport (Cathair na Mairt), positioned on the River Carrowbeg and the shores of Clew Bay, is easily Mayo's most beautiful town and a major tourist destination for visitors to this part of the country.

WHY THIS IS A GREAT TRIP
FIONN DAVENPORT, WRITER

Not only are you covering the spectacular landscapes of mountains and jagged coastlines of the Wild Atlantic Way, but you can also explore the modern incarnation of the country's earliest settlements, taking you from prehistoric monuments to bustling cities.

Top: Thatched cottage, Doolin
Left: Donkey, Inishmór
Right: Cliffs of Moher

It's a Georgian classic, its octagonal square and tidy streets lined with trees and handsome buildings, most of which date from the late 18th century.

The Drive » Follow the N84 as far as the outskirts of Galway city – a trip of about 100km. Take the N18 south into County Clare. At Kilcolgan, turn onto the N67 and into the heart of the Burren.

- - - - - - - - - - - - - - -

❼ The Burren

The karst landscape of the Burren is not the green Ireland of postcards. But there are wildflowers in spring, giving the 560-sq-km Burren brilliant, if ephemeral, colour amid its austere beauty. Soil may be scarce, but the small amount that gathers in the cracks and faults is well drained and nutrient-rich. This, together with the mild Atlantic climate, supports an extraordinary mix of Mediterranean, Arctic and alpine plants. Of Ireland's native wildflowers, 75% are found here, including 24 species of beautiful orchids, the creamy-white burnet rose, the little starry flowers of mossy saxifrage and the magenta-coloured bloody cranesbill.

The Drive » It's 36km southwest to Doolin along the R460 and R476 roads, which cut through more familiar Irish landscapes of green fields. The real pleasures along here are the villages – the likes of Kilfenora and Lisdoonvarna are great for a pit stop and even a session of traditional music.

----

8 Doolin

Doolin is renowned as a centre of Irish traditional music, but it's also known for its setting – 6km north of the Cliffs of Moher – and down near the ever-unsettled sea, the land is windblown, with huge rocks exposed by the long-vanished topsoil.

Many musicians live in the area, and they have a symbiotic relationship with the tourists: each desires the other and each year things grow a little larger. But given the heavy concentration of visitors, it's inevitable

DOOLIN'S MUSIC PUBS

Doolin's three main music pubs (others are recent interlopers) are, in order of importance to the music scene:

McGann's (www.mcgannspubdoolin.com; Roadford; ⏰10am-12.30am, kitchen 10am-9.30pm) McGann's has all the classic touches of a full-on Irish music pub; the action often spills out onto the street. The food here is the best of the trio.

Gus O'Connor's Pub (www.gusoconnorspubdoolin.net; Fisherstreet; ⏰9am-midnight) Right on the water, this sprawling favourite packs them in and has a rollicking atmosphere when the music and drinking are in full swing.

MacDiarmada's (Roadford; ⏰bar 11am-midnight, kitchen 9am-9.30pm) Also known as McDermott's, this simple red-and-white old pub can be the rowdy favourite of locals. When the fiddles get going, it can seem like a scene out of a John Ford movie.

that standards don't always hold up to those in some of the less-trampled villages in Clare.

🛏 p361

The Drive ≫ Ferries from Doolin to Inishmór take about 90 minutes to make the crossing.

`TRIP HIGHLIGHT`

9 Inishmór

A step (and boat- or plane-ride) beyond the desolate beauty of Connemara are the Aran Islands. Most visitors are satisfied to explore only Inishmór (Árainn) and its main attraction, **Dún Aengus** (Dún Aonghasa; www.heritageireland.ie/en/west/dunaonghasa/; adult/child €4/2; ⏰9.30am-6pm Apr-Oct, 9.30am-4pm Nov-Mar, closed Mon & Tue Jan & Feb),

the stunning stone fort perched perilously on the island's towering cliffs.

Powerful swells pound the 60m-high cliff face. A complete lack of rails or other modern additions that would spoil this amazing ancient site means that you can not only go right up to the cliff's edge but also potentially fall to your doom below quite easily. When it's uncrowded, you can't help but feel the extraordinary energy that must have been harnessed to build this vast site.

The arid landscape west of Kilronan (Cill Rónáin), Inishmór's main settlement, is dominated by stone walls, boulders, scattered buildings and the odd patch of deep-green grass and potato plants.

🛏 p327, p361

The Drive ≫ Once you're back on terra firma at Doolin, it's 223km to Dingle via the N85 through Ennis as far as Limerick City. The N69 will take you into County Kerry as far as Tralee, beyond which it's 50km on the N86 to Dingle.

----

10 Dingle

Unlike the Ring of Kerry, where the cliffs tend to dominate the ocean, it's the ocean that dominates the smaller Dingle Peninsula. The opal-blue waters surrounding the promontory's multihued landscape of green hills and golden sands give rise to aquatic adventures and to fishing fleets that haul in fresh seafood that appears on the menus of some of the county's finest restaurants.

Centred on charming Dingle town, there's an alternative way of life here, lived by artisans and idiosyncratic characters and found at trad sessions and folkloric festivals across Dingle's tiny settlements.

The classic loop drive around Slea Head from Dingle town is 50km, but allow a day to take it all in – longer if you have time to stay overnight in Dingle town.

✖ 🛏 p313, p327

The Drive » Take the N86 as far as Annascaul and then the coastal R561 as far as Castlemaine. Then head southwest on the N70 to Killorglin and the Ring of Kerry. From Dingle, it's 53km.

- - - - - - - - - - - - -

⓫ Ring of Kerry

The Ring of Kerry is the longest and the most diverse of Ireland's big circle drives, combining jaw-dropping coastal scenery with emerald pastures and villages.

The 179km circuit usually begins in Killarney and winds past pristine beaches, the island-dotted Atlantic, medieval ruins, mountains and loughs (lakes). The coastline is at

AN ANCIENT FORT

For a look at a well-preserved *caher* (walled fort) of the late Iron Age to early Christian period, stop at **Caherconnell Fort** (www.burrenforts.ie; R480; adult/ child €7/4, with sheepdog demo €9.60/5.60; ☺10am-6pm Jul & Aug, 10am-5pm Mar-Apr & Oct, 10am-5.30pm May, June & Sept), a privately run heritage attraction that's more serious than sideshow. Exhibits detail how the evolution of these defensive settlements may have reflected territorialism and competition for land among a growing, settling population. The drystone walling of the fort is in excellent condition. The top-notch visitor centre also has information on many other monuments in the area. It's about 1km south of Poulnabrone Dolman on the R480.

its most rugged between Waterville and Caherdaniel in the southwest of the peninsula. It can get crowded in summer, but even then the remote Skellig Ring can be uncrowded and serene – and starkly beautiful.

The Ring of Kerry can easily be done as a day trip, but if you want to stretch it out, places to stay are scattered along the route. Killorglin and Kenmare have the best dining options, with some excellent restaurants; elsewhere, basic (sometimes very basic) pub fare is the norm. The Ring's most popular diversion is the Gap of Dunloe, an awe-inspiring mountain pass at the western edge of Killarney National Park. It's signposted off the N72 between Killarney to Killorglin. The incredibly popular 19th-century

Kate Kearney's Cottage is a pub where most visitors park their cars before walking up to the gap.

- - - - - - - - - - - - -

⓬ Kenmare

If you've done the Ring in an anticlockwise fashion (or cut through the Gap of Dunloe), you'll end up in handsome Kenmare, a largely 18th-century town and the ideal alternative to Killarney as a place to stay overnight.

✖ 🛏 p313, p327

The Drive » Picturesque villages, a fine stone circle and calming coastal scenery mark the less-taken, 143km route from Kenmare to Cork city. When you get to Leap, turn right onto the R597 and go as far as Rosscarbery; or, even better, take twice as long (even though it's only 24km more) and freelance your way along narrow roads near the water the entire way.

LOCAL KNOWLEDGE: THE HEALY PASS

Instead of going directly into County Cork along the N71 from Kenmare, veer west onto the R571 and drive for 16km along the northern edge of the Beara Peninsula. At Lauragh, turn onto the R574 and take the breathtaking Healy Pass Road, which cuts through the peninsula and brings you from County Kerry into County Cork. At Adrigole, turn left onto the R572 and rejoin the N71 at Glengarriff, 17km east.

⑬ Cork City

Ireland's second city is first in every important respect, at least according to the locals, who cheerfully refer to it as the 'real capital of Ireland'. The compact city centre is surrounded by interesting waterways and is chock full of great restaurants fed by arguably the best foodie scene in the country.

✕ ⊨ p327

The Drive » It's only 60km to Ardmore, but stop off in Midleton, 24km east of Cork along the N25, and visit the whiskey museum. Just beyond Youghal, turn right onto the R671 for Ardmore.

TRIP HIGHLIGHT

⑭ Ardmore

Because it's off the main drag, Ardmore is a sleepy seaside village and one of the southeast's loveliest spots – the ideal destination for those looking for a little waterside R&R.

St Declan reputedly set up shop here sometime between AD 350 and 420, which would make Ardmore the first Christian bastion in Ireland – long before St Patrick landed. The village's 12th-century **round tower**, one of the best examples of these structures in Ireland, is the town's most distinctive architectural feature, but you should also check out the ruins of St Declan's church and well, on a bluff above the village.

Carrick-a-Rede Rope Bridge Tourists cross the 30m-high bridge

Eating & Sleeping

Dublin ❶

✕ Fade Street Social   Modern Irish €€

(📞01-604 0066; www.fadestreetsocial.com; 4-6 Fade St; mains €19-32, tapas €5-12; ⏱12.30-10.30pm Mon-Fri, 5-10.30pm Sat & Sun; 🛜; 🖥all city centre) Two eateries in one, courtesy of renowned chef Dylan McGrath: at the front, the buzzy tapas bar, which serves up gourmet bites from a beautiful open kitchen. At the back, the more muted restaurant specialises in Irish cuts of meat – from veal to rabbit – served with home grown, organic vegetables. There's a bar upstairs too. Reservations suggested.

⛺ Westbury Hotel   Hotel €€€

(📞01-679 1122; www.doylecollection.com; Grafton St; r/ste from €240/360; 🅿 @ 🛜; 🖥all city centre) Tucked away just off Grafton St is one of the most elegant hotels in town, although you'll need to upgrade to a suite to really feel the luxury. The standard rooms are perfectly comfortable but not really of the same theme as the luxurious public space – the upstairs lobby is a great spot for afternoon tea or a drink.

Belfast ❷

✕ Ginger   Bistro ££

(📞028-9024 4421; www.gingerbistro.com; 6-8 Hope St; mains lunch £10-12.50, dinner £16-24; ⏱5-9pm Mon, noon-3pm & 5-9.30pm Tue-Thu, noon-3pm & 5-10pm Fri & Sat; 🍴) Ginger is cosy and informal, but its food is anything but ordinary – the flame-haired owner/chef (hence the name) really knows what he's doing, sourcing top-quality Irish produce and creating exquisite dishes such as tea-smoked duck breast with ginger and sweet-potato puree.

⛺ Merchant Hotel   Hotel £££

(📞028-9023 4888; www.themerchanthotel.com; 16 Skipper St; d/ste from £200/300; 🅿 @ 🛜) Belfast's most flamboyant Victorian building (the old Ulster Bank head office) has been converted into the city's most flamboyant boutique hotel, a fabulous fusion of contemporary styling and old-fashioned elegance, with individually decorated rooms. Luxe leisure facilities at its gymnasium and spa include an eight-person rooftop hot tub. Its restaurant, **Great Room** (mains £19.50-28.50; ⏱7am-11pm), is magnificent.

Giant's Causeway ❸

✕ 55 Degrees North   International ££

(📞028-7082 2811; www.55-north.com; 1 Causeway St; mains £10-19; ⏱12.30-2.30pm & 5-8.30pm Mon-Fri, to 9pm Sat, noon-8.30pm Sun; 🍴🚼) Floor-to-ceiling windows allow you to soak up a spectacular panorama of sand and sea from this stylish restaurant. The food concentrates on clean, simple flavours.

Dunfanaghy ❹

✕ Cove   Modern Irish €€

(📞074-913 6300; www.thecoverestaurant donegal.com; off N56, Rockhill, Port-na-Blagh; dinner mains €17-25; ⏱1-4pm Sun, 6.30-9pm Tue-Sun Jul & Aug, shorter hours rest of year, closed Jan–mid-Mar) Owners Siobhan Sweeney and Peter Byrne are perfectionists who tend to every detail in Cove's art-filled dining room, and on your plate. The cuisine is fresh and inventive. Seafood specials are deceptively simple with subtle Asian influences. After dinner, enjoy the elegant lounge upstairs. Book ahead.

Sligo Town ❺

✕ Lyons Cafe   Modern European €

(📞071-914 2969; www.lyonscafe.com; Quay St; mains €7-15; ⏱9am-6pm Mon-Sat) Sligo's flagship department store, Lyons, opened in 1878 – with original leadlight windows and squeaky timber floors – and has been going strong since 1923. At its airy 1st-floor cafe, acclaimed chef (and cookbook author) Gary Stafford offers a fresh and seasonal menu.

🛏 Pearse Lodge B&B €€

(📞071-916 1090; www.pearselodge.com; Pearse Rd; s/d from €50/80; @ 🛜) Welcoming owners Mary and Kieron have four stylish guest rooms with hardwood floors. The breakfast menu includes smoked salmon and French toast with bananas. A sunny sitting room opens to a garden. It's 700m southwest of the centre.

Inishmór ❼

🛏 Kilmurvey House B&B €€

(📞099-61218; www.kilmurveyhouse.com; Kilmurvey; s/d from €50/90; 🕙mid-Apr–mid-Oct) On the path leading to Dún Aengus is this grand 18th-century stone mansion. It's a beautiful setting and the 12 rooms are well maintained. Hearty meals (dinner €30) incorporate vegetables from the garden, and local fish and meats. You can swim at a pretty beach that's a short walk from the house.

Dingle ❿

✖ Idás Irish €€€

(📞066-915 0885; John St; mains €27-31; 🕙5.30-9.30pm Tue-Sun) Chef Kevin Murphy is dedicated to promoting the finest of Irish produce, much of it from Kerry, taking lamb and seafood and foraged herbs from the Dingle peninsula and creating delicately flavoured concoctions such as braised John Dory fillet with fennel dashi cream, pickled cucumber, wild garlic and salad burnet. An early-bird menu offers two/three courses for €24.50/28.50.

🛏 Pax House B&B €€

(📞066-915 1518; www.pax-house.com; Upper John St; d from €120; 🕙Mar-Nov; P @ 🛜) From its highly individual decor to the outstanding views over the estuary from room balconies and terrace, Pax House is a treat. Choose from less expensive hill-facing accommodation, rooms that overlook the estuary, and two-room family suites opening onto the terrace. It's 1km southeast of the town centre.

Kenmare ⓬

✖ Tom Crean Fish & Wine Irish €€

(📞064-664 1589; http://tomcrean.ie; Main St; 2-/3-course menus €25/29, mains €16.50; 🕙5-9.30pm Thu-Sun late-Mar–Dec; 🛜) Named for Kerry's pioneering Antarctic explorer, and run by his granddaughter, this venerable restaurant uses only the best of local organic produce, cheeses and fresh seafood, all served in modern, low-key surrounds. The oysters *au naturel* capture the scent of the sea; the homemade ravioli of prawn mousse, and sesame seed-crusted Atlantic salmon with lime and coriander are divine.

🛏 Virginia's Guesthouse B&B €€

(📞064-664 1021; www.virginias-kenmare.com; Henry St; s/d from €40/75; 🛜) You can't get more central than this award-winning B&B, whose creative breakfasts celebrate organic local produce (rhubarb and blueberries in season, for example, as well as fresh-squeezed OJ and porridge with whiskey). Its eight rooms are super-comfy without being fussy.

Cork City ⓭

✖ Market Lane Irish, International €€

(📞021-427 4710; www.marketlane.ie; 5 Oliver Plunkett St; mains €10-25; 🕙noon-10pm Mon-Thu, noon-10.30pm Fri & Sat, 1-9pm Sun; 🛜♿) It's always hopping at this bright corner bistro. The menu is broad and hearty, changing to reflect what's fresh at the English Market: perhaps braised ox cheek in ale, or smoked haddock with bacon and cabbage? No reservations for fewer than six diners; sip a drink at the bar till a table is free.

🛏 Imperial Hotel Hotel €€

(📞021-427 4040; www.flynnhotels.com; South Mall; d €130-200; P @ 🛜) Having recently celebrated its bicentenary – Thackeray, Dickens and Sir Walter Scott have all stayed here – the Imperial knows how to age gracefully. Public spaces resonate with period detail, while the 130 bedrooms feature writing desks, understated decor and modern touches including a luxurious spa and a digital music library. Irish Free State commander-in-chief Michael Collins spent his last night alive here; you can ask to check into his room.

Ring of Kerry

24

Circumnavigating the Iveragh Peninsula, the Ring of Kerry is the longest and most diverse of Ireland's prized peninsula drives, combining jaw-dropping cliffs with soaring mountains.

TRIP HIGHLIGHTS

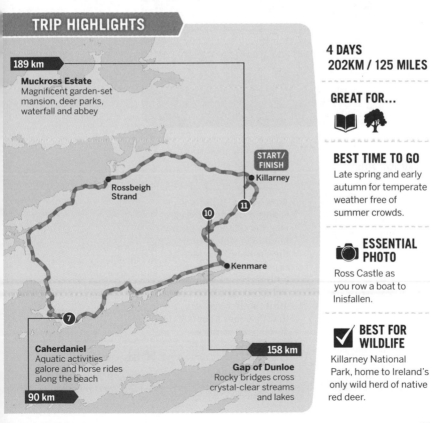

189 km

Muckross Estate
Magnificent garden-set mansion, deer parks, waterfall and abbey

START/FINISH

Killarney

Rossbeigh Strand

11

10

Kenmare

7

Caherdaniel
Aquatic activities galore and horse rides along the beach

90 km

158 km

Gap of Dunloe
Rocky bridges cross crystal-clear streams and lakes

4 DAYS
202KM / 125 MILES

GREAT FOR...

BEST TIME TO GO
Late spring and early autumn for temperate weather free of summer crowds.

ESSENTIAL PHOTO
Ross Castle as you row a boat to Inisfallen.

BEST FOR WILDLIFE
Killarney National Park, home to Ireland's only wild herd of native red deer.

Waterville County Coastal scenery

24 Ring of Kerry

You can drive the Ring of Kerry in a day, but the longer you spend, the more you'll enjoy it. The circuit winds past pristine beaches, the island-dotted Atlantic, medieval ruins, mountains and loughs, with the coastline at its most rugged between Waterville and Caherdaniel in the peninsula's southwest. You'll also find plenty of opportunities for serene, starkly beautiful detours, such as the Skellig Ring and the Cromane Peninsula.

1 Killarney

A town that's been practising the tourism game for more than 250 years, Killarney is a well-oiled machine driven by the sublime scenery of its namesake national park, and competition keeps standards high. Killarney nights are lively and most pubs put on live music.

Killarney and its surrounds have been inhabited probably since the Neolithic period and were certainly the site of some important Bronze Age settlements, based on the copper ore mined on Ross Island. Killarney changed hands between warring tribes, the most notable of which were the Fir Bolg ('Bag Men'), expert stonemasons who built forts and devised Ogham script. It wasn't until the 17th century that Viscount Kenmare developed the town as an Irish version of England's Lake District. Among its notable 19th-century tourists were Queen Victoria and Romantic poet Percy Bysshe Shelley, who began *Queen Mab* here.

The town can easily be explored on foot in an hour or two, or you can get around by taking a horse-drawn jaunting car.

✗ ⏢ p313, p339

The Drive » From Killarney, head 22km west to Killorglin

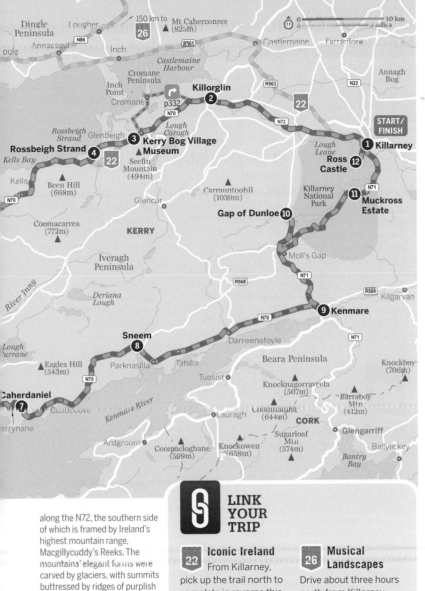

along the N72, the southern side of which is framed by Ireland's highest mountain range, Macgillycuddy's Reeks. The mountains' elegant forms were carved by glaciers, with summits buttressed by ridges of purplish rock. The name derives from the ancient Mac Gilla Muchudas clan; reek means 'pointed hill'. In Irish, they're known as Na Crucha Dubha (the Black Tops).

LINK YOUR TRIP

22 Iconic Ireland

From Killarney, pick up the trail north to complete in reverse this tour of the very best of Ireland's attractions.

26 Musical Landscapes

Drive about three hours north from Killarney to Galway to start a quest for County Clare's hottest trad music spots.

② Killorglin

Killorglin (Cill Orglan) is quieter than the waters of the River Laune that lap against its 1885-built eight-arched bridge – except in mid-August, when there's an explosion of time-honoured ceremonies at the famous **Puck Fair** (Aonach an Phuic; ☎066-976 2366; www.puck fair.ie), a pagan festival whose first recorded mention was in 1603. A statue of King Puck (a goat) peers out from the Killarney side of the river.

Killorglin has some of the finest eateries along the Ring. That said, there's not much competition along much of the route until you reach Kenmare.

🗙 🛏 p339

The Drive » Killorglin sits at the crossroads of the N72 and the N70; continue 13km along the N70 to the Kerry Bog Village Museum.

③ Kerry Bog Village Museum

Between Killorglin and Glenbeigh, the **Kerry Bog Village Museum** (www.kerrybogvillage.ie; Ballincleave, Glenbeigh; adult/child €6.50/4.50; ⊗8.30am-6pm; P ★) re-creates a 19th-century bog village, typical of the small communities that carved out a precarious living in the harsh environment of Ireland's ubiquitous peat bogs. You'll see the thatched homes of the turf cutter, blacksmith, thatcher and labourer, as well as a dairy, and meet rare Kerry Bog ponies.

The Drive » It's less than 1km from the museum to the village of Glenbeigh; turn off here and drive 2km west to unique Rossbeigh Strand.

④ Rossbeigh Strand

This unusual beach is a tendril of sand protruding into Dingle Bay, with views of Inch Point and the Dingle Peninsula. On one side, the sea is ruffled by Atlantic winds; on the other, it's sheltered and calm.

DETOUR: CROMANE PENINSULA

Start: ② Killorglin

Open fields give way to spectacular water vistas and multihued sunsets on the Cromane Peninsula, with its tiny namesake village sitting at the base of a narrow shingle spit.

Cromane's exceptional restaurant, **Jack's Coastguard Restaurant** (☎066-976 9102; http://jackscromane.com; 2-/3-course menus €33/39, dinner mains €16.50-32.50; ⊗6-9pm Wed-Sat, 1-3.30pm & 6-9pm Sun, hrs may vary; P ★), is a local secret and justifies the trip. Entering this 1866-built coastguard station feels like arriving at a low-key village pub, but a narrow doorway at the back of the bar leads to a striking, whitewashed contemporary space where lights glitter from midnight-blue ceiling panels, and there are stained glass and metallic fish sculptures, a pianist and huge picture windows overlooking the water. Seafood is the standout, but there's also steak, roast lamb and a veggie dish of the day.

Cromane is 9km from Killorglin. Heading southwest from Killorglin along the N70, take the second right and continue straight ahead until you get to the crossroads. Turn right; Jack's Coastguard Restaurant is on your left.

For more info on the area, visit www.cromane.net.

DETOUR:
VALENTIA ISLAND & THE SKELLIG RING

Start: ❺ Cahersiveen

If you're here between April and October, and you're detouring via Valentia Island and the Skellig Ring, a **ferry service** (📞087 241 8973; one way/return car €7/10, cyclist €2/3, pedestrian €1.50/2; ⏱7.45am-10pm Mon-Sat, 9am-10pm Sun Jul & Aug, 7.45am-9.30pm Mon-Sat, 9am-9.30pm Sun Apr-Jun, Sep & Oct) from Reenard Point, 5km southwest of Cahersiveen, provides a handy shortcut to Knightstown on Valentia Island. The five-minute crossing departs every 10 minutes. Alternatively, there's a bridge from Portmagee to Valentia Island.

Crowned by Geokaun Mountain, 11km-long Valentia Island (Oileán Dairbhre) makes an ideal driving loop, with some lonely ruins that are worth exploring. Knightstown, the only town, has pubs, food and walks.

The **Skellig Experience** (📞066-947 6306; www.skelligexperience.com; adult/child €5/3, incl cruise €30/17.50; ⏱10am-7pm Jul & Aug, to 6pm May, Jun & Sep, to 5pm Tue-Sat Mar, Apr, Oct & Nov; 🅿) heritage centre, in a distinctive building with turf-covered barrel roofs, has informative exhibits on the Skellig Islands offshore. From April to September, it also runs two-hour cruises around the Skelligs. If the weather's bad, there's often the option of a 90-minute mini-cruise (€22/11, including museum entry) in the harbour and channel.

Immediately across the bridge on the mainland, Portmagee's single street is a rainbow of colourful houses. On summer mornings the small pier comes to life with boats embarking on the choppy crossing to the Skellig Islands. Portmagee holds **set-dancing workshops** (www.moorings.ie) over the May bank holiday weekend, with plenty of stomping practice sessions in the town's **Bridge Bar** (⏱food noon-9pm), a friendly local gathering point that's also good for impromptu music year-round and more formal sessions in summer.

The wild and beautiful, 18km-long Skellig Ring road links Portmagee and Waterville via a Gaeltacht (Irish-speaking) area centred on Ballinskelligs (Baile an Sceilg), with the ragged outline of Skellig Michael never far from view.

The Drive ⟩⟩ Rejoin the N70 and continue 25km south to Cahersiveen.

- - - - - - - - - - - -

❺ Cahersiveen

Cahersiveen's population – over 30,000 in 1841 – was decimated by the Great Famine and emigration to the New World. A sleepy outpost remains, overshadowed by the 688m peak of **Knocknadobar**. It looks rather dour compared with the peninsula's other settlements, but the atmospheric remains of 16th-century **Ballycarbery Castle**, 2.4km along the road to White Strand Beach from the town centre, are well worth a visit.

Along the same road are two stone ring forts. The larger, **Cahergall**, dates from the 10th century and has stairways on the inside walls, a *clochán* (circular stone building shaped like an old-fashioned beehive) and the remains of a house. The smaller, 9th-century **Leacanabuile** has an entrance to an underground passage. Their inner walls and chambers give a strong sense of what life was like in a ring fort. Leave your car in the parking area next to a stone

WHY THIS IS A GREAT TRIP
CATHERINE LE NEVEZ, WRITER

In a land criss-crossed with classic drives, the Ring of Kerry is perhaps the most classic of all. Now a key stretch of the Wild Atlantic Way, the Ring showcases Ireland's most spectacular coastal scenery, its ancient and recent history, its low-ceilinged pubs with crackling turf fires and spontaneous, high-spirited trad-music sessions, and the Emerald Isle's most engaging asset: its welcoming, warm-hearted locals.

Above: Ross Castle, Killarney
Left: Killarney National Park
Right: Standing stones, Waterville

wall and walk up the footpaths.

The Drive » From Cahersiveen you can continue 17km along the classic Ring of Kerry on the N70 to Waterville, or take the ultrascenic route via Valentia Island and the Skellig Ring, and rejoin the N70 at Waterville.

- - - - - - - - - - - -

6 Waterville

A line of colourful houses on the N70 between Lough Currane and Ballinskelligs Bay, Waterville is charm-challenged in the way of many mass-consumption beach resorts. A statue of its most famous guest, Charlie Chaplin, beams from the seafront. The **Charlie Chaplin Comedy Film Festival** (http://chaplinfilmfestival.com) is held in August.

Waterville is home to a world-renowned **links golf course**. At the north end of Lough Currane, **Church Island** has the ruins of a medieval church and beehive cell reputedly founded as a monastic settlement by St Finian in the 6th century.

🛏 p339

The Drive » Squiggle your way for 14km along the Ring's most tortuous stretch, past plunging cliffs and soaring mountains, to Caherdaniel.

7 Caherdaniel

The scattered hamlet of Caherdaniel counts two of the Ring of Kerry's highlights: Derrynane National Historic Park, surrounded by sub-tropical gardens; and bar-restaurant **Scarriff Inn** (📞066-947 5132; http://scarriffinn.com; Caherdaniel; ⏰9am-9pm, kitchen hrs vary), with its picture windows framing what it plausibly claims is 'Ireland's finest view' over rugged cliffs and islands.

Most activity here centres on the Blue Flag beach. **Derrynane Sea Sports** (📞087 908 1208; www.derrynaneseasports.com; Derrynane Beach) organises sailing, canoeing, surfing, windsurfing and water-skiing (from €40 per person), as well as equipment hire (around €10 per hour). **Eagle Rock Equestrian Centre** (📞066-947 5145; www.eaglerockcentre.com; Bally-carnahan; per hr €35) offers beach, mountain and woodland horse treks for all levels.

The Drive ≫ Wind your way east along the N70 for 21km to Sneem.

8 Sneem

Sneem's Irish name, An tSnaidhm, translates to 'the knot', which is thought to refer to the River Sneem that swirls, knot-like, into nearby Kenmare Bay.

Take a gander at the town's two cute squares, then pop into the **Blue Bull** (📞064-664 5382; South Sq; mains €17-29; ⏰food noon-2pm & 6-9.30pm), a perfect little old stone pub, for a pint.

🛏 p339

The Drive ≫ Along the 27km drive to Kenmare, the N70 drifts away from the water to coast along under a canopy of trees.

9 Kenmare

The copper-covered lime-stone spire of Holy Cross Church, drawing the eye to the wooded hills above town, may make you forget for a split second that Kenmare is a seaside town. With rivers named Finnihy, Roughty and Sheen emptying into Kenmare Bay, you couldn't be anywhere other than southwest Ireland.

In the 18th century Kenmare was laid out to an X-shaped plan, with a triangular market square in the centre. Today the inverted V to the south is the focus. Kenmare Bay stretches out to the southwest, and there are glorious views of the mountains.

Signposted south-west of the square is an early Bronze Age **stone circle**, one of the biggest in southwest Ireland. Fifteen stones ring a boulder dolmen, a burial monument rarely found outside this part of the country.

✕ 🛏 p313, p339

The Drive ≫ The coastal scenery might be finished, but, if anything, the next 23km are even more stunning as you head north from Kenmare to the Gap of Dunloe on the vista-crazy N71, winding between rock and lake, with plenty of lay-bys (shoulders) to stop and admire the views (and recover from the switchback bends).

10 Gap of Dunloe

Just west of Killarney National Park, the Gap

✓ **TOP TIP:**
AROUND (AND ACROSS) THE RING

Tour buses travel anticlockwise around the Ring, and authorities generally encourage visitors to drive in the same direction to avoid traffic congestion and accidents. If you travel clockwise, watch out on blind corners. There's little traffic on the Ballaghbeama Gap, which cuts across the peninsula's central highlands and has some spectacular views.

KILLARNEY NATIONAL PARK

Designated a Unesco Biosphere Reserve in 1982, **Killarney National Park** (www. killarneynationalpark.ie) is among the finest of Ireland's national parks. And while its proximity to one of the southwest's largest and liveliest urban centres (including pedestrian entrances right in Killarney's town centre) is an ongoing threat due to high visitor numbers, it's an important conservation area for many rare species. Within its 102 sq km is Ireland's only wild herd of native red deer, which has lived here continuously for 12,000 years, as well as the country's largest area of ancient oak woods and views of most of its major mountains.

The glacial Lough Leane (the Lower Lake or 'Lake of Learning'), Muckross Lake and the Upper Lake make up about a quarter of the park. Their peaty waters are as rich in wildlife as the surrounding land: cormorants skim across the surface, deer swim out to graze on islands, and salmon, trout and perch prosper in a pike-free environment. Lough Leane has vistas of reeds and swans.

With a bit of luck, you might see white-tailed sea eagles, with their 2.5m wingspan, soaring overhead. The eagles were reintroduced here in 2007 after more than 100 years of local extinction. There are now more than 50 in the park and they're starting to settle in Ireland's rivers, lakes and coastal regions. And like Killarney itself, the park is also home to plenty of summer visitors, including migratory cuckoos, swallows and swifts.

Keep your eyes peeled, too, for the park's smallest residents – its insects, including the northern emerald dragonfly, which isn't normally found this far south in Europe and is believed to have been marooned here after the last ice age.

of Dunloe is ruggedly beautiful. In the winter it's an awe-inspiring mountain pass, overshadowed by Purple Mountain and Macgillycuddy's Reeks. In high summer it's a bottleneck for the tourist trade, with buses ferrying countless visitors here for horse-and-trap rides through the Gap.

On the southern side, surrounded by lush, green pastures, is **Lord Brandon's Cottage** (Gearhameen, Beaufort; dishes €3-8; ☺8am-3pm Apr-Oct), accessed by turning left at Moll's Gap on the R568, then taking the first right, another right at the bottom of the hill, then right again at the crossroads (about 13km from the N71 all up). A simple 19th-century hunting lodge, it has an open-air cafe and a dock for boats crossing Killarney National Park's Upper Lake. From here a (very) narrow road weaves up the hill to the Gap – theoretically you can drive this 8km route to the 19th-century pub **Kate Kearney's Cottage** (☎064-664 4146; www. katekearneyscottage.com; mains €11-23.50; ☺food noon-8pm; [P][🚲]) and back *but* only outside summer. Even then walkers and cyclists have right of way, and the precipitous hairpin bends are nerve-testing. It's worth walking or taking a jaunting car (or, if you're carrying two wheels, cycling) through the Gap, however: the scenery is a fantasy of rocky bridges over clear mountain streams and lakes. Alternatively, there are various options for exploring the Gap from Killarney.

The Drive ≫ Continue on the N71 north through Killarney National Park to Muckross Estate (32km).

- - - - - - - - - -

TRIP HIGHLIGHT

⑪ **Muckross Estate**

The core of Killarney National Park is Muckross

Estate, donated to the state by Arthur Bourn Vincent in 1932. **Muckross House** ([J]064-667 0144; www.muckross-house. ie; adult/child €9/6, incl Muckross Traditional Farms €15/10.50; ☺9am-7pm Jul & Aug, to 5.30pm Sep-Jun; [P]) is a 19th-century mansion, restored to its former glory and packed with period fittings. Entrance is by guided tour.

The beautiful **gardens** slope down, and a block behind the house contains a restaurant, craft shop and studios where you can see potters, weavers and bookbinders at work. Jaunting cars wait to run you through deer parks and woodland to **Torc Waterfall** and **Muckross Abbey** (about €20 each, return; haggling can reap discounts). The visitor centre has an excellent cafe.

Adjacent to Muckross House are the **Muckross Traditional Farms**

([J]064-663 0804; www. muckross-house.ie; adult/child €9/6, incl Muckross House €15/10.50; ☺10am-6pm Jun-Aug, 1-6pm May & Sep, 1-6pm Sat & Sun Apr & Oct). These reproductions of 1930s Kerry farms, complete with chickens, pigs, cattle and horses, re-create farming and living conditions when people had to live off the land.

The Drive ❯❯ Continuing a further 2km north through the national park brings you to historic Ross Castle.

- - - - - - - - - - -

⓲ Ross Castle

Restored by Dúchas, **Ross Castle** ([J]064-663 5851; www.heritageireland. ie; Ross Rd; adult/child €4/2; ☺9.30am-5.45pm early Mar-Oct; [P]) dates back to the 15th century, when it was a residence of the O'Donoghues. It was the last place in Munster to succumb to Cromwell's forces, thanks partly to its cunning spiral stair-

case, every step of which is a different height in order to break an attacker's stride. Access is by guided tour only.

You can hire boats (around €5) from Ross Castle to row out to **Inisfallen**, the largest of Killarney National Park's 26 islands. The first monastery on Inisfallen is said to have been founded by St Finian the Leper in the 7th century. The island's fame dates from the early 13th century when the Annals of Inisfallen were written here. Now in the Bodleian Library at Oxford, they remain a vital source of information on early Munster history. Inisfallen shelters the ruins of a 12th-century oratory with a carved Romanesque doorway and a monastery on the site of St Finian's original.

The Drive ❯❯ It's just 3km north from Ross Castle back to Killarney.

Eating & Sleeping

Killarney ❶

🛏 Aghadoe Heights Hotel
Luxury Hotel €€€

(📞064-663 1766; www.aghadoeheights.com; Aghadoe; d/f/ste from €249/319/390, bar mains €15-29.50; ⏰bar 11am-9.30pm; 🅿@🛜🏊) A huge, glassed-in swimming pool overlooking the lakes is the centrepiece of this stunning contemporary hotel, but you can also soak up the views from the **bar** and **Lake Room Restaurant** (mains €21-38; ⏰6.30-9.30pm; 🧑), both of which are open to nonguests, as is the decadent spa, with 11 treatment rooms and four-chamber thermal suite. Heavenly beds have memory foam mattresses.

Killorglin ❷

🍴 Bianconi
Irish €€

(📞066-976 1146; www.bianconi.ie; Bridge St; mains €14.50-25; ⏰8am-11.30pm Mon-Thu, 8am-12.30am Fri & Sat, 6-11pm Sun; 🛜🧑) Bang in the centre of town, this Victorian-style pub has a classy ambience and an equally classy menu. Its spectacular salads, such as Cashel blue cheese, apple, toasted almonds and chorizo, are a meal in themselves. Upstairs, newly refurbished guest rooms (doubles from €110) have olive and truffle tones and luxurious bathrooms (try for a roll-top tub).

🛏 Coffey's River's Edge
B&B €

(📞066-976 1750; www.coffeysriversedge.com; Lower Bridge St; s/d €50/70; 🅿🛜) You can sit out on the balcony overlooking the River Laune at this contemporary B&B with spotless spring-toned rooms and hardwood floors. Central location next to the bridge.

Waterville ❻

🛏 Brookhaven House
B&B €€

(📞066-947 4431; www.brookhavenhouse. com; New Line Rd; d €80-120; 🅿🛜) The pick of Waterville's B&Bs is the contemporary Brookhaven House, run by a friendly family, with spick-and-span rooms, comfy beds and a sunny sea-view breakfast room.

Sneem ❽

🛏 Parknasilla Resort & Spa
Hotel €€

(📞064-667 5600; www.parknasillaresort. com; Parknasilla; d/f/ste from €139/179/229; 🅿@🛜🏊) This hotel has been wowing guests (including George Bernard Shaw) since 1895 with its pristine resort on the tree-fringed shores of the Kenmare River with views to the Beara Peninsula. From the modern, luxuriously appointed bedrooms to the top-grade spa, private 12-hole golf course and elegant restaurant, everything here is done just right. It's 3km southeast of Sneem.

Kenmare ❾

🍴 Horseshoe
Pub Food €€

(📞064-664 1553; www.thehorseshoekenmare. com; 3 Main St; mains €14-26; ⏰kitchen 5-10pm Thu-Mon) Flower baskets brighten the entrance to this popular gastropub, which has a short but excellent menu that runs from Kenmare Bay mussels in creamy apple cider sauce to braised Kerry lamb on mustard mash.

🍴 Tom Crean Fish & Wine
Irish €€

(📞064-664 1589; http://tomcrean.ie; Main St; 2-/3-course menus €25/29, mains €16.50; ⏰5-9.30pm Thu-Sun late-Mar–Dec; 🛜) Named for Kerry's pioneering Antarctic explorer, and run by his granddaughter, this venerable restaurant uses only the best of local organic produce, cheeses and fresh seafood, all served in modern, low-key surrounds.

🛏 Virginia's Guesthouse
B&B €€

(📞064-664 1021; www.virginias-kenmare.com; Henry St; s/d from €40/75; 🛜) You can't get more central than this award-winning B&B, whose creative breakfasts celebrate organic local produce (rhubarb and blueberries in season, for example, as well as fresh-squeezed OJ and porridge with whiskey).

The North in a Nutshell

25

The North's must-do trip takes in unmissable cities and big-name sights. It also heads off the tourist trail, revealing secret beaches, quaint harbours, waterfalls and music-filled pubs.

TRIP HIGHLIGHTS

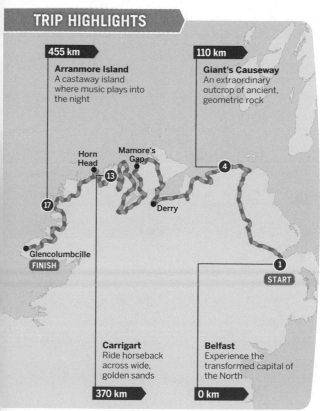

455 km
Arranmore Island
A castaway island where music plays into the night

110 km
Giant's Causeway
An extraordinary outcrop of ancient, geometric rock

Horn Head
Mamore's Gap
13
17
Derry
Glencolumbcille
FINISH
1
START
4

Carrigart
Ride horseback across wide, golden sands
370 km

Belfast
Experience the transformed capital of the North
0 km

10 DAYS
470KM / 292 MILES

GREAT FOR...

BEST TIME TO GO
March to June and September mean good weather but fewer crowds.

ESSENTIAL PHOTO
Crossing the Carrick-a-Rede Rope Bridge as it swings above the waves.

BEST FOR SCENERY
Stops 16 to 20 head into the heart of wild, wind-whipped Donegal.

Ballycastle Sunset on the harbour

The North in a Nutshell

On this road-trip-to-remember you'll drive routes that cling to cliffs, cross borders and head high onto mountain passes. You'll witness Ireland's turbulent past and its inspiring path to peace. And you'll also explore rich faith, folk and music traditions, ride a horse across a sandy beach, cross a swaying rope bridge and spend a night on a castaway island. Not bad for a 10-day drive.

❶ Belfast

In bustling, big-city Belfast, the past is palpably present – walk the city's former sectarian battlegrounds for a profound way to start exploring the North's story. Next, cross the River Lagan and head to the Titanic Quarter. Dominated by the towering yellow Harland and Wolff (H&W) cranes, it's where RMS *Titanic* was built. **Titanic Belfast** (www.titanicbelfast.com; Queen's Rd; adult/child £17.50/7.25; ☺9am-7pm Jun-Aug, to 6pm Apr, May & Sep, 10am-5pm Oct Mar) is a stunning multisensory experience: see bustling shipyards, join crowds at *Titanic's* launch, feel temperatures drop as she strikes that iceberg, and look through a glass floor at watery footage of the vessel today. Slightly to the west, don't miss the **Thompson Graving Dock** (www.titanicsdock. com; Queen's Rd; graving dock admission free, pump house adult/child £5/3.50; ☺10am-5pm Sat-Thu, 9.30am-5pm Fri), where you descend into the immense dry dock where the liner was fitted out.

The Drive ❯❯ As you drive the M3/M2 north, the now-familiar H&W cranes recede. Take the A26 through Ballymena; soon the Antrim Mountains loom large to the right. Skirt them along the A44 into Ballycastle, 96km from Belfast.

 p326

❷ Ballycastle

Head beyond the sandy beach to the harbour at the appealing resort of Ballycastle. From here, daily **ferries** (☎028-2076 9299; www.rathlinballycastle ferry.com; adult/child/bicycle return £12/6/3.30) depart for Rathlin Island, where you'll see sea stacks and thousands of guillemots, kittiwakes, razorbills and puffins.

🛏 p351

LINK YOUR TRIP

22 **Iconic Ireland**
Trip down to Dublin (four hours via the N3) to add the best of the south's attractions to your northern jaunt.

23 **The Long Way Round**
From Glencolumbcille head 53km west to Donegal to complete the west and south legs of this coastal tour of vibrant port cities and island treasures.

The Drive » Pick up the B15 towards Ballintoy, which meanders up to a gorse-dotted coastal plateau where hills part to reveal bursts of the sea. As the road plunges downwards, take the right turn to the Carrick-a-Rede Rope Bridge (10km).

❸ Carrick-a-Rede Rope Bridge

The **Carrick-a-Rede Rope Bridge** (www.nationaltrust. org.uk; Ballintoy; adult/child £5.90/3; ⏰9.30am-7pm Apr-Aug, to 6pm Mar, Sep & Oct, to 3.30pm Nov-Feb) loops across a surging sea to a tiny island 20m offshore. This walkway of planks and wire rope sways some 30m above the waves, testing your nerve and head for heights. The bridge was originally put up each year by salmon fishermen to help them set their nets, and signs along the 1km clifftop hike to the bridge detail the fascinating process. Declining stocks have

put an end to fishing, however.

The Drive » The B15, then the A2, snake west along clifftops and past views of White Park Bay's sandy expanse. Swing right onto the B146, passing Dunseverick Castle's fairy-tale tumblings, en route to the Giant's Causeway (11km).

TRIP HIGHLIGHT

❹ Giant's Causeway

Stretching elegantly out from a rugged shore, the **Giant's Causeway** (www. nationaltrust.org.uk; ⏰dawn-dusk) is one of the world's true geological wonders. Clambering around this jetty of fused geometric rock chunks, it's hard to believe it's not man-made. Indeed, legend says Irish giant Finn Mc-Cool built the Causeway to cross the sea to fight Scottish giant Benan-donner. More prosaically, however, scientists tell us the 60-million-year-old rocks were formed when a flow of molten basaltic lava cooled and

hardened from the top and bottom inwards. It contracted, and the hexagonal cracks spread as the rock solidified.

Entry to the Causeway site is free, but to use the National Trust car park you'll need to buy a ticket that includes entrance to the excellent new **Giant's Causeway Visitor Experience** (☎028-2073 1855; www. nationaltrust.org.uk; adult/child with parking £9/4.50, without parking £7/3.25; ⏰9am-7pm Apr-Sep, to 6pm Feb, Mar & Oct, to 5pm Nov-Jan).

✗ p326

The Drive » Continue west, through Bushmills, with its famous distillery, picking up the A2 Coastal Causeway route towards Portrush. You'll pass wind-pruned trees, crumbling Dunluce Castle and Portrush's long sandy beaches before arriving at Portstewart (16km).

❺ Portstewart

Time for some unique parking. Head through resort-town Portstewart, following signs for the **Strand** (beach). Ever-sandier roads descend to an immense shoreline that doubles as a car park for 1000 vehicles. It's a decidedly weird experience to drive and park (£5) on an apparently endless expanse of hard-packed sand. It's also at your own risk, which doesn't deter the locals (but do stick to central, compacted areas). Nearby, a 1km **walking**

CAUSEWAY COAST WALKS

The official **Causeway Coast Way** (www.walkni.com) stretches for 53km from Ballycastle to Portstewart, but individual chunks can be walked whenever you feel like stretching your legs. Day hikes include the supremely scenic 16.5km section between Carrick-a-Rede and the Giant's Causeway – one of the finest coastal walks in Ireland. Shorter options also abound, including a 2km ramble around Portrush, a 1.5km stroll on sandy White Park Bay and a 300m scramble around ruined Dunluce Castle.

trail meanders up a sand ladder, through huge dunes and past marram grass and occasional orchids.

🛏 p351

The Drive » Take the A2 west, through Coleraine towards Downhill. About 1km after the Mussenden Temple's dome appears, take the Bishop's Rd left up steep hills with spectacular Lough Foyle views. Descend, go through Limavady and onto the B68 (signed Dungiven). Soon a brown Country Park sign points to Roe Valley (42km).

⑥ Roe Valley

This beguiling **country park** (🕐9am-dusk) is packed with rich reminders of a key Irish industry: linen production. The damp valley was ideal for growing the flax that made the cloth; the fast-flowing water powered the machinery. The **Green Lane Museum** (🕐1-4.30pm Sat-Thu May-Aug, Sat & Sun Sep), near the car park, features sowing fiddles, flax breakers and spinning wheels. Look out for nearby watchtowers, built to guard linen spread out to bleach in the fields, and Scutch Mills, where the flax was pounded.

The Drive » Head back into Limavady to take the A2 west to Derry (28km). Green fields give way to suburbs, then city streets.

✓ TOP TIP: THE BORDER

Driving 20 minutes north out of Derry will see you entering another country: the Republic of Ireland. Be aware that road sign speed limits will suddenly change from mph to km/h, while wording switches from English to Irish and English. Stock up on euros in Derry or visit the first post-border ATM.

⑦ Derry

Northern Ireland's second city offers another powerful insight into the North's troubled past and the remarkable steps towards peace. It's best experienced on foot. Drop into the **Tower Museum** (www.derrycity.gov. uk/museums; Union Hall Pl; adult/child £4/2; 🕐10am-5.30pm): Its imaginative Story of Derry exhibition leads you through the city's history, from the 6th-century monastery of St Colmcille (Columba) to the 1960s Battle of the Bogside.

🍴 🛏 p351

The Drive » The A2 heads north towards Moville. Soon speed-limit signs switch from mph to km/h: welcome to the Republic of Ireland. Shortly after Muff take the small left turn, signed Iskaheen, up the hill. Park beside Iskaheen church (11km).

⑧ Iskaheen

It's completely off the tourist trail, but Iskaheen church's tiny **graveyard** offers evidence of two of

Ireland's most significant historical themes: the poverty that led to mass migration and the consequences of sectarian violence. One gravestone among many is that of the McKinney family, recording a string of children dying young: at 13 years, 11 months, nine months, and six weeks. It also bears the name of 34-year-old James Gerard McKinney, one of 13 unarmed civilians shot dead when British troops opened fire on demonstrators on Bloody Sunday, 1972.

The Drive » Rejoin the R238 north, turning onto the R240 to Carndonagh, climbing steeply into rounded summits. After quaint Ballyliffin and Clonmany, pick up the Inis Eoghain (Scenic Route) towards Mamore's Gap, before parking at the Glen House Tea Rooms (40km).

⑨ Glenevin Waterfall

Welcome to Butler's Bridge – from here a 1km trail winds beside a stream through a wooded glen to Glenevin

WHY THIS IS A GREAT TRIP
ISABEL ALBISTON, WRITER

Starting in Belfast, a city whose turbulent history seems finally to be coming second to its flourishing future, this trip gives a sense of the north's past and present while showcasing a stunning and ancient natural landscape – the striking hexagonal rocks of the Giant's Causeway date back 60 million years.

Top: Portstewart Strand
Left: Tower Museum, Derry
Right: Lighthouse, Arranmore Island

Waterfall, which cascades 10m down the rock face. It's an utterly picturesque, gentle, waymarked route that's the perfect spot for a leg stretch.

🛏 p351

The Drive » The Inis Eoghain snakes south up to Mamore's Gap, a high-altitude, white-knuckle mountain pass that climbs 260m on single-lane, twisting roads, past shrines to the saints. After a supremely steep descent (and glorious views), go south through Buncrana, and on to Fahan (37km), parking beside the village church.

❿ Fahan

St Colmcille founded a monastery in Fahan in the 6th century. Its creeper-clad ruins sit beside the church. Among them, hunt out the beautifully carved **St Mura Cross**. Each face of this 7th-century stone slab is decorated with a cross in intricate Celtic weave. The barely discernible Greek inscription is the only one known in Ireland from this early Christian period and is thought to be part of a prayer dating from 633.

The Drive » Take the N13 to Letterkenny, where you'll pick up the R245 to Rathmelton (aka Ramelton), a 10km sweep north through the River Swilly valley. Turn off for the village, heading downhill to park beside the water in front of you (50km).

11 Rathmelton

In this picture-perfect town, rows of Georgian houses and rough-walled stone warehouses curve along the River Lennon. Strolling right takes you to a string of three-storey, three-bay Victorian warehouses; walking back and left up Church Rd leads to the ruined **Tullyaughnish Church**, with its Romanesque carvings in the eastern wall. Walking left beside the river leads past Victorian shops to the three-arched, late-18th-century Rathmelton Bridge.

p351

The Drive » Cross the town bridge, turning right (north) for Rathmullan. The hills of the Inishowen Peninsula rise ahead and Lough Swilly swings into view – soon you're driving right beside the shore. At Rathmullan (11km), make for the harbour car park.

12 Rathmullan

Refined, tranquil Rathmullan was the setting for an event that shaped modern Ireland. In 1607 a band of nobles boarded a ship here, leaving with the intention of raising an army to fight the occupying English. But they never returned. Known as the Flight of the Earls, it marked the end of the Irish (Catholic) chieftains' power. Their estates were confiscated, paving the way for the Plantation of Ulster with British (Protestant) settlers. Beside the sandy beach, look for the striking modern **sculpture** depicting the departure of the earls, waving to their distressed people as they left.

The Drive » Head straight on from the harbour, picking up Fanad/Atlantic Dr, a rollercoaster road that surges up Lough Swilly's shore, round huge Knockalla, past the exquisite beach at Ballymastocker Bay and around Fanad Head. It then hugs the (ironically) narrow Broad Water en route to Carrigart (74km), with its village-centre horse-riding centre.

TRIP HIGHLIGHT

13 Carrigart

Most visitors scoot straight through laid-back Carrigart, heading for the swimming beach at Downings (there's also accommodation there; see p351). But they miss a real treat: a horse ride on a vast beach. The **Carrigart Riding Centre** (087 227 6926; per hr adult/child €20/15) is just across the main street from sandy, hill-ringed Mulroy Bay, meaning you can head straight onto the beach for an hour-long ride amid the shallows and the dunes. Trips go on the hour, but it's best to book.

The Drive » Head south for Creeslough. An inlet with a creamy, single-towered castle soon pops into view. The turn-off comes on the plain, where brown signs point through narrow lanes and past farms to Doe Castle (12km) itself.

14 Doe Castle

The best way to appreciate the charm of early-16th-century Doe Castle is to wander the peaceful grounds, admiring its slender tower and crenellated battlements. The castle was the stronghold of the Scottish MacSweeney family until

NORTH WEST 200 ROAD RACE

Driving this delightful coast can have its challenges, so imagine doing it at high speed. Each May the world's best motorcyclists do just that, going as fast as 300km/h in the **North West 200** (www.northwest200.org), which is run on a road circuit taking in Portrush, Portstewart and Coleraine. This classic race is Ireland's biggest outdoor sporting event and one of the last to take place on closed public roads anywhere in Europe. It attracts up to 150,000 spectators; if you're not one of them, it's best to avoid the area on the race weekend.

it fell into English hands in the 17th century. It's a deeply picturesque spot: a low, water-fringed promontory with a moat hewn out of the rock.

The Drive » Near Creeslough, the bulk of Muckish Mountain rears up before the N56 to Dunfanaghy undulates past homesteads, loughs and sandy bays. Once in Dunfanaghy, with its gently kooky vibe, welcoming pubs and great places to sleep (see p351), look out for the signpost pointing right to Horn Head (25km).

Belfast Titanic Belfast

🕔 Horn Head

This headland provides one of Donegal's best clifftop drives: along sheer, heather-clad quartzite cliffs with views of an island-dotted sea. A circular road bears left to the coastguard station – park to take the 20-minute walk due north to the signal tower. Hop back in the car, continuing east – around 1km later a viewpoint tops cliffs 180m high. There's another superb vantage point 1km further round – on a fine day you'll see Ireland's most northerly point, Malin Head.

The Drive » The N56 continues west. Settlements thin out, the road climbs and the pointed peak of Mt Errigal fills more and more of your windshield before the road swings away. At tiny Crolly, follow the R259 towards the airport, then turn right, picking up signs for Leo's Tavern (35km).

🕕 Meenaleck

You never know who'll drop by for one of the legendary singalongs at **Leo's Tavern** (☎074-954 8143; www.leostavern.com; off R259, Crolly; ⏰kitchen 1-8.45pm Jun-Sep, 5-8.45pm Thu-Fri, 1-8.45pm Sat, 1-8pm Sun Oct-May, 🔊🚻) in Meenaleck. It's owned by Bartley Brennan, brother of Enya and her siblings Máire, Ciaran and Pól (aka the group Clannad). The pub glitters with gold, silver and platinum discs and is packed with musical mementos – there's live music nightly in the summer.

The Drive » Continue west on the R259 as it bobbles and twists besides scattered communities and a boggy, then sandy, shore. Head on to the pocket-sized port of Burtonport, following ferry signs right, to embark for Arranmore Island (25km).

TRIP HIGHLIGHT

🕗 Arranmore Island

Arranmore (Árainn Mhór) offers a true taste of Ireland. Framed by dramatic cliff faces, cavernous sea caves and clear sandy beaches, this 9km-by-5km island sits 5km offshore. Here you'll discover a prehistoric triangular fort and an off-shore bird sanctuary fluttering with corncrakes, snipes and seabirds. Irish is the main language spoken, pubs put on turf fires, and trad-music sessions run late into the night. To get the full castaway experience, stay overnight (book). The **Arranmore Ferry** (☎074-952 0532; www.arranmoreferry.com; Burtonport; return adult/child/car & driver €15/7/30; ⏰4-8 daily sailings year-round) takes 20 minutes.

🛏 p351

DETOUR: FINTOWN RAILWAY

Start: ⑰ Arranmore Island (p349)

You've been driving for days now – time to let the train take the strain. The charming **Fintown Railway** (📞074-954 6280; www.antraen.com; off R250, Fintown; adult/child €8/5; ⏰11am-4pm Mon-Sat, 1-5pm Sun Jun–mid-Sep) runs along a rebuilt 5km section of the former County Donegal Railway track beside picturesque Lough Finn. It's been lovingly restored to its original condition, and a return trip in the red-and-white, 1940s diesel railcar takes around 40 minutes. To get to the railway, head east on the R252, off the N56 south of Dungloe. Then settle back to enjoy the ride.

The Drive >> The R259 bounces down to Dungloe, where you take the N56 south into a rock-strewn landscape that's backed by the Blue Stack Mountains. After a stretch of rally-circuit-esque road, the sweep of Gweebarra Bay emerges. Take the sharp right towards peaceful Narin (R261), following signs to the beach (*trá*), 45km from Arranmore Island.

⑱ Narin

You've now entered the beautiful Loughrea Peninsula, which glistens with tiny lakes cupped by undulating hills. Narin boasts a spectacular 4km-long, wishbone-shaped Blue Flag beach, the sandy tip of which points towards **Iniskeel Island**. You can walk to the island at low tide along a 500m sandy causeway. Your reward? An intimate island studded with early Christian remains: St Connell, a cousin of St Colmcille, founded a monastery here in the 6th century.

🛏 p351

The Drive >> Continue south on the R261 through tweed-producing Ardara. Shortly after leaving town, take the right, signed 'Waterfall', following a road wedged between craggy hills and an increasingly sandy shore. In time the Assarancagh Waterfall (14km) comes into view.

⑲ Assarancagh Waterfall

Step out of the car and you immediately feel what an enchanting spot this is. As the waterfall streams down the sheer hillside, walk along the road (really a lane) towards the sea. This 1.5km route leads past time-warp farms – sheep bleat and the tang of peat smoke scents the air. At tiny Maghera, head through the car park, down a track, over a boardwalk and onto a truly stunning expanse of pure-white sand. This exquisite place belies a bloody past. Some 100 villagers hid from Cromwell's forces in nearby caves – all except one were discovered and massacred.

The Drive >> Drive west through Maghera on a dramatic route that makes straight for the gap in the towering hills. At the fork, turn right, heading deeper into the remote headland, making for Glencolumbcille (20km).

⑳ Glencolumbcille

The welcome in the scattered, pub-dotted, bayside village of Glencolumbcille (Gleann Cholm Cille) is warm. This remote settlement also offers a glimpse of a disappearing way of life. **Father McDyer's Folk Village** (www.glenfolkvillage. com; Doonalt; adult/child €4.50/2.50; ⏰10am-6pm Mon-Sat, noon-6pm Sun Easter-Sep) took traditional life of the 1960s and froze it in time. Its thatched cottages re-create daily life with genuine period fittings, while the Craft Shop sells wines made from such things as seaweed, as well as marmalade and whiskey truffles – a few treats at your journey's end.

Eating & Sleeping

Ballycastle ❷

🛏 An Caislean Guesthouse
Guesthouse ££

(📞028-2076 2845; www.ancaislean.co.uk; 42 Quay Rd; s/d from £45/60; P 🛜) An Caislean has a luxurious lounge, a summer tea room and restaurant, and a welcoming atmosphere.It's just a few minutes' walk from the beach.

Portstewart ❺

🛏 Strandeen
B&B ££

(📞028-7083 3872; www.strandeen.com; 63 Strand Rd; d from £110) Set on a hilltop and more like a boutique hotel than a B&B, Strandeen has four beautiful rooms, scrumptious organic and/ or free-range breakfasts, bike rental (per day £15), and an ocean-facing terrace.

Derry ❼

🛏 Merchant's House
B&B ££

(📞028-7126 9691; www.thesaddlershouse. com; 16 Queen St; s/d/tr/f from £40/65/90/100; @ 🛜) This historic, Georgian-style town house has an elegant lounge and dining room and home-made marmalade at breakfast. Some rooms share a bathroom. Call at **Saddler's House** (36 Great James St) first to pick up a key.

Glenevin Waterfall ❾

🛏 Glen House
Guesthouse €€

(📞074-937 6745; www.glenhouse.ie; Straid, Clonmany; r €70-100; P 🛜) Despite the grand surroundings and luxurious rooms, you'll find neither pretension nor high prices at this gem of a guesthouse. The rooms are a lesson in restrained sophistication, and the setting is incredibly tranquil. The walking trail to Glenevin Waterfall starts next to the **Rose Tea Room** (mains from €6; 🕙10am-6pm daily Jul-Aug, Sat & Sun only Mar-Jun & Sep-Oct), which opens to a deck.

Rathmelton ⓫

🛏 Frewin House
B&B €€

(📞074-915 1246; www.frewinhouse.com; Rectory Rd; d €110-150; P) Set in secluded grounds, this fine Victorian rectory combines antique furniture with contemporary style. You can arrange for a communal dinner by candlelight.

Downings ⓭

🛏 Beach
Hotel €€

(Óstán na Trá; 📞074-915 5303; www.beachhotel. ie; s/d €80/120; P) Many of the bright, modern rooms at this large family-run hotel have ocean views. You can refuel in its restaurant (three courses for €27.50) or bar (mains €10 to €22). It's in Downings, 4km north of Carrigart.

Dunfanaghy ⓮

🛏 Corcreggan Mill
Guesthouse €

(📞074-913 6409; www.corcreggan.com; off N56; camp sites from €12, s/d from €60/75; @ 🛜) Spotless four-bed dorms and private guest rooms are tucked into cosy corners of this lovingly restored former mill house, Continental breakfast is included in the room rates. Some rooms have private bathrooms. The mill is 2.5km southwest of town on the N56.

Arranmore Island ⓱

🛏 Claire's Bed & Breakfast
B&B €

(📞074-952 0042; www.clairesbandb.wordpress. com; Leabgarrow; s/d €35/60; 🛜) This modern house with simple rooms is right by the ferry port.

Narin ⓲

🛏 Carnaween House
B&B €€

(📞074-954 5122; www.carnaweenhouse.com; Narin; s/d €60/120, cottage from €210, mains €15-25; 🕙kitchen 6-9pm Thu-Sun, 1-4pm Sun Jun-Sep, shorter hrs rest of year; 🛜) Carnaween House glows with brilliant white bedrooms in a luxury beach-house style. The restaurant serves modern Irish fare.

Musical Landscapes

26

From the busker-packed streets of Galway city, this rip-roaring ride takes you around County Clare and the Aran Islands to discover fine traditional-music pubs, venues and festivals.

TRIP HIGHLIGHTS

155 km

Inisheer
End-of-the-earth landscape and traditional drumming festival

START
Galway

Inishmór

9

FINISH

Doolin • **Lisdoonvarna**

Kilfenora

4

Miltown Malbay

2

Ennistymon
Country village with roaring Cascades and music at every turn

110 km

65 km

Ennis
Medieval town simply bursting with fine pubs featuring trad music

5 DAYS
155KM / 96 MILES

GREAT FOR...

BEST TIME TO GO

The summer months, for outdoor *céilidh* (traditional dancing) and music festivals.

ESSENTIAL PHOTO

Nightly set-dancing at the crossroads, in Vaughan's of Kilfenora.

BEST FOR SONG

Ennis, on summer nights, where local musicians ply their wares.

Doolin A musician performs at Gus O'Connor's Pub

353

26 Musical Landscapes

Pick the big bawdy get-togethers of Galway's always-on music scene, the atmospheric small pub sessions in crossroad villages like Kilfenora or Kilronan on the Aran Islands, where nonplaying patrons are a minority, or the rollicking urban boozers in Ennis. Whatever way you like it, this region is undeniably one of Ireland's hottest for traditional music.

❶ Galway City

Galway (Gaillimh) has a young student population and largely creative community that give a palpable energy to the place. Walk its colourful medieval streets, packed with heritage shops, sidewalk cafes and pubs, all ensuring there's never a dull moment. Galway's pub selection is second to none, and some swing to tunes every night of the week. **Crane Bar** (www.thecranebar.com; 2 Sea Rd; ⊘10.30am-11.30pm Mon-Fri, 10.30am-12.30am Sat, 12.30-11pm Sun), an atmospheric old pub west of the Corrib, is the best spot in Galway to catch an informal *céilidh* most

nights. Or for something more contemporary, **Róisín Dubh** (www. roisindubh.net; Upper Dominick St; ⊘5pm-2am Sun-Thu, till 2.30am Fri & Sat) is *the* place to hear emerging international rock and singer-songwriters.

🍴 🛏 p312, p361

The Drive » From Galway city centre, follow either the coast road (R338) east out of town, or the inner R446, signposted Dublin or Limerick, as far as the N18 and then cruise south to Ennis, where your great musical tour of Clare begins.

TRIP HIGHLIGHT

❷ Ennis

Ennis (Inis), a medieval town in origin, is packed with pubs featuring

trad music. **Brogan's** (24 O'Connell St; ⊘10.30am-11.30pm Mon-Thu, to 12.30am Fri & Sat, 12.30-11pm Sun), on the corner of Cooke's Lane, sees a fine bunch of musicians rattling even the stone floors almost every night in summer, and the plain-tile-fronted **John O'Dea** (66 O'Connell St; ⊘10.30am-11.30pm Mon-Thu,

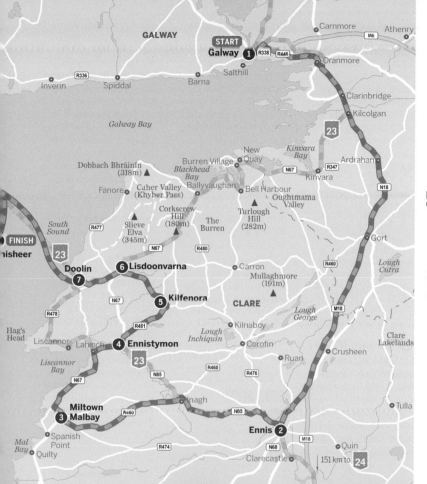

to 12.30am Fri & Sat, 12.30-11pm Sun) is a hideout for local musicians serious about their trad sessions. **Cois na hAbhna** (☎065-682 0996; www.coisnahabhna.ie; Gort Rd; ☺shop 9am-5pm, trad sessions 9pm Tue), a pilgrimage point for traditional music and culture, has frequent performances and a full

LINK YOUR TRIP

23 The Long Way Round

From Galway, pick up this trip north or south for crenellated coastlines, vibrant port cities and island treasures.

24 Ring of Kerry

Head south to Killarney via Limerick to encounter jaw-dropping scenery around the Iveragh Peninsula.

range of classes in dance and music; it's also an archive and library of Irish traditional music, song, dance and folklore. Traditional music aficionados might like to time a visit with **Fleadh Nua** (www.fleadhnua.com), a lively festival held in late May.

🍴 🛏️ p312, p361

The Drive » From the N85 that runs south of The Burren, you'll meet the smaller R460 at the blink-and-you'll-miss-it village of Inagh. Here you'll find the Biddy Early Brewery, which sells a draught ale, Red Biddy, made using local Burren plants and seaweeds for flavouring. Refuelled, it's a straight run into Miltown Malbay.

- - - - - - - - - - - -

❸ Miltown Malbay

Miltown Malbay was a resort favoured by well-to-do Victorians, though the beach itself is 2km south at **Spanish Point**. To the north of the Point, there are beautiful **walks** amid the low cliffs, coves and isolated beaches. A classically friendly place in the chatty Irish way, Miltown Malbay hosts the annual Willie Clancy Summer School, one of Ireland's great trad music events. **O'Friel's Bar** (Lynch's; The Square; ⊙2pm-midnight Sun-Wed, 6pm-1am Thu-Sat) is one of a couple of genuine old-style places with occasional trad sessions. The other is the dapper **Hillery's** (Main St; ⊙noon-12.30am Sun-Thu, to 1.30am Fri-Sat).

The Drive » Hugging the coast, continue north until you come to the small seaside resort of Lahinch, more or less a single street backing a wide beach renowned for its surfing. From here, it's only 4km up the road to the lovely heritage town of Ennistymon.

- - - - - - - - - - - -

TRIP HIGHLIGHT

❹ Ennistymon

Ennistymon (Inis Díomáin) is one of those country villages where people go about their business barely noticing the characterful buildings lining Main St. And behind this facade there's a surprise: the roaring **Cascades**, the stepped falls of the River Inagh. After heavy rain they surge, beer-brown and foaming, and you risk getting drenched on windy days in the flying drizzle. Not to be missed, **Eugene's** (Main St; ⊙10.30am-11.30pm Mon-Thu, 10.30am-12.30am Fri-Sat, 12.30-11pm Sun) is intimate and cosy and has a trademark collection of visiting cards covering its walls, alongside photographs of famous writers and musicians. The inspiring collection of whiskey (Irish) and whisky (Scottish) will have you smoothly debating their relative merits. Another great old pub is **Cooley's House** (☎065-707 1712; Main St; ⊙10.30am-11pm Mon-Sat, noon-11.30pm Sun), with music most nights in summer and on Wednesday (trad night) in winter.

🛏️ p361

The Drive » Heading north through a patchwork of green fields and stony walls on the R481, you'll land at the tiny village of Kilfenora, some 9km later. Despite its diminutive size, the pulse of Clare's music scene beats strongly in this area.

THE PIED PIPER

Half the population of Miltown Malbay seems to be part of the annual **Willie Clancy Irish Summer School** (☎065-708 4148; www.scoilsamhraidhwillieclancy.com; ⊙Jul), a tribute to a native son and one of Ireland's greatest pipers. The eight-day **festival**, now in its fourth decade, begins on the first Saturday in July, when impromptu sessions occur day and night, the pubs are packed and Guinness is consumed by the barrel – up to 10,000 enthusiasts from around the globe turn up for the event. Specialist workshops and classes underpin the event; don't be surprised to attend a recital with 40 noted fiddlers.

Kilfenora Kilfenora Cathedral

❺ Kilfenora

Underappreciated Kilfenora (Cill Fhionnúrach) lies on the southern fringe of The Burren. It's a small place, with a diminutive 12th-century cathedral, and is best known for its **high crosses**. The town has a strong music tradition that rivals that of Doolin but without the crowds. The **Kilfenora Céili Band** (www.kilfenoraceiliband. com) is a celebrated community that's been playing for 100 years; its traditional music features fiddles, banjos, squeeze boxes and more. **Vaughan's Pub** (www. vaughanspub.ie; Main St; mains €8-15; ⊘kitchen 10am-9pm) has music in the bar every night during the summer and terrific set-dancing sessions in its barn on Thursday and Sunday nights.

The Drive » From Kilfenora, the road meanders northwest 8km to Lisdoonvarna, home of the international matchmaking

WHY THIS IS A GREAT TRIP
FIONN DAVENPORT, WRITER

To witness a proper traditional session in one of the music houses of Clare or the fine old pubs of Galway can be a transcendent experience, especially if it's appropriately lubricated with a pint (or few) of stout. Sure, there'll be plenty of tourists about, but this is authentic, traditional Ireland at its most evocative.

Top: Abandoned cottage, Inishmór
Left: Eugene's, Ennistymon
Right: Musician, Galway

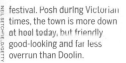

festival. Posh during Victorian times, the town is more down at hool today, but friendly good-looking and far less overrun than Doolin.

- - - - - - - - - - - -

❻ Lisdoonvarna

Lisdoonvarna (Lios Dún Bhearna), often just called 'Lisdoon', is well known for its mineral springs. For centuries people have been visiting the local spa to swallow its waters. Down by the river at **Roadside Tavern** (www. roadsidetavern.ie; Kincora Rd; mains €11.50-20; ☉noon-4pm & 6-9pm Mon-Fri, noon-9pm Sat, noon-8pm Sun), third-generation owner Peter Curtin knows every story worth telling. There are trad sessions daily in summer. Look for a trail beside the pub that runs 400m down to two **wells** by the river. One is high in sulphur, the other iron. Mix and match for a cocktail of minerals. Next door, **Burren Smokehouse** (☎065-707 4432; www.burren smokehouse.ie; Kincora Rd; ☉9am-7pm May-Aug, 9am-6pm Apr, 10am-5pm Mar & Sep-Oct, shorter hrs winter; ℗) is where you can learn about the ancient Irish art of oak-smoking salmon.

The Drive » Just under 10 minutes' drive west of here is the epicentre of Clare's trad music scene, at Doolin. Also known for its setting – 6km north of the Cliffs of Moher – what's called Doolin is really three small neighbouring villages. There's Fisherstreet, right on the water, Doolin itself, about 1km east on the little River Aille, and Roadford, another 1km east.

❼ Doolin

Doolin gets plenty of press as a centre of Irish traditional music, owing to a trio of pubs that have sessions through the year. **McGann's** (www.mcgannspubdoolin.com; Roadford; ⏲10am-12.30am, kitchen 10am-9.30pm) has all the classic touches of a full-on Irish music pub; the action often spills out onto the street. Right on the water, **Gus O'Connor's Pub** (www.gusoconnorspubdoolin.net; Fisherstreet; ⏲9am-midnight), a sprawling favourite, has a rollicking atmosphere. It easily gets the most crowded and has the highest tourist quotient. **MacDiarmada's** (Roadford; ⏲bar 11am-midnight, kitchen 9am-9.30pm), also known as McDermott's, is a simple and sometimes rowdy red-and-white old pub popular with locals. When the fiddles get going, it can seem like a scene out of a John Ford movie.

🛏 p361

The Drive » You'll need to leave your car at one of Doolin's many car parks to board the ferry to the Aran Islands.

❽ Inishmór

The Aran Islands sing their own siren song to thousands of travellers each year who find their desolate beauty beguiling. The largest and most accessible Aran, Inishmór, is home to ancient fort **Dún Aengus** (Dún Aonghasa; www.heritageireland.ie/en/west/dunaonghasa/; adult/child €4/2; ⏲9.30am-6pm Apr-Oct, 9.30am-4pm Nov-Mar, closed Mon & Tue Jan & Feb), one of the oldest archaeological remains in Ireland. The island also has some lively pubs and restaurants, particularly in the only town, Kilronan. Irish remains the local tongue, but most locals speak English with visitors. **Tí Joe Watty's Bar** (www.joewattys.com; Kilronan; ⏲kitchen 12.30-9pm) is the best pub in Kilronan, with traditional sessions most nights. Turf fires warm the air on the 50 weeks a year when this is needed. Informal music sessions, turf fires and a broad terrace with harbour views make **Tí Joe Mac's** (Kilronan) a local favourite, while jovial **Tigh Fitz** (Killeany), near the airport, has traditional sessions and set dancing every weekend. It's 1.6km from Kilronan (about a 25-minute walk).

🛏 p361

The Drive » Ferries can be picked up between Aran Islands but tickets must be prebooked.

TRIP HIGHLIGHT

❾ Inisheer

On Inisheer (Inis Oírr), the smallest of the Aran Islands, the breathtakingly beautiful end-of-the-earth landscape adds to the island's distinctly mystical aura. Steeped in mythology, traditional rituals are still very much respected here. Locals still carry out a pilgrimage with potential healing powers, known as the *Turas,* to the Well of Enda, an ever-burbling spring in the southwest. For a week in late June the island reverberates to the thunder of traditional drums during **Craiceann Inis Oírr International Bodhrán Summer School** (www.craiceann.com), which includes Bodhrán master classes, workshops and pub sessions as well as Irish dancing. Rory Conneely's atmospheric inn **Tigh Ruairí** (Strand House; ☎099-75020; www.tighruairi.com; r €50-90; @) hosts live music sessions and, here since 1897, **Tigh Ned** (meals €5-10) is a welcoming, unpretentious place, with harbour views and lively traditional music.

🛏 p361

Eating & Sleeping

Galway City

🛏 Heron's Rest   B&B €€

(📞091-539 574; www.theheronsrest.com;
16a Longwalk; s/d from €80/140; 🛜) Ideally
located in a lovely row of houses on the banks of
the Corrib, the thoughtful hosts here give you
deck chairs so you can sit outside and enjoy the
scene. Other touches include holiday-friendly
breakfast times (8am to 11am), decanters of
port (enough for a glass or two) and more.
Rooms are small and cute, with double-glazed
windows and water views.

Ennis ❷

🍴 Zest   Cafe €

(www.zestfood.ie; Market Pl; meals €5-10;
⏰8am-6pm Mon-Sat, 10.30am-4.30pm Sun)
Zest combines a deli, bakery, shop and cafe.
Excellent prepared foods from the region are
offered along with salads, soups and much
more. It's ideal for a coffee or lunch.

🛏 Old Ground Hotel   Hotel €€

(📞065-682 8127, www.flynnhotels.com;
O'Connell St; s/d from €120/150; P @ 🛜) A
seasoned, charming and congenial space of
polished floorboards, cornice-work, antiques
and open fires, the lobby is always a scene:
old friends sinking into sofas, deals cut at
the tables, and ladies from the neighbouring
church's altar society exchanging gossip over
tea. Parts of this smart and rambling landmark
date back to the 1800s. The 83 rooms vary
greatly in size and decor – don't hesitate to
inspect a few. On balmy days, retire to tables
on the lawn.

Ennistymon ❹

🛏 Falls Hotel   Hotel €€

(📞065-707 1004; www.fallshotel.ie; off N67;
r from €95; P 🛜 🏊) Built on the ruins of an
O'Brien castle, this handsome and sprawling
Georgian house was once Ennistymon House,
the family home of Caitlín MacNamara, who
married Dylan Thomas. With 140 modern
rooms and a large, enclosed pool, the hotel's
view of the Cascades from the entrance steps
is breathtaking, and there are 20 hectares of
wooded gardens.

Doolin ❼

🛏 Cullinan's Guesthouse   Inn €€

(📞065-707 4183; www.cullinansdoolin.com; d
from €100; P 🛜) Owned by well-known fiddle-
playing James Cullinan, the eight rooms at this
smart place on the River Aille are very good-
looking, with power showers and comfortable
fittings. A couple of rooms are slightly smaller
than the others, but are right on the water.
There's a lovely back terrace for enjoying the
views.

Inishmór ❽

🛏 Man of Aran Cottage   B&B €€

(📞099-61301; www.manofarancottage.com;
Kilmurvey; s/d from €55/80; ⏰Mar-Oct) Built
for the 1930s film of the same name, this
thatched B&B doesn't trade on past glories –
its authentic stone-and-wood interiors define
charming. The owners are avid organic
gardeners (the tomatoes are famous) and their
bounty can become your meal (mains €22).

Inisheer ❾

🛏 Fisherman's Cottage & South Aran House   B&B €€

(📞099-75073; www.southaran.com; Castle
Village; s/d €49/80; ⏰Apr-Oct; 🛜) Slow-food
enthusiasts run this sprightly B&B and cafe
that's a mere five-minute walk from the pier;
look for the lavender growing in profusion at
the entrance. Meals (dinner mains €12 to €20)
celebrate local seafood and organic produce.
Nonguests can enjoy cakes by day and dinner at
night, but will need to book. Rooms are simple
yet stylish. Kayaking and fishing are among the
activities on offer.

NEED TO KNOW

CURRENCY
Republic of Ireland: Euro (€); Northern Ireland: pound sterling (£)

LANGUAGES
English, Irish

VISAS
Generally not required by citizens of Europe, Australia, New Zealand, USA and Canada.

FUEL
Petrol (gas) stations are everywhere, but are limited on motorways. Expect to pay €1.30 per litre of unleaded (€1.20 for diesel) in the Republic and £1.15 for unleaded and diesel in Northern Ireland.

RENTAL CARS
Avis (www.avis.ie)
Europcar (www.europcar.ie)
Hertz (www.hertz.ie)
Thrifty (www.thrifty.ie)

IMPORTANT NUMBERS
Country code (☏353 Republic of Ireland, ☏44 Northern Ireland)

Emergencies (☏999)

Roadside Assistance (☏1800 667 788 Republic of Ireland, ☏0800 887 766 Northern Ireland)

Climate

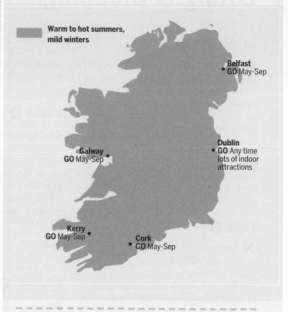

Warm to hot summers, mild winters

Belfast
GO May–Sep

Dublin
GO Any time lots of indoor attractions

Galway
GO May–Sep

Kerry
GO May–Sep

Cork
GO May–Sep

When to Go

High Season (Jun–mid-Sep)

» Weather at its best.

» Accommodation rates at their highest (especially in August).

» Tourist peak in Dublin, Kerry, southern and western coasts.

Shoulder Season (Easter to May, mid-Sep to Oct)

» Weather often good; sun and rain in May, 'Indian summers' and often warm in September.

» Summer crowds and accommodation rates drop off.

Low Season (Nov–Feb)

» Reduced opening hours from October to Easter; some destinations close.

» Cold and wet weather throughout the country; fog can reduce visibility.

» Big-city attractions operate as normal.

Daily Costs

Budget: Less than €60

» Dorm bed: €12–20

» Cheap meal in cafe or pub: €6–12

» Pint: €4.50–5 (more expensive in cities)

Midrange: €60–120

» Double room in hotel or B&B: €80–180 (more expensive in Dublin)

» Main course in midrange restaurant: €12–25

» Car rental (per day): from €25–45

Top End: More than €120

» Four-star hotel stay: from €150

» Three-course meal in good restaurant: around €50

» Top round of golf (midweek): from €90

Eating

Restaurants From cheap cafes to Michelin-starred feasts, covering all kinds of cuisines.

Cafes For all day breakfasts, sandwiches and basic dishes.

Pubs Pub grub ranges from toasted sandwiches to carefully crafted dishes.

Hotels All hotel restaurants take non-guests. They're a popular option in the countryside.

Eating price indicators represent the cost of a main dish:

Republic/Northern Ireland	
€/£	<€12/£12
€€/££	€12–25/£12–20
€€€/£££	>€25/£20

Sleeping

Hotels From chain hotels to Norman castles – with prices to match.

B&Bs Standards vary, but the B&B is the bedrock of Irish accommodation.

Hostels Feature clean dorms and wi-fi. Some have laundry and kitchen facilities.

Sleeping price indicators represent the cost of a double room in high season:

Republic/ Northern Ireland	
€/£	<€80/£50
€€/££	€80–180/£50–120
€€€/£££	>€180/£120

Arriving in Ireland

Dublin Airport

Rental cars The main rental agencies have offices at the airport.

Taxis Taxis to the city take 30 to 45 minutes and cost €20 to €25.

Buses Run every 10 to 15 minutes to the city centre (€7).

Cork Airport

Rental cars There are car-hire desks for the main companies.

Taxis A taxi to/from town costs €20 to €25.

Buses Run every half hour between 6am and 10pm to the train station (€7.40).

Dun Laoghaire Ferry Port

DART (Suburban rail); 25 minutes to the centre of Dublin.

Buses Take around 45 minutes to the centre of Dublin.

Mobile Phones

Phones from most other countries work in Ireland but attract roaming charges. Local SIM cards cost from €10; SIM and basic handsets around €40.

Internet Access

Most hotels, B&Bs, hostels, bars and restaurants offer free wi-fi access. Internet cafes charge up to €6/£5 per hour.

Money

ATMs are widely available. Credit and debit cards can be used in most places, but check first.

Tipping

Not obligatory, but 10% to 15% in restaurants; €1/£1 per bag for hotel porters.

Useful Websites

Entertainment Ireland (www.entertainment.ie) Countrywide listings for every kind of entertainment.

Failte Ireland (www.discoverireland.ie) Official tourist board website – practical info and a huge accommodation database.

Lonely Planet (www.lonelyplanet.com/ireland) Destination information, hotel bookings, traveller forums and more.

Northern Ireland Tourist Board (www.nitb.com) Official tourist site.

Language

Irish (Gaeilge) is the country's official language. In 2003 the government introduced the Official Languages Act, whereby all official documents and street signs must be either in Irish or in both Irish and English. Despite its official status, Irish is really only spoken in pockets of rural Ireland known as the Gaeltacht, the main ones being Cork (Corcaigh), Donegal (Dún na nGall), Galway (Gaillimh), Kerry (Ciarraí) and Mayo (Maigh Eo).

Ask people outside the Gaeltacht if they can speak Irish and nine out of 10 of them will probably reply, 'ah, cupla focal' (a couple of words), and they generally mean it – but many adults also regret not having a greater grasp of it. Irish is a compulsory subject in schools for those aged six to 15. In recent times, a new Irish curriculum has been introduced cutting the hours devoted to the subject but making the lessons more fun, practical and celebratory.

Irish divides vowels into long (those with an accent) and short (those without), and also distinguishes between broad (a, á, o, ó, u) and slender (e, é, i and i), which can affect the pronunciation of preceding consonants. Other than a few clusters, such as mh and bhf (both pronounced as w), consonants are generally pronounced the same as in English.

Irish has three main dialects: Connaught Irish (in Galway and northern Mayo), Munster Irish (in Cork, Kerry and Waterford) and Ulster Irish (in Donegal). Our pronunciation guides are an anglicised version of modern standard Irish, which is essentially an amalgam of the three – if you read them as if they were English, you'll be able to get your point across in Gaeilge without even having to think about the specifics of Irish pronunciation or spelling.

BASICS

Hello.
Dia duit.   deea gwit

Hello. (reply)
Dia is Muire duit.   deeas moyra gwit

Good morning.
Maidin mhaith.   mawjin wah

Good night.
Oíche mhaith.   eekheh wah

Goodbye. (when leaving)
Slán leat.   slawn lyat

Goodbye. (when staying)
Slán agat.   slawn agut

Yes.
Tá.   taw

No.
Níl.   neel

It is.
Sea.   sheh

It isn't.
Ní hea.   nee heh

Thank you (very) much.
Go raibh (míle)   goh rev (meela)
maith agat.   mah agut

Excuse me.
Gabh mo leithscéal.   gamoh lesh scale

I'm sorry.
Tá brón orm.   taw brohn oruhm

Do you speak (Irish)?
An bhfuil (Gaeilge) agat?   on wil (gaylge) oguht

I don't understand.
Ní thuigim.   nee higgim

What is this?
Cad é seo?   kod ay shoh

Want More?

For in-depth language information and handy phrases, check out Lonely Planet's *Irish Language & Culture*. You'll find it at **shop.lonelyplanet.com**, or you can buy Lonely Planet's iPhone phrasebooks at the Apple App Store.

Signs

Dúnta	Closed
Gardaí	Police
Leithreas	Toilet
Ná Caitear Tobac	No Smoking
Oifig An Phoist	Post Office
Oifig Eolais	Tourist Information
Oscailte	Open
Páirceáil	Parking
Fir	Men
Mná	Women

What is that?
Cad é sin? — kod ay shin

I'd like to go to ...
Ba mhaith liom — baw wah lohm
dul go dtí ... — dull go dee ...

I'd like to buy ...
Ba mhaith liom ... — bah wah lohm ...
a cheannach. — a kyanukh

another/one more
ceann eile — kyawn ella

nice
go deas — goh dyass

MAKING CONVERSATION

Welcome.
Ceád míle fáilte. — kade meela fawlcha
(lit: 100,000 welcomes)

Bon voyage!
Go n-éirí an bóthar leat! — go nairee on bohhar lat

How are you?
Conas a tá tú? — kunas aw taw too

I'm fine.
Táim go maith. — thawm go mah

... please.
... más é do thoil é. — ... maws ay do hall ay

Cheers!
Sláinte! — slawncha

What's your name?
Cad is ainm duit? — kod is anim dwit

My name is (Sean Frayne).
(Sean Frayne) is — (shawn frain) is
ainm dom. — anim dohm

Impossible!
Ní féidir é! — nee faydir ay

Nonsense!
Ráiméis! — rawmaysh

That's terrible!
Go huafásach! — guh hoofawsokh

Take it easy.
Tóg é gobogé . — tohg ay gobogay

DAYS OF THE WEEK

Monday	Dé Luaín	day loon
Tuesday	Dé Máirt	day maart
Wednesday	Dé Ceádaoin	day kaydeen
Thursday	Déardaoin	daredeen
Friday	Dé hAoine	day heeneh
Saturday	Dé Sathairn	day sahern
Sunday	Dé Domhnaigh	day downick

NUMBERS

1	haon	hayin
2	dó	doe
3	trí	tree
4	ceathaír	kahirr
5	cúig	kooig
6	sé	shay
7	seacht	shocked
8	hocht	hukt
9	naoi	nay
10	deich	jeh
11	haon déag	hayin jague
12	dó dhéag	doe yague
20	fiche	feekhe
21	fiche haon	feekhe hayin

STRETCH YOUR LEGS
DUBLIN

Start/Finish Trinity College

Distance 4.9km

Duration 3 hours

Dublin's most important attractions are concentrated on the south side of the Liffey, split between the older medieval town dominated by the castle and the two cathedrals, and the handsome 18th-century city that is a showcase of exquisite Georgian aesthetics.

Take this walk on Trips

Trinity College

Ireland's most prestigious **university** (☎01-896 1000; www.tcd.ie; College Green; ◷8am-10pm; ▣ all city centre) is a masterpiece of architecture and landscaping, and Dublin's most attractive bit of historical real estate, beautifully preserved in Georgian aspic.

The Walk ≫ From Trinity College, walk west along Dame St and turn into Dublin Castle.

Chester Beatty Library

The world-famous **library** (☎01-407 0750; www.cbl.ie; Dublin Castle; ◷10am-5pm Mon-Fri, 11am-5pm Sat, 1-5pm Sun year-round, closed Mon Nov-Feb, free tours 1pm Wed, 3pm & 4pm Sun; ▣ all city centre), in the grounds of Dublin Castle, houses the collection of mining engineer Sir Alfred Chester Beatty (1875–1968). Spread over two floors, the breathtaking collection includes more than 20,000 manuscripts, rare books, miniature paintings, clay tablets, costumes and other objects of historical and aesthetic importance.

The Walk ≫ Exit the castle and walk west; you'll see Christ Church Cathedral directly in front of you.

Christ Church Cathedral

Its hilltop location and eye-catching flying buttresses make this the most photogenic by far of Dublin's three **cathedrals** (Church of the Holy Trinity; www.christchurchcathedral.ie; Christ Church Pl; adult/student/child €6/4.50/2; ◷9am-5pm Mon-Sat, 12.30-2.30pm Sun year-round, longer hours Jun-Aug; ▣50, 50A, 56A from Aston Quay, 54, 54A from Burgh Quay) as well as one of the capital's most recognisable symbols. It was founded in 1030 on what was then the southern edge of Dublin's Viking settlement. The Normans rebuilt the lot in stone from 1172.

The Walk ≫ Go south along Nicholas St (which becomes New St); St Patrick's is 400m along.

St Patrick's Cathedral

Reputedly, it was at this **cathedral** (www.stpatrickscathedral.ie; St Patrick's Close;

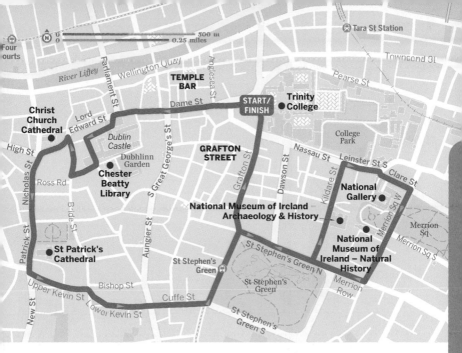

adult/student/child €6/5/free; ⏰9.30am-5pm
Mon-Fri, 9am-6pm Sat, 9-10.30am & 12.30-
2.30pm Sun; 🚌50, 50A, 56A from Aston Quay,
54, 54A from Burgh Quay) that St Paddy
himself dunked the Irish heathens into
the waters of a well. Although there's
been a church here since the 5th century, the present building dates from
1190 or 1225 (opinions differ).

The Walk » Just south of St Patrick's, turn left
onto Kevin St and keep going until you reach St
Stephen's Green; cross it and then turn onto
Kildare St.

National Museum of Ireland –
Archaeology & History

The star attraction of this branch of
the **National Museum of Ireland** (www.
museum.ie; Kildare St; ⏰10am-5pm Tue-Sat,
2-5pm Sun; 🚌all city centre) is the Treasury,
home to the finest collection of Bronze
Age and Iron Age gold artefacts in the
world, and the world's most complete
collection of medieval Celtic metalwork.

The Walk » Walk north on Kildare St and turn
right on Nassau St, then stay right on Clare St.

National Museum of Ireland –
Natural History

Dusty, weird and utterly compelling,
and a window into Victorian times, this
museum (Upper Merrion St; ⏰10am-5pm
Tue-Sat, 2-5pm Sun; 🚌7, 44 from city centre)
has barely changed since Scottish
explorer Dr David Livingstone opened
it in 1857 – before disappearing into
the African jungle for a meeting with
Henry Stanley.

The Walk » Turn right onto Merrion Row, skirt
St Stephen's Green and go right into Grafton St to
head back to Trinity College.

Spain

SPECTACULAR BEACHES, MOUNTAINTOP CASTLES, MEDIEVAL VILLAGES, STUNNING ARCHITECTURE and some of the most celebrated restaurants on the planet – Spain has an allure that few destinations can match.

There's much to see and do amid the enchanting landscapes that inspired Picasso and Velàzquez. You can spend your days feasting on seafood in coastal Galician towns, feel the heartbeat of Spain at soul-stirring flamenco shows or hike across the flower-strewn meadows of the mountains. The journeys in this region offer something for everyone: beach lovers, outdoor adventurers, family travellers, music fiends, foodies and those simply wanting to delve into Spain's rich art and history.

Costa del Sol Mijas
ALEX TIHONOVS/SHUTTERSTOCK ©

Spain

DON'T MISS

Cabo de Gata

A slice of arid coastline that the developers forgot. Fortunately, it's now a natural park and sports abundant flora and birdlife. Explore it on Trip 27

Orchidarium

Meander through Europe's largest orchid collection, in the Costa del Sol beach town of Estepona, on Trip 28

Covarrubias

Step behind the walls of this stunning riverside village and into another world on Trip 30

Wine Tasting

La Rioja is home to the best red wines in Spain – bodegas, tours, tastings and museums will inform as you consume on Trip 31

Gibraltar Upper Rock Nature Reserve

Mediterranean Meander

27

Follow the Mediterranean coast northeast out of Málaga and you'll be contemplating far more than just beach umbrellas. Roman ruins, heavyweight art, and fabulous festivals also pepper this surprisingly cultural coastline.

TRIP HIGHLIGHTS

1095 km
La Rambla
Stretch your legs on one of Europe's finest boulevards

Tarragona

12

FINISH

726 km
Ciudad de las Artes y las Ciencias
See Valencia's and Spain's new cutting edge in this futuristic complex

9

Xàtiva

Cartagena

START

1

Mojácar

4

Museo Picasso Málaga
Admire the greatest 20th-century master in the city of his birth

1 km

Cabo de Gata
Precious enclave of pure unblemished Mediterranean coastline

254 km

7 DAYS
1095 KM /
680 MILES

GREAT FOR...

BEST TIME TO GO
March to June is sunny, but not too hot, and there are plenty of festivals, including Las Fallas.

ESSENTIAL PHOTO
The chameleonic Sagrada Familia changes every time you visit.

BEST FOR OUTDOORS
Parque Natural de Cabo de Gata-Nijar.

27 Mediterranean Meander

From the Costa Daurada to the Costa del Sol, from Catalan pride in Sitges to Andalucian passion in Almería, from the Roman ruins of Tarragona to the Modernisme buildings of Barcelona: this drive proves that not all southern Spain is a beach bucket of cheesy tourist clichés. The full 1095km trajectory passes through four regions; two languages; Spain's second-, third- and sixth- largest cities; and beaches too numerous to count.

TRIP HIGHLIGHT

❶ Málaga

The Costa del Sol can seem wholly soulless until you fall gasping for a shred of culture into Málaga, an unmistakably Spanish metropolis curiously ignored by the lion's share of the millions of tourists who land annually at Pablo Ruíz Picasso International Airport.

Málaga is currently on the crest of a wave and is a great place to begin this epic 1000km-plus drive. The city that until 2003 lacked even a museum to its legendary native son, Picasso, is becoming an art heavyweight to rival Madrid or Barcelona. Recent gallery openings include the modernist Centre Pompidou and the evocative **Museo Ruso de Málaga** (www.coleccionmuseoruso.es; Avenida de Sor Teresa Plat 15; adult/child €8/free; ⊙11am-10pm Tue-Sun; P). They join over 20 established art nooks anchored by the distinguished **Museo Picasso Málaga** (www. museopicassomalaga.org; Calle San Agustín 8; admission €7; 10am-8pm Tue-Thu & Sun, to 9pm Fri & Sat) Moving with the times, Málaga is also developing its own arts district, Soho, transforming a former rundown area near the port with giant murals and groovy cafes.

✕ 🛏 p386

The Drive » Head east out of Málaga on the A7 motorway towards Almería. This is southern Spain's epic coastal road (also known as European route 15 or E15) and will be your companion for much of this trip. The coast gets ever

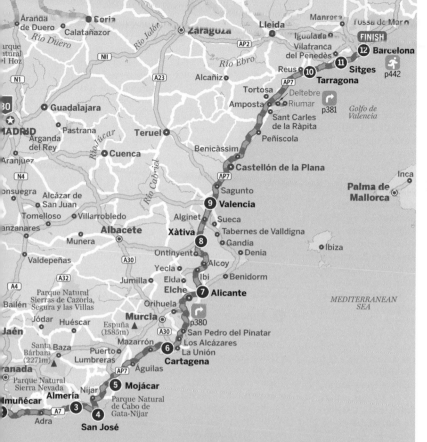

Aranda de Duero • Coria • Calatañazor • Zaragoza • Lleida • Manresa • Tossa de Mar
Río Jalón • Igualada • Vilafranca del Penedès • **FINISH** • **12 Barcelona**
urque atural l'Hoz • Río Duero • Río Ebro • AP2 • Reus • 10 • 11 • **Sitges** p442
N1 • NII • A23 • Alcañiz • AP7 • **Tarragona**
30 • Guadalajara • Tortosa • Deltebre • p381 • *Golfo de Valencia*
MADRID • Pastrana • Teruel • Amposta • Riumar • Sant Carles de la Ràpita
Arganda del Rey • Río Júcar • Cuenca • Benicàssim • Peñíscola
Aranjuez • N4 • **Castellón de la Plana** • AP7 • Inca
onsuegra • Alcázar de San Juan • Río Cabriel • Sagunto • **Palma de Mallorca**
Tomelloso • Villarrobledo • **9 Valencia**
anzanares • **Albacete** • Alginet • Sueca • Tabernes de Valldigna
Valdepeñas • Munera • **Xàtiva** • Gandia • Ibiza
A30 • Ontinyent • Alcoy • Denia
A4 • Yecla • Elda • **8** • Ibi • Benidorm • *MEDITERRANEAN SEA*
Bailén • Parque Natural Sierras de Cazorla, Segura y las Villas • Jumilla • **Elche** • Alicante
Jaén • Jódar • Huéscar • España ▲ (1585m) • Orihuela • **7 Alicante**
Santa Bárbara (2271m) ▲ • Baza • Espuña ▲ (1585m) • Puerto Lumbreras • **Murcia** • A30 • p380 • San Pedro del Pinatar
anada • AP7 • Mazarrón • **6** • Los Alcázares • La Unión
Parque Natural Sierra Nevada • Águilas • **Cartagena**
lmuñécar • Almería • **5 Mojácar**
Níjar • Parque Natural de Cabo de Gata-Níjar
Adra • A7 • **3** • **4** • **San José**

◉ N — 0 / 0 ——— 200 km / 100 miles

more precipitous as you enter Granada province. After 68km turn south on the N340 and follow it for 8km into Almuñécar.

----

2 Almuñécar

Granada province's cliff-lined, 80km-long coast has a hint of Italy's Amalfi about it, although it is definitively Spanish

LINK YOUR TRIP

27 Costa del Sol Beyond the Beaches

Can't get enough of the Mediterranean? Jump onto this trip in Málaga and head all the way down the coast to Gibraltar.

30 Historic Castilla y León

From Barcelona it's nearly six hours west to Madrid, but you'll encounter some of Spain's most captivating historic towns and villages.

when you get down to the nitty-gritty. Its warm climate – there's no real winter to speak of – lends it the name, Costa Tropical. The region's unofficial capital is Almuñécar, a fiercely traditional town that's a little rough around the edges, but very relaxed.

Dedicated to beach fun, Almuñécar's seafront is divided by a rocky outcrop, the Peñón del Santo, with pebbly Playa de San Cristóbal stretching to its west, and Playa Puerta del Mar to the east backed by a strip of cool cafes.

The **Museo Arqueológico** (Calle San Joaquín; adult/child €2.35/1.60; ⏱10am-1.30pm & 4-6.30pm Tue-Sat, 10.30am-1pm Sun) in the maze of the old town highlights Almuñécar's ancient Phoenician roots. Tickets include entry to the **Castillo de San Miguel** (Santa Adela Explanada; adult/child €2.35/1.60; ⏱10am-1.30pm &

4-6.30pm Tue-Sat, 10.30am-1pm Sun) at the top of a hill overlooking the sea, with fine views and another cleverly curated museum.

The Drive » After 20 years in the making, the final links of the A7 around Motril and Salobreña were established in 2015 after many delays. The *autopista* (toll way) takes drivers around the north of Motril, bypassing the older N340 in the south. As the landscape gets more arid you'll spy increasing numbers of commercial greenhouses punctuating the coastal landscape. Almería beckons. Distance from Almuñécar to Almería is 139km.

- - - - - - - - - - - -

❸ Almería

Don't underestimate sun-baked Almería, a tough waterside city with an illustrious history and a handful of important historical monuments to prove it. While the queues bulge outside Granada's Alhambra, mere trickles of

savvy travellers head for Almería's equally hefty Alcazaba fortress, which lords it over a city that once served as chief sea outlet for the 10th-century Córdoba caliphate.

Almería's old Moorish quarter that lies in the skirts of the Alcazaba hill hasn't been spruced up for the tourist hordes, meaning it is scruffy, but very real. Get Moorishly acquainted in the **Alcazaba** (Calle Almanzor; ⏱9am-7.30pm Tue-Sat Apr–mid-Jun, to 3.30pm Tue-Sat mid-Jun–mid-Sep, to 5.30pm Tue-Sat mid-Sep–Mar, to 3.30pm Sun all year), or the **Hammam Aire de Almería** (www.aire-dealmeria.com; Plaza de la Constitución 5; 1½hr session incl 15min aromatherapy €23; ⏱10am-10pm), a sanitised modern-day version of a Arabic bathhouse. The city's latest sight is the fantastic **Museo de la Guitarra** (📞950 27 43 58; Ronda del Beato Diego Ventaja; admission €3; ⏱10.30am-1.30pm Tue-Sun, 6-9pm Fri & Sat Jun-Sep, 10am-1pm Tue-Sun, 5-8pm Fri & Sat Oct-May), which documents Almería's understated role in the development of the iconic instrument.

🍴 p386

The Drive » Head east out of Almería on the N344. Cross the Río Andarax and pass the airport on your right. Fork right onto the ALP202 and at a T-junction turn right. Follow the road (AL3108) through low hills into the village of San José (total distance 40km).

✓ **TOP TIP: TOLL ROADS**

The AP7 (also known as E15), is a toll-charging *autopista* (motorway) that parallels much of Spain's southern coastline. You will have to stop periodically to pay a toll at manned booths. The total cost for the route highlighted here will be in the vicinity of €57. The confusingly named A7 follows a similar route to the AP7, but is toll-free. The N340 is a third road paralleling Spain's southern coast, although these days much of it has merged with the A7. Some of the N340 follows the route of the Roman Vía Augustus.

THE PICASSO TRAIL

Málaga and Barcelona are linked by more than Mediterranean beaches – both cities have strong Picasso connections. The great Andalucían painter was born in Málaga in 1881 and lived there until he was 10, while Barcelona served as his inspiration and muse in the late 1890s and early 1900s when he intermittently resided in the Catalan capital. As a result, the start and finish points of this trip stand as important way-stations in Picasso's illustrious career and are loaded with plenty of art and artefacts to investigate.

Málaga guards the painter's birth house, the diminutive **Casa Natal de Picasso** (www.fundacionpicasso.malaga.eu; Plaza de la Merced 15; admission €3; ⊘9.30am-8pm), which includes a replica of his father's erstwhile studio. Nearby, and run by the same foundation, is the **Museo Picasso Málaga** (⌨902 44 33 77; www.museopicassomalaga. org; Calle San Agustín 8; admission €7, incl temporary exhibition €10; ⊘10am-8pm Tue-Thu & Sun, to 9pm Fri & Sat), which opened in 2003. Barcelona hosts the **Museu Picasso** (⌨93 256 30 00; www.museupicasso.bcn.cat; Carrer de Montcada 15-23; adult/child €14/free, temporary exhibitions adult/child €6.50/free, 3-8pm Sun & 1st Sun of month free; ⊘Tue, Wed & Fri-Sun 9am-7pm, to 9.30pm Thu; MJaume I), which, with over 4000 exhibits, has one of the most complete Picasso collections in the world.

On a more modest scale, but also worth perusing as you pass through, is Alicante's **Museo de Arte Contemporáneo** (MACA; www.maca-alicante.es; Plaza Santa María 3; ⊘10am-8pm Tue-Sat, to 2pm Sun) displaying Picasso's *Portrait d'Arthur Rimbaud* (1960); and the **Museu Cau Ferrat** (www.museusdesitges.cat; Carrer de Fonollar) in Sitges, encased in the house of Picasso's friend, the late artist Santiago Rusiñol.

4 Cabo de Gata

If you can find anyone old enough to remember the Costa del Sol before the bulldozers arrived, they'd probably say it looked a bit like Cabo de Gata. Some of Spain's most beautiful and least-crowded beaches are strung between the grand cliffs and capes east of Almería City, where dark volcanic hills tumble into a sparkling turquoise sea.

Though Cabo de Gata is not undiscovered, it still has a wild, elemental feel and its scattered fish-ing villages (remember them?) remain low-key.

A good nexus is San José, with its secluded beaches, including Playa de los Genoveses just southwest of the village. Footpaths run along the coast in either direction, criss-crossing the protected Parque Natural de Cabo de Gata-Nijar. They're good for a short tentative stroll or a full-blown multiday excursion. The area is also one of the best places in Andalucía for diving. **Isub** (⌨950 38 00 04; www. isubsanjose.com; Calle Babor 8; ⊘8.30am-2pm & 4-7.30pm Mon-Sat, to 2pm Sun Mar-Dec) in San José offers a full range of courses.

The Drive » Follow the AL3108 inland from San José until you hit the A7 *autovia* (highway) just shy of Nijar. Head northeast towards Valencia for 43km until the exit for A370, signposted Mojácar.

5 Mojácar

Tucked away in an isolated corner of one of Spain's most traditional regions Mojácar was almost abandoned in the mid-20th century until a foresighted local mayor started luring artists and others with giveaway property offers. Although

WHY THIS IS A GREAT TRIP
BRENDAN SAINSBURY, AUTHOR

Growing up, I always imagined Spain's southern coast to be full of raucous resorts plying 18 to 30 holidays. When I eventually visited, I found that, in between the 'Benidorms', there was as much culture as after-hours cacophony. Where else can you find a city more innately Spanish than Málaga, a coast more unsullied than Cabo de Gata, or a Roman amphitheater more thrillingly sited than Tarragona's?

Top: Outdoor dining in Málaga
Left: Tarragona's Roman amphitheatre
Right: Cabo de Gata

the tourists have arrived, Mojácar has retained its essence.

There are actually two towns here: old Mojácar Pueblo, a jumble of white, cube-shaped houses on a hilltop 2km inland, and Mojácar Playa, a modern beach resort.

Exploring Mojácar Pueblo is mainly a matter of wandering the mazelike streets, with their bougainvillea-swathed balconies, stopping off at craft shops, galleries and boutiques. **El Mirador del Castillo**, at the top-most point, has a cafe-bar and magnificent views. The fortress-style **Iglesia de Santa María** (Calle Iglesia) dates from 1560 and may have once been a mosque.

South of Mojácar Playa, the beaches are quieter, and once you get to the fringes of town, there are a number of more secluded areas.

🛏 p386

The Drive ≫ Retrace your steps from Mojácar back to the A7 *autovia*. After 10km merge onto the AP7 near Vera. This is a toll road. Continue until the exit for Cartagena Oeste. At the roundabout take the N332 into the city. Mojácar to Cartagena is 134km.

- - - - - - - - - - - - -

❻ Cartagena

Cartagena's fabulous natural harbour has been used for thousands of years. Stand on the battlements of the castle that overlooks this city and you can literally see layer upon layer of history spread below you, from Phoenician traders through Roman legionaries, Islamic architects and the armies of the Christian Reconquista to the factories of the industrial age.

As archaeologists continue to reveal a long-buried, and fascinating, Roman and Carthaginian heritage, the city is finally starting to get the recognition it deserves. The **Museo Nacional de Arqueología Subacuática** (Arqua; http://museoarqua.mcu. es; Paseo del Muelle Alfonso XII 22; adult/child €3/free; ⊙10am-8pm or 9pm Tue-Sat,

to 3pm Sun) has lots of old pots, flashy lights, buttons to press, films to watch and a replica Phoenician trading ship, while the super **Museo del Teatro Romano** (www. teatroromanocartagena.org; Plaza del Ayuntamiento 9; adult/child €6/5; ⊙10am-6pm or 8pm Tue-Sat, to 2pm Sun) transports visitors via escalators and an underground passage to a magnificent, recently restored Roman theatre dating from the 1st century BC.

✖ p386

The Drive ❯❯ Get back on the AP7 towards Alicante (more tolls!). After 75km the *autovia* rejoins the (free) A7. Follow it for 32km before taking exit 17A signposted Alicante.

- - - - - - - - - - - -
❼ Alicante

Of all Spain's mainland provincial capitals, Alicante is the most influenced by tourism, thanks to the nearby airport and resorts. Nevertheless, this is a dynamic, attractive Spanish city with a castle, old quarter and long waterfront. The eating scene is exciting and the nightlife is absolutely legendary, whether you're chugging pints with the stag parties at 7pm or twirling on the dance floor with the locals seven hours later.

There are sweeping views over the city from the large 16th-century **Castillo de Santa Bárbara** (adult/child €3/1.50;

↱ DETOUR: ORIHUELA

Start: ❻ Cartagena (p379)

Beside the Río Segura and flush with the base of a barren mountain of rock, the historical heart of Orihuela, with superb Gothic, Renaissance and, especially, baroque buildings, well merits a detour. The old town is strung out between the river and a mountain topped by a ruined castle. The main sights are dotted along it, more or less in a line.

A few of the buildings are particularly worth looking out for. The **Convento de Santo Domingo** (Calle Adolfo Claravana; admission €2; ⊙9.30am-1.30pm & 4-7pm or 5-8pm Tue-Sat, 10am-2pm Sun) is a 16th-century convent with two fine Renaissance cloisters and a refectory clad in 18th-century tilework. One of the town's splendid ecclesiastical buildings is the 14th-century Catalan Gothic **Catedral de San Salvador** (Calle Doctor Sarget; ⊙10.30am-2pm & 4-6.30pm Tue-Fri, 10.30am-2pm Sat), with its three finely carved portals and a lovely little cloister. The Renaissance facade of **Iglesia de las Santas Justa y Rufina** (Plaza Salesas 1; ⊙10am-1pm & 4-6pm Mon-Fri) is worth admiring, and its Gothic tower is graced with gargoyles.

Orihuela is between the Cartagena and Alicante stops on this trip. To reach it branch west off the AP7 onto the CV91 around 70km north of Cartagena.

DETOUR: DELTA DE L'ERBE

Start: ❾ Valencia (p382)

The delta of the Río Ebre, formed by silt brought down by the river, sticks out 20km into the Mediterranean near Catalonia's southern border. Dotted with reedy lagoons and fringed by dune-backed beaches, this completely flat and exposed wetland, with **Parc Natural Delta de l'Ebre** comprising 77 sq km, is northern Spain's most important waterbird habitat. The migration season (October and November) sees the bird population peak, but they are also numerous in winter and spring. Even if you're not a twitcher, a visit here is worthwhile for the surreal landscapes alone. Tiny whitewashed farmhouses seem to float on little islands among green and brown paddy fields which stretch to the horizon. It's completely unlike anywhere else in Catalonia.

The scruffy, sprawling town of **Deltebre** is at the centre of the delta but push on from here to smaller villages such as **Riumar**, the coastal village at the delta's easternmost point, or **Poblenou del Delta**.

To reach Deltebre, branch off AP7 at exit 41, 180km north of Valencia. The town lies 13km to the east along TV3454.

🕑10am-10pm Apr-Sep, to 8pm Oct-Mar), which also houses a museum recounting the history of Alicante. If you're not up for the steep climb, the city has a couple of good free museums. The Museo de Arte Contemporáneo de Alicante (p377) displays Dalí, Miró and Picasso, among others. The **Museu de Fogueres** (Museo de las Hogueras; Rambla de Méndez Núñez 29; 🕑10am-2pm & 5-8pm or 6-9pm Tue-Sat) has photos, costumes and an audiovisual presentation of the Fiesta de Sant Joan.

✕ p386

The Drive » Leave Alicante on the A77 signposted Valencia. After 10km merge onto the A7. The autovia proceeds north, passing through a couple of tunnels and heading progressively downhill as it forges an inland route to Valencia. After 106km exit on the CV645 signposted Xàtiva. It's 5km to the town itself.

- - - - - - - - - -

❽ Xàtiva

Xàtiva (Spanish: Játiva) is often visited on an easy and rewarding 50km day trip from Valencia or – in this case – as a stop on the way north from Alicante. It has a small historic quarter and a mighty castle strung along the crest of the Serra Vernissa, at whose base the town snuggles.

The Muslims established Europe's first paper manufacturing plant in Xàtiva, which is also famous as the birthplace of the Borgia Popes Calixtus III and Alexander VI. The town's glory days ended in 1707 when Felipe V's troops torched most of the town.

What's interesting in Xàtiva lies south and uphill from the Alameda, including the **castle** (adult/child €2.40/1.20; 🕑10am-6pm or 7pm Tue-Sun), which clasps to the summit of a double-peaked hill overlooking the old town. Today, behind its crumbling battlements you'll find a mixture of flower gardens (bring a picnic), tumbledown turrets and towers, and an excellent museum on medieval life. The walk up to the castle is a long one, but the views are sensational.

The Drive » Use N340 to rejoin the A7 and head north to Valencia. Just outside the city when the A7 merges with the AP7, take the V31, Valencia's main southern access road for the final 18km into the city centre.

TRIP HIGHLIGHT

9 Valencia

Spain's third-largest city is a magnificent place, content for Madrid and Barcelona to grab the headlines while it gets on with being a wonderfully liveable city with thriving cultural, eating and nightlife scenes. Never afraid to innovate, Valencia has diverted its flood-prone river to the outskirts of town and converted the former riverbed into a wonderful green ribbon of park winding right through the city. On it are the strikingly futuristic buildings of the **Ciudad de las Artes y las Ciencias** (City of Arts & Sciences; www.cac. es; combined ticket for Oceanogràfic, Hemisfèric & Museo de las Ciencias Príncipe Felipe adult/child €36.25/27.55), designed by local-boy-made-good Santiago Calatrava. Other brilliant contemporary buildings grace the city, which also has a fistful of fabulous Modernista architecture, great museums and a large, characterful old quarter.

Valencia, surrounded by the fertile fruit-and-veg farmland La Huerta, is famous as the home of rice dishes such as paella, but its buzzy dining scene offers plenty more besides.

✗ ⨞ p387

The Drive » Leave Valencia on the V21 signposted Puçol. After 23km you'll rejoin your reliable old friend, the AP7. Get your toll money ready! The AP7 is your route for the next 200km, taking you into Catalonia. Take exit 38 and get on the A7 for the final 35km of the route into Tarragona.

10 Tarragona

The eternally sunny port city of Tarragona is an improbable mix of Mediterranean beach life, Roman history and medieval alleyways. As Spain's second-most important Roman site, Tarragona has a wealth of ruins, including a seaside amphitheatre where gladiators once hacked away at each other (or wild animals) to the death.

The Unesco-listed Roman sites are scattered around town. Entrance tickets can be acquired at the **Museu d'Historia de Tarragona** (MHT; www.museutgn.com; adult/child per site €3.30/free, all sites €11.05/free; ⊙ sites 9am-9pm Tue-Sat, 10am-3pm Sun Easter-Sep, 10am-7pm Tue-Sat, 10am-3pm Sun Oct-Easter).

The town's medieval heart is one of the most beautifully designed in Spain, its maze of narrow cobbled streets encircled by steep walls and crowned with a splendid **Catedral** (www.catedraldetarragona.com; Plaça de la Seu; adult/child €5/3; ⊙10am-7pm Mon-Sat mid-Mar–Oct, 10am-5pm Mon-Fri, 10am-7pm Sat Nov–mid-Mar). A lively eating and drinking scene makes for an enticing stop.

OSCAR SANCHEZ PHOTOGRAPHY / GETTY IMAGES ©

Sitges A seaside resort with great nightlife

✗ ⌘ p387

The Drive ≫ From Tarragona use the N240 to get back onto AP7 and head east towards Barcelona. After 23km take exit 31 onto the C32. Follow this road for 31km, crossing one viaduct and burrowing through two tunnels, to Sitges.

----

⑪ Sitges

This lovely fishing-village-turned-pumping-beach-resort town has been a favourite with upper-class Catalans since the late 19th century, as well as a key location for the burgeoning Modernisme movement which paved the way for the likes of Picasso. A famous gay destination, in July and August Sitges turns into one big beach party with a nightlife to rival Ibiza; the beaches are long and sandy, the tapas bars prolific and the Carnaval bacchanalian.

The main beach is flanked by the attractive seafront Passeig Maritim, dotted with *chiringuitos* (beachside bars) and divided into nine sections with different names by a series of breakwaters.

The art highlight is the recently refurbished

Museu Cau Ferrat (p377), built in the 1890s as a house-cum-studio by artist Santiago Rusiñol – a pioneer of the Modernista movement. The whitewashed mansion is full of his own art and that of his contemporaries, including his friend Picasso, as well as a couple of El Grecos.

The Drive » It's only 40km to Barcelona! Get back onto the C32 and pay your last cursed toll. Fly through a multitude of tunnels. After 30km of driving, take exit 168 and follow the signs for Barcelona, Gran Via and Centre Ciutat.

- - - - - - - - - - - -

TRIP HIGHLIGHT

⑫ Barcelona

Barcelona is a guidebook in itself and a cultural colossus to rival Paris or Rome, let alone Madrid. Take our 'stretch your legs' walk (p442) to bag some of its many highlights. The city's ever-evolving symbol is Gaudí's one-of-a-kind **Sagrada Família** (☑93 207 30 31; www.sagradafamilia. cat; Carrer de Mallorca 401; adult/child under 11yr/senior & student €14.80/free/12.80; ◷9am-8pm Apr-Sep, to 6pm Oct-Mar; ⓜSagrada Família), which rises like an unfinished symphony over L'Eixample district. The surounding grid is well known for the whimsical waves of Modernisme architecture, a style expounded most eleoquently in **La Pedrera** (Casa Milà; ☑90 220 21 38; www.lapedrera. com; Carrer de Provença

261-265; adult/student/child €20.50/16.50/10.25; ◷9am-8pm Mar-Oct, to 6.30pm Nov-Feb; ⓜDiagonal) with its rooftop chimney pots and statues of medieval knights. History lurks in the Barri Gòtic, home to **La Catedral** (☑93 342 82 62; www.catedralbcn.org; Plaça de la Seu; admission free, special visit €6, choir admission €2.80; ◷8am-12.45pm & 5.15-7.30pm Mon-Sat, special visit 1-5pm Mon-Sat, 2-5pm Sun & holidays; ⓜJaume I), while the modern hip crowd congregate in the Born, a subneighbourhood of La Ribera quarter.

A good orientation point in this complex city is the legendary (and much copied) **La Rambla** (ⓜCatalunya, Liceu or Drassanes), a tree-lined

---

LEGACY OF THE ROMANS

What did the Romans ever do for us? Well, quite a lot actually, an assertion that rapidly gains validity as you drive northeast up the Mediterranean coast of Spain.

The Roman colonies in Hispania (their name for the Iberian peninsula) lasted from around 400BC to 200BC and reminders of their existence are spread all along the coast from Andalucía up to Catalonia. The three main stops for Roma-philes are Málaga, Cartagena and Tarragona, all once flourishing Roman cities whose pasts equal or outweigh their present profiles in modern Spain. Málaga's **Roman amphitheatre** (☑951 50 11 15; Calle Alcazabilla 8), nestled beneath its Alcazaba, was rediscovered in 1951 and dates from the 1st century AD when the settlement was called Malaca. An adjacent interpretive centre has touch screens and displays artefacts dug up from the site. Cartagena (Carthago Nova to the Romans) has multiple Roman sights including villas, a theatre and parts of an old wall. The history is all pulled together at the new-ish Museo del Teatro Romano (p380), where you can buy a museum pass for all the sights. Tarragona (Tarraco) was once capital of Rome's Spanish provinces and has ruins to prove it, including an amphitheatre, a forum, street foundations and the **Aqüeducte Romà** (Pont del Diable; admission free; ◷9am-dusk), a glorious two-tiered aqueduct. Wonderful ocean-themed mosaics can be seen in the nearby **Museu Nacional Arqueològic de Tarragona** (www.mnat.cat; Plaça del Rei 5; adult/child €2.40/free; ◷9.30am-6pm Tue-Sat, 10am-2pm Sun).

LOCAL KNOWLEDGE: FESTIVALS

If you're undertaking this trip in February, March or August, look out for the following festivals.

Feria de Malaga (🕐mid-Aug) Málaga's nine-day *feria* (fair), launched by a huge fireworks display, is the most ebullient of Andalucía's summer *ferias*. It resembles a mad Rio-style street party with plenty of flamenco and *fino* (sherry); head for the city centre to be in the thick of it. At night, festivities switch to large fairgrounds and nightly rock and flamenco shows at Cortijo de Torres, 3km southwest of the city centre; special buses run from all over the city.

Las Fallas de San José (www.fallas.es; 🕐March) The exuberant, anarchic swirl of Las Fallas de San José – fireworks, music, festive bonfires and all-night partying – is a must if you're visiting the city of Valencia in mid-March. The *fallas* themselves are huge sculptures of papier mâché on wood built by teams of local artists. Each neighbourhood sponsors its own *falla*.

Sitges Carnaval (www.sitges.com/carnaval) Carnaval in Sitges is a week-long booze-soaked riot made just for the extroverted and exhibitionist, complete with masked balls and capped by extravagant gay parades held on the Sunday and the Tuesday night, featuring flamboyantly dressed drag queens, giant sound systems and a wild all-night party with bars staying open until dawn. Held in February/March; dates change from year to year.

pedestrian promenade which was made with the evening *paseo* (stroll) in mind. La Rambla divides the Barri Gòtic and La Ribera from El Raval. To the northeast lies the Modernisme-inspired L'Eixample quarter; to the south are the steep parks and gardens of Montjuïc, site of the 1992 Olympics.

🍴 🛏 p387

Eating & Sleeping

Málaga ❶

✗ El Mesón de Cervantes
Tapas, Argentinian €€

(📞952 21 62 74; www.elmesondecervantes.com; Calle Álamos 11; mains €13-16; ⏱7pm-midnight Wed-Mon) Cervantes started as a humble tapas bar run by expat Argentinian Gabriel Spatz (the original bar is still operating around the corner), but has expanded into plush spacious digs with an open kitchen, fantastic family-style service and incredible meat dishes.

🛏 Molina Lario
Hotel €€

(📞952 06 20 02; www.hotelmolinalario.com; Calle Molina Lario 20-22; r €116-130; ✲🛜🛗) Perfect for romancing couples, this hotel has a sophisticated contemporary feel with spacious rooms decorated in a cool palette of earthy colours. There are crisp white linens, marshmallow-soft pillows and tasteful paintings, plus a fabulous rooftop terrace and pool with views to the sea. Situated within confessional distance of the cathedral.

Almería ❸

✗ Casa Puga
Tapas €

(www.barcasapuga.es; Calle Jovellanos 7; wine & tapa €2.80; ⏱noon-4pm & 8pm-midnight Mon-Sat, closed Wed evening) The undisputed tapas champ (since it opened in 1870) is Casa Puga; make it an early stop, as it fills up fast. Shelves of ancient wine bottles, and walls plastered with everything from lottery tickets to ancient maps, are the backdrop for a tiny cooking station that churns out saucers of tasty stews and griddled meats, fish, mushrooms and shrimps.

Mojácar ❺

🛏 Hostal El Olívar
Hostal €

(📞950 47 20 02; www.hostalelolivar.es; Calle Estación Nueva 11, Mojácar Pueblo; s/d incl breakfast €38/59; ✲@🛜) A stylish and welcoming addition to the Mojácar Pueblo options, the Olívar has contemporary, pretty rooms with up-to-date bathrooms and tea/coffee sets. Some overlook a plaza, others the countryside. Breakfast is generous and you can take it on a panoramic terrace, when the weather is decent.

Cartagena ❻

✗ Techos Bajos
Seafood €€

(www.techosbajos.com; Calle Joaquín Madrid; dishes €7-16; ⏱9.30am-4pm Tue-Sun, plus 7pm-midnight Fri & Sat) Locals absolutely flood this large, no-frills kind of place at lunchtime for its well-priced portions of fresh fish and seafood. You'll find it down the hill from the bus station, right opposite the fishing port.

Alicante ❼

✗ Cervecería Sento
Tapas €

(Calle Teniente Coronel Chápuli 1; tapas €2-8; ⏱10am-5pm & 8pm-midnight Mon-Sat) Superb, quality *montaditos* (little rolls) and grilled things are the reason to squeeze into this brilliant little bar. Watching the nonstop staff in action is quite an experience too. They've got a bigger branch nearby, but this has the atmosphere.

Valencia ❾

✖ Delicat
Tapas, Fusion €€

(☎963 92 33 57; Calle Conde Almodóvar 4; mains €9-14; ☺1-4pm & 8.30-11.30pm Tue-Sat, 1-4pm Sun) At this particularly friendly, intimate option (there are only nine tables, plus the terrace in summer), Catina, up front, and her partner, Paco, on full view in the kitchen, offer an unbeatable-value, five-course menu of samplers for lunch and a range of truly innovative tapas anytime.

🛏 Caro Hotel
Hotel €€€

(☎963 05 90 00; www.carohotel.com; Calle Almirante 14; r €143-214; P ✳🏠) Housed in a sumptuous 19th-century mansion, this sits atop some 2000 years of Valencian history, with restoration revealing a hefty hunk of the Arab wall, Roman column bases and Gothic arches. Each room is furnished in soothing dark shades, has a great king-sized bed, and varnished cement floors. Bathrooms are tops. For that very special occasion, reserve the 1st-floor grand suite, once the ballroom. Savour, too, its excellent restaurant Alma del Temple.

Tarragona ❿

✖ AQ
Catalan €€

(☎977 21 59 54; www.aq-restaurant.com; Carrer de les Coques 7; degustation €40-50; ☺1.30-3.30pm & 8.30-11pm Tue-Sat) This is a bubbly designer haunt alongside the cathedral with stark colour contrasts (black, lemon and cream linen), slick lines and intriguing plays on traditional cooking. One of the two degustation menus is the way to go here, or the weekday lunch menú for €18.

🛏 Hotel Plaça de la Font
Hotel €€

(☎977 24 61 34; www.hotelpdelafont.com; Plaça de la Font 26; s/d €55/75; ✳🏠) Comfortable modern rooms, with photos of Tarragona monuments above the bed, overlook a bustling terrace in a you-can't-get-more-central-than-this location, right on the popular Plaça de la Font. The ones at the front are pretty well soundproofed and have tiny balconies for people-watching.

Barcelona ⓬

✖ Quimet i Quimet
Tapas €€

(☎93 442 31 42; Carrer del Poeta Cabanyes 25; tapas €4-11; ☺noon-4pm & 7-10.30pm Mon-Fri, noon-4pm Sat & Sun; Ⓜ Paral·lel) Quimet i Quimet is a family-run business that has been passed down from generation to generation. There's barely space to swing a *calamar* (squid) in this bottle-lined, standing-room-only place, but it is a treat for the palate, with *montaditos* made to order. Let the folk behind the bar advise you, and order a drop of fine wine to accompany the food.

✖ Tapas 24
Tapas €€

(☎93 488 09 77; www.carlesabellan.com; Carrer de la Diputació 269; tapas €4-9; ☺9am-midnight Mon-Sat; Ⓜ Passeig de Gràcia) Carles Abellan, master of Comerç 24 in La Ribera, runs this basement tapas haven known for its gourmet versions of old faves. Specials include the *bikini* (toasted ham and cheese sandwich – here the ham is cured and the truffle makes all the difference) and a thick black *arròs negre de sípia* (squid-ink black rice).

🛏 Five Rooms
Boutique Hotel €€

(☎93 342 78 80; www.thefiverooms.com; Carrer de Pau Claris 72; s/d from €155/165; ✳@🏠; Ⓜ Urquinaona) Like they say, there are five rooms (standard rooms and suites) in this 1st-floor flat virtually on the border between L'Eixample and the old centre of town. Each is different and features include broad, firm beds, stretches of exposed brick wall, mosaic tiles and minimalist decor. There are also two apartments.

🛏 DO
Boutique Hotel €€€

(☎93 481 36 66; www.hoteldoreial.com; Plaça Reial 1; s/d from €230/280; ✳🏠🍴; Ⓜ Liceu) Overlooking the magnificent plaza for which it is named, this 18-room property has handsomely designed rooms, set with beamed ceilings, wide plank floors and all-important soundproofing. The service is excellent, and the facilities extensive, with roof terrace (with bar in summer), dipping pool, solarium and spa. Its excellent market-to-table restaurants draw in visiting foodies.

Costa del Sol Beyond the Beaches

28

This coast-hugging trip travels via a sparkling tiara of holiday resorts, as well as some little known gems and a diamond of a capital: Málaga.

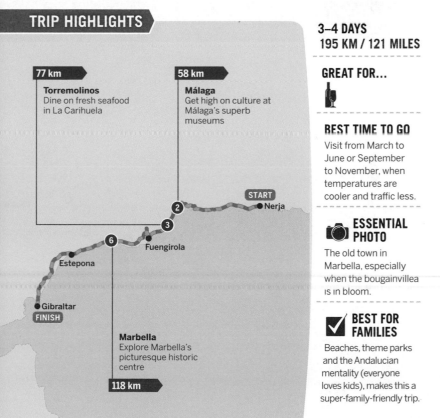

77 km

Torremolinos
Dine on fresh seafood in La Carihuela

58 km

Málaga
Get high on culture at Málaga's superb museums

START ● Nerja

②
③

⑥
Fuengirola

● **Estepona**

● **Gibraltar**
FINISH

Marbella
Explore Marbella's picturesque historic centre

118 km

**3–4 DAYS
195 KM / 121 MILES**

GREAT FOR...

BEST TIME TO GO

Visit from March to June or September to November, when temperatures are cooler and traffic less.

ESSENTIAL PHOTO

The old town in Marbella, especially when the bougainvillea is in bloom.

BEST FOR FAMILIES

Beaches, theme parks and the Andalucian mentality (everyone loves kids), makes this a super-family-friendly trip.

389

Málaga

28 Costa del Sol Beyond the Beaches

This drive, running from Nerja in the east to Gibraltar in the west, travels via a landscape that constantly shifts and changes: from orchards of subtropical fruit trees to shimmering white urbanisations; a culture-loving metropolis to the cobbled backstreets of a former fishing village. Be prepared for a journey that constantly challenges any preconceived ideas you may have about this, Spain's most famous, tourist-driven coast.

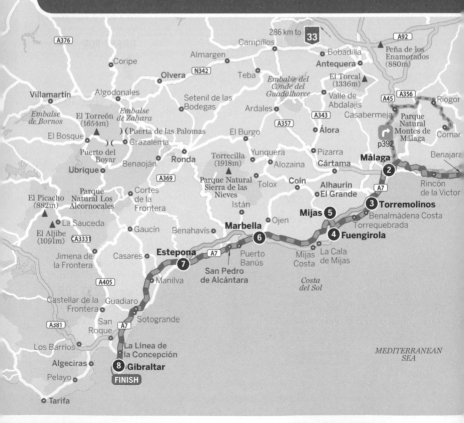

❶ Nerja

In a charmed spot sitting at the base of the Sierra Almijara peaks, this former fishing village has retained its low-rise village charm, despite the proliferation of souvenir shops and day trippers. At its heart is the Balcón de Europa, one of the most beautiful promenades on the Costa del Sol, built on the site of a Moorish castle. Grab a coffee at one of the terraced cafes before heading north of town to visit the extraordinary **Cueva**

de Nerja (www.cuevade nerja.es; adult/child €9/5; ⏰unguided visit 10am-1pm & 4-5.30pm Sep-Jun, 10am-6pm Jul & Aug; guided visit 1-2pm & 5.30-6.30pm Sep-Jun, 11am-noon & 6.30-7.30pm Jul & Aug), dating back a cool five million years: it's a 4km long theatrical wonderland of extraordinary rock formations, subtle shifting colours and stalactites and stalagmites.

✖ p397

↱ DETOUR.
FRIGILIANA

Start: ❶ Nerja

After the cavernous gloom of the Cueva de Nerja, consider heading inland to Frigiliana, a *pueblos blanco* voted as the prettiest in Andalucía by the Spanish tourism authority. It's well signposted: take the M5105 inland from Nerja, passing groves of mango and avocado trees and follow signs to the *casco historico* and car park. Frigiliana is famed for its sweet local wine and honey, which you can buy at small village shops. It is an enchanting place with a tangible Moroccan feel; read the plaques around town to learn why – the village stretches back to the time of the Moors.

The Drive » Consider taking the slightly slower, but more scenic, N340 to Rincón de la Victoria, then pick up the A7-E15 bypass to Málaga. This meandering coastal road passes through pretty agricultural land. Look for the centuries-old watchtowers from the days of Barbarian invaders. It's a total drive of 58km (1¼ hours).

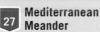
`TRIP HIGHLIGHT`

❷ Málaga

Book a one- or two-night stay here to experience the city's buzzing bar life

🔗 LINK YOUR TRIP

27 **Mediterranean Meander**

Málaga is the start of this east-coast ramble that takes in several of the most stunning cities in Spain, including its final destination: Barcelona.

33 **Alentejo & Algarve Beaches**

For more stunning coast, head west via Seville to the Portuguese border then on to Cacela Velha to do the Algarve trip in reverse. (349km).

and increasingly sophisticated foodie scene. Málaga has also emerged as a serious cultural capital, with some 30 museums, including the **Museo Carmen Thyssen** (www.carmenthyssenmalaga.org; Calle Compañía 10; admission €4.50, incl temporary exhibition €9; ☺10am-7.30pm Tue-Sun), the **Museo Ruso** (☎951 92 61 50; www.coleccionmuseo-ruso.es; Avenida de Sor Teresa Plat 15; adult/child €8/free; ☺11am-10pm Tue-Sun; P), and the **Museo del Vidrio y Cristal** (Museum of Glass & Crystal; ☎952 22 02 71; www.museovidrioycristalmalaga.com; Plazuela Santísimo Cristo de la Sangre 2; admission €5; ☺11am-7pm Tue-Sun), a private collection that concentrates on glass and crystal. Climb the tower for fabulous views from the landmark 16th-century **Catedral de Málaga** (☎952 21 59 17; Calle Molina Lario; cathedral & museum €5, tower €6; ☺10am-6pm Mon-Sat), then duck inside to admire the gorgeous retables and stash of 18th-century religious art. Travel further back in time by visiting the **Alcazaba** (Calle Alcazabilla; admission €2.20, incl Castillo de Gibralfaro €3.40; ☺9.30am-8pm Tue-Sun), a fascinating 11th-century Moorish palace-fortress. Across from the entrance – and **Roman Amphitheatre** (☎951 50 11 15; Calle Alcazabilla 8) – **Batik** (☎952 22 10 45; www.batikmalaga.com; Calle Alcazabilla 12; mains €12-20; ☺10am-midnight; 🛜) is an atmospheric place for a drink and innovative bite to eat.

✕ 🛏 p397

The Drive » Leaving Málaga, take the A7 in the direction of Algecíras, Torremolinos and Cádiz, then follow the MA20 signposted to Torremolinos.

This is a busy stretch of *autovia* (highway) that passes the airport. It's a drive of 18.5km or 25 minutes.

- - - - - - - - - -

TRIP HIGHLIGHT

❸ Torremolinos

Start your exploration in the centre of town with a meander down pedestrian **Calle San Miguel**, lined with shops, cafes and bars. Continue as the street winds down to steps which lead to Playamar, the main beach. Turn right for one of the most delightful walks on the Costa, round the rocky headland to **La Carihuela**; the former fishing *barrio* (neighbourhood) which is now, fittingly, home to some superb seafood restaurants such as **Casa Juan** (www.losmellizos.net; Calle San Ginés 20, La Carihuela; mains €13-20). This *paseo* (walk) continues to the

DETOUR: COMARÉS

Start: ❷ Málaga (p391)

Heading inland, northeast of Málaga, brings you to La Axarquía, a stunning rugged region, great for hiking, and stippled with pretty unspoiled *pueblos* (villages). A highlight of the area is, quite literally, Comarés which sits like a snowdrift upon a lofty mountain (739m) commanding spectacular views of the surrounding mountain range and coast. Wander the tangle of narrow lanes and don't miss the remarkable summit cemetery. There are also several walking trails that start from here; stop by the small *ayuntamiento* (town hall) on Plaza de la Axarquía for more information and maps. The village is home to several bars and a couple of restaurants, as well as a small supermarket for self-caterers. Get here via the A45 *autovia* (highway), direction Granada, Córdoba and Seville, take the Casabermeja exit and follow signs to Comarés via the A356 (through Riogordo) and the MA159. The journey totals 55km and should take you roughly one hour.

Puerto Deportivo de Benalmádena, striking for its Gaudí-cum-Asian-cum-Mr Whippy–style architecture, and large choice of bars, restaurants and shops overlooking the boats (one of which reputedly belongs to actor celeb and native *malagueño* Antonio Banderes).

✗ p397

The Drive ›› Continue on the N340, which hugs the coast and passes through the busy coastal resort of Benalmádena Costa. Note that there is a 50km speed limit on this scenic stretch.

---

④ Fuengirola

The appeal of Fuengirola lies in the fact that it is a genuine Spanish working town, as well as a popular resort. There is a large foreign resident population here as well, many of whom arrived here in the '60s and stayed after their ponytails went grey. Grab a (bar) chair in pretty flower-festooned Plaza de la Constitucíon, which is overlooked by the baroque facade of the church, then explore the surrounding narrow pedestrian streets flanked by idiosyncratic small shops and tapas bars. The excellent **Bioparc** (✆952 66 63 01; www.bioparcfuengirola.es; Avenida Camilo José Cela; adult/child €18/13; ☺10am-sunset; **P**), northwest of here, is the Costa's best zoo and treats its animals

TOP TIP: TOLL ROAD AP7

If you are travelling in July and August, consider taking the AP7 toll road, at least between Fuengirola and Marbella as the A7 can become dangerously congested. This particular A7 stretch (formerly part of the N340) used to be notorious for accidents; however, the situation has improved since the introduction of a 80km/h speed limit in former trouble spots.

very well, with no cages or bars, but, rather, spacious enclosures and conservation and breeding programs.

✗ p397

The Drive ›› From Fuengirola's central Renfe train station, take Avenida Alcalde Clemente Díaz Ruiz inland. Cross the *autovia* A7 and continue on the Carretera de Mijas. In Mijas follow signs to the underground carpark (€1 for 24 hours). This 7km journey should take around 10 minutes.

---

⑤ Mijas

The *pueblo blanco* (white village) of Mijas has retained its sugarcube cuteness despite being on the coach-tour circuit. Art buffs should check out the **Centro de Arte Contemporáneo de Mijas** (CAC; www.cacmijas.info; Calle Málaga 28; admission €3; ☺10am-7pm Tue-Sun) contemporary art museum, with its second-largest collection of Picasso ceramics in the world. Otherwise this village is all about strolling the narrow

cobbled streets, dipping into the tapas bars and shopping for souvenirs. Be sure to walk up to the **Plaza de Toros** (museum €3; ☺10am-8pm); an unusual square-shaped bullring at the top of the village, surrounded by lush ornamental gardens with spectacular views of the coast. Mijas also has a large foreign resident population and a vigorous calendar of events, including live flamenco shows in the main plaza every Wednesday at noon, an annual blues festival in July and regular concerts in the auditorium.

The Drive ›› Return to the A7 *autovia*. This double carriageway passes through the most densely built span of the entire Costa, with urbanisations such as Calahonda and Miraflores that date from the 1980s, when the Costa was at its peak of popularity and expansion. Continue west along here until you reach the exit for Marbella; a total drive of 33km or 25 minutes.

WHY THIS IS A GREAT TRIP
JOSEPHINE QUINTERO, AUTHOR

My home for two decades, the Costa del Sol is changing all the time and definitely for the better. Whatever you already know about this coast, one fact is for sure – it is extraordinary: both crazily diverse and supremely entertaining. In other words, I have ensured there's never a dull moment on this classic drive – and there shouldn't be dull weather either – it's called 'the sunshine coast' for good reason.

Top: Gibraltar ape perched high above the town
Left: Resort life in Marbella
Right: Estepona's pretty balconied houses

------- -------

TRIP HIGHLIGHT

⑥ Marbella

Marbella is the Costa del Sol's classiest 'rich and famous' resort and is a good choice for an overnight stop. This town has a magnificent natural setting, sheltered by the beautiful Sierra Blanca mountains, as well as a gorgeous old town with pristine white houses, narrow traffic-free streets and geranium-filled balconies. At its heart is picturesque **Plaza de los Naranjos**, dating back to 1485 with tropical plants, palms and orange trees. From here walk to the coastal promenade via the lush **Parque de la Alameda** gardens with its fountains and tiled seats. Next consider a gentle stroll east along the seafront towards the luxurious marina of Puerto Banús, past the five-star resorts of the Marbella Club and Puente Romano, the latter named after the still-standing Roman bridge, once part of the Via Augustus linking Càdiz to Rome. It's 6km in total to the port if you decide to stride out all the way.

✕ ⌅ p397

The Drive ≫ Continue due west on the A7 *autovia*, signposted to Algeciras and Cádiz. This stretch of highway is less built up and passes by San Pedro de la Alcántara, as well as five golf courses (they don't

395

nickname this the Costa del Golf for nothing!). It's a snappy 20 minutes or just 24km to your next stop: Estepona.

- - - - - - - - - - - -

❼ Estepona

This is the Costa del Sol resort which is most intrinsically Spanish, with a charming historic centre of narrow cobbled streets flanked by simple *pueblo* houses decorated by well-tended pots of geraniums. Make a beeline for the historic Plaza de las Flores square with its fountain centrepoint, orange trees and handy tourist office, where you can stop for a town map. Highlights here include the fabulous **Orchidarium** (www.orchidariumestepona.es; Calle Terraza 86; ⊘11am-2pm & 5-9pm Tue-Thu & Sun, to 11pm Fri & Sat), with the largest orchid collection in Europe, some 1500 species, plus subtropical plants, flowers and trees. A meandering path takes you through the exhibition space and past a dramatic 17m-high waterfall. Estepona's **Puerto Deportivo** is excellent for water sports, as well as bars and restaurants.

✗ p397

The Drive » For the final leg consider taking the AP7 toll road for the first 20km (12 minutes, €3.50) as the N340 coastal stretch here is very slow, with numerous roundabouts. At Guadiaro the AP7 merges with the A7 for the rest of the 34km journey. Consider a refreshment stop at swanky Sotogrande harbour; Sotogorande is also home to Spain's leading golf course, the Real Club Valderrama.

- - - - - - - - - - - -

❽ Gibraltar

Red pillar boxes, fish-and-chips shops, bobbies on the beat and creaky seaside hotels. Stuck strategically at the jaws of Europe and Africa, Gibraltar's Palladian architecture and camera-hogging Barbary apes create an interesting contrast and finale to your journey. Highlights on 'the Rock' include the **Upper Rock Nature Reserve** (adult/child incl attractions £10/5, vehicle £2, pedestrian excl attractions £0.50; ⊘9am-6.15pm, last entry 5.45pm), one of the most dramatic landforms in southern Europe. Entry tickets include admission to the extraordinary **St Michael's Cave** (St Michael's Rd; ⊘9am-5.45pm, to 6.15pm Apr-Oct), the Apes'

Den, the **Great Siege Tunnels** (⊘9.30am-6.15pm), the Moorish castle, the Military Heritage Centre, and the 100-tonne gun. The Rock's most famous inhabitants, however, are the tailless Barbary macaques. Some of the 200 apes hang around the top cable-car station while others are found at the Apes' Den. Most Gibraltar soujourns start in Grand Casemates Sq, a jolly place surrounded by bars and restaurants, but with a grim history as the site of public executions. Learn more about the Rock's history at the fine **Gibraltar Museum** (www.gibmuseum.gi; 18-20 Bomb House Lane; adult/child £2/1; ⊘10am-6pm Mon-Fri, to 2pm Sat); don't miss the well-preserved Muslim bathhouse and an intricately painted 7th-century-BC Egyptian mummy that washed up here in the late 1800s.

Eating & Sleeping

Nerja ❶

Oliva — Modern European €€€

(☎952 52 29 88; www.restauranteoliva.com; Calle Pintada 7; mains €19-23; ⏰1-4pm & 7-11pm) Impeccable service, single orchids, a drum-and-bass soundtrack and a charcoal-grey-and-green colour scheme; in short, this place has class. The menu is reassuringly brief and changes regularly according to what's in season. The inventive dishes combine unlikely ingredients such as pistachio falafel and mango panna cotta with black-olive caramel. Reservations recommended.

Málaga ❷

Uvedoble Taberna — Tapas €

(www.uvedobletaberna.com; Calle Císter 15; tapas €2.70; ⏰12.30-4pm & 8pm-midnight Mon-Sat; 📶) There's not much elbow room at this slick contemporary place, but this local tapas hotspot is planning to expand to meet the demand for their famously popular seafood-based tapas such as *fideos negro tostada con calamaritos* (toasted black noodles with baby squid), and grilled octopus with potatoes and chives.

El Hotel del Pintor — Boutique Hotel €€

(☎952 06 09 81; www.hoteldelpintor.com; Calle Álamos 27; s/d €59/70; ❄@📶) The red, black and white colour scheme of this friendly, small hotel echoes the abstract artwork of *malagueño* artist Pepe Bornov, whose paintings are on permanent display throughout the public areas and rooms. Although convenient for most of the city's main sights, pack your earplugs, as the rooms in the front can be noisy, especially on a Saturday night.

Torremolinos ❸

El Cordobes — Andalucian €€

(Playamar; mains €12-15; 👪) The best of the beachside *chiringuitos* (seafront restaurants), attracting a loyal Spanish clientele. Specialities include a delicious *salmorejo* (thick garlicky gazpacho), barbecued sardines, and *almejas* (clams) in a spicy paprika-based sauce. The terrace fronts onto the sand.

Fuengirola ❹

La Cepa — Seafood €

(Plaza Yate 21; tapas €3, mains €7-10; ⏰noon-4pm & 7-11pm Mon-Sat, to 3.30pm Sun) Hidden away on an attractive bar-and-restaurant-lined square, the menu concentrates on seafood, including such tentacle ticklers as fried squid, and prawns wrapped in bacon.

Marbella ❺

El Estrecho — Tapas €

(Calle San Lázaro; tapas €2.50-3.50; ⏰noon-midnight) It's always crammed, so elbow your way to a space in the small back dining room and order from a massive menu that includes tapas such as *salmorejo* (gazpacho) and seafood salad.

Hotel San Cristóbal — Hotel €€

(☎952 86 20 44; www.hotelsancristobal.com; Avenida Ramñon y Cajal 3; s/d incl breakfast €60/85; 📶) Dating back to the '60s, this solid midrange hotel has recently revamped rooms sporting tasteful pale-grey and cream decor contrasting with smart navy fabrics. Most rooms have balconies and a pool is being planned.

Estepona ❻

La Esquina del Arte — Tapas €

(Calle Villa; tapas €2-3; ⏰noon-midnight Mon-Sat; 📶) This place may be in the middle of the historic centre but there is nothing old fashioned about the creative tapas and *pintxos* (Basque tapas) here. Expect tasty bites such as prawns wrapped in flaky pastry, pâté with fig jam and peppers stuffed with salt cod. It has excellent wines by the glass.

Northern Spain Pilgrimage

29

Travel in the footprints of thousands of pilgrims past and present as you journey along the highroads and backroads of the legendary Camino de Santiago pilgrimage trail.

TRIP HIGHLIGHTS

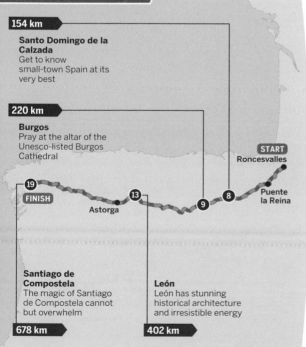

154 km

Santo Domingo de la Calzada
Get to know small-town Spain at its very best

220 km

Burgos
Pray at the altar of the Unesco-listed Burgos Cathedral

START
Roncesvalles

19
FINISH

13

9

8

Puente la Reina

Astorga

Santiago de Compostela
The magic of Santiago de Compostela cannot but overwhelm

678 km

León
León has stunning historical architecture and irresistible energy

402 km

5–7 DAYS
678 KM / 423 MILES

GREAT FOR...

BEST TIME TO GO
April to June for fields of poppies, September and October for golden leaves.

ESSENTIAL PHOTO

Standing outside the Cathedral de Santiago de Compostela.

BEST FOR CULTURE

Santiago de Compostela

Camino de Santiago Route marker

For over a thousand years pilgrims have marched across the top of Spain on the Camino de Santiago (Way of St James) to the tomb of St James the Apostle in Santiago de Compostela. Real pilgrims walk, but by driving you'll enjoy religious treasures, grand cathedrals, big skies and wide open landscapes — and no blisters.

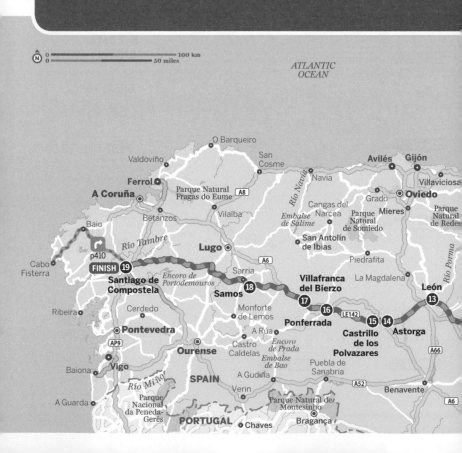

① Roncesvalles

Long a key stopping point on the Camino de Santiago, history hangs heavily in the air of the monastery complex of Roncesvalles, where pilgrims give thanks for a successful crossing of the Pyrenees. The main event here is the **monastery complex** (www.roncesvalles. es; adult/child €4.30/2.50; ☺10am-2pm & 3.30-7pm Apr-Oct, shorter hours Nov-Mar), which contains a number of different buildings of interest. The 13th-century Gothic **Real Colegiata de**

Santa María (admission free; ☺9am-8.30pm) houses a much revered, silver-covered statue of the Virgin beneath a modernist-looking canopy. There's also a statue of **Santiago** (St James) dressed as a pilgrim (with scallop shell and staff). Also of interest is the cloister, which contains the tomb of King Sancho VII (El Fuerte) of Navarra, the apparently 2.25m-tall victor in the Battle of Las Navas de Tolosa, fought against the Muslims in 1212. Nearby

LINK YOUR TRIP

31 Roving La Rioja Wine Region

Take a detour to enjoy wine and gourmet treats on this peaceful countryside circuit departing from Logroño.

30 Historic Castilla y León

Branch off at Burgos for a captivating tour around Spain's inland towns and villages.

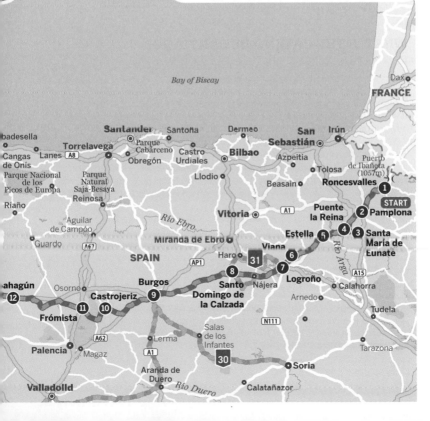

is the 12th-century **Capilla de Sancti Spiritus**.

If you need some exercise there's lots of good walking around here.

The Drive » It's basically 47km (one hour) downhill all the way from Roncesvalles to Pamplona. It's a pretty drive through mountainscapes, forests and gentle farmland. The N135 road passes through innumerable hamlets and villages painted in the red and white Basque colours and centred on old stone churches, many of which are crammed with religious treasures.

----

② Pamplona

Renowned across the world for the Sanfermines festival, when bulls tear through the streets at dawn causing chaos as they go (and alcohol-fueled revellers cause chaos for the remainder of the day – and night), Pamplona is a quiet and low-key city at any other time of the year. Animal rights groups oppose bullrunning as a cruel tradition and increasing left-wing influence in local government has called the future of Pamplona's bullrun into question. Pamplona's history stretches back to Roman times, and is best traced in the city's fantastic **Museo de Navarra** (www.cfnavarra.es/cultura/museo; Calle Cuesta de Santo Domingo 47; adult/student/child €2/1/free, free Sat afternoon & Sun; ⊙9.30am-2pm & 5-7pm Tue-Sat, 11am-2pm Sun), whose highlights include huge Roman mosaics. The **Catedral** (www.catedraldepamplona.com; Calle Dormitaleria; adult/child €5/3; ⊙10.30am-7pm Mon-Sat) is late-medieval Gothic with a neoclassical facade. The cathedral tour is a highlight and takes you up to the top of the bell tower, into the pretty cloisters and a museum with religious treasures, a Roman-era house and finishes all surreal with a room full of Virgins!

✗ 🛏 p412

WHAT IS THE CAMINO DE SANTIAGO?

The Camino de Santiago (Way of St James) originated as a medieval pilgrimage and ever since people have taken up the challenge of the Camino and walked to Santiago de Compostela. It all began back in the 9th century when a remarkable event occurred in the poor Iberian hinterlands: following a shining star, Pelayo, a religious hermit, unearthed the tomb of the apostle James the Greater (or, in Spanish, Santiago). The news was confirmed by the local bishop, the Asturian king and later the pope.

Compostela became the most important destination for Christians after Rome and Jerusalem. Its popularity increased with an 11th-century papal decree granting it Holy Year status: pilgrims could receive a plenary indulgence – a full remission of your life's sins – during a Holy Year. These occur when Santiago's feast day (25 July) falls on a Sunday: if you've been naughty then you'll need to wait until 2021 for the next one – but driving there doesn't count...

The 11th and 12th centuries marked the heyday of the pilgrimage. The Reformation was devastating for Catholic pilgrimages and by the 19th century the Camino had nearly died out. In its startling late-20th-century reanimation, which continues today, it's most popular as a personal and spiritual journey of discovery, rather than one primarily motivated by religion.

Today the most popular of the several *caminos* (paths) to Santiago de Compostela is the Camino Francés, which spans 783km of Spain's north and attracts walkers of all backgrounds and ages from across the world. It's the Council of Europe's first Cultural Itinerary and a Unesco World Heritage site but, for pilgrims, it's a pilgrimage equal to visiting Jerusalem, and by finishing it you're guaranteed a healthy chunk of time off purgatory.

The Drive >> Leave Pamplona on the A12 westbound and after about 10 minutes turn off at exit 9, onto the more driver-friendly NA1110. Drive through Astraín and continue along this peaceful country road for 10 minutes to Legarda, then to Muruzábal and, finally, 2km southeast to Santa María de Eunate.

---

3 Santa María de Eunate

Surrounded by cornfields and brushed by wildflowers, the near perfect octaganal Romanesque chapel of **Santa María de Eunate** (⊙10am-2pm & 4-7.30pm Tue-Sun) is one of the most picturesque chapels along the whole Camino. Dating from around the 12th century its origins – and the reason why it's located in the middle of nowhere – are something of a mystery.

The Drive >> From the chapel it's just a 5km drive along the NA6064 to gorgeous Puente la Reina.

---

4 Puente la Reina

The chief calling card of Puente la Reina (Basque: Gares), 22km southwest of Pamplona on the A12, is the spectacular six-arched **medieval bridge** that dominates the western end of town, but Puente la Reina rewards on many other levels. A key stop on the Camino de Santiago, the town's pretty streets throng

TOP TIP.
FUENTE DE VINO

Even the most adamant nonwalker might wish they'd donned hiking boots when they get to the Monasterio de Irache near Estella and find the **Fuente de Vino** (Spring of Wine), just behind the Bodega de Irache. Yes, it really is a spring of wine and yes, you really can drink some for free – though only if you're a pilgrim walking, not driving! – to Santiago.

with the ghosts of a multitude of pilgrims. Their first stop here is at the late-Romanesque **Iglesia del Crucifijo**, erected by the Knights Templar and still containing one of the finest Gothic crucifixes in existence.

The Drive >> The fastest way between Puente la Reina and Estella is on the A12 (20 minutes, 22km), but the more enjoyable drive is along the slower, more rural, NA1110, for which you should allow about half an hour. You'll probably spy a few Camino pilgrims trudging along.

---

5 Estella

Estella (Basque: Lizarra) was known as 'La Bella' in medieval times because of the splendour of its monuments and buildings, and though the old dear has lost some of its beauty to modern suburbs, it's not without charms. During the 11th century Estella became a main reception point for the growing flood of pilgrims along the Camino de Santiago. Today most

visitors are continuing that same plodding tradition. There's an attractive old quarter and a couple of notable churches, including the 12th-century **Iglesia de San Pedro de la Rúa**. It's cloisters are a fine example of Romanesque sculptural work. Across the river and overlooking the town is the **Iglesia de San Miguel**, with a fine Romanesque north door. Close to Estella are a couple of interesting monasteries: the **Monasterio de Irache** (⊙10am-1.15pm & 4-7pm Wed-Sun, closed 1-17 Jan) and **Monasterio de Iranzu** (www.monasterio-iranzu.com; admission €2.50; ⊙10am-2pm & 4-8pm).

The Drive >> It's a 40km (50 minute) drive from Estella to Viana. When you leave Estella take the A12 westward and turn onto the NA1110 at junction 58. Follow the NA1110 through the sleepy towns of Los Arcos, Sansol and Torres del Rio. In hillside Torres you'll find a remarkably intact eight-sided Romanesque chapel, the Iglesia del Santo Sepulcro.

WHY THIS IS A GREAT TRIP
STUART BUTLER, AUTHOR

This is a drive on an epic scale. The Camino de Santiago has been drawing people to northern Spain for a millennia, and although religion plays no part in it for me I still consider the Camino the ultimate way of seeing northern Spain. Drive it. Cycle it. Walk it. Just do it!

Top: Puente la Reina bridge
Left: Camino de Santiago
Right: Pilgrims near Burgos

DANIEL ACE EDD / GETTY IMAGES ©

➏ Viana

Overlooked by many nonpilgrim tourists, Viana, the last town in Navarra, started life as a garrison town defending the kingdom of Navarra from Castilla. Today, the old part of the town, which sits atop a hill, is still largely walled and is an interesting place to wander about for a couple of hours. The **Iglesia de Santa María** and **Iglesia de San Pedro** are the chief attractions. Work started on Santa María in the 13th century and it is one of the more impressive religious structures on this eastern end of the Camino. The Iglesia de San Pedro is today a ruin that hosts concerts and weddings. The former **bull ring** is today a plaza in the middle of town, where children booting footballs are considerably more common than bulls.

The Drive ➤➤ It's 10km and 20 minutes from Viana to Logroño. The first half of the drive is through open, big-sky countryside; the last part through the city suburbs. There's a large carpark underneath the main plaza by the old town.

➐ Logroño

Logroño, capital of La Rioja and Spain's wine-growing region par excellence, doesn't feel the need to be loud and brash. Instead it's a stately town with a heart of tree-studded squares, narrow streets, hidden corners and a monumentally good selection of *pintxos* (Basque tapas) bars. All up, this is the sort of place that you cannot help but feel contented in – and it's not just the wine. The superb **Museo de la Rioja** (Plaza San Agustin 23; ⊙10am-2pm & 4-9pm Tue-Sat, 10am-2pm Sun) in the centre of Logroño takes you on a wild romp through Riojan history and culture – from the days when dinner was killed with arrows to re-creations of the kitchens that many a Spanish granny grew up using. The other major attraction is the **Catedral de Santa María de la Redonda** (Calle de Portales; ⊙8am-1pm & 6-8.45pm Mon-Sat, 9am-2pm & 6.30-8.45pm Sun), which started life as a Gothic church before maturing into a full-blown cathedral in the 16th century.

✕ 🛏 p412, p435

The Drive » For the short 45km (35 minute) hop to Santo

Domingo de la Calzada, the Camino walking trail virtually traces the route of the fast, and dull, A12 motorway. There's really not much reason for you to veer off the motorway (none of the quieter, smaller roads really follow the Camino).

- - - - - - - - - - - - -

TRIP HIGHLIGHT

8 Santo Domingo de la Calzada

Santo Domingo is small-town Spain at its very best. A large number of the inhabitants continue to live in the partially walled old quarter, a labyrinth of medieval streets where the past is alive and the sense of community is strong. The **Catedral de Santo Domingo de la Calzada** (www.catedralsantodomingo. es; Plaza del Santo 4; adult/ student/child €4/3/free; ⊙10am-8.30pm Mon-Fri, 9am-7.10pm Sat, 9am-12.20pm & 1.45-7.10pm Sun Apr-Oct, shorter hours Nov-Mar) and its attached museum glitter with the gold that attests to the great wealth the Camino has bestowed on otherwise backwater towns. The cathedral's

most eccentric feature is the white rooster and hen that forage in a glass-fronted cage opposite the entrance to the crypt. Their presence celebrates a long-standing legend, the Miracle of the Rooster, which tells of a young man who was unfairly executed only to recover miraculously, while the broiled cock and hen on the plate of his judge suddenly leapt up.

The Drive » From Santo Domingo to Burgos it's just 57km and 50 minutes. Again you're sort of stuck with using the A12.

- - - - - - - - - - - - -

TRIP HIGHLIGHT

9 Burgos

On the surface, conservative Burgos seems to embody all the stereotypes of a north-central Spanish town, with sombre grey-stone architecture, the fortifying cuisine of the high *meseta* (plateau) and a climate of extremes. But Burgos is a city that rewards. The historic centre is austerely elegant, guarded by monumental gates and with the cathedral as its centrepiece. This Unesco World Heritage–listed Catedral is a masterpiece that originally started life as a modest Romanesque church, but over time became one of the most impressive cathedrals in a land of impressive cathedrals. For more on the Catedral

TOP TIP: PILGRIM HOSTELS

In towns and villages all along the Camino you will see very cheap pilgrim hostels. These are *only* for pilgrims travelling to Santiago by foot or bicycle (and able to prove it). As a driver you will be reliant on normal hotel-style accommodation.

WHO WAS ST JAMES THE APOSTLE?

St James, or James the Greater, was one of the 12 disciples of Jesus. He may even have been the first disciple. He was also the first to be martyred by King Herod in AD 44. So, if St James was living in the Holy Lands 2000 years ago, an obvious question persists: what were the remains of St James doing in northwest Spain a thousand years later? The accepted story (and we're not standing by its authenticity) suggests that two of St James's own disciples secreted his remains onto a stone boat which then set sail across the Mediterranean and passed into the Atlantic to moor at present-day Padrón (Galicia). Continuing inland for 17km, the disciples buried his body in a forest named Liibredon (present-day Santiago de Compostela). All was then forgotten until a thousand years later, when a religious hermit found the remains.

and the other stellar attractions of Burgos, see p422.

✕ ⛉ p412, p425

The Drive » It's 58km (45 minutes) from Burgos to little castle-topped Castrojeriz. Take the A12 out of town to junction 32 and turn off northwest along the minor BU400.

⑩ Castrojeriz

With it's mix of old and new buildings huddled around the base of a hill that's topped with what's left of a crumbling **castle**, Castrojeriz is your typical small *meseta* town. It's worth a climb up to the castle if only for the views. The town's church, **Iglesia de San Juan**, is worth a look as well.

The Drive » From Castrojeriz it's only 30km (35 minutes) along the BU403 and P432 to Frómista. The scenery is classic *meseta* and if you're lucky you'll catch a glimpse of such evocative sights as a flock of sheep being led over the alternately burning or freezing plateau by a shepherd.

⑪ Frómista

The main (and some would say only) reason for stopping here is the village's exceptional Romanesque church, the **Iglesia de San Martín** (admission €1; ◷9.30am-2pm & 4.30-8pm). Dating from 1066 and restored in the early 20th century, this harmoniously proportioned church is one of the premier Romanesque churches in rural Spain, adorned with a veritable menagerie of human and zoomorphic figures just below the eaves. The capitals within are also richly decorated.

The Drive » From Frómista to Sahagún is 59km (45 minutes) via the P980 to Carrión de los Condes, where the Camino basically starts following the major A231 road.

⑫ Sahagún

Despite appearances, Sahagún was an immensely powerful and wealthy Benedictine centre by the 12th century. The Mudéjar-influenced brick Romanesque churches merit a visit.

The Drive » The 59km (50 minute) stretch from Sahagún to León along the A231 and N601 isn't one of the more memorable driving moments of this route. Still, you have to feel for those walking the Camino as they're virtually walking along beside you (some pilgrims bus between Burgos and León because so much of the route is next to the motorway).

TRIP HIGHLIGHT

⑬ León

León is a wonderful city, combining stunning historical architecture with an irresistible energy. Its standout attraction is the 13th-century **Catedral** (⌨987 87 57 70; www. catedraldeleon.org; adult/ concession/child under 12yr €5/4/free; ◷9.30am-1.30pm & 4-8pm Mon-Sat, 9.30am-2.30pm & 5-8pm Sun), one of the most beautiful cathedrals in Spain. Whether spotlit by night or bathed in glorious sunshine, the cathedral, arguably Spain's premier Gothic masterpiece, exudes a glorious, almost luminous quality. The show-stopping facade has a radiant rose window, three richly sculpted doorways and two muscular towers. After going through the main entrance, lorded over by the scene of the Last Supper, an extraordinary gallery of *vidrieras* (stained-glass windows) awaits. Even older than León's cathedral, the **Real Basílica de San Isidoro** (⊙7.30am-11pm) provides a stunning Romanesque counterpoint to the former's Gothic strains, with extraordinary frescoes in the attached Panteón, the main highlight. Fernando I and Doña Sancha founded the church in 1063 to house the remains of the saint, as well as the remains of themselves and 21 other early Leónese and Castilian monarchs. The main basilica is a hotchpotch of styles, but the two main portals on the southern facade are pure Romanesque. Attached to the Real Basílica de San Isidoro, **Panteón Real** (admission €5; ⊙10am-1.30pm & 4-6.30pm Mon-Sat, 10am-1.30pm Sun) houses the remaining sarcophagi, which rest with quiet dignity beneath a canopy of some of the finest Romanesque frescoes in Spain. Motif

after colourful motif of biblical scenes drench the vaults and arches of this extraordinary hall.

🍴 🛏 p413

The Drive » Taking the N120 from León to Astorga will keep you on the route of the Camino. It's a 50km (one hour) drive. There's also the much faster AP71 motorway, but what's the point in coming all this way to drive on a road like that?!

---

⑭ Astorga

On a map of Spain, Astorga comes across as rather insignificant, but this medium-sized town has history and attractions totally out of proportion to its provincial status today.

The Drive » It's just a 7km (15 minute) drive from Astorga to Castrillo de los Polvazares along the rural LE142. Note that nonresidents are not allowed to drive into Castrillo de los Polvazares, so park up in one of the parking areas on the edge of the village.

---

⑮ Castrillo de los Polvazares

One of the prettiest villages along the Camino – if a little twee – is Castrillo de los Polvazares. It consists of little but one main cobbled street, a small church and an array of well-preserved 18th-century stone houses. If you can be here before or after all the tour buses have left then it's an absolute delight of a place and one in which the

spirit of the Camino can be strongly felt.

The Drive » Continue along the LE142 towards Ponferrada (one hour 20 minutes; 53km). The road runs pretty much beside the Camino and you'll pass through a string of attractive stone villages, most of which have churches topped with storks nests. It's worth stopping in Rabanal del Camino with its 18th-century Ermita del Bendito Cristo de la Vera Cruz (a hermitage).

Ponferrada Castillo Templario's imposing entrance

⑯ Ponferrada

Ponferrada is not the region's most enticing town, but its castle and remnants of the old town centre (around the stone clock tower) make it worth a brief stop. Built by the Knights Templar in the 13th century, the walls of the fortress-monastery **Castillo** **Templario** (adult/concession €4/2, Wed free; ⏰10am-2pm & 4.30-8.30pm Tue-Sat, 10am-2pm Sun) rise high over Río Sil, and the square, crenelated towers ooze romance and history. The castle has a lonely and impregnable air, and is a striking landmark in Ponferrada's otherwise bleak urban landscape.

Among Ponferrada's churches, the Gothic-Renaissance **Basílica de Nuestra Señora de la Encina** (☎987 41 19 78; ⏰9am-2pm & 4.30-8.30pm), up the hill past the tourist office, is the most impressive, especially its 17th-century painted wood altarpiece from the school of Gregorio Fernández.

The Drive » Take the NVI from Ponferrada to Villafranca del Bierzo (23km, 25 minutes), which runs almost right next to both the A6 motorway and the Camino.

⑰ Villafranca del Bierzo

Villafranca del Bierzo has a very well preserved old core and a number of interesting churches and other religious buildings. Chief among the sights are the **San Nicolás El Real**, a 17th-century convent with a baroque altarpiece, and the 12th-century **Iglesia de Santiago**. The northern doorway of this church is called the 'door of forgiveness'. Pilgrims who were sick, or otherwise unable, to carry onto Santiago de Compostela were granted the same Godly favours as if they'd made it all the way.

The Drive » The Camino, and the driving road, leaves Villafranca del Bierzo and starts to wind uphill before entering Galicia at tiny O Cebreiro, which at 1300m is the highest point on the whole Camino. From here continue to Samos. Total drive length is 90km (two hours) using the NVI, or reduce the journey time a little by taking the neighbouring A6.

⑱ Samos

Samos is built around the very fine Benedictine **Mosteiro de Samos** (www.abadiadesamos.com; tours €3; ⏱tours every 30min 10am-12.30pm Mon-Sat, 12.45-1.30pm Sun, 4.30-6.30pm daily). This monastery has two beautiful big cloisters (one Gothic, with distinctly unmonastic Greek nymphs adorning its fountain; the other neoclassical and filled with roses).

The Drive » Between Samos and Santiago de Compostela (136km 2½ hours on the LU633 and N547) there's a whole load of attractive little villages (Sarria, Portomarín and Melide) – there's not a lot to see at each, but it's worth an amble around any of them. Once in Santiago de Compostela dump the car and head to the cathedral.

TRIP HIGHLIGHT

⑲ Santiago de Compostela

This, then, is it. The end of The Way. And what a spectacular finish. Santiago de Compostela, with its granite buildings and frequent drizzle, is one of the most attractive cities in Spain. It goes without saying that your first port of call should be the **Catedral de Santiago de Compostela** (www.catedraldesantiago.es; Praza do Obradoiro; ⏱7am-8.30pm), which soars above the city centre in a splendid jumble of moss-covered spires and statues. Built piecemeal over several centuries, its beauty is a mix of the original Romanesque structure (built between 1075 and 1211) and later Gothic and baroque flourishes. The tomb of Santiago beneath the main altar is a magnet for all who come to the cathedral. The artistic high point is the Pórtico de la Gloria inside the west entrance, featuring 200 masterly Romanesque sculptures. After you've given thanks for a safe journey head to

---

DETOUR: CABO FISTERRA

Start: ⑲ Santiago de Compostela

In popular imagination Cabo Fisterra (86km, 1½ hours; take the AC441) is not just the western edge of Spain (it's not, that honour goes to Cabo da Nave, 5km north), but in the days way before sat-nav it was considered the very end of the world. This has long made it a popular extension to the Camino de Santiago. People today may not come here to ponder what might lie beyond the western horizon, but they do come with equal awe to watch the setting sun and admire the views from beside the powerful lighthouse that sits at the edge of these high cliffs. Fisterra itself is a fishing port with a picturesque harbour, and a tourist destination growing ever more popular among Camino pilgrims.

Santiago de Compostela The city's magnificent Catedral

the **Musco da Catedral**, which spreads over four floors and includes the cathedral's large, 16th-century Gothic/plateresque cloister. The **Grand Praza do Obradoiro**, in front of the cathedral's west facade, is traffic- and cafe-free and has a unique atmosphere. At its northern end, the Renaissance Hostal dos Reis Católicos (p413) was built in the early 16th century by order of the Catholic Monarchs, Isabel and Fernando, as a refuge for pilgrims and a symbol of the crown's power in this ecclesiastical city. Today it's a hotel, but its four courtyards and some other areas are open to visitors.

✕ ⮞ p413

411

Eating & Sleeping

Pamplona ➋

✖ Bar-Restaurante Gaucho — Pintxos €

(Travesía Espóz y Mina 7; pintxos €2-3; ⏰7am-3pm & 6.30-11pm) This bustling bar serves multi-award-winning *pintxos* that, despite some serious competition, many a local will tell you are the finest in the city – and we agree! Try the ones made of sea urchins or the crispy spinach and prawn caramel creations.

🛏 Palacio Guendulain — Historic Hotel €€€

(📞948 22 55 22; www.palacioguendulain. com; Calle Zapatería 53; s/d incl breakfast from €132/143; 🅿❄🛜) To call this stunning hotel, inside the converted former home of the viceroy of New Granada, sumptuous is an understatement. On arrival, you're greeted by a museum-piece 17th-century carriage and a collection of classic cars being guarded beside the viceroy's private chapel. The rooms contain *Princess and the Pea*-soft beds, enormous showers and regal armchairs.

Logroño ➐

✖ La Cocina de Ramon — Spanish €€€

(📞941 28 98 08; www.lacocinaderamon.es; Calle de Portales 30; menús €28-37; ⏰1-4pm & 8-11pm Tue-Sat, 1-4pm Sun) It looks unassuming from the outside, but Ramon's mixture of high-quality, locally grown market-fresh produce and tried-and-tested family recipes gives this place a lot of fans. But it's not just the food that makes it so popular: the service is outstanding, and Ramon likes to come and explain the dishes to each and every guest.

🛏 Hotel Calle Mayor — Boutique Hotel €€€

(📞941 23 23 68; www.hotelcallemayor.com; Calle Marqués de San Nicolás 71; r incl breakfast €120-160; 🅿❄🛜) This delicious hotel is *the* place to stay in Logroño. It has huge rooms with cheeky touches such as modern lamps atop ancient columns, it's bathed in light and simply oozes class. The staff are highly efficient.

Burgos ➒

✖ El Huerto de Roque — Contemporary Castilian €€

(www.elhuertoderoque.com; Calle de Santa Águeda 10; mains €10-12, menú del día €15; ⏰restaurant 1-4pm Tue-Sat, gastrobar 8pm-2am Thu-Sat; ✒) Come here for an inexpensive lunch with plenty of choice of dishes. The emphasis is on fresh market and ecological produce with typical plates including vegetable spring rolls with a sweet and sour sauce, and crab in a Thai green curry sauce. The atmosphere throughout is boho-rustic with original tiles, wooden furniture and edgy artwork.

🛏 Hotel Norte y Londres — Historic Hotel €€

(📞947 26 41 25; www.hotelnorteylondres.com; Plaza de Alonso Martínez 10; s/d €66/100; 🅿@🛜) Set in a former 16th-century palace and with understated period charm, this fine hotel promises spacious rooms with antique furnishings, polished wooden floors and pretty balconies; those on the 4th floor are more modern. The bathrooms are exceptionally large, the service exceptionally efficient.

León ❿

✖ Delirios   Contemporary Castilian €€

(☎987 23 76 99; www.restaurantedelirios.
com; Calle Ave Maria 2; mains €12-20; ⏱1.30-
3.30pm & 9-11.30pm Tue-Sat, 1.30-3.30pm
Sun) One of the city's more adventurous
dining options where innovative combinations
such as tuna tataki with orange and ginger,
and brie and foie gras with coconut hit the
mark virtually every time. Those with more
conservative taste buds can opt for dishes
such as steak with parsnip chips, while
the chocolate mousse with passionfruit is
designed to put a satisfied waddle in every
diner's step. Reservations recommended.

🛏 La Posada Regia   Historic Hotel €€

(☎987 21 31 73; www.regialeon.com; Calle de
Regidores 9-11; s/d incl breakfast from €54/59;
❄🛜) This place has the feel of a *casa rural*
(village accommodation) despite being in
the city centre. The secret is a 14th-century
building, magnificently restored (wooden
beams, exposed brick and understated antique
furniture), with individually styled rooms and
supremely comfortable beds and bathrooms.
As with anywhere in the Barri Gótic, weekend
nights can be noisy.

🛏 Hostal de San Marcos   Historic Hotel €€€

(☎987 23 73 00; www.parador.es; Plaza de San
Marcos 7; d incl breakfast from €134; ❄@🛜)
Despite the confusing '*hostal*' in the name,
León's sumptuous *parador* (state-owned
hotel) is one of the finest hotels in Spain. With
palatial rooms fit for royalty and filled with
old-world luxury and decor, this is one of the
Parador chain's flagship properties and as you'd
expect, the service and attention to detail are
faultless. It also houses the **Convento de
San Marcos**.

Santiago de Compostela ⓳

✖ O Curro da Parra   Contemporary Galician €€

(www.ocurrodaparra.com; Rúa do Curro da Parra
7; mains €17-23, tapas €4-8; ⏱1.30-3.30pm &
8.30-11.30pm Tue-Sat, 1.30-3.30pm Sun) With
a neat little stone-walled dining room upstairs
and a narrow tapas and wine bar below, O Curro
da Parra serves up a broad range of thoughtfully
created, market-fresh fare. You might go for
pork cheeks with apple purée and spinach – or
just ask what the fish and seafood of the day
are. On weekday lunchtimes there's a good-
value €12 *menú mercado* (market menu).

🛏 Hotel Costa Vella   Boutique Hotel €€

(☎981 56 95 30; www.costavella.com; Rúa
da Porta da Pena 17; s €59, d €81-97; ❄🛜)
Tranquil, thoughtfully designed rooms – some
with typically Galician *galerías* (glassed-in
balconies) – a friendly welcome and a lovely
garden cafe make this old stone house a
wonderful option, and the €6 breakfast is
substantial. Even if you don't stay, it's an ideal
spot for breakfast or coffee. Book ahead from
May to September.

🛏 Parador Hostal dos Reis Católicos   Historic Hotel €€€

(☎981 58 22 00; www.parador.es; Praza
do Obradoiro 1; r incl breakfast from €205;
🅿❄@🛜) Opened in 1509 as a pilgrims'
hostel, and with a claim to be the world's oldest
hotel, this palatial *parador* just steps from the
cathedral is Santiago's top hotel, with regal (if
rather staid) rooms. If you're not staying, stop
in for a **look round** (⏱noon-2pm & 4-6pm
Sun-Fri; admission €3) and coffee and cakes at
the elegant cafe.

Historic Castilla y León

This journey through Spain's Castilian heartlands takes in some of the country's most beguiling historic cities and larger towns with numerous time-worn pueblos (villages) en route.

TRIP HIGHLIGHTS

671 km

Covarrubias
One of Spain's most beautiful villages

631 km

Burgos
Arguably Spain's foremost Gothic cathedral

Valladolid

Aranda de Duero

Soria
FINISH

START
★ MADRID

Salamanca
Golden sandstone architecture without peer

254 km

Segovia
Disney castle, Roman aqueduct and lively streets

92 km

7 DAYS
782 KM / 486 MILES

GREAT FOR...

BEST TIME TO GO

Spring (March to May) and Autumn (September and October) to avoid extreme heat and cold.

ESSENTIAL PHOTO

Plaza Mayor, Salamanca, floodlit at night.

BEST FOR CULTURE

Irresistible Salamanca street life against a glorious architectural backdrop.

30 | Historic Castilla y León

From Segovia to Soria, the towns of Castilla y León rank among Spain's most appealing historic centres. Architecture may be central to their attraction, but these are no museum pieces. Instead, the relentless energy of life lived Spanish-style courses through the streets, all set against a backdrop of grand cathedrals and animating stately squares. Out in the countryside postcard-perfect villages complement the clamour of city life.

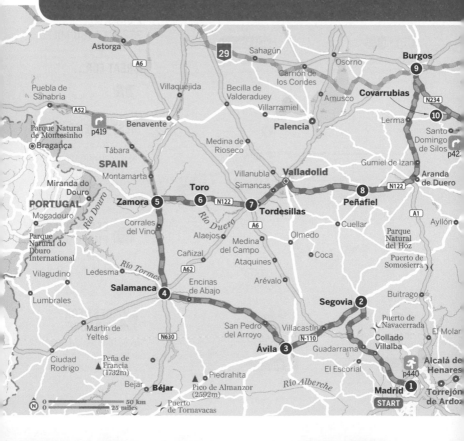

❶ Madrid

Madrid is the most Spanish of all Spanish cities. Its food culture, drawn from the best the country has to offer, makes it one of Europe's more underrated culinary capitals, while its nightlife and its irresistible joie de vivre exist like some Spanish stereotype given form. But there is more to Madrid than just nonstop colour and movement. This is one of the premier art cities on the continent, with three world-class galleries – the Prado, Thyssen and Reina Sofía – all clustered close to one of the city's main boulevards and a short walk from the Parque del Buen Retiro, one of the loveliest and most expansive monumental parks in Europe. In short, this is a city that rewards those who linger and love all things Spanish. To explore Madrid on foot, see p440.

The Drive » Getting out of Madrid can be a challenge, with a complicated system of numbered motorways radiating out from the city. Drive north along the Paseo de la Castellana, turn west along the M50 ring road, then take the A6, direction A Coruña. Of the two main roads to Segovia from the A6, the N603 is the prettier.

TRIP HIGHLIGHT

❷ Segovia

Unesco World Heritage-listed Segovia is a stunning confluence of everything that's good about the beautiful towns of Castilla. There are historic landmarks in abundance, among them the Roman **Acueducto**, the fairytale **Alcázar** (☎921 46 07 59; www.alcazardesegovia.com; Plaza de la Reina Victoria Eugenia; adult/concession/child under 6yr €5/3/free, tower €2, EU citizens free 3rd Tue of month; ⊙10am-6pm Oct-Mar, 10am-7pm Apr-Sep; 🚹), which is said to have inspired Walt Disney, and Romanesque gems such as the **Catedral** (☎921 46 22 05; Plaza Mayor; adult/concession €3/2, Sun morning free, tower €5; ⊙9.30am-5.30pm Oct-Mar, 9.30am-6.30pm Apr-Sep) or the **Iglesia de San Martín** (⊙before & after Mass). This is also one of the most dynamic towns in the country, a winning mix of local students and international visitors filling the city's bars and public spaces with an agreeable crescendo of noise. To cap it all, the setting is simply superb – a city strung out along a ridge, its warm terracotta and sandstone hues arrayed against a backdrop of Castilla's rolling hills and the often-snowcapped

LINK YOUR TRIP

31 Roving La Rioja Wine Region

Discover the wealth of the grape on this peaceful countryside drive, just an hour and a half north from Soria.

29 Northern Spain Pilgrimage

Crisscross the Camino de Santiago pilgrim route, two and a half hours north from Soria.

Sierra de Guadarrama. There are many vantage points to take in the full effect, but our favourite can be found anywhere in the gardens near the entrance to the Alcázar.

 p424

The Drive » It's 66km from Segovia to Ávila along the N110. The road runs southwest, parallel to the Sierra de Guadarrama, with some excellent views en route. At around the halfway mark, you'll cross the A6 motorway.

❸ Ávila

Ávila's old city, surrounded by imposing 12th-century *murallas* (walls) comprising eight monumental gates, 88 watchtowers and more than 2500 turrets, is one of the best-preserved medieval-walled cities in Spain. Two sections of the **Murallas** (muralladeavila.com; adult/child under 12yr

€5/free; ⏰10am-8pm Tue-Sun; 📷) can be climbed – a 300m stretch that can be accessed from just inside the Puerta del Alcázar, and a longer 1300m stretch that runs the length of the old city's northern perimeter. The best views are those at night from **Los Cuatro Postes**, a short distance northwest of the city. Ávila is also the home city of Santa Teresa, with the **Convento de Santa Teresa** (☎920 21 10 30; Plaza de la Santa; ⏰8.45am-1.30pm & 3.30-9pm Tue-Sun) as its centrepiece. Other important religious high points include the **Catedral del Salvador** (Plaza de la Catedral; admission €4; ⏰10am-7.30pm Mon-Fri, 10am-8pm Sat, noon-6.30pm Sun), the **Monasterio de Santo Tomás** (www.monasteriosantotomas.com; Plaza de Granada 1; admission €4; ⏰10am-1pm & 4-8pm) and

the sandstone **Basílica de San Vicente** (Plaza de San Vicente; admission €2; ⏰10am-6.30pm Mon-Sat, 4-6pm Sun).

🛏 p424

The Drive » The N501 runs northwest of Ávila to Salamanca, in the process traversing the pancake-flat high *meseta* (plateau) of central Spain and covering 96km en route.

- - - - - - - - - - - -

TRIP HIGHLIGHT

❹ Salamanca

Salamanca is a special place: its perfect mix of eye-catching architecture and animated streets make it one of our favourite cities in Spain. The city is at its best as day turns the corner into night.

🍴 🛏 p424

The Drive » The N630 runs due north from Salamanca to Zamora (67km), a relatively quiet road by Spanish standards

LOCAL KNOWLEDGE: FROG-SPOTTING IN SALAMANCA

Arguably a lot more interesting than trainspotting (and you don't have to wear an anorak and drink tea from a thermos flask), a compulsory task facing all visitors to Salamanca is to search out the frog sculpted into the facade of the **Universidad Civil** (Calle de los Libreros; adult/concession €4/2, Mon morning free; ⏰9.30am-1.30pm & 4-6.30pm Mon-Sat, 10am-1.30pm Sun). Once pointed out, it's easily enough seen, but the uninitiated can spend considerable time searching. Why bother? Well, they say that those who detect it without help can be assured of good luck and even marriage within a year. Some hopeful students see a guaranteed examination's victory in it. If you believe all this, stop reading now. If you need help, look at the busts of Fernando and Isabel. From there, turn your gaze to the largest column on the extreme right of the front. Slightly above the level of the busts is a series of skulls, atop the leftmost of which sits our little amphibious friend (or what's left of his eroded self).

DETOUR:
PUEBLA DE SANABRIA

Start: ❺ Zamora

Northwest of Zamora, close to the Portuguese border, this captivating village is a tangle of medieval alleyways that unfold around a 15th-century castle and trickle down the hill. This is one of Spain's loveliest hamlets and it's well worth the detour, or even stopping overnight: the quiet cobblestone lanes make it feel like you've stepped back centuries. Wandering the village is alone worth the trip here but a few attractions are worth tracking down. Crowning the village's high point and dominating its skyline for kilometres around, the **Castillo** (adult/child under 12yr €3/ free; ⊙11am-2pm & 4-8pm Mon-Sat, 4-7pm Sun; [P][🚻]) has some interesting displays on local history, flora and fauna and superb views from the ramparts. Also at the top of the village, the striking **Plaza Mayor** is surrounded by some fine historical buildings. The 17th-century *ayuntamiento* (town hall) has a lovely arched facade and faces across the square to **Iglesia de Nuestra Señora del Azogue** (admission free; ⊙11am-2pm & 4-8pm Sat & Sun), a pretty village church which was first built in the 12th century. If you're staying the night, the **Posada Real La Cartería** ([☎]980 62 03 12; www.lacarteria.com; Calle de Rúa 16; r from €81; [❄][@][📶]) captures the essence of Puebla de Sanabria's medieval appeal with both rooms and a restaurant.

and one that follows the contours of the rolling hill country of Castilla y León's west.

❺ Zamora

If you're arriving by road, first appearances can be deceiving and, as in so many Spanish towns, your introduction to provincial Zamora is likely to be nondescript apartment blocks. But persevere as the *casco historico* (old town) is hauntingly beautiful, with sumptuous medieval monuments that have earned Zamora the popular sobriquet 'Romanesque Museum'. Much of the old town is closed to motorised transport and walking is easily the best way to

explore this subdued encore to the monumental splendour of Salamanca. Zamora is also one of the best places to be during Semana Santa, with haunting processions of hooded penitents parading through the streets. Whatever time of year you're here, don't miss the **Museo de Semana Santa** ([☎]980 53 22 95; semanasantadezamora. com; Plaza de Santa María La Nueva; adult/child €4/1.50; ⊙10am-2pm & 5-8pm Tue-Sat, 10am-2pm Sun).

🍴 🛏 p424

The Drive » The A11 tracks east of Zamora – not far out along the sweeping plains that bake in summer, take the turn-off to Toro.

---

❻ Toro

With a name that couldn't be more Spanish and a stirring history that overshadows its present, Toro is your archetypal Castilian town. It was here that Fernando and Isabel cemented their primacy in Christian Spain at the Battle of Toro in 1476. The town sits on a rise high above the north bank of Río Duero and has a charming historic centre with half timbered houses and Romanesque churches. The high point, literally, is the 12th-century **Colegiata Santa María La Mayor** (Plaza de la Colegiata; admission €2; ⊙10.30am-2pm & 5.30-7.30pm Tue-Sun), which

WHY THIS IS A GREAT TRIP
ANTHONY HAM, AUTHOR

The towns north and west of Madrid are windows on the Spanish soul, each with their own distinctive appeal. Segovia, Ávila, Salamanca, Zamora and Burgos are all Spanish classics, dynamic cities with extraordinary architectural backdrops. Throw in some captivating, beautiful villages along the way and you've captured the essence of this remarkable country in just a week.

Top: Tordesillas reflected in the Rio Duero
Left: Diners in Covarrubias
Right: Ávila's fortified *murallas* (walls)

rises above the town and boasts the magnificent Romanesque-Gothic Pórtico de la Majestad.

The Drive » Return to the main east–west road that passes to the north of Toro (the A11, then E82), and continue east to Tordesillas.

❼ Tordesillas

Commanding a rise on the northern flank of Río Duero, this pretty little town has a historical significance that belies its size. Originally a Roman settlement, it later played a major role in world history when, in 1494, Isabel and Fernando, the Catholic Monarchs, sat down with Portugal here to hammer out a treaty determining who got what in Latin America. Portugal got Brazil and much of the rest went to Spain. Explaining it all is the excellent **Museo del Tratado de Tordesillas** (☏983 77 10 67; Calle de Casas del Tratado; ⊙10am-1.30pm & 5-7.30pm Tue-Sat, 10am-2pm Sun). Not far away, the heart of town is formed by the delightful porticoed and cobbled **Plaza Mayor**, its mustard-yellow paintwork offset by dark-brown woodwork and black grilles.

The Drive » From Tordesillas, E80 sweeps northeast, skirts the southern fringe of Valladolid and then continues east as the N122, through the vineyards of the Ribera del Duero wine region all the way into Peñafiel.

8 Peñafiel

Peñafiel is the gateway to the Ribera del Duero wine region and it's an appealing small town in its own right. At ground level, **Plaza del Coso** is one of Spain's most stunningly picturesque plazas. This rectangular 15th-century 'square' was one of the first to be laid out for this purpose and is considered one of the most important forerunners to the *plazas mayores* (main squares) across Spain. It's still used for bullfights on ceremonial occasions, and it's watched over by distinctive half-wooden facades. But no matter where you are in Peñafiel, your eyes will be drawn to the **Castillo de Peñafiel** (Museo Provincial del Vino; Peñafiel; castle €3, incl museum €7, audioguides €2; ☉11am-2.30pm & 4.30-8.30pm Tue-Sun), one of Spain's longest and narrowest castles (the walls and towers stretch over 200m but are little more than 20m across). Within the castle's crenulated walls is the state-of-the-art **Museo Provincial del Vino**, the local wine museum that tells a comprehensive story of the region's wines.

🛏 p425

The Drive » The N122 continues east of Peñafiel. At Aranda del Duero, turn north along the E5 and make for Lerma, an ideal place to stop for lunch – try the roast lamb at Asador Casa Brigant on Plaza Mayor. Sated, return to the E5 and take it all the way into Burgos.

TRIP HIGHLIGHT

9 Burgos

Dominated by its Unesco World Heritage–listed cathedral but with plenty more to turn the head, Burgos is one of Castilla y León's most captivating towns. The extraordinary Gothic **Catedral** (📞947 20 47 12; www.catedraldeburgos. es; Plaza del Rey Fernando; adult/child under 14yr incl multilingual audioguide €6/1.50; ☉10am-6pm) is one of Spain's glittering jewels of religious architecture and looms large over the city and skyline. Inside is the last place of El Cid and there are numerous extravagant chapels, a gilded staircase and a splendid altar. Some of the best cathedral views are from up the hill at the lookout, just below the 9th-century Castillo de Burgos. Elsewhere in town, two monasteries – the **Cartuja de Miraflores** (📞947 25 25 86; ☉10.15am-3pm & 4-6pm Mon, Tue & Thu-Sat, 11am-3pm & 4-6pm Sun) and the **Monasterio de las Huelgas** (📞947 20 16 30; www.monasteriodelashuelgas.org; guided tours €7, Wed free; ☉10am-1pm & 4-5.30pm Tue-Sat, 10.30am-2pm Sun) – are worth seeking out, while the city's eating scene is excellent.

🍴🛏 p412, p425

The Drive » Take the E5 south of Burgos but almost immediately after leaving the city's southern outskirts, take the N234 turnoff and follow the signs over gently undulating hills and through green valleys to the walled village of Covarrubias.

TRIP HIGHLIGHT

10 Covarrubias

Inhabiting a broad valley in eastern Castilla y León and spread out along the shady banks of Río Arlanza with a gorgeous riverside aspect, Covarrubias is only a short step removed from the Middle Ages. Once you pass beneath the formidable stone archways that mark the village's entrances, Covarrubias takes visitors within its intimate embrace with tightly huddled and distinctive, arcaded half-timbered houses opening out onto cobblestone squares. Simply wandering around the village is the main pastime, and don't miss the charming riverside pathways or outdoor tables that spill out onto the squares. Otherwise, the main attraction is the **Colegiata de San Cosme y Damián** (admission €2.50; ☉10.30am-2pm & 4-7pm Mon & Wed-Sat, 4.30-6pm Sun), which has the evocative atmosphere of a mini cathedral and Spain's oldest still-functioning church organ; note also the gloriously ostentatious altar, fronted by several Roman stone tombs, plus that of Fernán González, the 10th-century founder of Castilla. Don't miss the graceful cloisters and the sacristia with its vibrant 15th-century paintings by Van Eyck and tryptic *Adoracion de los Magis*.

The Drive ⟩⟩ The N234 winds southwest of Covarrubias through increasingly contoured country all the way to Soria. Along the way there are signs to medieval churches and hermitages marking many minor roads that lead off into the trees. In no time at all you'll see the turn-off to Santo Domingo de Silos.

- - - - - - - - - -

⓫ Soria

Small-town Soria is one of Spain's smaller provincial capitals. Set on Río Duero in the heart of backwoods Castilian countryside, it has an appealing and compact old centre, and a sprinkling of stunning monuments. The narrow streets of the town centre on Plaza Mayor, with its attractive Renaissance-era *ayuntamiento* and the **Iglesia de Santa María la Mayor**, with its unadorned Romanesque facade and gilt-edged interior. A block north is the majestic, sandstone, 16th-century **Palacio de los Condes Gomara** (Calle de Aguirre). Further

DETOUR: SANTO DOMINGO DE SILOS

Start: ⓾ Covarrubias

Nestled in the rolling hills just off the Burgos–Soria (N234) road, this tranquil, pretty village is built around a monastery with an unusual claim to fame: monks from here made the British pop charts in the mid-1990s with recordings of Gregorian chants. Notable for its pleasingly unadorned Romanesque sanctuary dominated by a multidomed ceiling, the **church** (◷6am-2pm & 4.30-10pm, chant 6am, 7.30am, 9am, 1.45pm, 4pm, 7pm & 9.30pm) is where you can hear the monks chant. The monastery, one of the most famous in central Spain, is known for its stunning **cloister** (admission €3.50; ◷10am-1pm & 4.30-6pm Tue-Sat, 4.30-6pm Sun), a two-storey treasure chest of some of Spain's most imaginative Romanesque art. Don't miss the unusually twisted column on the cloister's western side. For sweeping views over the town, pass under the Arco de San Juan and climb the grassy hill to the south to the Ermita del Camino y Via Crucis.

north is the beautiful Romanesque **Iglesia de Santo Domingo** (Calle de Santo Tomé Hospicio; ◷7am-9pm), with a small but exquisitely sculpted portal of reddish stone that seems to glow at sunset. Down the hill by the river east of the town centre, the 12th-century **Monasterio de San Juan de Duero** (Camino Monte de las Ánimas; admission €0.60, Sat & Sun free; ◷10am-2pm & 5-8pm Tue-Sat, 10am-2pm Sun) has many gracefully interlaced arches in the partially ruined cloister. A lovely riverside walk south for 2.3km will take you past the 13th-century church of the former Knights Templar, the Monasterio de San Polo (not open to the public), and on to the fascinating, baroque **Ermita de San Saturio** (Paseo de San Saturio; ◷10.30am-2pm & 4.30-7.30pm Tue-Sun).

✖ ⌂ p425

Eating & Sleeping

Segovia ❷

✕ Restaurante
El Fogón Sefardí   Sephardic €€

(📞921 46 62 50; www.lacasamudejar.com; Calle de Isabel la Católica 8; mains €15-25, tapas from €2.50; ⏱1.30-4.30pm & 5.30-11.30pm) Located within the Hospedería La Gran Casa Mudéjar, this is one of the most original places in town. Sephardic and Jewish cuisine is served either on the intimate patio or in the splendid dining hall with original, 15th-century Mudéjar flourishes. The theme in the bar is equally diverse. Stop here for a taste of the award-winning tapas. Reservations recommended.

⊨ Hospedería La Gran
Casa Mudéjar   Historic Hotel €€

(📞921 46 62 50; www.lacasamudejar.com; Calle de Isabel la Católica 8; r from €80; ✳@ 🛜) Spread over two buildings, this place has been magnificently renovated, blending genuine 15th-century Mudéjar carved wooden ceilings in some rooms with modern amenities. In the newer wing, the rooms on the top floors have fine mountain views out over the rooftops of Segovia's old Jewish quarter. Adding to the appeal, there's a small spa and the restaurant comes highly recommended.

Ávila ❸

⊨ Hotel El Rastro   Historic Hotel €

(📞920 35 22 25; www.elrastroavila.com; Calle Cepedas; s/d €35/55; ✳🛜) This atmospheric hotel occupies a former 16th-century palace with original stone, exposed brickwork and a natural earth-toned colour scheme exuding a calm understated elegance. Each room has a different form, but most have high ceilings and plenty of space. Note that the owners also run a marginally cheaper, same-name *hostal* (budget hotel) around the corner.

Salamanca ❹

✕ Mesón Cervantes   Castilian €€

(www.mesoncervantes.com; Plaza Mayor 15; menú del día €13.50, mains €10-22; ⏱10am-midnight) Although there are outdoor tables on the square, the dark wooden beams and atmospheric buzz of the Spanish crowd on the 1st floor should be experienced at least once; if you snaffle a window table in the evening, you've hit the jackpot. The food's a mix of *platos combinados* (meat-and-three-veg dishes), salads and *raciones* (large tapas servings).

⊨ Microtel
Placentinos   Boutique Hotel €€

(📞923 28 15 31; www.microtelplacentinos. com; Calle de Placentinos 9; s/d incl breakfast Sun-Thu €57/73, Fri & Sat €88/100; ✳🛜) One of Salamanca's most charming boutique hotels, Microtel Placentinos is tucked away on a quiet street and has rooms with stone walls and wooden beams. The service is faultless, and the overall atmosphere is one of intimacy and discretion. All rooms have a hydromassage shower or tub and there's a summer-only outside whirlpool spa.

Zamora ❺

✕ El Rincón
de Antonio   Contemporary Castilian €€€

(📞980 53 53 70; www.elrincondeantonio. com; Rúa de los Francos 6; mains €19.50-26, set menus €11-65; ⏱1.30-4pm & 8.30-11.30pm Mon-Sat, 1.30-4.30pm Sun) A fine place offering tapas in the bar, as well as sit-down meals in a classy, softly lit dining area. Amid the range of tasting menus there's one consisting of four tapas for €11, including a glass of wine. In the restaurant, dishes are classic with a contemporary twist, such as Galician scallops served in onion leaves. Reservations recommended.

Parador Condes de Alba y Aliste
Historic Hotel €€€

(☎980 51 44 97; www.parador.es; Plaza Viriato 5; r €100-168; ✳ @ 🛜 ☒) Set in a sumptuous 15th-century palace, this is modern luxury with myriad period touches (mostly in the public areas). There's a swimming pool and, unlike many *paradores* (luxurious state-owned hotels), it's right in the heart of town. On the downside, there is very limited parking available (just eight places). The **restaurant** (menú del día €33) is predictabe *parador* quality.

Peñafiel 🔘

Hotel Convento Las Claras
Historic Hotel €€

(☎983 87 81 68; www.hotelconventolasclaras. com; Plaza de los Comuneros 1; s €80-105, d €95-150; ✳ 🛜 ☒) This cool, classy hotel is an unexpected find in little Peñafiel. A former convent, the rooms are luxurious and there's a full spa available with thermal baths and treatments. There's also an excellent restaurant with, as you'd expect, a carefully chosen wine list. Lighter meals are available in the cafeteria.

Burgos 🔘

✕ Cervecería Morito
Tapas €

(Calle Sombrerería 27; tapas €3, raciones €5-7; ⏱12.30-3.30pm & 7-11.30pm) Cervecería Morito is the undisputed king of Burgos tapas bars and it's always crowded, deservedly so. A typical order is *alpargata* (lashings of cured ham with bread, tomato and olive oil) or the *pincho de morcilla* (small tapa of local blood sausage). The presentation is surprising nouvelle, especially the visual feast of salads.

Hotel La Puebla
Boutique Hotel €€

(☎947 20 00 11; www.hotellapuebla.com; Calle de la Puebla 20; r from €95; ✳ @ 🛜) This boutique hotel adds a touch of style to the Burgos hotel scene. The rooms aren't huge and most don't have views but they're softly lit, beautifully designed and supremely comfortable. Extra perks include bikes and a pillow menu, while, on the downside, some readers have complained about the level of street noise.

Soria ⓫

✕ Baluarte
Contemporary Castilian €€

(☎975 21 36 58; www.baluarte.info; Caballeros 14; mains €12-25, menú degustación €47; ⏱1.45-3.45pm & 9-11pm Tue-Sat, 1.30-3.30pm Sun) Oscar Garcia is one of Spain's most exciting new chefs and this venture in Soria appropriately showcases his culinary talents. Dishes are based on classic Castilian ingredients but treated with just enough foam and drizzle to ensure that they are both exciting and satisfying, without being too pretentious. Reservations essential.

Hotel Soria Plaza Mayor
Hotel €€

(☎975 24 08 64; www.hotelsoriaplazamayor. com; Plaza Mayor 10; s/d/ste €65/72/91; ✳ @) This hotel has terrific rooms, each with its own style of decor, overlooking either Plaza Mayor or a quiet side street. There are so many balconies that even some bathrooms have their own. The suites are *very* comfortable.

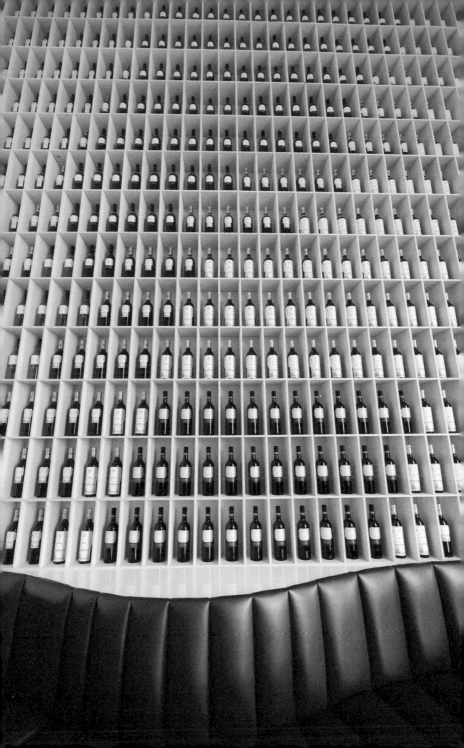

Roving La Rioja Wine Region

31

Learn all about the gift of the grape on this quiet road trip through vine-studded countryside. Along the way you can visit wine museums and bodegas and admire stunning architecture.

TRIP HIGHLIGHTS

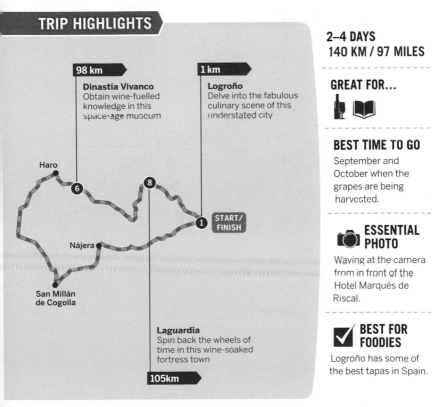

98 km

Dinastía Vivanco
Obtain wine-fuelled knowledge in this space-age museum

1 km

Logroño
Delve into the fabulous culinary scene of this understated city

Haro

⑥

⑧

Nájera

①

START/ FINISH

San Millán de Cogolla

Laguardia
Spin back the wheels of time in this wine-soaked fortress town

105km

2–4 DAYS
140 KM / 97 MILES

GREAT FOR...

BEST TIME TO GO
September and October when the grapes are being harvested.

ESSENTIAL PHOTO
Waving at the camera from in front of the Hotel Marqués de Riscal.

BEST FOR FOODIES
Logroño has some of the best tapas in Spain.

31 | Roving La Rioja Wine Region

La Rioja is home to the best wines in Spain and on this short and sweet road trip along unhurried back roads you'll enjoy gorgeous vine-striped countryside and asleep-at-noon villages of honey-coloured stone. But the real interest is reserved for food and drink: cutting-edge museums, bodega tours and some of the best tapas in Spain will make this drive an essential for any foodie.

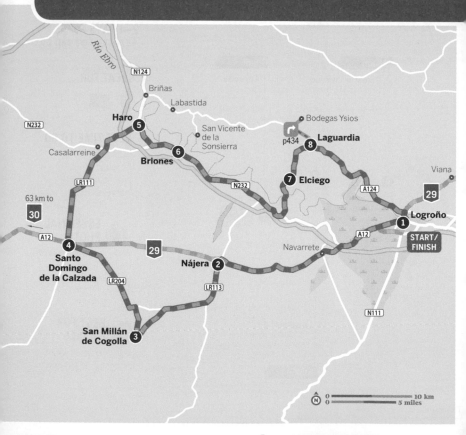

TRIP HIGHLIGHT

❶ Logroño

Small and low-key Logroño is the capital of La Rioja. The city doesn't receive all that many tourists and there aren't all that many things to see and do, but there is a monumentally good selection of tapas bars. In fact, Logroño is quickly gaining a culinary reputation to rival anywhere in Spain.

Based in the small village of Fuenmayor (10 minutes west of Logroño), **Rioja Trek** (941 58 73 54; www.riojatrek.com; wine experience €28 per person) offers three-hour wine 'experiences' where you visit a vineyard and bodega and participate in the process of actually making wine yourself. It also offers family-friendly wine-

LINK YOUR TRIP

29 **Northern Spain Pilgrimage**

Drive alongside pilgrims on the road to Santiago de Compostela. You can join 'the Way' in Logroño.

30 **Historic Castilla y León**

A quick skip south to Soria will let you do this captivating inland tour in reverse.

related activities. For more on things to see and do in Logroño, see p405.

📖 p412, p435

The Drive ⟫ It's only a short drive of 28km (25 minutes) from Logroño to Nájera along the N232, which transforms into the A12 motorway around the halfway point.

❷ Nájera

The main attraction of this otherwise unexciting town, which lies on the Camino de Santiago, is the Gothic **Monasterio de Santa María la Real** (admission €3; ⊙10am-1pm & 4-7pm Tue-Sat, 10am-12.30pm & 4-6pm Sun), in particular its fragile-looking, early-16th-century cloisters. The monastery was built in 1032, but was significantly rebuilt in the 15th-century.

The Drive ⟫ The dry landscapes around Nájera become greener and more rolling as you head southwest along the LR113 and LR205 for 18km (20 minutes) to San Millán de Cogolla. In the far distance mountains, which are snow-capped in winter, rise up.

❸ San Millán de Cogolla

The hamlet of San Millán de Cogolla is home to two remarkable monasteries, which between them helped give birth to the Castilian (Spanish) language. On account of their linguistic heritage and artistic beauty, they

have been recognised by Unesco as World Heritage sites.

The **Monasterio de Yuso** (941 37 30 49; www.monasteriodeyuso.org; adult/child €6/2; ⊙10am-1.30pm & 4-6.30pm Tue-Sun) contains numerous treasures in its museum. You can only visit as part of a guided tour. Tours last 50 minutes and run every half-hour or so. In August it's also open on Mondays.

A short distance away is the **Monasterio de Suso** (☏941 37 30 82; admission €4; ⊙9.30am-1.30pm & 3.30-6.30pm Tue-Sun). It's believed that in the 13th century a monk named Gonzalo de Berceo wrote the first Castilian words here. Again, it can only be visited on a guided tour. Tickets, which must be bought in advance, can be reserved by phone and can be picked up at the Monasterio de Yuso.

The Drive ⟫ It's a 23km (20 minute) drive along the delightfully quiet LR204 to Santo Domingo de la Calzada. The scenery is a mix of vast sunburnt fields, red tinged soils, vineyards and patches of forest.

❹ Santo Domingo de la Calzada

The small, walled old town of Santo Domingo is the kind of place where you can be certain that the baker knows all his customers by name and that everyone will turn up for María's christening. Santiago-bound pilgrims have long been a part of the fabric of this town, and that tradition continues to this day, with most visitors being foot-weary pilgrims. All this helps to make Santo Domingo one of the most enjoyable places in La Rioja. The biggest attraction in town, aside from the very worthwhile pursuit of just strolling the streets and lounging in the main old-town plaza, is a visit to the cathedral. See p406 for more.

p435

The Drive » The LR111 goes in an almost ruler-straight line across fields of crops and under a big sky to the workaday town of Haro (20km, 20 minutes).

----

❺ Haro

Despite its fame in the wine world, there's not much of a heady bouquet to Haro, the capital of La Rioja's wine-producing region. But the town has a cheerful pace and the compact old quarter, leading off Plaza de la Paz, has some intriguing alleyways with bars and wine shops aplenty.

There are plenty of wine bodegas in the vicinity of the town, some of which are open to visitors (almost always with advance reservation). One of the more receptive to visitors is the **Bodegas Muga** (📞941 30 60 60; www.bodegasmuga.com; Barrio de la Estación; winery tour €10), which is just after the railway bridge on the way out of town. It gives daily guided tours (except Sunday) in Spanish, and tastings. Although technically you should book in advance in high season, you can often just turn up and

💬 LOCAL KNOWLEDGE: TAPAS IN LOGROÑO

Make no mistake about it: Logroño is a foodie's delight. There are a number of very good restaurants, and then there are the tapas (which here are sometimes called by their Basque name of *pintxos*). Few cities have such a dense concentration of excellent tapas bars. Most of the action takes place on Calle Laurel and Calle de San Juan. Tapas cost around €2 to €4, and most of the bars are open from about 8pm through to midnight, except on Mondays. The following are some of our favourites.

Torrecilla (Calle Laurel 15; pintxos from €2) OK, we're going to stick our necks out here and say that this place serves the best *pintxos* in town. Go for the pyramid of *jamón* (cured ham) or the miniburgers (which come with mini bottles of ketchup!). In fact, what the heck, go for anything. It's all good!

Bar Soriano (Travesía de Laurel 2; pintxos from €2) The smell of frying food will suck you into this bar, which has been serving up the same delicious mushroom tapa, topped with a shrimp, for more than 30 years.

La Taberna de Baco (Calle de San Agustín 10; pintxos from €2) This place has a cracking list of around 40 different *pintxos*, including *bombitas* (potatoes stuffed with mushrooms) and a delightful mess of toast with pate, apple, goat cheese and caramel.

La Fontana (Calle Laurel 16; pintxos from €2) Another stellar *pintxo* bar with a welcoming atmosphere. This one's speciality is *sepia fontana*. And when you order this what emerges from the kitchen? A pile of egg, mushroom, aubergine and foie gras. The octopus isn't bad either.

THE WEALTH OF THE GRAPE

La Rioja, and the surrounding areas of Navarra and the Basque province of Álava, is Spain's best-regarded wine-producing region. La Rioja itself is further divided into three separate wine-producing areas: Rioja Alta, Rioja Baja and Rioja Alavesa. The principal grape of Rioja is the tempranillo. The first taste of a tempranillo is of leather and cherries and the wine lingers on the tongue.

The Riojans have had a long love affair with wine. There's evidence that both the Phoenicians and the Celtiberians produced and drank wine here and the earliest written evidence of grape cultivation in La Rioja dates to 873. Today, some 250 million litres of wine bursts forth from the grapes of La Rioja annually. Almost all of this (around 85%) is red wine, though some quality whites and rosés are also produced. The Riojan love of wine is so great that in the town of Haro they even have a fiesta devoted to wine. It culminates with a messy 'wine battle' in which thousands of litres of wine gets chucked around, turning everyone's clothes red in the process. This takes place on 29 June.

How to find a good bottle? Spanish wine is subject to a complicated system of classification, similar to the ones used in France and Italy. La Rioja is the only wine region in Spain classed as Denominación de Origen Calificada (DOC), the highest grade and a guarantee that any wine labelled as such was produced according to strict regional standards. The best wines are often marked with the designation 'Crianza' (aged for a year in an oak barrel), 'Reserva' (aged for two years, at least one of which is in an oak barrel) and 'Gran Reserva' (aged for two years in an oak barrel and three years in the bottle).

latch on to the back of a tour.

The Drive » Briones is almost within walking distance of Haro. It's just 9km away (10 minutes) along the N124.

- - - - - - - - - - -

TRIP HIGHLIGHT

❻ Briones

One man's dream has put the small, obscenely quaint village of Briones firmly on the Spanish wine and tourism map. The sunset-gold village crawls gently up a hillside and offers commanding views over the surrounding vine-carpeted plains. It's on these plains where you will find the fantastic **Dinastía Vivanco** (Museo de la Cultura del Vino; www.dinastiavivanco.com; adult/child €8/free; ◷11am-6pm Tue-Fri & Sun, 10am-8pm Sat Jul-Aug, shorter hours rest of year). Over several floors you will learn all about the history and culture of wine and the various processes that go into its production. All of this is done through interesting displays brought to life with computer technology. The treasures on display include Picasso-designed wine jugs; Roman and Byzantine mosaics; gold-draped, wine-inspired religious artifacts; and the world's largest collection of corkscrews. At the end of the tour you can enjoy some wine tasting, and by booking in advance, you can join a tour of the winery (€20 including museum entry; in Spanish only).

The Drive » It's 19km (25 minutes) along the N232 to Elciego. The scenery, which is made up of endless vineyards, will delight anyone who enjoys wide open spaces. In the distance are strange sheer-faced table-topped mountains.

- - - - - - - - - - -

❼ Elciego

When the owner of the Bodegas Marqués de Riscal, in the village of Elciego, decided he wanted to create something special, he didn't hold back. The

431

WHY THIS IS A GREAT TRIP
STUART BUTLER,
AUTHOR

How can anyone not love an area sloshing in wine?! Well, for me, wine is only a part of my love for this region. The light and huge skies is what draws me here. It's so very different to the often grey and damp north coast where I live. It feels so, well, Spanish!

Top: La Rioja vineyards
Left: Bodegas Palacio cellar, Laguardia
Right: Hotel Marqués de Riscal, Elciego

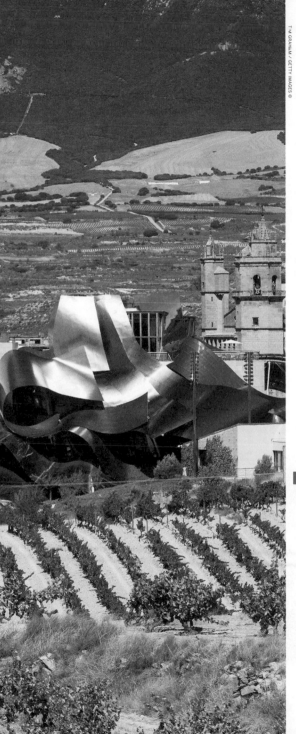

result in the spectacular Frank Gehry–designed Hotel Marqués de Riscal. Costing around €85 million, the building is a flamboyant wave of multicoloured titanium sheets that stands in utter contrast to the village behind. It's like a rainbow-flavoured Guggenheim museum (not surprisingly, perhaps, as that was also designed by Gehry). Casual visitors are not really welcome to look around the hotel, but there is an excellent wine shop and interesting **wine tours** (☎945 18 08 88; www.marquesderiscal. com; tour €11) take place – there's at least one English-language tour a day.

🛏p435

The Drive ⟫ It's only 15 minutes (9km) along the A3210 from Elciego to wonderful Laguardia, which rises up off the otherwise flat, vine-striped countryside.

- - - - - - - - - - -

TRIP HIGHLIGHT

8 Laguardia

It's easy to spin back the wheels of time in the medieval fortress town of Laguardia, or the 'Guard of Navarra' as it was once appropriately known, sitting proudly on its rocky hilltop. As well as memories of long-lost yesterdays, the town further entices visitors with its wine-producing present.

Bodegas Palacio (☎945 60 01 51; www.bodegas-palacio.com; Carretera de Elciego; tour €5; ⊙tours 11am & 1pm Mon & Sat, 4.30pm Tue-Fri, 1.30pm Sun, closed afternoons Jul & Aug) is only 1km from Laguardia on the Elciego road; reservations are not essential but are a good idea (especially out of season). Also just outside Laguardia is the **Centro Temático del Vino Villa Lucia** (☎945 60 00 32; www.villa-lucia. com; Carretera de Logroño; museum €11; ⊙11am-6.30pm Tue-Fri, 10.15am-6.30pm Sat, 11am-12.30pm Sun), a wine museum and shop. Museum visits are by

DETOUR: BODEGAS YSIOS

Start: ❽ Laguardia (p433)

Just a couple of kilometres to the north of Laguardia is the **Bodegas Ysios** (☎941 27 99 00; www.ysios.com; Camino de la Hoya, Laguardia; per person €10; ⊙tours 10.30am, 1pm & 3pm Mon-Fri, 10.30am & 1pm Sat & Sun, advance booking required). Architecturally it's one of the most gob-smacking bodegas in Spain. Designed by Santiago Calatrava as a 'temple dedicated to wine', it's wavelike roof made of aluminium and cedar wood matches the flow of the rocky mountains behind it. Daily tours of the bodega are an excellent introduction to wine production.

guided tour only and finish with a 4D film and wine tasting.

✕⊨ p435

The Drive » From Laguardia it's a short 18km (20 minutes) down the A124 back to Logroño and the start of this tour.

CARLOS SANCHEZ PEREYRA / GETTY IMAGES ©

Bodegas Ysios

Eating & Sleeping

Logroño ❶

⌷ Hotel Marqués de Vallejo
Design Hotel €€

(☎941 24 83 33; www.hotelmarquesdevallejo.com; Calle del Marqués de Vallejo 8; s/d from €50/75; P❄🛜) From the driftwood art to cow skins, beach pebbles and photographic flashlights it's clear that a lot of thought and effort has gone into the design of this stylish, modern and very well-priced hotel.

Santo Domingo de la Calzada ❹

⌷ Hostal R Pedro
Hotel €

(☎941 34 11 60; www.hostalpedroprimero.es; Calle San Roque 9; s/d €48/59; 🛜) This carefully renovated townhouse, which has terracotta-coloured rooms with wooden roof beams and entirely modern bathrooms, is a terrific deal.

⌷ Parador Santo Domingo
Historic Hotel €€

(☎941 34 03 00; www.parador.es; Plaza del Santo 3; r from €105; P🛜) The Parador Santo Domingo is the antithesis of the town's general air of piety. Occupying a 12th-century former hospital, opposite the cathedral, this palatial hotel offers anything but a frugal medieval-like existence. The in-house restaurant is reliably good.

⌷ Parador Santo Domingo Bernado de Fresneda
Hotel €€

(☎941 34 11 50; www.parador.es; Plaza de San Francisco 1; r from €90; P🛜) Just on the edge of the old town is the Parador Santo Domingo Bernado do Frocnoda, which occupies a former convent and pilgrim hostel, although quite honestly, with its divine beds and rooms that gush luxury, you probably wouldn't describe it as a 'hostel' anymore.

Elciego ❼

⌷ Hotel Marqués de Riscal
Design Hotel €€€

(☎945 18 08 80; www.hotel-marquesderiscal.com; Calle Torrea 1; r from €310; P❄🛜) When the owner of Elciego's Bodegas Marqués de Riscal decided he wanted to create something special, he didn't hold back. The result is the spectacular Frank Gehry–designed Hotel Marqués de Riscal. Costing around €85 million, the building is a wave of multicoloured titanium sheets that stand in utter contrast to the village behind.

Laguardia ❽

✗ Restaurante Amelibia
Spanish €€

(☎945 62 12 07; www.restauranteamelibia.com; Barbacana 14; menú del día €17; ⊘1-3.30pm Sun-Mon & Wed-Thu, 1-3.30pm & 9-10.30pm Fri & Sat) This classy restaurant is one of Laguardia's highlights: stare out the windows at a view over the scorched plains and mountain ridges while dining on sublime traditional Spanish cuisine.

⌷ Posada Mayor de Migueloa
Historic Hotel €€

(☎945 600 187; www.mayordemigueloa.com; Calle Mayor 20; s/d incl breakfast €99/105; ❄🛜) For the ultimate in gracious La Rioja living, this old mansion-hotel with its rickety rooms full of polished wood is irresistible. The in-house **restaurant** (menus from €24), which is open to nonguests, is recommended and offers original twists on local cuisine. Under the hotel is a small **wine bodega** (guided visits for non-guests €5).

⌷ Castillo el Collado
Historic Hotel €€€

(☎945 62 12 00; www.hotelcollado.com; Paseo el Collado 1; d €125-185; 🛜) Like a whimsical Disney dream castle, this place, which from the outside is all sturdy turrets and pretty flower gardens, is a truly unique place to stay. The half-dozen rooms are all different but combine quirky style with luxury living. The open-to-all **restaurant** (menus from €25) is also excellent.

NEED ^{TO} KNOW

CURRENCY
Euro (€)

LANGUAGE
Spanish (Castilian). Also Catalan, Basque and Galician.

VISAS
Generally not required for stays of up to 90 days (not at all for members of EU or Schengen countries). Some nationalities need a Schengen visa.

FUEL
Petrol stations (usually open 24 hours) can be found along major highways. Expect to pay €1.35 to €1.80 per litre.

RENTAL CARS
Auto Jardim (www.autojardim.com)

Hertz (www.hertz.com)

Holiday Autos (www.holidayautos.com)

Pepecar (www.pepecar.com)

IMPORTANT NUMBERS
Europe-wide emergencies (☏112)

International access code (☏00)

Country code (☏34)

Climate

- **Santiago de Compostela** GO May–Sep
- **Barcelona** GO year-round
- **Madrid** GO Mar–May, Sep & Oct
- **Valencia** GO year-round
- **Seville** GO Oct–Apr

- Dry climate
- Warm to hot summers, cold winters
- Mild to hot summers, cold winters
- Cold climate

When to Go

High Season (Jun–Aug, public holidays)
» Accommodation books out and prices increase by up to 50%.

» Low season in parts of inland Spain.

» Expect warm, dry and sunny weather; more humid in coastal areas.

Shoulder (Mar–May, Sep & Oct)
» A good time to travel: mild, clear weather and fewer crowds.

» Local festivals can send prices soaring.

Low Season (Nov–Feb)
» Cold in central Spain; rain in the north and northwest.

» Mild temperatures in Andalucía and the Mediterranean coast.

» This is high season in ski resorts.

» Many hotels are closed in beach areas but elsewhere prices plummet.

Daily Costs

Budget: Less than €80

» Dorm bed: €20–30

» Double room in *hostal* (budget hotel): €55–65 (more in Madrid and Barcelona)

» Self-catering and lunch *menú del día* (daily set menu): €10–15

» Use museum and gallery 'free admission' afternoons

Midrange: €80-175

» Double room in midrange hotel: €65–140

» Lunch and/or dinner in local restaurant: €20–40

» Car rental: per day from €25

Top End: More than €175

» Double room in top-end hotel: €140 and up (€200 in Madrid, Barcelona and the Balearics)

» Fine dining for lunch and dinner: €150–250

» Double room in *parador* (luxurious state-owned hotel): €120–200

Eating

Tapas Bar Tapas and drinks; open longer hours than restaurants.

Taberna Rustic place serving tapas and raciones (large tapas).

Panadería Bakery; good for pastries and coffee.

Vinoteca Wine bar where you order by the glass.

Cervecería Beerhall; the place to go for snacks and draft beer (*cerveza*).

Marisqueira Eatery specialising in seafood.

Price categories indicate the cost of a main course:

€	less than €10
€€	€10–20
€€€	more than €20

Sleeping

Casas Rurales Comfy village houses or farmhouses for hire in the countryside.

Hostales Simple guesthouses that have ensuite rooms.

Paradores State funded lodging often in castles, ex-monasteries or old mansions.

Pensión Inexpensive, extremely basic guesthouses, often with shared bathrooms.

Price categories indicate the cost of a double room with private bathroom in high season:

	BARCELONA & MADRID	ELSEWHERE
€	less than €75	less than €65
€€	€75–200	€65–140
€€€	more than €200	more than €140

Arriving in Spain

Barajas Airport (Madrid)

Rental cars Major car-rental agencies have desks in the airport at arrival terminals.

Metro & buses Cost around €5 and run every five to 10 minutes from 6.05am to 1.30am; 30 to 40 minutes to the centre.

Taxis Cost €30 and reach the centre in 20 minutes.

El Prat Airport (Barcelona)

Rental cars Major car-rental agencies have concessions at arrival terminals.

Buses Cost €5.90 and run every five to 10 minutes from 6.10am to 1.05am; it's 30 to 40 minutes to the centre.

Trains Cost €4.10 and run every 30 minutes from 5.42am to 11.38pm; it takes 25 to 30 minutes to reach the centre.

Taxis Cost €25 to €30 and reach the centre in 30 minutes.

Mobile Phones (Cell Phones)

Local SIM cards are widely available and can be used in European and Australian mobile phones, but are not compatible with many North American or Japanese systems.

Internet Access

Wi-fi is available in most lodgings and cafes (and is usually free). Internet cafes are rare.

Money

The most convenient way to bring your money is in the form of a debit or credit card, with some extra cash in case of an emergency.

Many credit and debit cards can be used for withdrawing money from *cajeros automáticos* (ATMs) that display the relevant symbols such as Visa, MasterCard, Cirrus etc. There is usually a charge (around 1.5% to 2%) on ATM cash withdrawals abroad.

Language

The pronunciation of most Spanish sounds is very similar to that of their English counterparts. If you read our coloured pronunciation guides as if they were English, you'll be understood. Note that kh is a throaty sound (like the 'ch' in the Scottish *loch*), r is strongly rolled, ly is pronounced as the 'lli' in 'million' and ny as the 'ni' in 'onion'. You may also notice that the 'lisped' th sound is pronounced as s in Andalucia. In our pronunciation guides stressed syllables are indicated with italics.

SPANISH BASICS

Hello.	*Hola.*	o·la
Goodbye.	*Adiós.*	a·dyos
How are you?	*¿Qué tal?*	ke tal
Fine, thanks.	*Bien, gracias.*	byen *gra*·syas
Excuse me.	*Perdón.*	per·*don*
Sorry.	*Lo siento.*	lo *syen*·to
Yes.	*Sí.*	see
No.	*No.*	no
Please.	*Por favor.*	por fa·*vor*
Thank you.	*Gracias.*	*gra*·syas
You're welcome.	*De nada.*	de *na*·da

My name is ...
Me llamo ...   me *lya*·mo ...

What's your name?
¿Cómo se llama Usted?   ko·mo se *lya*·ma oo·*ste* (pol)
¿Cómo te llamas?   ko·mo te *lya*·mas (inf)

Do you speak English?
¿Habla inglés?   a·bla een·*gles* (pol)
¿Hablas inglés?   a·blas een·*gles* (inf)

I don't understand.
No entiendo.   no en·*tyen*·do

DIRECTIONS

Where's ...?
¿Dónde está ...?   don·de es·*ta* ...

What's the address?
¿Cuál es la dirección?   kwal es la dee·*rek*·syon

Can you please write it down?
¿Puede escribirlo,   pwe·de es·kree·*beer*·lo
por favor?   por fa·*vor*

Can you show me (on the map)?
¿Me lo puede indicar   me lo pwe·de een·dee·*kar*
(en el mapa)?   (en el *ma*·pa)

EMERGENCIES

| Help! | *¡Socorro!* | so·*ko*·ro |

I'm lost.
Estoy perdido/a.   es·toy per·*dee*·do/a (m/f)

ON THE ROAD

I'd like to hire a ...	*Quisiera alquilar ...*	kee·*sye*·ra al·*kee*·lar ...
4WD	*un todo-terreno*	oon *to*·do·te·*re*·no
bicycle	*una bicicleta*	*oo*·na bee·see·*kle*·ta
car	*un coche*	oon *ko*·che
motorcycle	*una moto*	*oo*·na *mo*·to

Want More?

For in-depth language information and handy phrases, check out Lonely Planet's *Spanish Phrasebook*. You'll find them at **shop.lonelyplanet.com**.

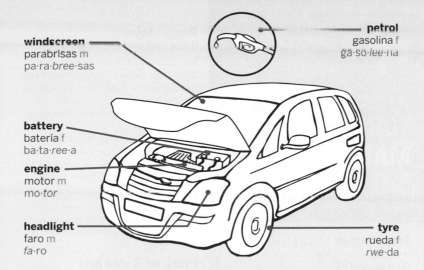

windscreen
parabrisas m
pa·ra·*bree*·sas

petrol
gasolina f
ga·so·*lee*·na

battery
batería f
ba·ta·*ree*·a

engine
motor m
mo·*tor*

headlight
faro m
fa·ro

tyre
rueda f
rwe·da

child seat	asiento de seguridad para niños	a·*syen*·to de se·goo·ree·*da* pa·ra *nee*·nyos
diesel	gasóleo	ga·*so*·le·o
helmet	casco	*kas*·ko
mechanic	mecánico	me·ka·*nee*·ko
petrol	gasolina	ga·so·*lee*·na
service station	gasolinera	ga·so·lee·*ne*·ra

How much is it per day/hour?
¿Cuánto cuesta por   *kwan*·to *kwes*·ta por
día/hora?   *dee*·a/o·ra

Is this the road to ...?
¿Se va a ... por esta   se va a ... por *es*·ta
carretera?   ka·re·*te*·ra

(How long) Can I park here?
¿(Por cuánto tiempo)   (por *kwan*·to *tyem*·po)
Puedo aparcar aquí?   *pwe*·do a·par·*kar* a·*kee*

The car has broken down (at ...).
El coche se ha averiado   el *ko*·che se a a·ve·*rya*·do
(en ...).   (en ...)

I have a flat tyre.
Tengo un pinchazo.   *ten*·go oon peen·*cha*·tho

I've run out of petrol.
Me he quedado sin   me e ke·*da*·do seen
gasolina.   ga·so·*lee*·na

Where's a petrol station?
¿Dónde hay una   *don*·de ai *oo*·na
gasolinera?   ga·so·lee·*ne*·ra

I had an accident.
He tenido un   e te·*nee*·do oon
accidente.   ak·thee·*den*·te

I need a mechanic.
Necesito un/una   ne·the·*see*·to oon/*oo*·na
mecánico/a. m/f   me·ka·*nee*·ko/a

Are there cycling paths?
¿Hay carril bicicleta?   ai ka·*reel* bee·thee·*kle*·ta

Is there bicycle parking?
¿Hay aparcamiento   ai a·par·ka·*myen*·to
de bicicletas?   de bee·thee·*kle*·tas

Signs

- - - - - - - - - - - - - - - - - - - -

Stop	Stop
Ceda el Paso	Give Way
Prohibido	No Entry
Acceso	Entrance
Peaje	Toll
Dirección Única	One Way
Vía Acceso	Freeway Exit
Aparcamiento	Parking
Prohibido Aparcar	No Parking

STRETCH YOUR LEGS
MADRID

Start/Finish: Plaza Mayor

Distance: 3.8km

Duration: Two to three hours

Madrid's compact and historic centre is ideal for exploring on foot. So much of Madrid life occurs on the streets and in its glorious plazas, and it all takes place against a spectacular backdrop of architecture, stately and grand.

Take this walk on Trip

30

Plaza Mayor

So many Madrid stories begin in Madrid's grand central square. Since it was laid out in 1619, the Plaza Mayor has seen everything from bullfights to the trials of the Spanish Inquisition. These days the grandeur of the plaza owes much to the warm colours of the uniformly ochre apartments, with 237 wrought-iron balconies offset by the exquisite frescoes of the 17th-century Real Casa de la Panadería (Royal Bakery).

The Walk » Walk down Calle de Postas off the plaza's northeastern corner, cross the endlessly busy Plaza de la Puerta del Sol, then continue east along Carrera de San Jerónimo. At elegant Plaza de Canalejas, turn right.

Plaza de Santa Ana

There are few more iconic Madrid squares than Plaza de Santa Ana, a local favourite since Joseph Bonaparte carved it out of this crowded inner-city neighbourhood in 1810. Surrounded by classic Madrid architecture of pastel shades and wrought-iron balconies, the plaza presides over the Barrio de las Letras and the outdoor tables are among the most sought-after in the city.

The Walk » Walking west, cross Plaza del Ángel, walk along Calle de la Bolsa, cross Calle de Toledo and make for Calle de la Cava Baja, a glorious, medieval street lined with tapas bars. Keep Iglesia de San Andrés on your right, and stroll down the hill to Plaza de la Paja.

Plaza de la Paja

Delightful Plaza de la Paja (Straw Sq) slopes down into the tangle of lanes that once made up Madrid's Muslim quarter. In the 12th and 13th centuries the city's main market occupied the square and it retains a palpable medieval air, and at times can feel like a Castilian village square. **Delic** (☎91 364 54 50; www.delic.es; Costanilla de San Andrés 14; ◷11am-2am Sun & Tue-Thu, 11am 2.30am Fri & Sat; Ⓜ La Latina), with tables on the square, is brilliant for a mojito, while the **Jardín del Príncipe Anglona** (Plaza de la Paja; ◷10am-10pm Apr-Oct, 10am-6.30pm Nov-Mar; Ⓜ La Latina),

a walled 18th-century garden, is a peaceful oasis in the heart of this most clamorous of cities.

The Walk ⟫ Take any lanes heading west through La Morería, the old Muslim quarter, to Calle de Bailén. Turn right, cross the Viaduct (with fine views on either side), pass the cathedral and continue on to Plaza de Oriente.

Plaza de Oriente

Cinematic in scope, Plaza de Oriente is grand and graceful. It's watched over by the **Palacio Real** (☏91 454 88 00; www.patrimonionacional.es; Calle de Bailén; adult/concession €11/6, guide/audioguide €4/4, EU citizens free last two hours Mon-Thu; ☺10am-8pm Apr-Sep, 10am-6pm Oct-Mar; MÓpera) and the **Teatro Real** (☏91 516 06 96; www.teatro-real.com; Plaza de Oriente; 50min guided tour adult/child under 7yr €8/free; ☺10.30am-1pm; MÓpera) – Madrid's opera house – by sophisticated cafes, and apartments that cost the equivalent of a royal salary. At the centre of the plaza is an equestrian statue of Felipe IV designed by Velázquez, and nearby are some 20 marble statues, mostly of an-cient monarchs. Local legend holds that these royals get down off their pedestals at night to stretch their legs.

The Walk ⟫ Return south along Calle de Bailén, then turn left (east) up Calle Mayor. After passing the intimate Plaza de la Villa on your right, Mercado de San Miguel appears, also on your right as you climb the hill.

Mercado de San Miguel

One of Madrid's oldest and most beautiful markets, the **Mercado de San Miguel** (www.mercadodesanmiguel.es; Plaza de San Miguel; tapas from €1; ☺10am-midnight Sun-Wed, 10am-2am Thu-Sat; MSol) is now one of the city's most exciting gastronomic spaces. Within the early-20th-century glass walls, all manner of stalls serve up tapas, from fishy *pintxos* (Basque tapas) atop mini toasts to *jamón* (cured ham) or other cured meats from Salamanca, cheeses, pickled goodies and fine wines.

The Walk ⟫ To get back to where you started, leave the market, walk down Calle de la Cava de San Miguel, turn left and climb the stairs through the Arco de los Cuchilleros to the Plaza Mayor.

STRETCH YOUR LEGS
BARCELONA

Start: Parc de la Ciutadella

Finish: Casa Batlló

Distance: 3.5km

Duration: Three hours

Packed with historic treasures and jaw-dropping architecture, Barcelona is a wanderer's delight. This stroll takes you through atmospheric medieval lanes and along elegant boulevards, leading you past Gothic cathedrals, lively tapas bars and picturesque plazas.

Take this walk on Trips

27

Parc de la Ciutadella

The handsomely landscaped Parc de la Ciutadella is a local favourite for a leisurely promenade. Start in the northeast corner, and descend past the monumental **Cascada** (waterfall), then stroll south across the park, passing a small lake and Catalonia's regional parliament.

The Walk » With your back to the park, cross Passeig de Picasso and walk along restaurant-lined Passeig del Born. According to legend, jousting matches were once held here.

Basílica de Santa Maria del Mar

Nothing prepares you for the singular beauty of **Basílica de Santa Maria del Mar** (☎93 310 23 90; Plaça de Santa Maria del Mar; ☺9am-1.30pm & 4.30-8.30pm, from 10.30am Sun; ⓂJaume I). Barcelona's most stirring Gothic structure, the 14th-century church was built in just 59 years. In contrast to the tight warren of neighbouring streets, a real sense of light and space pervades the entire sanctuary of the church.

The Walk » Leave via the main entrance and follow Carrer de l'Argenteria up to busy Via Laietana. Turn left onto Baixada de la Llibreteria, then right onto Carrer de la Freneria. After a few blocks, you'll see the massive cathedral on your left.

La Catedral

For centuries the spiritual heart of Barcelona, **La Catedral** (☎93 342 82 62; www.catedralbcn.org; Plaça de la Seu; admission free, special visit €6, choir admission €2.80; ☺8am-12.45pm & 5.15-7.30pm Mon-Sat, special visit 1-5pm Mon-Sat, 2-5pm Sun & holidays; ⓂJaume I) is at once lavish and sombre, anchoring the city in its past. Begun in the late 13th century and not completed until six centuries later, the cathedral is Barcelona's history rendered in stone.

The Walk » Turn left out of the main entrance and left again down Carrer del Bisbe. Just before reaching Plaça Sant Jaume, turn right onto Carrer del Call. Follow this narrow lane a few blocks, then turn left onto Carrer d'en Quintana. After two blocks, you'll reach the plaza.

Plaça Reial

One of the most photogenic squares in Barcelona, the Plaça Reial is not to be missed. Numerous eateries, bars and nightspots lie beneath the arcades of 19th-century neoclassical buildings, with a buzz of activity at all hours. The lamp posts by the central fountain are Antoni Gaudí's first known works in the city.

The Walk › Exit the square onto famous La Rambla, a bustling boulevard with a wide pedestrian-filled strip in the middle. Walk north a few blocks until you see the large cast-iron market off to your left.

Mercat de la Boqueria

This temple of temptation is one of Europe's greatest permanent **produce fairs** (☎93 318 25 84; www.boqueria.info; La Rambla 91; ☾8am-8.30pm Mon-Sat, closed Sun; ⓂLiceu). Step inside for a seemingly endless bounty of glistening fruits and vegetables, smoked meats, pungent cheeses and chocolate truffles. In the back, a handful of popular tapas bars serve up delectable morsels.

The Walk › Get back on La Rambla and continue north. You'll soon reach the spacious Plaça de Catalunya. Walk diagonally across this plaza, and turn left onto the grand boutique-lined Passeig de Gràcia, and walk up four blocks to the architectural treasures looming just past Carrer del Consell de Cent.

Casa Batlló

Even Gaudí outdid himself with this fantastical **apartment block** (☎93 216 03 06; www.casabatllo.es; Passeig de Gràcia 43; adult/concessions/child under 7yr €21.50/€18.50/free; ☾9am-9pm daily; ⓂPasseig de Gràcia): an astonishing confection of rippling balconies, optical illusions and twisted chimney pots along Barcelona's grandest boulevard. The facade, sprinkled with bits of blue, mauve and green tiles and studded with wave-shaped window frames and balconies, rises to an uneven blue-tiled roof with a solitary tower.

The Walk › Since it's a long walk back to the start, hop on the metro and head to Arc de Trionf station, a short stroll from Parc de la Ciutadella.

Portugal

PORTUGAL'S MIX OF THE MEDIEVAL AND THE MARITIME makes it a superb place to visit. A turbulent history involving the Moors, Spain and Napoleon has left the interior scattered with walled medieval towns topped by castles, while the pounding Atlantic has sculpted a coast of glorious sand beaches.

The nation's days of exploration and seafaring have created an introspective yet open culture with wide-ranging artistic influences. The eating and drinking scene here is a highlight, with several wine regions, and restaurants that are redolent with aromas of grilling pork or the freshest of fish.

Comparatively short distances mean that you get full value for road trips here: less time behind the wheel means you can take more time to absorb the atmosphere.

Douro Valley Vineyards along the Douro River
SIMON DANNHAUER/SHUTTERSTOCK ©

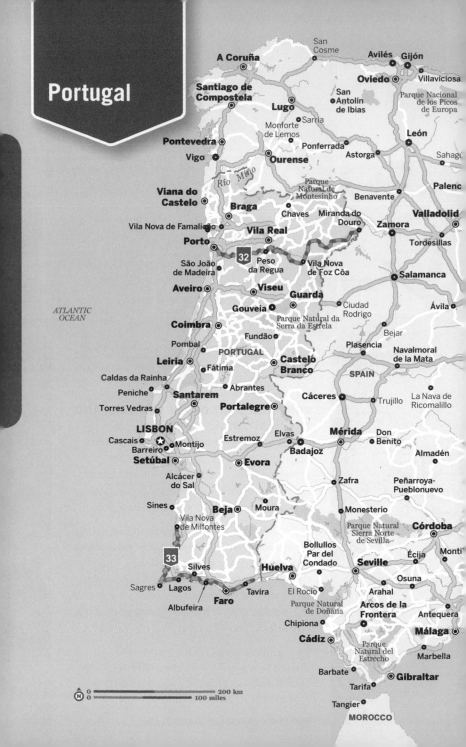

Carrapateira Praia do Amado

 Douro Valley Vineyard Trails 5–7 Days
Heartbreakingly beautiful river valley laced
with vines producing sensational ports and reds.
(p449)

Alentejo & Algarve Beaches 4–6 Days
Some of the world's great beaches and towns with
Moorish heritage. (p459)

✓ **DON'T MISS**

Surfing
Portugal is one of
Europe's surfing
hotspots: despite the
Mediterranean vibe,
this is the Atlantic, and
those are serious waves
on Trip 33

Wine Tasting
Often undererrated,
Portugal's wines are
among the region's
great pleasures. Visit
wineries and taste wines
and ports on Trip 32

Hiking
Jump out of the car for
some picturesque hill
walking on Trips 32 33

Douro Valley Vineyard Trails

32

The Douro is a little drop of heaven. Uncork this region on Porto's doorstep and you'll soon fall head over heels in love with its terraced vineyards, wine estates and soul-stirring vistas.

TRIP HIGHLIGHTS

193 km

Pinhão
Wine tastings and Douro cruises on a gorgeous bend in the river

171 km

Quinta do Crasto
Eyrie-like winery in the Unesco-listed Alto Douro region

FINISH
Miranda do Douro

START
1

Peso da Regua **7**
4 **8**

Vila Nova de Foz Côa

Porto
Medieval core, historic port lodges galore and a whole lotta soul

1 km

Casal de Loivos
Gasp-eliciting views of Douro vines cascading down the hillsides

197 km

5–7 DAYS
358KM / 222 MILES

GREAT FOR...

BEST TIME TO GO

Spring for wildflowers, early autumn for the grape harvest.

ESSENTIAL PHOTO

The staggering view of the Douro vineyards from Casal de Loivos miradouro.

✓ BEST FOR FOODIES

Chef Rui Paula keeps it regional at DOC, with vineyard and river views from its terrace.

449

Douro Valley Vineyards to the west of Porto

32 Douro Valley Vineyard Trails

You're in for a treat. This Unesco World Heritage region is hands down one of Portugal's most evocative landscapes, with mile after swoon-worthy mile of vineyards spooling along the contours of its namesake river and marching up terraced hillsides. Go for the food, the fabulous wines, the palatial *quintas,* the medieval stone villages and the postcard views on almost every corner.

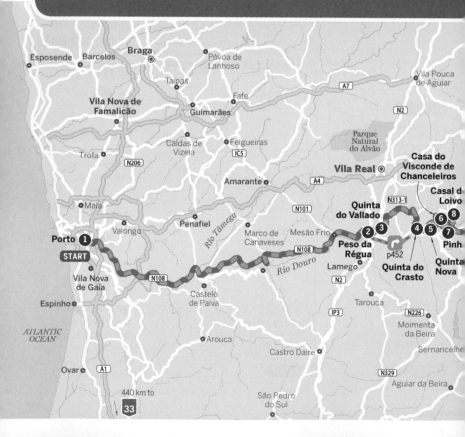

TRIP HIGHLIGHT

❶ Porto

Before kick-starting your road trip, devote a day or two to Porto, snuggled on banks of the Río Douro, where life is played out in the mazy lanes of the medieval Ribeira district. From here, the double-decker **Ponte de Dom Luís I**, built by an apprentice of Gustav Eiffel in 1877, takes the river in its stride. Cross it to reach Vila Nova de Gaia, where grand 17th-century port lodges march up the hillside. Many open their barrel-lined cellars for guided tours and tastings – usually of three different ports – that will soon help you tell your tawny from your late-bottled vintage. Top billing goes to British-run **Taylor's** (☏223 742 800; www.taylor.pt; Rua do Choupelo 250; tour €5; ◷10am-6pm Mon-Fri, to 5pm Sat & Sun) (don't miss the immense 100,000L barrel), **Graham's** (☏223 776 484; www.grahams-port.

LINK YOUR TRIP

33 **Alentejo & Algarve Beaches**

Do one trip in reverse: about four hours south from Porto are great beaches and towns with Moorish heritage.

30 **Historic Castilla y León**

For a taste of historic Spain, head east from Miranda do Douro across the border to Tordesillas, then southeast to Madrid (about 3 hours).

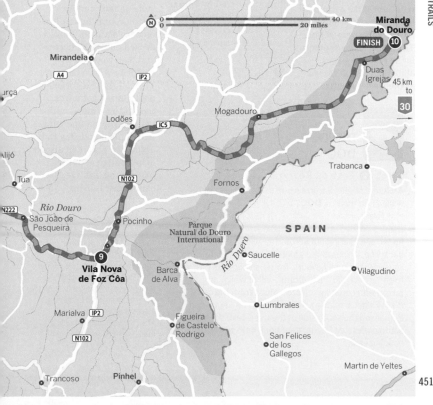

com; Rua do Agro 141; tour €5-20; ⏰9.30am-6pm Apr-Oct, to 5.30pm Nov-Mar) and **Calém** (☎223 746 672; www.calem.pt; Avenida Diogo Leite 344; Cellar visit & tasting adult/reduced/under 12 €5/2.50/free; ⏰10am-6.30pm).

The Drive » There are quicker ways of getting from A to B, sure, but for immersion in Douro wine country, you can't beat this three-hour (137km) drive east on the N108. The serpentine road shadows the Río Douro from Porto to Peso da Régua, with views of hillsides combed with vines, little chapels and woodlands spilling down to the sparkling river.

❷ Peso da Régua

Terraced hills scaled with vines like a dragon's backbone rise around riverside Peso da Régua. The sun-bleached town is the region's largest, abutting the Río Douro at the western end of the demarcated port-wine area. It grew into a major port-wine *entrepôt* in the 18th century. While not as charming as its setting, the town is worth visiting for its **Museu do Douro** (www.museudodouro. pt; Rua Marqués de Pombal; adult/concession €6/3; ⏰10am-6pm daily May-Oct, Tue-Sun Nov-Apr). Housed in a beautifully converted riverside warehouse, the museum whisks you through the entire wine spectrum, from impressionist landscapes to the remains of an old flat-bottomed port hauler. Down at the pier, you'll find frequent 50-minute boat trips to Pinhão, offered by **Tomaz do Douro** (☎222 081 935; www.viadouro-cruzeiros. com; cruises from €10), for instance.

🍴 🛏️ p457

DETOUR: DOC

Start: ❷ Peso da Régua

Architect Miguel Saraiva's ode to clean-lined, glass-walled minimalism, **DOC** (☎254 858 123; www.ruipaula. com; Folgosa; mains €27.50-29; ⏰12.30-3.30pm & 7.30-11pm) is headed up by Portuguese star chef Rui Paula. Its terrace peering out across the river is a stunning backdrop. Dishes give a pinch of imagination to seasonal, regional flavours, from fish *açordas* (stews) to game and wild mushrooms – all of which are paired with carefully selected wines from the cellar. It's in Folgosa, midway between Peso da Régua and Pinhão, on the south side of the river. Take the N2 south of Peso da Régua, then hook onto the N222 heading east.

The Drive » From Peso da Régua, take the first exit onto the N2 at the roundabout at the end of Rua Dr Manuel de Arriaga, then the third exit at the next roundabout to join the N313. Turn right onto the N313-1 when you see the yellow sign to Quinta do Vallado. It's around a 5km drive.

❸ Quinta do Vallado

Ah, what views! The vineyards spread picturesquely before you from **Quinta do Vallado** (☎254 318 081, 254 323 147; www.quintadovallado. com; Vilarinho dos Freires; r €120-180; [P][❄][📶][🐾]), a glorious 70-hectare winery. It brings together five rooms in an old stone manor and eight swank rooms in an ultra-modern slate building, decked out with chestnut and teak wood, each complete with a balcony. They all share a gorgeous pool. Guests get a free tour of the winery, with a tasting. Have a fine wine-paired meal and stay the night. The staff can also help arrange activities like cycling, hiking, fishing or canoeing – just ask.

The Drive » From Quinta do Vallado, the N313-2, CM1258 and N322-2 take you on a 29km drive east through the curvaceous wine terraces of the Alto Douro, past immaculately tended rows of vines and chalk-white hamlets, with tantalising glimpses of the river below. After Gouvinhas, the wiggling road takes you south to Quinta do Crasto.

❹ Quinta do Crasto

Perched like an eyrie on a promontory above the Río Douro and a spectacular ripple of terraced vineyards, **Quinta do Crasto** (📞934 920 024, 254 920 020; www.quintadocrasto.pt; Sabrosa, Gouvinhas; tours €18; ⏱9am-6pm Mon-Fri) quite literally takes your breath away. The winery is beautifully set amid the lyrical landscapes of the Alto Douro, a Unesco World Heritage site. Stop by for a tour and tasting or lunch. It produces some of the country's best drops – reds that are complex, spicy and smooth, with wild berry aromas, and whites that are fresh, with a mineral nose and tang of citrus and apples. Designed by Portuguese architect Eduardo Souto Moura, the plunge pool here appears to nosedive directly into the valley below.

The Drive » From Quinta do Crasto it's an easy 4km drive east along the mellow banks of the Río Douro to Quinta Nova via the N322-2 and CM1268.

❺ Quinta Nova

Set on a ridge, surrounded by 120 hectares of ancient vineyards, overlooking the Douro river with mountains layered in the distance, **Quinta Nova** (📞254 730 420, 254 730 430; www.quintanova.

com; s €134-152, d €152-173; 📶🍴) is simply stunning. Besides plush lodgings in a beautifully restored 19th-century manor, it offers romantic grounds, a pool gazing out across vines rolling into the distance, a restaurant, wine tours, tastings and some of the region's top walking trails – the longest of which is 2½ hours.

The Drive » It's a 10km drive east from Quinta Nova to Casa do Visconde de Chanceleiros on the CM1268, tracing the contours of the emerald-green vines unfurling around you

❻ Casa do Visconde de Chanceleiros

Fancy staying the night up in the hills of the sublime Alto Douro? **Casa do Visconde de Chanceleiros** (📞254 730 190; www.chanceleiros.com; s €130-140, d €135-170; 🅿🛏🍴) is a gorgeous 250-year-old manor house, with spacious standard and superior rooms featuring classic decor and patios. The expansive views of the valley and lush terraced gardens steal the show, but so does the outdoor pool, tennis court, Jacuzzi, and sauna in a wine barrel. Delicious dinners (€38) are served on request.

The Drive » A gentle 7.5km drive east along the M590, with spirit-lifting views across the terraced vineyards, the deep-green Douro and family-run *quintas*, brings you to Pinhão.

❼ Pinhão

Encircled by terraced hillsides that yield some of the world's best port – and some damn good table wines too – little Pinhão sits on a particularly lovely bend of the Río Douro. Wineries and their competing signs dominate the scene and even the delightful train station has *azulejos* (tiles) depicting the grape harvest. The town, though cute, holds little of interest, but makes a fine base for exploring the surrounding vineyards. From here, you can also cruise upriver into the heart of the Alto Douro aboard a traditional flat-bottomed port boat with **Douro-a-Vela** (📞918 793 792; www.douro-a-vela.pt; 1hr cruise €25). Catch the boat from the Folgosa do Douro pier. Or rewind to the early days of viniculture on a guided tour followed by a tasting at **Quinta Nova Wine Museum & Shop** (Aris Douro; 📞254 730 030; www.quintanova.com; Largo da Estacão 14; tours & tastings €5; ⏱tours 11am, 3pm & 5pm Mon-Sat, 11am & 3pm Sun Apr-Oct).

🍴🛏 p457

The Drive » Veer slightly west of Pinhão on the N323 and turn right onto the M585, following the sign for Casal de Loivos, 4.5km away. The country road that weaves up through

WHY THIS IS A GREAT TRIP
KERRY CHRISTIANI, AUTHOR

Step down a gear and enjoy the sweet life. Shadowing the bends in the river from Porto to the Spanish border, the Douro plays up romance, with its steeply climbing vines, giddy views and meandering roads leading to chalk-white hamlets, barrel-lined cellars and historic *quintas*, where fine meals and Portugal's best wines are served to the backbeat of cicadas.

Top: A boat cruises past the Douro's terraced vineyards
Left: Decorative tiles at Pinhão's train station
Right: The Rio Douro framed by surrounding hills

the vines, with the river below, later becomes the cobbled Rua da Calçada, passing *socalcos* (stone-walled terraced vineyards).

- - - - - - - - - -

TRIP HIGHLIGHT

8 Casal de Loivos

It's a tough call, but Casal de Loivos has hands down one of the most staggeringly beautiful views in the region. From the *miradouro* (viewpoint), the uplifting vista reduces the Douro to postcard format, taking in the full sweep of its stone-walled terraced vineyards, stitched into the hillsides and fringing the sweeping contours of the valley, and the river scything through them. To maximise on these dreamy views, stay the night at **Casa de Casal de Loivros** (☏254 732 149; www.casadecasaldeloivos.com; s/d €90/110; @ ☒). The elegant house has been in this winemaking family for nearly 350 years. The halls are enlivened by museum-level displays of folkloric dresses, and the perch – high above the Alto Douro – is spectacular. Swim laps in the pool while peering down across the vines spreading in all directions.

The Drive ≫ Backtrack on the N323, then pick up the N222 south of the river for the 64km drive southeast to Vila Nova de Foz Côa. The winding road takes you through some picture-book scenery, with whitewashed hamlets and *quintas* punctuating vines, orchards and olive groves.

❾ Vila Nova de Foz Côa

Welcome to the heart of the Douro's *terra quente* (hot land). This once-remote, whitewashed town has been on the map since the 1990s, when researchers, during a proposed project for a dam, stumbled across an astounding stash of Paleolithic art. Thousands of these mysterious rock engravings speckle the Río Côa valley. Come to see its world-famous gallery of rock art at the **Parque Arqueológico do Vale do Côa** (www.arte-coa. pt; Av Gago Coutinho 19 A, Foz Côa; park €10, museum €5 (on Sun afternoons €1), park & museum €12; ☺ museum 10am-1.30pm & 2-5.30pm Tue-Sun, park 9am-12.30pm & 2-5.30pm Tue-Sun). The three sites open to the public include Canada do Inferno, with departures at around 9.30am from the park museum in Vila Nova de Foz Côa, which is the ideal place to un-derstand just how close these aeons-old drawings came to disappearing.

The Drive » Wrap up your road trip by driving 120km northeast to Miranda do Douro via the N102, IP2 and IC5. The closer the Spanish border, the more you'll notice the shift in scenery, with lushness giving way to more arid, rugged terrain, speckled with vineyards and olive groves.

❿ Miranda do Douro

A fortified frontier town hunkering down on the precipice of the Río Douro canyon, Miranda do Douro was long a bulwark of Portugal's 'wild east'. While its crumbling castle and handsomely severe 16th-century cathedral still lend an air of medieval charm, modern-day Miranda now receives weekend Spanish tourists, as opposed to repelling Castillian attacks. For an insight on the region's border culture, including ancient rites such as the 'stick dancing' of the *paulitei-ros*, visit the **Museu da Terra de Miranda** (Praça de Dom João III; admission €2, Sun morning free; ☺9am-1pm & 2-6pm Wed-Sun, 2-6pm Tue). If you'd rather get a taste of the rugged nature on Miranda's doorstep, **Europarques** (☎273 432 396; www.europarques. com; adult/child under 10yr €16/8; ☺trips 4pm daily, plus 11am Sat & Sun) runs 1½-hour river boat trips along a dramatic gorge. Boats leave from beside the dam on the Portuguese side. Stop by the **Parque Natural do Douro Internacional Office** (☎273 431 457; Largo do Castelo; ☺9.30am-12.30pm & 2-5.30pm Mon-Fri) for the inside scoop on hiking among the woods and towering granite cliffs of the 832-sq-km park, home to bird species including black storks, Egyptian vultures, peregrine falcons, golden eagles and Bonelli's eagles.

✕ ⮕ p457

Eating & Sleeping

Peso da Régua ②

✖ Castas e Pratos   Portuguese €€€

(☎254 323 290; www.castasepratos.com; Av José Vasques Osório; mains €19.50-22.50; ⊙10.30am-11pm) The coolest dining room in town is set in a restored wood-and-stone railyard warehouse with exposed original timbers. You can order grilled *alheira* sausage or octopus salad from the tapas bar downstairs or have the seabass on seafood fumet with saffron filaments, or kid goat in port with fava beans in the mezzanine.

⊨ Hotel Régua Douro   Hotel €€

(☎254 320 700; www.hotelreguadouro.pt; Largo da Estação; s €91-96, d €112.50-152.50; P ❋ @ 🛜 ⊠) This industrial-sized hotel sits by the river and is steps from the train station. It has plush, carpeted rooms in ruby (or is that tawny?) colour schemes and windows overlooking the Douro. The pool is much appreciated on hot days.

Pinhão ❼

✖ Veladouro   Portuguese €

(☎254 738 166; Rua de Praia 3; mains €6-8; ⊙10am-11pm Mon-Sat) Simple Portuguese food, such as wood-grilled meats, is served inside this quaint schist building or outside under a canopy of vines. From the train station, turn left and go along the main road for 150m, then left again under a railway bridge, and right at the river.

⊨ Quinta de la Rosa   B&B €€

(☎254 732 254; www.quintadelarosa.com; d €80-120, ste €120-140, villa per week €750-1800) Sitting on the banks of the Douro, 2km west of Pinhão, this charming vineyard and winery runs hour-long tours (€3) followed by tastings at 11am daily. The bright, appealing rooms straddle different buildings and private villas are available for weekly rental. Three-course dinners (€25) are perfectly matched with wines, and during the autumn harvest you can even join in with grape-treading traditions.

⊨ Vintage House   Boutique Hotel €€€

(☎254 730 230; www.csvintagehouse. com; Lugar da Ponte; s €140-210, d €180-285; P ❋ @ 🛜 ⊠) Occupying a string of 19th-century buildings right on the river, this luxurious sleep is actually very modern once you get past the distinctly English facade (a reminder of the key role Brits played in the port trade). This is where BB King stayed when he rocked the Douro. All rooms have terraces or balconies with river views.

Miranda do Douro ❿

✖ São Pedro   Portuguese €€

(☎273 431 321; Rua Mouzinho de Albuquerque; mains €7.50-12.50; ⊙noon-3pm daily, 7-10pm Tue-Sun) This spacious restaurant, just in from the main old-town gate, serves up a fine *posta á São Pedro* (grilled veal steak dressed with garlic and olive oil). The €11 tourist menu comes with soup, main, dessert, wine and coffee.

⊨ Hotel Parador Santa Catarina   Hotel €€

(☎273 431 005; www.hotelparadorsantacatarina. pt; Largo da Pousada; s/d/tr/q €50/80/85/100; P ❋ 🛜) Every guest gets a private veranda with spectacular views of the gorge at this luxurious hotel perched on the canyon's edge. Rooms are a handsome mix of traditional and contemporary, with hardwood floors, flat-screen TVs and large marble bathrooms. The attached restaurant is the most upmarket in town.

Alentejo & Algarve Beaches

33

On this sunny coastal drive you'll experience some of Europe's finest beaches and explore the picturesque, formerly Moorish towns of Portugal's south.

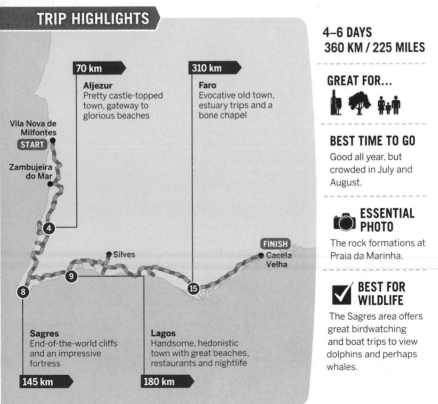

TRIP HIGHLIGHTS

70 km
Aljezur
Pretty castle-topped town, gateway to glorious beaches

310 km
Faro
Evocative old town, estuary trips and a bone chapel

Vila Nova de Milfontes
START

Zambujeira do Mar

4

Silves

FINISH
Cacela Velha

9

8

15

Sagres
End-of-the-world cliffs and an impressive fortress

145 km

Lagos
Handsome, hedonistic town with great beaches, restaurants and nightlife

180 km

4–6 DAYS
360 KM / 225 MILES

GREAT FOR...

BEST TIME TO GO
Good all year, but crowded in July and August.

ESSENTIAL PHOTO
The rock formations at Praia da Marinha.

BEST FOR WILDLIFE
The Sagres area offers great birdwatching and boat trips to view dolphins and perhaps whales.

Carvoeiro Rock arches at Praia da Marinha

459

33 Alentejo & Algarve Beaches

Portugal's southern coasts offer a Mediterranean ideal, with fragrances of pine, rosemary, wine and grilling fish drifting over some absolutely stunning beaches. Only this isn't the Med, it's the Atlantic, so add serious surfable waves, important maritime history and great wildlife-watching opportunities to the mix. This drive takes in some of the finest beaches in the region, and explores the intriguing towns, which conserve their tight-knit Moorish street plans.

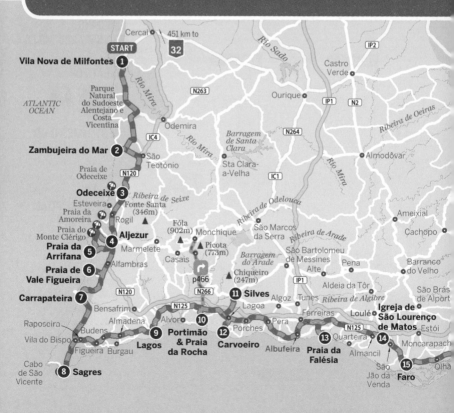

❶ Vila Nova de Milfontes

One of the loveliest towns along this stretch of the coast, Vila Nova de Milfontes has an attractive, whitewashed centre, sparkling beaches nearby and a laid-back population who couldn't imagine living anywhere else. Milfontes remains much more low-key than most resort towns, except in August when it's packed to the hilt with surfers and sun-seekers. It's located in the middle of the beautiful Parque Natural do Sudoeste Alentejano e Costa Vicentina and is still a port (Hannibal is said to have sheltered here) alongside a lovely, sand-edged limb of estuary.

Milfonte's narrow lanes, tiny plazas and beach harbour varied eating and drinking options. The town beach is sheltered but can get busy; the best strand in the vicinity is fantastic **Praia do Malhão**, backed by rocky dunes and covered in fragrant scrub, around 7km to the north.

The Drive » It's a 30km drive through protected parkland on the N393 south to Zambujeira.

❷ Zambujeira do Mar

Enchantingly wild beaches backed by rugged cliffs form the setting of this sleepy seaside village. The main street terminates at the cliff; paths lead to the attractive sands below. Quieter than Vila Nova, Zambujeira attracts a backpacker, surfy crowd, though in August the town is a party place and hosts the massive music fest, **Festa do Sudoeste**. The high-season crowds obscure Zambujeira's out-of-season charms: fresh fish in family-run restaurants, blustering cliff-top walks and a dramatic, empty coast.

🛏 p469

The Drive » Cutting back to the main road, you then head south on the N120. It's about 25km to Odeceixe through beautiful coastal woodland.

❸ Odeceixe

Located just as you cross into the Algarve from the Alentejo, Odeceixe is an endearing whitewashed village cascading down a hill below a picture-perfect windmill on the southern side of the Ribeira de Seixe valley. It's a sleepy town, except in summer, when it fills with people keen on its nearby beach. This tongue of

Parque Natural do Vale do Guadiana

São Domingos

IC27

ertola   Moreanes

Gundiana du Vale do atural Parque   *Embalse del Chanza*

Rio Guadiana   **SPAIN**

Pomarão   El Granado

PORTUGAL   Alcoutim

Ribeira da Foupana

Vaqueiros   Foz de Odeleite

Ribeira de Odeleite   Odeleite   30✶1km to

Azinhal   **28**

Miguel Anes (229m)   Vila Real de Santo António

E01   ⓱ **Cacela Velha**

Pedras d'el Rei   ⓰ **Tavira**   **FINISH**

Santa Luzia

Fuzeta

Ⓝ 0 ▬▬▬▬▬▬▬ 20 km
   0 ▬▬▬▬▬▬▬ 10 miles

❽ LINK YOUR TRIP

32 Douro Valley Vineyard Trails

Do one trip in reverse: about four hours north from Vila Nova de Milfontes is a beautiful river valley producing sensational ports and reds.

28 Costa del Sol Beyond the Beaches

For more stunning coast, head east across the Spanish border to Seville and on to Nerja (423km) or Gibraltar (349km).

sand is winningly set at a rivermouth and flanked by imposing schist cliffs (try saying that with a mouthful of porridge...). It's a particularly good option for families, as smaller children can paddle on the peaceful river side of the strand while older kids tackle the waves on the ocean side. The beach is 3.5km from Odeceixe itself along a charming country road. At the beach, a small village has eating and surfing options. The Rota Vicentina, a long-distance walking path that leads right to the southwestern tip of Portugal, passes through Odeceixe, and there are great day walks in the vicinity.

The Drive » It's an easy 15km down the N120 to Aljezur, through woodland and open shrubland patched with heather and gorse.

- - - - - - - - - - - - - - -

TRIP HIGHLIGHT

④ Aljezur

The old part of Aljezur is an attractive village with a Moorish feel. A collection of cottages winds down the hill below a ruined 10th-century hilltop **castle** (⊘24hr). Aljezur is close to some fantastic beaches, edged by black rocks that reach into the white-tipped, bracing sea – surfing hot spots. The handsomest beach in the Aljezur area, on the north side of the picturesque rivermouth and backed by wild dunes, is **Praia da Amoreira**. It's 9km by road from Aljezur, signposted off the main road north of town.

The Drive » A couple of kilometres south of Aljezur, the beaches of Monte Clérigo and Arrifana are signposted off to the right. At the top of the hill, head right (towards Monte Clérigo) for the full coastal panorama before winding your way south to Arrifana.

- - - - - - - - - - - - - - -

⑤ Praia da Arrifana

Arrifana is a seductive fingernail-shaped cove embraced by cliffs. Just to add to the picturesqueness, it also sports an offshore pinnacle and a petite traditional fishing harbour. The beach is wildly popular with surfers of all abilities and there are several surf schools in the area. The beach break is reliable, but there's also a right-hand reef break that can offer some of the Algarve's best surfing when there's a big swell. There's a small, very popular beachside restaurant, and clifftop eateries near the ruined fortress up above, which offers breathtaking vistas. Good diving is also possible here.

The Drive » Praia de Vale Figueira is reached by a rough road that runs some 5km from the main road at a point 10km south of Aljezur. Before reaching the turnoff, you must turn right off the N120 on to the N268

- - - - - - - - - - - - - - -

⑥ Praia de Vale Figueira

One of the remoter west coast beaches, this is a long, wide and magnificent stretch of whitish sand with an ethereal beauty, backed by stratified cliffs hazy in the ocean spray. It's reached by a rough, partly paved road. The beach, which has no facilities, faces due west and has pretty reliable surf, especially when a southeaster is blowing. It's one of those lonely, romantic beaches

---

✓ **TOP TIP: FAMILY ATTRACTIONS**

This central section of the Algarve coast is great for families, with numerous water parks and other attractions in the area. Two of the most popular are **Slide & Splash** (☑282 340 800; www.slidesplash.com; Estrada Nacional 125; adult/child 5-10yr €26/19; ⊘10am-5pm, 6pm or 6.30pm daily May-Sep, Mon-Sat Apr & Oct) and **Aqualand** (☑282 320 230; www.aqualand.pt; N125, Sítio das Areias, Alcantarilha; adult/child €22.50/16.50; ⊘10am-6pm Jul & Aug, to 5pm late Jun & early Sep).

that's great to stroll on even when the weather's nasty.

The Drive » Head back to the main road and turn right onto it. It's about 10km from here to Carrapateira.

7 Carrapateira

Surf-central Carrapateira is a tranquil, pretty, spread-out village offering two fabulous beaches with spectacular settings and turquoise seas. Bordeira is a mammoth swath of sand merging into dunes 2km from the north side of town. Amado, with even better surf, is at the southern end. The circuit of both from Carrapateira (9km) is a visually stunning hike (or drive), with lookouts over the beaches and rocky coves and cliffs between them. In town, the **Museu do Mar e da Terra** (282 970 000; Rua de Pescador; adult/child €2.70/1.10; 10am-5pm Tue-Sat) is an intriguing place to visit, with great views.

The Drive » The N268 barrels on right down to Portugal's tip at Sagres (22km), via the regional centre of Vila do Bispo.

TRIP HIGHLIGHT

8 Sagres

The small, elongated village of Sagres, with a rich nautical history, has an appealingly out-of-the-way feel. It sits on a remote peninsula amid picturesque seaside scenery with a sculpted coastline and stern **fortress** (282 620 140; http://www.monumentosdoalgarve.pt/pt/monumentos-do-algarve/fortaleza-de-sagres; adult/child €3/1.50; 9.30am-8pm May-Sep, to 5.30pm Oct-Apr) giving access to a stunning clifftop walk. It also appeals for its access to fine beaches and water-based activities; it's especially popular with surfers. Outside town, the striking cliffs of **Cabo de São Vicente** (lighthouse complex 10am-6pm Tue-Sun Apr-Sep, to 5pm Oct-Mar), the southwesternmost point of Europe, make for an enchanting visit, especially at sunset. Make sure you pop into the small **museum** (adult/child €1.50/1; 10am-6pm Tue-Sun Apr-Sep, to 5pm Oct-Mar) here, which has interesting background on the Algarve's starring role in the Age of Discoveries. From Sagres' harbour, worthwhile excursions head out to observe dolphins and seabirds. **Mar Ilimitado** (916 832 625; www.marilimitado.com; Porto da Baleeira) is a recommended operator.

p469

The Drive » Head back to Vila do Bispo and turn right onto the N125 that will take you to Lagos, a total drive of 34km. Promising beach detours include Zavial and Salema.

TOP TIP: THE SAGRES EAT SCENE

A closely packed string of surfer-oriented places on Rua Comandante Matoso offer a bit of everything, whether it's a coffee or a caipirinha you're after: they are cafes by day, restaurants serving international favourites whatever time hunger drags you away from the beach, and lively bars by night. Further down the same street, near the port, is a cluster of more traditional Portuguese restaurants.

TRIP HIGHLIGHT

9 Lagos

Touristy, likeable Lagos lies on a riverbank, with 16th-century walls enclosing the old town's pretty, cobbled streets and picturesque plazas. A huge range of restaurants and pumping nightlife add to the allure provided by fabulous beaches and numerous watery activities. Aside from the hedonism, there's plenty of history here: start by visiting the lovably higgledy-piggledy **Museu Municipal** (282 762 301; Rua General Alberto da Silveira; adult/concession €3/1.50; 10am-12.30pm &

WHY THIS IS A GREAT TRIP
ANDY SYMINGTON, AUTHOR

I can't think of a more impressive series of beaches than those of Portugal's south; they are simply magical. There's a wild and unspoiled romance to the seasprayed west-coast strands, while a succession of sun-baked golden sands in the south includes intriguing island beaches only reachable by boat. I love wandering the region's tight-knit old towns too, trying to detect which lane that delicious aroma of grilling fish is coming from...

Top: Sagres at sunset
Left: Faro's cobbled old town
Right: Sunbathers at Praia da Rocha

2-5.30pm Tue-Sun), which incorporates the fabulous baroque church **Igreja de Santo António** (Rua General Alberto da Silveira; adult/child incl museum €3/1.50; ☺10am-12.30pm & 2-5.30pm Tue-Sun). Heading out on to the water is a must, perhaps cetacean-spotting with **Algarve Dolphins** (☏282 788 513; www.algarve-dolphins.com; adult/child from €35/25), kayaking with **Axessextreme** (☏919 114 649; www.axessextreme.com; 3hr tour €25) or learning to surf with **Lagos Surf Center** (☏282 764 734; www.lagossurfcenter.com; Rua da Silva Lopes 31; 1-/3-/5-day courses €55/150/225). East of town stretch the long, golden sands of Meia Praia, backed by worth-while beach restaurants.

✗ p469

The Drive 》 Portimão is really just along the coast from Lagos, but it's a 24km detour inland via the N125 in a car.

- - - - - - - - - - - - - - - - -

❿ Portimão & Praia da Rocha

The Algarve's second-largest town, Portimão's history dates back to the Phoenicians before it became the region's fish-ing and canning hub in the 19th century. Though that industry has since declined, it's still an in-triguing port with plenty of maritime atmosphere. Learn all about the town's fishing heritage in the excellent **Museu de Portimão** (☏282 405 230;

www.museudeportimao.pt;
Rua Dom Carlos I; adult/child
€3/free; 🕐2.30-6pm Tue,
10am-6pm Wed-Sun Sep-Jul,
7.30-11pm Tue, 3-11pm Wed-
Sun Aug), **before strolling
through the no-frills
sardine restaurants of
the fishermen's quarter
of Largo da Barca near
the road bridge. At the
southern end of Portimão
stretches the impressive
resort beach of Praia da
Rocha, backed by numer-
ous restaurants and
nightlife options.**

The Drive » The N125 leads
you east to the junction with the
N124-1, that takes you south to
Silves. It's a drive of only 20km.

⓫ Silves

Silves is one of the
Algarve's prettiest towns
and replete with history:
it was an important
trading city in Moorish
times and preserves a

tightly woven medieval
centre. At the top of the
town, its sizeable **castle**
(📞282 445 624; adult/conces-
sion/under 10yr €2.80/1.40/
free, joint ticket with Museu
Municipal de Arqueologia
€3.90; 🕐9am-8pm Jun-Aug,
to 6.30pm Mar-May & Sep-Nov,
to 5pm Dec-Feb) **offers great
views from the ramparts.
Originally occupied in
the Visigothic period,
what you see today dates
mostly from the Moorish
era, though the castle
was heavily restored in
the 20th century. Below
this, the atmospheric
cathedral** (Rua da Sé; admission €1; 🕐9am-12.30pm &
2-5pm Mon-Fri, plus 9am-1pm
Sat Jun-Aug) **is the region's
best-preserved Gothic
church. The Museu
Municipal** (📞282 444
838; Rua das Portas de Loulé;
adult/under 10yr €2.10/
free, joint ticket with Castelo
€3.90; 🕐10am-6pm) **gives
good background on**

the city's history and is
built around a fascinat-
ing Moorish-era well,
complete with spiral
staircase. The old-town
streets are great for
strolling.

The Drive » Cruise 14km
straight down the N124-1 to the
beach at Carvoeiro.

⓬ Carvoeiro

Carvoeiro is a cluster of
whitewashed buildings
rising up from tawny,
gold and green cliffs and
backed by hills. This
diminutive seaside resort
is prettier and more
laid-back than many of
the bigger resorts. The
town beach is pretty
but small and crowded,
however, there are lots
of other excellent op-
tions in the area. The
most picturesque of
all, with stunning rock
formations, is **Praia da
Marinha**, best reached by
the **Percurso dos Sete
Vales Suspensos** clifftop
walk, beginning at Praia
Vale Centianes, 2.3km
east of town.

🛏 p469

The Drive » Head back
to Lagoa to join the N125
eastwards. After 25km, turn
right and head towards the
coast, emerging atop the long
beach. It's a 37km total drive.

⓭ Praia da Falésia

This long straight strip
of sand offers one of the
region's most impressive
first glimpses of coast as

↱ DETOUR: MONCHIQUE

**Start: ⓾ Portimão & Praia da Rocha
(p465)**

High above the coast, in cooler mountainous
woodlands, the picturesque little town of Monchique
makes a lovely detour, with some excellent options
for day hikes, including climbing the Algarve's highest
hills, Picota and Fóia, for super views over the coast.
Monchique and the surrounding area have some
excellent eating choices and nearby Caldas de
Monchique is a sweet little spa hamlet in a narrow
wooded valley.

The N266 heads north from the N124 north of
Portimão; it's a 27km drive from Lagos to Monchique,
then another 30km on to Silves.

you arrive from above. It's backed by stunning cliffs in white and several shades of ochre, gouged by weather into intriguing shapes and topped by typical pines. The areas near the car parks get packed in summer (especially as high tides cover much of the beach), but as the strip is over 3km long, it's easy enough to walk and find plenty of breathing room. It's a good beach for strolling, as the cliffscape constantly changes colours and shapes, and there's a surprising range of hardy seaside plants in the cracks and crevices.

The Drive » Head back to the N125 and continue eastwards. Just after bypassing the town of Almancil, there's an exit to 'Almancil, São Lourenço, praias'. The church is signposted from here.

14 Igreja de São Lourenço de Matos

It's worth stopping here to visit the marvellous interior of this small **church** (Church of St Lawrence; Rua da Igreja; admission €2; 10am-1pm & 3-5pm Mon-Sat), built over a ruined chapel after local people, while digging a well, had implored the saint for help and then struck water. The resulting baroque masterpiece, built by fraternal masterteam Antão and Manuel Borges, is wall-to-wall *azulejos* (painted tiles)

inside, with beautiful panels depicting the life of the Roman-era saint, and his death by barbecue. In the 1755 earthquake, only five tiles fell from the roof.

The Drive » Back on the N125, head eastwards and after 12km you're in Faro.

TRIP HIGHLIGHT

15 Faro

The capital of the Algarve has a distinctly Portuguese feel and plenty to see. Its evocative waterside old town is very scenic and has several interesting sights, including the excellent **Museu Municipal** (289 897 400; Praça Dom Afonso III 14; adult/student €2/1; 10am-7pm Tue-Fri, 11.30am-6pm Sat & Sun Jun-Sep, 10am-6pm Tue-Fri, 10.30am-5pm Sat & Sun Oct-May), set in a former convent. The area is centred around Faro's **cathedral** (289 823 018; www.paroquiasedefaro.org; Largo da Sé; adult/child €3/free; 10am-6.30pm Mon-Fri, to 1pm Sat Jun-Aug, to 5pm Mon-Fri, to 1pm Sat Sep-May),

built in the 13th century but heavily damaged in the 1755 earthquake. What you see now is a variety of Renaissance, Gothic and Baroque features. Climb the tower for lovely views across the walled town and estuary islands. These islands are part of the Parque Natural da Ria Formosa and can be explored on excellent boat trips run by **Formosamar** (918 720 002; www.formosamar. com; Clube Naval, Faro Marina). The cathedral has a small bone chapel, but much spookier is the one at the **Igreja de Nossa Senhora do Carmo** (Largo do Carmo; chapel €2; 9am-1pm & 3-5pm or 6pm Mon-Fri, 9am-1pm Sat, mass 9am Sun), built from the mortal remains of over a thousand monks.

✗ p469

The Drive » It's 35km east along the N125 to Tavira. Despite the road's proximity to the coast, you won't see much unless you turn off: Fuzeta is a pleasant waterside village to investigate, with boat connections to island beaches.

MANFRED GOTTSCHALK / GETTY IMAGES ©

Tavira Saturday street bazaar

16 Tavira

Set on either side of the meandering Río Gilão, Tavira is a charming town. The ruins of a hilltop **castle** (Largo Abu-Otmane; ⊙8am-5pm Mon-Fri, 9am-7pm Sat & Sun, to 5pm winter), **now housing a pleasant little botanic garden, the Renaissance Igreja da Misericórdia** (Rua da Galeria; ⊙9am-1pm & 2-6pm Mon-Sat), **and the Núcleo Islâmico** (Praça da República 5; adult/child €2/1, joint admission with Palácio da Galeria €3/1.50; ⊙10am-12.30pm & 3-6pm mid-Jun–mid-Sep, 10am-4.30pm Tue-Sat mid-Sep–mid-Jun)

museum of Moorish history are among the attractions. It's ideal for wandering; the warren of cobblestone streets hides pretty, historic gardens and shady plazas. Tavira is the launching point for the stunning, unspoilt beaches of the Ilha de Tavira, a sandy island that's another part of the Ria Formosa park.

⏾ p469

The Drive ❯❯ Cacela Velha is 14km east of Tavira: head along the N125 and you'll see it signposted; it's 1km off the road.

17 Cacela Velha

Enchanting, small and cobbled, Cacela Velha is a huddle of white-washed cottages edged with bright borders, and has a pocket-sized fort, orange and olive groves, and gardens blazing with colour. It sits above a gorgeous stretch of sea, with a character-ful local bar, plus other restaurants, a church and heart-lifting views. From nearby Fábrica, you can get a boat across to the splendid Cacela Velha beach, which has a low-key LGBT scene in summer.

Eating & Sleeping

Zambujeira do Mar ❷

🛏 Herdade do Touril — Rural Inn €€
(📞937 811 627; www.herdadedotouril.pt; r from €90; @🐾) Four kilometres north of Zambujeira do Mar is this upmarket *quinta* building with rooms and apartments of the fluffy-pillow variety. Some are located within the original building (built in 1826), others are converted farm cottages. The rustic and contemporary design of this tranquil place has an African safari-lodge feel – without the lions. Instead, storks nest in nearby cliffs (note, this area is not safe for children). There's a seawater pool, a buffet breakfast and free bikes. Good taste, good choice.

Sagres ❽

🍴 A Casínha — Portuguese €€
(📞917 768 917; www.facebook.com/acasinha. restaurantesagres; Rua de São Vicente; mains €12-18; ⊕dinner Mon, lunch & dinner Tue-Sat) This cosy terracotta-and-white spot – built on the site of the owner's grandparents' house – serves up some fabulous Portuguese cuisine, including standout barbecued fish, a good variety of *cataplanas* for two (€34) and *arroz de polvo* (octopus rice). High quality and a pleasant atmosphere.

🛏 Pousada do Infante — Luxury Hotel €€€
(📞218 442 001, 282 620 240; www.pousadas. pt; Rua Patrão António Faustino; s/d €215/225, superior €260/270; P🕸@🛜🐾) This modern *pousada* has large rooms in a great setting near the clifftop. Count on green or orange interiors, handsome public areas and picture-perfect views from the terraces. A well priced, quality pick.

Lagos ❾

🍴 A Forja — Portuguese €€
(📞282 768 588; Rua dos Ferreiros 17; mains €8-15; ⊕noon-3pm & 6.30-10pm Sun-Fri) The

secret is out. This buzzing place pulls in the crowds – locals, tourists and expats – for its hearty, top-quality traditional food served in a bustling environment at great prices. Plates of the day are always reliable, as are the fish dishes.

Carvoeiro ⓬

🛏 O Castelo — Guesthouse €€
(📞919 729 259; www.ocastelo.net; Rua do Casino 59; d without view €65, with view €90-110; 🕸🛜) To the west of the bay, behind the *turismo*, this standout guesthouse with a welcoming and justifiably proud owner is recently renovated and gleamingly well-maintained. Rooms are most inviting; some share a large terrace and sea views (with sunrises), while one has a private balcony. They get all the details right; it's a stunning outlook and a lovely, lovely place.

Faro ⓯

🍴 Faz Gostos — Portuguese, French €€
(📞289 878 422; www.fazgostos.com; Rua do Castelo 13; mains €14-20; ⊕lunch & dinner Mon-Fri, dinner Sat; 🛜) Elegantly housed in the old town, this offers high-class French-influenced Portuguese cuisine in a spacious, comfortably handsome dining area. There's plenty of game, fish and meat on offer with rich and seductive sauces, and a few set menus are available.

Tavira ⓰

🛏 Casa Beleza do Sul — Apartment €€
(📞960 060 906; www.casabelezadosul.com; Rua Dr Parreira 43; apt €90-120; 🛜) A gorgeous historic house in central Tavira is showcased to full advantage in this beautiful conversion. The result is a cute studio and three marvellous suites of rooms, all different with original tiled floors and modern bathrooms. All have a kitchenette and there are numerous decorative and thoughtful touches that put this well above the ordinary. Minimum stays apply. Breakfast available for an extra charge.

NEED ^{TO} KNOW

CURRENCY
Euro (€)

LANGUAGE
Portuguese

VISAS
Generally not required for stays of up to 90 days (not at all for members of EU or Schengen countries). Some nationalities need a Schengen visa.

FUEL
Petrol stations (usually open 24 hours) can be found along major highways. Expect to pay €1.35 to €1.80 per litre.

RENTAL CARS
Auto Jardim (www.autojardim.com)

Hertz (www.hertz.com)

Holiday Autos (www.holidayautos.com)

Pepecar (www.pepecar.com)

IMPORTANT NUMBERS
Europe-wide emergencies (☎112)

International access code (☎00)

Country code (☎351)

Climate

Warm to hot summers, mild winters

The Douro
GO May–Sep

The Beiras
GO Jun & Sep

Lisbon
GO May & Jun

The Alentejo
GO May–Sep

The Algarve
GO Jun & Sep

When to Go

High Season (Jul & Aug)
» Accommodation prices increase 30%.

» Expect big crowds in the Algarve and coastal resort areas.

» Sweltering temperatures are commonplace.

» Warmer ocean temperatures.

Shoulder (Apr–Jun & Sep–Nov)
» Wildflowers and mild days are ideal for hikes and outdoor activities.

» Lively festivals take place in June.

» Crowds and prices are average.

» Colder ocean temperatures.

Low Season (Dec–Mar)
» Shorter, rainier days with freezing temperatures at higher elevations.

» Lower prices, fewer crowds.

» Attractions keep shorter hours.

» Frigid ocean temperatures.

Daily Costs

Budget: Less than €50

» Dorm bed: €15–22

» Basic hotel room for two: from €30

» Lunch special at a family-run restaurant: €7–9

» Second-class train ticket from Lisbon to Faro: from €22

Midrange: €50–120

» Double room in a midrange hotel: €50–100

» Lunch and dinner in a midrange restaurant: €22–35

» Admission to museums: €2–6

Top End: More than €120

» Boutique hotel room: from €120

» Dinner for two in a top restaurant: from €80

» Three-day surf course: €150

Eating

Tapas Bar Tapas and drinks; open longer hours than restaurants.

Pasteleria Bakery; good for pastries and coffee.

Vinoteca Wine bar where you order by the glass.

Cervejaria Beerhall; the place to go for snacks and draft beer (cerveja)

Price categories indicate the cost of a main course:

€	less than €10
€€	€10–20
€€€	more than €20

Sleeping

Casa no Campo Comfy village houses or farmhouses for hire in the countryside.

Pousadas State funded accommodation, often in castles, converted monasteries and old mansions.

Pensão Inexpensive, extremely basic guesthouses, often with shared bathrooms.

Price categories refer to a double room with bathroom in high season. Unless otherwise stated, breakfast is included in the price:

€	less than €60
€€	€60–120
€€€	more than €120

Arriving in Portugal

Aeroporto de Lisboa (Lisbon)

Rental cars There is a wide choice of car-hire companies at the airport.

Metro €1.90 (including €0.50 Viva Viagem card); red line from Aeroporto station; transfer at Alameda for blue line to Rossio and Baixa-Chiado. It's 20 minutes to the centre; frequent departures from 6.30am to 1am.

AeroBus €3.50; every 20 minutes from 7.45am to 8.15pm.

Taxis €12–€16; around 20 minutes to the centre.

Aeroporto de Faro (Faro)

Rental cars Car-rental agencies have desks in the airport.

Buses €1.60; every 30 minutes weekdays, every two hours weekends.

Taxis €10–€14; around 20 minutes to the centre.

Mobile Phones (Cell Phones)

Local SIM cards are widely available and can be used in European and Australian mobile phones. Not compatible with many North American or Japanese systems.

Internet Access

Wi-fi is available in most lodgings and cafes (and is usually free). Internet cafes are rare.

Money

ATMs widely available, except in the smallest villages. Credit cards accepted in midrange and high-end establishments.

Tipping

Menu prices indicate a service charge. Most people leave small change if satisfied: 5% is fine, 10% is considered generous.

Useful Websites

Lonely Planet (www.lonelyplanet.com) Destination information, articles, hotel bookings, traveller forums and more.

Portugal Tourism (www.visitportugal.com) Portugal's useful and official tourism authority.

RAC (www.rac.co.uk/drivingabroad) Information for British drivers on driving in Spain and Portugal.

Language

Portuguese pronunciation is not difficult because most sounds are also found in English. The exceptions are the nasal vowels (represented in our pronunciation guides by ng after the vowel), which are pronounced as if you're trying to make the sound through your nose; and the strongly rolled r (represented by rr in our pronunciation guides). Also note that the symbol zh sounds like the 's' in 'pleasure'. The stress generally falls on the second-last syllable of a word. In our pronunciation guides stressed syllables are indicated with italics.

PORTUGUESE BASICS

Hello.	*Olá.*	o·*laa*
Goodbye.	*Adeus.*	a·de·*oosh*
How are you?	*Como está?*	ko·moo shtaa
Fine, and you?	*Bem, e você?*	beng e vo·*se*
Excuse me.	*Faz favor.*	faash fa·*vor*
Sorry.	*Desculpe.*	desh·*kool*·pe
Yes.	*Sim.*	seeng
No.	*Não.*	nowng
Please.	*Por favor.*	poor fa·*vor*
Thank you.	*Obrigado.* (m)	o·bree·*gaa*·doo
	Obrigada. (f)	o·bree·*gaa*·da
You're welcome.	*De nada.*	de *naa*·da

What's your name?
Qual é o seu nome? kwaal e oo se·oo *no*·me

My name is ...
O meu nome é ... oo *me*·oo *no*·me e ...

Do you speak English?
Fala inglês? faa·la eeng·*glesh*

I don't understand.
Não entendo. nowng eng·*teng*·doo

DIRECTIONS

Where's (the station)?
Onde é (a estação)? ong·de e e (a shta·*sowng*)

Can you show me (on the map)?
Pode-me mostrar po·de·me moosh·*traar*
(no mapa)? (noo *maa*·pa)

EMERGENCIES

Help!	*Socorro!*	soo·ko·*rro*

I'm lost.
Estou perdido. (m) shtoh per·*dee*·doo
Estou perdida. (f) shtoh per·*dee*·da

ON THE ROAD

I'd like to hire a ...	*Queria alugar ...*	ke·*ree*·a a·loo·*gaar* ...
bicycle	*uma bicicleta*	oo·ma bee·see·*kle*·ta
car	*um carro*	oong *kaa*·rroo
motorcycle	*uma mota*	oo·ma *mo*·ta
child seat	*cadeira de criança*	ka·*day*·ra de kree·*ang*·sa
helmet	*capacete*	ka·pa·*se*·te
mechanic	*mecânico*	me·*kaa*·nee·koo
petrol/gas	*gasolina*	ga·zoo·*lee*·na
service station	*posto de gasolina*	*posh*·too de ga·zoo·*lee*·na

Want More?

For in-depth language information and handy phrases, check out Lonely Planet's *Portuguese Phrasebook.* You'll find them at **shop.lonelyplanet.com**.

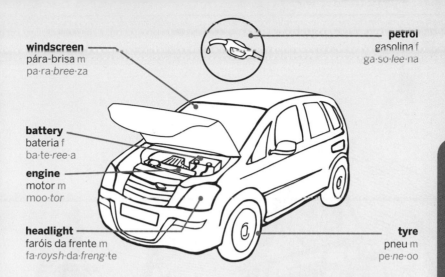

petrol
gasolina f
ga·so·lee·na

windscreen
pára-brisa m
pa·ra·bree·za

battery
bateria f
ba·te·ree·a

engine
motor m
moo·tor

headlight
faróis da frente m
fa·roysh·da·freng·te

tyre
pneu m
pe·ne·oo

How much for daily hire?
Quanto custa para   kwang·too koosh·ta pa ra
alugar por dia?   a·loo·gaar poor dee·a

How much for weekly hire?
Quanto custa para   kwang·too koosh·ta pa ra
alugar por semana?   a·loo·gaar poor se·ma·na

Do you have a road map?
Tem um mapa de   teng oong maa·pa de
estradas?   ·shtraa·dash

Is this the road to ...?
Esta é a estrada   esh·ta e a shtraa·da
para ...?   pa·ra ...

(How long) Can I park here?
(Quanto tempo)   (kwang·too teng·poo)
Posso estacionar   po·soo shta·see·oo·naar
aqui?   a·kee

What's the speed limit?
Qual é o limite de   kwaal e oo lee·mee·te de
velocidade?   ve·loo·see·daa·de

The car/motorbike has broken down (at ...).
O carro/A mota   oo kaa·rroo/a mo·ta
avariou-se (em ...).   a·va·ree·oh·se (eng ...)

I have a flat tyre.
Tenho um furo no   ta·nyoo oong foo·roo noo
pneu.   pe·ne·oo

I've run out of petrol.
Estou sem gasolina.   shtoh seng ga·zoo·lee·na

I need a mechanic.
Preciso de um   pre·see·zoo de oong
mecânico.   me·kaa·nee·koo

Can you fix it (today)?
Pode-se arranjar   po·de·se a·rrang·zhaar
(hoje)?   (o·zhe)

How long will it take?
Quanto tempo vai   kwang·too teng·poo vai
levar?   e·vaar

Signs

Pare	Stop
Dar Prioridade	Give Way
Proibido el Paso	No Entry
Entrada	Entrance
Portagem	Toll
Sentido Unico	One Way
Sair da Autoestrada	Freeway Exit

Germany

GRANDIOSE CITIES, STORYBOOK VILLAGES, VINE-STITCHED VALLEYS AND BUCOLIC LANDSCAPES that beg you to toot your horn, leap out of the car and jump for joy – road-tripping in Germany is a mesmerising kaleidoscope of brilliant landscapes and experiences.

The trips in this section take you for a spin from Germany's edgy cities to fabled Rhine vineyards and the medieval walled towns of Bavaria. Whether you want to cruise past castles, sample wine or climb into the foothills of the Alps, we have something for you.

Rothenburg ob der Tauber Traditional half-timbered buildings

Germany

Würzburg Residenz

DON'T MISS

Cologne
The star of the region, Cologne makes its statement from the moment you spot the twin spires of the legendary Dom. See it on Trip **34**

Wine Tasting
Learn to love Germany's often excellent white wines. Sip exquisite vintages at the source in cosy wineries amid the vineyards on Trip **34**

Würzburg Residenz
Ogle the world's largest fresco at Würzburg's magnificent Unesco-listed palace. Get your ticket as part of Trip **35**

Neuschwanstein Castle
The world's most famous castle inspired Walt Disney's citadel and strikes a fairytale pose against Alpine forests. Book your tour on Trip **35**

Romantic Rhine

34

After traversing powerhouse riverside cities Düsseldorf, Cologne and Bonn, watch epic scenery unfold as Germany's Romantic Rhine valley carves between towering cliffs clad in forest and capped by castles, to delightful Mainz.

TRIP HIGHLIGHTS

START
Düsseldorf

198 km

Rüdesheim
Escape the crowds by hiking into the picturesque vineyards

Cologne

Koblenz

7

Loreley

13

14 **FINISH**

Boppard
One of the Romantic Rhine's prettiest towns

155 km

Mainz
Home to rustic wine taverns and a magnificent cathedral

235 km

5–7 DAYS
235 KM / 146 MILES

GREAT FOR...

BEST TIME TO GO
April to October offers the best weather, but July and August can be crowded.

ESSENTIAL PHOTO
Boat-shaped toll castle Pfalzgrafstein on a Rhine island.

BEST FOR OUTDOORS
Hike through the vines above Rüdesheim.

34 Romantic Rhine

Boats gliding down the Rhine give passengers mesmerising views of the medieval villages, craggy hillsides, and castle after castle floating past. But on this trip you'll get up close to its mightiest sights, hike through its loftiest vineyards and discover hidden treasures and romantic hideaways you'd never see from the water. (Though you'll have plenty of opportunities en route to board a cruise, too.)

❶ Düsseldorf

Survey the mighty Rhine from Düsseldorf's **Medienhafen**. This old harbour area continues to attract red-hot restaurants, bars, hotels and clubs. Crumbling warehouses have transformed into high-tech office buildings and now rub shoulders with bold new structures designed by celebrated international architects, including Frank Gehry.

Of course, no visit to Düsseldorf is complete without exploring its **Altstadt** (old town), which claims to be the 'longest bar in the world'.

The Drive ❱❱ It's a 44km drive from Düsseldorf south via the B1 and the A57 to Cologne (fear not: although this section mainly travels through built-up areas and industrial estates, later stages of the drive become much more scenic).

❷ Cologne

A walking tour (see p522) is the best way to appreciate this engaging city (Germany's fourth-largest) on the Rhine.

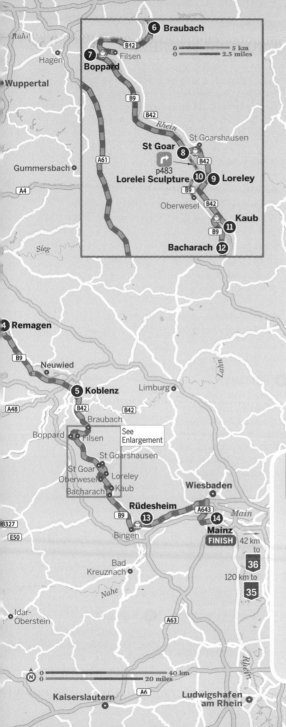

Must-sees include Cologne's world famous **Kölner Dom** (Cologne Cathedral; ☎0211-1794 0200; www.koelner-dom.de; tower adult/concession €4/2; ◷6am-9pm May-Oct, to 7.30pm Nov-Apr, tower 9am-6pm May-Sep, to 5pm Mar-Apr & Oct, to 4pm Nov-Feb), whose twin spires dominate the skyline, as well as superb museums such as the **Römisch-Germanisches Museum** (Roman Germanic Museum; ☎0221-2212 4438; www.museenkoeln.de; Roncalliplatz 4; adult/concession €9/5; ◷10am-5pm Tue-Sun); sculptures and ruins displayed outside its entrance are the overture to its symphony of Roman artefacts found along the Rhine.

The Drive » Drive south along the B51 along the Rhine's western bank before joining the A555 to bring you into Bonn (29km all-up).

LINK YOUR TRIP

36 German Fairy Tale Road

Get on the trail of the Brothers Grimm 65km west of Mainz in Hanau.

35 The Romantic Road

This ribbon of historical quaintness starts at Würzburg, two hours (154km) west from Mainz.

481

❸ Bonn

In a beautiful riverside setting, Ludwig van Beethoven's home town warrants a stop to visit the **Beethoven-Haus Bonn** (📞0228-981 7525; www.beethoven-haus-bonn.de; Bonngasse 24-26; adult/concession €6/4.50; ◷10am-6pm Apr-Oct, 10am-5pm Mon-Sat, 11am-5pm Sun Nov-Mar), where the great composer was born in 1770. Other landmarks include the soaring **Münster Basilica** (📞0228-985 880; www.bonner-muenster.de; Münsterplatz; ◷7am-7pm), built on the graves of the two martyred Roman soldiers who later became the city's patron saints.

Bonn's old government quarter dates from its time as West Germany's 'temporary' capital, between 1949 and 1991 (when a reunited German government decided to move to Berlin). For a romp through recent German history from the end of WWII, pop by the **Haus der Geschichte der Bundesrepublik Deutschland** (Museum of History; 📞0228-916 50; www.hdg.de; Willy-Brandt-Allee 14; ◷9am-7pm Tue-Fri, 10am-6pm Sat & Sun).

The Drive » From Bonn, take the B9 southeast for 24km to Remagen. When you leave the German state of North Rhine-Westphalia and enter Rhineland-Palatinate the road returns to the river's western bank; on your right-hand side, you'll see the hilly wildlife park Wildpark Rolandseck.

CROSSING THE RHINE

No bridges span the Rhine between Koblenz and Mainz; the only way to cross the river along this stretch is by **Autofähre** (car ferry). Prices vary slightly but you can figure on paying about €4.20 per car, including driver; €1.20 per car passenger; €1.30 per pedestrian (€0.80 for a child); and €2.50 for a bicycle, including the rider.

Bingen–Rüdesheimer (www.bingen-ruedesheimer.com; ◷5.30am-9.45pm Sun-Thu & 5.30am-12.50am Fri & Sat May-Oct, 5.30am-9.45pm Nov-Apr)

Boppard–Filsen (www.faehre-boppard.de; ◷6.30am-10pm Jun-Aug, 6.30am-9pm Apr, May & Sep, 6.30am-8pm Oct-Mar)

Niederheimbach–Lorch (www.mittelrhein-faehre.de; ◷6am-7.50pm Apr-Oct, 6am-6.50pm Nov-Mar)

Oberwesel–Kaub (www.faehre-kaub.de; ◷6am-8pm Mon-Sat & 8am-8pm Sun Apr-Sep, 6am-7pm Mon-Sat & 8am-7pm Sun Oct-Mar)

St Goar–St Goarshausen (www.faehre-loreley.de; ◷5.30am-midnight Mon-Sat, 6.30am-midnight Sun)

---

❹ Remagen

Remagen was founded by the Romans in AD 16 as Rigomagus, but the town would hardly figure in the history books were it not for one fateful day in early March 1945. As the Allies raced across France and Belgium to rid Germany of Nazism, the Wehrmacht tried frantically to stave off defeat by destroying all bridges across the Rhine.

But the Brücke von Remagen (the steel rail bridge at Remagen) lasted long enough for Allied troops to cross the river, contributing significantly to the collapse of Hitler's western front. One of the bridge's surviving basalt towers now houses the **Friedensmuseum** (Peace Museum; 📞218 63; www.bruecke-remagen.de; adult/child €3.50/1; ◷10am-5pm early Mar-mid-Nov, to 6pm May-Oct), with a well-presented exhibit on Remagen's pivotal role in WWII.

The Drive » Take the B9 southeast for 49km. The Rhine winds back and forth away from the road until you come to the city of Koblenz. Stay on the B9 until you've crossed the Moselle River to the town centre, or risk getting lost in a maze of concentric flyovers.

---

❺ Koblenz

Koblenz sits at the confluence of the Rhine and Moselle Rivers – marked by the expansive **Deutsches**

Eck (German Corner), adjoining flower-filled parks and promenades – and the convergence of three low mountain ranges (the Hunsrück, the Eifel and the Westerwald). Its roots date back to the Romans, who founded a military stronghold (Confluentes) here because of the site's supreme strategic value.

On the Rhine's right bank, the 118m-high fortress **Festung Ehrenbreitstein** (www. diefestungehrenbreitstein.de; adult/child €6/3, incl cable car €11.80/5.60; ☉10am-6pm Apr-Oct, to 5pm Nov-Mar) proved indestructible to all but Napoleonic troops, who levelled it in 1801. To prove a point, the Prussians rebuilt it as one of Europe's mightiest fortifications. It's acces-sible by car, on foot and by cable car.

Inside Koblenz' striking new glass **Forum Confluentes**, exhibits at the **Mittelrhein-Museum** (www.mittelrhein-museum. de; Zentralplatz 1; adult/child €10/7; ☉10am-6pm Tue-Sun) span 2000 years of the region's history, including 19th-century landscape paintings of the Romantic Rhine by German and British artists.

🛏 p489

The Drive ›› Take the B49 across the Rhine to its eastern bank and travel south on the B42; it's 13km to Braubach. At this point of the drive, you leave the cityscapes behind and enter an older world of cobblestones, half-timbered villages, densely forested hillsides and ancient vineyards.

⑥ Draubach

Framed by forest, vineyards and rose gardens, the 1300-year-old town of Braubach centres on its small, half-timbered **Marktplatz**.

High above Braubach are the dramatic towers, turrets and crenellations of the 700-year-old **Marksburg** (www.marksburg. de; adult/child €64; ☉10am-5pm mid-Mar–Oct, 11am-4pm Nov–mid-Mar), which is unique among the Rhine's fastnesses as it was never destroyed. The compulsory tour takes in the citadel, the Gothic hall and a grisly torture chamber. English tours depart at 1pm and 4pm from late March to October.

↱ DETOUR: OBERWESEL

Start: ⑧ St Goar (p486)

It's a quick 7.8km south from St Goar along the B9 to the village of Oberwesel.

Every April, Oberwesel crowns not a *Weinkönigin* (wine queen), as in most Rhine towns, but a *Weinhexe* (wine witch) – a good witch, of course – who is said to protect the vineyards. Photos of all the *Weinhexen* crowned since 1946 are displayed in the cellar of Oberwesel's **Kulturhaus** (www.kulturhaus-oberwesel.de; Rathausstrasse 23; adult/child €3/1; ☉10am-5pm Tue-Fri, 2-5pm Sat & Sun Apr-Oct), along with 19th-century engravings of the Romantic Rhine and models of Rhine riverboats.

Hidden sky-high up a vineyard-striped hillside, the flagstone terrace of **Günderode Haus** (www.guenderodefilmhaus.de; Siebenjungfrauenblick; ☉11am-6pm Sat-Thu, to 8pm Fri Apr-Oct, reduced hours Nov-Mar) is an incredible spot for a glass of wine, beer or brandy, with sweeping views over the Rhine. The adjacent 200-year-old half-timbered house was used as a film set for *Heimat 3* (2004), and now has a cinema room and hosts live music and literary events, as well as wine tastings. From Oberwesel, take the K93 east for 600m, turn right (north) onto the K95; after 1km, the car park's on your right.

WHY THIS IS A GREAT TRIP
CATHERINE LE NEVEZ, AUTHOR

The romance along this stretch of the Rhine is timeless. Poets and painters including Lord Byron and William Turner are among those who have been inspired by this castle-crowned, forest-and-vineyard-cloaked valley. A fabled stop on the original European Grand Tour, the riverscape here is now a designated Unesco World Heritage site. It doesn't get more classic than that.

Top: The Rhine and the town of Boppard on the bend
Left: Natascha Alexandrova's *Lorelei* sculpture
Right: Cologne's Kölner Dom illuminated at dusk

The Drive » Hug the eastern bank of the Rhine for 11km as it curves around to the car-ferry dock at Filsen. It's a five-minute crossing to charming Boppard.

- - - - - - - - -

TRIP HIGHLIGHT

❼ Boppard

Idyllically located on a horseshoe bend in the river, Boppard (pronounced 'bo-*part*') is one of the Romantic Rhine's prettiest towns, not least because its riverfront and historic centre are both on the same side of the railway tracks.

Boppard's riverfront promenade, the **Rhein-allee**, has grassy areas for picnicking and a children's playground.

Many of the town's half-timbered buildings house cosy wine taverns, including its oldest, **Weinhaus Heilig Grab** (www.heiliggrab.de; Zelkesgasse 12; ☺3pm-midnight Wed-Mon). In summer you can sip local rieslings under the chestnut trees, where live music plays on weekends.

Fantastic hiking trails fan out into the countryside, including the **Hunsrück Trails**, accessed by Germany's steepest scheduled railway route, the **Hunsrückbahn** (adult/child one-way €2.90/1.75; ☺hourly 10am-6pm Apr-Oct, to 4pm Nov-Mar). Around the **Vierseenblick** (Four-Lakes-View), a panoramic outlook reached by **Sesselbahn** (chair lift; http://sesselbahn-boppard.de; adult/child return €7.50/4.50, one-way €4.80/3; ☺10am-5pm Apr-Oct) creates the illusion that you're looking at four separate lakes rather than a single river.

The Drive » Take the B9 south from Boppard for 15km, passing Burg Maus across the river on the eastern bank near the village of Wellmich. Shortly afterwards, you'll spot Burg Rheinfels on the western bank above St Goar.

❽ St Goar

Lording over the village of St Goar are the sprawling ruins of **Burg Rheinfels** (www.st-goar. de; adult/child €5/2.50; ⏰9am-6pm mid-Mar–late Oct, 11am-5pm late Oct–mid-Nov), at one time the mightiest fortress on the Rhine. Built in 1245 by Count Dieter von Katzeneln-bogen as a base for his toll-collecting operations, its size and labyrinthine layout are astonishing. Kids (and adults) will love exploring the sub-terranean tunnels and galleries (bring a torch). From St Goar's northern edge, follow the Schloss-berg road to the castle.

✗ 🛏 p489

The Drive » At St Goar, take the five-minute car ferry across to the little village of St Goarshausen. From St Goarshausen's Marktplatz, follow the L338 as it twists steeply uphill through thick forest for 1.2km and turn right onto the K89 for 2.5km to reach Lorcley.

CAT & MOUSE

Two rival castles stand either side of the village of St Goarshausen. Burg Peterseck was built by the archbishop of Trier to counter the toll practices of the powerful Katzenelnbogen family. The latter responded by building a much bigger castle high on the other side of town, Burg Neukatzenelnbogen, which was dubbed **Burg Katz**, meaning 'Cat Castle'. Highlighting the obvious imbalance of power between the Katzenelnbogens and the archbishop, Burg Peterseck was soon nicknamed **Burg Maus** (Mouse Castle). Both are closed to the public.

❾ Loreley

The most storied spot along the Romantic Rhine, Loreley is an enormous, almost vertical slab of slate that owes its fame to a mythical maiden whose siren songs are said to have lured sailors to their death in the river's treach-erous currents. Heinrich Heine told the tale in his 1824 poem *Die Lorelei*.

On the edge of the plateau 4km southeast of the village of St Goar-shausen, visitor centre **Loreley Besucherzen-trum** (📞06771-599 093; www.loreley-besucherzentrum. de; Loreleyring 7; adult/child €2.50/1.50, parking €2; ⏰10am-6pm Apr-Oct, 10am-5pm Mar, 11am-4pm Sat & Sun Nov-Feb) covers the Loreley myth and local flora, fauna, shipping and winemaking traditions. A 300m gravel path leads to a **viewpoint** at the tip

of the Loreley outcrop 190m above the river.

The Drive » Return to the B42 at the bottom of the hill; on your left, you'll see Burg Katz. Travel south for 2km to the car park by the breakwater for the next stop, the Lorelei Sculpture.

❿ Lorelei Sculpture

At the tip of a narrow breakwater jutting into the Rhine, a bronze sculpture of Loreley's famous maiden perches lasciviously atop a rocky platform. From the car park, you can walk the 600m out to the sculpture, from where there are fantastic views of both riverbanks, but be aware that the rough path is made from jag-ged slate (wear sturdy shoes!) and the gentler sandy lower path is often underwater.

The Drive » Leaving the car park, take the B42 south for 8km to the little village of Kaub, and park next to the ferry dock.

⑪ Kaub

Kaub is the gateway to one of the river's iconic sights. Like something out of a fairy tale, 1326-built, boat-shaped toll castle **Pfalzgrafstein** (www.burg-pfalzgrafenstein.de; adult/child €3/2; ⏰10am-6pm Tue-Sun Apr-Oct, 10am-5pm Mar, 10am-5pm Sat & Sun Nov, Jan & Feb, closed Dec), with distinctive white-painted walls, red trim, and slate turrets, perches on a narrow island in the middle of the Rhine. A once-dangerous rapid here (since modified) forced boats to use the right-hand side of the river, where a chain forced ships to stop and pay a toll. The island makes for a fabulous picnic spot.

Alongside Kaub's car ferry dock you can hop on a little **Fährboot** (propelled boat; adult/child €2.50/1; ⏰every 30min 10am-6pm Tue-Sun Apr-Oct, 10am-5pm Mar, 10am-5pm Sat & Sun Nov, Jan & Feb, closed Dec) passenger ferry (it only runs from this side of the river).

The Drive » From Kaub, take the car ferry across to the Rhine's western bank and head south on the B9 for 3km to Bacharach.

⑫ Bacharach

Tiny Bacharach conceals its considerable charms behind a 14th-century wall. Enter one of the thick arched gateways under the train tracks and you'll find yourself in a medieval old town filled with half-timbered mansions.

It's possible to walk almost all the way around the centre on top of the walls. The lookout tower on the upper section of the wall affords panoramic views.

Dating from 1421, **Zum Grünen Baum** (www.weingut-bastian-bacharach.de; Oberstrasse 63; ⏰noon-midnight Apr-Oct, reduced hours Nov-Mar) serves some of Bacharach's best whites in rustic surrounds. Its nearby **Vinothèque** (www.weingut-bastian-bacharach.de/vinothek; Koblenzer Strasse 1;

CRUISING THE RHINE

If you'd like to let someone else drive for a while and get a different perspective of the Rhine, it's easy to park up and hop on a cruise boat.

From about Easter to October (winter services are very limited), passenger ships run by **KD** (Köln-Düsseldorfer; ☎0221-208 8318; www.k-d.com) link Rhine villages on a set timetable:

» You can travel to the next village or all the way between Mainz and Koblenz (one-way/return €50/55, downstream Mainz to Koblenz/upstream Koblenz to Mainz 5½/eight hours).

» Within the segment you've paid for (for example, Boppard–Rüdesheim, which costs €25.40/26.80 one-way/return), you can get on and off as often as you like, but make sure to ask for a free stopover ticket each time you disembark.

» Children up to the age of four travel free, while those up to age 13 are charged a flat fee of €6 regardless of distance.

» Return tickets usually cost only slightly more than one-way.

» To bring along a bicycle, there's a supplement of €2.80.

Several smaller companies also send passenger boats up and down the river:

Bingen-Rüdesheimer (www.bingen-ruedesheimer.com)

Hebel Linie (www.hebel-linie.de)

Loreley Linie (www.loreley-linie.com)

Rössler Linie (www.roesslerlinie.de)

⏱3-5pm Mon-Fri & 11am-6pm Sat & Sun Apr-Oct, 3-5pm Mon-Fri Nov-Mar), by contrast, is state of the art. Owner Friedrich Bastian is a renowned opera singer, so music (and culinary) events take place year-round, including on Bastian's private river island with its own vineyard.

🛏 p489

The Drive » Head south on the B9, passing Burg Reichenstein, then Burg Rheinstein, on your right. Then, on your left, in the river itself, you'll pass the Mäuseturm, a fortified tower used as a signal station until 1974. Drive through the busy working town of Bingen to the car-ferry dock at its eastern edge, and cross the river to Rüdesheim.

----

⑬ Rüdesheim

Depending on how you look at it, Rüdesheim's town centre – and especially its most famous feature, the tunnel-like medieval alley **Drosselgasse** – is either a touristy nightmare or a lot of kitschy, colourful fun. But there's also wonderful walking in the greater area, which is part of the Rheingau wine region, famed for its superior rieslings.

For a stunning Rhine panorama, head up the wine-producing slopes west of Rüdesheim to the **Niederwald Monument**. Erected between 1877 and 1883, this bombastic monument celebrates the

Prussian victory in the Franco-Prussian War and the creation of the German Reich, both in 1871. To save climbing 203 vertical metres, glide above the vineyards aboard the 1400m-long **Seilbahn** (Kabinenbahn; www.seilbahn-ruedesheim.de; Oberstrasse 37; adult/child one-way €5/2.50, return €7/3.50, with Sesselbahn €8/4; ⏱10am-5.30pm Mon-Fri, to 6pm Sat & Sun May-Sep, 10am-5pm Mon-Fri, to 5.30pm Sat & Sun Apr & Oct) cable car. A network of hiking trails extends from the monument.

🛏 p489

The Drive » From Rüdesheim, head east on the B42 for 23km and turn south on the A643 to cross the bridge over the Rhine. From here it's 13km southeast to the centre of Mainz.

----

⑭ Mainz

The Rhine River meets the Main at lively Mainz, which has a sizeable university, pretty pedestrian precincts and a *savoir vivre* dating from Napoleon's occupation (1797–1814).

Strolling along the Rhine and sampling local wines in an **Altstadt** tavern are as much a part of any Mainz visit as viewing the sights. Try the 1791 **Weinstube Hottum** (Grebenstrasse 3; ⏱4pm-midnight), serving wines purely from the Rheingau and Rheinhessen regions,

or vine-draped **Weingut Michel** (www.michel-wein.de; Jakobsbergstrasse 8; ⏱4pm-midnight), Mainz' only *Weingut* (winery) to exclusively serve its own wines.

Highlights you won't want to miss include the fabulous **Mainzer Dom** (📞06131-253 412; www.mainz-dom.de; Markt 10; ⏱9am-6.30pm Mon-Fri, to 4pm Sat, 12.45-3pm & 4-6.30pm Sun, shorter hours Nov-Feb), the ethereal windows of Chagall in **St-Stephan-Kirche** (www.st-stephan-mainz.de; Kleine Weissgasse 12; ⏱10am-5pm Mon-Sat, noon-5pm Sun Mar-Oct, 10am-4.30pm Mon-Sat, noon-4.30pm Sun Nov-Feb), and the first printed Bible in the **Gutenberg-Museum Mainz** (www.gutenberg-museum.de; Liebfrauenplatz 5; adult/child €5/2; ⏱9am-5pm Tue-Sat, 11am-5pm Sun). This museum commemorates native son Johannes Gutenberg who ushered in the information age here in the 15th century by perfecting movable type.

Also well worth a visit is the dungeon-like, brilliantly illuminated Roman archaeological site **Heiligtum der Isis und Mater Magna** (www.isis-mainz.de; Römer Passage 1; admission by donation; ⏱10am-6pm Mon-Sat). The easy-to-miss entrance is on the Römer Passage mall's ground floor just inside the western entrance.

🍴 p489

Eating & Sleeping

Koblenz ⑤

🛏 Hotel Stein · Boutique Hotel €€

(📞0261-963 530; www.hotel-stein.de; Mayener Strasse 126; s/d from €85/110; 🅿🛜) Decorated in zesty colours such as tangerine contrasted with dark timbers, Stein's 30 contemporary rooms are all soundproofed for a peaceful night's sleep. The hotel is situated across the Moselle River 2km north of Koblenz' city centre but you won't need to leave to dine: its superb gourmet restaurant Schiller's utilises premium ingredients like white aspargus, scampi, foie gras and truffles.

St Goar ⑧

🍴 Weinhotel Landsknecht · German €€

(📞06741-2001; www.hotel-landsknecht.de; Aussiedlung Landsknecht 4; mains €14-27.50, 4-course dinner menu €42; 🕙noon-2.30pm & 6-9pm Apr-Oct, noon-2.30pm & 6-9pm Wed-Sun Nov, Dec & Mar, closed Jan & Feb) The dining room and terrace at this wonderful spot 1.5km north of St Goar feel like being aboard a cruise boat, with close-up, uninterrupted river views. Sensational home cooking spans pickled salmon with quince mousse to schnitzel with mushroom and riesling sauce, and red-wine-marinated plums with rosemary-and-vanilla ice cream. Many of its rooms (doubles from €90) also have Rhine views.

🛏 Romantik Hotel Schloss Rheinfels · Historic Hotel €€€

(📞06741-8020; www.schloss-rheinfels.de; s/d weekday from €95/130, weekend €110/140; 🅿@🛜♨) Part of the Burg Rheinfels (p486) castle complex is occupied by a romantic hotel with 64 rooms and suites that range in size from tiny to palatial. All have antique-style furnishings; pricier rooms come with a river view. The hotel has three fine restaurants: one rustic, one semiformal and one gourmet.

Bacharach ⑫

🛏 Rhein Hotel · Hotel €€

(📞06743-1243; www.rhein-hotel-bacharach.de; Langstrasse 50; s €39-68, d €78-136; 🅿❄🛜) Right on the town's medieval ramparts, this welcoming family-run hotel has 14 well-lit rooms with original artwork. Rooms facing the river, and so the train tracks, have double-glazing Guests can borrow bikes for free. Its **Stübers Restaurant** (📞06743-1243; Langstrasse 50; mains €17-23; 🕙11.30am-2.15pm & 5.30-9.15pm Wed-Mon; 🍴) is top-notch.

Rüdesheim ⑬

🛏 Rüdesheimer Schloss · Boutique Hotel €€

(📞06722-905 00; www.ruedesheimer-schloss. com; Steingasse 10; s €95-115, d €125-155, ste €155-165; 🅿🛜) Truly good places to sleep and eat are thin on the ground in Rüdesheim, but this 18th-century building has 26 stunning contemporary rooms designed by local and regional artists. Its restaurant is excellent, serving dishes such as cheese and riesling soup, veal liver with truffled mash, and roast duck stuffed with dates and figs, with a live pianist and after-dinner dancing

Mainz ⑭

🍴 Zur Kanzel · German, French €€€

(📞06131-237 137; www.zurkanzel.de; Grebenstrasse 4; mains €8-23.50; 🕙kitchen 5-11pm Mon-Fri, noon-4pm & 6-11pm Sat) Germany meets France at this dark-timber-panelled *Weinstube* (wine bar) in dishes such as grilled tuna with riesling and sage sauce, garlic-crusted rack of lamb with wilted spinach, schnitzel with Frankfurt-style *Grüne Sosse* (green sauce) and rump steak with herb butter, as well as garlic snails. All ingredients are fresh, so the menu evolves with the seasons; there's a lovely summer courtyard. Cash only.

The Romantic Road

35

On this trip you'll experience the Germany of the bedtime story-book – medieval walled towns, gabled townhouses, cobbled squares and crooked streets, all preserved as if time has come to a standstill.

TRIP HIGHLIGHTS

0 km

Würzburg
One of Germany's finest baroque palaces is here

99 km

Rothenburg ob der Tauber
Wander the streets of this medieval marvel

149 km

Dinkelsbühl
The Romantic Road's quaintest town

350 km

Neuschwanstein & Hohenschwangau Castles
Two of Germany's finest castles

Nördlingen

Augsburg

Schongau

10 DAYS
350 KM / 218 MILES

GREAT FOR...

BEST TIME TO GO
Any time of year.

ESSENTIAL PHOTO
The half-timbered buildings of Rothenburg ob der Tauber's Plönlein.

BEST TWO DAYS
The stretch between stops 4 and 6 takes in the most romantic towns of the Romantic Road.

Dinkelsbühl Gabled houses

The Romantic Road

From the vineyards of Würzburg to the foot of the Alps, the Romantic Road (Romantische Strasse) is by far the most popular of Germany's touring routes. This well-trodden trail cuts through a cultural and historical cross-section of southern Germany, coming to a climax at the gates of King Ludwig II's crazy castles. The route links some of Germany's most picturesque towns, many appearing untouched since medieval times.

35 km to **36**
85 km to **34**
A3

Tauberbischofsheim B81
2

A81

Burg
Guttenberg

Heilbronn

Schwäbisch
Hall

Backnang

Ludwigsburg

Schwäbisc
Gmun

Stuttgart B29

Göppinge

Reutlingen

B311

Pfullendorf

Bad
Waldsee

Weingarten
Ravensburg

Meersburg

Friedrichshafen
Konstanz 31

Lindau
Lake Constance
Arbon
SWITZERLAND Bregenz

A1 St Gallen

TRIP HIGHLIGHT

❶ Würzburg

This scenic town in Bavaria's northeast corner straddles the Main River and is renowned for its art, architecture and delicate wines. A large student population keeps things lively and plenty of hip nightlife pulsates through its cobbled streets.

Top billing here goes to the **Würzburg Residenz** (www.residenz-wuerzburg.de; Balthasar-Neumann-Promenade; adult/concession/under 18yrs €7.50/6.50/free; ⊙9am-6pm Apr-Oct, 10am-4.30pm Nov-Mar, 45 min English tours 11am & 3pm, also 4.30pm Apr-Oct), a vast Unesco-listed palace, built by 18th-century architect Balthasar Neumann as the home of the local prince-bishops. It's one of Germany's most important and beautiful baroque palaces. The wonderful zigzagging Treppenhaus (Staircase) is capped by what is still the world's largest fresco, a masterpiece by Giovanni Battista Tiepolo depicting allegories of the four then-known continents (Europe, Africa, America and Asia). The recently renovated **Dom St Kilian** (www.dom-wuerzburg. de; Domstrasse 40; ⊙8am-7pm

Map Labels

Würzburg ① START

Main

Weikersheim ③

Rothenburg ob der Tauber ④

L1040

Dinkelsbühl ⑤

Nördlingen ⑥

Aalen

Harburg ⑦

Donauwörth ⑧

Donau

Augsburg ⑨

Landsberg am Lech ⑩

Schongau ⑪

Wieskirche ⑫

Füssen ⑬ ⑭ FINISH

Neuschwanstein & Hohenschwangau Castles

AUSTRIA

Erlangen
Fürth   **Nuremberg**
Schwabach
Ansbach
Altmühl
Gunzenhausen
Weissenburg

Eichstätt & the Altmühltal Nature Park
p498

Donau
Donau

Memmingen
Kaufbeuren
Leutkirch
Marktoberdorf
Kempten

Ammersee
Wurmsee
Weilheim
Staffelsee
Garmisch-Partenkirchen
Zugspitze (2962m) Mittenwald
Alpsee

0 — 40 km
0 — 20 miles

Mon-Sat, 8am-8pm Sun) is a highly unusual cathedral with a Romanesque core and the baroque Schönbornkapelle by Balthasar Neumann.

 p502

The Drive » The 37km between Würzburg and the next stop, Tauberbischofsheim, is best tackled in the following way: from the centre of Würzburg take the B19 south until it joins the A3 motorway; follow this until the junction with the B81, which goes all the way to Tauberbischofsheim.

- - - - - - - - - - -

② Tauberbischofsheim

The main town of the pretty Tauber Valley, this small settlement has a picturesque marketplace dominated by a neo-Gothic town hall and lined with typical half-timbered houses. Follow the remains of the medieval town walls

GERMANY **35** THE ROMANTIC ROAD

LINK YOUR TRIP

36 German Fairy Tale Road

Do one of the trips in reverse: the start of the Grimm Brothers' Fairy Tale Road is about an hour east from Würzburg.

34 Romantic Rhine

Würzburg is two hours (154km) from Mainz, at the end of this castle-lined riverside jaunt.

to the Kurmainzisches Schloss, which now houses the **Tauberfränkisches Landschaftsmuseum** (Schlossplatz; admission €2; ⊘2-4.30pm Tue-Sat, 10am-noon & 2-4.30pm Sun Easter-Oct), where you can learn more about Tauberbischofsheim's past.

The Drive » The 34km dash from Tauberbischofsheim to Weikersheim passes through Lauda-Königshofen, a pretty stop in the Tauber Valley.

- - - - - - - - - - -

❸ Weikersheim

Top billing in undervisited Weikersheim is **Schloss Weikersheim** (www.schloss-weikersheim.de; Marktplatz 11; adult/concession €6.50/3.30; ⊘9am-6pm Apr-Oct, 10am-noon & 1-5pm Nov-Mar), the finest palace on the entire Romantic Road. Renaissance to the core, it's surrounded by beautiful formal gardens inspired by Versailles. Highlights include the enormous Knights Hall dating from around 1600 and over 40m long. The rich decor here includes a huge painted ceiling, each panel depicting a hunting scene, and the amazingly ornate fireplace. The unforgettable rococo mirror cabinet, with its gilt-and-red decor, is also part of the guided tour, after which you can wander the elegantly laid-out gardens.

The Drive » The short 28km journey between Weikersheim and Rothenburg ob der Tauber

MUSEUM OF THE BAVARIAN KINGS

Palace-fatigued visitors often head straight for the bus stop, coach park or nearest beer after a tour of the castles, most overlooking the area's third attraction, the worthwhile **Museum der Bayerischen Könige** (Museum of the Bavarian Kings; www.museumderbayerischenkoenige.de; Alpseestrasse 27; adult/concession €9.50/8; ⊘10am-6pm), installed in a former lakeside hotel 400m from the castle ticket office (heading towards Alpsee Lake). The big-window views across the beautiful lake (a great picnic spot) to the Alps are almost as amazing as the Wittelsbach bling on show, including Ludwig II's famous blue-and-gold robe. The architecturally stunning museum is packed with historical background on Bavaria's first family and is well worth the extra legwork. A detailed audioguide is included in the ticket price.

follows minor country roads all the way, with the route passing through a rolling patchwork of fields. You could also detour via Creglingen, a minor stop on the Romantic Road.

- - - - - - - - - - -

TRIP HIGHLIGHT

❹ Rothenburg ob der Tauber

A well-preserved historical town, Rothenburg ob der Tauber is the most popular stop on the Romantic Road. But when you're finished with the main sights, there are a couple of less obvious attractions here.

You'll often see the **Plönlein** on the covers of brochures and tourist bumf, a gathering of forks in the cobbled road (Obere Schmiedgasse) occupied by possibly the quaintest, most crooked

half-timbered house you are ever likely to see.

Hidden down a little alley is the **Alt-Rothenburger Handwerkerhaus** (Alter Stadtgraben 26; adult/concession €3/2.50; ⊘11am-5pm Mon-Fri, from 10am Sat & Sun Easter-Oct, 2-4pm daily Dec), where numerous artisans – including coopers, weavers, cobblers and potters – have their workshops today, and mostly have had for the house's 700-plus-years existence. It's half museum, half active workplace and you can easily spend an hour or so watching the craftsmen at work.

✗ p502

The Drive » The quickest and simplest way between Rothenburg ob der Tauber and Dinkelsbühl is along the A7 motorway (50km). For a gentler, but slower and longer experience, follow the official Romantic Road route, which tacks along country roads via Schillingsfürst, another quaint halt.

- - - - - - - - - - - - -

TRIP HIGHLIGHT

5 Dinkelsbühl

Immaculately preserved Dinkelsbühl is arguably the Romantic Road's quaintest and most authentically medieval halt. Just like Rothenburg it is ringed by medieval walls, which boast 18 towers and four gates. The joy of Dinkelsbühl is aimless wandering through the crooked lanes, but for a lowdown on the town's history visit the **Haus der Geschichte** (Altrathausplatz 14; adult/child €4/2; ⏰9am-6pm Mon-Fri, 10am-5pm Sat & Sun May-Oct, 10am-5pm daily Nov-Apr), in the same building as the tourist office.

✗ 🛏 p502

The Drive » Just 32km separate Dinkelsbühl from Nördlingen along the B25; drivers are accompanied by the Wörnitz River for the first part of the journey. Just a few kilometres short of Nördlingen is Wallerstein, a small market town with the beautiful parish church of St Alban, also a Romantic Road stop.

- - - - - - - - - - - - -

6 Nördlingen

Charmingly medieval, Nördlingen lies within the Ries Basin, a massive impact crater gouged out by a meteorite more than 15 million years ago. The crater – some 25km in diameter – is one of the best preserved on earth,

---

ROTHENBURG'S SNOWBALLS

Where is it possible to get your hands on a snowball in July? Why, in Rothenburg ob der Tauber, of course! The town's speciality are *Schneeballen* (snowballs), ribbons of dough loosely shaped into balls, deep-fried then coated in icing sugar, chocolate and other dentist's foes. Some 24 types are produced at **Diller's Schneeballen** (Hofbronnengasse 16; ⏰10am-6pm); a more limited range can be enjoyed all over town.

---

and has been declared a special 'geopark'. Nördlingen's 14th-century walls, all original, mimic the crater's rim and are almost perfectly circular. The **Rieskrater Museum** (Eugene-Shoemaker-Platz 1; adult/concession €4.50/2.50, ticket also valid for Stadtmuseum; ⏰10am-4.30pm Tue-Sun, closed noon-1.30pm Nov-Apr) tells the story. Next door is the **Stadtmuseum** (Vordere Gerbergasse 1; adult/concession €4.50/2.50, ticket also valid for Rieskrater Museum; ⏰1.30-4.30pm Tue-Sun Mar-early Nov), which gives an interesting rundown of Nördlingen's story so far.

On a completely different note, the **Bayerisches Eisenbahnmuseum** (www.bayerisches-eisenbahnmuseum.de; Am Hohen Weg 6a; adult/child €6/3; ⏰noon-4pm Tue-Sat, 10am-5pm Sun May-Sep, noon-4pm Sat, 10am-5pm Sun Oct-Mar) near

---

the railway station is a retirement home for locos that have puffed their last. The museum runs steam trains up to Dinkelsbühl, Feuchtwangen and Gunzenhausen several times a year; see the website for details.

✗ 🛏 p503

The Drive » The 19km drive from Nördlingen to Harburg is a simple affair along the arrow-straight B25 all the way. The road crosses the flatlands created by the Ries meteorite, now fertile agricultural land.

- - - - - - - - - - - - -

7 Harburg

Looming over the Wörnitz River, the medieval covered parapets, towers, turrets, keep and red-tiled roofs of the 12th-century **Schloss Harburg** (www.burg-harburg.de; adult/child €5/3; ⏰10am-5pm Tue-Sun mid-Mar–Oct) are so perfectly

---

WILLY WONKA'S NÖRDLINGEN

If you've seen the 1970s movie *Willy Wonka & the Chocolate Factory*, you've already looked down upon Nördlingen, from a glass elevator – aerial shots of the town were used in the final sequences of the film.

WHY THIS IS A GREAT TRIP
MARC DI DUCA, AUTHOR

This 350km-long ribbon of historical quaintness is the Germany you came to see, but things can get crowded in the summer months, taking away a bit of the romance. Do the trip in winter when Bavaria's chocolate-box towns look even prettier under a layer of snow.

Top: The Main River in Würzburg with a fortress on the hilltop
Left: *Schneeballen* (snowballs), a traditional cake in Rothenburg ob der Tauber
Right: Franconia Fountain in front of Würzburg Residenz

preserved they almost seem like part of a film set Tours tell the Schloss' long tale and evoke the ghosts that are said to use the castle as a hang-out.

From the castle, the walk to Harburg's cute, half-timbered **Altstadt** (old town) takes around 10 minutes, slightly more the other way as you're heading uphill. A fabulous panorama of the village and castle can be admired from the 1702 stone bridge spanning the Wörnitz.

The Drive » A mere 12km separate tiny Harburg with its bigger neighbour Donauwörth. The route follows the B25 all the way across undulating farmland.

- - - - - - - - - - -

❽ Donauwörth

Sitting pretty at the confluence of the Danube and Wörnitz Rivers, the small town of Donau-wörth had its heyday as a Free Imperial City in the 14th century. WWII destroyed 75% of the medieval old town but three gates and five town-wall towers still guard it today. The main street is Reichsstrasse, which is where you'll discover the **Lieb-fraukirche** (Reichstrasse), a 15th-century Gothic church with original frescos and a curiously sloping floor that drops 120cm. Swabia's largest church bell (6550kg) swings in the belfry. The other major attraction in town is the **Käthe-Kruse-Puppenmuseum** (www.kaethe-kruse.de; Pflegstrasse 21a; adult/child €2.50/1.50; ☺11am-6pm Tue-Sun May-Sep, 2-5pm Thu-Sun Oct-Apr). In a former monastery, it's a nostalgia-inducing place full of old dolls and dollhouses from world-renowned designer Käthe Kruse (1883–1968).

The Drive » The quickest way between Donauwörth and the next stop in Augsburg 47km away is via the B2 and the A8 motorway. The scenic route via backroads east of the A8 passes close to the pretty town of Rain, another minor halt on the Romantic Road.

- - - - - - - - - - - - - -

❾ Augsburg

Augsburg is the Romantic Road's largest city and one of Germany's oldest, founded by the stepchildren of Roman emperor Augustus over 2000 years ago. This attractive city of spires and cobbles is an engaging stop, though one with a less quaint atmosphere than others along the route.

Augsburg's top sight is the **Fuggerei** (www.fugger.de; Jakober Strasse; adult/concession €4/3; ☺8am-8pm Apr-Sep, 9am-6pm Oct-Mar), Europe's oldest Catholic welfare settlement, founded by banker and merchant Jakob Fugger in 1521. Around 200 people inhabit the complex today; see how the residents of yesterday lived by visiting the **Fuggereimuseum** (Mittlere Gasse 14; admission incl with entry to the Fuggerei; ☺9am-8pm Mar-Oct, 9am-6pm Nov-Apr).

Two famous Germans have close associations with Augsburg. The Protestant Reformation leader Martin Luther stayed here in 1518 – his story is told at the **St Anna Kirche** (Im Annahof 2, off Annastrasse; ☺noon-5pm Mon, 10am-12.30pm & 3-5pm Tue-Sat, 10am-12.30pm & 3-4pm Sun). The birthplace of the poet and playwright Bertolt Brecht is now a museum called the **Bertolt-Brecht-Haus** (☎0821-324 2779; Auf dem Rain 7; adult/concession €2.50/2; ☺10am-5pm Tue-Sun).

✗ ⌂ p503

The Drive » The 41km drive from Augsburg to Landsberg am Lech is a simple affair along the B17. The route mostly follows the valley of the Lech River, which links the two towns. Look out for signs to the amusingly named town of Kissing!

- - - - - - - - - - - - - -

❿ Landsberg am Lech

A walled town on the River Lech, lovely Landsberg has a less commercial ambience than others on the route. Just like the Wieskirche further south, the small baroque **Johan-**

DETOUR: EICHSTÄTT & THE ALTMÜHLTAL NATURE PARK

Start: ❽ Donauwörth (p497)

A short 55km off the Romantic Road from Donauwörth lies the town of Eichstätt, the main jumping-off point for the serenely picturesque 2900-sq-km Altmühltal Nature Park, which follows the wooded valley of the Altmühl River. Canoeing the river is a top activity here, as is cycling the same route and camping. The park is an ideal break from the road and a relaxing place to spend a few days in unspoilt natural surroundings. Eichstätt itself has a wealth of architecture, including the richly adorned medieval **Dom** (www.bistum-eichstaett.de/dom; Domplatz; ☺7.15am-7.30pm), with its museum, the baroque **Fürstbischöfliche Residenz** (Residenzplatz; admission €1; ☺7.30am-noon Mon-Fri, 2-4pm Mon-Wed, 2 5.30pm Thu), where the local prince-bishops once lived it up, and the **Willibaldsburg** (☎08421-4730; Burgstrasse 19; adult/concession €4.50/3.50; ☺9am-6pm Tue-Sun Apr-Oct, 10am-4pm Tue-Sun Nov-Mar), a 14th-century castle that now houses a couple of museums.

TOP TIP: GUEST CARDS

Overnight anywhere in the Alps and your hotel should issue you with a free *Gästekarte,* which gives free bus travel as well as many other discounts on admission and activities.

niskirche (Vorderer Anger) is a creation by the baroque architect Dominikus Zimmermann, who lived in Landsberg and even served as its mayor. The town's **Neues Stadtmuseum** (www.museum-landsberg. de; Von-Helfenstain-Gasse 426; adult/concession €3.50/2; ☺2-5pm Tue-Fri, from 11am Sat & Sun May-Jan, closed Feb-Apr) tells Landsberg's tale from prehistory to the 20th century.

The Drive >> Still tracing the valley of the River Lech, the 28km drive along the B17 between Landsberg am Lech and Schongau shouldn't take more than 30 minutes. En route you pass through Hohenfurch, a pretty little town regarded as the gateway to the Pfaffenwinkel, a foothill region of the Alps.

- - - - - - - - - - - -

⑪ Schongau

One of the lesser-visited stops on the Romantic Road, the attractive town of Schongau is known for its largely intact medieval defences. The Gothic **Ballenhaus** (Marienplatz 2) served as the town hall until 1902 and has a distinctive stepped gable. It now houses a cafe. Other attractions include the **Church of Maria Him-**

melfahrt (Kirchenstrasse 23), which sports a choir by Dominikus Zimmermann.

The Drive >> To reach the next Romantic Road stop, the Wieskirche (21km away), take the B17 south until you reach Steingaden. From there country roads lead east and then south to Wies. This is where Bavaria starts to take on the look of the Alps, with flower-filled meadows in summer and views of the high peaks when the weather is clear.

- - - - - - - - - - -

⑫ Wieskirche

Located in the village of Wies, the **Wieskirche** (☎08862-932 930; www. wieskirche.de; ☺8am-8pm Apr-Oct, to 5pm Nov-Mar) is one of Bavaria's best-known baroque churches and a Unesco-listed site, the

monumental work of the legendary artist-brothers, Dominikus and Johann Baptist Zimmermann.

In 1730 a farmer in Steingaden claimed he'd witnessed the miracle of his Christ statue shedding tears. Pilgrims poured into the town in such numbers over the next decade that the local abbot commissioned a new church to house the weepy work. Inside the almost-circular structure, eight snow-white pillars are topped by gold capital stones and swirling decorations. The unsupported dome must have seemed like God's work in the mid-17th century, its surface adorned with a pastel ceiling fresco celebrating Christ's resurrection.

The Drive >> From the Wieskirche, the best way to reach the next stop at Füssen is to backtrack to Steingaden and rejoin the B17 there. The entire journey is 27km through the increasingly undulating foothills of the Alps, with some gorgeous views of the ever-nearing peaks along the way.

LANDSBERG'S DARK LITERARY CONNECTIONS

Landsberg am Lech can claim to be the town where one of the German language's best-selling books was written. Was it a work by Goethe, Remarque, Brecht? No, unfortunately, it was Adolf Hitler. It was during his 264 days of incarceration in a Landsberg jail, following the 1923 beer-hall putsch, that Hitler penned his hate-filled *Mein Kampf*, a book that sold an estimated seven million copies when published. The jail later held Nazi war criminals and is still in use.

⑬ Füssen

Nestled at the foot of the Alps, tourist-busy Füssen is all about the nearby castles of Neuschwanstein and Hohenschwangau, but there are other reasons to linger longer in the area. The town's historical centre is worth half a day's exploration and, from here, you can easily escape from the crowds into a landscape of gentle hiking trails and Alpine vistas. When you've had your fill of these, take an hour or two to drop by Füssen's very own castle, the **Hohes Schloss** (Magnusplatz 10; adult/concession €6/4; ☺galleries 11am-5pm Tue-Sun Apr-Oct, 1-4pm Fri-Sun Nov-Mar), today home to an art gallery.

✕ 🍴 p503

The Drive » To drive to King Ludwig II's castles, take the B17 across the river until you see the signs for Hohenschwangau. Parking is at a premium in summer. However, as the castles are a mere 4km from the centre of Füssen it's probably not worth driving at all. RVO buses 78 and 73 (www.rvo-bus.de) run there from Füssen Bahnhof (€4.40 return, eight minutes, at least hourly, buy tickets from the driver).

TRIP HIGHLIGHT

⑭ Neuschwanstein & Hohenschwangau Castles

The undisputed highlights of any trip to Bavaria, these two castles make a fitting climax to the Romantic Road.

Schloss Neuschwanstein (☎tickets 08362-930 830; www.neuschwanstein.de; Neuschwansteinstrasse 20; adult/concession €12/11, incl Hohenschwangau €23/21; ☺9am-6pm Apr–mid-Oct, 10am-4pm mid-Oct–Mar) was the model for Disney's *Sleeping Beauty* castle. King Ludwig II planned this fairy-tale pile himself, with the help of a stage designer rather than an architect. He envisioned it as a giant stage on which to recreate the world of Germanic mythology, inspired by the operatic works of his friend Richard Wagner.

PAUL BIRIS / GETTY IMAGES ©

✔ TOP TIP:
VISITING NEUSCHWANSTEIN & HOHENSCHWANGAU CASTLES

The castles can only be visited on guided tours (35 minutes). Buy timed tickets from the **Ticket Centre** (☎08362-930 830; www.hohenschwangau.de; Alpenseestrasse 12; ☺8am-5.30pm Apr–mid-Oct, 9am-3.30pm mid-Oct–Mar) at the foot of the castles. In summer, arrive as early as 8am to ensure you get in that day.

Bavaria Schloss Neuschwanstein

It was at nearby **Schloss Hohenschwangau** (📞08362-930 830; www.hohenschwangau.de; Alpseestrasse 30, adult/ concession €12/11, incl Neuschwanstein €23/21; ⊙8am-5.30pm Apr–mid-Oct, 9am-3.30pm mid-Oct–Mar) that King Ludwig II grew up and later enjoyed sum mers until his death in 1886. His father, Maximil ian II, built this palace in a neo-Gothic style atop 12th-century ruins. Less showy than Neuschwan stein, Hohenschwangau

Eating & Sleeping

Würzburg ❶

✗ Bürgerspital
Weinstube   Wine Restaurant €€

(☎0931-352 880; Theaterstrasse 19; mains €13-24; ⏰10am-11pm) If you are going to eat out just once in Würzburg, the aromatic and cosy nooks of this labyrinthine medieval place probably provide the top local experience. Choose from a broad selection of Franconian wines (some of Germany's best) and wonderful regional dishes and snacks, including *Mostsuppe* (a tasty wine soup).

🛏 Hotel Rebstock   Hotel €€

(☎0931-309 30; www.rebstock.com; Neubaustrasse 7; s/d from €92/113; ❄@🛜) Würzburg's top digs, in a squarely renovated rococo townhouse, has 70 unique, stylishly finished rooms with the gamut of amenities, impeccable service and an Altstadt location. A pillow selection and supercomfy 'gel' beds should ease you into slumberland, perhaps after a fine meal in the dramatic bistro or the slick Michelin-star restaurant.

Rothenburg ob der Tauber ❹

✗ Mittermeier   Bavarian €€

(☎09861-945 430; www.villamittermeier.de; Vorm Würzburger Tor 7; mains €12-19; ⏰6-10.30pm Tue-Sat; 🅿🛜) Supporters of the slow food movement and deserved holders of a Michelin Bib Gourmand, this hotel restaurant pairs punctilious craftsmanship with top-notch ingredients, sourced regionally whenever possible. There are five different dining areas including a black-and-white tiled 'temple', and alfresco terrace and a barrel-shaped wine cellar. The wine list is one of the best in Franconia.

✗ Zur Höll   Franconian €€

(☎09861-4229; www.hoell.rothenburg.de; Burggasse 8; mains €6.80-20; ⏰5-11pm) This medieval wine tavern is in the town's oldest original building, with sections dating back to the year 900. The menu of regional specialities is limited but refined, though it's the superb selection of Franconian wines that people really come for.

Dinkelsbühl ❺

✗ Haus
Appelberg   Franconian, International €€

(☎09851-582 838; www.haus-appelberg.de; Nördlinger Strasse 40; dishes €6-11; ⏰6pm-midnight Mon-Sat) At this 40-cover wine restaurant, the owners double up as cooks to keep tables supplied with traditional dishes such as local fish, Franconian sausages and *Maultaschen* (pork and spinach ravioli). On warm days swap the rustic interior for the secluded terrace, a fine spot for some evening idling over a Franconian white.

🛏 Dinkelsbühler
Kunst-Stuben   Guesthouse €€

(☎09851-6750; www.kunst-stuben.de; Segringer Strasse 52; s €60, d €80-85, ste €90; 😊@🛜) Personal attention and charm by the bucketload make this guesthouse, situated near the westernmost gate (Segringer Tor), one of the best on the entire Romantic Road. Furniture (including the four-posters) is all handmade by Voglauer, the cosy library is perfect for curling up in with a good read, and the suite is a matchless deal for travelling families. The artist owner will show his Asia travel films if enough guests are interested.

Nördlingen ⑥

✖ La Fontana
Italian €

(Bei den Kornschrannen 2; mains around €8; ⏱11am-11pm) Nördlingen's most popular restaurant is this large Italian pizza-pasta place occupying the terracotta Kornschrannen as well as tumbling tables out onto Schrannenstrasse. The menu is long, the service swift and when the sun is shining there's no lovelier spot to fill the hole.

🛏 Kaiserhof Hotel Sonne
Hotel €€

(☎09081-5067; www.kaiserhof-hotel-sonne.de; Marktplatz 3; s €55-75, d €80-120; [P]🛜) Right on the main square, Nördlingen's top digs once hosted crowned heads and their entourages, but have quietly gone to seed in recent years. However, rooms are still packed with character, mixing modern comforts with traditional charm, and the atmospheric regional restaurant downstairs is still worth a shot.

Augsburg ⑨

✖ August
International €€€

(☎0821-352 79; Frauentorstrasse 27; dinner €130; ⏱from 7pm Wed-Sat) Most Augsburgers have little inkling their city possesses two Michelin stars, both of which belong to chef Christian Grünwald. Treat yourself to some of Bavaria's most innovative cooking in the minimalist dining room, though with just 16 covers, reservations are essential.

✖ Bauerntanz
German €€

(Bauerntanzgässchen 1; mains €7-17; ⏱11am-11.30pm) Belly-satisfying helpings of creative Swabian and Bavarian food – *Spätzle* (a kind of soft egg noodle or dumpling) and more *Spätzle* – are plated up by friendly staff at this prim Alpine tavern with lace curtains, hefty timber interior and chequered fabrics. When the sun makes an appearance, everyone bails for the outdoor seating.

🛏 Dom Hotel
Hotel €€

(☎0821-343 930; www.domhotel-augsburg. de; Frauentorstrasse 8; s €70-150, d €95-190;

[P]😊@🛜📶) Augsburg's top choice packs a 500-year-old former bishop's guesthouse (Martin Luther and Kaiser Maxmilian I stayed here) with 57 rooms, all different but sharing a stylishly understated air and pristine upkeep; some have cathedral views. However, the big pluses here are the large swimming pool, fitness centre and solarium. Parking is an extra €6.

Füssen ⑬

✖ Zum Franziskaner
Bavarian €€

(Kemptener Strasse 1; mains €6-19.50; ⏱noon-11pm) This revamped restaurant specialises in *Schweinshaxe* (pork knuckle) and schnitzel, prepared in more varieties than you can shake a haunch at. There's some choice for non-carnivores such as *Käsespätzle* (rolled cheese noodles) and salads, and when the sun shines the outdoor seating shares the pavement with the 'foot-washing' statue.

✖ Zum Hechten
Bavarian €€

(Ritterstrasse 6; mains €8-19; ⏱10am-10pm) Füssen's best hotel restaurant keeps things regional with a menu of Allgäu staples like schnitzel and noodles, Bavarian pork-themed favourites, and local specialities such as venison goulash from the Ammertal. Post-meal, relax in the wood-panelled dining room caressing a König Ludwig Dunkel, one of Germany's best dark beers brewed by the current head of the Wittelsbach family.

🛏 Hotel Sonne
Design Hotel €€

(☎08362-9080; www.hotel-sonne.de; Prinzregentenplatz 1; s/d from €89/109; [P]🛜) Although traditional looking from outside, this Altstadt favourite offers an unexpected design-hotel experience within. Themed rooms feature everything from swooping bed canopies to big-print wallpaper, huge pieces of wall art to sumptious fabrics. The public spaces are littered with pieces of art, period costumes and design features – the overall effect is impressive and unusual for this part of Germany.

German Fairy Tale Road

36

You might just live happily ever after! You'll certainly end this trip happy, having explored a beautiful swath of Germany and learned the real stories behind Brothers Grimm fairy tales.

TRIP HIGHLIGHTS

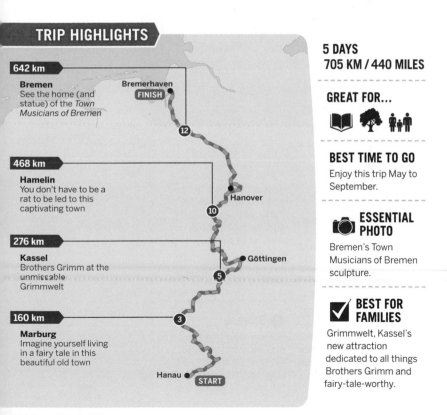

642 km

Bremen
See the home (and statue) of the *Town Musicians of Bremen*

Bremerhaven
FINISH

12

468 km

Hamelin
You don't have to be a rat to be led to this captivating town

Hanover

10

276 km

Kassel
Brothers Grimm at the unmissable Grimmwelt

Göttingen

5

160 km

Marburg
Imagine yourself living in a fairy tale in this beautiful old town

3

Hanau
START

**5 DAYS
705 KM / 440 MILES**

GREAT FOR...

BEST TIME TO GO
Enjoy this trip May to September.

ESSENTIAL PHOTO
Bremen's Town Musicians of Bremen sculpture.

BEST FOR FAMILIES
Grimmwelt, Kassel's new attraction dedicated to all things Brothers Grimm and fairy-tale-worthy.

Marburg St Elizabeth's Church

36 German Fairy Tale Road

Tirelessly roaming the villages and towns of 19th-century Germany, the Brothers Grimm collected 209 folk tales that had been passed down for countless generations. The stories they published often bear little resemblance to the sanitised versions spoon-fed to kids today; rather they are morality tales with blood, gore, sex, the supernatural, magic and much more. See the locations of the stories and learn about these remarkable brothers on this trip, which includes a few non-Grimm fairy-tale sights as well.

❶ Hanau

A mere 20km east of Frankfurt on the Main River, Hanau is the birthplace of the Brothers Grimm (Jacob in 1785 and Wilhelm in 1786) and is a perfect place to begin this trip. Not that their birth is especially com-memorated here...

Located within Philippsruhe Palace, dat-ing from the early 18th century, the **Historisches Museum Schloss Philipp-sruhe** (☎06181-295 564; www.hanau.de/kultur/museen/ hanau; Philippsruher Allee 45; adult/concession €4/3; ☉11am-6pm Tue-Sun) has displays on town history, and arts and crafts. The parks and gardens (free) are a beautiful stroll in snow or in summer.

The Drive » Hop on the A66 for a quick 50km run through the rolling hills to Steinau.

❷ Steinau

Steinau is situated on the historic trade road between Frankfurt and Leipzig. (Note that the full name of the town is

'Steinau an der Strasse', an important distinction when using your map app as there's another Steinau way up by the North Sea.)

The twin musuems, **Brüder Grimm-Haus and Museum Steinau** (☎06663-7605; www.brueder-grimm-haus.de; Brüder Grimm-Strasse 80, Steinau; adult/concession €6/3.50; ☺10am-5pm), inside the building where the Grimm family lived from 1791 to 1796, have exhibits on the brothers, their work and the history of Steinau.

The Drive » Exit Steinau to the west on the L3196 for 18km to the B276 where you'll turn north. Weave through the valleys for 64km until the junction with the L3166 and follow the Marburg signs along the L3127, L3089, L3048 and L3125 to your destination. Picnic spots abound along the route.

🔗 LINK YOUR TRIP

34 Romantic Rhine

Get your fill of castles and medieval villages: the end of the river trip is 65km east of Hanau.

35 The Romantic Road

Do one of the trips in reverse: the start of the quaint and historical Romantic Road is about an hour (110km) west from Hanau.

③ Marburg

Hilly, historic and delightful, the university town of Marburg is situated 90km north of Frankfurt. It's a delight to wander around the narrow lanes of the town's vibrant **Altstadt** (old town), sandwiched between a palace (above) and the spectacular Gothic church, St Elizabeth's (below). On the south side of the focal **Marktplatz** is the historic **Rathaus** (town hall), dating to 1512. At the base of the **Altstadt's** Reitgasse is the neo-Gothic **Alte Universität** (1891), still a well-used and well-loved part of Philipps-Universität – the world's oldest Protestant university. Founded in 1527, it once counted the Brothers Grimm among its students.

Perched at the highest point in town, a steep walk up from St-Marien-Kirche or the Marktplatz, is the massive **Landgrafenschloss** (🔊991 20; www.uni-marburg.de/uni-museum; Schloss 1; adult/concession €4/3; ⊙10am-6pm Tue-Sun), built between 1248 and 1300. It offers panoramic views of bucolic hills, jumbled Marburg rooftops and the **Schlosspark**.

✕ 🛏 p516

The Drive » Leave Marburg to the north on the B3, after 18km turn north on the L3073. Continue north for

DETOUR: FULDA

Start: ② Steinau (p506)

Although it's not quite on the Fairy Tale Road, photogenic Fulda is well worth a side trip for those interested in sumptuous baroque architecture, historic churches and religious reliquaries. A Benedictine monastery was founded here in 744, and today Fulda has its own bishop.

Inside the baroque **Dom zu Fulda** (🔊0661-874 57; www.bistum-fulda.de; Domplatz 1; ⊙10am-6pm Mon-Fri, to 3pm Sat, 1-6pm Sun), built from 1704 to 1712, you'll find gilded furnishings, plenty of *putti* (figures of infant boys), some dramatic statues (eg to the left of the altar) and the tomb of St Boniface, who died a martyr in 754.

Fulda's history started in **Michaelskirche** (Michaelsberg 1; ⊙10am-5pm). A still-standing reminder of the abbey that made this town, this remarkable church was the monastic burial chapel. Beneath classic witch's-hat towers, a Carolingian rotunda and crypt recall Fulda's flourishing Middle Ages, when the abbey scriptorium churned out top-flight illuminated manuscripts.

Don't miss Fulda's spectacular **Stadtschloss** (🔊0661-1020; adult/concession €3.50/2.30; ⊙10am-5pm Tue-Sun), built from 1706 to 1721 as the prince-abbots' residence. It now houses the city administration and function rooms. Visitors can enter the ornate **Historiche Räume** (historic rooms), including the grandiose banquet hall, and the octagonal **Schlossturm** (April to October) for great views of the town and magnificent **Schlossgarten** (palace gardens), where locals play *pétanque* (boules) and sunbathe in summer.

The palace's fairy-tale qualities capture the era's extravagance. Don't miss the amazing **Speigelkabinett** (Chamber of Mirrors) and grandiose **Fürstensaal**, a banquet hall decorated with reliefs of tipsy-looking wine queens. Also, there are pretty views from the **Green Room** over the gardens to the Orangerie.

Fulda is a mere 40km northeast of Steinau on the A66.

37km through Gemunden and Frankenau to Edertal where you'll find the park. Note how the forest gets thicker and darker as you go.

- - - - - - - - - - -

④ Kellerwald-Edersee National Park

Kellerwald-Edersee National Park (www.national park-kellerwald-edersee.de) encompasses one of the largest extant red-beech forests in Central Europe, the **Kellerwald**, and the **Edersee**, a serpentine artificial reservoir 55km northeast of Marburg and about the same distance southwest of Kassel. In 2011 this national park, along with Hainich National Park in Thuringia and a cluster of other parks and reserves with large beech forests, became a Unesco World Cultural Heritage site.

On a fairy-tale trip, it's fitting to wander into the deep woods, never forgetting that if your name is Grimm, nothing good is bound to happen. If you're lucky, you may see larger land animals including red deer; while overhead you might spot eagles and honey buzzards and, at night, various species of bat. (The brothers would approve of that.)

For information, head to the striking modern **visitors centre** (☎05635-992 781; www.nationalpark zentrum-kellerwald.de; B252, Vöhl-Herzhausen; e-bikes per day €20; ☺10am-6pm Apr-Oct,

to 5pm Nov-Mar) at the western end of the Edersee.

The Drive ›› Drive east on the L3332, B485 and the B253 for 28km until you reach the A49 autobahn and zip along northeast until you reach Kassel.

- - - - - - - - - - -

TRIP HIGHLIGHT

⑤ Kassel

Visitors to this culture-rich, sprawling hub on the Fulda River discover a pleasant, modern city.

Occupying a prime position atop the Weinberg bunker in the scenic Weinbergpark is the truly most unmissable attraction on this trip: Kassel's newest musuem, **Grimmwelt** (☎0561-598 610; www.grimmwelt.de; Weinbergstrasse; adult/concession €8/6; ☺10am-6pm Tue-Sun). It could be described as an architect-designed walk-in sculpture housing the most significant collection of Brothers Grimm memorabilia on the planet. Visitors are guided around original exhibits, state-of-the-art installations and fun, hands-on activities, aided by entries from the Grimms' German dictionary: there were more to these famous brothers than just fairy tales, didn't you know?

Billed as 'a meditative space for funerary art', the **Museum für Sepulkralkultur** (Museum of Sepulchral Culture; ☎0561-918 930; www.sepulkralmuseum.de; Weinbergstrasse 25-27; adult/concession €6/4; ☺10am-5pm

Tue & Thu-Sun, to 8pm Wed) aims at burying the taboo of discussing death.

✗ ⎩ p516

The Drive ›› Your shortest jaunt of the trip takes you 6km west through Kassel's leafy suburbs. Take Wilhelmshöher Allee.

- - - - - - - - - - -

⑥ Wilhelmshöhe

Wilhelmshöhe is the classy end of Kassel. You can spend a full day exploring the spectacular baroque parkland, **Bergpark Wilhelmshöhe** (www.museum-kassel.de; ☺9am-sunset), which takes its name from **Schloss Wilhelmshöhe** (☎0561-316 800; www.museum-kassel.de; Schlosspark 1; adult/concession €6/4, Weissenstein wing incl tour €4/3; ☺10am-5pm Tue & Thu-Sun, to 8pm Wed), the late-18th-century palace situated inside the expanse. Walk through the forest, enjoy a romantic picnic and explore the castles, fountains, grottoes, statues and water features: the **Herkules** (www.museum-kassel.de; Schlosspark Wilhelmshöhe 26, Herkules-Terrassen; adult/concession €3/2; ☺10am-5pm mid-Mar–mid-Nov) statue and Löwenburg castle are also here.

The palace could star in any fairy tale. Home to Elector Wilhelm and later Kaiser Wilhelm II, the opulent complex today houses one of Germany's best collections of Flemish and Dutch baroque

WHY THIS IS A GREAT TRIP
RYAN VER BERKMOES, AUTHOR

Did they give us nightmares or fantasies? Or both? Who can forget hearing the wild stories of the Brothers Grimm as a child? Evil stepmothers, dashing princes, fair maidens, clever animals, mean old wolves and more. With every passing year, these stories become more sanitised. But the real fairy tales are far more compelling, as you'll learn on this trip.

Top: Beech trees in Kellerwald-Edersee National Park
Left: Brothers Grimm sculpture in Hanau
Right: The exterior of an old building in Marburg

paintings, featuring works by Rembrandt, Rubens, Jordaens, Lucas Cranach the Elder, Dürer and many others in the Gemäldegalerie (painting gallery).

✗ 🛏 p516

The Drive ›› Retrace your 6km drive on Wilhelmshöher Allee into Kassel and take the busy A7 right up to Göttingen.

❼ Göttingen

With over 30,000 students, this historic town nestled in a corner of Lower Saxony near the Hesse border offers a good taste of university-town life in Germany's north. Since 1734, the Georg-August Universität has sent more than 40 Nobel Prize winners into the world. As well as all those award-winning doctors and scientists, it also produced the fairy-tale-writing Brothers Grimm (as German linguistic teachers).

Be sure to stroll around the pleasant **Markt** and nearby Barfüsser-strasse to admire the *Fachwerk* (half-timbered) houses.

The city's symbol, the **Gänseliesel** (little goose girl) statue on Markt is hailed locally as the most kissed woman in the world – not a flattering moniker, you might think, but enough to make her iconic.

✗ p517

The Drive » Take the L561 22km west to the B80, then head northwest for another 27km to Bad Karlshafen. You'll enjoy the curving panoramas as you follow the Weser River, which links several of the Fairy Tale Road towns and cities.

- - - - - - - - - -

❽ Bad Karlshafen

Bad Karlshafen's orderly streets and whitewashed baroque buildings were built in the 18th century for the local earl Karl by French Huguenot refugees. The town was planned with an impressive harbour and a canal connecting the Weser with the Rhine to attract trade, but the earl died before his designs were completed. The only re-minder of his grand plans is a tiny **Hafenbecken** (harbour basin) trafficked by white swans.

Take a stroll around the town centre, on the sinuous Weser River's south bank, with the Hafenbecken and surrounding square, **Hafenplatz**, at its western end.

The interesting **Deutsches Huguenotten Museum** (German Huguenot Museum; ☏05672-1410; www.huguenot-museum-germany.com; Hafenplatz 9a; adult/concession €4/2; ⊙10am-5pm Tue-Fri, 11am-6pm Sat & Sun mid-Mar–Oct, 10am-noon Mon-Fri Nov–mid-Mar) traces the history of the French Huguenot refugees in Germany, although it fails to mention how many were eaten by big bad wolves in the forest during the journey.

The Drive » Just stay on B83 for the 58km right to Bodenwerder. You'll enjoy Weser vistas for much of the journey – which might lure you to stop for a picnic.

- - - - - - - - - -

❾ Bodenwerder

If Bodenwerder's most famous son were to have described his little hometown, he'd probably have painted it as a huge, thriving metropolis on the Weser River. But then Baron Hieronymous von Münchhausen (1720–97) was one of history's most shameless liars (his whoppers were no mere

---

GRIMM FAIRY TALES

In the early 19th century the Brothers Grimm travelled extensively through central Germany documenting folklore. Their collection of tales, *Kinder- und Hausmärchen*, was first published in 1812 and quickly gained international recognition. It has 209 tales and includes such fairy-tale staples as:

» *Hansel and Gretel* – A mother tries to ditch her son and daughter, a witch tries to eat them and Gretal outsmarts her. Kids and father reunite and all are happy (the evil mum has died).

» *Cinderella* – The story that gave step-sisters a bad name. Still, when the prince fits the shoe onto our heroine, all is good with the world, although in the Grimm version, the step-sisters are blinded by vengeful doves.

» *Rapunzel* – An adopted girl with very long hair, a prince that goes blind and some evil older women are combined in this morality play that ends on a love note when the prince stumbles upon an outcast Rapunzel and his sight is restored. In the first edition of the Grimm's book, Rapunzel bore children out of wedlock.

For entertaining synopses of all the Grimm fairy tales, see www.shmoop.com/grimms-fairy-tales. One thing you'll note is that the Grimm original versions are much bloodier, more violent and earthier than the ultra-sanitised, Disneyfied versions today.

Although best known for their fairy tales, it should be be noted that the Brothers Grimm were serious academics who also wrote *German Grammar* and *History of the German Language*, enduring works that populate reference shelves to this day.

fairy tales). He inspired the Terry Gilliam cult film, *The Adventures of Baron Munchausen*.

Bodenwerder's principal attraction, the **Münchhausen Museum** (☏05533-409 147; Münchhausenplatz 1; adult/child €2.50/1.50; ☺10am-5pm Apr-Oct), tackles the difficult task of conveying the chaos and fun associated with the 'liar baron' – a man who liked to regale dinner guests with his Crimean adventures, claiming he had, for example, tied his horse to a church steeple during a snow drift and ridden around a dining table without breaking one teacup. Among other artefacts, it also has paintings and displays of Münchhausen books in many languages.

The Drive » The unofficial spine for some of the Fairy Tale Road route, the B83 again takes you north, for 23km from Bodenwerder to Hamelin.

TRIP HIGHLIGHT

⑩ Hamelin

According to the Brothers Grimm in *The Pied Piper of Hamelin*, in the 13th century the Pied Piper (*Der Rattenfänger*) was employed by Hamelin's townsfolk to lure its rodents into the river. When they refused to pay him, he picked up his flute and led their kids away. Today, the rats rule once again – fluffy and cute stuffed rats, wooden rats, and tiny

---

THE FAIRY TALE ROAD

The 600km **Märchenstrasse** (Fairy Tale Road; www.deutsche-maerchenstrasse.com/en) is one of Germany's most popular tourist routes, with over 60 stops along the way. It's made up of cities, towns and hamlets in four states (Hesse, Lower Saxony, North Rhine-Westphalia and Bremen), which can often be reached by using a choice of roads rather than one single route. The towns are associated in one way or another with the works of Wilhelm and Jacob Grimm. Although most towns can be easily visited using public transport, a car lets you fully explore the route.

---

brass rats adorn the sights around town.

Rodents aside, Hamelin (Hameln in German) is a pleasant town with half-timbered houses and opportunities for cycling along the Weser River, on the eastern bank of which lies Hamelin's circular **Altstadt**. The town's heart is its **Markt**.

Many of Hamelin's finest buildings were constructed in the Weser Renaissance style, which has strong Italian influences. Learn more at the town's revamped **Museum Hamelin** (☏05151-202 1215; www.museum-hameln.de; Osterstrasse 8-9; adult/concession €5/4; ☺11am-6pm Tue-Sun), which has historical displays.

🍴 🛏 p517

The Drive » Leave the pastoral charms of Hamelin as you drive 47km northwest on the B217 to the modern vibe of busy Hanover.

---

⑪ Hanover

Known for its huge trade shows, Hanover has a past: from 1714, monarchs from the house of Hanover also ruled Great Britain and the entire British Empire for over a century.

Let your hair down at the spectacularly baroque **Herrenhäuser Gärten** (☏0511-1683 4000; www.hannover.de/Herrenhausen; Herrenhäuser Strasse 4; general admission free; ☺9am-6pm, grotto to 5.30pm Apr-Oct, 9am-4.30pm, grotto to 4pm Nov-Mar; Ⓤ Hannover Herrenhäuser Gärten), the grandiose baroque Royal Gardens of Herrenhausen, which are considered one of the most important historic garden landscapes in Europe. Inspired by the gardens at Versailles, they're a great place to slow down and smell the roses for a couple of hours, especially on a blue-sky day. With its fountains, neat flowerbeds, trimmed hedges and shaped lawns, the 300-year-old **Grosser**

Garten (Great Garden) is the centrepiece of the experience.

The Drive >> Germany's famed autobahns make quick work of the 127km to Bremen: take the A352 16km to the A7, then shoot northwest on that road and the A27. It will feel like you've arrived before you left, unless you get caught in a *Stau* (traffic jam).

TRIP HIGHLIGHT

⑫ Bremen

Bremen is well known for its fairy-tale character, a unique expressionist quarter and (it must be said, because Bremeners are avid football fans) one of Germany's most exciting football teams.

With high, historic buildings rising up from this very compact square, Bremen's **Markt** is one of the most remarkable in northern Germany. The two towers of the 1200-year-old **Dom St Petri** (St Petri Cathedral; ☎0421-334 7142; www.stpetridom.de; Sandstrasse 10-12; tower adult/concession €1/0.70, museum €3/2; ⊙10am-5pm Mon-Fri, to 2pm Sat, 2-5pm Sun) dominate the northeastern edge, beside the ornate and imposing **Rathaus**, which was erected in 1410. The Weser Renaissance balcony in the middle, crowned by three gables, was added between 1595 and 1618.

In front of the Rathaus is one of the hallmarks of Bremen, the city's 13m-high Knight Roland statue (1404). As elsewhere, Roland stands for the civic freedoms of a city, especially the freedom to trade independently.

On the western side of the Rathaus you'll find the city's unmissable and famous symbol of the Grimm fairy tale: the **Town Musicians of Bremen** (1951) by the sculptor Gerhard Marcks. The story tells of a donkey, a dog, a cat and a rooster who know their time is up with their cruel masters, so set out for Bremen and the good life. On the way they encounter a forest cottage filled with robbers. They cleverly dispatch the crooks and, yes, live happily ever after. The statue depicts the dog, cat and rooster, one on top of the other, on the shoulders of the donkey. The donkey's nose and front legs are incredibly shiny having been touched by many visitors for good luck.

✕ ⪚ p517

The Drive >> Another quick shot up the autobahn, the A27, for 65km will bring you to Bremerhaven and the North Sea.

⑬ Bremerhaven

Anyone who has had the fairy-tale dream of running away to sea will love Bremerhaven's waterfront – part machinery of the trade, part glistening glass buildings pointing to a more recent understanding of its harbour as a recreation spot.

Bremerhaven has long been a conduit that gathered the 'huddled masses' from the verdant but poor countryside and poured them into the world outside. Of the millions who landed in America, a large proportion sailed from here, and an enticing exhibition at the **Deutsches Auswandererhaus** (German Emigration Centre; ☎0471-902

Bremen Knight Roland statue in the Markt

200; www.dah-bremerhaven. de; Columbusstrasse 65; adult/ concession €12.60/10.60; ☉10am 6pm Mar-Oct, 10am-5pm Nov-Feb), the city's prime attraction, allows you to share their history.

The museum stands exactly in the spot where 7.2 million emigrants set sail between 1830 and 1974. Your visit begins at the wharf where passengers gathered before boarding a steamer. You then get to visit passenger cabins from different periods (note the improving comfort levels) before going through the immigration process at Ellis Island.

Eating & Sleeping

Marburg ❸

✖ Bückingsgarten German €€

(☎06421-165 7771; www.bueckingsgarten-marburg.de; Landgraf-Philipp-Strasse 6; mains €8-24; ⊙noon-10pm) Choose from two separate menus at this historical restaurant with a spectacular hilltop position adjacent to the castle. Dine inside for more upscale ambience and fare, or enjoy a beer and casual meal in the beer garden: both have excellent views.

✖ Café Barfuss Cafe €

(☎06421-253 49; www.cafebarfuss.de; Barfüsserstrasse 33; meals €4-15; ⊙10am-1am; 🖋) A local institution, humble Barfuss is a no-fuss, offbeat place with a steady stream of sociable student diners who favour its diverse menu of hearty, healthy plates, including great breakfasts and a variety of vegetarian options.

🛏 Vila Vita Rosenpark Hotel €€

(☎06421-600 50; www.rosenpark.com; Anneliese Pohl Allee 7-17; s/d from €116/126; P❋@🛜🏊) Marburg's swankiest and priciest digs are in a lovely spot by the river, a short stroll from the station. If you're going to splurge, superior double rooms and suites offer better value at almost twice the size of classic single rooms. An expansive wellness centre, day spa and two restaurants come with the package.

🛏 Welcome Hotel Marburg Hotel €€

(☎06421-9180; www.welcome-hotel-marburg.de; Pilgrimstein 29; s/d from €93/122; ❋@🛜) Just below the Altstadt, this central hotel has 147 bright, spacious rooms with large windows. Ask for a quieter room at the rear of the building.

Kassel ❺

✖ Lohmann German €€

(☎0561-701 6875; www.lohmann-kassel.de; Königstor 8; mains €8-18; ⊙noon-11pm Sun-Fri, 5-11pm Sat) With roots that go back to 1888, this popular, family-run *Kneipe* (pub) has an old-style birch-and-maple-shaded beer garden with an outdoor grill. Schnitzel (always pork) features heavily on the menu.

🛏 Pentahotel Kassel Boutique Hotel €

(☎0561-933 9887; www.pentahotels.com; Bertha-von-Suttner Strasse 15; d from €55; P❋🛜) This modern, central hotel has compact, stylish rooms with ambient lighting, arty design elements and free high-speed wi-fi. There's a bar and restaurant and free late checkout of 3pm on Sundays (subject to availability).

Wilhelmshöhe ❻

✖ Matterhorn Stübli Swiss €€

(☎0561-399 33; www.matterhornstuebli.de; Wilhelmshöher Allee 326; mains €14-22; ⊙5.30-11pm Tue-Sat, noon-2pm & 5.30-11pm Sun; 🖋) If you love cheese, fondue, schnitzel, or all three, you're well advised to hotfoot it to this quaint Swiss restaurant. If you like mushrooms as well, try the *Original Züri Geschnätzläts:* veal escalopes served with mushrooms and crispy rösti.

🛏 Kurpark Hotel Bad Wilhelmshöhe Boutique Hotel €€

(☎0561-318 90; www.kurparkhotel-kassel.de; Wilhelmshöher Allee 336; s/d from €105/137; P❋🛜🏊) In an excellent location near the castle and train station, this stylish hotel offers well-appointed rooms and common areas, a restaurant and terrace, and an indoor pool.

Göttingen ❼

✗ Zum Szultenburger   German €€

(☎0551-431 33; Prinzenstrasse 7; mains €8-20; ⊙noon-2.30pm & 5.30-11pm Tue-Sat) This traditional German pub does things to the humble schnitzel that will make your mouth water. It's cosy and cheap, the varied menu is all kinds of delicious, and the staff seem happy to be here, which makes all the difference. Cash only.

Hamelin ❿

✗ Klütturm   Modern European €€

(☎05151-962 620; www.kluetturm-restaurant. de; Klütturm 1; mains €12-22) If you fancy a splurge, take a drive into the hills above Hamelin to this classy hotel-restaurant serving well-executed modern-European dishes. The setting is wonderful, with an expanisve terrace and magnificent views. If you find yourself in the mood, you can also stay the night.

✗ Rattenfängerhaus   German €€

(☎05151-3888; www.rattenfaengerhaus. de; Osterstrasse 28; mains €10-23; ⊙11am-10pm) One of Hamelin's finest ornamental Weser Renaissance–style buildings, the Rattenfängerhaus (from 1602) is also home to a favourite, unashamedly tourist-centric restaurant, which has been serving 'rats' tails' flambéed at your table since 1966; don't fret – it's all a pork-based ruse. Aside from the novelty dishes, standard schnitzels, herrings, vegie dishes, and 'rat killer' herb liquor are also offered.

⊨ Komfort-Hotel Garni
Christinenhof   Boutique Hotel €€

(☎05151-950 80; www.christinenhof-hameln. de; Alte Marktstrasse 18; s/d incl breakfast €90/115; P🛜🏊) Historic outside, modern in, this quaint hotel has some neat touches, such as a tiny swimming pool in the vaulted cellar, a sauna, compact but pleasant and uncluttered rooms, and a generous buffet breakfast.

⊨ Schlosshotel
Münchhausen   Hotel €€€

(☎05154-706 00; www.schlosshotel-muenchhausen.com; Schwöbber 9, Aerzen bei Hamelin; s/d tithe barn from €110/140, castle from €135/180, ste €345-445; P🌀❄🛜) Palatial Schlosshotel Münchhausen, 15km outside Hamelin, is a popular spot for weddings and high-end functions. Stylish, contemporary rooms in the main wing have historic touches, while the suites have tasteful period furnishings. Rooms in the adjacent Tithe barn are entirely modern. Two restaurants, lavish spa facilities and two golf courses set in 8 hectares of parkland round off this luxurious option.

Bremen ⓬

✗ Engel Weincafe   Cafe €

(☎0421-6964 2390; www.engelweincafe-bremen.de; Ostertorsteinweg 31; dishes €4-13; ⊙8am-1am Mon-Fri, 10am-1am Sat & Sun; 🛜🍴) Exuding the nostalgic vibe of a former pharmacy, this popular hang-out gets a good crowd no matter where the hands on the clock. Come for breakfast, a hot lunch special, crispy *Flammkuchen* (regional pizza), carpaccio or pasta, or just some cheese and a glass of wine.

✗ Ständige Vertretung   German €€

(☎0421-320 995; www.staev.de; Böttcherstrasse 3-5; mains €9-20; ⊙11.30am-11pm) An offshoot of Berlin's best-known restaurant for homesick Rhineland public servants, this large, bustling place thrives on its political theme and solid cuisine, washed down with Rhineland wines and beer.

⊨ Hotel Bölts am Park   Hotel €€

(☎0421-346 110; www.hotel-boelts.de; Slevogtstrasse 23;·s/d €65/85; P🛜) This cosy family-run hotel in a leafy neighbourhood has real character, from the wonderfully old-fashioned breakfast hall to its well-proportioned doubles.

⊨ Park Hotel Bremen   Hotel €€€

(☎0421-340 80; www.park-hotel-bremen.de; Im Bürgerpark; s/d from €129/149, ste from €635; P🌀@🛜🏊) Although it's exterior is certainly dated, this domed lakeside mansion, surrounded by parkland, impresses through its sheer extravagance and could be considered Bremen's only true five-star, grand hotel. It offers access to excellent spa, fitness and beauty facilities, a heated outdoor pool and views over the lake in a 'spa resort' ambience.

NEED TO KNOW

CURRENCY
Euro (€)

LANGUAGE
German

VISAS
Generally not required for stays of up to 90 days; some nationalities need a Schengen visa.

FUEL
Petrol stations are common on main roads and highways, and in larger towns. Unleaded costs around €1.50 per litre and diesel is €1.25.

RENTAL CARS
Auto Europe (www. autoeurope.com)

Avis (www.avis.com)

Europcar (www.europcar. com)

Hertz (www.hertz.com)

IMPORTANT NUMBERS
Europe-wide emergency covering police, fire and ambulance (☎112)

Climate

Warm to hot summers, mild winters
Warm to hot summers, cold winters
Mild summers, cold winters
Cold climate

Hamburg
GO May–Sep

Berlin
GO May, Jun, Sep & Oct

Frankfurt
GO May–Sep

Munich
GO Apr, May, Sep & Oct

Freiburg
GO Apr–Oct

When to Go

High Season (Jul & Aug)
» Busy roads and long lines at key sights.

» Vacancies at a premium and higher prices in seaside and mountain resorts.

» Festivals celebrate everything from music to wine, and sailing to samba.

Shoulder Season (Apr–Jun & Sep–Oct)
» Smaller crowds and lower prices, except on public holidays.

» Blooming flowers in spring; radiant foliage in autumn.

» Sunny, temperate weather ideal for outdoor pursuits.

Low Season (Nov–Mar)
» No queues, but shorter hours at key sights; some may close for the season.

» Theatre, concert and opera season in full swing.

» Ski resorts busiest in January and February.

Daily Costs

Budget: Less than €100

» Hostel, camping or private room: €15–30

» Up to €8 per meal or self-cater

» Take advantage of Happy Hours and free or low-cost museums and entertainment

Midrange: €100–200

» Private apartment or double room: €60–100

» Three-course dinner at nice restaurant: €30–40

» Couple of beers in a pub or beer garden: €8

Top End: More than €200

» Fancy loft apartment or double in top-end hotel: from €150

» Sit-down lunch or dinner at top-rated restaurant: €100

» Concert or opera tickets: €50–150

Eating

Cafes Coffee, drinks, snacks.

Bistros Light meals to full-blown dinners.

Restaurants Simple eateries to Michelin-starred temples.

Vegetarian Few wholly vegetarian places, limited choices on most menus.

The following prices indicate the cost of a two-course set menu.

€	less than €15
€€	€15–30
€€€	more than €30

Sleeping

Hotels From budget to luxury; breakfast included unless indicated.

Pensiones Rates always include breakfast.

Hostels In cities and large towns; private or HI-affiliated.

Price symbols indicate the cost of a double room with private bathroom in high season:

€	less than €80
€€	€80–160
€€€	more than €160

Arriving in Germany

Frankfurt Airport

S-Bahn Commuter rail lines S8 and S9 from Flughafen Regionalbahnhof to Frankfurt centre, 4.30am to 12.30am (€4.55, 15 minutes).

Taxis €25 to €35; 20 minutes to centre.

Mobile Phones (Cell Phones)

Most European and Australian phones function; turn off roaming to avoid data charges. Buy a local SIM for cheaper rates.

Internet Access

Wi-fi (usually free) is available to guests in most hotels, B&Bs and hostels. Also offered by many cafes, bars, train stations and other public spaces.

Money

ATMs widely available in cities and towns, rarely in villages. Cash is king almost everywhere; credit cards are not widely accepted.

Tipping

Restaurant and bar prices include a service charge, but locals still tip. Taxis expect 10%.

Useful Websites

Lonely Planet (lonelyplanet.com) Travel tips, accommodation, traveller forums and more.

Germany: The Travel Destination (www.germany. travel) German tourist board.

ADAC (www.adac.de) Driving information for Germany and neighbouring countries.

Language

German is easy for English speakers to pronounce because almost all of its sounds are also found in English. If you read our coloured pronunciation guides as if they were English, you'll have no problems being understood. Note that kh is like the 'ch' in 'Bach' or the Scottish 'loch' (pronounced at the back of the throat), r is also pronounced at the back of the throat (almost like a g, but with some friction), zh is pronounced as the 's' in 'measure', and ü as the 'ee' in 'see' but with rounded lips. The stressed syllables are indicated with italics.

GERMAN BASICS

Hello.	*Guten Tag.*	*goo*·ten tahk
Goodbye.	*Auf Wiedersehen.*	owf *vee*·der·zay·en
Yes./No.	*Ja./Nein.*	yah/nain
Please.	*Bitte.*	*bi*·te
Thank you.	*Danke.*	*dang*·ke
You're welcome.	*Bitte.*	*bi*·te
Excuse me.	*Entschuldigung.*	ent·*shul*·di·gung
Sorry.	*Entschuldigung.*	ent·*shul*·di·gung

Do you speak English?
Sprechen Sie Englisch? (pol) — *shpre*·khen zee *eng*·lish
Sprichst du Englisch? (inf) — shprikhst doo *eng*·lish

I don't understand.
Ich verstehe nicht. — ikh fer·*shtay*·e nikht

DIRECTIONS

Where's ...?
Wo ist ...? — vaw ist ...

How far is it?
Wie weit ist es? — vee vait ist es

Can you show me (on the map)?
Können Sie es mir (auf der Karte) zeigen? — *ker*·nen zee es meer (owf dair *kar*·te) *tsai*·gen

How can I get there?
Wie kann ich da hinkommen? — vee kan ikh dah *hin*·ko·men

Turn ...	*Biegen Sie ... ab.*	*bee*·gen zee ... ab
at the corner	*an der Ecke*	an dair *e*·ke
at the traffic lights	*bei der Ampel*	bai dair *am*·pel
left	*links*	lingks
right	*rechts*	rekhts

ACCOMMODATION

Do you have a ... room?	*Haben Sie ein ...?*	*hah*·ben zee ain ...
double	*Doppelzimmer*	*do*·pel·tsi·mer
single	*Einzelzimmer*	*ain*·tsel·tsi·mer
How much is it per ...?	*Wie viel kostet es pro ...?*	vee feel *kos*·tet es praw ...
night	*Nacht*	nakht
person	*Person*	per·*zawn*

Is breakfast included?
Ist das Frühstück inklusive? — ist das *frü*·shtük in·kloo·zee·ve

ON THE ROAD

I'd like to hire a ...	*Ich möchte ein ... mieten.*	ikh *merkh*·te ain ... *mee*·ten
4WD	*Allradfahrzeug*	*al*·raht·fahr·tsoyk
car	*Auto*	*ow*·to
motorbike	*Motorrad*	*maw*·tor·raht

Want More?

For in-depth language information and handy phrases, check out Lonely Planet's *German Phrasebook*. You'll find it at **shop.lonelyplanet.com**.

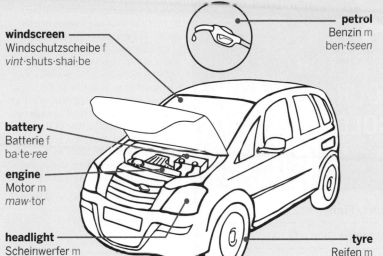

petrol
Benzin m
ben·*tseen*

windscreen
Windschutzscheibe f
vint·shuts·shai·be

battery
Batterie f
ba·te·*ree*

engine
Motor m
maw·tor

headlight
Scheinwerfer m
shain·ver·fer

tyre
Reifen m
rai·fen

How much is it per ...?	*Wie viel kostet es pro ...?*	vee feel *kos*·tet es praw ...
day	*Tag*	tahk
week	*Woche*	vo·khe

Does this road go to ...?
Führt diese Straße nach ...? — fürt dee·ze shtrah·se nahkh ...

(How long) Can I park here?
(Wie lange) Kann ich hier parken? — (vee lang·e) kan ikh heer par·ken

Where's a petrol station?
Wo ist eine Tankstelle? — vaw ist ai·ne tangk·shte·le

I need a mechanic.
Ich brauche einen Mechaniker. — ikh brow·khe ai·nen me·khah·ni·ker

My car/motorbike has broken down (at ...).
Ich habe (in ...) eine Panne mit meinem Auto/Motorrad. — ikh hah·be (in ...) ai·ne pa·ne mit mai·nem ow·to/maw·tor·raht

I've run out of petrol.
Ich habe kein Benzin mehr. — ikh hah·be kain ben·tseen mair

I have a flat tyre.
Ich habe eine Reifenpanne. — ikh hah·be ai·ne rai·fen·pa·ne

- - - - - - - - - - - - - - - - - - -

EMERGENCIES

Help!
Hilfe! — hil·fe

I'm lost.
Ich habe mich verirrt. — ikh hah·be mikh fer·irt

Call the police!
Rufen Sie die Polizei! — roo·fen zee dee po·li·tsai

Signs
- - - - - - - - - - - - - - - - - - - -

Einfahrt	Entrance
Ausfahrt	Exit
Einfahrt Verboten	No entry
Einbahnstraße	One way
Parkverbot	No Parking
Mautstelle	Toll

STRETCH YOUR LEGS COLOGNE

Start/Finish: Kölner Dom

Distance: 2km

Duration: Three hours

Cologne's history is everywhere, as you'll see on this walk, which circles through the heart of the bustling city. You can view Roman or medieval ruins, and you'll always be near somewhere to pause for refreshments.

Take this walk on Trips

Kölner Dom

Cologne's geographical and spiritual heart – and its single-biggest tourist draw – is the magnificent **Kölner Dom** (Cologne Cathedral; ☎0211-1794 0200; www. koelner-dom.de; tower adult/concession €4/2; ☺6am-9pm May-Oct, to 7.30pm Nov-Apr, tower 9am-6pm May-Sep, to 5pm Mar-Apr & Oct, to 4pm Nov-Feb), with its soaring twin spires, art and treasures. Climb the 533 steps up its south tower to the base of the steeple that dwarfed all European buildings until Eiffel built a certain tower in Paris. The underground Domforum visitor centre is a good source of info and tickets.

The Walk » There are large parking facilities around the Dom and the neighbouring Hauptbahnhof (just follow the signs). Then, after Kölner Dom, walk south across the Roncalliplatz to Am Hof, turn east then go south again on Bechergasse to the large, open Rathausplatz.

Altes Rathaus

Dating to the 15th century and much restored, the **old city hall** (Rathausplatz; ☺8am-4pm Mon, Wed & Thu, to 6pm Tue) has fine bells that ring daily at noon and 5pm. The Gothic tower is festooned with statues of old city notables.

The Walk » Walk to the west side of the Rathaus.

Archäologische Zone

Cologne used the construction of the U-Bahn line to also build this grand **Future Jüdisches Museum** (Archaeological Zone/Jewish Museum; ☎0221-2213 3422; Kleine Buden-gasse 2; adult/concession €3.50/3; ☺10am-5pm Tue-Sun) under the Rathausplatz. At the deepest level is the Praetorium, with relics of a Roman governor's palace. One level up are relics from the Middle Ages Jewish community.

The Walk » Cross the Marsplatz on the south side of the square to the museum.

Wallraf-Richartz-Museum

A famous collection of European paintings from the 13th to the 19th centuries, the **Wallraf-Richartz-Museum** (☎0221-2212 1119; www.wallraf.museum; Obenmarspforten; adult/concession €8/4.50; ☺10am-6pm Tue, Wed & Fri-Sun, to 9pm Thu) occupies a postmodern

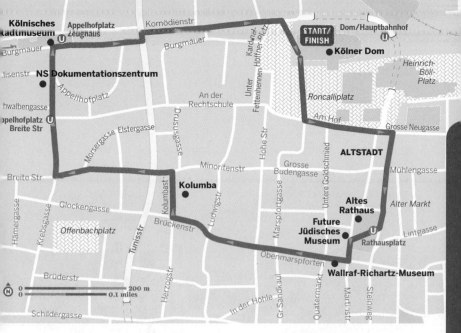

cube designed by OM Ungers. Works are presented chronologically, with the oldest on the 1st floor where stand-outs include examples from the Cologne School, known for its distinctive use of colour.

The Walk » Go west past the shops on Obenmarspforten for four streets, then turn north on Kolumbastrasse.

Kolumba

Art, history, architecture and spirituality form a harmonious tapestry in this spectacular collection of religious treasures of the Archdiocese of Cologne. Called **Kolumba** (☑0221-933 1930; www.kolumba.de; Kolumbastrasse 4; adult/child €5/free; ☺noon-5pm Wed-Mon), the building encases the ruins of the late-Gothic church of St Kolumba and layers of foundations going back to Roman times. Don't miss the 12th-century carved ivory crucifix.

The Walk » Walk west on commercial Breite Strasse, then turn north on Dumont-Strasse.

NS Dokumentationszentrum

Cologne's Third Reich history is poignantly documented in the **NS Documentation**

Centre (☑0221-2212 6332; www.museenkoeln. de; Appellhofplatz 23-25; adult/concession €4.50/2; ☺10am-6pm Tue-Fri, 11am-6pm Sat & Sun). In the basement of this otherwise mundane-looking building was the local Gestapo prison where scores of people were interrogated, tortured and killed.

The Walk » It's just a short jaunt north again along low-key Dumont-Strasse.

Kölnisches Stadtmuseum

The **Kölnisches Stadtmuseum** (Cologne City Museum; ☑0221-2212 2398; www.museenkoeln. de; Zeughausstrasse 1-3; adult/concession €5/3; ☺10am-8pm Tue, to 5pm Wed-Sun), in the former medieval armoury, explores all facets of Cologne history. There are exhibits on Carnival, *Kölsch* (the local beer), eau de cologne and other things that make the city unique. A **model** recreates the city of 1571; it's huge yet minutely detailed.

The Walk » Return to the Dom along Komödienstrasse, with the cathedral towers looming ever closer. Stop off for a much-deserved refreshment at Café Reichard, facing the Dom.

Switzerland

A PLACE OF HEART-STOPPING NATURAL BEAUTY AND HEAD-SPINNING EFFICIENCY, Switzerland lies in the centre of Europe yet exhibits a unique blend of cultures. Dazzling outdoor scenery, such as the ever-admired Alps, pristine lakes, lush meadows and chocolate-box chalets, combines with local traditions, cosmopolitan cities and smooth infrastructure.

In short, Switzerland makes it easy for you to dive deep into its heart: distances are manageable and variety is within easy reach. You can be perusing a farmers market for picnic provisions in the morning, then feasting on them on a mountaintop come lunchtime. At nightfall, try gazing at stars in the night sky from cosy digs or revelling in the cultural offerings of one of Switzerland's urbane cities.

Lucerne View of the Old Town

Switzerland

37 The Swiss Alps 7 Days
The greatest of the great outdoors: perfect peaks, gorgeous glaciers, verdant valleys. (p529)

38 Geneva to Zürich 7 Days
Mountains, pastures, lakes and small-town charm, book-ended by Switzerland's biggest cities. (p541)

The Matterhorn

Symbol of Switzerland, this magical mountain demands to be photographed. See it for yourself on Trip 37

Züri-West

Switzerland dispenses with its staid reputation in this hip Zürich neighbourhood full of great bars, clubs, cafes and restaurants. Explore it on Trip 38

Interlaken Lake Brienz

527

The Swiss Alps

37

From Arosa to Zermatt, this zigzagging trip is the A to Z of Switzerland's astounding Alpine scenery, with majestic peaks, formidable panoramas, cable-car rides and local charm.

TRIP HIGHLIGHTS

612 km

Zermatt
Switzerland's Alpine heart beats strongest here

77 km

Vals
A modern architectural jewel embellishes this remote spa town

Grindelwald

Schilthorn (2970m)

Andermatt

Arosa
START

2

11

12
FINISH

Aletsch Glacier
A mesmerising marvel, viewed from on-high

538 km

7 DAYS
612 KM / 382 MILES

GREAT FOR...

BEST TIME TO GO

This trip can be done year-round, although certain mountain passes may be closed to vehicular traffic.

ESSENTIAL PHOTO

The magical Matterhorn is the ultimate mountain photo op.

BEST FOR OUTDOORS

Whatever the season, the Alps offer activities galore.

37 The Swiss Alps

A natural barrier, the Alps are both a blessing and a burden when it comes to tripping around Switzerland. The soul-stirring views are stupendous, but you have to get over, around them or go through them to reach the next one. Starting in Graubünden's Arosa and finishing in Valais' Zermatt, this trip visits five cantons via hairpin bends, valley highways, tunnels, passes and cable cars to bring you the best.

① Arosa

Framed by the peaks of **Weisshorn**, **Hörnli** and moraine-streaked **Schiesshorn**, Arosa is a great Alpine all-rounder: perfect for downhill and cross-country skiing in winter, hiking and downhill biking in summer, and heaps of activities for families year-round. Although only 30km southeast of Chur (Switzerland's oldest city), getting here involves a series of 365 hairpin bends so challenging that Arosa cannot be reached by postal buses. Once here, you may want to revel in the beauty of the Mario Botta–designed **Tschuggen Bergoase Spa** (http://en.tschuggen.ch/spa; Tschuggen Grand Hotel; non-guest morning/evening pass Sfr65, massage from Sfr80; ⊙7am-9pm), an architectural statement built at the foot of the mountains. The recurring leaf-shaped motifs throughout the structures look particularly striking when illuminated at night.

✗ p539

The Drive ≫ The trip from Arosa to Vals takes 79km and 1¾ hours. First, head back towards Chur, then take Rte 19 to Ilanz, from where you drive a delightful road that passes through Uors and St Martin before arriving at Vals (1252m). About 2km short of the village, you emerge into Alpine pastures, liberally scattered with chalets and shepherds' huts.

② Vals

Shadowing the course of the babbling **Glogn** (Glenner) stream south, the luxuriantly green **Valsertal** (Vals Valley) is full of sleepy hamlets and thundering waterfalls, Vals stretches 2km along its glittering stream. The secret of this chocolate-box village and its soothing waters is out since Basel-born architect Peter Zumthor worked architectural magic to transform **Therme Vals** (☎081 926 89 61; www.therme-vals.ch; adult/child Sfr80/52, with Vals guest card Sfr45/30; ⊙11am-8pm) into a temple of cutting-edge cool.

Using 60,000 slabs of local quartzite, Zumthor created one of the country's most enchanting thermal spas. Aside from heated indoor and outdoor pools, this grey-stone labyrinth hides all sorts of watery nooks and crannies, cleverly lit and full of cavernous atmosphere. You can drift away in the bath-warm Feuerbad (42°C) and perfumed Blütenbad, sweat it out in the steam room and cool down in the teeth-chattering Eisbad.

🛏 p539

The Drive ≫ Take the road back to Ilanz, then continue on

LINK YOUR TRIP

38 **Geneva to Zürich**
Arosa is a two-hour drive southeast (147km) on the A3 from Zürich, the end point of this bucolic ramble between Switzerland's biggest cities.

2 **The Graceful Italian Lakes**
A scenic two-hour drive (143km) across the Simplon Pass into Italy gets you to Stresa in the glorious Lake Maggiore region.

Rte 19 until you reach Disentis/
Mustér (50km, 55 minutes).

❸ Disentis Abbey

Disentis/Mustér's
Benedictine monastery,
Kloster Disentis (www.
kloster-disentis.ch; Via Claustra
1, Disentis/Mustér; museum
adult/child Sfr7/3; ⊙museum
2-5pm Tue, Thu & Sat Jun-
Oct), which rises like a
vision above the town,
has a lavishly stuccoed
baroque church attached.
A monastery has stood
here since the 8th century,
but the present immense
complex dates from the
18th century. Left of the
church entrance is a door
to the **Klostermuseum**,
crammed with memora-
bilia. Head left upstairs
to the **Marienkirche**, a
chapel with Romanesque
origins filled with ex-voto
images from people in
need of (or giving thanks
for) a miraculous inter-
vention from the Virgin
Mary. If you're peckish,
a handy (and very good-
value) on-site cafe/
takeaway has soups, sal-
ads and specialities.

The Drive >> Disentis is
an exhilarating (40 minutes,
32km) drive along Rte 19 and
the twisting Oberalp Pass
(2044m), which connects
Graubünden and Uri cantons.
In winter, the Oberalp Pass is
closed to cars, but a car train
connects Sedrun on Rte 19
and Andermatt (three services
daily in winter, two in spring).
Reservations are essential. Call
☎027 927 77 40 or visit www.
matterhorngotthardbahn.ch.

LOCAL KNOWLEDGE: ZUMDORF

If the grand scale of this trip seems overwhelming,
the antidote surely lies in a quick detour to
Switzerland's smallest village, **Zumdorf** (Uri canton),
little more than a cluster of small buildings on the
Furkastrasse and a population that can be counted
on one hand. Despite its diminutive size, it has a
place to eat, **Restaurant Zum Dörfli** (☎041 887
01 32; www.zumdoerfli.ch; Furkastrasse; mains Sfr26-40),
specialising in Swiss dishes (especially rösti) and
venison (when in season). Find it 6km southwest of
Andermatt's centre.

TRIP HIGHLIGHT

❹ Andermatt

Blessed with austere
mountain appeal,
Andermatt (Uri canton)
contrasts low-key village
charm (despite a recent
five-star development)
with big wilderness. Once
an important staging-
post on the north–south
St Gotthard route, it's
now bypassed by the
tunnel, but remains a
major crossroads near
four major Alpine passes
(Susten, Oberalp, St Got-
thard and Furka), making
it a terrific base for **hiking**
and **cycling**. The tourist
office distributes free
booklets outlining these
opportunities.

One popular hike leads
from the Oberalp Pass to
sparkly **Lai da Tuma**, the
source of the Rhine; the
11km round trip takes
three to four hours, with
500m elevation gain.

A walk around and
along **Gotthardstrasse** reveals textbook dark-wood
central Swiss architecture,
often weighed down with
either geraniums or snow.

Skiers in the know flock
to 2963m **Gemsstock** (www.
skiarena.ch; cable car one-way/
return Sfr36/50) mountain,
reached by the Gemsstock-
bahn cable car (undergoing
a major overhaul at the
time of research), for the
snow-sure winter slopes.

🛏 p539

The Drive >> From Andermatt
to Engelberg, take Rte 2 to
Göschenen, then get on the A2/
E35 and follow the signs for
Lucerne. The road will skirt the
bottom of Lake Uri for some
lovely water views. Continue on
this road until you take exit 33
(Stans-Süd), then follow Rte 374
all the way to Engelberg (one
hour, 77km in total).

---

❺ Engelberg

Wonderful Engelberg (lit-
erally 'Angel Mountain'),
backed by the glacial

bulk of **Mt Titlis** (www.titlis. ch) – central Switzerland's tallest mountain – and frosted peaks, which feature in many a Bollywood production, is divine. After visiting the 12th-century Benedictine **Engelberg Monastery** (Kloster Engelberg; 041 639 61 19; www.kloster-engelberg. ch; church admission free, tours adult/child Sfr8/free; 1hr tour 10am & 4pm Wed-Sat), get closer to the heavens via the world's first revolving **cable car** (www.titlis. ch/en/tickets/cable-car-ride; adult/child return Sfr89/44.50; 8.30am-5pm). The cable car pirouettes over the dazzling **Titlis Glacier**, peaks rising like shark

fins ahead, before you step out onto Titlis station's **terrace** (3020m), with a panorama that stretches to Eiger, Mönch and Jungfrau in the Bernese Oberland. For even more thrilling views, step onto the adjacent **Cliff Walk** (www.titlis.ch/en/glacier/cliff-walk; 9.15am-4.45pm) – opened in 2012, this 100m-long, 1m-wide, cable-supported swinging walkway is Europe's highest suspension bridge.

There are some 360km of marked hiking trails in and around Engelberg. For gentle ambles and gorgeous scenery, head for **Brunni** on the opposite side of the valley. The

Brunni cable car (www. brunni.ch; cable car one-way/ return Sfr18/30, incl chairlift one-way/return Sfr26/42) goes up to Ristis at 1600m, where a chairlift takes you to the Swiss Alpine Club's refurbished **Brunni Hütte**. From here you can watch a magnificent sunset before spending the night, should you wish.

p539

The Drive » As Engelberg is a 'dead end' retrace your route back to the A2, heading west, before turning onto the A8 (direction Interlaken), and continuing alongside bright-blue Brienzersee to Giessbachfälle (one hour and 10 minutes, 71km).

AROUND GRINDELWALD: FIRST

From Grindelwald, a cable car zooms up to **First**, the trailhead for 100km of paths, half of which stay open in winter. From here, you can trudge up to **Faulhorn** (2681m; 2½ hours), even in winter, via the cobalt **Bachalpsee** (Lake Bachalp). As you march along the ridge, the unfolding views of the Jungfrau massif are entrancing. Stop for lunch and 360-degree views at Faulhorn. From here, you might like to continue on to Schynige Platte (another three hours) and return by train.

Other great walks head to **Schwarzhorn** (three hours), **Grosse Scheidegg** (1½ hours), **Unterer Gletscher** (1½ hours) and **Grindelwald** itself (2½ hours).

First has 60km of well-groomed pistes, which are mostly wide, meandering reds suited to intermediates. The south-facing slopes make for interesting skiing through meadows and forests. Freestylers should check out the kickers and rails at Bärgelegg or have a go on the superpipe at Schreckfeld station.

Faulhorn happens to be the starting point for **Europe's longest toboggan run**, accessible only on foot. Bring a sled to bump and glide 15km over icy pastures and through glittering woodlands all the way back down to Grindelwald via Bussalp. Nicknamed 'Big Pintenfritz', the track lasts around 1½ hours, depending on how fast you slide.

Year-round, you can get your pulse racing on the **First Flyer**, a staggeringly fast zip-line from First to Schreckfeld. The mountains are but a blur as, secure in your harness, you pick up speeds of around 84km/h.

Opened in 2015, the **First Cliff Walk** is a summit trail with a 40m-long suspension bridge, climbing stairs and an observation deck, with suitably impressive views of the local landscape and the jaw-dropping mountains.

WHY THIS IS A GREAT TRIP
SALLY O'BRIEN, AUTHOR

Even though I now call Switzerland home, the Alpine scenery still has an other-worldly effect on me. The abundance of snow-capped peaks, mountains with fairy-tale names that 'pop up' at numerous vantage points, time-defying glaciers, gravity-defying railways. And then there's the moment you catch sight of the Matterhorn...

Top: Mountain biking around Andermatt
Left: Climbers on the Matterhorn
Right: Aletsch Glacier

⑥ Giessbachfalle

Illuminating the fir forests like a spotlight in the dark, the misty **Giessbachfälle** (Giessbach Falls) plummet 500m over 14 rocky ridges. Europe's oldest **funicular**, dating to 1879, creaks up from the boat station (one-way/return Sfr5/10), but it's only a 15-minute walk up to the most striking section of the falls.

The Drive » Get back onto the A8 and follow the road along the Brienzersee until exit 25 (Wilderswil/Grindelwald), then continue as the road winds its way through rural countryside up to Grindelwald (39km, 45 minutes).

⑦ Grindelwald

Grindelwald's sublime natural assets are film-set stuff: the chiselled features of the north face of **Eiger**, the glinting tongues of **Oberer** and **Unterer Glaciers** and the crown-like peak of **Wetterhorn**. Skiers and hikers cottoned onto its charms in the late 19th century, which makes it one of Switzerland's oldest resorts. And it has lost none of its appeal, with geranium-studded Alpine chalets and verdant pastures aplenty.

Turbulent waters carve a path through the craggy glacier gorge known as **Gletscherschlucht** (Glacier Gorge; adult/child Sfr7/3.50; ⊙10am-5pm

May-Oct, to 6pm Jul & Aug), a 30-minute walk south of the centre. A footpath weaves through tunnels hacked into cliffs veined with pink and green marble. It's justifiably a popular spot for canyon and bungee-jumping expeditions.

Grindelwald is outstanding **hiking** territory, veined with trails that command arresting views to massive north faces, crevasse-filled glaciers and snow-capped peaks. High-altitude walks can be reached by taking cable cars from the village.

 p539

The Drive » From Grindelwald, follow the signs to Lauterbrunnen, which is 20km (15 minutes) away by car.

❽ Lauterbrunnen

Laid-back Lauterbrunnen's wispy **Staubbachfall**
(Staubbach Falls; ☺8am-8pm Jun-Oct) inspired both Goethe and Lord Byron to pen poems to their ethereal beauty. Today the postcard-perfect village, nestled deep in the valley of 72 waterfalls, including the **Trümmelbachfälle**
(Trümmelbach Falls; www. truemmelbachfaelle.ch; adult/ child Sfr11/4; ☺9am-5pm), attracts a less highfalutin crowd.

Hikes heading up into the mountains from the waterfall-laced valley include a 2½-hour uphill trudge to car-free **Mürren** and a more gentle 1¾-hour walk to **Stechelberg**. In winter, you can glide past frozen waterfalls on a well-prepared 12km cross-country trail.

The Drive » From Lauterbrunnen, head to Stechelberg (10 minutes, 6km), where you'll leave the car (paid parking available) and take the cable car to Schiltorn (adult/
child Stechelberg–Schilthorn return Sfr102/51).

❾ Schilthorn

There's a tremendous 360-degree, 200-peak panorama from the 2970m **Schilthorn** (www. schilthorn.ch), best appreciated from the **Skyline viewing platform** or **Piz Gloria revolving restaurant**. On a clear day, you can see from **Titlis** around to **Mont Blanc**, and across to the German Black Forest.

Some visitors seem more preoccupied with practising their delivery of the line, 'The name's Bond, James Bond', because a few scenes from *On Her Majesty's Secret Service* were shot here in 1968–69. The **Bond World 007** interactive exhibition gives you the chance to pose for photos secret-agent style and

LOCAL KNOWLEDGE: WINE TIME

The canton of Valais, which features so much of Switzerland's stunning Alpine scenery, is also the largest and best producer of wine in the country, so sampling it in situ at the end of a day's driving is a great idea.

Drenched in extra sunshine and light from above the southern Alps, much of the land north of the Rhône River in western Valais is planted with vines. Unique to the Valais are the bisses (narrow irrigation channels) that traverse the vineyards.

Dryish white Fendant, the perfect accompaniment to fondue and raclette, and best served crisp cold, is the region's best-known wine, accounting for two-thirds of Valais wine production. Dôle, made from Pinot noir and Garnay grapes, is the principal red blend and is full bodied, with a firm fruit flavour.

When ordering wine in a wine bar or restaurant, use the uniquely Swiss approach of deci (decilitre – ie a 10th of a litre) multiples. Or just order a bottle...

THE HIGH LIFE

Charming as Zermatt is, heading out of town and up to the mountains is a rush like no other.

Europe's highest cogwheel railway, the **Gornergratbahn** (www.gornergrat.ch; Bahnhofplatz 7; one-way adult/child Sfr42/21; ⊙7am-9.50pm), has climbed through picture-postcard scenery to Gornergrat (3089m) – a 30-minute journey – since 1898. Sit on the right-hand side to gawp at the Matterhorn. Tickets allow you to get on and off en route; there are restaurants at Riffelalp (2211m) and Riffelberg (2582m). In summer an extra train runs once a week at sunrise and sunset – the most spectacular trips of all.

Views from Zermatt's cable cars are all remarkable, but the **Matterhorn Glacier Paradise** (www.matterhornparadise.ch; adult/child Sfr99/49.50; ⊙8.30am-4.20pm) is the icing on the cake. Ride Europe's highest-altitude cable car to 3883m and marvel at 14 glaciers and 38 mountain peaks over 4000m from the Panoramic Platform (only open in good weather). Don't miss the Glacier Palace, an ice palace complete with glittering ice sculptures and an ice slide to swoosh down bum first. End with some exhilarating snow tubing outside in the snowy surrounds.

relive movie moments in a helicopter and bobsled.

The Drive » When you descend back to Stechelberg, head to Kandersteg via the road down to Interlaken. Get on the A8/Rte 11, then take exit 19 (direction Spiez/Kandersteg/ Adelboden). The 60km trip takes one hour.

⑩ Kandersteg

Turn up in Kandersteg wearing anything but muddy boots and you'll attract a few odd looks. Hiking is this town's raison d'être, with 550km of surrounding trails. An amphitheatre of spiky peaks studded with glaciers and jewel-coloured lakes such as **Blausee** (www.blausee.ch; adult/child Sfr7/3; ⊙9am-5pm) and **Oeschinensee** (www. oeschinensee.ch; cable-car one-way/return Sfr18/26; ⊙cable car 8am-6pm) creates a

sublime natural backdrop to the rustic village of dark-timber chalets.

In winter, there are more than 50km of cross-country ski trails, including the iced-over Oeschinensee. The limited 15km of downhill skiing is suited to beginners. Kandersteg's frozen waterfalls attract ice climbers and the village hosts the spectacular annual **Ice Climbing Festival** (⊙Jan).

The Drive » From Kandersteg, take the **BLS Lötschberg Tunnel** (www.bls.ch/e/ autoverlad/tickets-goppenstein. php), which connects with Goppenstein (in Valais) at regular intervals daily. The trip takes 15 minutes and costs from Sfr25 per car if booked online. From Goppenstein, head east from Rte 9. Once past Brig, the deep valley narrows and the landscape switches to rugged wilderness, with a string of bucolic villages of timber

chalets and onion-domed churches (47km).

TRIP HIGHLIGHT

⑪ Aletsch Glacier

The Aletsch Glacier is a seemingly never-ending, 23km-long swirl of ice with deep crevasses that slices past thundering falls, jagged spires of rock and pine forest. It stretches from Jungfrau in the Bernese Oberland to a plateau above the Rhône and is, justly so, a Unesco World Heritage site.

Picture-postcard riverside Fiesch on the valley floor is the best place to access it. From the village, ride the **cable car** (www.eggishorn. ch; adult/child 6-16yr return from Fiesch Sfr57/28.50) up to Fiescheralp and continue up to Eggishorn (2927m). Streaming down in a broad curve around the

Aletschhorn (4195m), the glacier is just like a frozen six-lane superhighway. In the distance to the north rise the glistening summits of Jungfrau (4158m), Mönch (4107m), Eiger (3970m) and Finsteraarhorn (4274m). To the southwest of the cable-car exit, you can spy Mont Blanc and the Matterhorn.

🛏 p539

The Drive » It takes one hour (56km) to get from Fiesch to Täsch via Rte 19 to Visp, then the winding rural road to Täsch itself. You'll park the car here before boarding the train to car-free Zermatt.

- - - - - - - - - - -

TRIP HIGHLIGHT

12 Zermatt

You can almost sense the anticipation on the train from Täsch. Then, as you arrive in car-free Zermatt, the pop-up-book effect of the one-of-a-kind **Matterhorn** (4478m) works its magic. Like a shark's fin it rises above the town, with moods that swing from

pretty and pink to dark and mysterious. Since the mid-19th century, Zermatt has starred among Switzerland's glitziest resorts. Today skiers cruise along well-kept pistes, spellbound by the scenery, while style-conscious darlings flash designer threads in the town's swish lounge bars.

Meander main-strip **Bahnhofstrasse** with its boutiques and stream of horse-drawn sleds or carriages and electric taxis, then head towards the noisy Vispa river along **Hinterdorfstrasse**. This old-world street is crammed with archetypal Valaisian timber granaries propped up on stone discs and stilts to keep out pesky rats; look for the fountain commemorating Ulrich Inderbinen (1900–2004), a Zermatt-born mountaineer who climbed the Matterhorn 370 times, the last time at age 90.

A walk in Zermatt's **Mountaineers' Cemetery** (Kirchstrasse) in the garden

of St Mauritius Church is sobering. Numerous gravestones tell of untimely deaths on Monte Rosa, the Matterhorn and Breithorn. In July 2015 a **memorial** to 'the unknown climber' was unveiled to mark the 150th anniversary of the Matterhorn's first ascent.

The **Matterhorn Museum** (☎027 967 41 00; www.matterhornmuseum.ch; Kirchplatz; adult/child Sfr10/5; ⏰11am-6pm Jul-Sep & mid-Dec–Apr, 3-6pm Oct–mid-Dec) provides a fascinating insight into Valaisian village life, the dawn of tourism in Zermatt and the lives the Matterhorn has claimed. Short films portray the first successful ascent of the Matterhorn on 14 July 1865, led by Edward Whymper, a feat marred by tragedy on the descent when four team members crashed to their deaths in a 1200m fall down the North Wall. The infamous rope that broke is on display.

✕ 🛏 p539

Eating & Sleeping

Arosa ❶

✖ Burestübli   Swiss €€

(☎081 377 18 38; Hotel Arlenwald, Prätschli; mains Sfr25-42; ⊙8am-midnight) This woodsy chalet has magical above-the-treetop views. Come winter, pots of gooey fondue and mugs of glühwein fuel floodlit dashes through the snow.

Vals ❷

🛏 Hotel Therme   Design Hotel €€€

(☎081 926 80 80; www.therme-vals.ch; Vals; s Sfr290-390, d Sfr390-590; P🖅) Peter Zumthor revamped many rooms at this famous spa hotel, with others given a Japanese touch (thanks to Tadao Ando and Kengo Kuma). The restaurants emphasise local and organic ingredients.

Andermatt ❹

🛏 River House
Boutique Hotel   Design Hotel €€

(☎041 887 00 25; www.theriverhouse.ch; Gotthardstrasse 58; s Sfr150-210, d Sfr200-280; P🖅) At this stylish eco-hotel in a 250-year-old building, the owners have created unique and beautiful rooms, some with river views. The excellent on-site restaurant features local produce and Swiss wines.

Engelberg ❺

🛏 Ski Lodge Engelberg   Hotel €€

(☎041 637 35 00; www.skilodgeengelberg.com; Erlenweg 36; s/d/tr/q Sfr150/270/360/450; P🖅) Run by sociable Swedish pro skiers, this delightful lodge fuses art-nouveau flair with 21st-century comfort. Après-ski activities include gazing at snowy peaks from an outdoor spa and chef Jonas' stellar New Nordic cuisine.

Grindelwald ❼

✖ C & M   Swiss €€

(☎033 853 07 10; Almisgässli 1; snacks Sfr5-9, mains Sfr29-49; ⊙8.30am-11pm Wed-Mon) Just as appetising as the seasonally inspired dishes are the stupendous views to Unterer Gletscher from this gallery-style cafe's sunny terrace.

🛏 Gletschergarten   Historic Hotel €€

(☎033 853 17 21; www.hotel-gletschergarten.ch; Obere Gletscherstrasse 1; s Sfr130-170, d Sfr230-300; P🖅) The sweet Breitenstein family make you feel at home in their timber heirloom-filled chalet. Rooms have balconies facing Unterer Gletscher and Wetterhorn.

Aletsch Glacier ⓫

🛏 Fiesch Youth Hostel   Hostel €

(www.youthhostel.ch/en/hostels/fiesch; Sport Ferien Resort; dm with shared bathroom per person from Sfr35, d with private bathroom per person Sfr50) This 1970s bunker-like complex plays host to 1001 activities and has spotless rooms (many recently updated).

Zermatt ⓬

✖ Snowboat   International €

(☎027 967 43 33; www.snowboat.ch; Vispastrasse 20; mains Sfr19-26; ⊙noon-midnight) This is a hybrid eating-drinking, riverside address with yellow deckchairs on its rooftop terrace. Head here for barbecue-sizzled burgers, creative salads and great cocktails.

🛏 Suitenhotel
Zurbriggen   Boutique Hotel €€

(☎027 966 38 38; www.zurbriggen.ch; Schluhmattstrasse 68; high season d/ste/apt from Sfr290/420/490) Owned by Swiss Alpine skiing legend Pirmin Zurbriggen, this modern hotel has a handy position near the cable-car station for Matterhorn Glacier Paradise. Suites have south-facing balconies and Matterhorn views, plus there's a wellness area.

Geneva to Zürich

38

Connect the dots between Switzerland's two biggest cities on a trip that takes you through its enigmatic heartland, historic cities, spine-tingling ascents and a world-famous mountain trio.

TRIP HIGHLIGHTS

0 km

Geneva
Cosmopolitan city and Old Town grace galore

481 km

Zürich
Culturally vibrant city with a post-industrial edge

FINISH
9

Lucerne

Bern

8

Fribourg

Stanserhorn
An open-air cable car; the perfect Lake Lucerne panorama

402 km

1
START

7 DAYS
481KM / 300 MILES

GREAT FOR...

BEST TIME TO GO
Late spring, summer and autumn, when the light and weather are best.

ESSENTIAL PHOTO
The verdant Emmental region exemplifies pastoral perfection.

BEST FOR CULTURE
Zürich's mighty museums and relentless nightlife are intoxicating.

Grindelwald Hiking at the foot of the Eiger

38 Geneva to Zürich

Rather than take a straight line from Geneva to Zürich, this trip gives you room to roam some of Switzerland's finest sights: small cities with charming Old Towns, heaven-sent lakes with dreamy views, winding roads through countryside that is by turns bucolic and wild, an adventure capital with the perfect setting, a train ride to the top of Europe and scenic ascents that will have you gasping, all book-ended by Switzerland's cultural capitals.

TRIP HIGHLIGHT

❶ Geneva

Cosmopolitan Geneva is a rare blend: a multicultural population chattering in every language under the sun, a distinctly French feel, one of the world's most expensive cities, a stronghold of the Protestant Reformation, a synonymity with numbered bank accounts and a humanitarian haven.

With a whole day and night, schedule time for Geneva's magnificent **Old Town**. Waterside attractions exert a strong pull, so make a beeline for the emblematic **Jet d'Eau** (Quai Gustave-Ador) and the egalitarian public swimming baths at **Bains des Pâquis** (☎022 732 29 74; www.bains-des-paquis.ch; Quai du Mont-Blanc 30; ☺9am-8pm mid-Apr–mid-Sep).

Plenty of museums will tempt you: among the best are the **Musée d'Art Moderne et Contemporain** (MAMCO; ☎022 320 61 22; www.mamco.ch; Rue des Vieux-Grenadiers 10; adult/child Sfr8/free; ☺noon-6pm Tue-Fri, 11am-6pm Sat & Sun) the **Musée International de la Croix-Rouge et du Croissant-Rouge** (International Red Cross & Red Crescent Museum; www.redcrossmuseum.ch; Av de la Paix 17; adult/child Sfr15/7; ☺10am-6pm Tue-Sun Apr-Oct, to 5pm Nov-Mar), the new **ICT Discovery** (☎022 730 61 55; www.ictdiscovery.org; Rue de Varembé 2; ☺10am-

1pm & 2-5pm Mon-Fri) and the lavish timepieces of **Patek Philipe Museum** (☎022 807 09 10; www.patekmuseum. com; Rue des Vieux-Grenadiers 7; adult/child Sfr10/free; ☺2-6pm Tue-Fri, 10am-6pm Sat).

If you're after a behind-the-scenes glimpse of the UN or the Large Hadron Collider, prebook a tour of the **Palais des Nations**

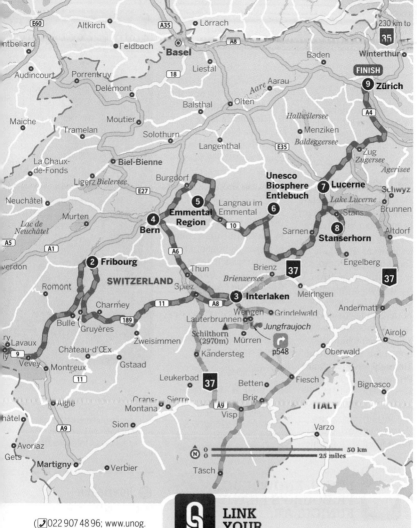

(📞022 907 48 96; www.unog.
ch; Av de la Paix 14; adult/child
Sfr12/7; 🕐10am-4pm Mon-Sat
Jul & Aug, 10am-noon & 2-4pm
Mon-Sat Sep-Jun) or **CERN**
(📞022 767 84 84; www.cern.
ch; Meyrin; 🕐guided tour 11am
Mon-Sat, 1pm Mon, Tue, Thu &
Fri), **respectively.**
   See also the Stretch
Your Legs walking tour
for Geneva on p552.

✕ p549

🔗 LINK YOUR TRIP

37 The Swiss Alps
It's a two-hour
(147km) drive southeast
from Zürich to Arosa,
the starting point of the
Swiss Alps whirl.

35 The Romantic Road
From Zurich, drive east
via the A1 to Füssen in
Germany, and do the
gorgeous Romantic Road
trip in reverse,

The Drive » From Geneva, head west via the A1 until the A9 (follow signs to Vevey/Montreux). Take exit 11 and follow signs for Lutry. From Lutry, take Rte 9 (direction Vevey) until Cully, then head up Rte de la Corniche to Chexbres. Next follow Rte du Genevrex and get on the A9, followed by the A12 to Fribourg (143km total).

② Fribourg

Nowhere is Switzerland's language divide felt more keenly than in Fribourg (Freiburg or 'Free Town'), a medieval city where the inhabitants on the west bank of the River Sarine speak French, and those on the east bank of the Sanne speak German. Sights that merit a look-see include the bohemian **Espace Jean Tinguely – Niki de Saint Phalle** (📞026 305 51 40; www.mahf.ch; Rue de Morat 2; adult/child Sfr6/free; ⏰11am-6pm Wed & Fri-Sun, to 8pm Thu), the evocative **Old Town** filled with Gothic

facades, the **Musée d'Art et d'Histoire** (📞026 305 51 40; www.mahf.ch; Rue de Morat 12; adult/child Sfr8/free; ⏰11am-6pm Tue, Wed & Fri-Sun, to 8pm Thu) and the outsize **Cathédrale de St Nicolas de Myre** (www.cathedrale-fribourg.ch; Rue des Chanoines 3; tower adult/child Sfr3.50/1; ⏰9.30am-6pm Mon-Fri, 9am-4pm Sat, 2-5pm Sun, tower 10am-noon & 2-5pm Mon-Fri, 10am-4pm Sat, 2-5pm Sun Apr-Oct) with its 74m-tall **tower**. Be sure to make time for a couple of the city's bohemian cafe-bars, such as Le Port (p549) or **Café Culturel de l'Ancienne Gare** (📞026 322 57 72; Esplanade de l'Ancienne-Gare 3; ⏰9am-11.30pm Mon-Thu, 9am-3am Fri, 1pm-3am Sat, 11am-midnight Sun).

🍴 🛏 p549

The Drive » We've chosen a longish (103km, one hour and 50 minutes) scenic route along winding roads through lovely small towns in Fribourg and Bern cantons, with unspoiled

countryside aplenty. Head first to the village of Charmey via Rte 189, then to Boltingen. Next take Rte 11 to Speiz on Lake Thun, from where you'll follow Rte 8 to Interlaken.

③ Interlaken

Once Interlaken made the Victorians swoon with mountain vistas from the chandelier-lit confines of grand hotels; today it makes daredevils scream with adrenaline-loaded adventures. Straddling the glittering Lakes Thun and Brienz and dazzled by the pearly whites of Eiger, Mönch and Jungfrau, the scenery is

---

◯ LOCAL KNOWLEDGE: FRIBOURG'S FILTHY FUNICULAR

Nowhere else in Europe does a funicular lurch up the mountainside with the aid of stinky sewage water (on certain days it smells as you'd expect). Constructed in 1899 and managed by the Cardinal Brewery until 1965 (when the municipality took over), the **Funiculaire de Fribourg** links the lower town with the upper. It runs every six minutes, and the ride in one of two counterbalancing water-powered carriages from the lower Pertuis station (121m; Place du Pertuis) to the upper station (618m; Rte des Alpes) takes two minutes.

Bern The city's Zytglogge (Clock Tower) is an important landmark

mind-blowing. Check out the views from **Harder Kulm** (www.harderkulm. ch), or do a daredevil activity with **Outdoor Interlaken** (☎033 826 77 19; www.outdoor-interlaken.ch; Hauptstrasse 15; ⏱8am-7pm), organised in advance. Leave the car in Interlaken after spending the night here and head to the Top of Europe (Jungfraujoch) very early the next morning.

🛏 p549

The Drive » From Interlaken to Bern is a one-hour (54km) drive via Lake Thun's Seestrasse, past turreted Schloss Oberhoffen and artnouveau-meets-neorenaissance Schloss Hünegg. After Thun, you'll get to the country's capital quickly via the A6.

- - - - - - - - - - -

❹ Bern

Wandering through the picture-postcard **Old Town**, with its laid-back, riverside air, it's hard to believe that Bern (Berne in French) is the Swiss capital, but it is, and a Unesco World Heritage site to boot. The flag-festooned, cobbled centre, rebuilt in distinctive grey-green sandstone after a devastating 1405 fire, is a delight, with 6km of covered arcades, cellar shops and bars, and fantastical folk figures frolicking on 16th-century fountains, such as the **Kindlifresserbrunnen** (Kornhausplatz). Be sure to visit Bern's **Münster** (www.berner muenster.ch; Münsterplatz 1; tower adult/child Sfr5/2; ⏱10am-5pm Mon-Sat, 11.30am-5pm Sun May–mid-Oct, noon-4pm Mon-Fri, 10am-5pm Sat, 11.30am-4pm Sun rest of year), the beautiful **Zytglogge** (Marktgasse), the famous **Bären Park** (Bear Park; www.baerenpark-bern.ch; ⏱9.30am-5pm), the architecturally daring **Zentrum Paul Klee** (☎031 359 01 01; www.zpk.org; Monument im Fruchtland 3;

ISLAND DINING

Genevan living is easy in summer when a constant crowd throngs the lakefront quays to hang out in pop-up terrace bars such as **La Terrasse** (www.laterrasse.ch; Quai du Mont-Blanc 31; ☺8am-midnight Apr-Sep), the fashionista spot by the water to see and be seen. Meander away from Quai du Mont-Blanc to uncover a brilliant trio of beloved summertime shacks on the water's edge – alfresco and effortlessly cool.

The right-bank address is refreshingly casual: Rhône-side **Terrasse Le Paradis** (☏079 665 35 73; www.terrasse-paradis.ch; Quai Turrettini; sandwiches & salads Sfr10-14; ☺10am-9pm Jun-Sep) is the type of cafe that practically begs you to pull out a book and stay all day in its deckchairs arranged down steps to the water while sipping beakers of homemade *citronnade* (lemonade). 'Paradise' does not serve alcohol, but the pots of green-mint tea flow and the wholly affordable sandwiches, salads and legendary *taboulé* hit the spot.

Le Bateau Lavoir (Passerelle des Lavandières; ☺11am-midnight Mon-Thu, 11am-2am Fri, 5pm-2am Sat May-Sep) is an eye-catching boat with rooftop terrace moored between the old market hall and Pont de la Coulouvrenière. Its cabin-size dining area cooks fondue and other basic local dishes, the crowd is hip and there is a 360-degree lake view. Its very design and name evokes the wash-house boats – yes, where undies et al were washed – that floated here in the 17th century.

Then there's **La Barje** (Terrasse des Lavandières; www.labarje.ch; Promenade des Lavandières; ☺11am-midnight Mon-Fri, 3pm-midnight Sat & Sun Apr-Sep), not a barge at all but a vintage caravan with tin roof and candy-striped facade, parked on the grassy banks of the Rhône near the Bâtiment des Forces Motrices. The beer and music are plentiful, outside concerts and art performances pull huge crowds, and proceeds go towards helping young people in difficulty.

---

adult/child Sfr20/7, audioguide Sfr6; ☺10am-5pm Tue-Sun) and the well-endowed **Kunstmuseum** (Museum of Fine Arts; ☏031 328 09 44; www.kunstmuseumbern.ch; Hodlerstrasse 8-12; adult/child Sfr7/free; ☺10am-9pm Tue, to 5pm Wed-Sun).

 p549

The Drive » Leave Bern via the A6 and take Krauchthalstrasse (35 minutes, about 24km) through verdant countryside to Burgdorf. From Burgdorf to Affoltern im Emmental, 6km to the east, is a scenic drive past old farmsteads proudly bedecked with flower boxes, neat woodpiles and kitchen gardens. Rte 23 between

Affoltern and Langnau im Emmental is 21km (25 minutes).

- - - - - - - - - - - - - - - -

❺ Emmental Region

After so much city time, the postcard-perfect landscapes of rural Switzerland beckon, with the bucolic idyll that is the Emmental region, where iconic and holey Emmental (Swiss) cheese is produced. To see how the cheese is made, head to **Emmentaler Schaukäserei** (☏034 435 16 11; www.showdairy. ch; Schaukäsereistrasse 6, Affoltern; ☺9am-6.30pm Apr-Oct, to 5pm Nov-Mar) in Affoltern.

The region's gateway towns of Burgdorf and Langnau im Emmental preside over a mellow patchwork of quiet villages, grazing cows and fabulous farm chalets with vast barns and overhanging roofs, strung out along the banks of the Emme river. Burgdorf (literally 'castle village') is split into an Upper and Lower Town. The natural highlight of the Oberstadt (Upper Town) is the 12th-century **Schloss** (castle), with its drawbridge, thick stone walls and trio of museums.

The Drive » From Langnau im Emmental, take Rte 10 for

30 minutes (23km), crossing over from Bern canton to Lucerne canton, until you reach Schüpfheim, the heart of the Entlebuch biosphere.

❻ Unesco Biosphere Entlebuch

The 39,000-plus-sq-km **Entlebuch area** (www.biosphaere.ch; a mixed mountain and highland ecosystem) was declared a Unesco Biosphere Reserve in 2001. Far from being a lonely wilderness outpost, the reserve is home to some 17,000 people keen to preserve their traditional dairy-farming lifestyle. The landscape of karst formations, sprawling moors (some 25% of the area), Alpine pastures and mountain streams, which rise from 600m to some 2350m above sea level, makes for some stirring scenery. The park office is in Schüpfheim.

The Drive » Driving through Entlebuch from Schüpfheim, you'll take the Panoramastrasse (which deserves to be more famous) to the town of Giswil (Obwalden canton; 50 minutes, 37km). Next, follow the signs to Lucerne (Luzern in German) along the A8 (30 minutes, 30km).

❼ Lucerne

Recipe for a gorgeous Swiss city: take a cobalt lake ringed by mountains of myth (Pilatus, Rigi), add a well-preserved medieval **Altstadt** (Old Town), then sprinkle with covered bridges **Kapellbrücke** (Chapel Bridge) and **Spreuerbrücke** (Spreuer Bridge; btwn Kasernenplatz & Mühlenplatz), sunny plazas, candy-coloured houses and waterfront promenades. Legend has it that an angel with a light showed the first settlers where to build a chapel in Lucerne, and today it still has amazing grace.

One minute it's nostalgic (its emotive **lion monument**; Löwendenkmal; Denkmalstrasse), the next highbrow, with concerts at acoustic marvel **Kultur und Kongresszentrum** (KKL; 🖉 tour reservations 041 226 79 50; www.kkl-luzern.ch; Europaplatz; guided tour adult/child Sfr15/9) and the peerless Picasso collection of **Museum Sammlung Rosengart** (🖉 041 220 16 60; www.rosengart.ch; Pilatusstrasse 10; adult/student Sfr18/16; ⊙10am-6pm Apr-Oct, 11am-5pm Nov-Mar). Crowd-pleasers such as **Verkehrshaus** (Swiss Museum of Transport; 🖉 041 370 44 44; www.verkehrshaus.ch; Lidostrasse 5; adult/child Sfr30/15; ⊙10am-6pm Apr-Oct, to 5pm Nov-Mar; 🚗) and the city's surrounding natural wonders never fail to impress, while balmy summers and golden autumns ensure this 'city of lights' shines constantly.

✕ 🛏 p549

The Drive » A fast 15-minute, 15km journey along the A2 will get you from Lucerne to Stans' Stansstaderstrasse 19, from where the journey up to Stanserhorn begins.

TRIP HIGHLIGHT

❽ Stanserhorn

Looming above the lake, 1898m **Stanserhorn** (www.stanserhorn.ch) boasts 360-degree vistas of **Lake Lucerne, Mt Titlis, Mt Pilatus** and the **Bernese Alps**, among others. Getting to the summit is half the fun. The journey starts with a ride on a vintage 19th-century funicular from Stans to Kälti; from here, the nearly transparent **CabriO** (🖉 041 618 80 40; www.cabrio.ch; Stansstaderstrasse 19, Stans; ticket office; all-inclusive funicular & cable-car fare adult/child one-way Sfr37/9.25, return Sfr74/18.50, online boarding pass Sfr5; ⊙mid-Apr–early Nov), launched in 2012 as the world's first cable car with an open upper deck, takes you the rest of the way, offering amazing on-the-go views.

On sunny days and when large numbers of travellers are expected, you'll need to book an online 'boarding pass' to confirm your time of departure and subsequent return.

At the summit there's the star-shaped **Rondorama**, the region's only revolving restaurant, which rotates 360 degrees every 43 minutes. Kids love the nearby **marmot park**, where the critters can be observed in a near-natural habitat.

DETOUR:
JUNGFRAUJOCH: THE TOP OF EUROPE

Presided over by monolithic **Eiger**, **Mönch** and **Jungfrau** (Ogre, Monk and Maiden), the crown jewels of Bernese Oberland's Alpine scenery, will make your heart skip a beat.

The 'big three' peaks have an enduring place in mountaineering legend, particularly the 3970m Eiger, whose fearsome north wall remained unconquered until 1938. Today, it takes only 2½ hours from Interlaken Ost (return fare Sfr204.40) by train to **Jungfraujoch** (3454m), Europe's highest station. From May through to October, the Good Morning Ticket costs Sfr145 if you take the first train (6.35am from Interlaken Ost) and leave the summit by 1pm.

From Kleine Scheidegg (the last stage of the journey), the train burrows through the Eiger before arriving at the Sphinx meteorological station. Opened in 1912, the tunnel took 3000 men 16 years to drill. Along the way, the Eigerwand and Eismeer stops have panoramic windows offering glimpses across rivers of crevassed ice. Good weather is *essential* for this journey; check beforehand on www.jungfrau. ch and always take warm clothing, sunglasses and sunscreen. Within the Sphinx weather station there's a nice sculpture gallery, restaurants, indoor viewpoints and a souvenir shop. Outside there are views of the 23km-long **Aletsch Glacier**. On cloudless days, the views stretch as far as the Black Forest in Germany.

When you tire (as if!) of the view, you can zip across the frozen plateau on a flying fox, dash downhill on a sled or snow disc, or enjoy a bit of tame skiing or boarding at the **Snow Park**. A day pass covering all activities costs adult/child Sfr45/25.

If you cross the glacier along the prepared path, in around an hour you reach the **Mönchsjochhütte** (☎033 971 34 72; www.moenchsjoch.ch; dm/d with half-board Sfr28/64; ⊙late Mar–mid-Oct) at 3650m, where hardcore rock climbers psyche themselves up to tackle the Eiger or Mönch.

The Drive ≫ Retrace your route along the A2 and head in the direction of Lucerne before changing to the A4 and following the signs to Zürich (50 minutes, 65km).

- - - - - - - - - -

TRIP HIGHLIGHT

⑨ Zürich

Culturally vibrant, efficiently run and attractively set at the meeting of river and lake, Zürich is constantly recognised as one of the world's most liveable cities. It's a savvy, hardworking financial centre, yet Switzerland's largest and wealthiest metropolis has an artsy, postindustrial edge. Much of the Old Town, with its winding lanes and quaint squares, is lovingly intact. Must-see sights include the glorious **Fraumünster** (www.frau muenster.ch; Münsterhof; ⊙9am-6pm Apr-Oct, 10am-4pm Nov-Mar), with its Marc Chagall stained-glass windows, the **Grossmünster** (www.grossmuenster.ch; Grossmünsterplatz; ⊙10am-6pm Mar-Oct, to 5pm Nov-Feb) with its salt-and-pepper-

shaker steeples, and the excellent **Kunsthaus** (☎044 253 84 84; www.kunsthaus.ch; Heimplatz 1; adult/child Sfr15/ free, Wed free; ⊙10am-8pm Wed-Fri, to 6pm Tue, Sat & Sun), which holds an impressive permanent collection. In summer, the fun revolves around the pools of the lake and river, such as **See-bad Utoquai** (☎044 251 61 51; Utoquai 49; adult/child Sfr7/3.50; ⊙7am-8pm mid-May–mid-Sep), **Frauenbad** (Stadthausquai) and **Männerbad** (Badweg 10).

✗ p549

Eating & Sleeping

Geneva ❶

✕ Brasserie des Halles de l'Île
European €€

(☎022 311 08 88; www.brasseriedeshallesdelile.ch; Place de l'Île 1; mains Sfr20-50; ☺10.30am-midnight Sun & Mon, to 1am Tue-Thu, to 2am Fri & Sat) An old market hall on an island, this industrial style venue produces a cocktail of aperitifs, after-dark DJs and fresh fare. Best seat in the house is a terrace hanging over the water.

Fribourg ❷

✕ Le Port
Cafe, Bar €€

(☎026 321 22 26; www.leport.ch; Planche-Inférieure 5; ☺10am-11pm Tue-Sun) In a former gas warehouse on the banks of the Sarine, the Port bursts with energy. Hang out on its shady riverside terrace enjoying lunchtime platters, or live bands and dancing at night.

⊨ Auberge aux 4 Vents
Boutique Hotel €€

(☎026 347 36 00; www.aux4vents.ch; Res Balzli Grandfrey 124; s Sfr130-170, d Sfr180-260, s/d/tr/q with shared bathroom Sfr65/130/170/200; P ✈) 'Stylish' scarcely does justice to this eight-room inn, with its dreamy Blue Room sporting a bathtub that rolls out on rails through the window for a soak beneath the stars.

Interlaken ❸

⊨ Victoria-Jungfrau Grand Hotel & Spa
Luxury Hotel €€€

(☎033 828 26 10; www.victoria-jungfrau.ch; Höheweg 41; d Sfr400-800, ste Sfr600-1000; P @ 🛜 ✈) The impeccable service here evokes a bygone era, with the perfect melding of well-preserved art-nouveau features, modern luxury, stellar dining and plum Jungfrau views.

Bern ❹

✕ Altes Tramdepot
Swiss €€

(☎031 368 14 15; www.altestramdepot.ch; Am Bärengraben; mains Sfr18-37; ☺11am-12.30am) At this cavernous microbrewery, Swiss staples compete against microbrews for your appetite.

⊨ Hotel Goldener Schlüssel
Hotel €€

(☎031 311 02 16; www.goldener-schluessel.ch; Rathausgasse 72; s Sfr148-185, d Sfr190-260; 🛜) This comfortable 500-year-old hotel has updated rooms in the Old Town.

Lucerne ❼

✕ Grottino 1313
Italian €€

(☎041 610 13 13; www.grottino1313.ch; Industriestrasse 7; 2-course lunch menu Sfr20; ☺11am-2pm & 6-11.30pm Mon-Fri, 6-11.30pm Sat, 9am-2pm Sun) A welcome escape, this relaxed yet stylish eatery with a candlelit interior serves seasonal menus featuring creative pasta dishes, meats cooked over an open fire and scrumptious desserts.

⊨ Château Gütsch
Hotel €€€

(☎041 289 14 14; www.chateau-guetsch.ch; Kanonenstrasse; d Sfr330-570, ste Sfr445-1260; 🛜) The setting is incomparable at this fairy-tale hilltop palace dating from 1888. Many rooms and suites enjoy sweeping views over Lake Lucerne, as do the bar and breakfast terrace. The decor features lavish details such as silver claw-footed bathtubs.

Zürich ❾

✕ Alpenrose
Swiss €€

(☎044 271 39 19; Fabrikstrasse 12; mains Sfr26-42; ☺11am-midnight Wed-Fri, 6.15-11pm Sat & Sun) With its timber-clad walls, 'No Polka Dancing' warning and multiregional Swiss cuisine, the Alpenrose exudes charm. Specialities include *Pizokel*, a savoury kind of *Spätzli* (egg noodles) from Graubünden.

NEED ^{TO} KNOW

CURRENCY
Swiss franc (official abbreviation CHF, also Sfr)

LANGUAGE
German (p520), French (p196), Italian (p110), Romansch

VISAS
Generally not required for stays of up to 90 days; some nationalities need a Schengen visa.

FUEL
Petrol stations are common on main roads and highways, and in larger towns. Unleaded costs around Sfr1.55 per litre and diesel is Sfr1.53.

RENTAL CARS
Auto Europe (www.autoeurope.com)

Avis (www.avis.com)

Europcar (www.europcar.com)

Hertz (www.hertz.com)

IMPORTANT NUMBERS
Europe-wide emergency covering police, fire and ambulance (☏112)

Climate

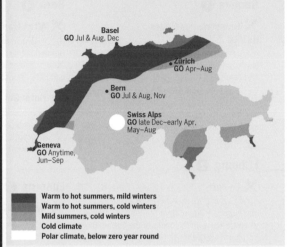

Basel
GO Jul & Aug, Dec

Zürich
GO Apr–Aug

Bern
GO Jul & Aug, Nov

Swiss Alps
GO late Dec–early Apr, May–Aug

Geneva
GO Anytime, Jun–Sep

Warm to hot summers, mild winters
Warm to hot summers, cold winters
Mild summers, cold winters
Cold climate
Polar climate, below zero year round

When to Go

High Season (Jul–Aug & Dec–Apr)
» In July and August walkers and cyclists hit high-altitude trails.

» Christmas and New Year see serious snow-sports action on the slopes.

» Late December to early April is high season in ski resorts.

Shoulder (Apr–Jun & Sep)
» Look for accommodation deals in ski resorts and traveller hotspots.

» Spring is idyllic with warm temperatures, flowers and local produce.

» Watch the grape harvest in autumn.

Low Season (Oct–Mar)
» Mountain resorts go into snooze mode from mid-October to early December.

» Prices are up to 50% less than in high season.

» Sights and restaurants are open fewer days and shorter hours.

Daily Costs

Budget: Less than Sfr200

» Dorm bed: Sfr30–60

» Free admission to some museums on first Saturday or Sunday of every month

» Lunch out (up to Sfr25) and self-cater after dark

Midrange: Sfr200–300

» Double room in two- or three-star hotel: Sfr200–350

» Dish of the day (*tageslteller, plat du jour, piatto del giorno*) or fixed two-course menu: Sfr40–70

Top End: More than Sfr300

» Double room in four- or five-star hotel: from Sfr350

» Lower rates Friday to Sunday in city business hotels

» Three-course dinner in an upmarket restaurant: from Sfr100

Eating

Cafes Coffee, drinks, snacks.

Bistros Light meals to full-blown dinners.

Restaurants Simple eateries to Michelin-starred temples.

Vegetarian Few wholly vegetarian places, limited choices on most menus.

The following prices indicate the cost of a two-course set menu.

€	less than Sfr25
€€	Sfr25–50
€€€	more than Sfr50

Sleeping

Hotels From budget to luxury; breakfast included unless indicated.

Pensiones Chambres d'hôte in French-speaking Switzerland; rates always include breakfast.

Hostels In cities and large towns; private or HI-affiliated.

Price symbols indicate the cost of a double room with private bathroom in high season:

€	less than Sfr170
€€	Sfr170–350
€€€	more than Sfr350

Arriving in Switzerland

Zürich Airport

Trains To Zürich centre, 6am to midnight (Sfr7, 14 minutes).

Taxis Sfr50 to Sfr70, 20 minutes to centre.

Mobile Phones (Cell Phones)

Most European and Australian phones function; turn off roaming to avoid data charges. Buy a local SIM for cheaper rates.

Internet Access

Wi-fi (usually free) is available to guests in most hotels, B&Bs and hostels. Also offered by many cafes, bars, train stations and other public spaces.

Money

ATMs widely available in cities and towns, rarely in villages. Cash is king almost everywhere; credit cards are not widely accepted.

Tipping

Tipping is not necessary, given that hotels, restaurants, bars and even some taxis are legally required to include a 15% service charge in bills.

You can round up the bill after a meal for good service, as locals do.

Hotel and railway porters expect a franc or two per bag.

Bargaining is non-existent.

Useful Websites

Lonely Planet (lonelyplanet.com) Travel tips, accommodation, traveller forums and more.

My Switzerland (www.myswitzerland.com) Swiss tourist board,

ADAC (www.adac.de) Driving information for Germany and neighbouring countries.

STRETCH YOUR LEGS
GENEVA

Start: Jardin Anglais

Finish: Place du Bourg-de-Four

Distance: 2km

Duration: Three hours

Geneva's beautiful Old Town (Vieille Ville) is the perfect spot for a charmingly edifying stroll, thanks to its mix of sights and a history lesson worthy of its status as one of the Protestant Reformation's key cities.

Take this walk on Trip

38

Jardin Anglais

Before strolling up the hill to the Old Town, visit the flower clock in Geneva's waterfront **garden** (Quai du Général-Guisan), landscaped in 1854 on the site of an old lumber-handling port and merchant yard. The **Horloge Fleurie** (Flower Clock), Geneva's most photographed clock, is crafted from 6500 plants and has ticked since 1955. Its second hand, 2.5m long, is claimed to be the world's longest.

The Walk » From the clock, cross Quai du Général-Guisan. Head south through the shopping district to Cour de St-Pierre, which faces the cathedral. It's about a seven-minute stroll.

Cathédrale St-Pierre

Begun in the 11th century, Geneva's **cathedral** (www.espace-saint-pierre.ch; Cour de St-Pierre; admission free, towers adult/child Sfr5/2; ☺9.30am-6.30pm Mon-Sat, noon-6.30pm Sun Jun-Sep, 10am-5.30pm Oct-May) is predominantly Gothic with an 18th-century neoclassical facade. Between 1536–64 Protestant John Calvin preached here; see his uncomfortable-looking seat in the north aisle. Inside the cathedral, 77 steps spiral up to the attic – a fascinating glimpse at its architectural construction – from where another 40 lead to the top of the panoramic **northern and southern towers** (adult/child Sfr5/2). Views of the Old Town and the Jet d'Eau are marvellous. In summer, free carillon (5pm) and organ (6pm) concerts fill the cathedral and its surrounding square with music.

The Walk » Exit the cathedral and head for the Site Archéologique de la Cathédrale St-Pierre; a few dozen footsteps should cover it.

Site Archéologique de la Cathédrale St-Pierre

This small **archaeological site** (☎022 310 29 29; www.site-archeologique.ch; Cour St-Pierre; adult/child Sfr8/4; ☺10am-5pm Tue-Sun) in the basement of Cathédrale St-Pierre has 4th-century mosaics in the Roman crypt and the tomb of an Allobrogian chieftain. Its

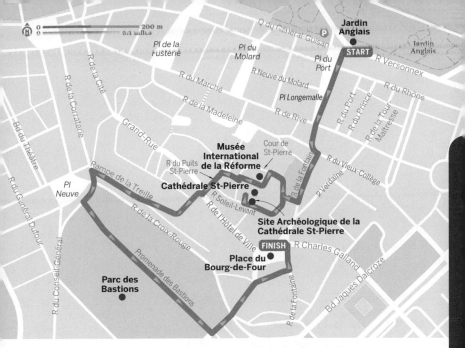

entrance is at the right of the cathedral's main portico.

The Walk » Head to the other side of the cathedral (a one-minute walk) to spend an hour at the Reformation Museum.

Musée International de la Réforme

This modern **museum** (☎022 310 24 31; www.musee-reforme.ch; Rue du Cloître 4; adult/child Sfr13/6; ⊙10am-5pm Tue-Sun) in an 18th-century mansion has state-of-the-art exhibits on the Reformation: printed bibles, the emergence of 16th-century Geneva as 'Protestant Rome', John Calvin and present-day Protestantism. A combined ticket covering the museum, Cathédrale St-Pierre and Site Archéologique de la Cathédrale St-Pierre is Sfr18/10 per adult/child.

The Walk » From Cour de St-Pierre, walk down Rue Otto Barblan. Turn left onto Rue du Puits-St-Pierre and continue past Maison Tavel (the city's longest-standing private residence, now a museum) to the bottom of Rue Henri Fazy, which overlooks Parc des Bastions and has the world's

longest bench. Turn down Rampe de la Treille and follow it to the park's gates.

Parc des Bastions

It's all statues – plus free life-size chess boards hosting lively games – in green Parc des Bastions. A laid-back stroll with locals along its tree-lined promenade reveals the 4.5m-tall po-faced figures of Bèze, Calvin, Farel and Knox on **Reformation Wall**, which stretches for 100m. There are play facilities for kids and a skating rink in winter.

The Walk » From Promenade des Bastion's eastern end, walk along Rue St-Léger. Continue under the bridge and ahead until Place du Bourg-de-Four ends at the fountained terrace area.

Place du Bourg-de-Four

Eateries, bars and locals crowd Place du Bourg-de-Four, Geneva's oldest square. In summer, it's filled to bursting with gossiping local denizens. Stalwart **La Clémence** (☎022 312 24 98; www.laclemence.ch; Place du Bourg-de-Four 20; ⊙7am-1am Mon-Thu & Sun, to 2am Fri & Sat) is a popular place to linger over a coffee.

Austria

AUSTRIA IS A ROAD-TRIPPERS FANTASY LAND. Not only are there spectacular backdrops of spellbinding landscapes and storybook architecture, but opportunities abound to get out and experience them. Along these routes, you can scale soaring peaks, ski year-round, raft white-water rapids and pelt down toboggan runs.

When you've had enough thrills and spills, Austria's multitude of cultural pursuits span medieval castles to monumental palaces, art-filled museums and magnificent churches. You can taste cheese at Alpine dairies, schnapps at distilleries, and beer and wine in monasteries where they're still made by monks. Or just hop aboard a horse-drawn carriage to clip-clop through cobbled, lamp-lit city streets.

Grossglockner Road Heiligenblut

39 **Grossglockner Road 5–7 Days**
Twist and turn along three of Austria's most spectacular mountain passes. (p559)

40 **Along the Danube 2–4 Days**
Follow the Danube River as it flows through forests and vineyards. (p569)

✓ **DON'T MISS**

Lake Swimming

Many of Austria's Alp-framed lakes reach temperatures of up to 28°C in summer. Dive into one on Trip **39**

Salzburg

Famed for its starring role in *The Sound of Music*, Salzburg's Unesco-listed Altstadt (old town) is a treasure. Visit on Trip **39**

Hiking

Through forests, up waterfall trails, down gorges, along wildflower-strewn meadows...You'll find some of Austria's best hiking on Trip **39**

Vienna

With its resplendent palaces, magnificent museums and opera house, Austria's capital is the belle of the country's ball. Waltz by on Trip **40**

Salzburg View over the city

Grossglockner Road

39

Austria's most exhilarating trip takes you on a wild roller-coaster drive over three legendary Alpine passes and packs in outdoor activities from year-round skiing to windsurfing and white-water rafting.

TRIP HIGHLIGHTS

335 km

Gerlos Alpine Road
Sing along the yodel hiking trail

START
Salzburg

FINISH
Bregenz

Innsbruck

7

4

Lienz

10

Silvretta High Alpine Road
Mountains reflect in the aquamarine reservoir

526 km

Grossglockner High Alpine Road
Traverse Austria's highest mountain

225 km

5–7 DAYS
644 KM / 401 MILES

GREAT FOR...

BEST TIME TO GO
The peak time to tackle this trip is midsummer.

ESSENTIAL PHOTO
Europe's highest waterfalls, the three-tiered Krimmler Wasserfälle.

BEST FOR DRIVERS
The Grossglockner's 36 heart-in-your-mouth hairpin bends.

Grossglockner High Alpine Road Alpine meadow

39 Grossglockner Road

Fair warning: if you're a faint-hearted driver (or passenger), this probably isn't the trip for you. (Take the gentler Tyrol & Vorarlberg route instead). But if you're up for a serious adventure, this Austrian classic provides an opportunity to experience epic scenery, invigorating Alpine sports, and dizzying mountain passes with so many switchbacks they're used by high-performance car manufacturers and championship race drivers as test tracks.

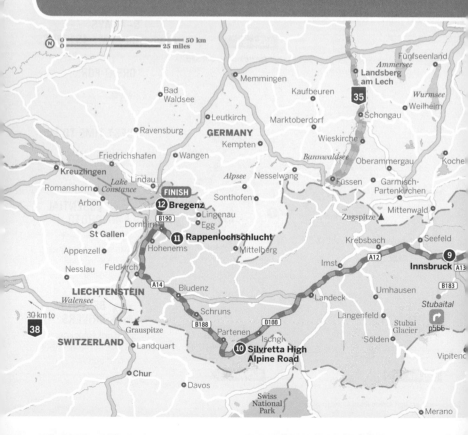

1 Salzburg

Salzburg's trophy sights huddle in the pedestrianised, Unesco World Heritage–listed **Altstadt** (old town). The tangled lanes are made for a serendipitous wander, leading to hidden courtyards and medieval squares framed by burgher houses and baroque fountains. You'll also see plenty of icons from the evergreen musical *The Sound of Music*.

Beyond city strolling, there are plenty of opportunities to get active, from swimming at **Freibad Leopoldskron** (Leopoldskronstrasse 50; adult/concession €4.60/2.60; ⊙9am-7pm May–mid-Sep), Salzburg's biggest lido, with diving boards, water slides and volleyball, to hiking up Salzburg's rival mountains, the 540m **Mönchsberg** and 640m **Kapuzinerberg**. Both mountains are thickly wooded and criss-crossed by walking trails, with photogenic views of the

LINK YOUR TRIP

35 The Romantic Road

Strike north after Innsbruck to find a ribbon of historical quaintness running through Bavaria's western reaches.

38 Geneva to Zürich

Mountains, pastures, lakes and small-town charm, book-ended by Switzerland's biggest cities..

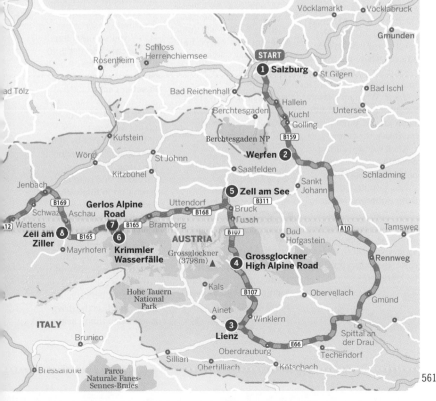

Altstadt's right bank and left bank, respectively.

The Drive » It's 47km south from Salzburg on the B159 to Werfen, mostly along the Salzach River. After passing through a wide valley, you'll enter a tight, steep gorge; follow it until Werfen.

❷ Werfen

More than 1000m above Werfen in the Tennengebirge mountains is **Eisriesenwelt** (www.eisriesen welt.at; adult/child €11/6, incl cable car €22/12; ☺8am-3.45pm May-Oct, to 4.45pm Jul & Aug). Billed as the world's largest accessible ice caves, this glittering ice spectacle spans 30,000 sq metres and 42km of narrow passages burrowing deep into the heart of the mountains. A highlight is the cavernous **Eispalast** (ice palace), where the frost crystals twinkle when a magnesium flare is held up to them. Wrap up warmly for subzero temperatures. Photography is not permitted inside the caves.

On a wooded clifftop beneath the majestic peaks of the Tennengebirge range, formidable fortress **Burg Hohenwerfen** (adult/child/family €11/6/26.50, incl lift €14.50/8/34.50; ☺9am-5pm Apr-Oct; 🚗) dates from 1077. Time your visit to be at the castle by 3.15pm for the falconry show.

🔖 p567

The Drive » Take the A10 south to the Millstätter See

(which you can visit on a trip through the Carinthian Lakes) and turn west onto the B100/E66 through the Drau Valley to Lienz (166km in total).

❸ Lienz

Ringed by Dolomite peaks blushing reddish-pink at sunset, Lienz straddles the Isel and Drau Rivers, and lies just 40km north of Italy. An ancient Roman settlement, today it's a famed ski town (for its Zettersfeld and Hochstein peaks, and especially its 100km of cross-country trails), but it has an energetic vibe year-round.

If you want to get up into the mountains, **Bergstatt** (☎0516-5835; www.bergstatt.at; Kranewitweg 5; rock climbing trips per adult/child from €75/55) has guides who can lead you on half-day, full-day and multiday rock-climbing, *via ferrata* or summit trips.

The Drive » Take the B107 north, passing picturesque villages including Winklern (with a wonderful Alpine hotel; p567) and Heiligenblut (look for the needle-thin spire of its pilgrimage church) to the Grossglockner High Alpine Road toll gates (43km in total).

TRIP HIGHLIGHT

❹ Grossglockner High Alpine Road

A stupendous feat of 1930s engineering, the 48km **Grossglockner Road** (www.grossglockner.at; Hwy 107; car/motorcycle

€34.50/24.50; ☺May-early Nov) swings giddily around 36 switchbacks, passing jewel-coloured lakes, forested slopes and above-the-clouds glaciers as it traverses the heart of the Hohe Tauern National Park, peaking at the bell-shaped **Grossglockner** (3798m), Austria's highest mountain.

En route, flag-dotted **Kaiser-Franz-Josefs-Höhe** (2369m) has memorable views of Grossglockner and the rapidly retreating Pasterze Glacier (best appreciated on the short and easy Gamsgrubenweg and Gletscherweg trails). Allow time to see the glacier-themed exhibition at the visitor centre and the crystalline Wilhelm-Swarovski observatory.

Get your camera handy for **Fuscher Törl** (2428m), with super views on both sides of the ridge, and **Fuscher Lacke** (2262m), a gemstone of a lake nearby. A small exhibition documents the construction of the road, built by 3000 men over five years during the Great Depression.

A 2km side road corkscrews up to **Edelweiss Spitze** (2571m), the road's highest viewpoint. Climb the tower for 360-degree views of more than 30 peaks topping 3000m.

Between toll gates, all attractions are free. Check the forecast before you hit the road, as the drive is not much fun in heavy fog, snow or a storm. It's often bumper-to-bumper by noon, especially in July and August; beat the crowds by setting out early.

The Drive » Descend the Grossglockner on the B107 to Bruck and take the B311 northeast to Zell am See.

⑤ Zell am See

Resort town Zell am See's brightly painted chalets line the shore of the deep-blue Zeller See, framed by the Hohe Tauern's snowcapped peaks.

Mountain breezes create ideal conditions for windsurfing on the lake; **Windsurfcenter Zell Am See** (📞0664-644 36 95; http://windsurfcenter.members.cablelink.at; Seespitzstrasse 13; windsurfing/SUP/wetsuit rental per hr €10/8/3; ⏰dawn-dusk May-Sep) rents equipment and runs courses.

The Drive » From the lake, it's 54km to the Krimmler Wasserfälle. Head west on the B168 and B165 to Krimml; when you arrive in the town the waterfalls come into view.

⑥ Krimmler Wasserfälle

Europe's highest falls, at 380m, are the thunderous, three-tier **Krimmler Wasserfälle** (Krimml Falls; www.wasserfaelle-krimml.at; adult/child €3/1; ⏰ticket office 8am-6pm mid-Apr–Oct). The **Wasserfallweg** (Waterfall Trail), which starts at the ticket office and weaves uphill through mixed forest, has up-close viewpoints.

It's 4km one way (about a 2½-hour round-trip walk).

The Drive » From the falls, it's 7.7km (and eight hairpin bends) to the Gerlos Alpine Road toll gates.

TRIP HIGHLIGHT

⑦ Gerlos Alpine Road

Open year-round, the **Gerlos Alpine Road** (www.gerlosstrasse.at; toll per car/motorcycle €8.50/5.50) winds 12km through high moor and spruce forest, reaching an elevation of 1630m. The lookout above the turquoise Stausee (reservoir) is a great picnic stop, with a tremendous vista of the Alps.

If you have the urge to burst out into song as you skip through wildflower-strewn meadows, take the 4.8km-long **Jodel Wanderweg** (Yodel Hiking Trail; 📞06565-82 43; www.jodelweg.at) in Königsleiten. You can go it alone and practise your high notes at eight stops with giant cowbells, alpine horns and listen-repeat audio clippings. Alternatively, join a free guided sing 'n' stroll hike with trail founder Christian Eder. The three-hour ambles

begin at 10.30am every Wednesday from late June to mid-September at the **Dorfbahn** (adult/child €9/4.50) cable-car station; reserve by 5pm the previous day by phone.

The Drive » Continue west on the B165, passing the reservoir Durlassboden, before descending to Zell am Ziller along six hairpin bends (63km in total).

⑧ Zell am Ziller

At the foot of knife-edge Reichenspitze (3303m), Zell am Ziller is a former gold-mining centre and popular ski base.

Year-round, you can take a wild toboggan ride on the 1.45km-long **Arena Coaster** (www.zillertalarena.com; Zillertal Arena; adult/child coaster only €4.80/2.90, incl cable car €20.90/10.40; ⏰9.30am-6pm late Jun-early Sep, shorter hours rest of year; ♿), which incorporates both a 360-degree loop and a 540-degree loop. It's accessible by cable car, or a steep 1.5km walk.

Aktivzentrum Zillertal (📞0664-505 95 94; www.aktivzentrum-zillertal.at; Freizeitpark Zell; ♿) offers

WHY THIS IS A GREAT TRIP
CATHERINE LE NEVEZ, WRITER

Awe-inspiring mountainscapes and adrenaline-pumping activities abound on this alpine itinerary, but the ultimate draw is the drive itself, peaking with its trio of dizzying high-altitude switchback passes – the Grossglockner High Alpine Road, Gerlos Alpine Road and Silvretta High Alpine Road. This is a route that reminds you that the highlight of road-tripping isn't the destination but the journey.

Top: Racing along Grossglockner High Alpine Road
Left: Bergisel ski jump in Innsbruck
Right: Krimmler Wasserfälle (Krimml Falls)

paragliding (€55 to €130), white-water rafting on the Ziller (€35), canyoning (€35 to €65), *via ferrata* climbing (€45 to €85) and llama trekking (€20).

🛏 p567

The Drive » Zell am Ziller sits 60km from Innsbruck. Take the B169 north then the A12 west.

❾ Innsbruck

Hit Innsbruck's cultural attractions, then head up to its ski jump, the **Bergisel** (www.bergisel.info; adult/child €9.50/4.50; ⏰9am-6pm), for a spectacular city and mountain panorama. Rising above Innsbruck like a celestial staircase, the glass-and-steel structure was designed by Iraqi architect Zaha Hadid.

Hadid also designed the space-age funicular **Nordkettenbahnen** (www.nordkette.com; one-way/return to Hungerburg €4.60/7.60, Seegrube €16.50/27.50, Hafelekar €18.30/30.50; ⏰Hungerburg 7am-7.15pm Mon-Fri, 8am-7.15pm Sat & Sun, Seegrube 8.30am-5.30pm daily, Hafelekar 9am-5pm daily), which whizzes from the Congress Centre to the slopes every 15 minutes. Walking trails head off in all directions from Hungerburg and Seegrube.

✕ 🛏 p567

The Drive » Leave Innsbruck on the westbound A12 and veer southwest on the B188, passing a string of ski towns, to the Silvretta High Alpine Road toll gates (118km all up).

TRIP HIGHLIGHT

⑩ Silvretta High Alpine Road

Silhouetted by the Silvretta range and crowned by the 3312m arrow of Piz Buin, the Montafon Valley remains one of the most serene and unspoilt in the Austrian Alps.

The 23km-long **Silvretta High Alpine Road** (www.silvretta-bielerhoehe. at; car/motorcycle €15/12; ☺early Jun-late Oct) twists and turns beneath peaks rising to well over 2500m before climbing over the 2036m Bielerhöhe Pass via 34 tight switchbacks. At the top of the pass, the **Silvretta Stausee** (2030m), an aquamarine reservoir, mirrors the surrounding peaks on bright mornings.

The Drive ❯❯ It's 100km to Rappenlochschlucht. Continue on the B188 and join the A14 at aromatic Bludenz. Continue northwest to Dornbirn, from where Rappenlochschlucht is 4km southeast on Gütlestrasse.

⑪ Rappenloch-schlucht

The **Rappenlochschlucht** (Rappenloch Gorge; www. rappenlochschlucht.at) was gouged out by the thundering Dornbirner Ache. From the car park, there's a 375m trail to the **Staufensee**, a turquoise lake ringed by forest.

At the bottom of the Rappenlochschlucht, a 19th-century cotton mill is the unlikely home of the world's largest collection of Rolls-Royces at the **Rolls-Royce Museum** (www. rolls-royce-museum.at; Gütle 11a; adult/child €9/4.50; ☺10am-6pm daily Jul & Aug, 10am-6pm Tue-Sun Feb-Jun & Sep-Nov).

The Drive ❯❯ Return to Dornbirn and head north on the B190 for 16km to Bregenz.

⑫ Bregenz

Bregenz sits on the shores of Lake Constance (in German, Bodensee), Europe's third-largest lake. The views here are extraordinary: before you the mirror-like lake; behind you, 1064m-high mountain the Pfänder, to the right,

DETOUR: STUBAITAL

Start: ⑨ Innsbruck (p565)

Slip out of sandals and into skis at year-round skiing magnet, Stubai Glacier. A one-day summer **ski pass** (www.stubaier-gletscher.com) costs €43/21.50 per adult/child and covers 26 lifts accessing 62km of slopes. Ski or snowboard and boot rental costs around €30/15 per adult/child. Summer skiing is between 2900m and 3300m and is dependent on weather conditions.

Lower down in the Stubai Valley, the **Wildewasserweg** waterfall trail wends for 9.2km (one way) to Sulzenau Glacier. En route, it passes the spectacular Grawa falls; there's a cafe with a panoramic viewing deck at its base.

The Stubai Glacier is just 38km south of Innsbruck. Take the A13 south to the toll gates (per car including passengers €3); keep right to take the B183 southwest along the valley.

Germany, to the left, Switzerland.

A **cable car** (www. pfaenderbahn.at; Steinbruchgasse 4; one-way adult/child €7.10/5.70, return €12.20/9.80; ☺8am-7pm Dec-Oct) glides up the Pfänder. At the top, a 30-minute circular trail brings you close to deer, wild boar, ibex and whistling marmots at the year-round **Alpine Game Park Pfänder** (www.pfaender. at; Pfänder; ☺sunrise-sunset).

Some 5km south of central Bregenz is the nature reserve **Rheindelta** (www. rheindelta.org). Its mossy marshes, reeds and woodlands attract more than 300 bird species, including curlews, grey herons and rare black-tailed godwits.

✕ 🛏 p567

Eating & Sleeping

Werfen ❷

🛏 **Weisses Rössl** Pension €

(📞06468-5268; Markt 39; s/d €30/52) In the village centre, this good-value pension has great views of the fortress and the Tennengebirge from its rooftop terrace. Rooms are a blast from the 1970s, but all are large and cosy with sofas and cable TV.

Winklern

🛏 **Hotel Tauernstern** Chalet €€

(📞04822-7205; www.tauernstern.at; Winklern 24, Winklern; s/d from €49/98; P 🛜) Sweeping valley views extend from the timber balconies of this mountain-set gem. Four-poster pine-and-stone beds, in-room fridges, a sauna and spa built from local wood and slate, and an exceptional gourmet restaurant using ingredients from local farms all make Tauernstern a fabulous pit stop before tackling the Grossglockner High Alpine Road.

Zell am Ziller ❽

🛏 **Hotel Englhof** Boutique Hotel €€

(📞05282-3134; www.englhof.at; Zellbergeben 28; s/d/tr/ste from €55/103/153/110; 🛜) Beautiful blond-wood-panelled, white-linen-dressed rooms (many with balconies) and amenities like free DVD rental make Englhof a superb place to stay. But what really seals the deal is its in-house gourmet restaurant and world-class cocktail bar with Austria's second-largest collection of spirits (over 1400 varieties), mixing incredible cocktails like a Bloody Mary with frozen cherry tomatoes and barbecued black-pepper seasoning.

Innsbruck ❾

🍴 **Die Wilderin** Austrian €€

(📞0512-56 27 28; www.diewilderin.at; Seilergasse 5; mains €11-18; ⏰5pm-2am Tue-Sat, 4pm-midnight Sun) Take a gastronomic walk on the wild side at this modern-day hunter-gatherer of a restaurant, where chefs take pride in local sourcing and using top-notch farm-fresh and foraged ingredients. The menu sings of the seasons, be it asparagus, game, strawberries or winter veg. The vibe is urbane and relaxed.

🛏 **Weisses Rössl** Guesthouse €€

(📞0512-58 30 57; www.roessl.at; Kiebachgasse 8; s €70-110, d €100-160; @ 🛜) An antique rocking horse greets you at this 16th-century guesthouse. The vaulted entrance leads up to spacious rooms recently revamped with blond wood, fresh hues and crisp white linen. The owner is a keen hunter and the restaurant (mains €10 to €18) has a meaty menu.

Bregenz ⓬

🍴 **Gebhardsberg** Austrian €€

(📞05574-908 61 60; www.greber.cc; Gebhardsbergstrasse 1; mains €14-26.50; ⏰11.30am-10pm daily May-Sep, 11.30am-10pm Tue-Sun Oct-Apr) Sweeping lake views taking in Switzerland and Germany extend from the dining room and terrace of this hilltop castle 1km south of the centre. Local specialities include *Käsespätzle* (hand-rolled noodles with cheese) with traditional apple sauce and fried onions, Lake Constance trout with almond butter and parsley potatoes, and white cheese strudel for dessert.

🛏 **Schwärzler** Hotel €€

(📞05574-4990; http://schwaerzler.s-hotels.com; Landstrasse 9; s/d from €122/153; P 🛜 🛗) This turreted, ivy-clad place is a far cry from your average business hotel. Contemporary rooms are done out in earthy hues and blond wood, with comforts including bathrobes, flat-screen TVs and minibars. Regional produce from organic farms features on the breakfast buffet, and there's a 400-sq-metre pool and a sauna area. Parking costs €7.

Along the Danube

40

Follow the beautiful Danube River as it flows from the German city of Passau by the Austrian border through farmland, forest and vineyard-streaked hillsides to Austria's majestic capital, Vienna.

TRIP HIGHLIGHTS

205 km

Dürnstein
Richard the Lionheart was imprisoned here in a now-ruined castle

293 km

Vienna
View Vienna by foot, horse-drawn carriage or Ferris wheel

START
Passau

Linz

Krems an der Donau

7

4

9

Melk

10 **FINISH**

St Florian
Visit the abbey's exuberant basilica

92 km

Stift Göttweig
This Unesco-listed abbey serves its own monk-made wines

219 km

2–4 DAYS
293 KM / 182 MILES

GREAT FOR...

BEST TIME TO GO
Aim for summer: many places close between November and March.

ESSENTIAL PHOTO
St Florian's dazzling interior.

BEST FOR ART
Linz's contemporary Lentos gallery.

Passau Cruising the Danube River

40 Along the Danube

Immortalised in the stirring *Blue Danube* waltz by Austrian composer Johann Strauss II, this magnificent river ripples with the reflections of green forests, hilltop castles, and ribbons of vineyards, particularly on its prettiest stretch, the Wachau, between Melk and Krems an der Donau. Along the river's course are plenty of surprises too, including the cutting-edge city of Linz, and two monasteries producing, respectively, sublime beer and wine.

❶ Passau

Just inside the German border, Passau's pastel-shaded **Altstadt** (old town) sits atop a narrow peninsula jutting into the confluence of three rivers: the Danube, the Inn and the Ilz. Christianity generated prestige as Passau evolved into the largest bishopric in the Holy Roman Empire, as testified by the mighty cathedral **Dom St Stephan** (www.bistum-passau.de; Domplatz; ⊗6.30am-7pm).

Stroll the old town, which remains much as

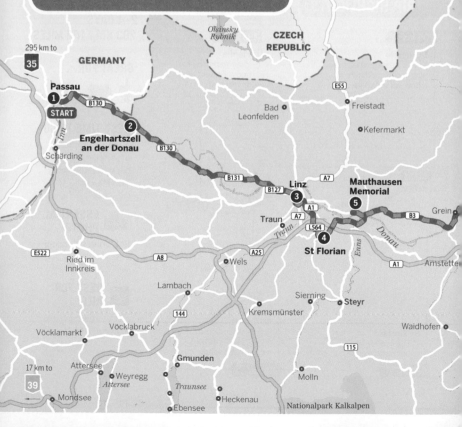

it was when the powerful prince-bishops built its tight lanes, tunnels and archways with an Italianate flourish.

✕ 🛏 p575

The Drive » Cross the Inn River where it joins the Danube and head east on ST2125 which, 3.3km later, becomes the B130 on entering Austria, and follows the Danube's southern bank. On your right, you'll pass Burg Krempelstein, built on the site of a Roman watch house. It's 26km all up to Engelhartszell an der Donau.

- - - - - - - - - -
❷ Engelhartszell an der Donau

The little riverside village of Engelhartszell an der Donau is home to one of only eight licensed Trappist breweries outside Belgium, and the only one in Austria. At the 1293-founded abbey **Engelszell** (www.stift-engelzell.at; Stiftstrasse 6; ⏱ church 8am-7pm Apr-Oct, to 5pm Nov-Mar, shop 9am-5pm Apr-Oct, 10-11.30am & 2.30-4pm

LINK YOUR TRIP

35 The Romantic Road

Head west, skirting Munich, to this ribbon of historical quaintness running through Bavaria's western reaches.

39 Grossglockner Road

A hop and a skip south and you can twist and turn along three of Austria's most spectacular montian passes.

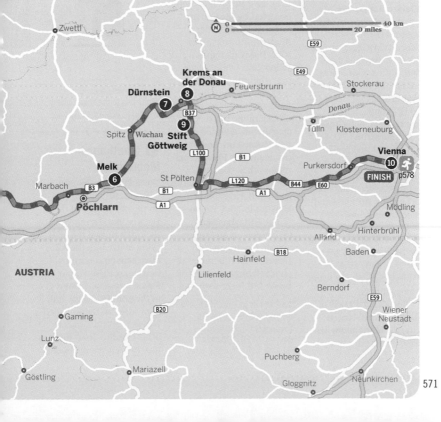

Sat & Sun Nov-Mar), you can purchase monk-made brews (dark Gregorius, amber Benno, and blond Nivard); the shop also sells liqueurs and cheeses produced here. Adjoining the shop is the abbey's gorgeous rococo church, completed in 1764.

The Drive ⟫ Take the B130; at Aschach an der Donau, cross the river on the B131, and continue east to Ottensheim to join the B127 to Linz (52km in total).

- - - - - - - - - - - - - - - -

③ Linz

The Austrian saying *In Linz beginnt's* (It begins in Linz) sums up this technology trailblazer. Its leading-edge **Ars Electronica Center** (www. aec.at; Ars Electronica Strasse 1; adult/child €8/6; ◷9am-5pm Tue-Fri, to 9pm Thu, 10am-6pm Sat & Sun) has labs for interacting with robots, animating digital objects, converting your name to DNA and (virtually) travelling to outer space. After dark, the LED glass skin kaleidoscopically changes colour. Directly across the Danube is Linz's world-class contemporary-art gallery, the glass-and-steel **Lentos** (www.lentos. at; Ernst-Koref-Promenade 1; adult/child €8/4.50, guided tours €3; ◷10am-6pm Tue-Sun, to 9pm Thu), with works by Warhol, Schiele and Klimt, among others.

But it's not all new in Austria's third-largest city: the **Mariendom** (Her-renstrasse 26; ◷7.30am-7pm

Mon-Sat, 8am-7.15pm Sun) is a neo-Gothic giant of a cathedral with a riot of pinnacles, flying buttresses and filigree traceried windows.

🍴 🛏 p575

The Drive ⟫ Take the A1 southeast to Ebelsberg, then continue on the L564 to St Florian (21km all up).

- - - - - - - - - - - - - - - -

TRIP HIGHLIGHT

④ St Florian

Rising like a vision above St Florian is its magnificent abbey, **Augustiner Chorherrenstift** (www. stift-st-florian.at; Stiftstrasse 1; tours €8.50; ◷11am, 1pm & 3pm May-early Oct). Dating to at least 819, it has been occupied by the Canons Regular, living under Augustinian rule, since 1071. Today its imposing yellow-and-white facade is overwhelmingly baroque.

Compulsory guided tours of the abbey's interior take in the resplendent apartments adorned with rich stuccowork and frescos, including 16 emperors' rooms (once occupied by visiting popes and royalty) and a galleried library housing 150,000 volumes.

The **Stiftsbasilika** (◷7am-dusk) is an exuberant affair with an altar carved from 700 tonnes of pink Salzburg marble, and a gold 18th-century organ.

The Drive ⟫ Head northeast on the L566 to join the B1. Follow it for 7.5km then turn east on the B123 to cross the Danube, before turning west

on the B3. After 2.4km take the L1411 for 2.5 signposted kilometres to the Mauthausen Memorial (22km in total).

- - - - - - - - - - - - - - - -

⑤ Mauthausen Memorial

Nowadays Mauthausen is a peaceful small town on the north bank of the Danube, but during WWII the Nazis turned the quarrying centre into the **KZ Mauthausen** concentration camp. Prisoners were forced into slave labour in the granite quarry and many died on the so-called *Todesstiege* (stairway of death) leading from the quarry to the camp. Some

St Florian The beautiful pipe organ on display in the Stiftsbasilika

100,000 prisoners perished or were executed in the camp between 1938 and 1945. The complex is now a **memorial** (www.mauthausen-memorial.at; Erinnerungsstrasse 1; admission incl guided tour €5, audioguide €3; ☻9am-5.30pm Mar-early Jul, 9am-5.30pm Tue-Sun early Jul-Oct, 9am-3pm Tue-Sun Nov-Feb); English-language audioguides relate its sobering history. It's not recommended for under 14s.

The Drive ❯❯ Travelling east for 76km brings you to Melk. Along the river at Grein, look out for the dramatic castle Greinburg rising to your left.

❻ Melk

Historically, Melk was of great importance to the Romans and later to the Babenbergs, who built a castle here. In 1089 the Babenberg margrave Leopold II donated the castle to Benedictine monks, who converted it into the fortified **Stift Melk** (Benedictine Abbey of Melk; www.stiftmelk.at; Abt Berthold Dietmayr Strasse 1; adult/child €10/5.50, with guided tour €12/7.50; ☻9am-5.30pm May-Sep, tours 11am & 2pm Oct-Apr). Fire destroyed the original edifice; today its monastery church dominates the complex with its twin spires and

high octagonal dome. The baroque-gone-barmy interior has regiments of cherubs, gilt twirls and polished faux marble. The theatrical high-altar scene depicts St Peter and St Paul (the church's two patron saints).

The Drive ❯❯ The Wachau is the loveliest along the mighty river's length: both banks here are dotted with ruined castles and terraced with vineyards. From Melk, follow the river northeast along the nothern bank for 28km, passing medieval villages Spitz, Wösendorf in der Wachau and Weissenkirchen, to reach Dürnstein.

✓ **TOP TIP: DANUBE CRUISES**

Floating past vine-covered banks crowned by castles gives you a different perspective of the river. From Passau, **Wurm + Köck** (☎0851-929 292; www.donauschiffahrt.de; Höllgasse 26) operates cruises between Regensburg, Germany, and Vienna from March to early November. One-way/return tickets for one stop start from €10.50/11.50; 10-stop tickets start from €26/29.

TRIP HIGHLIGHT

❼ Dürnstein

Picturesque Dürnstein is best known for the **Kuenringerburg** – the now-ruined castle above the town where Richard the Lionheart (Richard I of England) was imprisoned from 1192 to 1193, before being moved to **Burg Trifels** (p178) in Germany.

Of the 16th-century buildings lining Dürnstein's hilly, cobbled streets, the **Chorherrenstift** (www.stiftduernstein.at; Stiftshof; adult/child €3/1.50; ☺9am-6pm Mon-Sat, 10am-6pm Sun Apr-Oct) is the most impressive. It's all that remains of the former Augustinian monastery originally founded in 1410, and received its baroque facelift in the 18th century.

The Drive » Head east along the river on the B3 for 7.5km to reach Krems an der Donau.

❽ Krems an der Donau

Against a backdrop of terraced vineyards, Krems has an attractive cobbled centre and gallery-dotted **Kunstmeile** (Art Mile; www.kunstmeile-krems.at). Its flagship is the **Kunsthalle** (www.kunsthalle.at; Franz-Zeller-Platz 3; admission €10; ☺10am-5pm Tue-Sun), a collection of galleries and museums, with changing exhibitions.

🛏 p575

The Drive » Leave Krems an der Donau on the B37 and cross the southbound L100. Stift Göttweig is well signposted (9km altogether from Krems).

TRIP HIGHLIGHT

❾ Stift Göttweig

Surrounded by grape-laden vines, Unesco World Heritage–listed **Stift Göttweig** (Göttweig Abbey; ☎02732-855 81-0; www.stift-goettweig.at; Furth bei Göttweig; adult/child €7.50/4; ☺9am-6pm Jun-Sep, 10am-6pm Oct-May) was founded in 1083, but the abbey you see today is mostly baroque. Highlights include the Imperial Staircase with a heavenly ceiling fresco painted by Paul Troger in 1739, and the over-the-top baroque interior of the Stiftskirche (which has a Kremser Schmidt work in the crypt). Best of all is the opportunity to sip wine made here by the monks – including an exquisite Messwein rosé – on the panoramic garden terrace above the valley (you can also buy it at the abbey's shop).

The Drive » From Stift Göttweig, it's 79km to Vienna. The most scenic route, through farmland and forest, is south on the L100 to St Pölten, then east on the L120 to join the eastbound B44 at Ebersberg. Continue through the Wienerwald to the Austrian capital.

TRIP HIGHLIGHT

❿ Vienna

Renowned for its imperial palaces, baroque interiors, opera houses and magnificent squares, Vienna is also one of Europe's most dynamic urban spaces. The best way to experience its blend of old and new is on a walking tour (p578).

A wonderfully atmospheric (if touristy) alternative is aboard a **Fiaker** (up to 4 passengers 20min/40min/1hr tour €55/80/110), which is a traditional-style open carriage drawn by a pair of horses. Drivers point out places of interest en route. Lines of horses, carriages and bowler-hatted drivers can be found at Stephansplatz, Albertinaplatz and Heldenplatz at the Hofburg.

Or survey the city from Vienna's 65m-high, 1897-built Ferris wheel, the **Riesenrad**. It's located at

Eating & Sleeping

Passau ❶

✗ Heilig-Geist-Stifts-Schenke
Bavarian €€

(📞0851-2607; www.stiftskeller-passau.de; Heilig-Geist-Gasse 4; mains €10-20; ⏱11am-11pm, closed Wed; 🛜) Not only does this historical inn have a succession of walnut-panelled ceramic-stove-heated rooms, a candlelit cellar (from 6pm) and a vine-draped garden, but the food is equally inspired. Amid the river fish, steaks and seasonal dishes there are quite gourmet affairs such as beef fillet in flambéed cognac sauce. Help it all along with one of the many Austrian and German wines in stock.

🛏 Hotel Schloss Ort
Boutique Hotel €€

(📞0851-340 72; www.hotel-schloss-ort.de; Im Ort 11; s €68-121, d €9/-184; 🅿🛜) This 800-year-old medieval palace by the Inn River conceals a tranquil boutique hotel, stylishly done out with polished timber floors, crisp white cotton sheets and wrought-iron bedsteads. Many of the 18 rooms enjoy river views and breakfast is served in the vaulted restaurant. Parking is an extra €4.

Linz ❸

✗ k.u.k. Hofbäckerei
Cafe €

(Pfarrgasse 17; coffee & cake €3-6; ⏱6.30am-6.30pm Mon-Fri, 7am-12.30pm Sat) The Empire lives on at this gloriously stuck-in-time cafe. Here Fritz Rath bakes the best *Linzer Torte* in town – rich, spicy and with lattice pastry that crumbles just so.

🛏 Hotel am Domplatz
Design Hotel €€

(📞0732-77 30 00; www.hotelamdomplatz.at; Stifterstrasse 4; d €125-145, ste €300; ❄@🛜) Sidling up to the neo-Gothic Neuer Dom, this glass-and-concrete cube reveals streamlined interiors in pristine whites and blond wood that reveal a Nordic-style aesthetic. Wind down with a view at the rooftop spa.

Krems an der Donau ❽

🛏 Arte Hotel Krems
Design Hotel €€

(📞02732-711 23; www.arte-hotel.at; Dr-Karl-Dorrek-Strasse 23; s/d €109/159; 🅿🛜) This cutting-edge art hotel has 91 large, well-designed rooms scattered with big retro prints and patterns complementing the funky '60s-style furniture.

Vienna ❿

✗ Bierhof
Austrian €

(📞01-533 44 28; http://bierhof.at; 01, Haarhof 3; mains €10-19; ⏱11.30am-11.30pm; 🛜; Ⓜ Herrengasse) A narrow passageway opens to a courtyard where umbrella-shaded tables beneath the trees make a charming spot to dine on homemade classics like *Eiernockerl* (flour-and-egg dumplings), *Tiroler Groest'l* (pork, potatoes and bacon, topped with a fried egg), *Tiroler Leber* (liver dumplings with apple sauce and green beans) and *Weiner Schnitzel* with parsley potatoes. The bar stays open until late.

🛏 Hotel Capricorno
Hotel €€

(📞01-533 31 04-0; www.schick-hotels.com/hotel-capricorno; 01, Schwedenplatz 3-4; s/d from €120/150; 🅿🛜; Ⓜ Schwedenplatz) Behind an unpromising mid-20th-century facade, Hotel Capricorno was stunningly made over in 2015 in lustrous velveteens in zesty lime, orange, lemon and aubergine shades. Most of its 42 rooms have balconies (front rooms overlook the Danube Canal but rear rooms are quieter). Rare-for-Vienna parking is available for just €23 per day. It's a 10-minute walk from the Stephansdom.

NEED ^{TO} KNOW

CURRENCY
Euro (€)

LANGUAGE
German (see p520)

VISAS
Generally not required for stays of up to 90 days; some nationalities need a Schengen visa.

FUEL
Petrol stations are common on main roads and highways, and in larger towns. Unleaded costs around €1.50 per litre and diesel is €1.25.

RENTAL CARS
Auto Europe (www. autoeurope.com)

Avis (www.avis.com)

Europcar (www.europcar. com)

Hertz (www.hertz.com)

IMPORTANT NUMBERS
Europe-wide emergency covering police, fire and ambulance (☏112)

Climate

Mild to hot summers, cold winters
Warm to hot summers, mild winters
Mild year-round
Cold climate

Vienna
GO Late Mar–Oct

Kitzbühel
GO Jun–Sep & Dec–Mar

Salzburg
GO Jul & Aug

Innsbruck
GO Jun–Sep & Dec–Mar

Graz
GO Apr–Oct

When to Go

High Season (Apr–Oct)
» High season peaks from July to August.

» In lake areas, the peak is June to September.

» Prices rise over Christmas and Easter.

» Salzburg is busiest in July and August for the Salzburg Festival.

Shoulder (late Mar–May & late Sep–Oct)
» The weather's changeable, the lakes are chilly and the hiking's excellent.

» Sights are open and less crowded.

Low Season (Nov–Mar)
» Many sights are closed.

» There's a cultural focus in Vienna and the regional capitals.

» Ski resorts open from mid-December.

» High season for skiing is mid-December to March.

Daily Costs

Budget: Less than €80

» Dorm beds or cheap doubles: €25 per person

» Self-catering or lunch specials: €6–12

» Cheap museums: €4

Midrange: €80–160

» Hotel singles: €60–90 per person

» Two-course meal with glass of wine: €30

» High-profile museums: €12

Top end: More than €160

» Plush suites and doubles in major cities: from €200

» Pampering at spa facilities: €40–100

» Fine dining and wine pairing: €70

Eating

Cafes Coffee, drinks, snacks.

Bistros Light meals to full-blown dinners.

Restaurants Simple eateries to Michelin-starred temples.

Vegetarian Few wholly vegetarian places, limited choices on most menus.

The following prices indicate the cost of a two-course set menu:

€	less than €15
€€	€15–30
€€€	more than €30

Sleeping

Hotels From budget to luxury; breakfast included unless indicated.

Pensiones Rates always include breakfast.

Hostels In cities and large towns; private or HI-affiliated.

Price symbols indicate the cost of a double room with private bathroom in high season:

€	less than €80
€€	€80–160
€€€	more than €160

Arriving in Austria

Vienna Airport

Train & S-Bahn To city centre every 30 minutes, 6am to 11.30pm (€4 to €12, 15 to 30 minutes).

Taxis €35 to €50; 30 minutes to centre.

Mobile Phones (Cell Phones)

Most European and Australian phones function; turn off roaming to avoid data charges. Buy a local SIM for cheaper rates.

Internet Access

Wi-fi (usually free) is available to guests in most hotels, B&Bs and hostels. Also offered by many cafes, bars, train stations and other public spaces.

Money

ATMs are widely available. Maestro direct debit and Visa and MasterCard credit cards are accepted in most hotels and in midrange restaurants. Expect to pay cash elsewhere. Travellers cheques are not accepted.

Tipping

Restaurant and bar prices include a service charge but locals still tip. Taxis expect 10%.

Useful Websites

Lonely Planet (lonelyplanet.com) Travel tips, accommodation, traveller forums and more.

Austria (www.austria.info) Austrian tourist board.

ADAC (www.adac.de) Driving information for Germany and neighbouring countries.

STRETCH YOUR LEGS
VIENNA

Start/Finish: Café Central

Distance: 3.4km

Duration: Four hours

Vienna's grandeur unfolds in all its glory on this city stroll, from the timeless elegance of its *Kaffeehäuser* (coffee houses) to its monumental Hofburg palace, museums, parks and opulent opera house, as well as magnificent churches.

Take this walk on Trip

40

Café Central

Park just around the corner on Freyung and fortify yourself with coffee and a slice of *Altenbergtorte* cake at grand **Café Central** (www.palaisevents.at/cafecentral.html; 01, Herrengasse 14; ⏰7.30am-10pm Mon-Sat, 10am-10pm Sun; 📶; Ⓜ Herrengasse).

The Walk » Walk southeast on Herrengasse for 350m, then through the Michaelertor palace gate to the imposing Hofburg.

Hofburg

Nothing symbolises Austria's culture and heritage more than the **Hofburg** (Imperial Palace; www.hofburg-wien.at; 01, Michaelerkuppel; 🚌1A, 2A Michaelerplatz, Ⓜ Herrengasse, 🚃D, 1, 2, 71, 46, 49 Burgring), seat of the Habsburgs from 1273 to 1918. Its oldest section is the 13th-century **Schweizerhof** (Swiss Courtyard). The palace owes its size and architectural diversity to one-upmanship; sections were added by new rulers, including the Gothic Burgkapelle (Royal Chapel), early baroque Leopold Wing, 16th-century Amalia Wing and 18th-century Imperial Chancery Wing.

The Walk » It's a 750m stroll southwest through Heldenplatz, passing the twin museums Naturhistorisches and Kunsthistorisches on Maria-Theresien-Platz, to the MuseumsQuartier.

MuseumsQuartier

The **MuseumsQuartier** (Museum Quarter; www.mqw.at; 07, Museumsplatz; ⏰information & ticket centre 10am-7pm; Ⓜ Museumsquartier, Volkstheater) is a remarkable ensemble of museums, cafes, restaurants and bars inside former imperial stables. With over 60,000 sq metres of exhibition space, the complex is one of the world's most ambitious cultural spaces.

The Walk » Head southeast through the MuseumsQuartier's arched laneways to Mariahilfer Strasse. Turn left and continue 350m northeast to the Burggarten.

Burggarten

The **Burggarten** (Castle Garden; www.bundesgaerten.at; 01, Burgring; ⏰6am-10pm Apr-Oct, 7.30am-5.30pm Nov-Mar; Ⓜ Museumsquartier, 🚃D, 1, 2, 71) is a leafy oasis amid the city's hustle and bustle. The marble statue of Mozart is the park's most famous tenant,

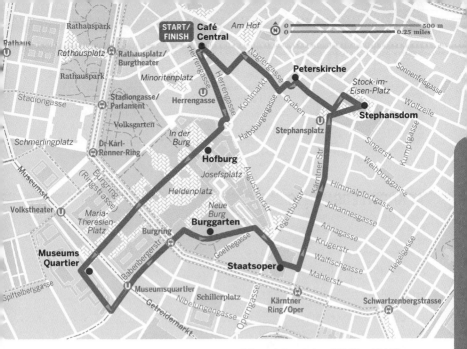

but there's also a statue of Emperor Franz Josef. Don't miss the **Schmetterlinghaus** (butterfly house), and the **Palmenhaus** bar, housed in a beautifully restored *Jugendstil* (art-nouveau) palm house.

The Walk » From the garden's northeastern edge, walk southeast on Hanuschgasse for 200m to the city's opera house, the Staatsoper.

Staatsoper

The neo-Renaissance **Staatsoper** (www.wiener-staatsoper.at; 01, Opernring 2; ⓂKarlsplatz, 🚋D, 1, 2, 71) is Vienna's foremost opera and ballet venue. Built between 1861 and 1869, it initially appalled the Viennese public, earning the nickname 'stone turtle'. Performances here are unforgettable; you also can visit its museum and/or take a guided tour.

The Walk » Head north on Kärntner Strasse for 600m to the Stephansdom, and pause to check out the glorious tiled roof.

Stephansdom

Vienna's soaring, filagreed Gothic masterpiece, the **Stephansdom** (St Stephan's Cathedral; www.stephanskirche.at; 01, Stephansplatz; ◷6am-10pm Mon-Sat, from 7am Sun; main nave

& Domschatz audio tours 9-11.30am & 1-4.30pm Mon-Sat, 1-3.30pm Sun; ⓂStephansplatz), is locally – and ironically – nicknamed Steffl (Little Stephan). A church has stood here since the 12th century; reminders include the Romanesque Riesentor (Giant Gate) and Heidentürme. Inside, a magnificent stone pulpit, sculpted in 1515, presides over the main nave.

The Walk » Take Goldschmiedgasse northwest for 230m to Petersplatz and the domed Peterskirche.

Peterskirche

The **Peterskirche** (Church of St Peter; www. peterskirche.at; 01, Petersplatz; ◷7am-8pm Mon-Fri, 9am-9pm Sat & Sun; ⓂStephansplatz) was built in 1733 according to plans by the celebrated baroque architect Johann Lukas von Hildebrandt. Interior highlights include a fresco on the dome painted by JM Rottmayr and a golden altar depicting the martyrdom of St John of Nepomuk.

The Walk » Head northwest on Graben and Naglergasse for 200m. Turn left onto Haarhof for 90m, then right onto Wallnerstrasse for 80m; Café Central is in front of you.

BEHIND THE SCENES

SEND US YOUR FEEDBACK

We love to hear from travellers – your comments help make our books better. We read every word, and we guarantee that your feedback goes straight to the authors. Visit **lonelyplanet. com/contact** to submit your updates and suggestions.

Note: We may edit, reproduce and incorporate your comments in Lonely Planet products such as guidebooks, websites and digital products, so let us know if you don't want your comments reproduced or your name acknowledged. For a copy of our privacy policy visit lonelyplanet.com/privacy.

ACKNOWLEDGMENTS

Climate map data adapted from Peel MC, Finlayson BL & McMahon TA (2007) 'Updated World Map of the Köppen-Geiger Climate Classification', *Hydrology and Earth System Sciences*, 11, 1633-44.

Front cover photographs: (top) Neuschwanstein Castle, Courtesy of the Bavarian Palace Department, Noppasin/Shutterstock© (right) Marble statue, mrivserg/Shutterstock© (left) Citroen Dolly, Ken Scicluna/AWL©

Back cover photograph: Cypress trees and red poppies, Tuscany, Buena Vista Images/Getty©

THIS BOOK

This 1st edition of Lonely Planet's *Europe's Best Trips* guidebook was curated by Belinda Dixon and researched and written by Isabel Albiston, Oliver Berry, Stuart Butler, Kerry Christiani, Fionn Davenport, Belinda Dixon, Marc Di Duca, Peter Dragicevich, Duncan Garwood, Anthony Ham, Paula Hardy, Catherine Le Nevez, Sally O'Brien, Josephine Quintero, Daniel Robinson, Brendan Sainsbury, Andy Symington, Ryan Ver Berkmoes, Nicola Williams and Neil Wilson.

This guidebook was produced by the following:

Destination Editors Jo Cooke, Helen Elfer, Gemma Graham, Lorna Parkes, James Smart, Anna Tyler

Product Editor Tracy Whitmey

Senior Cartographer Valentina Kremenchutskaya

Book Designer Clara Monitto

Cover Researcher Naomi Parker

Thanks to Bridget Blair, Victoria Harrison, Monique Perrin, Kirsten Rawlings, Alison Ridgway, Luna Soo, Tony Wheeler

INDEX

NICOLA WILLIAMS

British writer Nicola Williams has lived in France and written about it for more than a decade. From her hillside house on the southern shore of Lake Geneva, road trips beckon to Provence, Paris, the Dordogne and onwards to the Atlantic Coast where she has spent endless years revelling in its extraordinary landscapes, architecture and seafaring cuisine. Nicola has worked on numerous Lonely Planet titles, including *Discover France* and *Paris*. Find her on Twitter and Instagram at @Tripalong.

Read more about Nicola at: https://auth.
lonelyplanet.com/profiles/nicolawilliams

NEIL WILSON

Neil was born in Scotland and has lived there most of his life. Based in Perthshire, he has been a full-time writer since 1988, working on more than 80 guidebooks, including the Lonely Planet guides to Scotland, England, Ireland and Prague. An outdoors enthusiast since childhood, Neil is an active hill-walker, mountain-biker, sailor, snowboarder, fly-fisher and rock-climber, and has climbed and tramped in four continents, including ascents of Jebel Toubkal in Morocco, Mount Kinabalu in Borneo and the Old Man of Hoy in the Orkney Islands.

Read more about Neil at https://auth.lonelyplanet.
com/profiles/neilwilson

DANIEL ROBINSON

Co-author (with Tony Wheeler) of Lonely Planet's first *Paris* guide, Daniel has been writing about France for over 25 years. Passionate about history, he is always moved by the grand châteaux of the Loire, the sombre cemeteries of the Somme, and the dramatic and tragic events that both embody. Daniel's travel writing has appeared in the *New York Times*, *National Geographic Traveler* and many other publications and has been translated into 10 languages. He holds degrees in history from Princeton and Tel Aviv University.

BRENDAN SAINSBURY

Originally from Hampshire, England, Brendan first went to Spain on an Inter-rail ticket in the 1980s. He went back as a travel guide several years later and met his wife-to-be in a small village in rural Andalucía in 2003. He has been writing books for Lonely Planet for a decade, including four previous editions of the *Spain* and *Andalucía* guides. Brendan loves Granada, the writing of Federico Lorca, cycling along via verdes, and attending as many flamenco shows as his research allows.

Read more about Brendan at: https://auth. lonelyplanet.com/profiles/brendansainsbury

ANDY SYMINGTON

Though he hails from Australia, Andy's great-grandfather emigrated to Portugal in the 19th century and that side of his family still calls the country home. This connection means that he has been a frequent visitor to the country since birth, and now nips across the border very frequently from his home in Spain. Andy has authored and co-authored numerous Lonely Planet and other guidebooks.

RYAN VER BERKMOES

Ryan once lived in Germany. He spent three years in Frankfurt, during which time he edited a magazine until he got a chance for a new career with... Lonely Planet. One of his first jobs was working on Lonely Planet's Germany coverage. He loves smoked fish, which serves him well in the north, and he loves beer, which serves him well everywhere in Germany. Follow him at ryanverberkmoes.com and @ryanvb.

Read more about Andy at: https://auth. lonelyplanet.com/profiles/andysymington

Read more about Ryan at: https://auth. lonelyplanet.com/profiles/ryanvb

PAULA HARDY

From the slopes of Valpolicella to the shores of Lake Como and the spritz-fuelled bars of Venice and Milan, Paula has been contributing to Lonely Planet Italian guides for over 15 years, including previous editions of *Venice & the Veneto, Pocket Milan, The Italian Lakes, Sicily, Sardinia, Puglia & Basilicata* and *Italy*. When she's not scooting around the *bel paese,* she writes for a variety of travel publications and websites. Currently she divides her time between London, Italy and Morocco, and tweets her finds @paula6hardy.

Read more about Paula at: https://auth. lonelyplanet.com/profiles/paulahardy

CATHERINE LE NEVEZ

Catherine's wanderlust kicked in when she roadtripped across Europe aged four. She's been hitting the road at every opportunity since, completing her Doctorate of Creative Arts in Writing, Masters in Professional Writing, and post-graduate qualifications in editing and publishing along the way. Over the last dozen-plus years she's written scores of Lonely Planet guides, along with numerous print and online articles, covering destinations all over Europe and far beyond.

Read more about Catherine at: https://auth. lonelyplanet.com/profiles/catherine_le_nevez

SALLY O'BRIEN

Australian-born Sally, a Lonely Planet writer since 2001, has called Switzerland home since 2007. Swapping her surfboard for a snowboard, the beach for the lake and the barbecue for the *caquelon,* she loves exploring Switzerland's charming cities, the sublime Alps and lakes, and catching cable cars and trains to stunning vantage points. It's only fitting that she became a naturalised Swiss citizen while on the road for this guide. She lives with her husband, Denis, and their sons in the Lake Geneva region. Sally tweets @swissingaround.

JOSEPHINE QUINTERO

Spain is Josephine's favourite country on earth and she has lived in Málaga province on the Costa del Sol for over 20 years. As well as co-authoring four editions of the Lonely Planet *Spain* title, she has worked on the *Andalucía* regional guide and numerous other Lonely Planet titles. For this book her highlight was discovering still more fine dining venues in the cobbled Marbella backstreets.

Read more about Josephine at: https://auth. lonelyplanet.com/profiles/josephinequintero

MARC DI DUCA

A well-established travel guide author, Marc has explored many corners of Germany over the last 25 years but it's to the quirky variety and friendliness of Bavaria that he returns most willingly. When not hiking Alpine valleys, eating snowballs in Rothenburg ob der Tauber or brewery hopping in Bamberg, he can be found in Sandwich, Kent, where he lives with his wife, Tanya, and their two sons.

Read more about Marc at: https://auth. lonelyplanet.com/profiles/Madidu

PETER DRAGICEVICH

After a successful career in niche newspaper and magazine publishing, both in his native New Zealand and in Australia, Peter finally gave into Kiwi wanderlust, giving up staff jobs to chase his diverse roots around much of Europe. Over the last decade he's written literally dozens of guidebooks for Lonely Planet on an oddly disparate collection of countries, all of which he's come to love. He once again calls Auckland, New Zealand his home – although his current nomadic existence means he's hardly ever there.

Read more about Peter at https://auth. lonelyplanet.com/profiles/peterdragicevich

DUNCAN GARWOOD

A Brit travel writer based in the Castelli Romani hills just outside Rome, Duncan has clocked up tens of thousands of kilometres driving through Italy and exploring its far-flung reaches. He's co-author of the *Rome* city guide and has contributed to a host of Lonely Planet guidebooks including *Italy, Piedmont, Sicily, Sardinia,* and *Naples and the Amalfi Coast*. He has also written on Italy for newspapers, websites and magazines.

Read more about Duncan at: https://auth. lonelyplanet.com/profiles/duncangarwood

ANTHONY HAM

In 2001, Anthony fell in love with Madrid on his first visit to the city. Less than a year later, he arrived on a one-way ticket, with not a word of Spanish and not knowing a single person. After ten years living in the city, he recently returned to Australia with his Spanish-born family, but he still adores his adopted country as much as the first day he arrived. When he's not writing for Lonely Planet, Anthony writes about and photographs Spain, Scandinavia, the Middle East, Australia and Africa for newspapers and magazines around the world. See www.anthonyham.com.

Read more about Anthony at: https://auth. lonelyplanet.com/profiles/anthonyham

OLIVER BERRY

Oliver Berry has explored nearly every corner of France for Lonely Planet, travelling all the way from the mountains of Corsica to the beaches of Normandy. He has also photographed and written about France for many newspapers, magazines and online publications. When not in France, he can usually be found wandering the beaches and clifftops of his home county, Cornwall. His latest work is published at oliverberry.com.

Read more about Oliver at: https://auth. lonelyplanet.com/profiles/oliverberry

STUART BUTLER

Stuart's first childhood encounters with Spain came on a school trip to the far south of Spain and family holidays along the north coast. These left lasting impressions and when he was older he spent every summer on the Basque beaches, until one day he found he was unable to tear himself away – he's been in the region ever since. His travels for Lonely Planet, and a wide variety of magazines, have taken him beyond Spain, to the shores of the Arctic, the mountains of Asia and the savannahs of Africa. His website is www.stuartbutlerjournalist.com.

Read more about Stuart at: https://auth. lonelyplanet.com/profiles/stuartbutler

KERRY CHRISTIANI

Kerry's research for this guide included parts of Portugal and France. Her love affair with Portugal began as a child clambering along the cliffs of the Algarve. She later fell for the rest of the country – its captivating landscapes, super-friendly locals, fresh seafood and photogenic light. She's been travelling in her beloved France since she first visited in her school days to brush up her *français*, which she went on to study to MA level. Kerry authors a number of Lonely Planet's central and southern European titles and tweets @kerrychristiani.

Read more about Kerry at: https://auth. lonelyplanet.com/profiles/KerryChristiani

FIONN DAVENPORT

Irish by birth and conviction, Fionn has been writing about his native country for more than two decades. He's come and gone over the years, pulled abroad to escape Dublin's comfortable stasis and by the promise of adventure, but it has cemented his belief that Ireland remains his favourite place to visit, if not always live in. These days, he has a weekly commute home to Dublin from Manchester, where he lives with his partner Laura and their car, Trevor. In Dublin he presents *Inside Culture* on RTE Radio 1 and writes travel features for a host of publications, including *The Irish Times*.